The Rough Guide to

Amsterdam

There are more than one hundred and fifty Rough Guide titles
covering destinations from Amsterdam to Zimbabwe

Forthcoming titles include

Argentina • Croatia • Ecuador • Southeast Asia

Rough Guide Reference Series

Classical Music • Country Music • Drum 'n' Bass • English Football
European Football • House • The Internet • Jazz • Music USA • Opera
Reggae • Rock Music • Techno • Unexplained Phenomena • World Music

Rough Guide Phrasebooks

Czech • Dutch • Egyptian Arabic • European Languages • French
German • Greek • Hindi & Urdu • Hungarian • Indonesian • Italian
Mandarin Chinese • Mexican Spanish • Polish • Portuguese • Russian
Spanish • Swahili • Thai • Turkish • Vietnamese

Rough Guides on the Internet

www.roughguides.com

Rough Guide Credits

Text Editor:	Andrew Tomičić
Series Editor:	Mark Ellingham
Editorial:	Martin Dunford, Jonathan Buckley, Jo Mead, Kate Berens, Amanda Tomlin, Ann-Marie Shaw, Paul Gray, Helena Smith, Judith Bamber, Orla Duane, Olivia Eccleshall, Ruth Blackmore, Sophie Martin, Geoff Howard, Claire Saunders, Gavin Thomas, Alexander Mark Rogers, Polly Thomas, Joe Staines, Lisa Nellis, Richard Lim, Claire Fogg, Duncan Clark, Peter Buckley (UK); Andrew Rosenberg, Mary Beth Maioli, Don Bapst, Stephen Timblin (US)
Online Editors:	Kelly Cross (US)
Production:	Susanne Hillen, Andy Hilliard, Link Hall, Helen Ostick, Julia Bovis, Michelle Draycott, Katie Pringle, Robert Evers, Niamh Hatton, Mike Hancock
Cartography:	Melissa Baker, Maxine Repath, Nichola Goodliffe, Ed Wright
Picture Research:	Louise Boulton, Sharon Martins
Finance:	John Fisher, Gary Singh, Edward Downey, Mark Hall, Tim Bill
Marketing & Publicity:	Richard Trillo, Niki Smith, David Wearn, Jemima Broadbridge (UK); Jean-Marie Kelly, Myra Campolo, Simon Carloss (US)
Administration:	Tania Hummel, Charlotte Marriott, Demelza Dallow

Acknowledgements

Many thanks for help with this edition to the Amsterdam Tourist Board and Marlien Meijer at the Netherlands Tourist Board in London; Fred Bönnekamp for his invaluable knowledge of the city; Ton Geelhoed, Hermen Maat and Matthew Teller for their support and feedback; Laurence Larroche for proof-reading; Stratigraphics for cartography; and Robert Mackey and Alistair McDermott. At Rough Guides thanks to Andrew for his attentive editing and Robert Evers for typesetting.

The publishers and authors have done their best to ensure the accuracy and currency of all information in *The Rough Guide to Amsterdam*; however, they can accept no responsibility for any loss, injury, or inconvenience sustained by any traveller as a result of information or advice contained in the guide.

This sixth edition published May 2000 by Rough Guides Ltd, 62–70 Shorts Gardens, London WC2H 9AB.

Distributed by the Penguin Group:

Penguin Books Ltd, 27 Wrights Lane, London W8 5TZ.

Penguin Putnam Inc, 375 Hudson Street, New York, NY 10014, USA.

Penguin Books Australia Ltd, 487 Maroondah Highway, PO Box 257, Ringwood, Victoria 3134, Australia.

Penguin Books Canada Ltd, 10 Alcorn Avenue, Toronto, Ontario M4V 1E4, Canada.

Penguin Books (NZ) Ltd, 182–190 Wairau Road, Auckland 10, New Zealand.

Printed in England by Clays Ltd, St Ives Plc

Typography and original design by Jonathan Dear and The Crowd Roars.

Illustrations throughout by Edward Briant.

A catalogue record for this book is available from the British Library. ISBN 1-85828-512-7

The Rough Guide to

Amsterdam

Written and researched by
Martin Dunford and Jack Holland

With additional accounts and research by
Phil Lee and Malijn Maat

ROUGH GUIDES

Help us update

We've gone to a lot of trouble to ensure that this sixth edition of *The Rough Guide to Amsterdam* is accurate and up-to-date. However, things inevitably change, and if you feel we've got it wrong or left something out, we'd like to know: any suggestions, comments or corrections would be much appreciated. We'll credit all contributions and send a copy of the next edition – or any other Rough Guide if you prefer – for the best correspondence.

Please mark letters "Rough Guide to Amsterdam" and send to:
Rough Guides, 62–70 Shorts Gardens, London WC2H 9AB or
Rough Guides, 4th Floor, 345 Hudson St, New York, NY 10014.

Email should be sent to:
mail@roughguides.co.uk

Online updates about Rough Guide titles can be found on our Web site at *www.roughguides.com*

The Authors

Martin Dunford and **Jack Holland** first met at the University of Kent at Canterbury. Following jobs as diverse as insurance collection, beer-barrel rolling and EFL teaching in Greece they co-founded the Rough Guides in the mid-1980s. After co-authoring several other titles, Martin is now editorial director of Rough Guides and Jack lives in the Cotswolds.

Readers' letters

We'd like to thank all those readers who wrote in with comments and updates to the previous edition: Dr & Mrs E.S. Bechler, Sarah Bickford, Christopher Birch, Alan Bradley, J.W. Brown, B.W. Chambers, N.G. Clark, Sandra Clements & Steve Bishop, Albert Coo, Jim Doherty, Kelly Dunn, Lewis Edwards, Gerri Eickhof, Møyfrid Engeset, Chris Eyre, Neil Finer, Patricia Gilligan, Joy Glazener, M. Gordon, Andrew Haigh, Paul Hammond, David Hannam & Gillian Morgan, J. Herne, Sonia Kells, David Leslie, Alistair MacDonald & Lis Boulton, Tony McGardle, Treadwell Merrill, Daniel J. Mitchell, Kelvin Morton, Peter Moskos, Grace Mugadza, Jan Nevill, Adam Nightingale, Anne O'Byrne, John Ollerton, Ginny Oxley, Pauline Paddon, Graham & Melinda Paine, Mike & Eileen Pennington, Iwan Phillips, Lynn Polley, Philip Pool, Gabriela Rieberer, Pat Riley, Jesper Romers, Ian Saxby, Tamasa Sherwood, Toni Simon, Claire Smith, Nicola Smith, Monica Staaf, R.E. Swanepoel, Shelley Swillingham & Phil Guild, David Teale, M.C. Tomkins & B. Struggles, Liz Watson, Pat Wright.

Rough Guides

Travel Guides • Phrasebooks • Music and Reference Guides

We set out to do something different when the first Rough Guide was published in 1982. Mark Ellingham, just out of University, was travelling in Greece. He brought along the popular guides of the day, but found they were all lacking in some way. They were either strong on ruins and museums but went on for pages without mentioning a beach or taverna. Or they were so conscious of the need to save money that they lost sight of Greece's cultural and historical significance. Also, none of the books told him anything about Greece's contemporary life – its politics, its culture, its people, and how they lived.

So with no job in prospect, Mark decided to write his own guidebook, one which aimed to provide practical information that was second to none, detailing the best beaches and the hottest clubs and restaurants, while also giving hard-hitting accounts of every sight, both famous and obscure, and providing up-to-the-minute information on contemporary culture. It was a guide that encouraged independent travellers to find the best of Greece, and was a great success, getting shortlisted for the Thomas Cook travel guide award, and encouraging Mark, along with three friends, to expand the series.

The Rough Guide list grew rapidly and the letters flooded in, indicating a much broader readership than had been anticipated, but one which uniformly appreciated the Rough Guides' mix of practical detail and humour, irreverence and enthusiasm. Things haven't changed. The same four friends who began the series are still the caretakers of the Rough Guide mission today: to provide the most reliable, up-to-date and entertaining information to independent-minded travellers of all ages, on all budgets.

We now publish 150 titles and have offices in London and New York. The travel guides are written and researched by a dedicated team of more than 100 authors, based in Britain, Europe, the USA and Australia. We have also created a unique series of phrasebooks to accompany the travel series, along with the acclaimed series of music guides, and a best-selling pocket guide to the Internet and World Wide Web. We also publish comprehensive travel information on our Web site: *www.roughguides.com*

Contents

List of maps

MAP SYMBOLS

————	Road	⊠	Post office
▓▓▓▓	Pedestrianized road	▉	Building
– – –	Footpath	⊕	Church
════	Waterway	✡	Synagogue
──•──	Railway	ⵎ	Gardens
────	Chapter division boundary	†₊†	Cemetery
✕	Airport		Park
◉	Hotel		

Introduction

Amsterdam is a compact, instantly likeable capital. It's appealing to look at and pleasant to walk around, an intriguing mix of the parochial and the international; it also has a welcoming attitude towards visitors and a uniquely youthful orientation, shaped by the liberal counterculture of the last three decades. It's hard not to feel drawn in by the buzz of open-air summer events, by the intimacy of the clubs and bars, or by the Dutch facility with languages: just about everyone you meet in Amsterdam will be able to speak near-perfect English, on top of their own native Dutch and fluent German and French.

The city's layout is determined by a web of **canals** radiating out from a historical core to loop right around the centre: these planned, seventeenth-century extensions to the medieval town make for a uniquely elegant urban environment, with tall, gabled houses reflected in their still, green water. With its tree-lined canals, cobbled streets, tinkling bicycle bells and stately architecture, Amsterdam is a world away from the traffic and noise of other European city centres – modern and quiet, while still retaining a perfectly preserved 400-year-old centre.

The conventional sights are for the most part low-key – the **Anne Frank House** being a notable exception – but, thanks to an active and continuing government policy of supporting the arts, Amsterdam has developed a world-class group of museums and galleries. The **Van Gogh Museum** is, for many people, reason enough to visit the city; add to it the **Rijksmuseum**, with its collections of medieval and seventeenth-century Dutch paintings, the contemporary and experimental **Stedelijk Museum**, and hundreds of smaller galleries, and the quality and range of art on display is evident.

However, it's Amsterdam's **population and politics** that constitute its most enduring characteristics. Celebrated during the 1960s and 1970s for its radical permissiveness, the city mellowed only marginally during the 1980s, and, despite the inevitable gentrification of the last decade, it retains a laid-back feel. It is, however, far from being as cosmopolitan a city as London or Paris: despite the huge numbers of immigrants from former colonies in Surinam and Indonesia, as well as Morocco and Turkey (among other places), almost all live and work outside the centre and can seem almost invisible to the casual visitor. Indeed there is an ethnic and social homogeneity in the city-centre population that seems to run counter to everything you might have heard of Dutch integration.

This apparent contradiction embodies much of the spirit of Amsterdam. The city is world famous as a place where the possession and sale of cannabis are effectively legal – and yet, for the most part, Amsterdammers themselves can't really be bothered with the stuff. And while Amsterdam is renowned for its tolerance towards all styles of behaviour and dress, a more prim, correct-thinking capital city, with a more mainstream dress sense, would be hard to find. Behind the cosy cafés and dreamy canals lurks the suspicion that Amsterdammers' hearts lie squarely in their wallets. And while new-comers might see the city as a haven of liberalism and tolerance, Amsterdammers can seem just as indifferent to this as well.

In recent years, increasingly hard-line city mayors have taken this conservatism on board and seem to have embarked on a generally successful – if unspoken – policy of quashing Amsterdam's image as a counterculture icon and depicting it instead as a centre for busi-ness and international high finance. Most of the inner-city squats – which once defined Amsterdam's people-power for locals and visi-tors alike – are now either empty or legalized. Coffeeshops are now forced to choose between selling dope or alcohol, and, if only for economic reasons, many are switching to the latter. Such shifts in attitude, combined with alterations to the city's landscape, in the form of large-scale urban development projects on the outskirts and an almost continuous modernization of buildings and infrastructure in the historic centre, together generate an unmistakeable feeling that Amsterdam and its people are busy reinventing themselves, writ-ing off their hippyish adventures and returning to earlier, more respectable days.

Perhaps mercifully, this hasn't happened yet, and Amsterdam remains a casual and intimate place, modern and innovative yet comfortably familiar. Amsterdammers themselves make much of their city and its attractions being *gezellig*, a rather overused Dutch word roughly corresponding to a combination of "cosy", "lived-in" and "warmly convivial". The city's unparalleled selection of *gezellig* drinking places is a delight, whether you choose a traditional, bare-floored **brown café** or one of the many designer bars or "grand cafés". Amsterdam's unique approach to combating hard-drug abuse – embodied in the effective decriminalization of cannabis – has led to a large number of **coffeeshops**, which sell coffee only as a sideline to high-quality marijuana and hashish. The city's wide range of **entertainment** possibilities means you need never wonder what to do: **multimedia complexes** like the Melkweg are at the fore-front of contemporary European film, dance, drama and music, while dozens of other venues present live music from all genres (the Dutch have a particular soft spot for jazz), and, resident in the world-famous Concertgebouw concert hall, Amsterdam has one of the world's leading classical **orchestras**. The **club** scene, on the other hand, is subdued by the standards of other capital cities, dom-inated by more or less mainstream house music, and with the emphasis far more on dancing than on posing. **Gay** men, however, will discover that Amsterdam has Europe's most active nightlife net-work, although women might be disappointed at the exclusivity of the proclaimed "Gay Capital of Europe".

When to go

Whether you're coming for canals and architecture, or sex and drugs, Amsterdam is a delight at any time of year. In high **summer**, the city parks are packed and every pavement, doorway and stretch of canalside becomes a choice spot for lazy hanging-out. **Spring** and **autumn** are particularly beautiful, with mist hanging over the canals until late morning and low sunlight piercing through the cloud cover. The flatness of the surrounding countryside means that the weather is always changeable, and it's common at any time of year for heavy morning clouds to be blown away to reveal a sunny afternoon. It's never too hot, though, and, save for **January** and **February**, when icy winds blow off the canals, the weather is rarely so relentlessly mis-erable as to ruin a visit – the persistent winter rain can give the city a romantic cast, with wet cobbles glistening under the street-lights and the canals rippled by falling raindrops. But whatever the time of year, you should bear two things in mind: firstly, there are plenty of remarkably hardy mosquitoes living on the canals, at their friskiest in the hot summer evenings, although still a nuisance as late as October; and secondly, the few square kilometres of central Amsterdam comprise one of the most densely populated urban areas in the world – space is at a premium, and you should always book accommodation before leaving home.

Getting out of Amsterdam

Finally, don't fall into the trap of thinking that there's nothing to the Netherlands beyond Amsterdam. Although Amsterdam utterly dis-proves the theory that a capital city is a microcosm of the nation, there is plenty to see and do outside the city. In spring and early sum-mer the famous **bulbfields** are in full bloom, and the Randstad cities to the south of Amsterdam, such as **Haarlem** and **Leiden**, are worth a visit at any time of the year. Although there isn't much wild nature to be found in the Netherlands, there's some pleasant hiking to be had in the dunes near Bloemendaal-aan-Zee, and it's a quick train ride to the popular beach resort of **Zandvoort**. Indeed, just about everywhere can be reached quickly and painlessly by public transport – where the trains fizzle out the buses take over.

Average Maximum Temperatures												
	Jan	Feb	Mar	April	May	June	July	Aug	Sept	Oct	Nov	Dec
Min °C	-0.2	-0.5	1.5	3.8	7.5	10.5	12.5	12.5	10.5	7.3	3.8	1.1
Min °F	32	31	35	39	46	51	55	55	51	45	39	34
Max °C	4.3	4.9	8.1	11.6	16.0	19.1	20.5	20.5	18.3	14.0	8.8	5.7
Max °F	40	41	47	53	61	66	69	69	65	57	48	42

The Basics

Getting There from Britain

There are many ways to reach Amsterdam, but basically it comes down to deciding between a low-cost but time-consuming journey by bus, or ferry and train, and a swift but slightly more expensive flight. However, travelling by train through the Channel Tunnel is an attractive alternative, little cheaper than a flight, but with the advantage of taking you direct from London to the heart of Amsterdam. Whichever method you opt for, you'll find a variety of competitive fares.

By Air

There are plenty of direct flights to **Amsterdam Schiphol** (*skip-oll*) from the UK, either from London or a large number of UK regional airports. Flights take between an hour (from London) and ninety minutes (from Scotland and the north of England), representing a huge saving in time compared with other ways of getting there. Both British Airways and KLM run a large number of daily **scheduled flights** from London, while regional airports are well served by KLM uk and British Midland, who fly at least twice a day from those given in the box above. Of the **smaller operators**, EasyJet's budget, ticketless service operates three or four flights daily from Luton, plus two or three from Liverpool; ScotAirways has two or three daily flights on weekdays from Cambridge and Southampton, with a reduced service at the weekend; and Transavia flies from Gatwick at least twice a day. You may also find **long-haul airlines** offering reasonable prices on the London–Amsterdam route, as they stop off on their way to more distant destinations: Air Kenya, Cathay Pacific and Quantas are three such operators.

The large number of flights to Schiphol has led to a price war between the airlines. As as result it's reasonably easy to find **return fares** from London for £70 to £120. Flights from regional airports are likely to be around twice the price, with the exception of those operated by EasyJet,

■ BY AIR

Airlines and Routes

British Airways ☎ 0345/222111, *www.british-airways.com*
London (Heathrow and Gatwick), Birmingham and Manchester to Amsterdam Schiphol.
British Midland ☎ 0870/607 0555, *www.britishmidland.com*
London Heathrow, East Midlands, Edinburgh, Glasgow, Leeds/Bradford, Manchester and Teeside to Amsterdam Schiphol.
EasyJet ☎ 0870/600 0000, *www.easyjet.com*
Luton and Liverpool to Amsterdam Schiphol.
KLM Royal Dutch Airlines ☎ 0870/507 4074, *www.klm.com*

London Heathrow and Gatwick to Amsterdam Schiphol.
KLM uk ☎ 0870/507 4074, *www.klmuk.com*
London City and Stansted, Aberdeen, Birmingham, Bristol, Cardiff, Edinburgh, Glasgow, Humberside, Leeds/Bradford, Manchester, Newcastle, Norwich and Teeside to Amsterdam Schiphol.
ScotAirways ☎ 0870/606 0707, *www.scotairways.co.uk*
Cambridge and Southampton to Amsterdam Schiphol.
Transavia ☎ 01293/596650
London Gatwick to Amsterdam Schiphol.

Discount Flight Agents

Alpha Flights, 37 Kings Exchange, Tileyard Rd, London N7 9AH ☎ 020/7609 8188.
Reliable discount flight agents.

APA Travel, 138 Eversholt St, London NW1 1BL ☎ 020/7388 1732.
Efficient discount flight agents.

North South Travel, Moulsham Mill Centre, Parkway, Chelmsford, Essex CM2 7PX ☎ 01245/608291.
Friendly, competitive travel agency, offering discounted fares worldwide – profits are used to support projects in the developing world, especially the promotion of sustainable tourism.

STA Travel, 86 Old Brompton Rd, London SW7 3LQ; 117 Euston Rd, London NW1 2SX; 38 Store St, London WC1 (all: Europe ☎ 020/7361 6161, worldwide ☎ 020/7361 6262); 38 North St, Brighton ☎ 01273/728 282; 25 Queens Rd, Bristol BS8 1QE ☎ 0117/929 4399; 38 Sidney St, Cambridge CB2 3HX ☎ 01223/366966; 75 Deansgate, Manchester M3 2BW ☎ 0161/834 0668; 78 Bold Street, Liverpool L1 4HR ☎ 0151/707 1123; 88 Vicar Lane, Leeds LS1 7JH ☎ 0113/244 9212; 9 St Mary's Place, Newcastle-upon-Tyne NE1 7PG ☎ 0191/233 2111; 36 George St, Oxford OX1 2OJ ☎ 01865/792800; 27 Forrest Rd, Edinburgh ☎ 0131/226 7747; 184 Byres Rd, Glasgow G1 1JH ☎ 0141/338 6000; 30 Upper Kirkgate, Aberdeen ☎ 0122/465 8222; and branches on university campuses in London, Birmingham, Bristol, Canterbury, Cardiff, Coventry, Durham, Glasgow, Leeds, Loughborough, Nottingham, Sheffield and Warwick; *www.statravel.co.uk*
Worldwide specialists in low-cost flights and tours for students and under-26s, though other customers welcome.

Travel CUTS, 295a Regent St, London W1R 7YA ☎ 020/7255 1944; 33 Prince's Square, London W2 4NG ☎ 020/7792 3770;

www.travelcuts.co.uk
British branch of Canada's main youth and student travel specialist.

Trailfinders, 1 Threadneedle Street, London EC2R 8JX (all destinations ☎ 020/7628 7628); 42–50 Earls Court Rd, London W8 6FT (long-haul ☎ 020/7938 3366); 194 Kensington High St, London W8 7RG (long-haul ☎ 020/7938 3939); 215 Kensington High St, London W8 6BD (transatlantic and European ☎ 020/7937 5400); 58 Deansgate, Manchester M3 2FF ☎ 0161/839 6969; 254–284 Sauchiehall St, Glasgow G2 3EH ☎ 0141/353 2224; 22–24 The Priory Queensway, Birmingham B4 6BS ☎ 0121/236 1234; 48 Corn St, Bristol BS1 1HQ ☎ 0117/929 9000; 7–9 Ridley Place, Newcastle NE1 8 JQ ☎ 0191/261 2345; *www.trailfinder.com*
One of the best-informed and most efficient agents for independent travellers; their Web site offers best-buy information, provides a brochure ordering service and sells travel insurance.

The Travel Bug, 125 Gloucester Rd, London SW7 4SF ☎ 020/7835 2000; 597 Cheetham Hill Rd, Manchester M8 5EJ ☎ 0161/721 4000; *www.travel-bug.co.uk*
Large range of discounted tickets; the Web site offers a flight price "wizard" as well as a brochure request service.

UsitCAMPUS, 52 Grosvenor Gardens, London SW1W 0AG ☎ 020/7730 3402; 541 Bristol Rd, Selly Oak, Birmingham B29 6AU ☎ 0121/414 1848; 61 Ditchling Rd, Brighton BN1 4SD ☎ 01273/570226; 39 Queen's Rd, Clifton, Bristol BS8 1QE ☎ 0117/929 2494; 5 Emmanuel St, Cambridge CB1 1NE ☎ 01223/324283; 53 Forrest Rd, Edinburgh EH1 2QP ☎ 0131/668 3308; 105–106 St Aldates, Oxford OX1 1BU ☎ 01865/484730; *www.usitcampus.co.uk*
Student/youth travel specialists, with branches also in YHA shops and on university campuses all over Britain.

---

which start at around £60 return, plus airport tax. **Apex** fares are around £150, with a maximum return fare of £210 direct from Heathrow. To help you find the best bargains, all major airlines have **Web sites** providing the latest information about timetables and fares, and, increasingly, an online booking service. There are also a growing number of flight agents' Web sites offering

instant access to the best deals; while we've listed some of these opposite, others can be found through the online service Cheapflights, at *www.cheapflights.co.uk*, which will signpost you to the booking agent or airline offering the lowest prices.

Alternative sources of **discounted tickets** include Ceefax, which hosts a large number of

Telephone and online Discount Agents

Dial-a-Flight ☎0870/333 4488,
www.dialaflight.com
Telephone sales of scheduled flights, with a Web site useful for tracking down bargains.
Expedia UK *expedia.co.uk*
Microsoft's venture into the Internet travel market, with a "flight wizard" listing many (but not all) airline options, its own "special fares" and an online booking service.

Flightline ☎01702/715151,
www.flightline.co.uk
Another telephone-based outfit offering online searches for cheap charter and scheduled flights.
Lastminute.com *www.lastminute.com*
Vast Web site selling everything from holidays to mobile phones, but with a particular emphasis on cheap travel.

travel agents touting last-minute deals, the weekend travel sections of the quality newspapers, or, if you live in London, the back pages of the listings magazine *Time Out* or the *Evening Standard*. Alternatively, contact a **discount flight agent** such as STA Travel, Trailfinders or UsitCAMPUS, who specialize in youth flights and, if you're under 26 (or a student under 32), can offer substantial savings; they also sell ordinary discounted tickets to non-students.

By Train

The simplicity of the Eurostar passenger service is likely to make it the first choice for anyone travelling by **train** to Amsterdam, though there are a couple of other, rather more convoluted possibilities, the best of which uses the very competitively priced Stena Line fast ferry.

The routes

Eurostar's rapid passenger service from London through the Channel Tunnel can cut the journey time to Amsterdam to a manageable six hours, with a change at Brussels Midi station for the last leg of the journey (the London–Brussels leg takes a little less than three hours). The Eurostar service from **London Waterloo** to **Brussels** runs roughly ten times a day from Monday to Saturday, and eight times on Sunday, usually stopping at Ashford in Kent and always at Lille, France (if you need a visa to visit France, you'll have to get one in order to use the Eurostar). Travel is simple: you're required to check in twenty minutes before departure, passports are checked on the train, and when you get to Brussels the onward connection to Amsterdam runs hourly.

There are a wide range of **fares** on Eurostar, which start at around £70 return if you're under 26 (no single fare), but can cost up to £250 for a

standard return (£125 one-way). The standard ticket offers you travel between Monday and Friday with flexible return dates and ticket exchanges or refunds for up to two months after departure. One way of reducing the cost is to take advantage of **economy deals** such as the "Excursion" and "Leisure Return" tickets; at around half the price of the standard return (£100 for an Excursion and £130 for a Leisure return ticket) you can travel any day, are required to stay a minimum of one Saturday night before returning (or alternatively three nights, for the Leisure Return) and you cannot exchange or refund your return ticket after departure.

If you're planning to take a **bicycle**, Eurostar will charge £20 per journey to carry it as "registered baggage"; you can retrieve it at Brussels, but not at intermediate stations. It's possible to check your bike in up to ten days in advance, to ensure it's waiting for you on arrival; if you check it in on the day of travel Eurostar only guarantees that you will be reunited within 24 hours, which obviously poses problems if you're travelling on to Amsterdam.

The longer, but cheaper route is available through **Stena Line**, in conjunction with a handful of local rail operators – Scotrail, Anglia, First North Western, First Great Western and Virgin – and utilises the fast **Harwich** to **Hook of Holland** ferry crossing (3hr 40min). The London Liverpool Street to Amsterdam journey takes around eight hours and operates twice daily. Prices from London start at £50 return for a three-day APEX fare, which must be booked at least a week in advance, with the return journey being made within three days. A standard return costs £60 with a young person's railcard, £80 for an adult. Tickets can be purchased from Rail Europe or any principal train station.

Rail passes

If you're intending to travel around the Netherlands, there are a number of discount **rail pass** options. The **Euro Domino** pass (also called the "Freedom" pass) is valid for unlimited travel within a single country, though you can buy several to run concurrently in different countries. There are no residence requirements or age restrictions and these can be remarkably good value. Euro Dominos are valid for between three and eight days' travel within any one month, with three categories of pass – youth (under-26), first- and second-class: **prices** for a three-day pass in the Netherlands are £29, £59 and £39, for a five-day pass £49, £99 and £59, and for an eight-day pass, £79, £149 and £99, respectively. An equivalent national discount card, the **Holland Rail Pass**, enables unlimited travel within the Netherlands during either a three- or five-day period in a given month; the cost is the same as for a Euro Domino pass except for additional discounts on the cost of a second pass for two people travelling together, and an extra "senior" category, which enables people aged over 60 to purchase the pass for the same price as the youth option.

If the Netherlands is only part of your travel plans, and you would like to go further afield, there are a number of different passes available. The **InterRail** pass, available to European residents only, provides unlimited rail travel on national rail networks across Europe (though supplements are often payable on high-speed trains). The price of the pass depends on whether you're under or over 26 (the former faring considerably better), as well as the number of zones you wish to travel in; Europe is divided into eight zones, the Netherlands falling into Zone E, along with France, Belgium and Luxembourg, and the neighbouring zones, C and B, comprising Germany, Austria, Denmark and Switzerland, and Norway, Sweden and Finland, respectively. A pass enabling travel within a single zone for a 22-day period costs £159 for under-26s, £229 or more for over-26s; all other passes last a full month, with a two-zone pass costing £209 (£279), a three-zone £229 (£309) and an all-zone pass £259 (£349). If you're over 26, the **InterRail 26-Plus** pass covers some, but not all, of the countries in the scheme, including the Netherlands, Denmark, Norway, Sweden, Finland and Germany, but excluding France or Belgium. Passes can be bought from larger train stations, student/youth travel agents, or at a discounted price, online at *www.inter-rail.co.uk*. It's worth noting that, whilst not entitling UK and Irish nationals to free rail travel within Britain and Ireland, the InterRail pass does entitle the holder to discounted fares en route to the continent via rail/ferry routes.

One of the most popular deals if you're under 26 is to purchase a **BIJ ticket** (International Youth Ticket), which gives around a thirty-percent discount on city-to-city fares, allowing as many stopovers as you like within a two-month period. Tickets are available either direct from the rail operators, or from youth and student travel agents. Alternatively, if you're sixty or over, the **Rail Europe Senior Card** gives up to thirty percent discounts on any journeys which cross international boundaries (but not on journeys within countries) in most of western Europe. You can get one free if you have a Senior Citizen Rail Card (£18 from any UK train station).

By Bus

Travelling by long-distance **bus** is generally the cheapest way of reaching Amsterdam, but it takes ten hours and more to get there from London. There are three **Eurolines** coaches daily from **London Victoria** Coach Station to Amsterdam's **Amstel** Station, southeast of the city centre, leaving at 8.30am, 8pm and 10.30pm, and crossing the Channel with Eurotunnel. Prices for under-26s and over-60s are £42 return (£28 one-way) and £47 return (£31 one-way) standard fare.

Alternatively, if you prefer to travel by **ferry** there are services both from Newcastle to IJmuiden and Hull to Rotterdam Europoort. At both destination ports, coaches meet the ferries and leave for Amsterdam Centraal Station. Combined ferry and coach tickets are available from the ferry operator. A return trip from Newcastle to Amsterdam, via IJmuiden, costs around £70 in low season (£100 in high season) and takes approximately fifteen hours; travelling from Hull to Amsterdam via the Rotterdam Europoort will take around the same time, including the hour's coach journey, and cost roughly £86 in low season (£104 in high season).

By Car: the Channel Tunnel and Ferries

If you're looking to travel to the Netherlands by car, your options are either to take the **train**

Train and Bus Information

Busabout, 258 Vauxhall Bridge Rd, London SW1V 1BS ☎ 020/7950 1661, *www.busabout.com*
European coach operator.

Deutsche Bahn UK, 18 Conduit St, London W1R 9TD ☎ 020/7317 0919, *www.db-ag.de*
European rail tickets and passes including Scanrail.

Eurolines, 52 Grosvenor Gardens, London SW1W 0AU ☎ 0990/808080, *www.eurolines.co.uk*
European coach operator, offering scheduled coach services to European cities as well as passes for Europe-wide travel.

Eurostar, Eurostar House, Waterloo International Station, London SE1 8SE; 102–104 Victoria St, London SW1E 5JL

(☎ 0990/186186); ticket purchase also available at Ashford International and principal train stations; *www.eurostar.com*
Channel tunnel services to Paris or Brussels via Lille.

Eurotunnel, PO Box 300, Dept 302, Folkestone, Kent CT19 4QD (reservations ☎ 0990/353535, recorded information 0891/555566); *www.eurotunnel.co.uk*
Shuttle train via the Channel Tunnel for passengers and their vehicles.

Rail Europe, 179 Piccadilly, London W1V BA ☎ 08705/848848, *www.raileurope.co.uk*
European rail tickets and passes.

Wasteels, by platform 2, Victoria Station, London SW1V 1JT ☎ 020/7834 7066.
Youth train and coach ticket specialists.

through the Channel tunnel, or to opt for one of the many **ferry** routes.

Eurotunnel operates the car-carrying rail service which runs between **Folkestone** and **Coquelles**, near Calais, through the Channel tunnel. From Calais, it's over 300 miles (around 500km) to Amsterdam. The train journey takes around 35 minutes, and trains run three times an hour during the day and once hourly at night. Tickets can be bought on arrival, but advance booking (by phone or via the Internet) is advised at peak times. The recommended check-in time is 25 minutes before departure, with final boarding ten minutes before departure. Prices vary seasonally, but more noticeably depending on the time of day, with the cheapest fares available on journeys made between 10pm and 6am. Prices are charged per vehicle, with no additions for passengers, and one-way fares are charged at half the price of an economy return. Return trips made within five days entitle you to mini-break prices which, for a **car**, range from around £140 taking a night train to £170 (£215 in high season) during the day; for a **motorbike** the corresponding prices are £80 and £125 (£160) respectively. If you wish to stay longer, an economy return (the confusing name for the standard return ticket) by car will cost £220 for overnight travel and £250 (£330) by day; for a motorbike it's £120 and £190 (£250). A trailer or caravan costs more or less the equivalent of another car; bicycles and foot passengers are not carried on Eurotunnel.

There are three direct **ferry** crossings into Holland: the twice-daily Stena Line route from **Harwich** to the **Hook of Holland** (3hr 40min), which leaves you with roughly an hour's drive to Amsterdam; the DFDS Seaways route, sailed three times weekly from **Newcastle** to **IJmuiden** (pronounced "EYE-mao-dn"; 14hrs), which is twenty minutes' drive from Amsterdam; and the once-daily **Hull** to **Rotterdam** (Europoort) crossing (13hrs) with P&O North Sea Ferries, again an hour's drive away. P&O also operate a **Hull** to **Zeebrugge** service, leaving you with a drive of around two to three hours to Amsterdam. The prices, perhaps surprisingly given the differing lengths of the crossings, are broadly similar. The cost of a return for a single person and car taking the Stena Line route from Harwich varies from £160 (low season) to £260 (high season), with additional passengers charged at £10 per person. On the two longer routes, the price of a return crossing for a car and two people in a basic two-berth cabin will work out at between £235 (low season) and £390 (high season) with DFDS Seaways, although there's a discount of up to £30 per passenger for those under 26 or over 60, and, if there are more than two of you travelling together, the larger cabins and "all-in-a-car" offers can further reduce the price. The P&O North Sea Ferries routes will cost around £265 return from October to June and £325 from July to September, with reductions of up to £42 for each person under 26 or over 60; it also has an all-in one price

---

Ferry Operators

DFDS Seaways, Scandinavia House, Parkeston Quay, Harwich, Essex CO12 4QG ☎ 0990/333000; 15 Hanover St, London W1R 9HG ☎ 020/7409 6060; Tyne Commission Quay, North Shields, NE29 6EA ☎ 0191/296 0101; *www.dfdsseaways.com Newcastle to IJmuiden.*
Hoverspeed, ☎ 08705/240241, *www. hoverspeed.co.uk Dover to Oostende and Calais.*
P&O North Sea Ferries, King George Dock, Hedon Rd, Kingston-upon-Hull HU9 5QA ☎ 01482/377177, *www.ponsf.com*

Hull to Rotterdam and Zeebrugge.
P&O Stena Line, Channel House, Channel View Road, Dover CT17 9TJ ☎ 08706/000611, *www.posl.com Dover to Calais.*
Seafrance, Eastern Docks, Dover, Kent CT16 1JA ☎ 08705/711711, *www.seafrance.com Dover to Calais.*
Stena Line, Charter House, Park St, Ashford, Kent TN24 8EX ☎ 0990/707070, *www. stenaline.co.uk Harwich to Hook of Holland.*

---

that includes the cost of the car and up to four people. If you're looking for a short break, all three companies offer 5-day/night deals that bring down the cost of the crossing again.

If you want to spend less time on the sea, **Hoverspeed** "fly" from Dover to Oostende in Belgium. Otherwise there are countless Channel crossings to France, but you'll need to consider the additional time and cost involved in making your way north. If you're planning to take your bike, Stena Line charge just £5, while DFDS Seaways and P&O North Sea Ferries make no charge at all. For more on cycles and cycling see p.51.

Inclusive holidays

Don't dismiss the idea of going on a **package holiday**; most consist of no more than travel and accommodation (from two nights to two weeks or more) and can work out an easy way of cutting costs and hassle. Short breaks to Amsterdam on Eurostar giving two nights' accommodation with breakfast in a two-star hotel start at around £170 per person. The same package with return flights from a London airport works out around the same, with supplements of £10–50 for a flight from a regional airport. Operators can also arrange accommodation plus ferry tickets if you want to design your own self-drive package (both P&O North Sea Ferries and DFDS Seaways – see above – offer inclusive short breaks). **Day-trips** to Amsterdam, available through the Amsterdam Travel Service, cost between £120 and £185. The price includes a return flight and the trains between Schiphol and the city.

Selected Tour Operators

Amsterdam Travel Service, Bridge House, 55–59 High Rd, Broxbourne, Herts EN10 7DT ☎ 01992/456056, *www.bridge-travel.co.uk The largest collection of Amsterdam holidays, and a variety of short breaks, including cycling breaks.*
Cresta Holidays, Tabley Court, Victoria Street, Altrincham, Cheshire WA14 1EZ ☎ 0161/927 7000.
Popular short-break specialists with a broad

range of Amsterdam packages.
Inntravel, Hovingham, York YO62 4JZ ☎ 01653/628811, *www.inntravel.co.uk Classy short breaks, by air, rail or car.*
Stena Line Holidays, Charter House, Park Street, Ashford, Kent TN24 8EX ☎ 0990/747474, *www.stenaline.co.uk A reasonable selection of Amsterdam package holidays, along with eight other Dutch city destinations.*

Getting There from Ireland

Taking into account the time and inconvenience of crossing the UK and then the Channel, travelling by air is by far the simplest way to reach Amsterdam from Ireland. Unless you're on the tightest of budgets, the extra money spent on a flight is well worth it given the savings in time and hassle.

By Air

Aer Lingus flies direct from **Dublin** to Amsterdam, with around five flights daily, and connections from Cork, Galway, Kerry, Shannon and Sligo. Ordinary scheduled **Apex** fares can work out at about IR£200 from Dublin, a little more from regional airports. There are no direct flights from **Belfast**, but British Midland operate around three flights daily via London Heathrow, from around £160 plus tax.

Other flight options also involve **transfers** in the UK, which almost always mean switching carriers for the second leg of your journey. However flying with Ryanair to London Stansted, then with KLM uk to Amsterdam, can work out cheaper than a direct Aer Lingus flight. UsitNOW, or any of the discount agents listed in the box on p.10 can advise you on the best deals to be had.

By Train

The train journey between Dublin and Amsterdam is a real endurance test. There are three daily departures, taking between seventeen and 24 hours. The favoured route is Dublin to Holyhead on the ferry; then a train from Holyhead to London Euston (changing at Crewe or Birmingham). From London Euston, you must

---

AIRLINES

Aer Lingus, 40/41 Upper O'Connell St, Dublin 1 ☎01/705 3333; 46/48 Castle St, Belfast BT1 1HB ☎0845/9737747; 2 Academy St, Cork ☎021/327 155; 136 O'Connell Street, Limerick ☎061/474 239; *www.aerlingus.ie*
Direct flights from Dublin to Amsterdam, code-sharing with KLM uk, plus flights via Dublin from Cork, Shannon, Gaway, Sligo and Kerry.

British Midland, Nutley, Merrion Rd, Dublin 4

☎01/283 8833; Suite 2, Fountain Centre, College St, Belfast 1 ☎0870/6070555; *www.britishmidland.com*
Belfast and Dublin to Amsterdam via London Heathrow and East Midlands.

Ryanair, Phoenix House, Conyngham Rd, Dublin ☎01/609 7800, *www.ryanair.ie*
From Dublin, Cork, Knock and Kerry to London Stansted.

BUS COMPANY

Bus Éireann, Busáras, Store St, Dublin 1 ☎01/830 2222, *www.buseireann.ie*

Irish Eurolines agents.

FERRY COMPANIES

DFDS Seaways, c/o Stena Line, Ferry Terminal, Dún Laoghaire ☎01/204 7777; c/o SeaCat, SeaCat Terminal, Donegal Quay, Belfast BT1 3AL ☎0128/9031 4918.
Dún Laoghaire to Holyhead, Rosslare to Fishguard, and Belfast to Stranraer.

Irish Ferries, 2–4 Merrion Row, Dublin 2 ☎01/638 3333 or ☎01/661 0715; St Patrick's Buildings, Cork ☎021/551995; *www.irishferries.ie*
Rosslare to Roscoff and Cherbourg, or Dublin to Holyhead.

TRAIN COMPANY

Iarnród Éireann, Connolly Station, Amiens St, Dublin 1 ☎1-850/366222, *www.irishrail.ie*

National rail company.

---

make your own way across the city to Waterloo station to catch the **Eurostar** train through to Brussels, with another connecting train to Amsterdam. The cost of the ticket, available from Iamród Éireann and inclusive of the ferry, is a little less than the IR£200 cost of an Interrail pass.

There's a great variety of **InterRail passes** on offer, but bear in mind that to travel from Ireland you must buy a pass for two zones in order to cover travel across the UK. For under-26s resident in Ireland who buy the pass before they leave, an InterRail giving a month's unlimited travel throughout Zone A (UK) and Zone E (France, Belgium, Luxembourg and the Netherlands) costs around IR£200; this also gives reductions on the ferries. Those **over 26** buy a two-zone InterRail pass for IR£275, but it cannot be used in Belgium or France, which means that the only way of getting there from the UK is by taking a ferry route directly into Holland.

Another possibility is a **Euro Domino pass** (see p.6), to cover train travel within the Netherlands only – holders are entitled to reductions on ferries to and from, as well as train journeys across, the UK.

By Bus

The **bus** journey from Dublin to Amsterdam takes around 25 hours, but it's cheap enough to appeal to those watching every punt. The best way to reach Amsterdam by bus is to use the twice-daily **Eurolines** service. Starting at Dublin's Busáras, the route will take you across the Irish

Sea by ferry to Holyhead, the Eurotunnel via London, Antwerp, Rotterdam and The Hague, before reaching Amsterdam. From Dublin, a standard adult return costs IR£83 (IR£99 high season), with an under-26 ticket at IR£77 (IR£94); prices from elsewhere in Ireland are fixed at IR£103 (IR£119) for an adult, IR£94 (IR£108) if you're under 26. Alternatively, you could try the Busabout service, which provides a series of bus routes intended to link major European cities – the bus equivalent of the Interrail and Euro Domino passes. Bookings can be made through UsitNOW.

By Ferry

There are no ferries direct from Ireland to either Belgium or the Netherlands – the nearest ferries get is the northwest of France. However, Irish Ferries will arrange your travel via the UK, if you want to travel from Dublin to Holyhead, then head across land to Hull, to pick up the P&O North Sea Ferries route to Rotterdam or Zeebrugge. Obviously, any such routing is both time-consuming and comparatively expensive.

Inclusive holidays

Package holidays – which can simply mean flights plus accommodation – are a feasible and sensible method of eliminating snags, and can easily cut costs as well. Both KLM uk and Aer Lingus offer several different "weekend break" packages to suit various budgets and styles; trav-

---

Travel Agents

Aran Travel, Granary Hall, 58 Dominick St, Galway ☎091/562595, *arantvl@iol.ie*
General budget fares agent.
Dial-a-Flight Ireland, 11/12 Warrington Place, Dublin 2 ☎01/662 9933.
Good for cheap flights.
Joe Walsh Tours, 8–11 Baggot St, Dublin 2 ☎01/676 3053; 117 St Patrick St, Cork ☎021/277 959.
General budget fares and holiday package agent.
Thomas Cook, 11 Donegal Place, Belfast BT1 5AJ ☎028/9024 0833; 118 Grafton St, Dublin ☎01/677 1360; *www.thomascook.com*
Package holiday and flight agent, with occasional discount offers.

Twohigs Travel, 8 Burgh Quay, Dublin ☎01/677 2666; 13 Duke Street, Dublin ☎01/670 9750.
Reliable travel agent.
UsitNOW, O'Connell Bridge, 19–21 Aston Quay, Dublin 2 ☎01/602 1600; Fountain Centre, Belfast BT1 6ET ☎028/9032 4073; 66 Oliver Plunkett St, Cork ☎021/270900; 33 Ferryquay St, Derry ☎028/7137 1888; Victoria Place, Eyre Sq, Galway ☎091/565177; Central Buildings, O'Connell St, Limerick ☎061/415064; 36–37 Georges St, Waterford ☎051/872601; *www.usitnow.com*
Ireland's main student and youth travel specialists.

el agents should have the relevant brochures, or you can call the airlines direct for information.

Many travel agents can also give deals on city breaks in Amsterdam (see box opposite).

Getting There from the USA and Canada

Amsterdam's Schiphol airport is among the most popular and least expensive gateways to Europe from North America, and getting a convenient and good-value flight is rarely a problem. Virtually every region of the United States and Canada is well served by the major airlines, though only two scheduled carriers offer nonstop flights – KLM/Northwest Airlines and Delta. The rest fly via London and other European centres. Look out, too, for deals offered by the Dutch charter company Martinair, which offers mid-priced seats on nonstop flights from a number of cities in the USA and Canada.

Shopping for tickets

Barring special offers, the cheapest fare is usually an **Apex** ticket, although this will carry certain restrictions: you have to book – and pay – at least fourteen days in advance (more often 21 days), spend at least seven days abroad (maxi-

mum stay three months), and you tend to get penalized if you change your schedule. On transatlantic routes, there are also winter **Super Apex** tickets, sometimes known as "Eurosavers" – slightly cheaper than an ordinary Apex, but limiting your stay to between seven and 21 days. Some airlines also issue **Special Apex** tickets to people younger than 24, often extending the maximum stay to a year. Many airlines offer youth or student fares to **under-25s**; a passport or driver's licence is sufficient proof of age, though these tickets are subject to availability and can have eccentric booking conditions. It's worth remembering that most cheap return fares will only give a percentage refund if you need to cancel or alter your journey, so make sure you check the restrictions carefully before buying.

You can normally cut costs further by going through a **specialist flight agent** – either a **consolidator**, who buys up blocks of tickets from the airlines and sells them at a discount, or a **discount agent**, who wheels and deals in tickets offloaded by the airlines, and often offers special student and youth fares and a range of other travel-related services, such as travel insurance, car rental and tours. Bear in mind, though, that the penalties for changing your plans can be stiff. Remember too that these companies make their money by dealing in bulk, so don't expect them to answer lots of questions. Some agents specialize in **charter flights**, which may be cheaper than any scheduled flight available, but again departure dates are fixed and withdrawal penalties are high (check the refund policy). If you travel a lot, **discount travel clubs** are another option – the annual membership fee may be worth it for benefits such as cut-price air tickets and car rental.

A further possibility is to see if you can arrange a **courier flight**, although the hit-and-miss nature of these makes them most suitable for the single traveller who travels light and has a very flexible schedule. In return for shepherding a package through customs and possibly giving up your baggage allowance, you can expect to get a heavily discounted ticket. See opposite or, for more options, consult *A Simple Guide to Courier Travel* (Pacific Data Sales Publishing).

Regardless of where you buy your ticket, the fare will depend on the **season**. Fares are highest in December, June, July and August, and fares during these months can cost between $100 and $300 more, depending on the airline. Flying on weekends can add $100 to the cost of a return ticket; prices quoted below assume midweek travel. In addition, any Apex fares quoted entail a maximum stay of thirty days.

Flights from the USA

KLM and Northwest Airlines, which operate a joint service from the United States and Canada to Amsterdam, offer the widest range of flights, with nonstop or direct services from eleven US cities on KLM and connections from dozens more via Northwest. Their Apex fares are usually identical to those offered by other carriers, so for convenience at least, KLM/Northwest is your best bet. It's also worth looking into deals offered by the Dutch carrier, **Martinair**, which flies regularly scheduled nonstop flights from five US cities –

though note that three of them are served in summer only.

One-way fares are rarely good value, but if you're set on one, the best source is the seat consolidators that advertise in the back pages of the travel sections of the major Sunday newspapers – or see the box on p.14.

Travelling from the **East Coast**, KLM's nonstop flights out of New York JFK start at around $400 in low season, rising by around $150 in May and peaking at around $780 in July and August. Nonstop fares out of Washington DC, Atlanta, Detroit, Chicago and Minneapolis typically cost $50–100 more; connecting flights from other major cities are usually thrown in for free. Delta has similar fares on its nonstop flights out of New York and Atlanta, as does United from Washington DC, and most carriers match these prices on their flights via London Heathrow. Especially during winter, many airlines have special offers that can reduce fares to well under $500 return, and discount travel agents and consolidators can often find you fares as low as $350 (low season) or $650 (high season). Martinair also offers good deals in the summer out of Newark, with fares as low as $640 at the height of the peak season, and a year-round service from Miami (six days a week) and Orlando (four days per week) with similarly low prices.

As for the **West Coast**, KLM/Northwest Airlines' round-trip Apex fares on nonstop flights out of Los Angeles start at around $570 in low season, rising to $700 in May and $1200 in July and August. Consolidators can probably get you a seat for less than $550 (low season) or $750 (high season). Fares from San Francisco or Seattle usually cost $50–100 more and most international carriers charge similar prices. Special offers sometimes bring the fares down to under $500, though these are usually only available during winter.

Martinair's service from the west coast is now limited to flights from Los Angeles (three weekly) and Oakland (two weekly), and is only available between April and October, but if you are willing to work within these restrictions, the reward is low fares – with flights from either LA or Oakland to Amsterdam for as little as $538 (April to mid-June). Even their peak fare (mid-June to August) is low at $768.

Round-the-World tickets and courier flights

If you plan to visit Holland as part of a major world trip, then you might want to think about getting a **round-the-world ticket** that includes the city as one of its stops. A sample route from the West Coast, using a combination of airlines, might be Los Angeles–Hong Kong–Bangkok–Amman–Cairo–Amsterdam–New York–Los Angeles, which costs $1677. A ticket covering the same route from the East Coast (New York) costs $1536. See the box on p.14 for details of agents specializing in round-the-world tickets.

Return **courier flights** to Amsterdam from major US cities are available for around $200–250, with last-minute specials, booked within three days of departure, going for as little as $100. For more information about courier flights, contact The Air Courier Association or Now Voyager (see box on p.14).

Flights from Canada

KLM/Northwest Airlines has the best range of routes from Canada, with nonstop flights from all the major airports, and fares approximately the same as those from the USA. Return tickets out of **Toronto** start at around CDN$708 in the low season, stepping up to CDN$1000 in May and CDN$1300 in July and August. Fares from **Vancouver** start at around CDN$900, climbing to CDN$1400 and CDN$1700.

Canadian **charter** operations, such as Air Transat and Fiesta West/Canada 3000 offer some of the best deals on spring through fall travel,

with fares as low as CDN$659 from Toronto and CDN$819 from Vancouver and Calgary. Neither Air Canada nor Canadian Airlines serves Amsterdam, though Martinair flies nonstop charters out of Toronto, Vancouver, Calgary and Edmonton (April–Oct): low-season fares from Toronto start at CDN$620, rising to CDN$820 in high season.

Canadian departures for **round-the-world** tickets can usually be arranged for around CDN$150 more than the US fare (see above).

Travelling via Europe

Even though many flights from North America to Holland are routed via London, because of the various special fares it's often cheaper to stay on the plane all the way to Amsterdam. In general you can't stop over and continue on a later flight, as US and Canadian airlines are not allowed to provide services between European cities.

However, if you want to combine a trip with visits to other European cities, **London** makes the best starting point, as onward flights are relatively inexpensive. Besides having the best range of good-value transatlantic flights (New York to London is the busiest and cheapest route), London also has excellent connections on to Amsterdam. **Paris**, too, is becoming a popular gateway to Europe. United and American Airlines, as well as British Airways and the British carrier Virgin Atlantic, all have frequent flights to London from various parts of the US, BA flying from Canada too; Air France, United and American fly daily to Paris. See "Getting there from Britain", p.3, for details on travel from Britain to Amsterdam and other Dutch cities.

Rail passes

If you intend Amsterdam to form just part of your European travels, or envisage using the European rail network extensively, then you should consider investing in a **Eurail train pass**. These are good for unlimited travel within seventeen European countries, including Holland, and they should be purchased before you leave, as they cost ten percent more in Europe: you can get them from most travel agents in the USA and Canada or from Rail Europe (US: ☎1-800/438-7245; Canada ☎1-800/361-7245; *www.raileurope.com*), who can also supply you with up-to-date information and fares). The **standard** Eurail pass is valid for unlimited first-class travel on consecutive days for periods of fifteen days

Discount Flight Agents, Travel Clubs and Consolidators

Air Brokers International, 323 Geary St, Suite 411, San Francisco, CA 94102 ☎1-800/883-3273, *www.airbrokers.com*
Consolidator and specialist in round-the-world tickets.

Air Courier Association, 15000 W. 6th Ave, Suite 203, Golden, CO 80401 (☎1-800/282-1202 or 303/279-3600), *www.aircourier.org*
Courier flight broker – $25 membership plus $39 annual fee.

Airhitch, 2641 Broadway, New York, NY 10025 (☎1-800/326-2009 or 212/864-2000), *www.airhitch.org*
Standby-seat broker. For a set price, they guarantee to get you on a flight as close to your preferred destination as possible, within a week.

Council Travel, 205 E 42nd St, New York, NY 10017 ☎1-800/226-8624, *www.counciltravel.com*
Agent specializing in student/budget fares, with branches in forty US cities.

Encore Short Notice, 4501 Forbes Blvd, Lanham, MD 20706 ☎1-800/444-9800, *www.emitravel.com*
East Coast travel club – $69 membership fee.

Flight Centre, 3030 S Granville St, Vancouver, BC V6H 3J9 ☎604/739-9539
Discount air fares from Canadian cities.

High Adventure Travel Inc., 442 Post St., Suite 400, San Francisco, CA 94102 ☎1-800/350-0612, *www.airtreks.com*
Round-the-world tickets.

Interworld Travel, 3400 Coral Way, Miami FL 33145 ☎1-800/468-3796 or 305/443-4929, *www.interworld.com*
Southeastern US consolidator.

Last-Minute Travel Club, 132 Brookline Ave, Boston, MA 02215 ☎617/267-9800 or 1-800/LAST-MIN.
Package tour specialist.

Nouvelles Frontières US: 12 E 33rd St, New York NY 10016 ☎1-800/366-6387 or 212/779-0600; Canada: 1000 Sherbrook East, Suite 720, Montréal, H2L 1L3 ☎514/871-3060, *www.new-frontiers.com*
Main US and Canadian branches of the French discount travel outfit. Other branches in LA, San Francisco and Québec City.

Now Voyager, 74 Varick St, Suite 307, New York NY 10013 ☎212/431-1616, *www.nowvoyagertravel.com*
Courier flight broker and consolidator.

Overseas Tours, 199 California Drive, 188 Millbrae, CA ☎1-800/323-8777, *www.overseastours.com*
Discount agent.

Pan Express Travel, 65 Wellesely St East, Suite 401, Toronto M4Y 1H6 ☎416/964-6888.
Discount travel agent.

Rebel Tours, 25050 Avenue Kearny, Suite 215, Valencia, CA 91355 ☎1-800/227-3235 or 661/294-0900, *www.rebeltours.com*
Good source of deals with Martinair.

STA Travel, 10 Downing St, New York, NY 10014 ☎1-800/777-0112 or 212/627-3111, *www.sta-travel.com*
Worldwide discount firm specializing in student/youth fares, student IDs, travel insurance, car rental and rail passes. Other branches in the Los Angeles, San Francisco, Minneapolis, Chicago, Philadelphia and Boston areas.

TFI Tours, 34 W 32nd St, 12th Floor, New York, NY 10001 ☎1-800/745-8000 or 212/736-1140.
Consolidator with the very best East Coast deals, especially if you only want to fly one-way.

Travac, 989 6th Ave, 16th Floor, New York NY 10018 ☎1-800/872-8800, fax 1-888-872-8327, *www.thetravelsite.com*
Consolidator and charter broker. They will fax current fares from their fax line.

Travel CUTS, 187 College St, Toronto ON M5T 1P7 ☎416/979-2406, *www.travelcuts.com*
Main office of the Canadian student travel organization. Many other offices nationwide.

Travelers Advantage, 3033 S Parker Rd, Suite 1000, Aurora, CO 80014 ☎1-800/548-1116, *www.travelersadvantage.com*
Reliable discount travel club; annual membership of $59.95 required.

Travel Avenue, 10 S Riverside Plaza, Suite 1404, Chicago, IL 60606 ☎1-800/333-3335 or 312/876-6866, *www.tipc.com*
Discount travel agent.

Travelocity *www.travelocity.com*
Online consolidator.

Unitravel, 11737 Administration Dr, Suite 120, St Louis ☎1-800/325-2222, *www.flightsforless.com*
Reliable consolidator.

($554), 21 days ($718), one month ($890), two months ($1260), or three months ($1558). If you're **under 26** the Eurail Youthpass allows second-class rail travel, the prices for which, respectively, are $388, $499, $623, $882 or $1089. There's also the Eurail **Flexipass**, which may be a better buy, as it allows for a certain number of non-consecutive days travel within a two-month period, and also comes in first-class/under-26 versions: ten days costs $654/$458, and fifteen days, $862/$599. Parties of between two and five can save fifteen percent with the Eurail **Saver Flexipass**, allowing for travel within a two-month period on ten days ($556) or fifteen days ($732).

If you intend to move about within the Netherlands only there's also a **Holland Railpass** which might be worth purchasing. It can be purchased in 1st/2nd-class forms, with travel on any three days in a month costing $98/$65; and five days $147/$98. The discount offered for two adults travelling together brings the price for three days, each, down to $73/$49; and five days down to $110/$73 each. The under-26 version of this pass costs $52 for three days and $79 for five days. If you're planning to cross over into Holland's immediate neighbours as well, you might want to consider the **Benelux Tourrail Pass** (for unlimited travel in Belgium, the

Specialist Tour Operators

Abercrombie & Kent ☎1-800/323-7308, www.abercrombiekent.com
Six-night river and canal cruising tours from Amsterdam to Bruges starting at $1100. Airfare extra.

AESU Travel ☎1-800/638-7640, www.aesu.com
Tours, independent city stays, discounted air fares. 37-day "Grand Europe" tour includes one day in Amsterdam (with biking and a visit to a diamond-cutting factory) and a stop in Brussels; $3300 plus airfare.

Air Transat Holidays ☎604/688-3350.
Canadian charter company offering discount fares from major Canadian cities, tours and fly-drive trips. Contact travel agents for brochures.

American Airlines Vacations ☎1-800/321-2121, www.aavacations.com
Package tours and fly-drive programmes.

British Airways Holidays ☎1-800/359-8722, www.british-airways.com/vacations
Package tours and fly-drives.

Canada 3000/FiestaWest
Discount charter flights, car rental, accommodation and package tours. Book through travel agents or by calling BCAA TeleCentre in Canada: ☎1-800/663-1956.

CBT Bicycle Tours ☎1-800/736-BIKE, www.biketrip.net
Affordable tours in Holland, Belgium and Luxembourg. Two-week Amsterdam to Brussels trip, with one week in each country, starts at $2395. A one week tour through

Holland during the tulip season (May) costs $1565. Airfare extra. Available through travel agents.

Contiki Tours ☎1-800/CONTIKI, www.contiki.com
Budget tours to Europe for those aged 18 to 35, including a large number of multi-country tours with stops in Holland. A twenty-day tour of eleven countries, including two days in Amsterdam, starting in London, costs $1390.

Euro Bike Tours ☎1-800/321-6060, www.eurobike.com
Upscale cycling tours: fourteen days in Holland, Belgium, Luxembourg and Germany starts at $3095; and eight days in Holland, including Amsterdam, for $1995. Airfare extra.

Europe Through the Back Door ☎425/771-8303, www.ricksteves.com
Small-group travel off the beaten track, with an enthusiastic guide team. 21-day "Best of Europe" Tour, including stops in Amsterdam and Haarlem, costs $2700.

Kemwel's Premier Selections ☎1-800/234-4000, www.premierselections.com
Rail journeys and barge cruises – also a discount auto rental agency.

KLM/Northwest World Vacations ☎1-800/447-4747, www.nwa.com
Hotel and sightseeing packages and escorted tours.

United Vacations ☎1-800/538-2929, www.ual.com
Flight and hotel packages.

Netherlands and Luxembourg), which can be purchased in similar variations, with travel on any five days in a month going for $217/$155, the discounted ticket for two adults costing $163/$116.50 and for under-26s $104.

Inclusive tours

There are any number of **packages and organized tours** from North America to Amsterdam and elsewhere in Holland. Prices vary, with some operators including the air fare, while others cover just accommodation, sightseeing, and activities such as cycling or hiking. In addition, many airlines offer fly-drive deals that include a week's hotel accommodation, but again the prices vary according to season and can even change daily.

You'll find that most European tours include Amsterdam on their itineraries, too. Among the best of the Europe-wide operators are Europe Through the Back Door, a specialist in independent budget travel, with an emphasis on simple accommodation and meeting local people.

Getting There from Australia and New Zealand

There is no shortage of flights to Amsterdam from Australia and New Zealand, though all of them involve at least one stop. When buying a ticket, as well as the price, you might want to take into account the airline's route – whether, for example, you'd rather stop in Moscow or Bali. Some of the airlines allow free stopovers (see the box opposite).

Air fares to Amsterdam vary significantly with the season: low season runs from mid-January to the end of February and during October and November; high season runs from mid-May to the end of August and December to mid-January; the rest of the year is counted as shoulder season. Tickets purchased direct from the airlines tend to be expensive, with published fares ranging from A$2000/NZ$2500 (low season) to A$2500–3000/NZ$3000–3600 (high season).

Travel agents offer better deals on fares to Amsterdam and have the latest information on special deals, such as free stopovers en route and fly-drive-accommodation packages. Flight Centres and STA generally offer the best discounts, especially for students and those under 26. For a **discounted ticket** from Sydney, Melbourne or Auckland, expect to pay A$1600–2500/NZ$2000–2700. Fares from Perth and Darwin are slightly cheaper via Asia, rather more expensive via Canada and the US, and fares from Christchurch and Wellington are around NZ$150–300 more than those from Auckland.

If you want to combine Amsterdam with a stay in another European city, the lowest fares are with Britannia to London, during its limited charter season (Nov–March), when you can expect to pay A$1000–1600/NZ$1200–1900; from London you could pick up a cheap flight to Amsterdam or consider going overland (see "Getting There from Britain", p.3). For a scheduled flight, including any connections, count on paying A$1500–2260/NZ$1900–2800 on Alitalia or KLM; A$1900–2500/NZ$2280–3000 on SAS, Thai Airways and Lufthansa; A$2400–2850/NZ$2700–3400 on British

Airlines

Aeroflot, 44 Market St, Sydney ☎02/9262 2233. *Four flights a week to Amsterdam from Sydney via Moscow. There is a code-sharing arrangement with Qantas to either Bangkok or Singapore for the first leg.*

Air New Zealand Australia: 90 Arthur St, North Sydney ☎13/2476; NZ: Customs/Albert St Auckland ☎0800/737000); *www.airnz.co.nz Daily flights to London or Frankfurt via LA, from where you can get a connecting flight.*

Alitalia Australia: 118 Albert St, Milsons Point, Sydney ☎1300/653757; NZ: 229 Queen St, Auckland ☎09/379 4457; *www.alitalia.it Six flights a week from Sydney, with Ansett connections from the other major cities, direct to Amsterdam (code-sharing with KLM) or via Milan.*

Britannia Airways Australia: c/o UK Flight Shop, 7 Macquarie Place, Sydney ☎02/9247 4833; *www.ukflightshop.com.au*; NZ: c/o World Aviation, Trustbank Building, 229 Queen St, Auckland ☎09/308 3355. *Charter flights to London from Sydney and Auckland via Indonesia and Abu Dhabi (both stops for refuelling only).*

British Airways Australia: Level 4, 50 Franklin St, Melbourne ☎03/9603 1133; 70 Hunter St, Sydney ☎02/8904 8800; *www.british-airways. com.au*. NZ: 154 Queen St, Auckland ☎09/356 8690; *www.british-airways.com.nz Daily to London from Sydney, Perth or Brisbane with onward connections to Amsterdam.*

Cathay Pacific Australia: 8 Spring St, Sydney ☎13/1747; NZ: Floor 11, 205 Queen St, Auckland ☎09/379 0861. *Several flights a week from major Australasian cities via Hong Kong. Code-sharing with Qantas for the Australia–Hong Kong leg of the journey.*

Garuda Indonesia Australia: 55 Hunter St, Sydney ☎1300/365330; NZ: Westpac Trust Tower, 120 Albert St, Auckland ☎09/366 1862. *Three flights a week to Amsterdam from Bali and Jakarta, both of which are connected to major Australian and New Zealand cities by regular flights.*

KLM Australia: Nauru House, 80 Collins St, Melbourne ☎03/9654 5222, toll-free ☎1800/500 747; 5 Elizabeth St, Sydney ☎02/9231 6333, toll-free ☎1800/500747; *www.klm.com.au*. NZ: 369 Queen St, Auckland ☎09/309 1782. *Six times a week from Sydney to Amsterdam, with Ansett connections from other major*

Australasian cities. There may be some code-sharing with Alitalia.

Lauda Air, Level 7, 84 William St, Melbourne ☎03/9600 4000, toll-free ☎1800/642438; Level 11, 143 Macquarie St, Sydney ☎02/9251 6155, toll-free ☎1800/642438; *www.laudaair.com Four departures a week from Sydney and three from Melbourne, both via Vienna to Amsterdam.*

Lufthansa Australia: 143 Maxquarie St Sydney ☎1300/655727; NZ: 36 Kitchener St, Auckland ☎0800/945220 (toll-free); *www.lufthansa.com Daily flights from major cities via Bangkok or Singapore and Frankfurt. Code-share with Thai or Singapore Airlines for the first leg.*

Malaysia Airlines Australia: 16 Spring St, Sydney ☎13/2627; NZ: 12th Floor, 12–26 Swanson St, Auckland ☎09/373 2741, toll-free ☎0800/777747. *Daily flights to Amsterdam from major Australian cities and five flights a week from Auckland with a transfer or stopover in Kuala Lumpur.*

Olympic Airways, 37 Pitt St, Sydney (☎02/9251 2044, toll-free ☎1800/221663). *Three flights a week to Amsterdam from Sydney and Melbourne, with a transfer or stopover in Athens.*

Qantas Australia: 70 Hunter St, Sydney ☎13/1313; *www.qantas.com.au*. NZ: 154 Queen St, Auckland (☎09/357 8900, toll-free ☎0800/808767). *Daily from major cities with code-sharing arrangements via Asian gateway cities, or European cities with connections to Amsterdam.*

SAS, Level 15, 31 Market St, Sydney ☎02/9299 9800; *www.flysas.com No flights from Australia or New Zealand, but can organize connections through other airlines to Amsterdam via Bangkok, Beijing, Singapore or Tokyo and Copenhagen.*

Singapore Airlines Australia: 17 Bridge St, Sydney ☎13/1011; West Plaza Building, Fanshawe/Albert St, Auckland ☎09/303 2129, toll-free ☎0800/808909; *www.singaporeair.com Daily flights to Amsterdam via Singapore from most major Australasian cities.*

Thai Airways Australia: 75 Pitt St, Sydney ☎1300/651960; NZ: 22 Fanshawe St Auckland ☎09/377 3886; *www.thaiairways.com Daily flights to Amsterdam from Sydney and Auckland via Bangkok.*

Airways, Qantas, Singapore Airlines, Air New Zealand and Canadian Airways depending on the season. See the box on p.17 for a full run-down of airlines and routes.

Round-the-world tickets

For extended trips, **round-the-world tickets**, valid up to a year, can be good value. These are mileage-based tickets used with a combination of airlines – which airlines you use depends to a degree on your route, but al`so on seat availability. The cheapest tickets usually involve three to four stopovers, with prices rising the further you travel or the more stops you add – you can back-track as much as you like within the mileage of the ticket. RTW tickets can be booked through any of the partner airlines, or through travel agents, who may have cheaper deals. Those that take in Amsterdam include the "Star Alliance"

(Ansett, Air Canada, Air New Zealand, Lufthansa, SAS, Thai and United Airlines) which starts at A$2800/NZ$3350, and the One World Alliance "Global Explorer" (American, British Airways, Canadian, Cathay, Finnair, Iberia and Qantas) which starts at A$2400–2900/NZ$2900–3400.

Rail passes

If you're planning to travel around the Netherlands or the rest of Europe by train, then it's best to get hold of a rail pass before you go. Eurail passes are available through most travel agents or specialist operators like CIT or Thomas Cook (see box), and there are various kinds.

The **Eurail Youthpass** for under-26s is available in 15-day, 21-day, one-month, two-month and three-month versions and varies in price from A$615/NZ$765 for the fifteen-day pass to A$1730/NZ$2135 for the three-month one; if

---

Discount Travel Agents

Anywhere Travel, 345 Anzac Parade, Kingsford, Sydney ☎02/9663 0411, *anywhere@ozemail.com.au*

Budget Travel, 16 Fort St, Auckland ☎09/366 0061; other branches around the city ☎0800/808040 (toll-free), *www.budgettravel.co.nz*

CIT, 422 Collins St, Melbourne ☎03/9650 5510; 263 Clarence St, Sydney ☎02/9267 1255; also Brisbane, Adelaide and Perth.

Destinations Unlimited, 3 Milford Rd, Milford, Auckland ☎09/373 4033.

European Travel Office (ETO), 122 Rosslyn St, West Melbourne ☎03/9329 8844; 20th Floor, 133 Castlereagh St, Sydney ☎02/9267 7727.

Flight Centre Australia: branches nationwide; phone ☎13/1600 (24hr) for your nearest office. NZ: National Bank Towers, 205–225 Queen St, Auckland ☎0800/354 448 9 (toll-free), plus branches nationwide; *www.flightcentre.com*

Harvey World Travel, 631 Princes Highway, Kogarah, Sydney ☎02/9567 6099 or ☎13/2757, plus branches nationwide; *www.harveyworld.com.au*

Northern Gateway, 22 Cavenagh St, Darwin ☎08/8941 1394.

Passport Travel Suite 11, 401 St Kilda Rd, Melbourne ☎03/9867 3888, toll-free ☎1800/337031, *www.travelcentre.com.au*

STA Travel Australia: nationwide ☎1300/360960; 256 Flinders St, Melbourne ☎03/9654 7266; 855 George St, Sydney ☎02/9212 1255; toll-free 1800/637444, plus other offices in state capitals and major universities; *www.statravelaus.com.au*. NZ:

Travellers' Centre, 10 High St, Auckland ☎09/309 0458; 90 Cashel St, Christchurch ☎03/379 9098; 130 Cuba St, Wellington ☎04/385 0561, plus offices in Dunedin, Palmerston North, Hamilton and major universities; *www.statravel.co.nz*

Thomas Cook Australia: 257 Collins St, Melbourne ☎03/9282 0222 or ☎13/1771; 175 Pitt St, Sydney ☎02/9231 2877, toll-free ☎1800/801002; branches in other state capitals. NZ: 159 Queen St, Auckland ☎09/379 3924, toll-free ☎0800/353535; plus other branches.

Topdeck Travel, 65 Glenfell St, Adelaide ☎08/8232 7222.

Trailfinders, 8 Spring St, Sydney ☎02/9247 7666, *www.trailfinders.com.au*

Travel.com, 80 Clarence St, Sydney ☎02/9290 1500, *www.travel.com.au*

Tymtro Travel, 428 George St, Sydney ☎02/9223 2211.

UTAG Travel, 122 Walker St, North Sydney ☎02/9956 8399 or ☎13/1398, plus offices nationwide; *www.utag.com.au*

Specialist Operators

Adventure World Australia: 73 Walker St, North Sydney ☎02/9956 7766, toll-free ☎1800/221931, plus branches in Adelaide, Brisbane, Melbourne and Perth; *www.adventureworld.com.au*. NZ: 101 Gt South Rd, Remuera, Auckland ☎09/524 5118, *www.adventureworld.co.nz*
Agents for a vast array of international adventure travel companies.

CIT, 422 Collins St, Melbourne ☎03/9650 5510; 263 Clarence St, Sydney ☎02/9267 1255, plus branches in Brisbane, Adelaide and Perth; *www.cittravel.com.au*
City tours and accommodation packages, and also handles Eurail passes.

Eurolynx, 20 Fort St, Auckland ☎09/379 9716.
National World Travel, Level 1, 1 Mclaren St North, Sydney ☎13/1435, *www.natworldtravel.com.au*

Travel Plan, 118 Edinburgh St, Castlecraig, Sydney ☎02/9438 1333, *www.travelplan.com.au*

YHA Travel Centre, 38 Stuart St, Adelaide ☎08/8231 5583; 154 Roma St, Brisbane ☎07/3236 1680; 191 Dryandra St, O'Connor, Canberra ☎02/6248 0177; 69a Mitchell St, Darwin ☎08/8981 2560; 28 Criterion St, Hobart ☎03/6234 9617; 83 Hardware Lane, Melbourne ☎03/9670 9611; 236 William St Northbridge, Perth ☎08/9227 5122; 422 Kent St, Sydney ☎02/9261 1111; *www.yha.com.au*
Budget accommodation throughout Europe for YHA members.

UsitBEYOND (formerly YHA Travel), Shortland St/Jean Batten Place, Auckland ☎09/379 4224, plus offices in Hamilton, Palmerston North, Wellington and Christchurch; *www.usitbeyond.co.nz*

you're **over 26** you have to buy a first-class pass, which has the same options and costs between A\$880/NZ\$1090 for fifteen days and A\$2475/NZ\$3055 for three months. A **Eurail Flexipass** is good for a certain number of travel days in a two-month period and also comes in youth/first-class versions: ten days cost A\$725/1040 (NZ\$900/1285); and fifteen days, A\$950/1370 (NZ\$1175/1700). A scaled-down version of the Flexipass, the **Europass** allows travel in France, Germany, Italy, Spain and

Switzerland for (youth/first-class) A\$370/550 (NZ\$460/675) for five days in two months, or up to A\$815/1155 (NZ\$1020/1435) for fifteen days in two months; you also have the option of adding adjacent "associate" countries. There are also "**saver**" versions of all three passes, which are first-class passes valid for between two and five people who must be travelling together on all journeys.

Once you get to the Netherlands, you can also buy a **Euro Domino** pass – see p.6.

Visas and Red Tape

Citizens of Britain, Ireland, Australia, New Zealand, Canada and the USA need only a valid passport to stay for three months in the Netherlands. On arrival, be sure to have enough money to convince officials you can support yourself. Poorer-looking visitors are often checked out, and if you come from outside the EU and can't flash a credit card, or a few travellers' cheques or notes, you may not be allowed in.

If you want to stay longer than three months, you need a *verblijfsvergunning* or residence permit from the Aliens' Police. Even for **EU citizens**, however, this is far from easy to obtain (impossible if you can't show means of support), and the bureaucracy involved is byzantine.

Non-EU nationals should always have their documents in order, but even so the chance of gaining legal resident's status in the Netherlands without pre-arranged work is extremely slim. To

Dutch Embassies and Consulates

Australia

Embassy: 120 Empire Circuit, Yarralumla, Canberra ACT 2600 ☎02/6273 3111, *nlgovcan@ozemail.com.au*; *Consulates-general*: 499 St Kilda Rd, Melbourne ☎03/9867 7933; 500 Oxford St, Bondi Junction, Sydney ☎02/9387 6644.

Canada

Suite 2020, 350 Albert St, Ottawa, On. K1R 1A4 ☎613/237 5030, *nlgovott@netcom.ca*

Ireland

160 Merrion Road, Dublin 4 ☎01/269 3444, *nethemb@indigo.ie*

New Zealand

Embassy: Investment House, Featherston/Ballance St, Wellington ☎04/471 6390, *nlgovwel@compuserve.com*; *Consulates*: 1st Floor, 57 Symonds St, Auckland ☎09/379 5399; 161–163 Kilmore St, Christchurch ☎03/366 9280.

UK

38 Hyde Park Gate, London SW7 5DP ☎0207/590 3200, *london@netherlands-embassy.org.uk*

USA

4200 Linnean Ave, NW Washington DC 20008 ☎202/244 5300, *www.netherlands-embassy.org*

---

work legally, non-EU nationals need a work permit (*werkvergunning*), and these are even harder to get than a residence permit. EU citizens take priority in the job market, the only exceptions being Australians and New Zealanders aged between 18 and 25, who are eligible to apply for year-long Working Holiday visas (which vary slightly between the two countries). The process of applying for residency and work permits is described in "Long-Term Stays", p.37, along with tips on finding jobs and rented accommodation.

Customs

Within the EU, **EU nationals** can take goods for personal consumption across international borders without incurring duty, as long as they've paid the local tax imposed at the place of purchase. However, **duty-free goods** as such no longer exist. Instead, shop owners at Amsterdam Schiphol airport have come up with a discount "See Buy Fly" scheme, in which the businesses pre-pay the duty (the only exceptions being alcohol and cigarettes, for which you pay local prices). Call ☎1-020/312 7447 or have a look at the airport's Web site, *www.schiphol.nl*, for further details.

For **non-EU nationals**, the following export/import limits apply: 200 cigarettes or 250g tobacco or 50 cigars; 1 litre spirits or 2 litres fortified wine or 2 litres sparkling wine; and 60cl perfume. Non-EU nationals who spend more than ƒ300 in one shop in one day, and then export the goods within 3 months of purchase, can reclaim the VAT (sales tax); shops displaying the "Tax Free for Tourists" logo will help with the formalities, or alternatively check out the Web site *www.globalrefund.com*.

Foreign Embassies in the Netherlands

Australia

Carnegielaan 4, 2517 KH The Hague ☎070/310 8200.

Britain

Embassy: Lange Voorhout 10, 2514 ED The Hague ☎070/427 0427; *Consulate-General*: Koningslaan 44, 1075 AE Amsterdam ☎020/676 4343.

Canada

Sophialaan 7, 2514 JP The Hague ☎070/361 1600, *hague@hague01.x400.gc.ca*

Ireland

Dr Kuyperstraat 9, 2514 BA The Hague ☎070/363 0993, *postbus@irish.embassy.demon.nl*

New Zealand

Carnegielaan 10, 2517 KH The Hague ☎070/365 8037.

USA

Embassy: Lange Voorhout 102, 2514 EJ The Hague ☎070/310 9209, *www.usemb.nl*; *Consulate-General*: Museumplein 19, 1071 DJ Amsterdam ☎575 5309.

Information and Maps

Information on Amsterdam is easy to get hold of, either via the Internet, from the Netherlands Board of Tourism or, after arrival, from any of the city's four tourist offices (see p.49).

Information

It's not essential, but before you leave for Amsterdam, you might consider contacting the **Netherlands Board of Tourism** (see box) as they issue (or sell) a number of glossy leaflets on the city in particular and the Netherlands in general. One of their most useful publications is their country-wide *Accommodation* guide, complete with hotel prices, addresses, phone numbers, email addresses and Internet sites, as well as photographs of the hotels and brief (if sometimes rather flattering) descriptions.

It's also well worth accessing the Internet prior to travelling. There are many **Web sites** providing tourist information about Amsterdam, several of which are excellent – accurate, up-to-date, with comprehensive and clearly presented information. We've given a selection of sites in the box on p.23, all of which have English-language options.

Maps

Our **maps** are adequate for most purposes, but if you need one on a larger scale, or with a street index, there is lots of choice. Most good bookshops sell Geocart's clear and easy-to-use *Amsterdam Tourist Special* (1:10,000), whilst the pick of several handily compact, spiral-bound street atlases is produced by Falk (Suburbs: 1:12,500; centre 1:7500). An even wider range of city maps is available in Amsterdam and prices are very reasonable: the Falk street atlas, for example, costs just ƒ12, and the Amsterdam tourist office also sells an easy-to-use map with an index for ƒ4 – see p.22 for map outlets in the city.

Netherlands Board of Tourism Offices

Britain
18 Buckingham Gate, London SW1E 6LB
☎ 0906/871 7777, *goholland.co.uk*

Canada
25 Adelaide St East, Suite 710, Toronto, Ont M5C 1Y2 ☎ 416/363-1577, fax 1470, *goholland.com*

USA
355 Lexington Ave, 21st floor, New York, NY 10017 ☎ 212/370-7360, *goholland.com*

There are no offices in Australia or New Zealand.

MAP OUTLETS

BRITAIN AND IRELAND

Blackwell's Map and Travel Shop, 53 Broad St, Oxford OX1 3BQ ☎01865/792792, *bookshop.blackwell.co.uk*

Daunt Books, 83 Marylebone High St, London W1M 3DE ☎020/7224 2295; 193 Haverstock Hill, London NW3 4QL ☎020/7794 4006.

Easons Bookshop, 40 O'Connell St, Dublin 1 ☎01/873 3811, *www.eason.ie*

Fred Hanna's Bookshop, 27–29 Nassau St, Dublin 2 ☎01/677 1255, *www.hannas.ie*

Heffers Map and Travel, 3rd Floor, in Heffers Stationery Department, 19 Sidney St, Cambridge, CB2 3HL ☎01223/568467, *www.heffers.co.uk*

Hodges Figgis Bookshop, 56–58 Dawson St, Dublin 2 ☎01/677 4754, *www.hodgesfiggis.ie*

James Thin Melven's Bookshop, 29 Union St, Inverness, IV1 1QA ☎01463/233500, *www.jthin.co.uk*

National Map Centre, 22–24 Caxton St, London SW1H 0QU ☎020/7222 2466, *www.mapsworld.com*

Newcastle Map Centre, 55 Grey St, Newcastle upon Tyne, NE1 6EF ☎0191/261 5622, *nmc@enterprise.net*

John Smith and Sons, 57–61 St Vincent St, Glasgow, G2 5TB ☎0141/221 7472, *www.johnsmith.co.uk*

Stanfords, 12–14 Long Acre, WC2E 9LP ☎020/7836 1321; within Campus Travel at 52 Grosvenor Gardens, London SW1W 0AG ☎020/7730 1314; within the British Airways offices at 156 Regent St, London W1R 5TA ☎020/7434 4744; 29 Corn Street, Bristol BS1 1HT ☎0117/929 996, *www.stanfords.co.uk*

The Travel Bookshop, 13–15 Blenheim Crescent, London W11 2EE ☎020/7229 5260, *www.thetravelbookshop.co.uk*

Waterstone's, 91 Deansgate, Manchester, M3 2BW ☎0161/837 3000; Queens Bldg, 8 Royal Ave, Belfast BT1 1DA ☎01232/247 355; 7 Dawson St, Dublin 2 ☎01/679 1415; 69 Patrick St, Cork ☎021/276 522, *www.waterstones.co.uk*

USA AND CANADA

The Complete Traveler Bookstore, 199 Madison Ave, New York, NY 10016 ☎212/685-9007; 3207 Fillmore St, San Francisco CA 94123 ☎415/923-1511; *www.CompleteTraveler.com*

Curious Traveler Travel Bookstore, 101 Yorkville Ave, Toronto, ON M5R 1C1 ☎1-800/268 4395.

Elliott Bay Book Company, 101 S Main St, Seattle WA 98104 ☎206/624-6600, *www.elliottbaybook.com*

Map Link, 30 S La Petera Lane, Unit #5, Santa Barbara, CA 93117 ☎805/692-6777, *www.maplink.com*

The Map Store Inc., 1636 1st St, Washington DC 20006 ☎202/628 2608.

Open Air Books and Maps, 25 Toronto St, Toronto, ON M5R 2C1 ☎416/363-0719.

Phileas Fogg's Books & Maps, #87 Stanford Shopping Center, Palo Alto, CA 94304 ☎1-800/533-FOGG.

Rand McNally, 444 N Michigan Ave, Chicago, IL 60611 ☎312/321-1751; 150 E 52nd St, New York, NY 10022 ☎212/758-7488; 595 Market St, San Francisco, CA 94105 ☎415/777-3131; call ☎1-800/333-0136 (ext 2111) for other locations, or for maps by mail order, *www.randmcnally.com*

Traveler's Choice Bookstore, 22 W 52nd St, New York, NY 10019 ☎212/941-1535.

Ulysses Travel Bookshop, 4176 St-Denis, Montréal ☎514/843-9447, *www.ulysses.ca*

World Wide Books and Maps, 552 Seymour St, Vancouver, BC V6B 3J5 ☎604/687-3320, *www.itmb.com*

AUSTRALIA AND NEW ZEALAND

Map Land, 372 Little Bourke St, Melbourne ☎03/9670 4383, *mapland@lexicon.net*

Map World, 371 Pitt St, Sydney ☎02/9261 3601.

Mapworld, 173 Gloucester St, Christchurch ☎03/374 5399, *www.mapworld.co.nz*

Perth Map Centre, 884 Hay St, Perth ☎09/9322 5733, *www.perthmap.co.au*

Speciality Maps, 58 Albert St, Auckland ☎09/307 2217.

The Map Shop, 16a Peel St, Adelaide ☎08/8231 2033, *www.mapshop.net.au*

Travel Bookshop, Shop 3, 175 Liverpool St, Sydney ☎02/9261 8200.

Worldwide Maps and Guides, 187 George St Brisbane ☎07/3221 4330, *www.powerup.com.au/~wwmaps*

Amsterdam on the Net

Official city Web site

www.amsterdam.nl

The city's official Web site contains a raft of information about the operation of local government, but is elegantly presented and has an extremely useful map facility, which allows you to pinpoint and print out a map for any address in the city. It also links you to a host of other sites, including the main tourist information sources.

Tourist Board

www.visitamsterdam.nl

Produced by the Amsterdam Tourist Board and Netherlands Board of Tourism, this comprehensive and sophisticated city guide is less turgid than many official guides – presenting information under headings like "see", "shop", "relax", "avoid" etc, as well as providing a useful accommodation database.

Amsterdam Hotspots

www.amsterdamhotspots.nl

A clearly presented and well informed guide, including maps, with a particular emphasis on events listings, particularly music and the club scene. The site is kept bang up-to-date and offers the latest on the gay scene, coffeeshops and Red Light District, as well as the more usual information.

De Museumserver

www.museumserver.nl

This site is designed as a platform for Dutch museums represented on the Internet, giving details of over 250. Although the English text disappears at times (work is still in progress on the English version of the site), it's an excellent and fascinating resource.

Buiten Beelden Binnen Amsterdam

www.afk.nl/beelden

This site provides a comprehensive listing of the city's 2000 sculptures, with maps detailing where they are and an image and account of each one (not all in English).

De Digital Stad (Digital City)

www.dds.nl

One of the reasons for the high level of Internet access in Amsterdam is this site, the result of a plan to create a digital city. A number of themed pages, sharing a geometrical layout, guide the city's "residents" to information on subjects from Books to Education to Technology. Although much of the site is in Dutch, squares (sections) with English content include Sport, Politics, Film and the Gay Scene.

Royal Concertgebouw Orchestra

www.concertgebouworkest.nl

Providing a listing of the world-renowned orchestra's concert's, and enabling online ticket reservation.

Official Ajax Web site

www.ajax.nl

As its name suggests, the virtual home of the world-famous football team, giving you fixture information and allowing the purchase of replica shirts etc, but not match tickets, which are only sold to Club Card holders.

Health and Insurance

As a member of the European Union, the Netherlands has free reciprocal health agreements with other member states. To take advantage, British and Northern Ireland citizens will need form E111, available over the counter from most post offices, which entitles you to free treatment within the Netherlands' public health care system; other EU nationalities need comparable documentation. Australians are able to receive treatment through a reciprocal arrangement with Medicare (check with your local office for details). Anyone planning to stay for three months or more is required by Dutch law to have private health insurance.

Taking out your own **private medical insurance** means you will cover the cost of items not within the EU's scheme, such as dental treatment and repatriation on medical grounds. It will usually also cover your baggage and tickets in case of theft, as long as you get a crime report from the local police. **Non-EU residents**, apart from Australians, will need to insure themselves against all eventualities, including medical costs. In the case of major expense the more worthwhile policies promise to sort matters out before you pay rather than after, but if you do have to pay upfront, get and keep the receipts.

Health

If you should fall ill, **minor ailments** can be remedied at a **drugstore** (*drogist*). These sell non-prescription drugs as well as toiletries, tampons, condoms and the like. A **pharmacy** or *apotheek* (open Mon–Fri 9.30am–6pm; often closed Mon mornings) is where you go to get a prescription filled. There aren't any 24-hour pharmacies, but the 24-hour Afdeling Inlichtingen Apotheken helpline (☎694 8709) will supply addresses of ones that are open late. Most of the better hotels will have these details too.

In more serious cases, you can get the address of an English-speaking **doctor** from your local pharmacy, tourist office or hotel. There's also a 24-hour medical helpline, **Centrale Doktorsdienst** (☎0900/503 2042), where you can seek general advice about medical symptoms and get the details of duty doctors. If you're entitled to free treatment under EU health agreements, double-check that the doctor is both working within, and regarding you as a patient of, the public health care system; bear in mind, though, that even within the EU agreement you may still have to pay a significant portion of the prescription charges (senior citizens and children are exempt). Most private health insurance policies don't help cover prescription charges either, and although their "excesses" are usually greater than the cost of the medicines, it's worth keeping receipts just in case.

Minor accidents can be treated at the outpatients department of most hospitals (*ziekenhuis*); the most central one is the Onze Lieve Vrouwe Gasthuis, east of the city centre at Eerste Oosterparkstraat 179 (open 24hr; ☎599 9111; tram #3, #6, #10 or metro Wibautstraat). In **emergencies**, telephone ☎112. Again if you're reliant on free treatment within the EU health scheme, try to remember to make this clear to the ambulance staff, and, if you're whisked off to hospital, to the medic you subsequently encounter. If possible, it's a good idea to hand over a photocopy of your E111 on arrival at the hospital to ensure your non-private status is clearly understood. In terms of describing symptoms, you can anticipate that someone will speak English. Without an E111 you won't be turned away from a hospital, but you will have to pay for any treatment you receive and should therefore get an official receipt, a necessary pre-amble to the long-winded process of trying to get at least some of the money back.

Dental treatment is not within the scope of the EU's health agreements. To find an English-speaking dentist, ask at the local tourist office or, if you're staying in a good hotel, inquire at reception. For urgent dental treatment, ring the Dentist Administration Bureau on ☎06/821 2230. This costs about ƒ1 a minute, but they can find a den-tist (*tandarts*) for you 24 hours a day.

Information and anonymous testing for **sexually transmitted diseases** is available at the GG&GD (Municipal Health Department) clinic at Groenburgwal 44, near Waterlooplein; a walk-in service operates (Mon–Fri 8–10.30am & 1.30–3.30pm, Thurs also 7–8.30pm), but it's bet-ter to call ☎555 5822 first to make an appoint-ment. The SAD Schorerstichting runs a clinic offer-ing STD and HIV testing for gay men at the same address (Fri 7–9pm only; for more information, see *Gay and Lesbian Amsterdam*, p.274). The free national AIDS helpline is open Mon–Fri 2–10pm on ☎0800/022 2220, and there's also an HIV Plus line (☎685 0055; Mon, Wed & Fri 1–4pm, Tues & Thurs 8–10.30pm). For details of how to get contraceptives or the morning-after pill, see p.278.

Insurance

In Britain and Ireland, **travel insurance** schemes (around £20–40 per person for a fortnight, £30–50 for a month) are sold by almost every travel agent and bank, and direct by several spe-cialist insurance firms. These policies are usually reasonably good value, though as ever you should check the small print. It's also worth com-paring the price of an annual multi-trip policy with single trip cover, as these can start as low as £50 per year. If you feel the cover is inadequate, or you want to compare prices, any travel agent, insurance broker or bank should be able to help.

It's also a good idea to check the details of your existing policies; if you have a good "all risks" **home insurance** policy it may well cover your possessions against loss or theft even when overseas, and many private medical schemes also cover you when abroad – make sure you know the procedure and the helpline number. Additionally, some bank and credit cards have medical or other insurance included, which come into effect when you pay for your trip with them

– again check with your bank or credit card com-pany.

If you plan to participate in water sports or any other potentially **hazardous activity**, you'll prob-ably have to pay an extra premium; check care-fully that any insurance policy you are consider-ing will cover you in case of an accident. Note also that very few insurers will arrange on-the-spot payments in the event of a non-medical major expense or loss; you will usually be reim-bursed only after going home. In all cases of loss or theft of goods, you will have to contact the local police to have a report made out so that your insurer can process the claim. Get the crime report number if possible.

North American cover

Before buying an insurance policy, check that you're not already covered: **Canadians** are usually covered for medical mishaps overseas by their provincial health plans; official stu-dent/teacher/youth **card holders** are entitled to accident coverage and hospital in-patient benefits; **students** will often find that their stu-dent health coverage extends during the vaca-tions and for one term beyond the date of last enrolment; and **homeowners' or renters'** insurance often covers theft or loss of docu-ments, money and valuables while overseas, although conditions and maximum amounts vary from company to company.

After checking the above possibilities, you might want to contact a specialist **travel insurance company**; your travel agent can usually recom-mend one or alternatively try those listed in the box below. Premiums vary, and although policies are generally comprehensive maximum payouts tend to be meagre. The best deals are usually those offered by student/youth travel agencies – STA Travel for instance, offers insurance for trav-ellers of all ages: coverage is worldwide and comes in packages covering seven days ($35), fif-teen days ($55), one month ($115), 45 days ($155), two months ($180), and a year ($730).

Cover in Australia and New Zealand

Travel insurance is available from most travel agents or direct from insurance companies, for periods ranging from a few days to a year or even longer. Most policies are similar in premium and coverage. A typical policy covering medical costs, lost baggage and personal liability, for

Europe, will cost about A$130/NZ$150 for two weeks, A$200/NZ$230 for one month, though these are over-the-counter prices – online prices are roughly A$30/NZ$40 cheaper.

TRAVEL INSURANCE COMPANIES
BRITAIN AND IRELAND

Columbus Travel Insurance, 17 Devonshire Square, London EC2M 4SQ ☎ 020/7375 0011, *www.columbusdirect.co.uk*

Endsleigh Insurance, 97–107 Southampton Row, London WC1B 4AG ☎ 020/7436 4451, *www.endsleigh.co.uk*

Frizzell Insurance, Frizzell House, County Gates, Bournemouth, Dorset BH1 2NF ☎ 01202/292 333.

STA Travel, 86 Old Brompton Rd, London SW7 3LQ; 117 Euston Rd, London NW1 2SX; 38 Store St, London WC1 (all ☎ 020/7361 6161); 25 Queens Rd, Bristol BS8 1QE ☎ 0117/929 4399; 38 Sidney St, Cambridge CB2 3HX ☎ 01223/366966; 75 Deansgate, Manchester M3 2BW ☎ 0161/834 0668; 88 Vicar Lane, Leeds LS1 7JH ☎ 0113/244 9212; 36 George St, Oxford OX1 2OJ ☎ 01865/792800; and branches in Birmingham, Canterbury, Cardiff, Coventry, Durham, Glasgow, Loughborough, Nottingham, Warwick and Sheffield; *www.statravel.co.uk*

UsitCAMPUS, 52 Grosvenor Gardens, London SW1W 0AG ☎ 020/7730 3402; 541 Bristol Rd, Selly Oak, Birmingham B29 6AU ☎ 0121/414 1848; 61 Ditchling Rd, Brighton BN1 4SD ☎ 01273/570226; 39 Queen's Rd, Clifton, Bristol BS8 1QE ☎ 0117/929 2494; 5 Emmanuel St, Cambridge CB1 1NE ☎ 01223/324283; 53 Forrest Rd, Edinburgh EH1 2QP ☎ 0131/668 3308; 105–106 St Aldates, Oxford OX1 1BU ☎ 01865/484730; *www.usitcampus.co.uk Student specialists*.

UsitNOW, O'Connell Bridge, 19–21 Aston Quay, Dublin 2 ☎ 01/602 1600; Fountain Centre, Belfast BT1 6ET ☎ 028/9032 4073; 66 Oliver Plunkett St, Cork ☎ 021/270900; 33 Ferryquay St, Derry ☎ 028/7137 1888; Victoria Place, Eyre Square, Galway ☎ 091/565177; Central Buildings, O'Connell St, Limerick ☎ 061/415064; 36–37 Georges St, Waterford ☎ 051/872601; *www.usitnow.ie*

USA AND CANADA

Access America ☎ 1-800/284-8300, *www.accessamerica.com*

Carefree Travel Insurance ☎ 1-800/323-3149.

Desjardins ☎ 1-800/463-7830 (Canada only).

STA Travel Insurance ☎ 1-800/777-0112, *www.statravel.com*

Travel Guard ☎ 1-800/826-1300, *www.noelgroup.com*

AUSTRALIA AND NEW ZEALAND

AFTA, 144 Pacific Highway, North Sydney ☎ 02/9956 4800.

Cover More, Level 9, 32 Walker St, North Sydney ☎ 02/9202 8000, *www.covermore.com.au*

Ready Plan, 141 Walker St, Dandenong, Melbourne (☎ 03/9771 4000, nationwide ☎ 1300/555018); 63 Albert St, Auckland ☎ 09/300 5333.

Travel.com, 80 Clarence St, Sydney ☎ 02/9290 1500, *www.travel.com.au*

Money, Banks and Costs

The Netherlands is a cash society; as a general rule, people prefer to pay for most things with notes and coins. Indeed, quite a lot of smaller shops and a surprising number of restaurants still refuse all other forms of payment, though most hotels and the larger shops almost invariably take one or other of the major credit cards.

Money

Until the fully-fledged introduction of the EU's "Euro", the Dutch **currency** remains the **guilder**, generally indicated by "*f*" or "fl" ("guilders" were originally "florins"); other abbreviations include "Hfl", "Dfl" and, increasingly, "NLG". Each guilder is divided into 100 cents. There are notes of *f*1000, *f*250, *f*100, *f*50 and *f*10; coins come as *f*5 (thick bronze), *f*2,50, *f*1, 25c, 10c (all silver) and 5c (thin bronze). As in the rest of Europe, decimal points are indicated by a comma, thousands by a full stop. Thus "*f*2,50" means two guilders and fifty cents; "*f*2.500" means two thousand five hundred guilders. Round figures are often indicated with a little dash: "*f*3,-" means three guilders exactly. Although some prices (mostly in supermarkets) are still marked in individual cents, these are always rounded up or down to the nearest 5c.

Guilders are available in advance from any high street bank: current **exchange rates** are around *f*3,20 (€1.45) to £1, *f*2,20 (€1) to US$1, and there are no restrictions on bringing currency into the country.

Travellers' cheques, ATMs and credit cards

The safest way to carry your funds is in **travellers' cheques**; the usual fee for their purchase is one percent of face value. Make sure you keep the purchase agreement and a record of cheque serial numbers safe and separate from the cheques themselves. In the event that cheques are lost or stolen, the issuing company will expect you to report the loss forthwith; consequently, when you buy your travellers' cheques, ensure you have details of the company's emergency contact numbers or the addresses of their local offices. Most companies claim to replace lost or stolen cheques within 24 hours. American Express cheques are sold through most North American, Australasian and European banks, and they are the most widely accepted cheques in Amsterdam. When you cash your cheques, you'll find that almost all banks make a percentage charge per transaction on top of a basic minimum charge. Note also that there is no charge for American Express cheques cashed at either of their Amsterdam offices (see box on p.28 for addresses).

The euro

The Netherlands is one of eleven countries who have opted to join the European Monetary Union, and as a result have been phasing in the single European currency, the **euro**, since January 1, 1999. The exchange rate is fixed at one guilder to 0.45 euros, but at the moment it's only possible to make paper transactions in the new currency (if you have, for example, a Euro bank or credit-card account); euro notes and coins are scheduled to be issued at the beginning of 2002, with the guilder eventually phased out by the end of that year.

If you have an ordinary British/EU bank account you can use **Eurocheques** (with the respective guarantee card) in many banks, as well as in most shops and hotels up to a value of around ƒ450. In terms of exchange rates, this works out slightly more expensive than travellers' cheques, but can be more convenient; bear in mind also that you nearly always need to have your passport with you as well as the Eurocheque card.

Most Eurocheque cards, many Visa, Mastercard and British bank/cash cards, as well as cards in the Cirrus or Plus systems, can also be used for withdrawing cash from **ATMs**, often the quickest and easiest way of obtaining money. There are dozens dotted across Amsterdam, which usually give instructions in a variety of languages. Check with your bank to find out about reciprocal arrangements.

Credit cards are predictably useful for car rental, cash advances (though these attract a high rate of interest from the date of withdrawal) and hotel bills, and of course shopping. American Express, Visa and Mastercard are all widely accepted in Amsterdam.

Changing money

If you need to change money, Amsterdam's **banks** usually offer the best deals. Hours are Monday to Friday 9am to 4pm, with a few banks also open Thursday until 9pm or on Saturday morning; all are closed on public holidays (see p.34). Outside these times, you'll need to go to one of the many bureaux de change scattered around town. GWK, whose main 24-hour branches are at Centraal Station and Schiphol Airport, offers competitive rates, as does Thomas Cook. Beware of other agencies though, as some offer great rates but then slap on an extortionate commission, or, conversely, charge no commission but give bad rates. The VVV tourist office also changes money.

Wiring money

Having money wired from home is never convenient or cheap, and should only be considered as a last resort. One option is to have your own **bank** send the money through, and for that you need to nominate a receiving bank in Amsterdam – any local branch will do. Naturally, you need to confirm the cooperation of the local bank before you set the wheels in motion back home. The sending bank's fees are geared to the amount being transferred and the urgency of the service you require – the fastest transfers, taking two or three days, start at around £20/$32 for the first £300–400/$450–600.

You can also have money wired via **American Express**, with the funds sent by one office and available for collection at the company's local office in Amsterdam within minutes. All transactions are done in US dollars and the service is only open to American Express card holders.

BANKS AND BUREAUX DE CHANGE

These are some of the handiest of the many city-centre places where you can change money; for full listings, consult the Yellow Pages (*Gouden Gids*).

ABN-Amro Dam 2; Leideseplein 25; Rozengracht 88; Rokin 80.
American Express Damrak 66 (Mon–Fri 9am–5pm, Sat 9am–noon; ☎504 8777); Van Baerlestraat 39 (Mon–Fri 9am–5pm, Sat 9am–noon; ☎673 8550).
Change Express Damrak 86 (daily 8am–midnight; ☎624 6681); Leideseplein 1 (daily 8am–midnight; ☎622 1425; Kalverstraat 150 (daily 8am–8pm; ☎627 8087).

GWK Centraal Station; Schiphol Airport (both 24hr).
ING Bank Damrak 80; Herengracht 580 (near Amstel).
Thomas Cook Dam 23 (daily 9am–6pm; ☎625 0922); Damrak 1–5 (daily 8am–8pm; ☎620 3236); Leidseplein 31 (daily 9am–6pm; ☎626 7000).
VSB Bank Singel 548, near Muntplein.

EMERGENCY NUMBERS FOR LOST AND STOLEN CARDS AND CHEQUES

Access/Mastercard/Eurocard ☎030/283 5888
American Express
cards ☎504 8000 before 6pm,
☎504 8666 after 6pm

travellers' cheques ☎0800/022 0100
Diners Club ☎557 3557
Visa ☎660 0789

Again, charges depend on the amount being sent, but as an example, wiring $400 from Britain to Amsterdam will cost $20, $5000 about $190.

Costs

In terms of **accommodation**, Amsterdam is, by western European standards at least, moderately expensive, though this is partly offset by low-priced public transport and the availability of inexpensive cafés. More precise costs for places to stay and eat are given in the Guide, and you should consult the box on p.168 for general guidelines on accommodation prices.

On average, if you're prepared to buy your own picnic lunch, stay in youth hostels, and stick to the less expensive bars and restaurants, you could get by on around £25/US$40 a day. Staying in two-star hotels, regularly eating out in medium-range restaurants and going to bars, you'll get through at least £70/$110 a day, the main variable being the cost of your room. On £100/$160 a day and upwards, you'll be limited only by your energy reserves – though if you're planning to stay in a five-star hotel and have a big night out, this still won't be enough. **Restaurants** don't come cheap, but costs remain manageable if you avoid the extras and concentrate on the main courses, for which around £10/$14 will normally suffice – twice that with a drink, starter and dessert. You can, of course, pay a lot more – a top restaurant can be twice as expensive again, and then some. As always, if you're travelling alone you'll spend much more on accommodation than you would in a group of two or more: most hotels do have single rooms, but they're fixed at about 75 percent of the price of a double.

As for **incidental expenses**, ƒ2,75 buys a cup of coffee, a small glass of beer or a wedge of apple cake; today's English newspaper costs ƒ7; and developing a roll of film an outrageous ƒ35. **Museum admission** prices hover around the ƒ5–15 mark. Just so you know, hashish and marijuana both come in ƒ10 and ƒ25 bags; the more powerful it is, the less you get.

Post, Phones and Media

Holland in general (and Amsterdam in particular) has an efficient postal system and a first-rate telephone network. Telephone and mail boxes are liberally distributed across the city and charges are reasonable.

Post

Amsterdam's main **post office** (Mon–Fri 9am–6pm, Thurs till 8pm, Sat 10am–1.30pm) is at Singel 250, on the corner with Raadhuisstraat; a second major post office (Mon–Fri 9am–9pm, Sat 9am–noon) is at Oosterdokskade 5, a couple of hundred metres east of Centraal Station. For the record, **postal charges** right now are: ƒ1 for an airmail letter (up to 20g) to anywhere within the EU; ƒ1,60 airmail to the rest of the world (ƒ1,20 by surface mail); postcards to all destinations cost ƒ1. Stamps are sold at a wide range of outlets including many shops and hotels. **Postboxes** are everywhere, but be sure to use the correct slot – labelled *overige* for destinations other than Amsterdam. To receive mail **poste restante**, letters should be addressed to you at "Poste Restante, Hoofdpostkantoor PTT, Singel 250, 1012 SJ Amsterdam, Netherlands". The poste restante section, along with the postboxes, has a separate street entrance from the main

Selected city centre post offices

Singel 250, corner with Raadhuisstraat.
Oosterdokskade 5, east of Centraal Station.
St Antoniebreestraat 16, near Nieuwmarkt.
Keizersgracht 757, corner with Amstel.

Kerkstraat 167, corner with Nieuwe Spiegelstraat.
Waterlooplein, in the Stadhuis.
Plantage Middenlaan 167, corner with Pl.
Kerklaan.

office, to the left and down the stairs; to pick up mail you'll need your passport. Holders of Amex cards can have mail sent to – and pick up mail from – either of the city's American Express offices (see box on p.28); you need your card and some form of ID to collect.

Telephones

Although there are some coin-operated public **telephones**, the vast majority only take phone cards and often credit cards too. **Phone cards** can be bought at many outlets, including post offices, tobacconists and VVV offices, in denominations of ƒ10 and ƒ25. Brightly-coloured public phones are both easy to spot and use: the bulk are multilingual, switching between different languages, including English, when you press the appropriately labelled button. International direct dialling is straightforward – just follow the instructions. The cheap rate period for international calls is between 8pm and 8am during the week and all day at weekends. All the more expensive hotel rooms also have phones, but note that there is nearly always an exorbitant surcharge for their use.

All **Amsterdam phone numbers** are made up of seven digits. In addition, Amsterdam's area code is ☎020 (note that Schiphol Airport falls within the city's boundaries). Calling from abroad, dial your international access number (☎00 in the UK, ☎011 in the US), followed by ☎3120, then the seven-digit number. ☎0800 numbers are freephone, while Dutch premium lines are usually prefixed by ☎0900; at the start of these premium calls, a pre-recorded message warns you of the tariff applied, but it's usually only in Dutch. The multilingual international operator (see box) is able to place collect calls. Note also that various telephone companies, including British Telecom, issue phone cards to their subscribers for use abroad: you tap in an account and PIN number on any phone (or extension) and the subsequent call is automatically billed to your home telephone number; for further details, ask your phone company.

Internet and email

One area where the Dutch lead Europe is in computer literacy: from the earliest days of the **Internet** Amsterdam has been a node for transatlantic data interchange and today computers are omnipresent in the city. Most Internet **cafés** will charge around ƒ2,50 for every 20min spent online. A good central option is at Martelaarsgracht 11, and you can use the facilities at the *In de Waag* café-restaurant at Nieuwmarkt 4 (which are supplied by the Society

---

INTERNATIONAL DIALLING CODES

To Amsterdam	☎00 3120		
From Amsterdam			
Australia	☎00 61	UK	☎00 44
Ireland	☎00 353	USA and Canada	☎00 1
New Zealand	☎00 64		

USEFUL NUMBERS

Operator (domestic and international)
☎0800/0410; free
Domestic directory enquiries   ☎0900
8008; 60c per call

International directory enquiries
☎0900/8418; ƒ1,05 per call
Emergencies (Police, Ambulance, Fire
Brigade) ☎112

for Old and New Media housed in the same building) for the price of a drink.

Media

There's no difficulty in finding British **newspapers** – they are on sale almost everywhere in the city on the day of publication, as is the *International Herald Tribune*. Places with a good selection of international publications include the Centraal Station shop, the Athenaeum Nieuwscentrum and the American Book Center (see p.256).

Of the Dutch newspapers *NRC Handelsblad* is a right-of-centre paper that has perhaps the best news coverage and a liberal stance on the arts; *De Volkskrant* is a progressive, leftish daily; the popular right-wing *De Telegraaf* boasts the highest circulation figures in the country and has a well-regarded financial section; *Algemeen Dagblad* is a right-wing broadsheet, while the middle-of-the-road *Het Parool* ("The Password") and the news magazine *Vrij Nederland* ("Free Netherlands") are the successors of underground resistance newspapers printed during wartime occupation. The Protestant *Trouw* ("Trust"), another former underground paper, is centre-left in orientation with a focus on religion. Bundled in with the weekend *International Herald Tribune* is *The Netherlander*, a small but useful business-oriented review of Dutch affairs in English.

For information about **what's on**, non-Dutch readers have to grapple with the fact that there isn't a single English-language magazine in print in the city. There are some listings sources available, but they're all published by various interested parties, and so none of them can provide totally objective information. The Amsterdam Uitburo (AUB), the cultural office of Amsterdam's city council, publishes the *Uitkrant*, a monthly newspaper in Dutch (free from cafés, bars, libraries, etc), which gives interpretable listings of places and events, though with little or no information attached. The VVV tourist office issues the blandest, most basic listings guide imaginable, *What's On In Amsterdam* monthly, which you can either pick up directly from their offices for ƒ4, or free from selected hotels, hostels and restaurants. For other, more specific listings publications see *Entertainment and Nightlife*, p.229.

TV and Radio

Dutch **TV** isn't up to much, although the quantity of English-language programmes broadcast are high. If you're staying somewhere with cable TV (which covers almost 90 percent of Dutch households), it's also possible to find many foreign TV channels: Britain's BBC1 and BBC2 are available everywhere, along with TV10 Gold, which shows reruns of old British sitcoms and dramas. There's also a host of German, French, Spanish, Italian, Turkish and Arabic stations, some of which occasionally show undubbed British and American movies. Most hotels also pick up some European-wide cable and satellite stations, such as MTV Europe and CNN International. Other Dutch and Belgian TV channels, cable and non-cable, regularly run English-language movies with Dutch subtitles.

As for **Dutch radio**, Radio Honderd at 98.3FM is a stalwart of the squat movement and has an eclectic programming style – world music and dance rubbing shoulders with hardcore noise and long sessions of beat-free bleeps. Radio London (90.4FM) has no discernible English connection, but does have a play-list covering Latin, reggae and African music. Jazz Radio, at 99.8FM, speaks for itself. The Dutch Classic FM, at 101.2FM, like the British version, has bits of well-known classical music jumbled together, with jazz after 10pm. There's next to no English-language programming, but the **BBC** World Service broadcasts practically all day in English on 648kHz (medium wave), with occasional news in German; between 2am and 7am it also occupies 198kHz (long wave).

Police, Crime and Personal Safety

There's little reason why you should ever come into contact with Amsterdam's police force (*politie*), a laid-back bunch in dodgem-sized patrol cars or on bicycles. Few operate on the beat, and in any case Amsterdam is one of the safer cities in Europe: bar-room brawls are highly unusual, muggings uncommon, and street crime much less conspicuous than in many other capitals.

Petty crime

Almost all the problems tourists encounter in Amsterdam are to do with **petty crime** – pickpocketing and bag-snatching – rather than more serious physical confrontations, so it's as well to be on your guard and know where your possessions are at all times. Thieves often work in pairs and, although **theft** is far from rife, you should be aware of certain ploys, such as: the "helpful" person pointing out "birdshit" (actually shaving cream or similar) on your coat, while someone else relieves you of your money; being invited to read a card or paper on the street to distract your attention; someone in a café moving for your drink with one hand while the other is in your bag as you react; and if you're in a crowd of tourists, watch out for people moving in unusually close.

Sensible **precautions** against petty crime include: carrying bags slung across your neck and not over your shoulder; not carrying anything in pockets that are easy to dip into; having photocopies of your passport, airline ticket and driving licence, and leaving the originals in your hotel safe; and noting down travellers' cheque and credit card numbers. When you're looking for a hotel room, never leave your bags unattended, and similarly if you have a car, don't leave anything in view when you park: vehicle theft is still fairly uncommon, but luggage and valuables do make a tempting target. Again, if you're using a bicycle, make sure it is well locked up – **bike theft** and resale is a big deal here.

If you are robbed, you'll need to go to the **police** to report it, not least because your insurance company will require a police report; remember to make a note of the report number – or, better still, ask for a copy of the statement itself. Don't expect a great deal of concern if your loss is relatively small – and don't be surprised if the process of completing forms and formalities takes ages.

Personal safety

Although it's generally possible to walk around the city without fear of harassment or assault, certain parts of Amsterdam are decidedly shady, and wherever you go at night it's always better to err on the side of caution. You'd be well advised to avoid walking round the very rough area known as **"De Pijp"**, south of the Sarphatipark, and note also that one or two parts of the **Red Light District** have an unpleasant, threatening undertow, with hang-around junkies concentrated on the narrow streets between the Oude Kerk and Zeedijk: again, play safe and avoid these streets if you can. As general **precautions** avoid unlit or empty streets, don't go out brimming with valuables, and try not to appear hopelessly lost – doubly so if you're travelling alone. Using public transport, even late at night, isn't usually a problem, but if in doubt take a taxi.

Emergencies ☎112

Selected city-centre police stations
HQ: Elandsgracht 117
Amstel: Prinsengracht 1109
De Pijp: Pieter Aertszstraat 5
Dam Square: N.Z. Voorburgwal 104
Jordaan: Lijnbaansgracht 219
Red Light District: Warmoesstraat 44

In the unlikely event that you are **mugged**, or otherwise threatened, never resist, and try to reduce your contact with the robber to a minimum; either just hand over what's wanted, or throw money in one direction and take off in the other. Afterwards go straight to the police, who will be much more sympathetic and helpful on these occasions. Most police officers speak at least some English.

Drugs

Thousands of visitors come to Amsterdam just to get stoned. It's the one Western city where the purchase of **cannabis** is entirely legal, and the influx of people drawn solely by this fact itself creates problems: many Amsterdammers get mightily hacked off with "**drug tourism**".

However, the Dutch government's attitude to soft drugs is actually much more complex than you would think. The use of cannabis is tolerated but not condoned, with the result a rather complicated set of **rules and regulations**. The local administration sanctions the sale of cannabis at a few dozen coffeeshops, but these are not allowed to sell alcohol (or hard drugs) or sell drugs to under-18s, and neither are they allowed to advertise. Furthermore, over-the-counter sales of cannabis are limited to 5g (under one-fifth of an ounce) per purchase – sold in ƒ10 and ƒ25 bags (the more powerful it is, the less you get); possession of over 30g (1oz) is illegal. In practice, the 5g and 30g laws are pretty much unenforceable and busts are rare, but note that if the police search you they are technically entitled to confiscate any quantity they find, regardless of whether or not it's less than the legal limit. Outside of the coffeeshops, it's acceptable to smoke in some bars, but many are strongly against it so don't make any automatic assumptions. If in doubt, ask the barperson. "**Space cakes**" (cakes baked with hashish and sold by the slice), although widely available, count as hard drugs and are illegal; if you choose to indulge, spend a few days working your way up to them, since the effect can be exceptionally powerful and long-lasting (and you can never be sure what's in them anyway). And a word of warning: since all kinds of cannabis are so widely available in coffeeshops, there's no need to buy any on the street – if you do, you're asking for trouble.

Dutch drug law is the same throughout the **rest of the country**, but only in the cities can you anticipate the same relaxed attitude from the police. Needless to say, the one thing you shouldn't attempt to do is take cannabis out of the country – a surprising number of people think (or claim to think) that if it's bought in Amsterdam it can be taken back home legally; Customs officials and drug enforcement officers never believe this story.

As far as **other drugs** go, the Dutch law surrounding magic mushrooms is that you can legally buy and possess any amount so long as they are fresh, but as soon as you tamper with them in any way (dry or process them, boil or cook them), they become as illegal as crack. Conscious Dreams, at Kerkstraat 117 (among other shops), has sold mushrooms openly for years, and continues to do so – see box on p.267. Despite the existence of a lively and growing trade in cocaine and heroin, possession of either could mean a stay in one of the Netherlands' lively and growing jails. And Ecstasy, acid and speed are as illegal in the Netherlands as they are anywhere else.

For drug-related problems, Jellinek Clinic (office ☎570 2355) operates a Drugs Prevention Centre at Keisergracht 812 (☎626 7176); they can provide advice and help in English.

Being arrested

If you're **detained** by the police, you don't automatically have the right to a phone call, although in practice they'll probably phone your consulate for you – not that they have a reputation for excessive helpfulness. If your alleged offence is a minor matter, you can be held for up to six hours without questioning; if it is more serious, you can be detained for up to 24 hours.

Opening Hours and Public Holidays

Although there's recently been some movement towards greater flexibility, opening hours for shops, businesses and tourist attractions – including museums – remain a little restrictive. Travel plans can be disrupted on public holidays, when most things close down, apart from restaurants, bars and hotels, and public transport is reduced to a Sunday timetable.

The Amsterdam weekend fades painlessly into the working week with many smaller **shops and businesses**, even in the centre, staying closed on Monday mornings until noon. Normal **opening hours** are, however, Monday to Friday 8.30/9am to 5.30/6pm and – for shops not businesses – Saturday 8.30/9am to 4/5pm. That said, shops are allowed to open seven days a week from 9am–10pm and an increasing number are doing so; where this isn't the case, many open late on Thursday or Friday evenings. A handful of night shops – *avondwinkels* – stay open round the clock; see p.264 for a list.

Museums, especially those that are state-run, tend to follow a pattern: closed on Monday, open Tuesday to Saturday from 10am to 5pm, and from 1 to 5pm on Sunday and public holidays, though things are slowly changing in favour of seven-day opening. Though closed on December 25 and 26 and January 1, the state-run museums

adopt Sunday hours on the remaining public holidays, when most shops and banks are closed. **Galleries** tend to be open from Tuesday to Saturday noon to 6pm, plus noon to 5pm on the first Sunday of the month. For precise details of opening hours, see the Guide.

Most **restaurants** are open for dinner from about 5 or 6pm, and though many close as early as 9pm, a few stay open past 11pm. **Bars**, **cafés** and **coffeeshops** are either open all day from around 10am or don't open until about 5pm; both varieties close at 1am during the week and 2am at weekends. **Nightclubs** generally function from 11pm to 4am during the week, staying open until 5am at weekends.

Public Holidays (Nationale Feestdagen)

Jan 1, New Year's Day
Good Friday (many shops open)
Easter Sunday and Monday
April 30, the Queen's Birthday
May 5, Liberation Day
Ascension Day
Whit Sunday and Monday
Dec 25, Christmas Day
Dec 26 Boxing Day

Travellers with Disabilities

Despite its social progressiveness in general, Amsterdam is far from well equipped to deal with the particular requirements of people with mobility problems. The most obvious difficulty you'll face is in negotiating the cobbled streets and narrow, often broken pavements of the central part of the city. Similarly, provision on the city's public transport for people with disabilities is only average, although in fairness it is improving. And yet, while it can be difficult to simply get around, practically all public buildings, including museums, theatres, cinemas, concert halls and hotels, are obliged to provide access, and do (though it is worth bearing in mind that a lot of the older hotels are not allowed to install lifts, so check first).

In terms of travel outside of the city, most **airlines** are now reasonably accommodating of wheelchair users and if you're thinking of travelling on Eurostar, their Web site, *www.eurostar.com*, is likely to provide much of the information you'll need. If you're planning to use the Dutch **train** network at all during your stay, it is well worth calling the Head Office of Netherlands Railways (☎030/235 5555) in Utrecht at least 24 hours beforehand; as well as producing informative leaflets on train travel for people with disabilities, they can provide practical help during your journey.

Access in the City

Once in Amsterdam, you'll find the **metro** is accessible, with lifts at every station; you have to press a button to open the train doors. Each stop is normally announced over the PA by the conductor. However, it's the trams that are most useful for getting around, and it's the **trams** that are all but inaccessible to wheelchairs – with their high steps, they may cause problems for those with limited mobility as well. Some more modern trams, however, have their central doors positioned at pavement level. Outside the rush hour, and with a little help to negotiate the gap between kerb and tram, you might just be able to squeeze your wheelchair on board. One thing you can probably count on if you attempt this is a reasonably enlightened attitude from fellow travellers.

If you can't get around without your **car**, bear in mind all the expense and hassle parking in Amsterdam can involve – see "City Transport" (p.50) for details. Regular **taxis** can only take wheelchairs if they are folded. If you need to travel in your wheelchair, contact the private taxi company Boonstra (Koningsbergerstraat 79 ☎613 4134), which has specially designed wheelchair taxis that cost around the same as normal taxis – a relatively steep *f*3 or so per kilometre within the city. You need to book at least a day ahead.

One hazard particular to the city are the thousands of *Amsterdammertjes* lining every street – small bollards set into both sides of the roadway, which do a double job of keeping cars off the pavements and out of the canals. Unfortunately, streets in the touristy part of central Amsterdam are so narrow that sometimes you'll find the *Amsterdammertjes* positioned uncomfortably close to the house-fronts; if someone has chosen to chain up their bicycle in the narrow gap, the pavement may well become impassable to a wheelchair. Again, one thing to take comfort from is the fact that the generally calm local drivers are well used to dealing with bicycles on narrow streets, and should certainly be able to take a slow-moving wheelchair in their stride.

USEFUL CONTACTS

NETHERLANDS

Mobility International Nederland,
Nijmeegsebaan 9, 6561 KE Groesbeek
☎ 243/997138.
Mobility specialists.

Stichting Informatie Gehandicapten (SIG),
Zakkedragershof 34–44, Postbus 70, 3500 AB
Utrecht ☎ 030/316416.
General disability information.

UK AND IRELAND

Holiday Care Service, 2nd floor, Imperial
Building, Victoria Rd, Horley, Surrey RH6 9HW
☎ 01293/774535.
Information on all aspects of travel.

Irish Wheelchair Association, Blackheath
Drive, Clontarf, Dublin 3 ☎ 01/833 8241.
*National organisation working for people
with disabilities; related services for holidaymakers.*

RADAR, 12 City Forum, 250 City Rd, London
EC1V 8AS (☎ 020/7250 3222, minicom
☎ 020/7250 4119).
*An excellent source of advice on holidays and
travel abroad.*

Tripscope, The Courtyard, Evelyn Rd, London
W4 5JL (☎ 020/8994 9294, minicom
☎ 08457/585 641).
*A national telephone information service
offering free transport and travel advice.*

US AND CANADA

Directions Unlimited, 720 N Bedford Rd,
Bedford Hills, NY 10507 ☎ 1-800/533 5343.
*Travel agency specializing in custom tours
for people with disabilities.*

Jewish Rehabilitation Hospital, 3205 Place
Alton Goldbloom, Chomedy Laval, Québec H7V
1RT ☎ 450/688-9550 (ext. 226).
Guidebooks and travel information.

**Society for the Advancement of Travel for
the Handicapped (SATH)**, 347 5th Ave, Suite
610, New York, NY 10016 ☎ 212/447-0027, fax
212/725 8253, *www.sath.org*
*Non-profit travel-industry referral service that
passes queries on to its members as appropriate; allow plenty of time for a response.*

Travel Information Service, Moss
Rehabilitation Hospital, 1200 West Tabor Rd,
Philadelphia, PA 19141 ☎ 215/456-9600,
www.mossresourcenet.org/travel.htm

*Telephone service, plus an excellent Web site
offering information and resources, including
travel agents, tourist offices and airline information.*

Twin Peaks Press, Box 129, Vancouver, WA
98666-0129 (☎ 360/694-2462 or freephone ☎ 1-
800/637-2256); *www.pacifier.com/twinpeak*
*Publisher of the Directory of Travel Agencies for
the Disabled, listing more than 350 agencies
worldwide, and Travel for the Disabled which
lists many free access guides; plus the Directory
of Accessible Van Rentals and Wheelchair
Vagabond, loaded with personal tips.*

Wheels Up!, PO Box 5197, Plant City, FL 33564
☎ 1-888/389-4335, *www.wheelsup.com*
*Provides discounted airfare, tour and cruise
prices for disabled travellers. Also publishes a
free monthly newsletter and has a comprehensive Web site.*

AUSTRALIA AND NEW ZEALAND

**ACROD (Australian Council for
Rehabilitation of the Disabled)**, PO Box 60,
Curtin, ACT 2605 ☎ 06/682 4333; 24 Cabarita
Road, Cabarita NSW 2137 ☎ 02/9743 2699; 55
Charles St, Ryde ☎ 02/9809 4488; PO Box 8136,
Perth Business Centre, Perth, WA 6849
☎ 08/9221 9066.
*Provides lists of travel agencies and tour
operators for people with disabilities.*

Barrier Free Travel, 36 Wheatley St, North
Bellingen, NSW 2454 ☎ 02/6655 1733.

Disability Information & Resource Centre,
195 Gilles St, Adelaide, SA 5000 ☎ 08/8223
7522, *www.dircsa.org.au*
*Provides details of organizations offering hol-
iday and travel information.*

Disabled Persons Assembly (DPA), Level 4,
Wellington Trade Centre, 173–175 Victoria St,
Wellington ☎ 04/801 9100.

Wheelchair Travel, 29 Ranelagh Dr, Mt Eliza
VIC 3930 ☎ 03/9787 8861, toll-free
☎ 1800/674468, *www.travelability.com*

Long-term Stays

Many people come to Amsterdam for a visit and decide to stay. This isn't particularly advised, and in any case only EU and US citizens are eligible to look for work once in the Netherlands. However, if you are keen to stay in the city for a prolonged period of time, the following should provide you with a few basic pointers to how to go about it.

Residency and work permits

The first thing that both EU and non-EU nationals should know is that the law on foreigners working in the Netherlands has been significantly tightened up. On September 1, 1995, the Wet Arbeid Vreemdelingen (Employment of Foreigners Act) came into force, with the explicit aim of bringing about a decrease in the number of foreigners coming to the Netherlands to work. Work permits and residence permits are now issued with even less willingness than before.

Anyone who wants to stay in the Netherlands for more than three months must apply for **residency**. To do this, you need four things: a full passport, evidence of health insurance, your original birth certificate, and proof of a regular income that the Aliens' Police think sufficient to support you. The Dutch authorities require that birth certificates issued by both the UK and the US (check with the Population Registry for other nationalities; ☎ 551 9911) be authenticated by means of an apostille, or seal. In the UK this can be done by the Legalisation Office, Foreign and Commonwealth Office, 20 Victoria St, London, SW1H 0NZ ☎ 020/7210 2521; an apostille costs £12. In the US, apply to the Secretary of State's office in your home state. UK citizens should also bear in mind that the short version of your birth certificate, even though original, is not acceptable – you need the full version.

One characteristic liberality in the Dutch laws surrounding residency is that anyone – EU or non-EU – who is in a **permanent relationship** with someone who already has Dutch resident status can apply for residency while in the Netherlands – no marriage certificate is needed (in fact, an "affirmation of single status" is), and the only requirement is that the Dutch resident be

able to support both partners. This puts unmarried couples and same-sex couples on the same footing as married couples in the eyes of the Aliens' Police. At heart, the single most important criterion for gaining residency in the Netherlands is that you be financially self-supporting.

For help and advice, the **Information Centre** and **Municipal Service Centre** in the Stadhuis on Waterlooplein (Mon–Fri 9am–5pm; ☎ 624 1111) provides information on all municipal policies and answers general questions about living in Amsterdam. You can also pick up various helpful brochures and leaflets from them, including *Amsterdam Information*, which has details on the job market, social security, housing, health care, education and the like, though it hasn't been revised since 1991. *What Every Amsterdammer Should Know* lists the functions and phone numbers of every conceivable municipal department in the city, from the Mayor's Office to the City Pawn Shop. If still in doubt, the **Sociaal Raadslieden** (Citizens' Advice Bureau – see address on p.41) at the Stadhuis offers free personal – and confidential – advice on a wide range of issues. If you can't or don't want to go into the office they also give advice on the phone (Mon, Tues, Thurs & Fri 2–4pm; ☎ 625 8347).

EU nationals

EU nationals do not require a work permit – a *werkvergunning* – in order to work legally in the Netherlands; however, if you want to stay for more than three months, you must have a **residence permit** – a *verblijfsvergunning* – and you won't get a residence permit without a job or some other means of support. However, with the integration of the European Community, and since EU passports are never stamped on arrival at Schiphol or at land borders, officials are generally relaxed about the three-month stipulation. If you do arrive with the intention of staying, though, it's best to begin the whole tortuous process as soon as possible.

First of all, you need to report to the Aliens' Police (Vreemdelingenpolitie – address on p.41). Here you should get a stamp in your passport to prove you've been given your automatic three months' legal residency, pick up the so-called *EEG brief* ("EU letter"), which states that you have the right to look for work, and collect a yellow form to apply for a residence permit (entitled "We Will Help You"). Then take your passport and *EEG brief* to the Tax Office (Belastingdienst – address on p.41), who will issue you with a social-fiscal (SOFI) number, without which you cannot work legally. Once you've found work (see the section opposite), fill in the yellow residency form and send it back to the Aliens' Police, together with photocopies of your health insurance details, your apostilled birth certificate, the pages of your passport with the Aliens' Police stamp and your personal details, two identical photos (they say ones from a machine aren't suitable), and a *werkgeversverklaring* or written statement from your employer. The Aliens' Police will make an appointment to see you (with your original documents) in five or six weeks' time. At this appointment, after you've paid a processing fee of ƒ35, and assuming they're satisfied, they'll grant you a residence permit either for the duration of your job or for five years, if your job contract is for more than a year. At the same time, you'll also have to visit the aliens' department of the Population Registry (Bevolkingsregister), in the same building: almost all employers require you to have a bank account, and you need to be registered at the Bevolkingsregister before you can get one. All your details will be entered on their computer, which is linked to City Hall and the Tax Office; a week or so later, you have to go to City Hall (the Stadhuis) at Waterlooplein (☎551

Since 1998 non-EU recipients of residence permits are obliged to enrol onto a one-year Dutch-language and social science course, held at the ROC Amsterdam on Elisabeth Wolfstraat 2 ☎607 7575 (tram #12, #13 or #14 to De Clerqstraat). ROC also run inexpensive and very popular Dutch-language courses twice a year, for which enrolling times are on Mon, Tues, Thurs & Fri 9–11am (you normally need to enrol one or two weeks in advance). Otherwise, the cheapest place to study Dutch is the Volksuniversiteit, Rapenburgerstraat 73 (☎626 1626), which does full- and part-time courses in all sorts of other subjects, too; call or drop in for their prospectus, published twice a year.

9052) and pay ƒ11 for a computer-printed extract (*uittreksel*) of your details, which you then send off to the bank to open an account.

Other nationalities

US citizens, uniquely among non-EU nationals, are legally permitted to arrive in the Netherlands as tourists, and then look for work while they're here. However, there's a catch to this. Nobody can work legally in the Netherlands without a social-fiscal (SOFI) number, but the Tax Office won't issue a SOFI number to non-EU nationals without a residence permit, and the Aliens' Police won't issue a residence permit to anyone without a SOFI number. These regulations are designed to make things difficult, but there do seem to be two ways around them. The first relies on the slim chance that you can find an employer in the first three months of your stay who is prepared to give a written statement to both the Aliens' Police and Immigration Department that you alone are the right person for the job (see below); if an employer will do this, and you apply for residency at the same time that your work permit is being processed, then – assuming you're granted the work permit – you'll be given residency and a SOFI number to start work with. The second way around the catch is that if you live with either a Dutch citizen or an EU national, you can gain residency (and thus a SOFI number) without having a job on the grounds of "setting up a family with a partner", as long as the Aliens' Police are satisfied that your partner is earning enough to support both of you. Bear in mind that the processing fee for a residence permit for US nationals is ƒ130. Once this is all done, you can look for work, but when you've found an employer you still need to go through the process of getting a work permit before you can begin earning legally.

For all **other nationals**, the whole situation is more fraught still. If you want to work in the Netherlands, or stay more than three months, you need to have an official work permit before you arrive. Except for certain very specialized jobs, you're only granted this, along with the resulting MVV (Machtiging tot Voorlopig Verblijf, "Authorization for Temporary Residence") once you have a job already set up with a Dutch employer. However, for all non-EU nationals (US included), the new Employment of Foreigners Act means that work permits are granted only on certain stringent conditions. Any job must be advertised first throughout the country, then throughout Europe, and only if no EU citizen who applies for it turns out to be suitable can the employer then ask for a work permit on your behalf – so you'll only get one if nobody in Europe can do what you can do. If you do manage to find someone who is willing to employ you, they must apply for the work permit for you before you arrive in the Netherlands, while you must also start your own application to the Dutch embassy or consulate in your home country. Needless to say, even if an employer is willing to go through with the whole process, it can take months, and at the end of it all a work permit is far from even a probability. The only exceptions to this long-winded process are **Australians** and **New Zealanders** aged between 18 and 25, who are eligible to apply for year-long Working Holiday visas prior to leaving (the procedures vary slightly between countries); contact the relevant embassies or consulates listed on p.20.

Finding work in Amsterdam

On top of all this, actually **finding a legal job** is hard and getting harder. Bear in mind that, before you begin, you need the *EEG brief* described above, a SOFI number and a bank account. In previous years **temp agencies** (*uitzendburos*) were the main source of casual, quasi-legal work for EU nationals, but nowadays most of them won't even register you unless you speak some Dutch. If you do, or if you find an agency with less strict conditions – and you're prepared to tramp around to their offices twice a day and to take any job they give you – you may come up with something, especially if you're under 23 (by law, employers have to pay substantially more to older individuals). The sort of jobs you'll find in this way vary enormously: in the summer there's some demand in the hotel and catering industry – though you may do better applying directly to tourist establishments; it's rare, though, for people to pick up secretarial jobs without some Dutch. You could try scanning the newspapers, though this isn't much use save for irregular adverts from *uitzendburo's* and cleaning agencies. A slightly better bet is to head for the main **Arbeidsburo** (Job Centre – address on p.41); they'll register you on their books and talk through job possibilities with you. They have a large file of continuously updated job openings, but you can always just wander in and scan the

boards without registering if you prefer. They have been known to find work for non-Dutch speakers, mainly as skilled manual workers – although this, too, seems to have dried up considerably.

As for **working illegally**, there's no greater chance of finding work in Amsterdam than in any other European city; less, in fact, since most Amsterdammers speak near-perfect English and there is practically no chance of work in language teaching. Places such as coffeeshops, bars, cafés and hostels are obvious choices, the closer in to the centre the better; foot-slogging and luck'll be your only hope, though if you're aiming to spend the summer in Amsterdam, be warned that whatever jobs there are will probably have been taken by May. Summer work in the glasshouses and bulbfields outside Amsterdam can occasionally be found; the best way of doing so is to head down to Aalsmeer and the bulb areas around Haarlem, although bear in mind that these kinds of jobs are generally low-paid and exploitative.

It's worth being aware that, even once you're working, an alarmingly large chunk of your wages will vanish into the highly supportive Dutch welfare system: the basic rate of **income tax** in the Netherlands is 37.5 percent, and compulsory **health insurance**, either through a local *ziekenfonds* (state-controlled fund) or through a private company, can be several dozen guilders a month on top.

Finding accommodation

Reasonably priced **rented accommodation** in Amsterdam is in desperately short supply, and flat-hunting requires a determined effort. Before you begin you'll need to have access to enough money to cover the first month's rent, a deposit of a similar amount, and any possible *overname* (see p.41) – a realistic sum would be upwards of ƒ2000. With the exception of tiny apartments, and places in Amsterdam Zuid-Oost (Southeast), most of the housing with a monthly rent of under ƒ700 is controlled by the **council**, and can only be rented with a Housing Permit (*woonruimteverklaring*), and in most cases a Certificate of Urgency (*urgentiebewijs*) too. These documents are issued by the **Municipal Housing Office** (Stedelijke Woningdienst – address on p.41), where you'll find all kinds of information on housing in Amsterdam, including the addresses of non-commercial letting agencies. However, you will only be issued a housing permit or *urgentiebewijs* if you have been registered as living in Amsterdam for four years. Anyone planning to stay a while should therefore register at the **Bevolkingsregister** (see p.38; address opposite) as quickly as possible after arriving, since it's this date that counts as the official beginning of your stay in Amsterdam. You should only do this, however, once you've registered with the Aliens' Police, and you must remember to keep both places informed of any change of address during the four-year period, or they'll lose track of you.

In the meantime, though, you're forced to seek accommodation in other ways, which can prove difficult and expensive. One way of cutting costs is to look for a place in **Amsterdam Zuid-Oost**, an unpopular and somewhat notorious concrete extension to the city that is a great deal cheaper than any other neighbourhood. That said, the apartments are spacious and generally in good condition, with rents of ƒ500–600 a month; and although you're a long way out of the centre, there is a fast metro link. The Housing Office can give you details of letting agencies down there, or try contacting the **Nieuw Amsterdam agency** (☎567 5100), which handles accommodation exclusively in Bijlmermeer, a particularly unpopular high-rise corner of Amsterdam Zuid-Oost (look in the phone book under "*woning*" for other agencies). The rents in **Amsterdam Noord** (North), across the River IJ, are also cheaper than in central Amsterdam; this is more brick-and-concrete territory, with sparse public transport and only the ferry (or car tunnel) to link you to the city.

Otherwise, in the **private sector**, the cardinal rules to remember are that Amsterdam is a landlord's market (although the law is definitely protenant), and that the city runs very much on word-of-mouth. If you're looking for a place to live, tell absolutely *everybody* you meet. An easily legible notice pinned up on a noticeboard, with a contact phone number, is a worthwhile investment – good noticeboards to use and scan can be found at the main library, all Albert Heijn supermarkets, small neighbourhood cafés such as *Gary's Muffins* and the *Vliegende Schotel*, and other English-speaking outlets such as the American Book Center; the student mensas can also be a good way of finding cheap accommodation in student dorms.

Be aware that, if you're looking for a permanent, contracted apartment, there's little chance of finding anything for much under ƒ850 a month,

higher the closer in you get. However, if you're prepared (and you may have to be) to settle for a temporary **sublet** of someone else's apartment while they're away – this is legal in Amsterdam – you can cut costs and improve your chances no end, although you will lose out on a contract, and thus legitimacy of residence. Again, word-of-mouth is the key: the waitress who just served you that coffee might have a friend whose next-door neighbours might be looking for someone trustworthy to take care of the cat while they're on holiday. Far and away your next best bet is to buy a pocket Dutch dictionary to decipher the *Via Via*, Amsterdam's **free-ads paper**, which costs ƒ4,50 and is packed with hundreds of ads for contract apartments, sublets and the occasional flatshare, along with computers, old Osmonds' LPs and everything else. It's published every Tuesday and Thursday, but anything remotely interesting will have gone by 10am – you'll need to get the first one off the pile at Centraal Station when the kiosk opens at 6.30am to stand a chance. A recent innovation is for people to avoid advertising their phone number in the *Via Via*: instead they rent a ☎06 number from the paper, which means that every call you make will cost you ƒ1 a minute – galling, but unavoidable.

Otherwise, the **newspapers** *De Telegraaf* and *De Volkskrant* are a must, with large "For Rent" (*Te Huur*) sections, particularly on Friday and Saturday – though it's well worth buying them every morning (again at the crack of dawn for any sort of chance; look out in bars for roving sellers of the Saturday edition on Friday night).

A slim possibility lies in the fact that some of the old warehouse buildings around the central harbour area have been converted into small studios and rooming houses, which are comparatively cheap, if a little tacky.

Apartment-finding **agencies** advertise regularly in the newspapers and the *Via Via*, and are another useful source if you can afford the fee – normally one or two months' rent for finding a place – but beware of agencies that ask for money before they hand out an address, since fly-by-night operators are common. If you're really desperate, try some of the agencies advertising short-term holiday rentals for tourists – many of them are located on or near the Damrak – although the places they show you won't be cheap. Bear in mind, too, that whether you rent through an agency or direct from the paper, many people will slap an *overname* (pronounced "oh-fer-nah-meh") charge on you – this is key-money which they paid to the previous tenant to cover fixtures and fittings, and which they in turn charge you. These vary tremendously and can be exorbitant (four figures is common), but they're usually unavoidable and can only be recovered by continuing the vicious circle and charging them to the next tenant when you move out. Landlords also often ask for a *borgsom* – a refundable security deposit – of one, two or three months' rent up front.

Squatting

From the heady days of the early 1980s, when the **squatting** movement in Amsterdam was at its zenith, things have changed dramatically, and what squats are left survive only by the skin of their teeth and in the face of a sea-change in public perception and governmental policy. Successive administrations in the city council – and the national government – have taken an

ever-stronger line with surviving squats, with a less and less impassioned response from Amsterdammers themselves. Public policy in Amsterdam has slowly been changing the city (and its self-image) away from the freewheeling bastion of anarchistic hippiedom that it still was in the late 1970s towards the image of an ambitious, dynamic centre for international business that it hankers after today. One consequence of this has been a fading in the significance and popularity of overt signs of "people power", such as the values borne out in the few remaining big community squats. For established and committed Dutch political activists, for whom squatting is part of a way of life, times are hard enough; a foreign visitor looking to solve a short-term housing problem by squatting can expect little sympathy from locals and extremely short shrift from the Dutch authorities.

Useful addresses

Aliens' Police (Vreemdelingenpolitie)
Johan Huizingalaan 757 ☎ 559 6300; tram #2, stop Aletta Jacobslaan. Mon–Fri 8am–5pm. Arrive early and expect to wait, the queues can be enormous.

Citizens' Advice Bureau (Sociaal Raadslieden)
Stadhuis, Waterlooplein ☎ 552 2537. Mon–Fri 9am–noon, Mon & Tues also 1–4pm, Thurs also 1–4pm & 5–7pm. At 8.50am and 12.50pm queue numbers will be distributed: make sure you get there well in advance because there are only a certain number allocated. Phone consultations Mon, Tues, Thurs & Fri 2–4pm: ☎ 625 8347 & ☎ 624 6940. Free advice on all subjects.

Information Centre (Voorlichtingscentrum)
Stadhuis, Waterlooplein ☎ 624 1111. Mon–Fri 9am–5pm. Can't solve your problems, but can tell you the phone number of the person who can.

Job Centre (Arbeidsburo)
Westeinde 26 (near Frederiksplein) ☎ 553 3444. Mon–Fri 9am–5pm. Anyone is free to walk in and scan the boards.

Legal Aid Office (Bureau voor Rechtshulp)
Spuistraat 10 ☎ 626 4477. Mon–Thurs 9am–12.30pm &1.30–5pm, Thurs also 5–7pm (appointments only), Fri 9am–12.30pm. Free

30min of legal advice on housing, unemployment, social security, welfare, immigration and consumer rights – either on the phone or at a pre-arranged appointment.

Main Public Library (Openbare Bibliotheek)
Prinsengracht 587 ☎ 523 0900. Mon 1–9pm, Tues–Thurs 10am–9pm, Fri & Sat 10am–5pm; Oct–March also open Sun 1–5pm.

Municipal Housing Office (Stedelijke Woningdienst)
Stadhuis, Waterlooplein ☎ 581 0800. Mon–Fri 9am–noon and 1–4pm.

Nieuw Amsterdam
Letting office for Bijlmermeer ☎ 567 5100. Mon–Fri 9am–4pm.

Population Registry (Bevolkingsregister)
Amstel 1 ☎ 551 9911. Mon–Fri 8.30am–3.30pm, Thurs also 5–7pm.

Tax Office (Belastingdienst)
Kingsfordweg 1, near Sloterdijk Station (second-to-last stop on tram #12) ☎ 687 7777. Mon–Fri 8.30am–4pm.

Wijkcentrum d'Oude Stadt
Doelenstraat 55 ☎ 638 2205. Community centre for old-city inhabitants; no information desk, but they do publish an annual district guide with the details of all local services, which you pick up at the above address.

The City

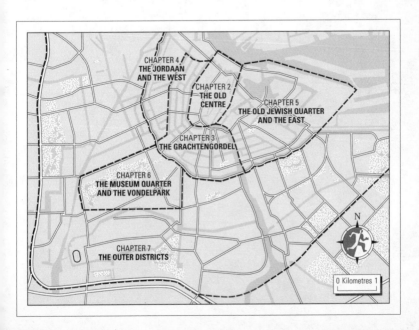

Introducing the City

A msterdam's compact centre, confined by the Singelgracht, contains almost all the city's leading attractions and only takes about forty minutes to stroll from one end to the other. Centraal Station, where you're likely to arrive, lies on the centre's northern edge, its back to the River IJ: from the station, the city fans south in a web of concentric canals, surrounded by expanding suburbs. The centre is short of landmarks and does not readily divide into distinct neighbourhoods, with one district merging seamlessly into the next, so the chapters in this Guide follow the city's historic development: Chapter 1 is devoted to the Old Centre, while subsequent chapters describe those areas added as the city grew. However, these divisions are to a certain extent arbitrary and our suggested itineraries need not be followed slavishly – just wandering around to get the flavour of Amsterdam is often the most enjoyable way to experience this unusual place.

Orientation

Butting up to the River IJ, the medieval town or **Old Centre** (Chapter 2) spreads south from Centraal Station, revolving around the main streets of Damrak and Rokin, which lead into and out of the Dam, at the very heart of the city. This area is Amsterdam's commercial centre, with the best of its bustling street life, home to shops, many bars and restaurants and, not least, the Red Light District, just to the east of Damrak. The Old Centre is bordered by the first of the major canals, the Singel, followed closely by the Herengracht, Keizersgracht and Prinsengracht – collectively known as the **Grachtengordel**, or "Girdle of Canals" (Chapter 3). These canals were part of a major seventeenth-century urban extension and, with the interconnecting radial streets, form the city's distinctive web shape. This is the Amsterdam you see in the brochures: still, dreamy canals, crisp reflections of seventeenth-century town houses, cobbled streets, railings with chained bicycles – an image which, although a little too familiar, is still utterly authentic.

Beyond the Grachtengordel, the **Jordaan** (Chapter 4) to the west grew up as a slum and immigrant quarter and remains the traditional heart of working-class Amsterdam, though in recent years it has experienced a measure of gentrification. The Jordaan adjoins the **Western Islands**, dredged out of the river to create more dock and shipbuilding space during the city's Golden Age; the shipping industry has long since gone, but now these islands are undergoing something of a revival as a riverside residential district. On the other side of town is the **Old Jewish Quarter** (Chapter 5), which, along with the adjacent **Plantagebuurt**, was once home to the city's thriving Jewish community. Since World War II of course this area has changed more than any other – its population gone and landscape altered through the construction of the metro and Town Hall. Just to the north the former docklands of the **Eastern Islands** too are undergoing renewal, but in all three areas strong cultural ties remain, evident through a number of fascinating museums.

The last of the Grachtengordel canals is Singelgracht, just beyond which lies the cluster of world-class museums on **Museumplein**, a cultural prelude to the sprawling greenery of the **Vondelpark** (Chapter 6). Otherwise, the residential suburbs – or **Outer Districts**

Amsterdam's addresses

Addresses are written as, for example, "Kerkstr. 79 II", which means the second-floor apartment at number 79, Kerkstraat. The ground floor is indicated by **hs** (*huis*, "house") after the number; the basement is **sous** (*sousterrain*).

For some reason, the Dutch ran out of ideas for street names, and many streets share the same name. To differentiate between them, **1e** or **2e** is placed in front: these are abbreviations for *Eerste* ("first") and *Tweede* ("second") – first and second streets of the same name. Thus, "1e Vogelstraat 10" is a completely different address from "2e Vogelstraat 10". There are plenty of **3e** (*Derde*, or "third"), and occasionally **4e** (*Vierde*, "fourth") streets too.

To confuse matters even more, many **side streets** take the name of the main street they run off, with the addition of the word *dwars*, meaning "crossing": Palmdwarsstraat is a side street off Palmstraat. Additionally, for no apparent reason, some dead-straight cross-streets can also change their name – so that, for instance, in the space of about 300m, 1e Bloemdwarsstraat becomes 2e Leliedwarsstraat, 3e Egelantiersdwarsstraat and so on.

T/O (*tegenover*, or "opposite") in an address shows that the address is a boat: hence "Prinsengracht T/O 26" would indicate a boat to be found opposite building no. 26 on Prinsengracht.

The main canals begin their **numbering** from the top left at Brouwersgracht and increase as they progress counterclockwise. By the time they reach the Amstel, Herengracht's house numbers are in the 600s, Keizersgracht's in the 800s and Prinsengracht's in the 1100s.

Dutch **post codes** – made up of four figures and two letters – can be found in the directory kept at post offices.

(Chapter 7) – spreading beyond Singelgracht are relatively short of attractions, one notable exception being the wooded parkland of the Amsterdamse Bos. The Netherlands has an outstanding public transport system, whose trains and buses put Amsterdam within easy reach of a large slice of the country. Consequently, the choice of possible **day-trips** (Chapter 8) from Amsterdam is extensive, but we've selected seven destinations – the towns of **Leiden, Haarlem** and **Alkmaar**, the old Zuider Zee ports of **Marken** and **Volendam**, and two villages, pretty **Edam** and the recreated seventeenth-century Dutch hamlet of **Zaanse Schans**.

Arrival

Centraal Station, the city's international train station, is both a quick and convenient train ride away from Schiphol, Amsterdam's international airport, and a ten-minute metro ride from Amstel Station, the terminus for long-distance and international buses. It is also the hub of an excellent public transport network, whose trams, buses and metro combine to delve into every corner of the city.

By air

Amsterdam's international airport, **Schiphol**, is located about 18km southwest of the city centre. The Arrivals hall, arranged around a large plaza, has all the standard facilities, including a VVV **tourist office** (daily 7am–10pm), two **bureaux de change** – the GWK (24hr) and ABN/Amro bank – plus **left luggage** facilities. Most of the major **car rental** companies are represented – Hertz, Avis, Budget, National and Europcar – and there's an NS railway ticket office. You'll find several credit-card-operated cash dispensers on the plaza too.

From the airport, **trains** run to Amsterdam's Centraal Station (often abbreviated to C.S.) – a fast service leaving every fifteen minutes during the day, and every hour at night (1–6am); the journey takes between fifteen and twenty minutes and costs just ƒ6,50. There are also trains from Schiphol to most of the suburban stations around Amsterdam, although not all of these stop at Centraal Station – check the signs on the platforms. Getting into the city by train is

---

Travel Information

Schiphol Airport	**NS** (Netherlands Railways)
General information	Domestic services
☎601 9111	☎0900/9292
Flights and arrivals	International services
☎0900/0141	☎0900/9296
	Eurolines (International buses)
	Rokin 10 ☎421 2738

---

the obvious choice, but alternatively there are a number of hotel shuttle **buses** departing from the stops outside the Arrivals hall, the most useful of which is KLM's "Hotel Bus Service" (☎649 5651), which operates on two routes, dropping passengers at around twenty of the larger hotels. The buses run every half an hour or hour (6am–9pm) and a one-way ticket costs ƒ17,50 (return ƒ30). The **taxi** fare from Schiphol to the city centre is around ƒ60 to ƒ65.

By train

Centraal Station (C.S.), Amsterdam's international train station, has regular connections with key cities in Germany, Belgium and France, as well as all the larger towns and cities of the Netherlands. Amsterdam also has several suburban train stations, but these are principally for the convenience of commuters. Centraal Station's facilities include a GWK bank and **bureau de change** (24hr), a VVV **tourist office** on platform 2 (see box opposite), coin-operated luggage lockers, a staffed **left-luggage** office (daily 6.30am–11.30pm) and **ATMs**. If you arrive late at night, it's best to take a taxi to your hotel or hostel – and you should certainly avoid wandering aimlessly around the station: it's not a dangerous place by any means, but there are too many shifty characters to make hanging around advisable.

There's a **metro** station inside the complex and city **trams** depart from the stands just outside, and to either side of, the main entrance on Stationsplein: trams #4, #9, #16, #20, #24 and #25 head south along Damrak and the first part of Rokin. City **buses** leave from the stands beyond the trams to the east of the main entrance, and there's a **taxi** rank outside the main entrance too. Stationsplein also possesses a second VVV office (see box opposite) and a GVB public transport office. For further details of city transport, see pp.50–54.

By bus

Eurolines long-distance, international buses arrive at **Amstel Station**, about 3.5km to the southeast of Centraal Station. The station concourse has a GWK bank, **bureau de change** (Mon–Sat 7.30am–9pm, Sun 10am–6pm) and ATMs, as well as a GVB municipal transport office. The metro journey to Centraal Station takes about ten minutes.

By car

Coming in on either the A4 (E19) from The Hague or the A2 (E35) from Utrecht, you should experience few traffic problems, and the city centre is clearly signposted as soon as you approach Amsterdam's southern reaches. Both the A4 and the A2 lead to the A10 (E22) ring road; on its west side, leave the A10 at either the Osdorp or Geuzenveld exits for the city centre. However, be warned

that driving in central Amsterdam – never mind parking – is extremely difficult; if you are travelling by car the best thing is to use the
city's "Park and Ride" scheme – for more on driving in Amsterdam,
see p.52.

Information

The Amsterdam Tourist Board runs three **tourist offices** (see box
below) in the city centre. These offices, known here as elsewhere in
the Netherlands as the **VVV** (pronounced "fay-fay-fay"), offer a wide
range of services and issue a comprehensive assortment of literature
(though few publications are free) – the bad news is that they are
amazingly popular, so come early if you want to beat the queues,
especially in the summer. In addition they operate a **money
exchange** and an excellent **hotel reservation** service, which costs ƒ6
(plus a refundable deposit which is subtracted from your final hotel
bill) and is especially useful in the summer when accommodation
gets mighty tight, and sell telephone cards, maps and guidebooks, as
well as tickets for public transport and canal cruises.

In terms of the city's cultural **events**, the VVV sells a comprehensive, but bland, monthly listings magazine, *What's On in
Amsterdam* (ƒ4), detailing everything from theatre and ballet
through to rock concerts. They also operate a premium-rate **information line** on ☎0900/400 4040, and sell **tickets** for concerts,
museums and the theatre. Another source of tickets for events is the
Amsterdam's Uitburo, or AUB, part of the city council, which has a
walk-in booking centre tucked away in a corner at Leidseplein 25
(☎621 1211).

You can also buy **tourist passes** at the VVV. The "Amsterdam
Pass" (ƒ39,50) contains 31 coupons providing a range of discounts
at museums, on boat trips and at several restaurants. Its lead feature
is free entry to either the Rijksmuseum or the Van Gogh Museum, but
all in all you'll need to be quite diligent to recoup your outlay.
Another option is the *Museumjaarkaart* ("museum year-card"),
which gives free entry to most museums in the country for a year; it
costs ƒ45 and there are concessionary rates for senior citizens and
the under-18s.

VVV Offices in central Amsterdam

On platform 2, Centraal Station
(Mon–Sat 8am–8pm, Sun
9am–5pm).

On Stationsplein, across from the
entrance to Centraal Station (daily
9am–5pm).

On Leidsestraat, just off the
Leidseplein (daily 9am–5pm,
Thurs–Sat till 7pm).

City transport

*There's a map
of Amsterdam's
public trans-
port routes in
the colour
insert at the
back of this
book.*

Almost all of Amsterdam's leading attractions are clustered in or near the city centre, within easy walking distance of each other. For longer jaunts, the city has an excellent **public transport system**, the mainstay of which is its trams. It also has a good bus network, which is supplemented by a modest metro and four passenger ferries across the river to the northern suburbs. Centraal Station is the hub of the transit system, which is operated by a publicly owned company, GVB. Amsterdam's **canals** present yet more possibilities for travelling between attractions by boat.

Trams, buses and the metro

The city centre is crisscrossed by **trams**, which operate on about twenty different routes. For the tourist, the most useful service is **Circle Tram #20** (daily 9am–7pm; every 10min); this links all the main attractions, running south from Centraal Station along Damrak and Rokin before threading east across Waterlooplein, southwest via Museumplein to Leidseplein, and then back to the station. For the most part, trams are entered at the rear doors (push the button). If the doors start to close before you've got on, put your foot on the bottom step, which will keep them open. To signal to the driver that you want to get off, push one of the buttons dotted at regular intervals down the length of the cars. This is especially important out in the suburbs or after dark, when drivers will blithely keep driving until someone tells them to stop. To get on a tram after dark, hold out your hand.

Buses, which are always entered at the front, are mainly useful for going to the outskirts, and the same applies to the **metro**, which has just two downtown stations, Nieuwmarkt and Waterlooplein. The metro is clean, modern and punctual, but the number of dodgy characters on it at night can make it a bit intimidating. The same operating hours (Mon–Fri 6am–midnight, Sat 6.30am–midnight, Sun 7.30am–midnight) apply to the bulk of the transport system, supplemented by a limited number of nightbuses (*nachtbussen*). All tram and bus stops display a detailed map of the network. For further details on all services, head for the main **GVB information office** (April–Sept Mon–Fri 7am–9pm, Sat & Sun 8am–9pm; Oct–March Mon–Fri 7am–7pm, Sat & Sun 8am–7pm) in front of Centraal Station. Their free, English-language *Tourist Guide to Public Transport* is very helpful.

Tickets

The most common type of ticket, used on all forms of GVB transport, is the **strippenkaart** – a piece of card divided into strips. On the city's trams, unless there's a conductor, you insert your *strippenkaart* into the on-board franking machine: fold it over to expose only the last of the strips required for your journey before doing so. One person making a journey within a zone costs two strips – one for the passenger and one for the journey. On the metro, the franking machines are on the station concourse and on the buses the driver does the job. To complicate matters, Amsterdam's public transport system is divided into eleven **zones**; the "Centre" zone covers the city centre and its immediate surroundings (well beyond Singelgracht), but for longer journeys you'll have to dock your *strippenkaart* one additional strip for each zone you cross (thus a journey across two zones requires three strips, and so on). More than one person can use a *strippenkaart*, as long as the requisite number of strips is stamped; once this has been done, it can be used to transfer between trams, buses and the metro for up to an hour.

Currently, a two-strip *strippenkaart* costs ƒ3, a fifteen-strip ƒ11,75, and a 45-strip ƒ34,50. The last two are available at a wide variety of outlets including tobacconists, the GVB, the VVV, post offices and metro station ticket offices – the two-strip is generally available at most of these locations too, but not always. Most tram drivers will only issue the two-strip *strippenkaart*, and the same applies to bus drivers within the city, though on longer distances (beyond the city limits), you can expect the fifteen-strip to be on sale. To avoid all this stamping, you can instead opt for a *dagkaart* or "day ticket", which gives unlimited access to the GVB system for as many days as you need, up to a maximum of nine. Prices start at ƒ10 for one day and ƒ15 for two, going up in multiples of four to ƒ43 for nine days. For long-term stays, you might consider a season ticket, valid for a month or a year. For further details and advice visit the GVB office, whose operatives usually speak English.

Finally, note that the city has been cracking down on fare dodgers (known as *zwartrijders* – "black riders"), and wherever you're travelling, and at whatever time of day, there's a reasonable chance you'll have your ticket checked. If caught riding "black", you're liable for a ƒ60 fine (plus the price of the ticket you should have bought), payable on the spot.

*For a list of
useful cycling
terms see
"Language",
p.335.*

Bikes

One of the most agreeable ways to explore pancake-flat Amsterdam is by **bicycle**. The city has an excellent network of designated bicycle lanes (*fietspaden*) and for once cycling isn't a fringe activity – there are cyclists everywhere. Much to the chagrin of the city's taxi drivers, the needs of the cyclist often take precedence over those of the motorist and if there's a collision, by law it's always the driver's fault. Despite this, no one blames the taxi drivers for the high incidence of **bike theft** in the city – this is a real problem, and you should lock up your bike thoroughly whenever it's not in use.

Bike **rental** is straightforward. There are lots of rental companies (*fietsen-verhuur*) but the benchmark is set by NS railways, who have outlets at over 80 stations, including Amsterdam Centraal – current rates are ƒ9,50 per day and ƒ38 per week, with substantial discounts for most rail ticket holders. For a list of other outlets see the *Directory*, p.294. Before renting, make sure you check the return time, the bike's age and condition, and any special discounts offered for longer rental periods. All firms, including NS, ask for some type of security, in the form of a cash deposit (some will take credit card imprints) and/or passport. Remember that you are legally obliged to have reflector bands on both wheels.

If you want to **buy** a bike, a well-worn bone-shaker will set you back about ƒ50, while ƒ120 should get you quite a decent machine – see p.256 for a list of bike shops. Bicycle locks are sold at all the city's flea markets.

Taxis

Taxis are plentiful in Amsterdam; they can be found in ranks on the main squares or by phoning the 24-hour radio-controlled central office on ☎677 7777 – you can't hail them on the street. Most drivers know their way around fairly well, though rates are pricey by any standards – a ƒ5,80 flat fee, plus ƒ2,85 per kilometre during the day, ƒ3,25 between midnight and 6am.

Cars

The centre of Amsterdam is geared up for trams and bicycles rather than cars as a matter of municipal policy. While pedestrianized zones as such are not extensive, motorists still have to negotiate a convoluted one-way system, not to mention herds of cyclists and fast-moving trams. It's also official policy to limit parking spaces in favour of bicycle racks, and zealous traffic police roam the city ready to clamp or tow away any vehicle that breaks the rules. What's more, the limited street spaces available are expensive: a fixed tariff applied across the city centre of ƒ4,75 per hour (Mon–Sat 9am–7pm) or ƒ2,75 per hour (Mon–Sat 7–11pm & Sun noon–11pm) – between 11pm and 9am it's free. City-centre car parks charge similar rates, the idea being to encourage drivers to use the free "**Park and Ride**" (P&R) service – watch for the signs as you approach the city. Otherwise, **parking permits** can be bought in person from the Parking Control offices (Dienst Stadstoezicht) listed in the *Directory* (see p.296) for ƒ28,50 per day (9am–7pm), or ƒ142,50 for a week (9am–7pm). Note also that a number of the better hotels offer guests special parking permits for up to three days at ƒ30 a day.

Parking fines

If you have not deposited the correct parking fee for your car, it will be clamped and a sticker on the windscreen will tell you where to pay the ƒ130 fine; once you've done this, return to your car and the traffic police will come and remove the clamp. If you don't pay your fine within 24 hours, your car will be towed away – as it will for all other parking violations. The 24-hour car pound is way out in the northeast of the city at Cruquiuskade 25 (bus #7 or #10 from Leidseplein); reclaiming costs a minimum of ƒ300 if you do it promptly, but there are steep surcharges the longer you leave it. Take your passport, licence number and enough cash – or check that they will accept your credit card. For information about parking tariffs, plus clamped and towed vehicles, contact the Parking Control Department (☎553 0333).

Car rental

All the major car **rental agencies** are represented in Amsterdam (see *Directory*, p.294), although the best deals are often with local operators, whose prices start at ƒ60–80 per day, plus around 35c per kilometre over 100km or 200km. Special weekend deals can bring the rates down further. The maximum speed limit within the city is 50kph and seatbelts must be worn by all drivers and front-seat passengers.

Canal transport

Apart from choosing one of the many organized boat cruises available (see box on p.54), the best way to get around Amsterdam's canals is to take the **Canal Bus** (☎623 9886). The bus operates on three circular routes, which meet once, at the jetty opposite Centraal Station beside Prins Hendrikkade. Two of the three routes also meet on the Singelgracht (opposite the Rijksmuseum), at Leidseplein and beside the Town Hall on Waterlooplein. There are eleven stops in all and together they give easy access to all the major sights. Boats leave from opposite Centraal Station (every 10–20min; 10am–5pm) and at least every half hour from any other jetty. A day ticket for all three routes, allowing you to hop on and off as many times as you like, costs ƒ22 per adult, ƒ15 for children (4–12 years old); it's valid until noon the following day and entitles the bearer to significant discounts at several museums. A similar boat service, **Museumboot** (☎530 1090) calls at six jetties located at or near eighteen of the city's major attractions, departing from opposite Centraal Station (every 30–45min; 10am–5.30pm). A come-and-go-as-you-please day ticket costs ƒ25.

Another waterborne "travel" option is **Canal Bikes**, four-person pedaloes which seem to take a lifetime to get anywhere, but are nevertheless good fun, particularly in the summer. Canal Bike (☎626 5574) rent their pedaloes out at four central locations: on the Singelgracht opposite the Rijksmuseum; the Prinsengracht outside the Anne Frank House; on Keizersgracht at Leidsestraat; and near the *American* hotel beside Leidseplein. Rental prices per hour, each, are ƒ10 (3–4 people) or ƒ12,50 (1–2 people), and there's a refundable

Canal Cruises and Guided Tours

Canal Bus, opposite Centraal Station ☎623 9886.

A "Canals and All That Jazz" cruise (April–Oct Sat 8–10pm), with a live jazz band and unlimited drinks and snacks. Tickets cost ƒ57 for adults, ƒ37 for children (4–12 year olds). Departs from the jetty opposite the Rijksmuseum; advance booking required.

Holland International, Damrak 90 ☎625 3035.

Large tour operator running a wide range of bus trips from city sightseeing tours (1 daily; 3hr 30min; ƒ48) to a gallop through Holland on their "Grand Holland Tour" (1 daily except Sat; 9hr; ƒ75). The same company also does canal cruises, beginning with the basic one-hour sightseeing trip round the city centre for ƒ15 per adult. Boats leave every 15min (9am–6pm) and every 30min (6–10pm) from the jetty at the foot of Damrak, facing Centraal Station.

Let's Go, VVV Tourist Offices (group bookings ☎600 1809), *come.to/letsgo*

VVV tour operator with various well-organized bike tours around Amsterdam, including one to Edam and Volendam (see p.157 and p.156), from April to October (6hr 30min; ƒ45, not including train fare), plus a "Mystery

Walking Tour" around the centre (April–Oct; 2hr; ƒ17,50). You can book at any of the VVV offices (phone for large bookings) and all tours leave from the VVV office opposite Centraal Station.

Mee in Mokum, Hartenstraat 18 ☎625 1390.

Two- to three-hour guided walking tours of the older parts of the city provided by long-time Amsterdam residents. Tours once daily; ƒ5 per person.

P. Kooij, on the Rokin, opposite the east end of Spui ☎623 3810.

Arguably the best of the major boat tour operators, this company offers hour-long canal cruises for ƒ15 with live commentary (daily: April–Oct 9.30am–10pm; Nov–March 10am–5pm; every 30min). Also two-hour "Cheese and Wine" canal cruises daily at 9pm for ƒ50.

Yellow Bike Tours, Nieuwezijds Kolk 29, off Nieuwezijds Voorburgwal ☎620 6940.

This efficient company organizes three-hour guided cycling tours around the city centre (1 or 2 daily; April–Oct). Tours cost ƒ30 per person, including the bike. They also do a full-day bike tour of the Waterland to the north of Amsterdam for ƒ45 per person. In both cases, advance reservations are required.

deposit of ƒ50. The Canal Bikes can be picked up at one location and left at any of the others; a map showing five possible routes between the jetties costs ƒ3,50.

Organized tours

No one could say that the Amsterdam tourist industry doesn't make the most of its canals; **cruises** are its staple diet. Right throughout the year, and especially in the summer, an armada of glass-topped **boats** powers along the waterways, offering everything from a quick hour-long excursion to a fully fledged dinner cruise. There are dozens of operators, several of which crowd the dock beside the Damrak, near Centraal Station. Excursion **prices** vary according to the season, but the boat companies keep to a similar tariff: for the one-hour tour reckon on ƒ15 per adult, ƒ7,50 per child (4–12 years old); ƒ50 (ƒ25) for a two-hour candlelit cruise – we've given a selection in the box opposite. Bear in mind that boat rides are popular and long queues commonplace in the summer. Many visitors find canal trips delightful, but the commentary can sometimes be tedious, and the views disappointing. That said, it's certainly true that Amsterdam can look enchanting at night when the bridges are illuminated.

As for **land-based tours**, as you might expect there's a wide choice, from a quick zip round the city by tram through to leisurely bus and boat tours out into the Dutch countryside. Again, we've given a selection in the box opposite, but the Amsterdam VVV also issues a comprehensive brochure detailing all the various guided tours on offer. More unusual options include guided tours of the city's museums, walks and city-centre cycle tours; the VVV will make the necessary bookings on your behalf for free. They also have an extensive list of recommended guides, some of whom have tempting specialisms in such subjects as Dutch architecture and art.

Chapter 2

The Old Centre

Amsterdam's most vivacious district, the Old Centre, is an oval-shaped affair whose jumble of antique streets and narrow canals are confined to the north by the River IJ and in the south by the first of several canals – the Singel – that once girdled the entire city. This was where Amsterdam began, starting out as a humble fishing village at the marshy mouth of the River Amstel before the local lord gave it some significance by building a castle here in 1204. Sixty years later, the Amstel was dammed (leading to the name Amstelredam) and the village began to flourish as a trading centre, receiving its municipal charter from a new feudal overlord, the Count of Holland, in about 1300. Thereafter, the city developed in stages, each of which was marked by the digging of new canals to either side of the main canal linking the River IJ with Dam square, along today's Damrak. Time and again, the wooden canalside buildings of medieval Amsterdam went up in smoke, but finally, after a particularly severe fire in 1452, timber was banned in favour of stone – and it's the handsome stone buildings of subsequent centuries, especially the seventeenth, which provide the Old Centre with most of its architectural highlights.

A map of the Old Centre appears in the colour insert at the back of the book.

Given the dominance of **Centraal Station** on most transport routes, this is where you'll almost certainly arrive. Immediately outside, on **Stationsplein** – home of the main tourist and transport information offices (see p.49) – you'll be thrust into the city centre's heaving streetlife of buskers and bicycles, trams and tourists. From here a stroll across the bridge will take you into **Damrak**, which once divided the "Old Side" of the medieval city to the east from the **"New Side"** to the west, and leads you into the heart of the Old Centre, **Dam square**. This is flanked by two of the city's most impressive buildings, the Koninklijk Paleis (Royal Palace) and the Nieuwe Kerk.

To the east of Damrak is the **Red Light District**, which stretches across two canals, Oudezijds Voorburgwal and Oudezijds Achterburgwal, and up to Nieuwmarkt. It's here you'll find many of the city's finest buildings, though the seediness of the tentacular red light zone dulls many charms. That said, with or without the industrialized eroticism of the "hookahs", be sure to spare time for the delightful **Amstelkring**, a clandestine Catholic church dating from the seventeenth century, and the charming Gothic architecture of the **Oude Kerk**.

Just beyond the reach of the Red Light district is druggy **Nieuwmarkt**, an unappetizing start to the **Kloveniersburgwal** which – together with Groenburgwal – forms one the most beguiling parts of the Old Centre, with a medley of handsome old houses lining the prettiest of canals. From here, it's a short walk south to the **Muntplein**, a busy square that boasts a floating **flower market** and the distinctive **Munttoren** ("Mint Tower"). Muntplein lies at the end of the **Rokin**, a shopping boulevard that runs north to Dam square. Near the Rokin, you'll find a clutch of good museums, but the prime target is arguably the secluded **Begijnhof**, a circle of dignified old houses originally built as a sanctuary for Catholic women in the middle of the fourteenth century.

Damrak and the New Side

The street leading from Centraal Station to Dam square, the **Damrak**, was the medieval city's main artery, with boats sailing up its canal to discharge their goods right in the centre of town on the square itself. In 1672, the canal was filled in and the function of both changed dramatically: the Damrak became a busy commercial drag, as it remains today, and the Dam became the centre of municipal power.

To the west of the Damrak lies the Old Centre's "**New Side**", whose outer boundary was marked in the 1500s by a defensive wall, hence the name of its principal avenue, **Nieuwezijds Voorburgwal** ("In Front of the Town Wall on the New Side"). The wall itself disappeared as the city grew, and in the nineteenth century the canal that ran

---

Junkies in the Old Centre

The hang-around **junkies** of the Old Centre are not generally considered dangerous, but they are certainly disconcerting where and whenever they gather in groups – especially when the streets are quiet. It frequently changes, but the edgiest area is generally regarded as being just to the east of the Oude Kerk (see p.65) on O. Z. Voorburgwal and Achterburgwal. It goes without saying that cutting any kind of drug deal with a street dealer is crazy and illegal.

---

through the middle of the street was filled in, leaving the unusually wide swathe that you see today. This area has been badly mauled by the developers, the only attraction of any note being the **Lutherse Kerk**.

Centraal Station and around

With its high gables and cheerful brickwork, the neo-Renaissance **Centraal Station** is an imposing prelude to the city. At the time of its construction in the 1880s, it aroused much controversy because it was seen to separate the centre from the River IJ, source of the city's wealth, for the first time in Amsterdam's long history. There was controversy about the choice of architect too. The man chosen, Petrus J.H. Cuypers, was a Catholic, and in powerful Protestant circles there were mutterings about the vanity of his designs (he had recently completed the Rijksmuseum – see p.117) and their unsuitability for Amsterdam. In the event, the station was built to Cuypers' design, but it was to be his last major commission; thereafter he spent most of his time building parish churches.

*For the open-
ing times of
the VVV on
Stationsplein,
see p.49.*

Outside the station, **Stationsplein** is a messy open space, edged by ovals of water, packed with trams and dotted with barrel organs and chip stands – in the summer street performers vying for attention complete the picture. Across the water, to the southeast on Prins Hendrikkade, rise the whopping twin towers and dome of **St Nicolaaskerk** (Mon–Sat 11am–4pm; free), the city's foremost Catholic Church. Dating back to the 1880s, the cavernous interior holds some pretty dire religious murals, mawkish concoctions only partly relieved by swathes of coloured brickwork. Above the high altar is the crown of the Habsburg Emperor Maximilian, very much a symbol of the city and one you'll see again and again. Amsterdam had close ties with Maximilian: in the late fifteenth century he came here as a pilgrim and stayed on to recover from an illness. The burghers funded many of his military expeditions and, in return, he let the city use his crown in its coat of arms – a practise which, rather surprisingly, survived the seventeenth-century revolt against Spain.

*St Nicolaaskerk
is just a few
metres from
Zeedijk, which
runs to the
Nieuwmarkt –
see p.67 for
further details.*

Just to the east of St Nicolaaskerk, at the top of Geldersekade, is the squat **Schreierstoren** ("Weepers' Tower"), which was originally part of the city's medieval walls. Overlooking the River IJ, its name derives from its use by women as a place to watch the ships of their menfolk sail away, a fact recalled by an old stone plaque inserted in its wall. There's another, much more recent plaque too, recalling the departure of Henry Hudson from here in 1609. On this particular voyage Hudson stumbled across the "Hudson" river and an island the locals called Manhattan. Hudson founded a colony there and called it New Amsterdam, a colonial possession that was re-named New York after the English seized it in 1664.

Along Damrak

From Stationsplein, **Damrak**, a wide but unenticing avenue lined
with tacky restaurants, bars and bureaux de change, storms south
into the heart of the city.

After passing an inner harbour crammed with the bobbing canal
boats of Amsterdam's considerable tourist industry, you'll come to
the **Sexmuseum Venustempel** (daily 10am–11.30pm; ƒ4,50) on the
right hand side of the street at Damrak 18. Displaying erotic pictures, statues, cartoons and examples of early pornographic films,
this museum is kitsch and tacky, and frankly not worth bothering
with. Much more interesting is the nearby old Stock Exchange, or
Beurs (Tues–Sun 10am–4pm; ƒ6) – known as the "Beurs van
Berlage" – a seminal work designed at the turn of the century by the
leading light of the Dutch Modern movement, Hendrik Petrus
Berlage (1856–1934). Berlage re-routed Dutch architecture with the
building, forsaking the historicism that had dominated the nineteenth century, and whose prime practitioner had been Cuypers (see
opposite). Instead he opted for a style with cleaner, heavier lines,
inspired by the Romanesque and the Renaissance, but with a minimum of ornamentation – and in so doing anticipated the
Expressionism that swept northern Europe from 1905 to 1925. The
Beurs has long since lost its commercial function and nowadays
holds a modest exhibition on the history of the exchange, but the
building is the main event, from the graceful exposed ironwork and
shallow-arched arcades of the main hall through to a fanciful frieze
celebrating the stockbroker's trade. Just behind the Beurs, the much
duller **Effectenbeurs**, flanking the eastern side of Beursplein, is the
home of today's stock exchange.

Just up Damrak, on the left hand side, the enormous and long-
established **De Bijenkorf** – literally "beehive" – department store
extends south as far as the Dam. Amsterdam's answer to Harrods, De
Bijenkorf posed all sorts of problems for the Germans when they
occupied the city in World War II. It was a Jewish concern, so the
Nazis didn't really want their troops shopping here, but it was just
too popular to implement a total ban; the bizarre solution was to pro-
hibit German soldiers from shopping on the ground floor, where the
store's Jewish employees were concentrated, as they always had
been, in the luxury goods section.

*For more on De
Bijenkorf, and
Amsterdam's
other depart-
ment stores,
see Shops and
Markets, p.261.*

The New Side

Running parallel to and just to the west of the Damrak, **Nieuwezijds
Voorburgwal** begins with the **Crowne Plaza Hotel**, at no. 5, formerly the Holiday Inn, built on the site of an old tenement building called
Wyers. The 1985 clearance of squatters from Wyers ranks among
the most infamous of that decade's anti-squatting campaigns, involving a great deal of protest (and some violence) throughout the city.

*For more on
the history of
Amsterdam's
squatting
movement,
see p.41.*

The squatters had occupied the building in an attempt to prevent yet another slice of the city being converted from residential use and handed over to a profit-hungry multinational. Although widely supported by the people of Amsterdam, they could not match the clout of the American hotel company and the riot police were sent in; construction of the hotel followed soon after.

From the hotel, it's a short walk along Hekelveld and a right turn down Kattengat to the **Lutherse Kerk**, a whopping seventeenth-century edifice whose copper-green dome gives this area its nickname, **Koepelkwartier** ("Dome Neighbourhood"). It's a grand, self-confident building, seen to best advantage from the Singel canal, but it has been dogged by bad luck: in 1882 the interior was gutted by fire and, although it was repaired, the cost of maintenance proved too high for the congregation, who decamped in 1935. After many years of neglect, the adjacent *Renaissance Hotel* bought the church and have since turned it into a conference centre.

Doubling back to Nieuwezijds Voorburgwal, you soon reach **Nieuwezijds Kolk**, where the angular, glassy and ultra modern building is testament to the recent large-scale construction work going on hereabouts. When the underground car park was being dug here, workers discovered archeological remains dating back to the thirteenth century; this turned out to be the castle of the "Lords of Aemstel", which, it is thought, had occupied the site when it was open marshland, even before the Amstel was dammed. Blemished by this and other new complexes, the patchwork of pedestrianized **alleys** that extend east from Nieuwezijds Voorburgwal to the Damrak, previously filled with quirky shops, small bars and homes, are now without charm, largely given over to chain stores and businesses, with the exception of a few cobbled back lanes near the Dam which retain a medieval eccentricity. Better to stay on Nieuwezijds Voorburgwal as it threads its way south from here, its trees partly concealing a series of impressive canal houses, though these fizzle out as you approach the square.

Dam Square

Situated at the heart of the city, **Dam square** gave Amsterdam its name: in the thirteenth century the River Amstel was dammed here, and the fishing village that grew around it became known as "Amstelredam". Boats could sail into the square down the Damrak and unload right in the middle of the settlement, which soon prospered by trading herrings for Baltic grain. In the early fifteenth century, the building of Amsterdam's principal church, the Nieuwe Kerk, and thereafter the town hall (now the Royal Palace), formally marked the Dam as Amsterdam's centre, but since World War II it has lost much of its dignity. Today it's as much a choked traffic junction as a square, but it does possess the main municipal **War Memorial**, a prominent stone tusk alongside twelve urns filled with soil from each of the Netherlands' provinces (plus the ex-colony of Indonesia). The memorial was designed by Jacobus Johannes Pieter Oud (1890–1963), a De Stijl stalwart who thought the Expressionism of Berlage (see p.59) much too flippant. The Amsterdam branch of **Madame Tussaud's** waxworks is on the Dam too, at no. 20 (daily: July–Aug 9.30am–7.30pm; Sept–June 10am–5.30pm; ƒ19,50, children ƒ16).

The Royal Palace

Dominating the Dam is the **Koninklijk Paleis**, the Royal Palace (guided tours daily: June & July 10am–6pm; Aug 12.30–5pm; ƒ7). The title is deceptive, given that the vast sandstone structure started out as the city's Stadhuis (town hall) in the mid-seventeenth century, and only had its first royal occupant when Louis Bonaparte moved in during the French occupation (1795-1813). At the time of the building's construction, Amsterdam was at the height of its powers. The city was pre-eminent amongst Dutch towns, and had just resisted William of Orange's attempts to bring it to heel; predictably, the council craved a residence that was a declaration of the city's municipal power and opted for a startlingly progressive design by Jacob van Campen, who proposed a Dutch rendering of the classical principles revived in Renaissance Italy. Initially, there was opposition to the plan from the council's Calvinist minority, who pointed out that the proposed Stadhuis would dwarf the Nieuwe Kerk (see p.62), to them an entirely inappropriate ordering of earthly and spiritual values. However, when the Calvinists were promised a new church spire (it was never built) they promptly fell in line and in 1648 work started on what was then the largest town hall in Europe, supported by no less than 13,659 wooden piles driven into the Dam's sandy soil – a number every Dutch schoolchild remembers by adding a "1" and a "9" to the number of days in the year. The poet Constantijn Huygens called the new building "The world's Eighth Wonder / With so much stone raised high and so much timber under".

The Royal Palace also holds temporary exhibitions – contact the VVV for more information.

The Stadhuis received its royal designation in 1808, when Napoleon's brother Louis, who had recently been installed as king, commandeered it as his residence. Lonely and isolated, Louis abdicated in 1810 and high-tailed it out of the country, leaving behind a large quantity of Empire furniture, most of which is exhibited in the rooms he converted. Possession of the palace subsequently reverted to the city, who sold it to the state in 1935, since when it has been used by royalty on very rare occasions.

The **exterior** of the Stadhuis is very much to the allegorical point: pediments depict Amsterdam as a port adored by maritime gods on one side and by river deities on the other, while above are representations of the values the city council espoused – Prudence, Justice and Peace, plus Temperance and Vigilance to either side of a muscular, globe-carrying Atlas. One deliberate precaution, however, was the omission of a central doorway – just in case the mob turned nasty (as they were wont to do) and stormed the place.

The building's **interior** similarly proclaims the pride and confidence of the Golden Age; the **Citizen's Hall** contains the enthroned figure of Amsterdam, sumptuously inlaid with brass and marble, looking down on the world and heavens laid out at her feet. A good-natured and witty symbolism pervades the building: cocks fight above the entrance to the Court of Petty Affairs, while Apollo, god of the sun and the arts, brings harmony to the disputes; and a plaque above the door of the Bankruptcy Chamber aptly shows the Fall of Icarus, surrounded by marble carvings depicting hungry rats scurrying around an empty chest and unpaid bills. On a more sober note, death sentences were pronounced at the High Court of Justice at the front of the building, and the condemned were executed in full view on a scaffold outside. Among the **paintings** dotted around the building, most are large-scale historical canvases of little distinction, with the exception of Ferdinand Bol's glossy *Moses the Lawgiver*. The situation could have been very different had Rembrandt, whose career was waning, not had his sketches rejected by the city council – a decision which must rank pretty high in any league of major mistakes.

Opposite the Royal Palace, you'll spy the **Magna Plaza** shopping mall, housed in the old neogothic post office of 1899. A municipal heavyweight, the post office was never very popular despite its whimsical embellishments, which continued the town's tradition of plonking towers on every major building partly as a matter of civic pride, and partly to make the city seem less flat.

The Nieuwe Kerk

Vying for importance with the Royal Palace is the adjacent **Nieuwe Kerk** (usually daily 10am–5pm; free, but admission charged during exhibitions; recorded information ☎638 6909). Despite its name (literally "new church"), it's an early fifteenth-century structure built in a late flourish of the Gothic style, with a forest of pinnacles and high, slender gables. Badly damaged by fire on several occasions and unceremoniously stripped of most of its fittings by the Calvinists, the **interior** is a hangar-like affair of dour demeanour, whose sturdy compound pillars soar up to support the wooden vaulting of the ceiling. Amongst a scattering of decorative highlights, look out for an extravagant, finely-carved mahogany **pulpit** that was fifteen years in the making, a cleverly worked copper **chancel screen** and a flashily Baroque **organ case**. Behind the high altar there's also the spectacularly vulgar tomb of Admiral **Michiel de Ruyter** (1607–1676), complete with trumpeting angels, conch-blowing Neptunes and cherubs all in a tizzy. In a long and illustrious naval career Ruyter trounced in succession the Spaniards, the Swedes, the English and the French,

Gravenstraat, one of the cluster of medieval lanes in the shadow of the Nieuwe Kerk, holds several of the city's most characterful bars – see Eating and Drinking for more details.

and his rise from deck hand to Admiral-in-Chief is the stuff of national legend. His most famous exploit was a raid up the River Thames to Medway in 1667 and the seizure of the Royal Navy's flagship, *The Royal Charles*; the subsequent Dutch crowing almost drove Charles II to distraction. Ruyter was buried here with full military honours and the church is still used for state occasions – the coronations of queens Wilhelmina, Juliana and, in 1980, Beatrix, were all held here.

The Red Light District

The whole area to the east of Damrak, between Warmoesstraat, Nieuwmarkt and Damstraat, is the **Red Light District**, known locally as the "De Walletjes" – since this was where the old city walls ran. It stretches across the two canals that marked the eastern edge of medieval Amsterdam, Oudezijds Voorburgwal and Oudezijds Achterburgwal, both of which are now seedy and seamy, though the legalized prostitution here is world renowned and has long been one of the city's most distinctive and popular draws. The two canals, with their narrow connecting passages, are thronged with "window brothels" and at busy times the crass, on-street haggling over the price of various sex acts is drowned out by a surprisingly festive atmosphere – entire families grinning more or less amiably at the women in the windows or discussing the specifications (and feasibility) of the sex toys in the shops. Groups of men line the streets hawking the peep shows and "live sex" within – and, unlike in London or New York, there actually is live sex within. There's a nasty undertow to the district too, oddly enough sharper during the daytime, when the pimps hang out in shifty gangs and drug addicts wait anxiously, assessing the chances of scoring their next hit.

Dodging the dealers, the district also contains two prime attractions, the medieval **Oude Kerk** and the clandestine **Amstelkring** Catholic church.

Tucked into one of the old ecclesiastical buildings adjoining the Nieuwe Kerk, 't Nieuwe Kafé serves excellent coffee and delicious lunches.

Amsterdam's prostitutes are camera shy: if you've got a camera don't even think about taking a picture of a "window brothel" unless you're prepared for some major grief.

Warmoesstraat

Soliciting hasn't always been the principal activity on sleazy **Warmoesstraat**. It was once one of the city's most fashionable streets, home to Holland's foremost poet, **Joost van den Vondel** (1587–1679), who ran his hosiery business from no. 110, in between writing and hobnobbing with the Amsterdam elite.

Vondel is a kind of Dutch Shakespeare: his *Gijsbrecht van Amstel*, a celebration of Amsterdam during its Golden Age, is one of the classics of Dutch literature, and he wrote regular, if ponderous, official verses, including well over a thousand lines on the inauguration of the new town hall. He had more than his share of hard luck too. His son frittered away the modest family fortune and Vondel lived out his last few years as doorkeeper of the pawn shop on

The Red
Light
District

One of the highlights of Warmoesstraat is the Condomerie, at no. 141, which specializes in every imaginable design of condom, in sizes ranging from the small to the remarkable.

Oudezijds Voorburgwal (see p.70), dying of hypothermia at what was then the remarkable age of 92. Witty to the end, his own suggested epitaph ran:

Here lies Vondel, still and old
Who died – because he was cold.

Vondel's Warmoesstraat house was knocked down decades ago, but the street does have two minor attractions, the Prostitution Information Centre, at Enge Kerksteeg 3 (see box), and the **Geels & Co. Koffie- en theemuseum** at Warmoesstraat 67 (Tues & Fri 2–4pm, Sat 2–4.30pm; free), which displays assorted paraphernalia related to the consumption of coffee and tea in tiny premises above the Geels & Co. shop.

Oude Kerk

Just to the east of Warmoesstraat, the handsome facades of
Oudezijds Voorburgwal are also reminders of ritzier days before the
prostitutes took up residence, when this was one of the wealthiest
parts of the city, richly earning its nickname the "Velvet Canal". The
canal's northern reaches are overlooked by the **Oude Kerk**
(April–Nov Mon–Sat 11am–5pm, Sun 1–5pm; Dec–March Mon–Fri &
Sun 1–5pm, Sat 11am–5pm; ƒ5), an attractive Gothic structure with
high-pitched gables and finely worked lancet windows. There's been
a church on this site since the mid-thirteenth century, but most of the
present building dates from the mid-fourteenth, funded by the pilgrims who came here in their hundreds following a widely publicized
miracle. The story goes that, in 1345, a dying man regurgitated the
Host he had received at Communion, which, when it was then thrown
on the fire, did not burn. The unburnable Host was placed in a chest
(now in the Amsterdam Historical Museum) and installed in a long-
lost chapel somewhere off Nieuwezijds Voorburgwal, before finally
being transferred to the Oude Kerk a few years later. It disappeared
during the Reformation, but to this day thousands of the faithful still
come to take part in the annual Stille Omgang, a silent nocturnal procession terminating at the Oude Kerk.

The Protestants cleared the church of almost all of its ecclesiastical tackle during the Reformation, but its largely bare **interior** does
hold several interesting features. These include some fruity and
folksy misericords, a few faded vault paintings recovered from
beneath layers of whitewash in the 1950s and the unadorned memorial tablet of Rembrandt's first wife, Saskia van Uylenburg. Better
still are the three beautifully coloured **stained-glass windows** beside
the ambulatory in the Lady Chapel. Dating from the 1550s, two of
the three depict Biblical scenes, while the third is both a later and –
as a sign of changing times – secular work, celebrating the Treaty of
Munster of 1648, which wrapped up the Thirty Years' War and recognized Dutch independence from the Habsburgs. All the windows
show their characters in classical gear with togas and sandals, but for
different reasons: Biblical figures were usually clad in Greco-Roman
clothes because this was thought to be accurate, whereas, a century
later, the point was to emphasize the dignity of the treaty signers and
their symbolic significance.

*During the
summer, the
Oude Kerk
holds a series
of "walking"
concert
evenings; see
Entertainment
and Nightlife,
p.235.*

The Amstelkring

A short walk from the Oude Kerk, towards the northern end of
Oudezijds Voorburgwal at no. 40, the clandestine **Amstelkring**
(Mon–Sat 10am–5pm, Sun 1–5pm; ƒ7,50) was once the principal
Catholic place of worship in the city and is now one of Amsterdam's
most enjoyable museums. In 1578, the city finally forsook the
Catholic Habsburgs and declared for the Protestant rebels in what

was known as the Alteratie (Alteration). Broadly speaking, the new regime treated its Catholics well – commercial pragmatism has always outweighed religious zeal here – but there was a degree of discrimination; Catholic churches were recycled for Protestant use and their members no longer allowed to practise openly. The result was an eccentric compromise: Catholics were allowed to hold services in any private building providing that the exterior revealed no sign of their activities – hence the development of the city's clandestine churches (*schuilkerken*), amongst which the Amstelkring is the only one to have survived intact.

The Amstelkring, more properly Ons Lieve Heer Op Solder ("Our Dear Lord in the Attic"), occupies the loft of a wealthy merchant's house and is perfectly delightful, with a narrow nave skilfully shoe-horned into the available space. Flanked by elegant balconies, the nave has an ornately carved organ at one end and a mock-marble high altar, decorated with Jacob de Wit's mawkish *Baptism of Christ*, at the other. Even the patron of the church, one Jan Hartman, clearly had doubts about de Wit's efforts – the two spares he procured just in case are now displayed behind the altar. The rest of the house has been left untouched, its original furnishings reminiscent of interiors by Vermeer or De Hooch. Amstelkring, meaning "Amstel Circle", is the name of the group of nineteenth-century historians who saved the building from demolition.

Spinhuis

From the Amstelkring head down Lange Niezel and turn left into Oudezijds Achterburgwal, where, at no. 28, you'll find the **Spinhuis**, once a house of correction for "fallen women," who were put to work here on the looms and spinning wheels. Curiously, workhouses like this used to figure on tourist itineraries: for a small fee the public were allowed to watch the women at work, and at carnival times admission was free and large crowds came to jeer and mock. The justification for this was that shame was supposed to be part of the reforming process – and shame there was – but in fact the municipality unofficially tolerated brothels and the incarcerated women had simply been singled out for exemplary punishment. As the eighteenth-century commentator Bernard de Mandeville observed, "The wary magistrates preserve themselves in the good opinion of the weaker sort of people, who imagine the government is always trying to suppress those [brothels] it really tolerates." The Spinhuis has been turned into offices, but the facade remains pretty much intact, with an inscription by the seventeenth-century Dutch poet Pieter Cornelisz Hooft: "Cry not, for I exact no vengeance for wrong but to force you to be good. My hand is stern but my heart is kind."

Zeedijk

The Red
Light
District

Curving southeast from the northern end of Oudezijds Voorburgwal, **Zeedijk** was originally just that – a dike to hold back the sea – and the wooden house at no. 1 is one of the oldest in the city, built as sailors' lodgings around 1550. As in other such places, sailors could pay their bill by barter here (having usually whored or gambled away their money), and for some unknown reason, trading in pet monkeys was particularly popular – hence the name *In't Aepjen* ("In the Monkeys"), retained by the café currently occupying the premises. As for the rest of Zeedijk, it begins promisingly with a huddle of antique buildings, but soon descends into seediness, with junkies and dealers hanging about in ramshackle doorways, altogether threatening enough to make you hurry on to the open spaces of Nieuwmarkt.

Kloveniersburgwal and around

The outermost of the three eastern canals of fifteenth-century Amsterdam, **Kloveniersburgwal** is a long, dead-straight waterway, with dignified facades jostling each other the whole way down. At its northern end is the old market square of **Nieuwmarkt**, now rather run-down, while in the opposite direction the canal leads to one of the most appealing parts of the city, a small pocket of dreamy waterways and handsome old canal houses along and around Groenburgwal.

Nieuwmarkt to the Oude Schans

Nieuwmarkt was long one of the city's most important markets and the place where Jews (from the nearby Jewish Quarter – see Chapter 5) and Gentiles traded. However, during World War II the Germans cordoned it off with barbed wire and turned the square into a holding pen, after which its old exuberance never returned. These days the market has all but vanished, though there are small markets for organic food on Saturdays (9am–5pm) and for antiques on Sundays (May–Sept 9am–5pm), with a few stalls selling fish, fruit and vegetables during the week.

For more on Amsterdam's markets, see pp.268–269.

Lokaal 't Loosje, with a terrace on Nieuwmarkt, is a fine place to while away a sunny afternoon – see p.197.

The focus of the square, the sprawling multi-turreted **Waag**, dating from the 1480s, has had a chequered history. Built as one of the city's fortified gates, Sint Antoniespoort, Amsterdam's expansion soon made it obsolete and the ground floor was turned into a municipal weighing-house (*waag*), with the rooms upstairs taken over by the surgeons' guild. It was here that the surgeons held lectures on anatomy and public dissections, the inspiration for Rembrandt's *Anatomy Lesson of Dr Tulp*, displayed in the Mauritshuis Collection in The Hague. Abandoned by the surgeons and the weigh-masters in the nineteenth century, the building served as a furniture store and fire station before falling into disuse, though it has recently been ren-

Klovenniers-
burgwal and
around

From
Nieuwmarkt
it's a quick
stroll southeast
along St
Antoniebree-
straat to the
Old Jewish
Quarter – see
pp.100–114.

ovated to house an excellent café-bar and restaurant, *In de Waag*
(see p.221 for further details).

Strolling along Rechtboomsloot from the northeast corner of
Nieuwmarkt, it only takes a couple of minutes to reach the
Montelbaanstoren, a sturdy tower dating from 1512 that overlooks
the **Oude Schans**, a canal dug around the same time to improve the
city's shipping facilities. The tower was built to protect the city's
eastern flank but its decorative spire was added later, when the city
felt more secure, by Hendrik de Keyser (1565–1621), the architect
who did much to create Amsterdam's prickly skyline.

At the top of the canal, turning left along busy Prins Hendrikkade
takes you to the unusual **Scheepvaarthuis** ("Shipping Building"), on
the left at no. 108, next to tiny Buiten Bantammerstraat. Completed
in 1917, this is the flashiest of the buildings designed by the
Amsterdam School of architecture, the work of Johann Melchior van
der Mey (1878–1949). An almost neurotic edifice, covered with a
welter of decoration celebrating the city's marine connections, the
facade is shaped like a prow and is surmounted by statues of
Poseidon, Amphitrite, his wife, and female representations of the
four points of the compass. Slender turrets and Expressionistic carving add to the effect and inside there's more nautical playfulness with
sea horses and dolphins, ships and anchors decorating everything
from the skylights to the doors.

Along Kloveniersburgwal

Heading along Kloveniersburgwal from Nieuwmarkt, it's a pleasant
walk to the **Trippenhuis**, at no. 29, a huge overblown mansion complete with Corinthian pilasters and a grand frieze built for the Trip
family in 1662. One of the richest families in Amsterdam, the Trips
were a powerful force among the **Magnificat**, the clique of families
(Six, Trip, Hooft and Pauw) who shared power during the Golden
Age. One part of the Trip family dealt with the Baltic trade, another
with the manufacture of munitions (in which they had the municipal
monopoly), but in addition to this they also had trade interests in
Russia and the Middle East, much like the multinationals of today. In
the nineteenth century, the Rijksmuseum collection was displayed
here, but the house now contains the Dutch Academy of Sciences.

De Engelbe-
waarder at
Klovenniers-
burgwal 59 is
an attractive
brown café,
with live jazz
on Sundays.

Directly opposite, on the right bank of the canal, there's a very different house that gives an idea of the sort of resentment such ostentatious displays of wealth engendered. Legend asserts that Mr Trip's
coachman was so taken aback by the size of the new family residence
that he exclaimed he would be happy with a home no wider than the
Trips' front door – which is exactly what he got: at a metre or so
across the **Kleine Trippenhuis**, Kloveniersburgwal 26, is one of the
narrowest houses in Amsterdam.

Further along the canal, on the corner of Oude Hoogstraat, is the
former headquarters of the Dutch East India Company, the

Oostindisch Huis, a monumental red-brick structure built in 1605 shortly after the founding of the company. It was from here that the Company organized and regulated its immensely lucrative trading interests in the Far East, importing shiploads of spices, perfumes and exotic woods. This trade underpinned Amsterdam's Golden Age, but predictably the people of what is now Indonesia, the source of most of the raw materials, received little in return. However, despite the building's historic significance, it's of little interest today, being occupied by offices and the university.

From the Oostindisch Huis, you can either proceed up Oude Hoogstraat to the Hash Museum (see below) or keep straight for the huddle of narrow streets and picturesque drawbridges edging the south end of Kloveniersburgwal. This is one of the prettiest corners of the Old Centre, especially among the old facades of Staalstraat, along the narrow **Groenburgwal** canal and amidst the Victorian pomp of Nieuwe Doelenstraat. Also here is **Oudemanhuispoort**, a passage leading through to Oudezijds Achterburgwal which was once part of an almshouse for elderly men (hence the strange name), but is now lined by secondhand bookstalls.

Around the Oostindisch Huis

At the other end of tiny Oude Hoogstraat, close to the Oostindisch Huis at Oudezijds Achterburgwal 148, the **Hash Marihuana Hemp Museum** (daily 11am–10pm; ƒ8) is still going strong despite intermittent battles with the police. As well as featuring displays on the various types of dope and numerous ways to smoke it, the museum has a live indoor marijuana garden, samples of textiles and paper made with hemp, and pamphlets explaining the medicinal properties of cannabis. There's also a shop selling pipes, books, videos and plenty of souvenirs. Amsterdam's reliance on imported dope ended in the late 1980s when it was discovered that a reddish weed bred in America – "skunk" – was able to flourish under artificial lights; over half the dope sold in the coffeeshops is now grown in Holland, a change that has helped minimize the role of organized crime in the supply chain. For more information on drugs in Amsterdam see the box on pp.70–71.

The triangular parcel of land at the southern end of Oudezijds Achterburgwal is packed with university buildings, mostly modern or nineteenth-century structures built in a vernacular Dutch style. Together they form a pleasant urban ensemble, but the red-shuttered, seventeenth-century **Huis op de Drie Grachten**, the "House on the Three Canals", stands out in particular, sitting prettily on the corner of Oudezijds Achterburgwal and Oudezijds Voorburgwal. Close by, through an ornate gateway at Oudezijds Voorburgwal 231, is the **Agnietenkapel** (St Agnes Chapel; Mon–Fri 9am–5pm; ƒ2,50), originally part of a Catholic convent, but now owned by the university. Upstairs the chapel has a good-looking, first-floor auditorium dating from the fifteenth century; it's used for temporary exhibitions mainly

---

Drugs in Amsterdam

Amsterdam's liberal policies on commercial sex (see p.64) are similarly
extended to **soft drugs**, and the city has an international reputation as a
haven for the dope-smoker, though, in fact, this confuses toleration with
approval. Many visitors are surprised to find that all drugs, hard and soft,
are technically illegal in Amsterdam, the caveat being that since 1976 the
possession of small amounts of cannabis (up to 30g/1oz) has been ignored
by the police. This pragmatic approach has led to the rise of "smoking"
coffeeshops, selling bags of dope much in the same way as bars sell glasses of beer.

From its inception, there have been problems with this policy. In part,
this is because the Dutch have never legalized the cannabis supply chain –
or more specifically that section of it within their national borders – and
partly because the 30g-rule has proved difficult to enforce. Other compli-
cations have arisen because of the difference between Holland's policy and
that of its European neighbours. Inevitably, the relative laxity of the Dutch
has made the country in general and Amsterdam in particular attractive to
soft (and arguably hard) **drug dealers**. The Dutch authorities have tried
hard to keep organized crime out of the soft drug market, but drug dealing
and drug tourism – of which there is an awful lot – irritate many
Amsterdammers no end.

In recent years, the French and German governments have put pressure on the Dutch to bring their drug policy into line with the rest of
Europe – one recent concession obliged coffeeshops to choose between
selling dope or alcohol, and many chose the latter. Overall however, while
the Dutch have found it prudent to keep a rigorous eye on the coffeeshops
and emphasize their credentials in the fight against hard drugs, they have

---

devoted to the university's history. Roughly opposite, the building at
Oudezijds Voorburgwal 300 has been known for years as **ome Jan**
("Uncle John's") for its former function as central Amsterdam's pawn
shop, though now it's the back of a bank. The poet Vondel ended his
days working here, and a short verse above the entrance extols the
virtues of the pawn shop and the evils of usury.

Ome Jan is on the corner of a passage that cuts through to Nes, a
long, narrow street leading to the Dam (see p.60); or you can make
your way down the Oudezijds Voorburgwal canal past the **Galerie
Mokum**, named for the old Jewish nickname for the city. From here,
it's just a few yards to the trams and traffic of Rokin.

The Rokin and around

The **Rokin** is the focus of the southeast corner of the Old Centre and
the narrow streets immediately to its west hold several leading
attractions, notably the **Amsterdam Historical Museum** and the
cloistered tranquillity of the **Begijnhof**. Here also is pedestrianized
Kalverstraat, one of the city's main shopping streets, far from the

stuck to their liberal guns on cannabis. As justification, they cite the lack of evidence to link soft- and hard-drug use and indeed, the country's figures for hard-drug addiction are actually among the lowest in Europe.

Furthermore, by treating drugs as a medical rather than criminal problem, Amsterdam's authorities have been able to pioneer positive responses to **drugs' issues**. The council operates a system of free needle exchanges and – more unusually – has even set up tables at nightclubs where its employees have chemically analyzed Ecstasy, testing its purity and, thereby, its toxicity, for clubbers. It also runs a wide range of rehabilitation programmes, although it recently decided to overhaul the methadone programme it introduced for heroin addicts in 1979. Here as elsewhere, methadone is now largely discredited as a means of weaning addicts off the drug and as a result the Dutch began issuing free heroin in tightly controlled quantities to users in 1998, a nationwide trial whose results are eagerly anticipated.

Nevertheless, for the casual visitor the main blot on the Amsterdam landscape is the groups of **hang-around junkies** who gather in and near the Red Light District, especially amongst the narrow streets and canals immediately to the east of the Oude Kerk (see p.65). The police estimate that there are around 1000 hard-drug users who, as they put it, "cause nuisance," and although the addicts are unlikely to molest strangers, they are a threatening presence, especially if you're travelling alone. In fairness, however, the police have done their best to clean things up, dramatically improving the situation on the Zeedijk and Nieuwmarkt, which were once notorious for hard drugs, and at the canal bridge on Oude Hoogstraat, formerly nicknamed the "Pillenbrug" – "Pill Bridge." You can read about the city government's regulations and attitude towards cannabis online on the Honest Cannabis information site, *www.thc.nl*

seediness of the Red Light District, but a mundane thoroughfare nonetheless – though the justifiably popular floating **flower market**, at its southern end by Muntplein, largely redeems matters.

Along the Rokin

The **Rokin** picks up where the Damrak (see p.57) leaves off, cutting south in an elegant sweep following the former course of the River Amstel. This wide boulevard was the business centre of the nineteenth-century city and although it has lost much of its prestige, grandiose old mansions like Sotheby's, at no. 102, and the elaborate *fin-de-siècle* Maison de Bonneterie clothes store, at no. 140, are reminders of more elegant times. The Rokin hits the city's canal system at Lange Brugsteeg and close by, beside the water at Oude Turfmarkt 127, the **Allard Pierson Museum** (Tues–Fri 10am–5pm, Sat & Sun 1–5pm; *f*9,50) holds Amsterdam's archeological collection. Highlights of this small and modest museum include a remarkably well-preserved assortment of Coptic clothes, plus Etruscan sculpture, Greek pottery and jewellery and a number of scale models – the Egyptian pyramids and such like – as well as a life-size model of a Greek chariot.

The Rokin and around

For coffee and bagels, avoid the tackier places beside the flower market and head instead to Gary's Muffins, one street south of the Singel at Reguliersdwarsstraat 53.

Rokin ends at Muntplein, where the **Munttoren** ("Mint Tower") was originally a mint that formed part of the old city walls, a plain brick structure to which Hendrik de Keyser, in one of his last commissions, added a flashy spire in 1620. A few metres away, the floating **Bloemenmarkt**, or flower market (daily 9am–6pm), extends along the southern bank of the Singel west as far as Koningsplein. Popular with locals and tourists alike, the market is the main supplier of flowers to central Amsterdam, its thousands of blooms now sharing stall space with souvenir clogs, garden gnomes and Delftware.

From Muntplein, seedy Reguliersbreestraat leads east to the bars and restaurants of **Rembrandtplein**, while Koningsplein, at the western end of the flower market, is within easy walking distance of the Spui (see opposite).

Kalverstraat and the Amsterdams Historisch Museum

Running parallel to, and just to the west of Rokin, pedestrianized **Kalverstraat** has been a commercial centre since it was used to host a calf market in medieval times. It's now a run-of-the-mill shopping street, but halfway down, a lopsided gateway at no. 92 forms an unexpected entrance to the **Amsterdams Historisch Museum** (Amsterdam Historical Museum; Mon–Fri 10am–5pm, Sat & Sun 11am–5pm; ƒ11), the main entrance being on St Luciensteeg, a sidestreet off Kalverstraat.

Housed in the restored seventeenth-century buildings of the municipal orphanage, the museum attempts to survey the city's development with a scattering of artefacts and lots of paintings from the thirteenth century onwards. It's a garbled collection, lacking continuity and poorly labelled, but a reorganization is underway and in the meantime highlights include several rooms, each containing **paintings** that illustrate a particular civic theme. One room has works relating to the surgeons' guild – notably Rembrandt's wonderful *Anatomy Lesson of Dr Jan Deijman* – while another depicts the regents of several orphanages, self-contented bourgeoisie in the company of the grateful poor. The orphanage's own Regents' Room, or office, dating from the seventeenth century, has survived too, but the most diverting part of the museum is the **Schuttersgalerij** – the Civic Guard Gallery – which occupies the glassed-in passageway immediately outside the museum. Access to this is free and exhibited here are a group of huge militia portraits, from serious-minded paintings of the 1540s through to lighter affairs from the seventeenth century.

The most famous Civic Guard portrait is The Nightwatch by Rembrandt, exhibited in the Rijksmuseum (see p.120).

The Begijnhof

Close to the Historical Museum along narrow Gedempte Begijnensloot, the **Begijnhof** (daily 10am–5pm; free) was founded in the fourteenth-century as a home for the *beguines* – members of a Catholic sisterhood living as nuns, but without vows and with the right of return to the secular world.

The original medieval complex comprised a series of humble brick cottages looking onto a central green, their backs to the outside world. These cottages were mostly replaced by larger, grander houses after the Reformation, but the secretive, enclosed design survived, totally removed from the bustle of the surrounding city. However a couple of pre-Reformation buildings do remain, including the **Houten Huys**, which, constructed in 1477, is the oldest house in Amsterdam, erected before the city forbade the construction of wooden houses as an essential precaution against fire. The **English Reformed Church**, which takes up one side of the Begijnhof, is of medieval construction too, but it was taken from the *beguines* and given to Amsterdam's English community during the Reformation. Plain and unadorned, the church is of interest for its pulpit panels, several of which were designed by a youthful Piet Mondriaan (1872–1944), the leading De Stijl artist. After they had lost their church, and in keeping with the terms of the Alteratie (see p.65), the *beguines* were allowed to celebrate Mass inconspicuously in the clandestine **Catholic chapel** (Mon 1–6pm, Tues–Sun 9am–6pm; free), which they established in the house opposite their old church. It's still used today, a homely little place with some terribly sentimental religious paintings, one of which – to the left of the high altar – depicts the miracle of the unburnable Host (see p.65).

There's an entrance to the Begijnhof on the west side of the Spui – look for the ornate gateway.

Spui

Emerging from the south side of the Begijnhof, you hit the **Spui** (rhymes with "cow"), a long and slender open space flanked by bookshops and fashionable café-bars. In the middle is a cloying statue of a young boy, known as 't Lieverdje ("Little Darling" or "Loveable Scamp"), a gift to the city from a cigarette company in 1960. It was here in the mid-1960s, with the statue seen as a symbol of the addicted consumer, that the playful **Provos** (see box on p.74) organized some of their most successful *ludiek* ("pranks").

One block south of the Spui, Heiligeweg, or "Holy Way", now an uninspiring extension to Kalverstraat, was once part of a much longer route used by pilgrims heading into Amsterdam. Every other religious reference disappeared centuries ago, but there is one interesting edifice here, the fanciful gateway of the old **Rasphuis** ("House of Correction") that now fronts a shopping mall near the corner with Kalverstraat. The gateway is surmounted by a sculpture of a woman punishing two criminals chained at her sides above the single word Castigatio ("punishment"). Beneath is a carving by Hendrik de Keyser showing wolves and lions cringing before the whip; the inscription reads "It is a virtue to subdue those before whom all go in dread".

The Rokin
and around

The Provos and the Kabouters

Amsterdam's reputation as a wacky, offbeat city largely rests on the events of the 1960s, when the social and political discontent that was fermenting all over Western Europe and North America began to coalesce here into direct opposition to many of the city council's redevelopment plans. Influenced by contemporary movements in France and the U.S., Dutch protesters adopted a playful stance, punctuating their protests with theatrical events, and, partly as a consequence, garnering substantial public support. At issue was the post-war consensus over **redevelopment**. In the 1950s and early 1960s, in the aftermath of World War II, every western government, including the Dutch, was committed to the construction of large-scale public works, and initially there were few dissenting voices; the tunnel under the IJ and a number of massive new housing projects were thus constructed without a fuss.

However, for complex reasons, towards the mid-Sixties the support such large-scale projects enjoyed withered away right across western Europe. The discontent was amorphous, partly fuelled by a resurgent, anti-capitalist left, and partly by a more general rejection by the young of what they considered an overly materialistic society. In Amsterdam, the key manifestation of this restlessness was the popular movement co-ordinated by **Roel van Duyn**, a philosophy student at the university. Duyn took to holding small "happenings" around the *'t Lieverdje* statue (see p.73) in central Amsterdam, which soon mushroomed into major events with the participation of activists known as **Provos** (as in "provocation"). In 1965, a clumsy attempt by the police to break up one of these happenings provoked a riot, but this disturbance was nothing compared with the scenes a few months later when, in March 1966, Princess (now Queen) Beatrix married an ex-Nazi, Claus von Amsberg. The Provos objected to the massive cost of the event as well as the Fascist connection and while the wedding procession was passing through the city, rioters clashed with police amidst smoke bombs and tear gas. Amsberg himself was jeered with the refrain "Give us back the bikes," a reference to the commandeering of hundreds of bikes by the retreating German army in 1945. The rioting continued throughout the summer, prompting Amsterdam's police chief to resign, followed by the mayor.

That same year, the Provos won over two percent of the vote in municipal elections, and gained a seat on the city council. They brought with them their wide-ranging and imaginative **White Plans**, whose most famous proposal was to ban cars from the centre of Amsterdam and provide 20,000 white bicycles instead. These bicycles were to be distributed for people to use free of charge, leaving them at their journey's end for someone else, but trials didn't really work and the plan was never implemented. By 1967, the Provos' plans for the rejuvenation of Amsterdam had become over-idealistic and unmanageable, and the group broke apart. Van Duyn promptly founded a group called the **Kabouters**, after a helpful gnome in Dutch folklore. The Kabouters' manifesto described their form of socialism as "not of the clenched fist, but of the intertwined fingers, the erect penis, the escaping butterfly . . ." In the local elections of 1970, they met with some success, taking five council seats, but once again implementation of the White Plans proved problematic. The Kabouters modified the White Bicycle Plan into a similar idea involving small, economical white cars, but trials in 1974 received poor public support and the plan was abandoned. In 1981, after ten years or so on the margins of Amsterdam politics, the Kabouters finally disintegrated; Van Duyn, though, has continued his involvement in local politics, and is still on the council, as a member of the Green Party.

Chapter 3

The Grachtengordel

Medieval Amsterdam was enclosed by the Singel, part of the city's protective moat, but this is now just the first of five canals that reach right around the city centre, extending anti-clockwise from Brouwersgracht to the River Amstel in a "girdle of canals" or Grachtengordel. These were dug in the seventeenth century as part of a comprehensive plan to extend the boundaries of a city no longer able to accommodate its burgeoning population. The idea was that the council would buy up the land around the city, dig the canals, and lease plots back to developers. The plan was passed in 1607 and work began six years later, against a backdrop of corruption – Amsterdammers in the know buying up the land they thought the city would soon have to purchase.

Increasing the area of the city from 450 to 1800 acres was a monumental task, and the conditions imposed by the council were strict. The three main waterways, Herengracht, Keizersgracht and Prinsengracht, were set aside for the residences and businesses of the richer and more influential Amsterdam merchants, while the radial canals were reserved for more modest artisans' homes; immigrants newly arrived to cash in on Amsterdam's booming economy were housed in much less commodious quarters beyond Prinsengracht in the Jordaan (see Chapter 4). Everyone, even the wealthiest merchant, had to comply with a set of rules when building their house. In particular, the council prescribed the size of each building plot – the frontage was set at thirty feet, the depth two hundred – and although there was a degree of tinkering, the end result was the loose conformity you can see today: tall, narrow residences, whose individualism is mainly restricted to decorative gables and the occasional facade stone to denote name and occupation. Even the colour of the front doors was once regulated, with choice restricted to a shade that has since become known as "Amsterdam Green" – even now, difficult to find outside Holland. It was almost the end of the century before the scheme was finished – a time when, ironically, Amsterdam's decline had already begun – but it remains to the council's credit that it was executed with such success.

See Contexts, p.301, for a history of Amsterdam.

Of the three main canals, **Herengracht**, the "Gentlemen's Canal", was the first to be dug, followed by the **Keizersgracht**, the "Emperor's Canal" named after the Holy Roman Emperor and fifteenth-century patron of the city, Maximilian. Further out still, the **Prinsengracht**, the "Princes' Canal", was named in honour of the princes of the House of Orange. The merchants who dominated Amsterdam soon lined the three with their mansions, the grandest concentrated on Herengracht, where the stretch of water between Leidsestraat and the Amstel was soon nicknamed the "Golden Bend" (De Gouden Bocht).

The Grachtengordel is the most charming part of Amsterdam, its lattice of olive-green waterways and dinky humpback bridges overlooked by street upon street of handsome seventeenth-century houses. It's a subtle cityscape too – full of surprises, with an unusual facade stone here, a bizarre carving there – and one whose overall atmosphere appeals rather than any specific sight. Nevertheless there are one or two obvious targets, principally the **Anne Frank House**, where the young – and now internationally famous – Jewish diarist hid from the Germans in World War II, and the ever popular **Heineken Brewery**.

> This chapter covers the full sweep of the *grachtengordel*, from Brouwersgracht in the north to the Amstel in the south, but for ease of reference, we've considered it as two areas – **Grachtengordel West** and **Grachtengordel South** – divided at roughly the halfway point by Leidsegracht. The *Accommodation* and *Eating and Drinking* listings chapters later in the book follow this division too.

Grachtengordel West

Stretching south from the Brouwersgracht to the Leidsegracht, **Grachtengordel West** contains a fine selection of seventeenth-century canal houses, at their prettiest at its southern end along the **Leidsegracht**, close to which the **Biblical Museum** is one of the city's real curiosities. However, easily the most popular attraction hereabouts is the **Anne Frank House**, on Prinsengracht, which is itself close to the soaring architecture of the **Westerkerk** and the enjoyable **Theatermuseum**.

Brouwersgracht

Running west to east along the northern edge of the three main canals is leafy **Brouwersgracht**, one of the most peaceful and picturesque waterways in the city. In the seventeenth century, Brouwersgracht lay at the edge of Amsterdam's great harbour. This was where many of the ships returning from the East unloaded their

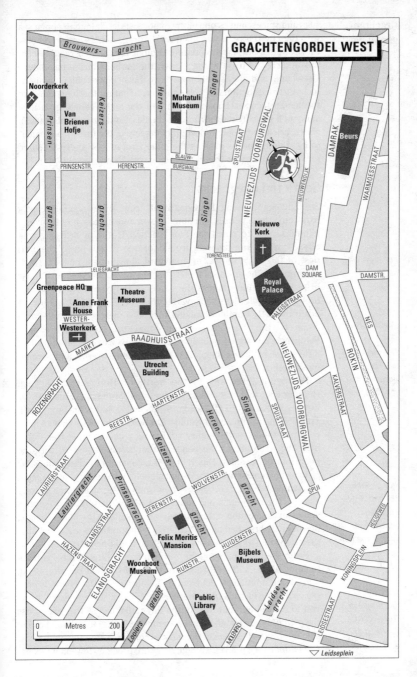

GRACHTENGORDEL WEST

Noorderkerk

Van Brienen Hofje

Multatuli Museum

Beurs

Nieuwe Kerk

Royal Palace

Greenpeace HQ

Theatre Museum

Anne Frank House

Westerkerk

RAADHUISSTRAAT

Utrecht Building

Felix Meritis Mansion

Woonboot Museum

Bijbels Museum

Public Library

▽ Leidseplein

0   Metres   200

silks and spices, and as one of the major arteries linking the open sea with the city centre, it was lined with storage depots and warehouses. Breweries flourished here too, capitalizing on their ready access to shipments of fresh water. Today, the harbour bustle has moved elsewhere, and the warehouses have been converted into apartments, their functional architecture interrupting the long ranks of residential facades. Look down any of the major canals from here and you'll see why visitors admire the city for its gentle interplay of water, brick and stone. Indeed, picking any of the three main canals to head down means missing the other two, unless you're prepared to weave a circuitous route, beginning with Prinsengracht.

South to Leliegracht

Strolling south along **Prinsengracht** from Brouwersgracht, past handsome canal houses and tumbledown houseboats, it only takes a minute or two to reach the **Van Brienen Hofje**, at Prinsengracht 89–133, which you can walk around for free. This is one of the prettiest of the city's *hofjes*, or courtyard almshouses, built in 1804, according to the entrance tablet, "for the relief and shelter of those in need." Opposite, across the canal, is the Noorderkerk, a dour brown-brick pile designed by Hendrick de Keyser just before his death in 1621. Continue walking for a few metres more and you'll come to the first cross-street connecting the main canals, **Prinsenstraat**, which quickly runs into **Herenstraat**, an appealing little street of flower shops and cafés, greengroceries and second-hand clothes shops.

For more on hofjes, see p.93.

For more on the Noorderkerk, see The Jordaan and the West, p.91.

Nearby, a little way to the north of Herenstraat between Herengracht and the Singel is the tiny **Multatuli Museum**, at Korsjespoortsteeg 20 (Tues 10am–5pm, Sat & Sun noon–5pm; free). This was the birthplace of **Eduard Douwes Dekker**, Holland's most celebrated nineteenth-century writer and a champion of free thinking, who wrote under the pen name Multatuli. Disgusted with the behaviour of his fellow Dutch in their colonies in the East Indies, he returned home to enrage the establishment with his elegantly written satirical novel *Max Havelaar*, now something of a Dutch literary classic. The museum's one room is filled with letters, first editions and a small selection of his furnishings, including the chaise longue on which he breathed his last. There's no information in English, but the attendant can tell you everything you might need to know.

For possibly the best apple cake in Amsterdam, and a fine cup of coffee to wash it down with, try Villa Zeezicht, on the Singel at Torensteeg, just east of Leliegracht.

From the museum continue through to the Singel; the red-brick building at **no. 140–142** was once home of Captain Banning Cocq, one of the militiamen depicted in Rembrandt's *The Night Watch* (see p.120). Cut back on to Herengracht, and a short walk will bring you to the **Leliegracht**, one of the tiny radial canals that cut across the *grachtengordel*, and home to a number of bookshops and canal-side bars, as well as one of the most exclusive restaurants in the city, *Christophe* (see p.221). Though there are precious few extant examples of Art Nouveau and Art Deco architecture in Amsterdam, one of the finest is the tall and striking building at the Leliegracht-Keizersgracht junction. The building was designed by Gerrit van Arkel in 1905, and added to in the late 1960s; it is now **Greenpeace's world headquarters**.

The Anne Frank House

In 1957, the Anne Frank Foundation set up the **Anne Frank House** (daily: April–Aug 9am–9pm; Sept–March 9am–7pm; closed Yom Kippur; ƒ10) in the house at Prinsengracht 263, close to the Leliegracht, where the young diarist used to listen to the Westerkerk bells until they were taken away to be melted down for the German war effort. Since the posthumous publication of her diaries, Anne Frank has become extraordinarily famous, in the first instance for recording the iniquities of the Holocaust, and latterly as a symbol of the fight against oppression and, in particular, racism. The house is now one of the most popular tourist attractions in town.

The story of Anne, her family and friends, is well known. Anne's father, **Otto Frank**, was a well-to-do Jewish businessman who ran a successful spice-trading business and lived in the southern part of the city. After the German occupation of the Netherlands, he felt – along with many other Jews – that he could avoid trouble by keeping his head down, but by 1942 it was clear that this would not be possible: Amsterdam's Jews were isolated and conspicuous, being confined to certain parts of the city and forced to wear a yellow star – roundups, too, were becoming increasingly common. In desperation, Otto Frank decided – on the advice of two Dutch friends, Mr Koophuis and Mr Kraler – to move the family into the unused back of their warehouse on the Prinsengracht. The Franks went into hiding in July 1942, along with a Jewish business partner and his family, the Van Daans. They were separated from the eyes of the outside world by a bookcase that doubled as a door. As far as everyone else was concerned, they had fled to Switzerland.

So began the two-year occupation of the *achterhuis*, or back annexe. The two families were joined in November 1942 by a Mr Dussel, a dentist friend. Koophuis and Kraler, who continued working in the front office, regularly brought supplies and news of the outside world. In her diary Anne Frank describes the day-to-day lives of the inhabitants of the annexe: the quarrels, frequent in such a claustrophobic environment; celebrations of birthdays, or of a piece of good news from the Allied Front; and her own, slightly unreal, growing up (much of which, it's been claimed, was deleted by her father).

Two years later, the atmosphere was optimistic: the Allies were clearly winning the war and liberation seemed within reach. It wasn't to be. One day in the summer of 1944 the Franks were betrayed by a Dutch collaborator and the Gestapo arrived and forced Mr Kraler to open up the bookcase. Thereafter, the occupants of the annexe were

*Related muse-
ums include
the Resistance
Museum
(p.110); the
Hollandsche
Schouwburg
(p.109); and
the Jewish
Historical
Museum
(p.108).*

all arrested and quickly sent to Westerbork – the transit camp in the north of the country where all Dutch Jews were processed before being moved to Belsen or Auschwitz. Of the eight from the annexe, only Otto Frank survived; Anne and her sister died of typhus within a short time of each other in Belsen, just one week before the German surrender.

Anne Frank's **diary** was among the few things left behind in the annexe. It was retrieved by one of the people who had helped the Franks and handed to Anne's father on his return from Auschwitz; he later decided to publish it. Since its appearance in 1947, it has been constantly in print, translated into 54 languages, and has sold millions of copies worldwide. The rooms the Franks lived in for two years are left much the same as they were during the war, even down to the movie star pin-ups in Anne's bedroom and the marks on the wall recording the children's heights. A number of other rooms offer background detail on the war and occupation: one presents a video biography of Anne, from her frustrated hopes in hiding up until her death in 1945; another details the gruesome atrocities of the Holocaust, and gives some up-to-date examples of fascism and anti-Semitism in Europe, drawing pertinent parallels with the war years. Anne Frank was only one of about 100,000 Dutch Jews who died during World War II, but this, her final home, provides one of the most enduring testaments to its horrors. Her diary has been a source of inspiration to many, including Nelson Mandela.

Westerkerk and Westermarkt

Just to the south of the Anne Frank House, the **Westerkerk** (Mon–Fri 10am–4pm, Sat 10am–1pm; free) dominates the district, its 85-metre tower (April–Sept Mon–Sat 10am–4pm; ƒ3) – without question Amsterdam's finest – soaring graciously above the gables of Prinsengracht. On its top perches the crown of Emperor Maximilian, a constantly recurring symbol of Amsterdam (see p.58) and the finishing touch to what was only the city's second place of worship built expressly for Protestants. The church was designed by Hendrick de Keyser and completed in 1631 as part of the general enlargement of the city, but whereas the exterior is all studied elegance, the interior – as required by the Calvinist congregation – is bare and plain.

The church is also the reputed resting place of **Rembrandt**, though the location of his pauper's tomb is not known. Instead, the painter is commemorated by a small memorial in the north aisle, close to which his son Titus is buried. Rembrandt adored his son – as evidenced by numerous portraits – and the boy's death dealt a final crushing blow to the ageing and embittered artist, who died just over a year later. During renovation of the church in the early 1990s, bones were unearthed that could have been those of Rembrandt – a possibility whose tourism potential excited the church authorities. The obvious way to prove it was through a chemical analysis of the bones' lead content, expected to be unusually high in an artist as the metal was a major ingredient of paint. The bones were duly taken to the University of Groningen for analysis, but, due to lack of public funds, the testing was never begun, and the bones – whoever they belonged to – remain there still.

Westermarkt, an open square in the shadow of the Westerkerk, possesses two evocative statues. At the back of the church, beside Keizersgracht, are the three pink granite triangles (one each for the past, present and future) of the **Homo-Monument**. The world's first memorial to persecuted gays and lesbians, commemorating all those who died at the hands of the Nazis, it was designed by Karin Daan and recalls the pink triangles the Germans made homosexuals sew onto their clothes during World War II. The monument has now become a focus for the city's gay community and the site of ceremonies and wreath-laying throughout the year, most notably on Queen's Day (April 30), Coming-Out Day (Sept 5) and World AIDS Day (Dec 1). The monument's inscription, by the Dutch writer Jacob Israel de Haan, translates as "Such an infinite desire for friendship". Nearby, on the south side of the church by Prinsengracht, is a small but beautifully crafted **statue of Anne Frank** by the gifted Dutch sculptor Mari Andriessen (1897–1979), who is also the creator of the dockworker statue outside Amsterdam's Portuguese Synagogue (see p.107). Incidentally, Westermarkt was for a while the home of French philosopher René Descartes, who lodged at no. 6. Happy that the Dutch were indifferent to his musings, he wrote "Everybody except me is in business and so absorbed by profit-making I could spend my entire life here without being noticed by a soul."

From Westermarkt, a five-minute walk east along Raadhuisstraat will bring you to Dam square (see p.160).

The Theatre Museum

A few metres from the Westermarkt at Herengracht 168, the **Theatermuseum** (Theatre Museum: Tues–Fri 11am–5pm, Sat–Sun 1–5pm; f7,50) holds an enjoyable collection of theatrical bygones, from props through to stage sets, with a particularly good selection of costumes and posters. Occupying a pair of fine old mansions – the restrained neoclassicism of no. 168 contrasting with the flashy neo-Renaissance facade of the (Hendrick de Keyser-designed) house next door – the museum runs a lively programme of temporary exhibitions. At times however, the sumptuousness of the interior decoration almost overwhelms the displays, not least with the eighteenth-century ceiling paintings by Jacob de Wit, the extravagant stucco work and, most dramatic of all, the slender and ornate spiral staircase.

Raadhuisstraat to Leidsegracht

Westermarkt adjoins **Raadhuisstraat**, the principal thoroughfare into the Old Centre, which runs east past the elegant curve of the nineteenth-century Art Nouveau **Utrecht Building**. South of here the main canals are less appealing than the narrow **cross-streets**, many of which are named after animals whose pelts were used in the local tanning industry; there's Reestraat ("Deer Street"), Hartenstraat (Hart), Berenstraat (Bear), Wolvenstraat (Wolf), Elandsstraat (Elk) and Hazenstraat (Hare), as well as Runstraat (a "run" is a bark used in tanning), Huidenstraat ("Street of Hides") and Looiersgracht ("Tanners' Canal"). The tanners are (maybe thankfully) long gone, but they've been replaced by some of the most pleasant shopping streets in the city – the shops here sell everything from carpets to handmade chocolates, toothbrushes to beeswax candles. The area's southern boundary is marked by **Leidsegracht**, a mostly residential canal, lined with chic town houses and a medley of handsome gables, though its tranquillity is often interrupted by flat-topped tourist boats, who use the stretch as a short cut and billow out diesel fumes as they rev their engines to make the tight turn into Prinsengracht. Although there are no real sights as such, this section of the *gracht-engordel* offers two places of interest: the Felix Meritis Mansion and the Biblical Museum.

Stroll along Leidsegracht and you can easily thread through to Leidseplein – see p.89.

The Felix Meritis Mansion

One block west of the Felix Meritis build-ing, on Prinsengracht at the foot of Elandsgracht, the Woonboot-museum (Tues–Sun 10am–5pm; ƒ4) is a Dutch houseboat that is open to visi-tors.

The **Felix Meritis Mansion** at Keizersgracht 324, near the corner with Berenstraat, is definitely worth a second look. A neoclassical monolith built in the late eighteenth century to house the artistic and scientific activities of the society of the same name, the mansion was very much the cultural focus of the city's upper crust – not that Dutch pretensions impressed everyone (the building's concert hall was notorious among musicians for its appalling acoustics, though this didn't stop it being used as a model for the later Concertgebouw). It's said that when Napoleon visited the city the entire building was redecorated for his reception, only to have him stalk out in disgust, claiming that the place stank of tobacco. Oddly enough, it later became the headquarters of the Dutch Communist Party, but they sold it to the council who now lease it to the Felix Meritis Foundation, a centre for experimental and avant-garde arts.

The Biblical Museum

One of Amsterdam's best bakeries, specializing in sourdoughs and whole-grain breads, is Paul Année, at Runstraat 25.

Cross the Keizersgracht from here and you'll quickly reach the **Bijbels Museum** (Biblical Museum; Mon–Sat 10am–5pm, Sun 1–5pm; ƒ5), which occupies a pair of splendid seventeenth-century stone mansions frilled with tendrils, carved fruit and scrollwork at Herengracht 366, near the corner with Leidsegracht. Built for one of Amsterdam's wealthy merchant families, the Cromhouts, the houses were designed by Philips Vingboons, arguably the most inventive of the architects who worked on the Grachtengordel during the city's expansion. The **interior** is comparatively plain, but the main hall does sport an extravagant painted ceiling portraying classical gods and goddesses – the work of Jacob de Wit – and at the back of the building is a fine, old Dutch kitchen. In these proud premises are exhibited the **bibles** gathered together over a lifetime by a nineteenth-century vicar, one Leendert Schouten. Amongst them is the first Dutch-language bible ever printed, dating from 1477, and several exquisite illuminated bibles from as early as the tenth century. There's also a scattering of archeological items from Palestine and Egypt and several models of the temples of Solomon and Herod. Attempts to reconstruct these Biblical temples were something of a cottage industry in Holland, with scores of Dutch antiquarians beavering away, bible in one hand and modelling equipment in the other, but Schouten himself went one step further and made his own version of the Tabernacle, on display here too.

A couple of doors down from the Bijbels Museum is **Herengracht 380**, a copy of a Loire valley chateau. This handsome stone building is ornately dressed, its main gable embellished with reclining figures and the bay window by cherubs, mythical characters and an abundance of acanthus leaves, and serves as a prelude to the string of impressive mansions which line the Herengracht further east on the so-called Golden Bend (see p.85). More or less adjacent to no. 380, the bridge at the end of Leidsegracht provides a delightful view of the leafy radial canal cutting across the *grachtengordel*. Continue east from the bridge and you'll arrive at busy Leidsestraat.

Grachtengordel South

The southern reaches of the Grachtengordel, **Grachtengordel South**, contain the city's proudest and most touted mansions, clustered along the "Golden Bend" – the curve of Herengracht between Leidsestraat and the Amstel. It's on this stretch that the merchant oligarchy abandoned the material modesty of their Calvinist forebears, indulging themselves with lavish mansions, whose fancy facades more than hinted at the wealth within. In the eighteenth century, this elite forsook brick for stone and the restrained details of traditional Dutch architecture for an overblown neoclassicism, defeat of the Spanish Habsburgs and their commercial success prompting them to compare themselves with the Greeks and Romans. In the event, it was all an illusion – the bubble burst when Napoleon's army arrived in 1793 – and, although the opulent interiors of two old mansions, the **Museum Willet-Holthuysen** and the **Van Loon Museum**, still give the flavour of those heady days, for the most part all that's left – albeit a substantial legacy – are the wonderful facades.

Grachtengordel South also contains some rather less savoury areas, where ill-considered twentieth-century development has blemished the city – from the seediness of the Rembrandtplein to the mediocrity of Vijzelstraat and Leidseplein, though the former does lead to a popular tourist attraction, the **Heineken Brewery**.

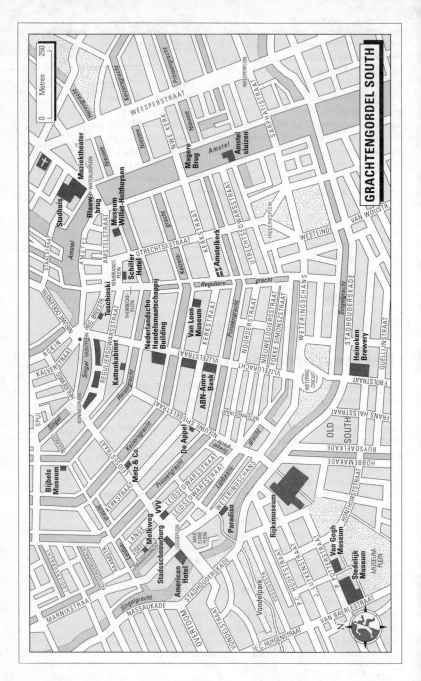

GRACHTENGORDEL SOUTH

The Golden Bend

Strolling east from Leidsestraat, the elegant sweep of **Herengracht**
unravels in the so-called "**Golden Bend**" (De Gouden Bocht), where
the canal is overlooked by a long sequence of double-fronted mansions, some of the most opulent dwellings in the city. Most of the
houses here date from the eighteenth century, with double stairways
leading to the entrance, underneath which the small door was for the
servants, and the lightly ornamented cornices that were fashionable
at the time. Classical references are common too, both in form – pediments, columns and pilasters – and decoration, from scrolls and
vases through to geometric patterns inspired by ancient Greece. One
of the first buildings to look out for on the north side of the canal is
no. 475, an extravagant edifice surmounted by a slender French-
style balustrade and a coat of arms, whilst the owners of the comparable residence at **no. 493** opted to finish off their house with a
grandly carved pediment. A couple of doors on at no. 497 a rather
more modest mansion is home to the peculiar **Kattenkabinet** (Cats'
Cabinet; Mon–Fri 10am–2pm, Sat & Sun 1–5pm; ƒ10), an enormous
collection of art and artefacts relating to cats installed by a Dutch
financier, whose own cherished moggy, John Pierpont Morgan, died
in 1984; feline fanatics will be delighted. The house also contains a
number of paintings by Jacob de Wit.

Across the canal, the facades of nos. 458–462 are soft and finely
decorated affairs, typical of such double-fronted mansions, whereas
those at nos. 504–508 are big and flashy, their balustrades decorated by dolphins and an imperious Neptune (the two-columned portal
next door at no. 502 indicates the mayor's official residence).
Finally, take a look at **no. 507**, just opposite: an imposing building,
all neoclassical pilasters and slender windows, it was once the home
of Jacob Boreel, the one-time major whose attempt to impose a burial tax prompted a riot during which the mob ransacked his house.

The Museum Willet-Holthuysen

Further along the Herengracht, near the Amstel, the **Museum
Willet-Holthuysen** (Mon–Fri 10am–5pm, Sat & Sun 11am–5pm;
ƒ7,50), at no. 605, is billed as "a peep behind the curtains into an
historic Amsterdam canal house", which just about sums it up. The
house itself dates from 1685, but the interior was remodelled by
successive members of the coal-trading Holthuysen family until the
last of the line, Sandra Willet-Holthuysen, gifted her home and its
contents to the city in 1895. Renovated a number of years ago,
most of the public rooms, notably the **Blue Room** and the **Dining
Room**, have now been returned to their original eighteenth-
century rococo appearance – a flashy and ornate style copied from
France, which the Dutch merchants held to be the epitome of
refinement and good taste. The chandeliers are gilded, heavy
affairs, the plasterwork neat and fancy, and graceful drapes hang to

either side of long and slender windows. At the back of the house are the formal **gardens**, a neat pattern of miniature hedges graced by the occasional stone statue. The museum's collection of fine and applied arts belongs to Sandra's husband, Abraham Willet; its forte is glass, silver and ceramics, including a charming selection of Chinese porcelain exhibited in the Blue Room.

Rembrandtplein and around

Just west of the museum is **Rembrandtplein**, a dishevelled bit of greenery that was formerly Amsterdam's butter market, renamed in 1876; today it claims to be one of the city's nightlife centres, though the crowded restaurants are firmly tourist-targeted. Rembrandt's pigeon-spattered statue stands in the middle, his back wisely turned against the square's worst excesses, which include live (but deadly) outdoor musak. Of the prodigious number of cafés and bars here, only the bar of the **Schiller Hotel** at no. 26 stands out, with an original Art Deco interior reminiscent of an ocean liner.

*The Tuschinski
shows all the
latest general
releases – ring
☎ 626 2633
for more
details.*

The narrow streets edging Rembrandtplein are even less endearing. The crumbling alleys to the north contain several of the city's raunchier gay bars, whilst the supremely tacky **Reguliersbreestraat** leads west to Muntplein (see p.72). Nevertheless, tucked in among Reguliersbreestraat's slot-machine arcades and sex shops at nos. 26–28, is the **Tuschinski** (guided tours July & Aug daily 10.30am; ƒ10), the city's most extraordinary cinema, with a marvellously well-preserved Art Deco interior. Opened in 1921 by a Polish Jew, Abram Tuschinski, the cinema boasts Expressionist paintings, coloured marbles and a wonderful carpet, handwoven in Marrakesh to an original design. Tuschinski himself died in Auschwitz in 1942, and there's a plaque in the cinema's foyer in his memory. The network of alleys behind the Tuschinski was once known as **Duivelshoek** ("Devil's Corner"), and, although it's been tidied up and sanitized, enough backstreet seediness remains to make it a spot to be avoided at night.

*The best-value
street food in
the city is to be
had at Maoz
on Reguliers-
breestraat,
where ƒ5 buys
you a high-
quality falafel
sandwich and
all the salad
you can eat.*

At the southern end of Rembrandtplein is pedestrianized **Thorbeckeplein**, which takes you back down to Herengracht. From the junction with the canal there's a delightful view down Reguliersgracht, the prettiest of the three surviving radial canals that cut across the *grachtengordel* – its dainty humpback bridges and greening waters overlooked by charming seventeenth- and eighteenth-century canal houses. Thorbeckeplein itself is a poor memorial to Rudolf Thorbecke (1798–1872), a far-sighted liberal politician and three times Dutch premier whose reforms served to democratize the country in the aftermath of the Europe-wide turmoil of 1848. Thorbecke's statue now oversees a tawdry assortment of bars and restaurants as well as a modest Sunday art market (10.30am–6pm).

The Amstel to the Van Loon Museum

Herengracht comes to an abrupt halt beside the wide and windy
River Amstel, which was long the main route into the interior, with
goods arriving downstream to be traded for the imported materials
held in Amsterdam's many warehouses. Turning left here takes you
to the Blauwbrug ("Blue bridge") and the Old Jewish Quarter (see
p.102), whilst in the opposite direction the **Magere Brug** ("Skinny
Bridge") is the most famous and arguably the cutest of the city's
many swing bridges. Legend has it that the current bridge, which
dates back to about 1670, replaced an even older and skinnier version, originally built by two sisters who lived on either side of the
river and were fed up with having to walk so far to see each other. It's
a few metres further south along the Amstel to the **Amstel sluizen**,
the Amstel Locks. Every night, the municipal water department closes these locks to begin the process of sluicing out the canals. A huge
pumping station on an island out to the east of the city then starts to
pump fresh water from the IJsselmeer into the canal system; similar
locks on the west side of the city are left open for the surplus to flow
into the IJ and, from there, out to sea via the North Sea Canal. The
watery contents of the canals is thus refreshed every three nights –
though, what with three centuries of algae, prams, shopping trolleys
and a few hundred rusty bikes, the water is appealing just as long as
you're not in it.

Doubling back along the Amstel, turn down **Keizergracht** and
you'll soon reach **Utrechtsestraat**, a tram-lined street renowned for
its pleasant restaurants and lively mix of bars and bookshops.
Slightly further on is **Reguliersgracht**, at a point where its humpback bridges are overlooked by several fine facades: nos. 37 and 39
have the classic neck gables popular with the merchants of the day,
as do the slightly more ornate nos. 17–21. Numbers 11 and 13 are
different again, these two buildings possessed of the plain spout
gables, external pulleys and shuttered windows used in the construction of the city's seventeenth-century warehouses. Nearby, just
south along Reguliersgracht between Kerkstraat and Prinsengracht,
is the small open space of the **Amstelveld**, an oasis of calm that
rarely sees visitors, and on the corner of which is the **Amstelkerk**,
a plain seventeenth-century white wooden church with a nineteenth-
century neogothic interior.

*The Seven
Bridges,
Reguliersgracht
31, is one of the
most appealing
hotels in the
city. See p.179
for further
details.*

The Van Loon Museum

Returning to Keizersgracht, it's just a few metres more to the **Van
Loon Museum** at no. 672 (Fri–Mon 11am–5pm; $f7,50$), which has
perhaps the finest accessible canal house interior in Amsterdam.
Built in 1672, the first tenant of the property was the artist Ferdinand
Bol, who seems to have been one of the few occupants to have avoided some sort of scandal. The Van Loons, who bought the house in
1884 and stayed until 1945, are a case in point. The last member of

Grachten-
gordel South

the family to live here was Willem van Loon, a banker whose wife, Thora van Loon-Egidius, was *dame du palais* to Queen Wilhelmina. Of German extraction, Thora was proud of her roots and allegedly entertained high-ranking Nazi officials here during the occupation – a charge of collaboration that led to the Van Loons being shunned by polite society.

Recently renovated, the **interior** of the house has been returned to its eighteenth-century appearance, a bright and breezy Rococo style of stucco, colourful wallpaper and rich wood panelling. Look out for the ornate copper **balustrade** on the staircase, into which is worked the name "Van Hagen-Trip" (former owners of the house); the Van Loons later filled the spaces between the letters with fresh iron curlicues to prevent their children falling through. The top-floor landing has several pleasant Grisaille **paintings** sporting Roman figures and one of the bedrooms – the "painted room" – is literally decorated with a Romantic painting of Italy, depicting the overgrown classical ruins and diligent peasants that were a favourite theme in Amsterdam from around 1750 to 1820. The oddest items are the fake bedroom doors: the eighteenth-century owners were so keen to avoid any lack of symmetry that they camouflaged the real bedroom doors and created imitation, decorative doors in the "correct" position instead.

Vijzelstraat and the Heineken Brewery

A short walk west along Keizersgracht from the Van Loon Museum will bring you to **Vijzelstraat**, which slices right through the middle of the *grachtengordel*'s southern portion. The northwest corner of its intersection with Keizersgracht is dominated by the **Nederlandsche Handelsmaatschappij** building, a heavyweight structure with Expressionistic flourishes that is now owned by the **ABN-AMRO Bank**. On the southern side of the canal, the bank weighs in again with a much uglier structure, a glum and low-slung office building of 1960s cubist design, whose construction was the subject of one of Amsterdam's earliest property skirmishes. Spanning Kerkstraat, the building altered the flavour of this part of Vijzelstraat – hence the opposition – but ABN-AMRO had more than enough clout to make sure it got its way.

Continuing west along Keizersgracht from Vijzelstraat will take you up to Leidsestraat (see p.90).

Below Prinsengracht, Vijzelstraat becomes Vijzelgracht, which culminates at the **Wetering circuit** roundabout with its two low-key **memorials** to World War II. On the southwestern corner of the roundabout, by the canal, is a sculpture of a wounded man holding a bugle: it was here, on March 12, 1945, that thirty people were shot by the Germans in reprisal for acts of sabotage by the Dutch Resistance – given that the war was all but over it's hard to imagine a crueller or more futile action. Across the main street, the second memorial commemorates H.M. van Randwijk, a Resistance leader. The restrained wording on the monument translates as:

When to the will of tyrants,
A nation's head is bowed,
It loses more than life and goods –
Its very light goes out.

Heineken Brewery

Looming on the far side of the Singelgracht canal – on the northern edge of the De Pijp district (see p.129) – is the **Heineken Brouwerij** (Heineken Brewery; tours Mon–Fri 9.30am & 11am; June–Sept also at 1pm & 2.30pm; July & Aug also Sat noon & 2pm; over-18s only; *f*2), one of the city's best-known attractions (tours are often sold out so try and get tickets in advance). The site had been devoted to brewing for almost 300 years before it was bought by Adriaan Heineken in 1864 as his company's headquarters. In 1988, the company was restructured and brewing was moved to a more efficient location out of town, but Heineken has developed the site as a tourist attraction with displays on the history of beer-making in general and Heineken in particular. The old brewing facilities are included on the tour, but the main draw is the snacks and **free beer**; as you'd imagine, the atmosphere is highly convivial when there are 200 people downing as much beer as they can reasonably stomach.

To get to Leidseplein from the brewery you can either take the more pleasant route, by doubling back along Vijzelgracht and heading west along Prinsengracht, or the direct route, by taking a left at the Wetering circuit roundabout down busy and unappealing Weteringschans.

Leidseplein and around

Leidseplein, lying at the western edge of Grachtengordel South, is the bustling hub of Amsterdam's nightlife, a rather cluttered and disorderly open space that has never had much character. The square once marked the end of the road in from Leiden and, as horse-drawn traffic was banned from the centre long ago, it was here that the Dutch left their horses and carts – a sort of equine car park. Today, it's quite the opposite: continual traffic made up of trams, bikes, cars and pedestrians gives the place a frenetic feel. This is supplemented by the dozens of bars, restaurants and clubs on the square and surrounding sidestreets – a bright jumble of jutting signs and neon lights – which include the famous Melkweg venue, housed in a converted dairy, and the Boom Chicago café-theatre. Given the proximity of these places to one another, it's not surprising that on a good night Leidseplein can be Amsterdam at its carefree, exuberant best.

Leidseplein also contains two buildings of some architectural note. The first is the grandiose **Stadsschouwburg**, a neo-Renaissance edifice dating from 1894 which was so widely criticized for its clumsy vulgarity that the city council of the day withheld the

For reviews of the bars and clubs on and around Leidseplein, see pp.204–208 and pp.240–242.

From Leidseplein, it's a short walk west across the Singelgracht and along Vondelstraat to Amsterdam's main park, the Vondelpark (see p.126).

Grachten-gordel South

From the Spiegel-kwartier, it's a brief and pleasant walk south to the Rijksmuseum – indeed, this is easily its most agreeable approach.

In the web of tiny streets east of Spiegelgracht, Café de Wetering, at Weteringstraat 37, is a wonderfully atmospheric brown café.

money for decorating the exterior. Home to the National Ballet and Opera until the Muziektheater (see p.105) was completed on Waterlooplein in 1986, it is now used for theatre, dance and music performances. However, its most popular function is as the place where the Ajax football team (see p.286) gather on the balcony to wave to the crowds whenever they win anything – as they often do.

Close by, just beside the square at Leidsekade 97, is the four-star **American Hotel**. One of the city's oddest buildings, it's a monumental and slightly disconcerting rendering of Art Nouveau, with angular turrets, chunky dormer windows and fancy brickwork. Completed in 1902, the present structure takes its name from its demolished predecessor, which was – as the stylistic peccadillo of its architect, W. Steinigeweg – decorated with statues and murals of North American scenes. Inside the present hotel is the *Café Americain*, once the fashionable haunt of Amsterdam's literati, but now more a mainstream location for high tea. The Art Nouveau decor is well worth a look – an array of stained glass, shallow brick arches and heavy-duty chandeliers.

Heading northeast from Leidseplein is **Leidsestraat**, one of Amsterdam's principal shopping streets – a long, slender gauntlet of fashion and shoe shops of little distinction. However, at its junction with Keizersgracht, you'll find **Metz & Co**, the city's most prestigious department store, with its fancy corner dome by Gerrit Rietveld, and a top-floor restaurant with one of the best views of the city centre. One block east of Leidseplein is Nieuwe Spiegelstraat, an appealing mixture of bookshops and corner cafés that extends south into Spiegelgracht to form the **Spiegelkwartier**. The district is home to the pricey end of Amsterdam's antiques trade and **De Appel**, a lively centre for contemporary art at Nieuwe Spiegelstraat 10 (Tues–Sun noon–5pm; ƒ2,50).

Chapter 4

The Jordaan and the West

L ying to the west of the city centre, bordered by Prinsengracht on one side and Lijnbaansgracht on the other, the Jordaan is a likeable and easily explored area of slender canals, narrow streets and simple but architecturally varied houses. Traditionally the home of Amsterdam's working class, it has recently experienced a transformation into one of the city's most attractive and sought-after residential neighbourhoods. Well into the twentieth century, the Jordaan's inhabitants were primarily stevedores and factory workers, earning a crust amongst the docks, warehouses and boat-yards that extended north beyond Brouwersgracht, the Jordaan's northern boundary. These extensive maritime facilities survive, albeit in diminished form, and divide into two zones, the first of which – between Brouwersgracht and the Haarlemerpoort – com-prises the Shipping Quarter (Scheepvaartsbuurt), and beyond that the artificial Western Islands, dredged out of the river to provide extra warehousing and dock space in the seventeenth century. In both zones, the maritime bustle has all but disappeared, but this atmospheric, admittedly down-at-heel segment of the city is rapidly finding new life as a chichi residential quarter. Specific sights here-abouts are few and far between – the best you'll do is the contempo-rary arts of the Jordaan's Stedelijk Museum Bureau – but it's still a delightful area to wander.

The Jordaan

In all probability the **Jordaan** takes its name from the French word *jardin* ("garden"), since the area's earliest settlers were French Protestant Huguenots, who fled here to escape persecution in the sixteenth and seventeenth centuries. Another possibility is that it's a corruption of the Dutch word for Jews, *joden*. Whatever the truth, the Jordaan developed from largely open country – hence the num-ber of streets and canals named after flowers and plants – into a refugee enclave: a teeming, cosmopolitan quarter beyond the pale of

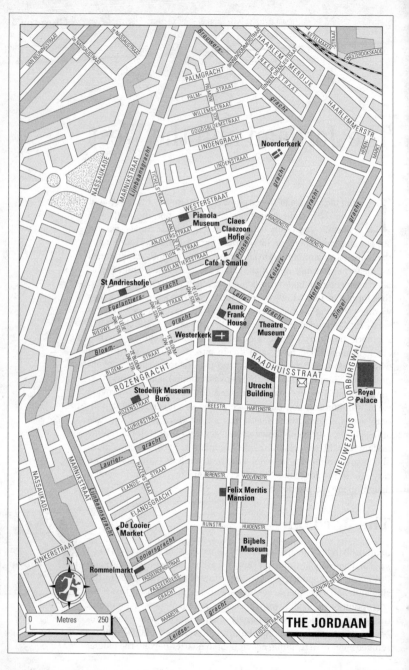

THE JORDAAN

bourgeois respectability. Indeed, when the city fathers planned the expansion of the city in 1610, they made sure the Jordaan was kept outside the city boundaries – even though Amsterdam was tolerant by contemporary standards. Consequently, the Jordaan was not subject to the rigorous planning restrictions of the main *grachten* – Herengracht, Keizersgracht and Prinsengracht – and its cobweb of narrow streets followed the lines of the original polder drainage ditches rather than any municipal outline. This gives the district its distinctive, mazy layout – and much of its present appeal.

By the late nineteenth century, the Jordaan had become one of Amsterdam's toughest neighbourhoods, a stronghold of the city's industrial working class, mostly crowded together in cramped and insanitary housing. Unsurprisingly, it was a highly politicized area, where protests against poor conditions were frequent, often coordinated by the Communist Party. In the post-war period, the slums were cleared or renovated, but rocketing property prices in the smarter parts of the city pushed middle-class professionals into the Jordaan from the early 1980s. This process of gentrification was at first much resented, but today the Jordaan is home to many young and affluent "alternative" Amsterdammers, who rub shoulders more or less easily with working-class Jordaaners with longstanding local roots.

The Jordaan's hofjes

Most notable among the Jordaan's low-key pleasures are its **hofjes** – almshouses built around a central courtyard for the city's elderly and needy, mostly in the seventeenth and eighteenth centuries. There were – and are – *hofjes* all over the city (most famously the Begijnhof – see p.72), but there's a scattering in the Jordaan, and it is worth looking in on a courtyard or two as you come across them: many have real charm. Bear in mind, though, that most are still lived in, so be discreet.

Leidsegracht to Elandsgracht

The southern boundary of the Jordaan is generally held to be the **Leidsegracht**, though it's open to debate; according to dyed-in-the-wool locals the true Jordaaner is born within earshot of the Westerkerk bells – and you'd be hard pushed to hear the chimes this far south. The narrow streets and canals just to the north of the Leidsegracht are mostly modern affairs, but **Looiersgracht** (pronounced "lawyers-gracht") retains a cluster of tumbledown cottages and, at no. 38, the indoor **Rommelmarket** (daily except Fri 11am–5pm), a vast, permanent flea market and jumble sale. You can pick up all sorts of stuff here, but if you're on the lookout for something specific, Monday is coins and stamps day, Tuesday is records and books, and Thursday is clothes; on other days, and in any spare

The Jordaan

Amsterdam has numerous markets, selling everything from tulips to flared trousers; you'll find them all listed in Shops and Markets, on pp.268–269.

space at any time, there's masses of general junk, ranging from worm-eaten wooden clogs to African masks.

Slightly further up, at Elandsgracht 109, is the rather more sophisticated **De Looier antiques market** (daily except Fri 11am–5pm, Thurs till 9pm), which – if you can manage to find your way in (the market takes up a whole row of shop fronts and the entrance isn't obvious) – is good for picking up Dutch bygones such as tiles and ceramics, with a few stalls dealing in particular items or styles such as silver trinkets or delftware. Footballophiles will also want to take a peek at the shop at Elandsgracht 96, where **Johan Cruyff** – star of Ajax in the 1970s and one of the footballing greats – bought his first pair of boots.

Elandsgracht to Rozengracht

The streets heading north from Elandsgracht are unremarkable, and easily the most agreeable route is along **Lijnbaansgracht** (literally "Tightrope-walk Canal"). This slender canal threads its way round most of the city centre and here – in between Looiersgracht and Rozenstraat – it's quiet, cobbled and leafy, the sleepy waters flanked by old brick buildings. On Rozenstraat itself, at no. 59, is an annexe of the Stedelijk Museum (see p.125), the **Stedelijk Museum Buro Amsterdam** (Tues–Sun 11am–5pm; free), which provides space for up-and-coming Amsterdam artists, with exhibitions, installations and occasional lectures and readings.

Circle Tram #20 (see p.50) runs along Rozengracht, as do trams #13, #14 and #17.

One block further north, **Rozengracht** lost its canal years ago and is now a busy main road of no particular merit. Rembrandt spent the last ten years of his life here at no. 184, but his old home is long gone too, and today only a plaque marks the spot. Rembrandt's last years were scarred by the death of his wife Hendrickje in 1663 and his son Titus five years later. Nevertheless, it was in this period that he produced some of his finest work, including *The Return of the Prodigal Son*, which is displayed in the Hermitage, Leningrad, and *The Jewish Bride*, a touchingly warm and heartfelt portrait of a bride and her father completed in 1668 and now housed in the Rijksmuseum (see p.115). The other place of interest on this street is a shop at no. 54 called 1001 Kralen, which is something of an Amsterdam institution – *kralen* means "beads", but there are a lot more than 1001 in its floor-to-ceiling collection.

From Rozengracht, the Westerkerk (see p.80) is just steps away.

Rozengracht to Westerstraat

The streets and canals extending north from Rozengracht form the heart of the Jordaan. Beyond Rozengracht, the first canal is the **Bloemgracht** ("Flower Canal"), a small and leafy waterway lined with houseboats. With its maze of cross-streets, the Bloemgracht, along with **Egelantiersgracht** ("Rose-Hip Canal") immediately to the north, exemplifies the new-found fashionableness of the Jordaan. Tiny streets filled with cafés, bars and odd little shops generate a warm, relaxed community atmosphere and murals have been graffitied onto blank walls with care. There are several attractive old houses on Bloemgracht too, especially nos. 87–91 with their dinky step gables and distinctive facade stones, depicting a *steeman* ("city-dweller"), *landman* ("farmer") and *seeman* ("sailor") living side by side.

A couple of streets up, tucked away down an alley on Egelantiersgracht between nos. 107 and 114, is one of the Jordaan's hidden *hofjes* – the **St Andrieshofje**, a small, quiet courtyard surrounded by antique houses, its entranceway lined with Delft tiles. Not far away, at no. 12, **Café 't Smalle** is one of Amsterdam's oldest cafés, opened in 1786 as a *proeflokaal*, a tasting house for the adjacent gin distillery. In the eighteenth century, when there were no quality controls, each batch of *jenever* (Dutch gin) could turn out differently, so customers were loath to part with their money until they had tasted the gin. As a result, each distillery ran a *proeflokaal* offering free samples. The *'t Smalle*'s waterside terrace is one of the most pleasant spots in the city to take a tipple – though nowadays it's not for free. Near here also, at 1e Egelantiersdwarsstraat, a sidestreet at the east end of Egelantiersgracht, is the pretty **Claes Claeszoon Hofje**, originally built as an almshouse for poor widows in 1616, but now occupied by the Amsterdam Conservatory of Music. It only takes a couple of minutes to walk from Egelantiersgracht to **2e Tuindwarsstraat** and its continuation **2e Anjeliersdwarsstraat**, which together hold many of the Jordaan's trendier stores and clothing shops as well as some of its liveliest bars and cafés.

At the end of 2e Anjeliersdwarsstraat is workaday **Westerstraat**, one of the district's main thoroughfares. The street has little going for it except for the small but fascinating **Pianola Museum** (Sun 1–5pm; *f*7,50) at no. 106, whose collection of pianolas and automatic music-machines dates from the beginning of the twentieth century. Fifteen have been restored to working order. These machines, which work on rolls of perforated paper, were the jukeboxes of their day, and the museum has a vast collection of 14,000 rolls of music, some of which were "recorded" by famous pianists and composers – Gershwin, Debussy, Scott Joplin, Art Tatum and others. The museum runs a regular programme of pianola music concerts, where the rolls are played back on restored machines.

The Noorderkerk and around

At the east end of Westerstraat, by Prinsengracht, is Hendrik de Keyser's **Noorderkerk** (March–Nov Sat 11am–1pm; free). This church, finished in 1623, was the architect's last creation, and

One of the most characterful cheap restaurants in the city, De Vliegende Schotel ("The Flying Saucer"), at Nieuwe Leliestraat 162, one block north of Bloemgracht, serves great food in huge portions at inexpensive prices.

See p.46 for an explanation of Amsterdam's street names.

Café Nol, at Westerstraat 109, is a traditional old Jordaan bar, complete with oom-pah-pah music and much heartiness. For more of the same, nip round the corner to the Twee Zwaantjes, at Prinsengracht 114, or the quieter De Tuin, on 2e Tuindwarsstraat.

probably his least successful. A bulky, overbearing building of brown and grey, it represented a radical departure from the conventional church designs of the time, having a symmetrical Greek cross floor plan, with four equally proportioned arms radiating out from a steepled centre. Uncompromisingly dour, it proclaimed the serious intent of the Calvinists who worshipped here, but this is the kindest thing to be said about it – and it's hard to understand quite how Keyser, who designed such elegant structures as the Westerkerk (see p.80), could have ended up building this.

The Lunchcafé Winkel, on the edge of the Noordermarkt at the corner with Westerstraat, sells huge wedges of apple cake, which Jordaaners swear is the best in the city.

The **Noordermarkt**, the forlorn square outside the church, holds a **statue** of three figures clinging to each other, a poignant tribute to the bloody Jordaanoproer riot of 1934, part of a successful campaign to stop the government cutting unemployment benefit during the Depression. The inscription reads "The strongest chains are those of unity". The square also hosts two of Amsterdam's best open-air markets: an antiques and general household goods market on Monday mornings (9am–1pm), and the popular Saturday farmers' market, the **Boerenmarkt** (9am–3pm), a lively affair selling organic fruit and vegetables, as well as freshly-baked breads and a plethora of oils and spices. Cross an unmarked border though and you'll find yourself in the middle of the bird market, which operates on an adjacent patch at much the same time, and, if you're at all squeamish, is best avoided – brightly coloured birds squeezed into tiny cages are not for everyone.

Just to the north of the Noorderkerk, **Lindengracht** ("Canal of Limes") lost its waterway decades ago, but has had a prominent role in local folklore since the day in 1886 when a policeman made an ill-advised attempt to stop an eel-pulling contest. Horrible as it sounds, eel-pulling was a popular pastime hereabouts with tug-o'-war teams holding tight to either end of the poor creature, which was smeared with soap to make the entertainment last a little longer. The crowd unceremoniously bundled the policeman away, but when reinforcements arrived, the whole thing got out of hand and there was a full-scale riot, which lasted for three days and cost 26 lives.

The Shipping Quarter and Western Islands

Brouwersgracht, one of Amsterdam's prettier canals, marks the northern boundary of the Jordaan and the beginning of a district loosely known as the **Shipping Quarter** – the Scheepvaartsbuurt – which focuses on the Haarlemmerdijk, a long, rather ordinary thoroughfare good for cheap restaurants and offbeat shops. In the seventeenth century this district boomed from its location between the city centre and the **Western Islands**, a narrow rectangle dredged out of the River IJ immediately to the north. The construction of these artificial islands, with their docks, warehouses and shipyards, took the pressure off Amsterdam's congested maritime facilities and was necessary to sustain the city's economic success. By then, Amsterdam's wharves stretched right along the south bank of the River IJ and functioned as the heartbeat of the city until the late nineteenth century. Thereafter, the city's shipping facilities began to drift away from the centre, a process that was accelerated by the construction of Centraal Station, slap in the middle of the old quayside in the 1880s. The Western Islands and the Shipping Quarter hung on to some of the marine trade until the 1960s, but today – bar the odd small boatyard – industry has pretty much disappeared and the area is busy re-inventing itself. There is still an air of faded grittiness here, but the old forgotten warehouses – within walking distance of the centre – are rapidly being turned into bijou studios and dozens of plant-filled houseboats are moored alongside the tiny streets.

The Shipping Quarter and Western Islands

The Haarlemmerdijk and around

Before World War II the **Haarlemmerdijk** was a bustling main street, but the trams that ran here were rerouted and now it is really rather ordinary. The only redeeming feature is the meticulously restored Art Deco **The Movies** cinema (see p.239), near the west end of the street

For cinema listings, see p.238.

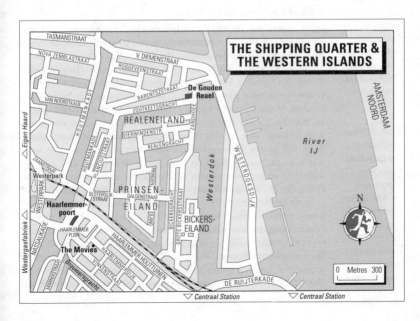

*For listings
details of the
Westergas-
fabriek, see
Entertainment
and Nightlife.
For informa-
tion on the
popular café-
cum-nightclub
here, the Café
West Pacific,
see p.209.*

*Padi, at
Haarlemmer
dijk 50, is a
small, relaxing
Indonesian
eethuis, with a
good selection
of dishes at rea-
sonable prices.*

*Tram #3 runs
south along
Houtmankade
before rum-
bling round
the edge of the
city centre via
Marnixstraat
and Frederik
Hendrikstraat
and the Van
Gogh Museum
(see p.124).*

at no. 161, which provides a spark of architectural interest, and there's an appealing café-bar here too. Haarlemmerdijk ends just twenty metres on from the cinema at the busy Haarlemmerplein traffic junction. Here, the grandiose neoclassical **Haarlemmerpoort** was built on the site of a medieval gateway in 1840 for the new king William II's triumphal entry into the city. Unfortunately the euphoria didn't last long. William was a distinguished general, who had been wounded at Waterloo, but he proved to be a crusty reactionary as a king, only accepting mild liberal reforms after extensive rioting in Amsterdam and elsewhere.

Beyond the Haarlemmerpoort, barely five minutes' walk away to the west, is an entrance to the **Westerpark**, one of the city's smaller and more enticing parks. At the far end of the park you get a good view of the old gas factory, the **Westergasfabriek**, across the canal footbridge to the south at Haarlemmerweg 8–10. Dating from 1884, the gas factory had a brief reincarnation as the city's prime venue for Acid House parties in the early 1990s, but is now a centre for performance art, exhibitions, music and culture. The *Panorama of the West* is the title of a permanent installation on the site, clearly signposted near the Ketelhuis no. 2. Basically a huge slide inside a viewing box, it was devised by artist Siebe Swart, with photographs illustrating the development of the Westergasfabriek from industrial lynchpin to cultural adornment.

The Western Islands

Duck under the railway lines beside the Haarlemmerpoort and you enter the **Western Islands**, bounded by Houtmankade in the west and Van Diemenstraat to the north. Take the first right – along Sloterdijkstraat – and you'll soon reach **Galgenstraat** ("Gallows Street"), so called because the city gallows were once visible from here just across the river. Galgenstraat bisects the nearest of the Western Islands, pint-sized **Prinseneiland**, which is, with its canals and houseboats, old dwellings and renovated warehouses, one of the most appealing parts of Amsterdam. Turn left at the east end of Galgenstraat and it's a short walk north to the bridge leading over to **Realeneiland** and another 400m or so to the junction of Zandhoek and Zoutkeetsgracht. Here, the **De Gouden Reael** restaurant is identifiable by the gold coin on its facade stone. Before Napoleon introduced a system of house numbers, these stones were the principal way that visitors could recognize one house from another, and many homeowners went to considerable lengths to make theirs unique. Jacob Real, the Catholic tradesman who owned this house, used the image of a *real* – a Spanish coin – to also discreetly advertise his sympathies for the Catholic Spanish cause during their war with the Dutch.

From the restaurant, it's a short walk south along the quayside back to Centraal Station, or you can walk west along Zoutkeetsgracht to the tram #3 terminus on Houtmankade. If you stroll south down Houtmankade and then follow the train tracks west along Zaanstraat, it takes about fifteen minutes to reach Spaarndammerplantsoen and the **Eigen Haard** complex, a good example of the work of the Amsterdam School of architecture. Seven years in the making, from 1913 to 1920, this housing project was designed by Michel de Klerk, who reacted strongly against the influence of H.P. Berlage, whose style – exemplified by the Beurs (see p.59) – emphasized clean lines and functionality. De Klerks' style was more playful and Eigen Haard is distinguished by its sweeping brick facades, soft angles, bulging windows and balconies, and needle-like spires.

The Shipping Quarter and Western Islands

For a description of De Klerk's De Dageraad housing project and an overview of the Amsterdam School of architects, see p.134.

Chapter 5

The Old Jewish Quarter and the East

O riginally one of the marshiest parts of Amsterdam, prone to regular flooding, the narrow slice of land sandwiched between the curve of the Amstel, Kloveniersburgwal and the Nieuwe Herengracht was the home of Amsterdam's Jews from the sixteenth century up until World War II. By the 1920s, this Old Jewish Quarter, focusing on Waterlooplein and Jodenbreestraat and often called the Jodenhoek ("Jews' Corner"), was crowded with tenement buildings and smoking factories, but in 1945 it lay derelict – and neither has post-war redevelopment treated it kindly. Waterlooplein has been overwhelmed by a whopping town and concert hall complex, which caused much controversy at the time of its construction, and the Jodenbreestraat is now bleak and very ordinary – with Mr Visserplein, at its east end, now one of the city's busiest traffic junctions. Picking your way round these obstacles is not much fun, but persevere – amongst all the cars and concrete are several moving reminders of the Jewish community that perished in the war. For reasons that remain unclear, the Germans did not destroy all the Jodenhoek's synagogues, and the late seventeenth-century Portuguese synagogue is one of the finest buildings in the city. Close by, four other synagogues have been merged into the fascinating Jewish Historical Museum, celebrating Jewish culture and custom. Rembrandt spent the best years of his life living in the Jodenhoek and the restored Rembrandt House contains a large collection of his etchings.

The eastern section of Amsterdam's centre is made up of the **Plantagebuurt** and the **Eastern Islands**. The backbone of Plantagebuurt is Plantage Middenlaan, a wide boulevard stretching east from the Old Jewish Quarter, constructed in the mid-nineteenth century as part of the creation of a smart, leafy suburb – one of Amsterdam's first. The avenue borders the city's largest botanical gardens, the **Hortus Botanicus**, and the zoo (see p.281) and runs close to the first-rate **Dutch Resistance Museum**. Just slightly to the

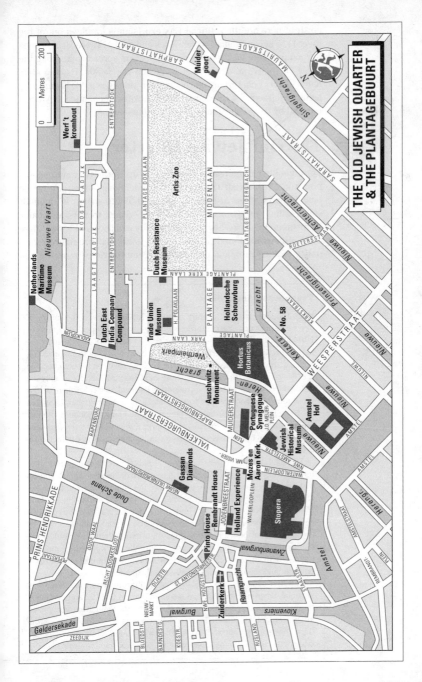

THE OLD JEWISH QUARTER & THE PLANTAGEBUURT

Metres 0 — 200

N

Labels on map:

SARPHATISTRAAT
Muiderpoort
MAURITSKADE
Werf 't kromhout
Singelgracht
Nieuwe Vaart
HOOGTE KADIJK
ENTREPOTDOK
LAAGTE KADIJK
Plantage Doklaan
Artis Zoo
MIDDENLAAN
SARPHATISTRAAT
1e Achtergracht
Netherlands Maritime Museum
Dutch Resistance Museum
PLANTAGE KERK LAAN
RUYTERSS
Nieuwe Achtergracht
KADIJKSPLEIN
Dutch East India Company Compound
Trade Union Museum
H. POLAKLAAN
PLANTAGE
Plantage Muidergracht
Hollandsche Schouwburg
No. 58
KERKSTRAAT
PARK LAAN
PLANTAGE MUIDERGRACHT
Prinsengracht
Wertheimpark
Hortus Botanicus
Heren
Keizers
gracht
NIEUWE
WEESPERSTRAAT
Auschwitz Monument
RAPENBURGERSTRAAT
RAPENBURG
MUIDERSTRAAT
Nieuwe Herengracht
Amstel Hof
AMSTEL
VALKENBURGERSTRAAT
Mr VISSER
PLEIN
J.D. MEIJER-PLEIN
Portuguese Synagogue
Jewish Historical Museum
NIEUWE AMSTELSTR
Gassan Diamonds
NIEUWE UILENBURGERSTRAAT
NWE AMSTELSTR
PRINS HENDRIKKADE
Oude Schans
Rembrandt House
Mozes en Aaron Kerk
WATERLOOPLEIN
Stopera
PETERSTRAAT
OUDE WAAL
RECHT BOOMSSLOOT
Pinto House
JODENBREESTRAAT
Holland Experience
Zwanenburgwal
Amstel
Het ENGL
AMSTELSTRAAT
PLEIN
RAMBRAND
DIJKSTR
ST. ANTONIESBREESTR
NW HOOGSTR
Raamgracht
RUSLAND
AMSTEL
GELDERSEKADE
ZEEDIJK
NIEUW-MARKT
Burgwal
Zuiderkerk
Klovenlers
AMSTELSTRAAT
BLOEDSTG
BARNDESTG
KOESTR
PETERSTRAAT

north of here are the artificial **Eastern Islands**, dredged out of the River IJ to accommodate warehouses and docks. These islands once formed part of a vast maritime complex that spread right along the River IJ. Industrial decline set in during the 1880s, but the area, much like its counterpart on the western side (see p.96) is currently being redefined as a residential district, whilst its nautical heyday is recalled by the **Netherlands Maritime Museum**.

The Old Jewish Quarter

Throughout the nineteenth century and up to the German occupation, the **Old Jewish Quarter** – the Jodenhoek – was one of the busiest parts of town, its main streets holding scores of open-air stalls selling everything from pickled herrings to pots and pans. Unfortunately, it was also surrounded by canals – and it was these the Germans exploited to create the ghetto that pre-figured their policy of starvation and deportation. They restricted movement in

---

The Jews in Amsterdam

From the late sixteenth century onwards, Amsterdam was the refuge of Jews escaping persecution throughout the rest of Europe. The **Union of Utrecht**, ratified in 1579, signalled the start of the influx. Drawn up by the largely Protestant northern Dutch provinces in response to the invading Spanish army, the treaty combined the United Provinces (later to become the Netherlands) in a loose federation, whose wheels could only be greased by a degree of religious toleration then unknown elsewhere across the continent. Whatever the Protestants may have wanted, they knew that the Catholic minority (around 35 percent) would only continue to support the rebellion against the Spanish Habsburgs if they were treated well – the Jews benefited by osmosis and consequently immigrated here in their hundreds.

The toleration, however, did have its limits: Jewish immigrants were forced to buy citizenship; Christian-Jewish marriages were illegal; and, as with the Catholics, they were only allowed to practise their religion discreetly behind closed doors. A proclamation in 1632 also excluded them from most guilds – effectively withdrawing their right to own and run businesses. This forced them either to excel in those trades not governed by the guilds or introduce new non-guild ones into the city, the result being that by the middle of the eighteenth century the city's Jewish community was active in almost every aspect of the economy, with particular strongholds in bookselling, tobacco, banking and commodity futures.

The first major Jewish influx was of **Sephardic** Jews from Spain and Portugal, where persecution had begun in earnest in 1492 and continued throughout the sixteenth century. In the 1630s, the Sephardim were joined in Amsterdam by hundreds of (much poorer) **Ashkenazi** Jews from German-speaking central Europe. The two groups established separate synagogues and, although there was no ghetto as such, the vast majority

and out of the quarter by raising most of the swing bridges (over the Nieuwe Herengracht, the Amstel and the Kloveniersburgwal) and imposing stringent controls on the rest. The Jews, readily identifiable by the yellow Stars of David they were obliged to wear, were not allowed to use public transport or to own a telephone, and were placed under a curfew. Roundups and deportations began shortly after the Germans arrived and continued well into 1945. At the end of the war, the Jodenhoek lay deserted and, as the need for wood and raw materials intensified in the cold winter that followed, many of the houses were dismantled for fuel, a process of destruction that was completed in the 1970s when the metro was sunk beneath Waterlooplein. By these means, pre-war Jodenhoek disappeared almost without trace, the notable exception being the imposing **Portuguese Synagogue** and the four connected synagogues of the Ashkenazi Jews, now the **Jewish Historical Museum**. The district's other main sight is the **Rembrandt House**, crammed with the artist's etchings.

settled on and around what is now Waterlooplein, then a distinctly unhealthy tract of marshland subject to regular flooding by the River Amstel. Initially known as **Vlooyenburg**, this district was usually referred to as the **Jodenhoek** (pronounced "yo-den-hook"), or "Jews' Corner", though this was not, generally speaking, a pejorative term – Rembrandt, for instance, was quite happy to live here and frequently painted his Jewish neighbours. Indeed, given the time, the most extraordinary feature of Jewish settlement in Amsterdam was that it occasioned mild curiosity rather than outright hate, as evinced by contemporary prints of Jewish religious customs, where there is neither any hint of stereotype nor discernible demonization.

The restrictions affecting both Jews and Catholics were removed during Napoleon's occupation of the United Provinces, when the country was temporarily renamed the Batavian Republic (1795-1806). Freed from official discrimination, Amsterdam's Jewish community flourished and the Jewish Quarter expanded, nudging northwest towards Nieuwmarkt and east across Nieuwe Herengracht, though this was just the focus of a community whose members lived in every part of the city. In 1882, the dilapidated houses of the Vlooyenburg were razed and several minor canals filled in to make way for **Waterlooplein**, which became a largely Jewish marketplace, a bustling affair that sprawled out along St Antoniesbreestraat and Jodenbreestraat. At the turn of the twentieth century, there were around 60,000 Jews living in Amsterdam, but refugees from Hitler's Germany swelled this figure to around 120,000 in the 1930s. The disaster that befell this community during the German occupation in World War II is hard to conceive, but the bald facts speak for themselves: when Amsterdam was liberated, there were only 5000 Jews left and the Jodenhoek was, to all intents and purposes, a ghost town. At present, there are about 25,000 Jews resident in the city, but while Jewish life in Amsterdam has survived, its heyday is gone forever.

St Antoniesbreestraat

Stretching southwest from Nieuwmarkt, **St Antoniesbreestraat** once linked the city centre with the Jewish quarter, but its huddle of shops and houses was mostly demolished in the 1980s to make way for a main road. The plan was subsequently abandoned, but the modern buildings that now line most of the street hardly fire the soul, the only bearable feature being the sharp, angular lines of the apartment blocks. One of the few survivors of all this municipal shenanigans is the **Pintohuis** (Pinto House; Mon & Wed 2–8pm, Fri 2–5pm, Sat 11am–2pm; free), at no. 69, which is now a public library. Easily spotted by its creamy Italianate facade, the mansion is named after Isaac De Pinto, a Jew who fled Portugal to escape the Inquisition and subsequently became a founder of the East India Company (see p.111). Pinto bought this property in 1651 and promptly had it remodelled in grandiose style, the facade interrupted by six lofty pilasters, which lead the eye up to the blind balustrade. The mansion was the talk of the town, even more so when Pinto had the interior painted in a similar style to the front – pop in to look at the birds and cherubs of the original painted ceiling.

There are two good but very different bars at the junction of St Antoniebree-straat and Jodenbree-straat. The first is the chic split-level Tisfris, at St Antoniebree-straat 142, the second is Café 't Sluyswacht, a traditional brown bar in an old brick building by the canal just opposite.

Across the street, through the old archway, the **Zuiderkerk** (centre: Mon–Wed & Fri 9.30am–5pm, Thurs noon–8pm, free; tower: June–Sept only Wed–Sat 2–4pm; ƒ3), dating from 1611, was the first church built in the city specifically for the Protestants. It was designed by Amsterdam's flashy architect and sculptor, Hendrick de Keyser (1565–1621), whose distinctive – and very popular – style extrapolated elements of traditional Flemish design, with fanciful detail and frilly towers added wherever possible. The basic design of the Zuiderkerk is firmly Gothic, but the soaring tower, which you can climb up during the summer, is typical of his work, complete with balconies and balustrades, arches and columns. Now deconsecrated, the church has been turned into a municipal information centre with displays on housing and the environment, plus temporary exhibitions revealing the city council's plans for future development.

Jodenbreestraat and the Rembrandt House

St Antoniesbreestraat runs into **Jodenbreestraat**, the "Broad Street of the Jews", at one time the Jodenhoek's principal market and centre of Jewish activity. Badly served by post-war development, this ancient thoroughfare is now short on charm, with the exception of the modern symmetries – and cubist, coloured panels – of the apartment blocks that spill along part of the street. In these unlikely surroundings stands **Het Rembrandthuis**, at no. 6 (Rembrandt House; Mon–Sat 10am–5pm, Sun 1–5pm; ƒ7,50, more during exhibitions), its slender facade decorated by pretty wooden shutters and a dinky pediment. Rembrandt bought this house at the height of his fame and popularity, living here for over twenty years and spending a fortune on furnishings – an expense that ultimately contributed to his bankruptcy. An inventory made at the time details a huge collection of paintings, sculptures and art treasures he'd amassed, almost all of which was confiscated after he was declared insolvent and forced to move to a more modest house on Rozengracht in the Jordaan in 1658. The city bought the artist's Jodenbreestraat house in 1907 and then had it renovated. It now holds an extensive collection of Rembrandt's **etchings** as well as several of the original copper plates on which he worked. The biblical illustrations attract the most attention, though the studies of tramps and vagabonds are equally appealing. An accompanying exhibit explains Rembrandt's engraving techniques and there are temporary exhibitions focusing on various aspects of Rembrandt's life and times.

Next door, the multimedia **Holland Experience** (daily 10am–6pm; ƒ17,50, under-16s ƒ15) is a kind of sensory-bombardment movie about Holland and Amsterdam, with synchronized smells, a moving floor and a simulation of a violent thunderstorm. From here, it's a couple of minutes' walk to **Gassan Diamonds** (daily 9am–5pm; free), which occupies a large and imposing brick building dating from 1897 on Nieuwe Uilenburgerstraat. Before World War II, many local Jews worked as diamond cutters and polishers, though there's little sign of the industry here today, this factory being an exception.

The Old Jewish Quarter

There's an unrivalled collection of Rembrandt's works in the Rijksmuseum, covered on pp.115–123.

Near Gassan Diamonds is Amsterdam's finest jazz club, the Bimhuis, at Oude Schans 73–77; see p.233 for full details.

Waterlooplein

Jodenbreestraat runs parallel to the **Stadhuis en Muziektheater** (Town Hall and Concert Hall), a sprawling complex whose indeterminate modernity dominates **Waterlooplein**, a rectangular parcel of land that was originally swampy marsh. This was the site of the first Jewish Quarter, but by the late nineteenth century it had become an insanitary slum, home to the poorest of the Ashkenazi Jews. The slums were cleared in the 1880s and thereafter the open spaces of the Waterlooplein hosted the largest and liveliest marketplace in the city, the place where Jews and Gentiles met to trade. In the war, the Germans used the square to round up their victims, but despite these ugly connotations the Waterlooplein was revived in the 1950s as the site of the city's main **flea market**. Unfortunately though it was only a stopgap as far as the city council was concerned; a depopulated Jodenhoek was, they felt, ideal for redevelopment. For starters whole streets were demolished to make way for the motorist – with Mr Visserplein, for example, becoming little more than a traffic intersection (see p.106) – and then, warming to their theme in the late 1970s, the council announced the building of a massive new concert-and-city-hall complex on Waterlooplein. Opposition was immediate and widespread, but attempts to prevent the building failed, and the Muziektheater opened in 1986, since when it has established a reputation for artistic excellence. One of the story's abiding ironies is that

For further details of Amsterdam's flea markets, see pp.268–269.

the title of the protest campaign – "**Stopera**" – has passed into common usage to describe the complex.

In the public **passageway** between the theatre and town hall a series of glass columns give a salutary lesson on the fragility of the Netherlands: two contain water indicating the sea levels in the Dutch towns of Vlissingen and IJmuiden (below knee-level), while another records the levels experienced during the 1953 flood disaster (way above head-height). Downstairs a plaque shows what is known as "Normal Amsterdam Level" (NAP), originally calculated in 1684 as the average water level in the river IJ and still the basis for measuring altitude above sea level across Europe.

It's not much, but there are a couple of **memorials** to the city's Jews in and around the complex. The most striking is the bronze cast of a Jewish violinist that bursts through the floor tiles in the foyer of the Muziektheater. Outside, at the very tip of Waterlooplein, where the River Amstel meets the Zwanenburgwal canal, there is also a black stone memorial to the dead of the Jewish Resistance; the passage from Jeremiah translates as:

> *If my eyes were a well of tears, I would cry*
> *day and night for the fallen fighters of my*
> *beloved people.*

Waterlooplein has one other minor attraction, the **Arcam Galerie** (Tues–Sat 1–5pm; free), at no. 213, which houses changing exhibitions on the city's architecture.

Mr Visserplein

Just behind the Muziektheater, on the corner of Mr Visserplein, is the **Mozes en Aaron Kerk**, a rather glum neoclassical structure built on the site of a clandestine Catholic church in the 1840s. It takes its unusual name from a pair of facade stones bearing effigies of the two prophets that decorated the earlier building. Earlier still, this site contained the house where the philosopher and theological writer Spinoza was born in 1632. Of Sephardic descent, Spinoza's pantheistic views soon brought him into conflict with the elders of the Jewish community. At the age of 23, he was excommunicated and forced out of the city, moving into a small village where he survived by grinding lenses. After an attempt on his life, Spinoza moved again, eventually ending up in The Hague, where his free-thinking proved more acceptable. He produced his most famous treatise, *Ethics Demonstrated in the Geometrical Order* in 1674, three years before his death.

Next door to the church, **Mr Visserplein** is a busy junction for traffic speeding towards the IJ tunnel. It takes its name from Mr Visser, President of the Supreme Court of the Netherlands in 1939. He was dismissed the following year when the Germans occupied the country, and became an active member of the Jewish resistance, working for the illegal underground newspaper *Het Parool* ("The Password") and refusing to wear the yellow Star of David. He died in 1942, a few days after publicly – and famously – denouncing all forms of collaboration.

The Portuguese Synagogue

Unmissable on the corner of Mr Visserplein is the brown and bulky brickwork of the **Esnoga** or **Portugees synagoge** (Portuguese Synagogue; April–Oct Mon–Fri & Sun 10am–4pm; Nov–March Mon–Thurs 10am–4pm, Fri 10am–3pm, Sun 10am–noon; closed Yom Kippur; ƒ7,50), completed in 1675 for the city's Sephardic Jews. One of Amsterdam's most imposing buildings, the central structure, with its grand pilasters and blind balustrade, was built in the broadly neoclassical style that was then fashionable in Holland. It is surrounded by a courtyard complex of small outhouses, where the city's Sephardim have fraternized for centuries. Barely altered since its construction, the synagogue's lofty interior follows the Sephardic tradition in having the Hechal (the Ark of the Covenant) and *tebah* (from where services are led) at opposite ends. Also traditional is the seating, with two sets of wooden benches (for the men) facing each other across the central aisle – the women have separate galleries up above. A set of superb brass chandeliers holds the candles that remain the only source of artificial light. When it was completed, the synagogue was one of the largest in the world, its congregation almost certainly the richest; today, the Sephardic community has dwindled to just sixty members, most of whom live outside the city centre. In one of the outhouses, a video sheds light on the history of the synagogue and Amsterdam's Sephardim; the mystery is why the Germans left it alone, and no one knows for sure, but it seems likely that they intended to turn it into a museum once all the Jews had been eradicated.

Jonas Daniel Meijerplein

Next to the synagogue, on the south side of its retaining wall, is **Jonas Daniel Meijerplein**, a scrawny triangle of lawn named after the eponymous lawyer, who in 1796, at the remarkable age of sixteen, was the first Jew to be admitted to the Amsterdam Bar. It was here in February 1941 that around 400 Jewish men were forcibly loaded up on trucks and taken to their deaths at Mauthausen concentration camp, in reprisal for the killing of a Dutch Nazi during a street fight. The arrests sparked off the **February Strike** (Februaristaking), a general strike in protest against the Germans' treatment of the Jews. It was organized by the outlawed Communist Party and spearheaded by Amsterdam's transport workers and dockers – a rare demonstration of solidarity with the Jews in occupied Europe and the Netherlands, where the majority of people had done

**The Old
Jewish
Quarter**

little to protest against the actions of the SS. The strike was quickly suppressed, but is still commemorated by an annual wreath-laying ceremony on February 25, as well as by Mari Andriessen's statue of the **Dokwerker** ("dockworker") here on the square.

Jewish Historical Museum

Across the square, on the far side of the main road, the **Joods Historisch Museum** (Jewish Historical Museum; daily 11am–5pm; closed Yom Kippur; ƒ8) is cleverly housed in four Ashkenazi synagogues dating from the late seventeenth century. For years after the war these buildings lay abandoned, but they were finally refurbished – and connected by walkways – in the 1980s to accommodate a wide-ranging collection that covers most aspects of Dutch Jewish life and beliefs. The Nieuwe Synagoge of 1752 is the starting point of the self-guided tour and displays memorabilia from the long history of the Jews in the Netherlands as well as a poignant section on the war, complete with several especially moving photographs. In addition, there's a display of the powerful autobiographical paintings of Charlotte Salomon, who was killed in the Auschwitz concentration camp at the age of 26. Further on, the ground floor of the capacious Grote Synagoge of 1671 focuses on religious practise and beliefs, while the upper level holds a finely judged social history of the city's Jews, tracing their prominent role in a wide variety of industries, both as employers and employees.

For more on Amsterdam during the German occupation, visit the Dutch Resistance Museum (see p.110).

The Plantagebuurt

Developed in the middle of the nineteenth century, the **Plantagebuurt**, with its comfortable streets bordering Plantage Middenlaan, was built as part of a concerted attempt to provide good quality housing for the city's expanding middle classes. Although it was never as fashionable as the older residential parts of the *gracht-engordel*, the new district did contain elegant villas and spacious terraces, making it a first suburban port-of-call for many aspiring Jews. Nowadays, the Plantagebuurt is still one of the more prosperous parts of the city, in a modest sort of way, and boasts two especially enjoyable attractions – the **Hortus Botanicus** botanical gardens and the **Dutch Resistance Museum**.

South of Nieuwe Herengracht

With the second phase of the digging of the *grachtengordel*, the three main canals that ringed the city centre were extended beyond the River Amstel up to the docks along the River IJ – hence "Nieuwe" Herengracht, Keizersgracht and Prinsengracht. At first, takers for the new land were few and far between and the city had no option but to offer it to charities at discount prices. One result was the establishment of the whopping **Amstel Hof**, a former *hofje* and a stern and especially dreary building, which still stretches out along the Amstel between Nieuwe Herengracht and Nieuwe Keizersgracht. Later, things picked up as many better-off Jews escaped the crowded conditions of the Old Jewish Quarter to live along the new canals, but this community did not of course survive World War II. One painful reminder of the occupation still stands at **Nieuwe Keizersgracht 58**, on the opposite side of Weesperstraat to the Amstel Hof. From 1940, this house, with its luxurious neoclassical doorway, was the headquarters of the Judenrat (Jewish Council), through which the Germans ran the ghetto and organized the deportations. The role of the Judenrat is extremely controversial. Many have argued that they were base collaborators, who hoped to save their own necks by working with the Germans and duping their fellow Jews into thinking that the deportations were indeed – as Nazi propaganda insisted – about the transfer of personnel to new employment in Germany. Just how much the council leaders knew about the gas chambers remains unclear, but after the war the surviving members of the Jewish Council successfully defended themselves against charges of collaboration, claiming that they had been a buffer against the Germans rather than their instruments.

The Plantage-buurt

Beginning at Centraal Station, Circle Tram #20 (see p.50) runs along the northern part of Plantage Middenlaan, passing by – or within easy walking distance of – all the Plantage-buurt's main attractions.

Plantage Middenlaan

From Mr Visserplein, it's a short walk east along Muiderstraat to the lush **Hortus Botanicus** (April–Sept Mon–Fri 9am–5pm, Sat & Sun 11am–5pm; Oct–March Mon–Fri 9am–4pm, Sat & Sun 11am–4pm; *f*7,50), a pocket-sized botanical garden at the corner of Plantage Middenlaan and Plantage Parklaan. Founded in 1682, the gardens contain 6000 plant species (including various carnivorous varieties) on display both outside and in a series of hothouses, including a Three-Climates Glasshouse, where the plants are arranged according to their geographical origins. The garden makes a relaxing break on any tour of central Amsterdam and you can stop off for coffee and cakes in the orangery. Across the street, in the small **Wertheimpark** beside the Nieuwe Herengracht canal, is the **Auschwitz monument**, designed by the Dutch writer Jan Wolkers. It's a simple affair with symbolically broken mirrors and a cracked urn containing the ashes of some of the Jews who died in Buchenwald. The inscription reads *Nooit meer Auschwitz* ("Auschwitz – Never Again").

Continue down the right-hand side of Plantage Middenlaan to reach another sad relic of the war at no. 24, **De Hollandsche Schouwburg** (daily 11am–4pm except Yom Kippur; free), a predominantly Jewish theatre that became the main assembly point for Dutch Jews prior to their deportation. Inside, there was no daylight and families were interned in conditions that foreshadowed those of the camps they would soon be taken to. The building has recently been refurbished to house a small exhibition on the plight of

Amsterdam's Jews, but the old auditorium out at the back has been left as an empty, roofless shell. A memorial column of basalt on a Star of David base stands where the stage once was, an intensely mournful monument to suffering of unfathomable proportions.

*For a full
account on the
zoo see p.281.*

The Dutch Resistance Museum

From De Hollandsche Schouwburg, it'a brief walk northeast along Plantage Kerklaan to both the **Artis Zoo** and the excellent **Verzetsmuseum**, at no. 61 (Dutch Resistance Museum; Tues–Fri 10am–5pm, Sat & Sun noon–5pm; ƒ8). The museum outlines the development of the Dutch Resistance from the German invasion of the Netherlands in May 1940 to the country's liberation in 1945. Thoughtfully presented, the main gangway examines the experience of the majority of the population, dealing honestly with the fine balance between co-operation and collaboration. Side rooms are devoted to aspects of the movement, from the brave determination of the Communist Party, who went underground as soon as the Germans arrived, to more ad hoc responses like the so-called Milk Strike of 1943, when hundreds of milk producers refused to deliver. Interestingly, the Dutch Resistance proved especially adept at forgery, forcing the Germans to make the identity cards they issued more and more complicated – but without much success. In English and Dutch, the text to all the exhibits is illustrated by fascinating old photographs and a host of original artefacts, from examples of illegal newsletters to signed German death warrants. Apart from their treatment of the Jews, which is also detailed here, perhaps the most chilling feature of the occupation was the use of indiscriminate reprisals to terrify the population. For the most part it worked, though there were always a minority courageous enough to resist. The museum has dozens of little metal sheets providing biographical sketches of the members of the Resistance – and it's this mixture of the general and the personal that is its real strength.

*One of the
least-known
brown cafés in
the city is the
friendly De
Druif ("The
Grape"), a
five-minute
walk north of
the Dutch
Resistance
Museum at
Rapenburger-
plein 83.*

*The
Muiderpoort
gateway,
standing at the
east end of
Plantage
Middenlaan,
marks the
start of the
multi-cultural
Oost (East)
district outside
the centre,
with the
Tropen-
museum and
the pretty
Oosterpark
just steps away
(see The Outer
Districts chap-
ter, pp.129-
163)*

The Trade Union Museum

Doubling back along Plantage Kerklaan, take the first right down Henri Polaklaan for the **Vakbondsmuseum**, at no. 9 (Trade Union Museum; Tues–Fri 11am–5pm, Sun 1–5pm; ƒ5). The museum contains a small exhibition of documents, cuttings and photos relating to the Dutch labour movement, with a section devoted to Henri Polak, the leader of the Diamond Workers' Union and the man responsible for co-ordinating the successful campaign for the eight-hour working day. However, the building is actually rather more interesting than the exhibition. Built by Berlage for the Diamond Workers' Union in 1900, it was designed in a distinctive style that incorporated Romanesque features – such as the castellated balustrade and the deeply recessed main door – within an Expressionist framework. The striking, brightly-coloured interior develops these themes with a beautiful mixture of stained glass windows, stone arches, painted brickwork and patterned tiles. From the outside, the building looks like a fortified mansion, hence its old nickname the Rode Burgt ("Red Stronghold"). This design was not just about Berlage's whims. Acting on behalf of the employers, the police – and sometimes armed scabs – were regularly used to break strikes, and the union believed members could retreat here to hold out in relative safety. Indeed on a number of occasions this proved to be the case, leading the idea to be copied elsewhere, especially in Berlin, where it had disastrous consequences for the left: in the 1930s the National Socialists simply surrounded the trade union strongholds and captured many of the leading activists in one fell swoop.

The Eastern Islands

Just to the north are the **Eastern Islands**, a network of artificial islands dredged out of the River IJ to increase Amsterdam's shipping facilities in the seventeenth century. By the 1980s, this mosaic of docks, jetties and islands had become something of a post-industrial eyesore, but since then an ambitious redevelopment programme has turned things around and the area is now reckoned to be one of the most up-and-coming in the city. The obvious sight here is the **Netherlands Maritime Museum**.

Entrepotdok

At the northern end of Plantage Kerklaan, just beyond the Dutch Resistance Museum, a footpath and bridge lead over to the first, and most interesting, of the Eastern Islands, **Entrepotdok**. On the far side of the bridge old brick warehouses stretch right along the quayside, distinguished by their spout gables, multiple doorways and overhead pulleys. Built by the **Dutch East India Company** in the eighteenth century, they were once part of the largest warehouse complex in continental Europe, a gigantic customs-free zone established for goods in transit. On the ground floor, above the main entrance, each warehouse sports the name of a town or island; goods for onward transportation were stored in the appropriate warehouse until there were enough to fill a boat or barge. The warehouses have been tastefully converted into offices and apartments, a fate that must surely befall the central East India Company **compound**, whose grand neo-classical entrance is at the west end of Entrepotdok on Kadijksplein. Founded in 1602, the Dutch East India Company was the chief pillar of Amsterdam's wealth for nearly two hundred years. Its high-percentage profits came from importing spices into Europe, and to secure them the company's ships ventured far and wide, establishing trading links with India, Sri Lanka, Indo-China, Malaya, China and

Next to the Muiderpoort, at Sarphatistraat 126, De Groene Olifant ("The Green Elephant") is a characterful old wood-panelled brown café.

Entredok, at Entrepotdok 64, is a friendly local bar, with sunny seating on the water-side.

Japan, though modern-day Indonesia was always the main event. Predictably, the company had a cosy relationship with the merchants who steered the Dutch government: the company was granted a trading monopoly in all the lands east of the Cape of Good Hope and could rely on the warships of the powerful Dutch navy if they got in difficulty. Neither was their business purely mercantile: the East India Company exercised unlimited military, judicial and political powers in those trading posts it established, the first of which was Batavia in Java in 1619. In the 1750s, the Dutch East India Company went into decline, partly because the British expelled them from most of the best trading stations, but mainly because the company over-borrowed. The Dutch government took it over in 1795.

From Kadijksplein, it's a couple of minutes' walk to the Netherlands Maritime Museum.

The Netherlands Maritime Museum

The **Nederlands Scheepvaartsmuseum** (Netherlands Maritime Museum; Tues–Sun 10am–5pm; mid-July to mid-Sept also Mon 10am–5pm; ƒ14,50) occupies the old arsenal of the Dutch navy, a vast sandstone structure built on the edge of the Oosterdok on Kattenburgerplein. It's underpinned by no less than 18,000 wooden piles driven deep into the river bed at enormous expense in the 1650s. The building's four symmetrical facades are dour and imposing despite the odd stylistic flourish, principally some dinky dormer windows and neoclassical pediments, and they surround a central,

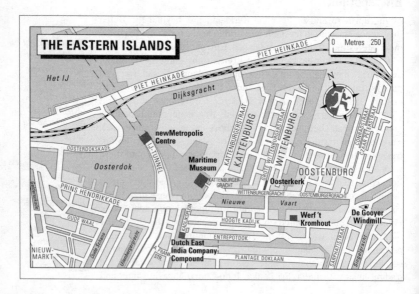

cobbled courtyard. It's the perfect location for a Maritime Museum – or at least it would be if the museum's collection, spread over three floors, was larger – in the event it seems a little forlorn, rattling around a building that's just too big.

The ground floor displays a flashy gilded barge built for King William I in 1818 and is used to host temporary exhibitions. The next floor up, devoted to shipping in the seventeenth and eighteenth centuries, is the most diverting. It includes garish ships' figureheads, examples of early atlases and navigational equipment, and finely detailed models of the clippers of the East India Company, then the fastest ships in the world. Contemporary shipbuilders tried hard to make the officers' quarters as domestic as possible – literally a home-from-home – and the fancifully carved, seventeenth-century stern which dominates one of the rooms comes complete with a set of dainty mullion windows. There are oodles of nautical paintings too, some devoted to the achievements of Dutch trading ships, others showing heavy seas and shipwrecks and yet more celebrating the successes of the Dutch Navy. Honed by the long and bloody struggle with Habsburg Spain, the Dutch navy was arguably the most powerful fleet in the world for about thirty years – from the 1650s to the 1680s. Commanded by a series of brilliant admirals – principally Tromp and De Ruyter – the Dutch even inflicted several defeats on the British navy, infuriating Charles II by a spectacular raid up the Thames in 1667 (see p.63). **Willem van de Velde II** (1633–1707) was the most successful of the Dutch marine painters of the period and there's a good sample of his work here – canvases that emphasize the strength and power of the Dutch warship, often depicted in battle. The final floor is devoted to the nineteenth and twentieth centuries and, compared with the one below, fails to excite. There are, however, a whole bunch of minutely precise ships' models, including one of the shipyard on the old Zuider Zee island of Urk and a salvaged radio cabin.

There are more paintings by Willem van de Velde II in the Rijksmuseum (see p.115), including perhaps his most famous canvas, The Gust of Wind.

Outside, moored at the museum jetty, is a full-scale replica of an East Indiaman, the *Amsterdam*. It's crewed by actors, and another set of nautical thespians will be needed when the 78-metre *Stad Amsterdam* clipper is completed in the next couple of years. Work is well under way on another of the museum's jetties.

From the Maritime Museum, there's a choice of routes: if you're heading west the Canal Bus (see p.53) will return you to Centraal Station via the newMetropolis centre, or you can walk back to the station along Prins Hendrikkade (see p.68) in about fifteen minutes. Alternatively, diligent sightseers can venture further east to the Werf 't Kromhout shipyard and the De Gooyer windmill.

The newMetropolis Centre

Strolling west along the waterfront from the Maritime Museum along Prins Hendrikkade, the foreground is dominated by a massive

elevated hood that rears up above the entrance to the IJ tunnel. This
hood is occupied by the large and lavish **newMetropolis Science
and Technology Centre** (Tues–Sun 10am–6pm; ƒ4 – see also
p.251) – follow the signs for the ground-floor entrance and on your
way, along the quayside, you'll pass a long line of retired canal
boats, low, wide and powerful-looking. Billing itself as the "centre
for human creativity", the newMetropolis is geared towards kids,
and has five interrelated exhibition areas – Technology, Energy, The
Lab, Humanity and Science – spread over six floors. The focus is
very much on interactive displays, the idea being to make learning
fun, with exhibits along the lines of huge soap bubbles you have to
get into and boats and planes you can set in motion using a light
beam. In addition there's a Glass Hall for temporary exhibitions, a
cinema, a theatre and a Children's World. The centre is very popular with school groups.

Pushing on west along Prins Hendrikkade, it's a brief walk to the
Oude Schans canal, once one of the city's busiest waterways.
Beyond is the Old Centre (see Chapter 2).

The Kromhout shipyard and De Gooyer windmill

Heading east from the Maritime Museum along Kattenburgergracht,
you soon reach the **Oosterkerk**, built for local shipyard workers and
sailors in the seventeenth century. Nearby, a bridge spans the
Nieuwe Vaart to reach Hoogte Kadijk, where – by the water's edge at
no. 147 – you'll find the **Werf 't Kromhout** (Mon–Fri 10am–4pm;
free), one of the city's few remaining shipyards. In their heyday, the
Eastern Islands were littered with shipyards like this one. The first
major contraction came at the back end of the nineteenth century
when steel and steam replaced timber and few of the existing yards
were big enough to make the switch successfully. A number struggled on, including this one, by concentrating on the repair and construction of smaller inshore and canal boats. Even so, 't Kromhout
almost went bust in 1969 and was only saved by turning into a combination of operating shipyard and tourist attraction; these days,
having given up its official museum function, it is more the former
than than the latter, but visitors are still welcome to come and see the
restoration in progress and soak up the atmosphere, which makes a
wonderfully refreshing change from much of the tackiness elsewhere
in the centre.

Continuing east along Hoogte Kadijk from the Kromhout, it's
about 500m to the **De Gooyer windmill**, constructed here beside a
long and slender canal at Funenkade 5. Like the shipyards, there
used to be far more mills like this at one time, used for pumping
water and grinding corn. This is one of the few survivors, an eighteenth-century grain mill now converted into a brewery called 't IJ,
though its sails still turn on the first Saturday of the month – wind
permitting.

Chapter 6

The Museum Quarter and Vondelpark

During the nineteenth century, Amsterdam burst out of its restraining canals, gobbling up the surrounding countryside. These new outlying neighbourhoods are mostly described in Chapter 7, but Amsterdam's leading museums, packed into a relatively small area around the edge of Museumplein, deserve their own chapter. The largest of the museums is the Rijksmuseum, which occupies a huge late nineteenth-century edifice overlooking the Singelgracht. Possessing an exceptional collection of Dutch paintings from the fifteenth to the seventeenth century, it is perhaps best-known for its series of paintings by Rembrandt. Close by, the Van Gogh Museum boasts the finest assortment of Van Gogh paintings in the world, whilst the Stedelijk Museum focuses on modern and contemporary art. The three museums together justifiably form one of Amsterdam's biggest pulls.

Museumplein itself, extending south from Stadhouderskade to Van Baerlestraat, is Amsterdam's largest open space, its wide lawns used for a variety of outdoor activities, from visiting circuses to political demonstrations. There's a war **memorial** here too: the group of slim steel blocks about halfway down the Museumplein commemorates the women of the wartime concentration camps, particularly the thousands who died at Ravensbruck. The text on the right reads: "For those women who defied fascism until the bitter end". A few minutes' walk to the northwest of Museumplein lies the sprawling greenery of the **Vondelpark**, Amsterdam's loveliest park, while its south side is overlooked by the **Concertgebouw**, the city's most prestigious classical music concert hall.

The Rijksmuseum

At the head of Museumplein, but facing onto the Singelgracht, the **Rijksmuseum** (daily 10am–5pm; ƒ15) is an imposing pile, built in an

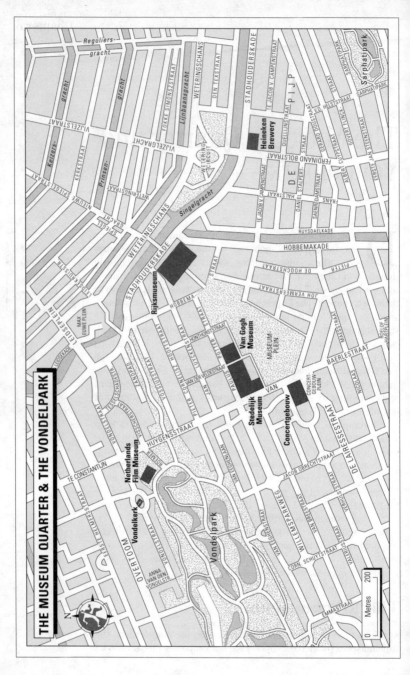

THE MUSEUM QUARTER & THE VONDELPARK

Reguliers-gracht

Reguliersgracht

VIJZELSTRAAT

Keizers-gracht

Prinsen-gracht

NIEUWE SPIEGELSTRAAT

Kerkstraat

SPIEGEL-GRACHT

FOKKE SIMONSZSTRAAT

Lijnbaansgracht

WETERINGSCHANS

VIJZELGRACHT

WETERINGSTRAAT

WETERINGSCHANS

DEN TEKSTRAAT

STADHOUDERSKADE

D E P I J P

TE JACOB V. CAMPENSTRAAT

QUELLIJNSTRAAT

FERDINAND BOLSTRAAT

GERARD DOUSTRAAT

ALBERT CUYPSTRAAT

GOVERT FLINCK STRAAT

EERSTE JAN STEENSTRAAT

SARPHATISTRAAT

SARPHATIPARK

Sarphatipark

Heineken Brewery

D E

-FRANS HALSSTRAAT

DANIEL STALPERT.

-SAENREDAMSTRAAT

TE JACOB V. CAMPENSTRAAT

Singelgracht

WETERINGSCHANS

STADHOUDERSKADE

RUYSDAELKADE

HOBBEMAKADE

DE HOOCHSTRAAT

JOH VERMEERSTRAAT

PIETER

LEIDSEPLEIN

LEIDSEKADE

FERDINAND

EERSTE C. HUYGENSSTR.

MAX EUWE PLEIN

Rijksmuseum

HOBBEMA

STRAAT

ROELOF HARTPLEIN

ROELOF HARTSTRAAT

Van Gogh Museum

MUSEUM-PLEIN

BAERLESTRAAT

MAESSTRAAT

NICOLAAS

JAN LUYCKENSTRAAT

HONTHORSTSTRAAT

PAULUS POTTER STRAAT

CORNELIS SCHUYTSTRAAT

VAN DE VELDESTRAAT

PIETER CORNELISZ. HOOFTSTRAAT

VOSSIUSSTRAAT

ZANDPAD

TESSELSCHADESTR.

VONDELSTRAAT

VAN

Stedelijk Museum

Concertgebouw

CONCERT-GEBOUW-PLEIN

DE LAIRESSESTRAAT

JACOB OBRECHTSTRAAT

BANSTRAAT

VAN BREESTRAAT

JAN WILLEM BROUWERSTRAAT

HUYGENSSTRAAT

Netherlands Film Museum

TE CONSTANTIJN HUYGENSSTRAAT

EERSTE HELMERSSTRAAT

OVERTOOM

Vondelkerk

ANNA VAN DEN VONDELSTR.

VONDELSTRAAT

VAN EEGHENLAAN

VAN EEGHENSTRAAT

WILLEMSPARKWEG

CORN. SCHUYTSTRAAT

VALERIUSSTRAAT

VERHULSTSTRAAT

Vondelpark

EMMASTRAAT

0   Metres   200

N

inventive historic style by Petrus Josephus Hubertus Cuypers, also the creator of Centraal Station (see p.58), in the early 1880s. The leading Dutch architect of his day, Cuypers (1827–1921) specialized in neogotic churches, but this commission called for something more ambitious; the result is a permutation of the neo-Renaissance style then popular in Holland, an intricate structure complete with towers and turrets, galleries, dormer windows and medallions. Inside, the museum possesses one of the most comprehensive collections of seventeenth-century **Dutch paintings** in the world, with twenty or so of Rembrandt's works, plus a healthy sample of canvases by Steen, Hals, Vermeer and their leading contemporaries. There are also representative displays of every other pre-twentieth-century period of Dutch and Flemish painting, along with an outstanding medieval Sculpture and Decorative Arts section.

The sections are clearly labelled, but the museum is labyrinthine, so be sure to pick up a free **floor plan** at the entrance. The other problem is that the collection's organization leaves something to be desired: works by the same artist can be distributed in several different rooms, which is frustrating, although in fairness this is partly because the sheer size of some of the canvases limits the display options. More helpfully, the **labelling** is both in Dutch and English.

The collection is too large to absorb in one visit, so if time is limited it's best to be content with the core paintings supplemented by a few selective forays into other sections. All the major works are described in detail in the *Treasures of the Rijksmuseum* (ƒ35), on sale at the museum shop, while the much more affordable – and very useful – *A Walk featuring highlights of the Dutch Golden Age*, a pamphlet costing just ƒ1, is sold at the first-floor information desks. It is worth bearing in mind that, since the museum's paintings are on a continual rotation system, some of the works mentioned in the account below may not always be on display.

The Rijks-museum

For details of the museum's concessionary rates see p.252.

Circle Tram #20 passes close by the Rijksmuseum, stopping on Hobbemastraat.

Fifteenth- and sixteenth-century paintings

Beginning beside the top-floor shop, the Rijksmuseum's collection of early Flemish – or more properly Netherlandish – paintings runs chronologically through the eastern wing. First off are the highly stylized works of the pre-Renaissance painters, traditionally known as the "**Flemish Primitives**", whose preoccupations were exclusively religious. Depicting biblical figures or saints, these paintings are devotional snapshots, dotted with symbols that provided a readily-understood lexicon for the medieval onlooker. Thus, in the *Madonna Surrounded by Female Saints*, painted by an unknown artist referred to thereafter as the **Master of the Virgin Among Virgins**, each of the saints wears a necklace that contains her particular symbol – St Barbara the tower of her imprisonment; St Catherine the wheel on which she was martyred; the organ of St Celicia and the wounded heart of St Ursula. However, the most striking paintings in

this section are by **Geertgen tot Sint Jans**. His *Holy Kindred*, painted around 1485 and displayed in Room 201, is a skilfully structured
portrait of the family of Anna, Mary's mother, in which the
Romanesque nave represents the Old Testament, the Gothic choir the
New. Mary and Joseph in the foreground parallel the figures of Adam
and Eve behind by the altar and Joseph holds a lily, emblem of purity, over Mary's head. Alongside are Geertgen's *Adoration of the
Magi*, full of humility and with an engaging fifteenth-century backdrop of processions, castles and mountains, and Jan Mostaert's *Tree
of Jesse*, crammed with tumbling, dreamlike, medieval characters. An
even clearer picture of the Low Countries in the Middle Ages appears
in *The Seven Works of Charity* by the **Master of Alkmaar**. Originally
hung in St Laurenskerk in the town of Alkmaar (see p.160), each
panel shows the charitable acts expected of those with sufficient piety
(and cash): alms are doled out to the poor with medieval Alkmaar as
the backcloth.

The collection moves into the sixteenth century with the work of
Jan van Scorel, represented here by a voluptuous *Mary Magdalen*,
next to which is his pupil **Maerten van Heemskerck**'s portrait of the
master of the Mint *Pieter Bicker*, shiftily counting out the cash.
There's also a memorable *Carrying of the Cross* by **Quinten
Matsys**, long Antwerp's leading painter and a transitional figure in so
far as he was one of the first Netherlandish artists to be influenced by
the Italian Renaissance.

Paintings of the Dutch Golden Age

Beyond the early Netherlandish works lie the classic paintings of the
Dutch Golden Age, beginning in Rooms 208 and 209 with several
wonderful canvases by **Frans Hals**, most notably his expansive
Marriage Portrait of Isaac Massa and Beatrix Laen. Relaxing
beneath a tree, a portly Isaac glows with contentment as his new wife
sits beside him in a suitably demure manner. An intimate scene, the
painting also carries a detailed iconography: the ivy at Beatrix's feet

*See Contexts
on pp.312–316
for a full run-
down on the
major artists
of the Dutch
Golden Age.*

symbolizes her devotion to her hubby, the thistle faithfulness, the
vine togetherness and in the fantasy garden behind them the peacock
is a classical allusion to Juno, the guardian of marriage. Here also is
Dirck van Baburen's sensational *Prometheus in Chains* – a work
from the Utrecht School, which used the paintings of Caravaggio as
its model – and in the small circular gallery (Room 207) are displayed the miniatures of **Hendrick Avercamp**, noted for their folksy
and finely detailed skating scenes.

Moving on, there are more thoroughly Dutch works in, for
instance, the soft, tonal river scenes of the Haarlem artist **Salomon
van Ruysdael** and the cool church interiors of **Pieter Saenredam**.
Search out especially the latter's *Old Town Hall of Amsterdam*
(Room 214), a characteristic work in which the tumbledown predecessor of the current building (now the Royal Palace) witnesses the

comings and goings of black-hatted townsmen in the stilted manner of a Lowry work. Beyond this is a mixed selection of canvases by some of Rembrandt's better-known pupils, including **Ferdinand Bol**'s *Portrait of Elizabeth Bas* (Room 215), long thought to be a Rembrandt until the director of the Rijksmuseum proved it otherwise in 1911. Perhaps the most talented of the master's pupils was **Carel Fabritius**, who was killed in 1654 at the age of thirty-two, when Delft's powder magazine exploded. His *Portrait of Abraham Potter* (Room 215), a restrained, skilful work of soft, delicate hues, contrasts heavily with the same artist's earlier *The Beheading of St John the Baptist* (Room 222), where the head is served on a platter in grisly style. Mingling with these works are several paintings by **Rembrandt** himself – later works, for the most part, from the artist's mature period, notably a late *Self-Portrait*, caught in mid-shrug as the Apostle Paul, a self-aware and defeated old man. There's also the finely detailed *Portrait of Maria Trip*, a wonderfully expressive portrait of his first wife *Saskia* and the emotional subtlety of *The Staalmeesters*.

The next rooms (Rooms 216–220) take you into the latter half of the seventeenth century, and include works ranging from **Gerrit Berckheyde**'s crisp depictions of Amsterdam and Haarlem to the carousing peasants of **Jan Steen**. Steen's *Feast of St Nicholas*, with its squabbling children, makes the festival a celebration of disorderly greed, while the drunken waywardness of his *Merry Family* and *The Drunken Couple* verge on the anarchic. Steen knew his bourgeois audience well: his caricatures of the proletariat blend humour with moral condemnation – or at least condescension – a mixture perfectly designed to suit their tastes. Steen was also capable of more subtle works, a famous example being his *Morning Toilet*, which is full of associations, referring either to sexual pleasures just had or about to be taken. For example, the woman is shown putting on a stocking in a conspicuous manner, the point being that the Dutch word for stocking, *kous*, is also a slang word for a woman's genital parts. By contrast, **Willem van de Velde II**'s preoccupations were nautical, his canvases celebrating either the power of the Dutch navy or the seaworthiness of the merchant marine, as in the churning seas of *The Gust of Wind* (Room 220).

Room 221A focuses on **Vermeer**, whose *Love Letter* reveals a tension between servant and mistress – the lute on the woman's lap was a well-known sexual symbol – and *The Kitchen Maid*, an exquisitely observed domestic scene, literally right down to the nail – and its shadow – on the background wall. Similarly, in the precise *Young Woman Reading a Letter*, the map behind her hints at the far-flung places her loved one is writing from. **Gerard ter Borch** also depicted innocent scenes, both in subject and title, but his *Woman at a Mirror* glances in a meaningfully anxious manner at her servants, who look on with delicate irony from behind dutiful

exteriors; equally, Borch's blandly named *Interior Scene* is set in a
brothel. The paintings of **Pieter de Hooch** are less symbolic, more
exercises in lighting, but they're as good a visual guide to the everyday life and habits of the seventeenth-century Dutch bourgeoisie as
you'll find. So, too, with **Nicholas Maes**, whose caring *Young
Woman by the Cradle* (Room 222) is not so much a didactic
tableau as an idealization of motherhood.

The Gallery of Honour

Room 223, a small side room at the end of this part of the museum,
provides an introduction to one of the Rijksmuseum's greatest treasures, Rembrandt's **The Night Watch** of 1642. This is the most
famous and most valuable of all the artist's pictures, restored after
being slashed in 1975, and hung – as architect Cuypers intended – at
the end of the so-called **Gallery of Honour**, the museum's stately,
top-floor centrepiece. The painting is of a Militia Company and as
such celebrates one of the companies formed in the sixteenth century to defend the United Provinces against Spain. As the Habsburg
threat receded, so the militias became social clubs, gatherings of the
well-heeled and well-connected who were eager to commission their
own group portraits as signs of their prestige. Rembrandt's militia
painting, of the Amsterdam Kloveniersdoelen company, was erro-
neously tagged *The Night Watch* in the eighteenth century. This was
largely due to misinterpretation of the background darkness, but
also because the grime that had by then accumulated on the surface
obscured matters further – the painting had been hung in the dining
hall of the Kloveniersdoelen and then the town hall, before being
moved to the Rijksmuseum shortly after it opened. There were other
misconceptions about the painting too, most notably that it was this
work that led to the downward shift in Rembrandt's standing with the
Amsterdam elite; in fact, there's no evidence that the militia men
weren't pleased with the picture, or that Rembrandt's commissions
flowed in any more slowly after it was completed.

*An extensive
collection of
Rembrandt's
drawings and
etchings is on
display in the
artist's house,
now a museum
– see p.104.*

Though not as subtle as much of the artist's later work, *The Night
Watch* is an adept piece, full of movement and carefully arranged.
Paintings of this kind were collections of individual portraits as much
as group pictures, and for the artist their difficulty lay in including
each single face while simultaneously producing a coherent group
scene. Rembrandt opted to show the company preparing to march
off, a snapshot of military activity in which banners are unfurled,
muskets primed and drums rolled. There are a couple of allegorical
figures as well, most prominently a young, spotlight woman who has
a bird hanging from her belt, a reference to the Kloveniersdoelen's
traditional emblem of a claw. *The Night Watch* is surrounded by several other militia paintings, two of which are by **Bartholomeus van
der Helst**: the one on the left of *The Night Watch* is perhaps the best
of them – it's lively and colourful, but its arrangement and lighting

are static. Van der Helst's painting to the right includes, as was commonplace, a self-portrait (on the far left), as does the one by **Govert Flinck** (on the top far right of his picture). It seems that Rembrandt didn't insert his likeness in *The Night Watch*, though some art historians insist that the pudgy-faced figure peering out from the back between the gesticulating militiamen is indeed the man himself.

Elsewhere, the Gallery of Honour houses a healthy sample of large-scale Dutch paintings, though admittedly some are notable only for their size. Two of Rembrandt's better-known pupils crop up here: **Nicholas Maes**, with one of his typically intimate scenes in *An Old Woman at Prayer*, and **Ferdinand Bol**, with his flashy and fleshy *Venus and Adonis*. Bol's dashing *Self-Portrait* is here too, a forceful, rich and successful character leaning on a sleeping Cupid. Nearby is Rembrandt's touching depiction of his cowled son, *Titus*, and *The Jewish Bride*, one of his very last pictures, finished in 1667. No one knows who the people are, nor whether they are actually married (the title came later), but the painting is one of Rembrandt's most telling, the paint dashed on freely and the hands touching lovingly, as Kenneth Clark wrote, in a "marvellous amalgam of richness, tenderness and trust".

Sculpture and Applied Art

The Rijksmuseum owns a vast hoard of **applied art**, but unless your stamina is limitless, it's wise to restrict yourself to a single period. The most impressive section is the top-floor **Medieval and Renaissance** collection, which occupies Rooms 238 to 261 on the other (west) side of the Gallery of Honour. Room 238 kicks off with a handful of Byzantine trinkets and a glass case crammed with beautiful Limoges enamels, whilst Room 239 holds the magnificent *Ten Mourners*, sensitive and finely detailed fifteenth-century carvings taken from the Antwerp tomb of Isabelle de Bourbon, wife of Charles the Bold. Contemporaneous with these is a whole raft of religious carvings amongst which are a number of wonderful altar pieces, or **retables**. Thousands of these were produced in the Low Countries from the end of the fourteenth century up until the Reformation, their manufacture partly mechanized, with panel and cabinet makers, wood carvers, painters and goldsmiths (for the gilding) working on several altarpieces at any given time. The standard format was to create a series of mini-tableaux illustrating Biblical scenes with medieval characters and landscapes, but above all it's the extraordinary detail that impresses. Few of the wood carvers of the period are known by name, but one exception is **Adriaen van Wesel** of Utrecht, several of whose works are displayed here (for example, the *Meeting of the Magi*) in all their lively, crowded dynamism.

Room 248 marks the start of the Renaissance section, whose wide-ranging exhibits include everything from tapestries and cabinets to beds and porcelain. In particular there are three rooms (Rooms

255–257) devoted to **delftware**, the blue-and-white ceramics to which Delft gave its name in the seventeenth century. The original designs were stylized copies of Chinese ceramics imported by the Dutch East India Company, but the patterns soon changed to depict more traditional Dutch landscapes, animals and comic figures. By the early years of the eighteenth century, Delft's craftsmen had become confident enough to create vases, jars and even musical instruments in polychrome as well as the traditional blue and white – and examples of each and every period are on display.

There's another Sculpture and Applied Art section below on the ground floor, this time focusing on the seventeenth and eighteenth centuries, and yet another in the basement, where there's more Dutch porcelain and a couple of rooms devoted to Art Nouveau.

Dutch History

The ground-floor **Dutch History** section (Rooms 102–112) starts promisingly with exhibitions depicting aspects of life in the Golden Age, focusing, not surprisingly, on the naval might that brought Holland its wealth. **Model ships** impress with their compulsive detail, but more revealing of everyday life are the maritime odds and ends retrieved from the wreck of the *Witte Leeuw* ("White Lion"), an East Indian vessel, laden with a cargo of pepper and Chinese porcelain, which sank in 1613. The galleries off this room, however, are for the most part uninspired, filled with relics from Holland's naval and colonial past. The prize for the most conspicuous exhibit goes to **Willem Pieneman** for his painting of the *Battle of Waterloo*, a vast canvas that took six years to complete. All the big names of the battle are there (the artist spent two years on the portrait studies alone), but it's a laboured and rather arid piece nonetheless.

The South Wing

Four years ago, the **South Wing** of the Rijksmuseum reopened after a renovation and restoration project funded to the tune of ƒ23 million. Originally cobbled together by Cuypers – the architect of the main building – from fragments of walls and buildings sent in to Amsterdam from all over the country, the South Wing had remained largely as it was since it opened in 1898. The remodelled version can now be reached through a passageway from the main building and also has its own entrance at Hobbemastraat 19, round the back of the main building. There are two floors: on the ground floor is the **Asiatic Art** section while up above the top floor is primarily devoted to eighteenth- and nineteenth-century paintings.

Eighteenth- and nineteenth-century paintings

The South Wing's collection of **eighteenth- and nineteenth-century Dutch paintings** picks up chronologically where the Gallery of

Honour leaves off, beginning with the work of **Cornelis Troost**, whose eighteenth-century comic scenes earned him the dubiously deserved title of the "Dutch Hogarth". More enduring are the later pictures, notably the pastels of **Pierre-Paul Prud'hon** and **Jan Ekels'** *The Writer* – small and simple, its lighting and attention to detail reminiscent of Vermeer.

After this, rooms follow each other in haphazard fashion, containing sundry landscapes and portraiture from the lesser nineteenth-century artists. **Jan Jongkind** is the best of the bunch, his murky *River Landscape in France* typical of the Impressionist style that was developing in the nineteenth century. The chief proponents of Dutch Impressionism originated from or worked in The Hague, and the **Hague School** label covers a variety of styles and painters who shared a clarity and sensitivity in their depiction of the Dutch landscape. Of the major Hague School painters, the Rijksmuseum collection is strongest on the work of **Jan Weissenbruch**, whose land- and seascapes, such as *View near the Geestbrug*, hark back to the compositional techniques of Van Ruisdael and the Maris brothers. **Jacob Maris's** sultry landscapes are the most representative of the School, while the works of the younger **Willem Maris** are more direct and approachable – his *Ducks* is a good example. **Anton Mauve's** work is similar, his *Morning Ride on the Beach* filled with shimmering gradations of tone that belie the initial simplicity of the scene.

While members of the Hague School were creating gentle landscapes, a younger generation of Impressionist painters working in Amsterdam – the **Amsterdam School** – was using a darker palette to capture city scenes. By far the most important work from this turn-of-the-century group is **G.H. Breitner's** *Singelbrug near Paleisstraat in Amsterdam*, a random moment in the street recorded and framed with photographic dispassion. Breitner worked best when turning his attention to rough, shadowy depictions of the city, as in *Rokin* and *Damrak*. **Josef Israëls'** work is lighter in tone and mood, with canvases like *Donkey Rides on the Beach* showing his affinities with the French Impressionists of the period.

The Asiatic collection

Holland's colonial and commercial links with the Far East are the source of the South Wing's ground-floor **Asiatic collection**. Of the different cultures, **China** and **Japan** are best represented: the striking twelfth-century *Statue of Avalokiteshvara* and graceful *Paintings* by Kao Ch'i-p'ei, drawn with his fingernails, are the highlights of the Chinese works, while the seventeenth-century **ceramics** and **lacquerwork** are the best of the Japanese. If you're interested, you'll find much more here, from twelfth-century Indonesian gold jewellery to Cambodian carving.

The Van Gogh Museum

For details of
the museum's
concessionary
rates see
p.253.

Circle Tram
#20 passes
close by the
Van Gogh
Museum, stop-
ping on Van
Baerlestraat.

Vincent van Gogh (1853–1890) is arguably the most popular, most reproduced and most talked about of all modern artists, so it's not surprising that the **Van Gogh Museum** (daily 10am–6pm; ƒ12,50) comprising a fabulous collection of the artist's work, is one of Amsterdam's top tourist attractions. Housed in an angular building designed by a leading light of the De Stijl movement, Gerritt Rietveld, and opened to the public in 1973, it's a well-conceived and beautifully presented introduction to the man and his art, with the kernel of the collection inherited from Vincent's art-dealer brother Theo. It's located a brief walk west of the Rijksmuseum on the north edge of Museumplein.

The collection

The museum starts on the ground floor with a group of works by some of Van Gogh's well-known friends and contemporaries, many of whom influenced his work – Gauguin, Millet, Adolph Monticelli and others. It then moves on to the works of the man himself, presented for the most part chronologically on the first floor. The first paintings go back to the artist's **early years** in Nuenen, southern Holland, where he was born: dark, sombre works in the main, ranging from an assortment of drab grey and brown still-lifes to the gnarled faces and haunting, flickering light of *The Potato Eaters* – one of Van Gogh's best-known paintings, and the culmination of hundreds of studies of the local peasantry.

Across the hall, the sobriety of these early works is easily transposed onto the **Parisian** urban landscape, particularly in the *View of Paris*, where the city's domes and rooftops hover below Montmartre under a glowering, blustery sky. But before long, under the sway of fellow painters and – after the bleak countryside of North Brabant – the sheer colour of the city itself, his approach began to change. This is most noticeable in the views of Montmartre windmills, a couple of self-portraits, and the pictures from Asnières just outside Paris, where the artist used to travel regularly to paint. Look out also for *A Pair of Shoes*, a painting that used to hang in the house Van Gogh shared with Gauguin in Arles, the dazzling movement of *Wheatfield with a Lark* and the almost neurotic precision of his *Flowerpot with Chives*.

In February 1888, Van Gogh moved to **Arles**, inviting Gauguin to join him a little later. With the change of scenery came a heightened interest in colour, and the predominance of yellow as a recurring motif: it's represented best in such paintings as *Van Gogh's Bedroom* and the *Harvest at La Crau*, and most vividly in *The Yellow House*. A canvas from the artist's *Sunflowers* series is justly one of his most lauded works, intensely, almost obsessively, rendered in the deepest oranges, golds and ochres he could find.

Gauguin told of Van Gogh painting these flowers in a near trance; there were usually sunflowers in jars all over their house.

At the asylum in **St Rémy**, where Van Gogh committed himself in 1889 after snipping off part of his ear and offering it to a local prostitute, his approach to nature became more abstract: trees bent into cruel, sinister shapes and skies coloured purple and yellow, as in the *Garden of St Paul's Hospital*. Van Gogh is at his most expressionistic here, the paint applied thickly, often with a palette knife, especially in the final, tortured paintings done at **Auvers**, where Van Gogh lodged for the last three months of his life. It was at Auvers that he painted the frantic *Ears of Wheat* and *Wheatfield with a Reaper*, in which the fields swirl and writhe under weird, light-green, moving skies. It was a few weeks after completing these last paintings that Van Gogh shot and fatally wounded himself.

The two floors above provide a back-up to the main collection: the second floor has a study area with PC access to an excessively detailed computerized account of Van Gogh's life and times, and the third features a changing selection from the museum's vast stock of Van Gogh **drawings** and less familiar paintings, plus notebooks and letters. This floor also affords space to relevant temporary exhibitions illustrating Van Gogh's artistic influences, or his own influence on other artists. There's much more temporary exhibition space in the new, ultra-modern annexe reached via the first-floor escalator. Completed in 1998 and partly underground, the annexe was financed by a Japanese insurance company – the same conglomerate who paid $35 million for one of Van Gogh's *Sunflowers* canvases in 1987. The museum also has a shop and café, both located on the ground floor beside the main entrance.

The Stedelijk Museum

Amsterdam's number one venue for modern art, the **Stedelijk Museum** (daily: April–Sept 10am–6pm; Oct–March 11am–5pm; ƒ9), next door to the Van Gogh Museum, is still at the cutting edge after a hundred years or more. Its permanent collection is wide-ranging and its temporary exhibitions – based both on its own acquisitions and on loaned pieces, and regularly extending to photography and installations – are usually of international standard. It's housed in a grand neo-Renaissance building dating from 1895, but the interior is very modern and a new wing was added in the 1950s.

For the museum's concessionary rates see p.252.

Circle Tram #20 passes close by, stopping on Van Baerlestraat.

The collection

The museum's ground floor is usually given over to **temporary exhibitions**, often by living European artists. Contemporary Dutch art is a particular favourite, so keep an eye out for the work of such painters as Jan Dibbets, Rob Scholte and Marlene Dumas. Also on

*You can see
many more
works by
Appel and
other expo-
nents of the
CoBrA School
at the CoBrA
museum
– see p.249.*

the ground floor are a couple of large-scale permanent attractions –
Karel Appel's *Bar* in the foyer, installed in the 1950s, and the same
artist's wild daubings in the restaurant. But perhaps the most interesting permanent exhibit is **Ed Kienholz**'s *Beanery* (1965), in the
basement: modelled on his local bar in Los Angeles, the tableau's
clock-faced figures, combined with the music and hum of conversation, create a nervous, claustrophobic background to the horror of
the newspaper headline in the vending machine – "Children Kill
Children in Vietnam Riots". For Kienholz, this is *real* time, and time
inside the bar is "surrealist time . . . where people waste time, lose
time, escape time, ignore time".

Upstairs, the first floor is given over to a changing selection drawn
from the museum's **permanent collection**. Broadly speaking, this
starts off with drawings by Picasso, Matisse and their contemporaries, and moves on to paintings by major Impressionists (Manet,
Monet, Bonnard) and Post-Impressionists (Ensor, Van Gogh,
Cézanne). Further on, Mondriaan holds sway among the De Stijl
group, from his early, muddy-coloured abstractions to the cool, bold-
ly coloured rectangular blocks for which he's most famous. Kasimir
Malevich is similarly well represented, his dense attempts at Cubism
leading to the dynamism and bold, primary tones of his
"Suprematist" paintings – slices, blocks and bolts of colour that shift
around as if about to resolve themselves into some complex computer graphic. Elsewhere, depending on what's on show, you may
come across some of the Stedelijk's wide collection of Marc Chagall
paintings, and a number of pictures by American Abstract
Expressionists Mark Rothko, Ellsworth Kelly and Barnett Newman,
in addition to the odd work by Lichtenstein or Warhol. Jean
Dubuffet, too, with his swipes at the art establishment, may well have
a profile, and you might catch Matisse's large cutout, *The Parakeet
and the Mermaid*.

The Vondelpark and around

Amsterdam is desperately short of green spaces, which makes the
leafy expanses of the Vondelpark, just northwest of Museumplein,
doubly welcome. This is easily the largest and most popular of the
city's parks, its network of footpaths used by a healthy slice of the
city's population. In the northeast corner of the park stands the
Netherlands Film Museum, noted for its programme of international cult and arthouse films, and, further south along Van Baerlestraat,
is Amsterdam's renowned concert hall, the **Concertgebouw**.

The Vondelpark

Vondelpark, the city's most enticing chunk of greenery, dates back
to 1864, when a group of leading Amsterdammers clubbed together

to transform the soggy marshland that lay beyond the Leidsepoort into a landscaped park. The group, who were impressed by the contemporary English fashion for natural (as distinct from formal) landscaping, gave the task of developing the new style of park to the Zocher family, big-time gardeners who set about their task with gusto, completing their work in 1865. Named after the seventeenth-century poet Joost van den Vondel, the park proved an immediate success and was expanded to its present size (45 hectares) in 1877. It now possesses over 100 species of tree, a wide variety of local and imported plants, and – amongst many incidental features – a **bandstand** and excellent **rose garden**. Neither did the Zochers forget their Dutch roots: the park is latticed with ponds and narrow waterways, home to many sorts of wildfowl. There are other animals too: cows, sheep, hundreds of squirrels plus, bizarrely enough, a large colony of bright-green parakeets. The Vondelpark has several different children's **play areas** and during the summer regularly hosts free **concerts** and theatrical performances, mostly in its own specially designed open-air theatre.

Other pleasant city parks include the Sarphatipark (see p.131), the Westerpark (see p.98), the Beatrixpark (see p.133) and the Amsterdamse Bos (see p.133), all of which are open daily from dawn to dusk. For a full listing of Amsterdam's parks and their relevant tram routes see the Directory, p.296.

The Netherlands Film Museum and Vondelkerk

Housed in a grand pavilion on the northern edge of the Vondelpark is the **Nederlands Filmmuseum** (Netherlands Film Museum; box office Mon–Fri 9am–10pm, Sat & Sun 1–10pm; ☎589 1400). It's really more an arthouse cinema (with two screens) than a museum, a showcase for avant-garde films – most of which are shown in their original language, plus subtitles in Dutch (and occasionally English). There are several screenings nightly, plus a matinée on Wednesday afternoons, and the programme often follows a prescribed theme or subject. Look out for news of the free screenings of classic movies on Saturday nights in summer. Round the corner, the museum's film **library**, at Vondelstraat 69 (Tues–Fri 10am–5pm, Sat 11am–5pm) has a well-catalogued collection of books, magazines and journals, some in English, though they are for reference only and are not loaned out.

Just west of the museum, perched in the middle of a roundabout on Vondelstraat, is the **Vondelkerk**, which has had more than its share of bad luck. Work on the church, which was designed by Cuypers – the architect of Centraal Station and the Rijksmuseum – began in 1872, but finances ran out the following year and the building was not completed until the 1880s. Twenty years later it was struck by lightning and in the ensuing fire its tower was burnt to a cinder – the present one was added much later. The church always struggled to find a decent-size congregation, but limped on until it was finally deconsecrated in 1979, being turned into offices thereafter.

The Vondelpark and around

Attached to the Netherlands Film Museum, Café Vertigo is a wonderful place to while away an easy afternoon.

The Concertgebouw

*For
Concertgebouw
box office
details, see
p.234.*

*Keyser, at Van
Baerlestraat
96, is a long-
established
and elegant
place for a
quick drink or
a full meal.*

A ten-minute walk from the Vondelpark's southern edge, along Van Baerlestraat, will bring you to the **Concertgebouw** (Concert Hall), home of the famed – and much recorded – Royal Concertgebouw Orchestra. When the German composer Brahms visited Amsterdam in the 1870s he was scathing about the locals' lack of culture and, in particular, their lack of an even halfway suitable venue for his music. In the face of such ridicule, a consortium of Amsterdam businessmen got together to fund the construction of a brand-new concert hall and the result was the Concertgebouw, completed in 1888. An attractive structure with a pleasingly grand neoclassical facade, the Concertgebouw has become renowned among musicians and concert-goers for its marvellous acoustics, though it did have to undergo major repairs when it was discovered that the wooden piles on which it rested were rotting away. The overhaul included the addition of a new, largely glass wing that contrasts nicely with the red brick and stone of the rest of the building. Although the Concertgebouw attracts the world's best orchestras and musicians, ticket prices can be surprisingly inexpensive – the venue operates an arts-for-all policy – and from September to May there are often free walk-in concerts at lunchtime.

Chapter 7

The Outer Districts

A
msterdam is a small city, and most of its residential outer districts are easily reached from the city centre. The south holds
most interest, with the raucous "De Pijp" quarter, the 1930s
architecture of the New South, which also contains the enjoyable
woodland area of the Amsterdamse Bos, and the occasional municipal park more than justifying the walk or tram ride. As for the other
districts, you'll find a good deal less reason to make the effort.
Multicultural influences in the east give it some diversity, and it also
holds the Tropenmuseum, but otherwise it's of little appeal, and the
west has nothing special at all. Finally, Amsterdam north, across the
IJ, is entirely residential and only relevant if you're cycling through
it on the way to open country; the "highlight" of a visit is the short
(free) ferry ride there from behind Centraal Station.

The Old South: De Pijp

Across the canal to the east of Museumplein, away from the money,
lies the busy heart of the Old South (Oud Zuid) – the district known
as "**De Pijp**" ("The Pipe"), Amsterdam's first suburb. New development beyond the Singelgracht began around 1870, but after laying
down the street plans, the city council left the actual house-building
to private developers. They made the most of the arrangement and
constructed long rows of cheaply built and largely featureless five-
and six-storey buildings and it is these which still dominate the area
today. The district's name comes from the characteristically narrow
terraced streets running between long, sombre canyons of brick ten-
ements: the apartments here were said to resemble pipe-drawers,
since each had a tiny street frontage but extended deep into the
building. De Pijp remains one of the city's more closely-knit communities, with a large proportion of new immigrants – Surinamese,
Moroccan, Turkish and Asian, and although it's fine to wander
around during the day, at night it should be avoided, particularly the
area south of Sarphatipark.

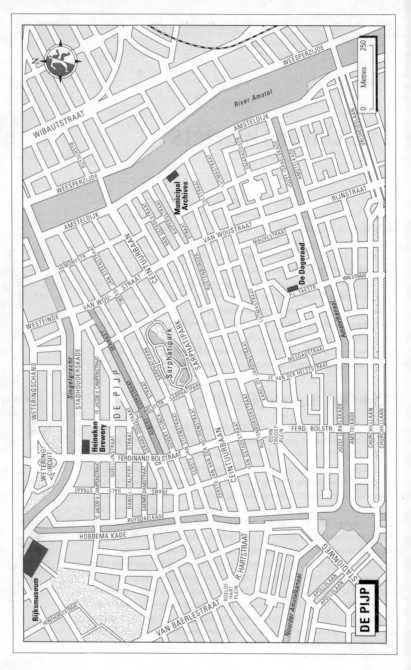

Albert Cuypstraat, the Sarphatipark and around

Ferdinand Bolstraat, running north–south, is the district's main street, but the long, slim east–west thoroughfare of **Albert Cuypstraat** (pronouced "cowp-straat") is its heart. The daily general **market** held here – which stretches for over a kilometre between Ferdinand Bolstraat and Van Woustraat – is the largest in the city, with a huge array of stalls selling everything from cut-price carrots and raw-herring sandwiches to saucepans and day-glo thongs. Check out, too, the bargain-basement and ethnic shops that flank the market on each side, and the Indian and Surinamese restaurants down the side streets – they're often cheaper than their equivalents in the city centre.

A couple of blocks south of the Albert Cuypstraat market is the small but pretty **Sarphatipark**, a welcome splash of greenery amongst the surrounding brick and concrete. The park, complete with footpaths and a sinewy lake, was laid out before the construction of De Pijp got underway, and was initially intended as a place for the bourgeoisie to take a stroll.

Heading east from the Sarphatipark, the main **Ceintuurbaan** artery crosses **Van Woustraat** – a long, unremarkable shopping street, though with a number of speciality ethnic food shops – before it reaches the River Amstel. At the river, turn right along Amsteldijk for the short walk south to the **Gemeentearchief** (Municipal Archives; daily 11am–5pm during exhibitions, otherwise Mon–Fri 10am–5pm; ☎572 0202; free), on the corner with Rustenburgerstraat. Housed in a flashy neogothic structure built as the district's town hall in 1895, the archives provide extensive research facilities: all births, marriages and deaths from the early sixteenth century onwards are on record here, and there's also an enormous collection of newspapers, posters, plans and documents. Of more general interest are the temporary exhibitions on the city's past held here twice a year.

The New South

Southwest of De Pijp and the Old South, the **New South** (Nieuw Zuid) encompasses the whole area south of the Noorder Amstel canal to the railway tracks, as well as the old Rivierenbuurt district wedged in between the railway track, the River Amstel and the Amstel canal. Contrasting heavily with the Old South, this was the first properly planned extension to the city since the concentric canals of the seventeenth century. The Dutch architect Hendrik Petrus Berlage (1856–1934) was responsible for the overall plan, but much of the implementation passed to a pair of prominent architects of the Amsterdam School, Michael de Klerk (1884–1923) and Piet Kramer (1881–1961). By the 1890s, Berlage had broken away

Bagels & Beans, at Ferdinand Bolstraat 70, is a perfect place to sip a good cup of coffee before heading into the Albert Cuyp market.

Beginning at Centraal Station, tram #4 runs the length of Van Woustraat; Circle-Tram #20 scuttles along the northern part of Van Woustraat before turning west along Ceintuurbaan; trams #12 and #25 travel along Ferdinand Bolstraat.

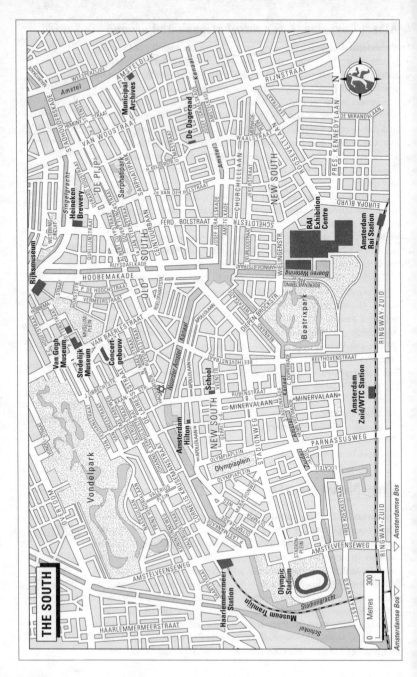

THE SOUTH

Municipal Archives

De Dageraad

Amstel

Amsteldijk

WEESPERZIJDE

HEMONYLAAN

VAN WOUSTRAAT

DE PIJP

Sarphatipark

GERARD DOUSTRAAT

STADHOUDERSKADE

WETERINGCIRCUIT

Singelgracht

Heineken Brewery

Rijksmuseum

HOOBEMAKADE

RUYSDAELKADE

SOUTH

CEINTUURBAAN

Ze VAN DER HELSTRAAT

1e KELISSTRAAT

SARPHATIKADE

Amstel

AMSTELDIJK

JOSEF ISRAELS KADE

SKATE

Kanaal

JOSEF ISRAELS KADE

RIJNSTRAAT

DE MIRANDALAAN

WAALSTRAAT

CHURCHILLLAAN

NEW SOUTH

ROOSEVELTLAAN

PRES. KENNEDYLAAN

EUROPA BLVD

RAI Exhibition Centre

Amsterdam Rai Station

Boeren Wetering

RINGWAY-ZUID

FERD. BOLSTRAAT

AMSTE KADE

JOSEF ISRAELS MASKADE

SCHELDESTR

SCHELDESTR

WIELINGENSTR

MARINGPLEIN STRAAT

BOEREN WETERING

PAD

Beatrixpark

P. DE HOOCHSTRAAT

VERMEERSTRAAT

HORSTR

MUSEUM PLEIN

ROELOFHARTSTR

APOLLOLAAN

DIEPEN BROCKSTR

BERNARD

BEETHOVENSTRAAT

Van Gogh Museum

Stedelijk Museum

Concert gebouw

VAN BAERLESTRAAT

Noorder Amstel Kanaal

APOLLOLAAN

RUBENSTRAAT

C. DUPPERKADE

Amsterdam Zuid/WTC Station

Vondelpark

J. OBRECHTSTR

School

MINERVALAAN

MINERVALAAN

BEETHOVENSTRAAT

STADIONKADE

PARNASSUSWEG

LOCATELLI

OVERTOOM

Amsterdam Hilton

NEW SOUTH

GERRIT

STADIONWEG

OLYMPIAPLEIN

Olympiaplein

OLYMPIAPLEIN

CORNELIS KRUSEMANSTRAAT

LAIRESSE PLEIN

PRINS VAN

AMSTELVEENSEWEG

HAARLEMMERMEERSTRAAT

OLYMPIA

STADION PLEIN

FRED ROESKESTRAAT

AMSTELVEENSEWEG

RINGWAY-ZUID

IJSBAANPAD

Haarlemmermeer Station

Olympic Stadium

Stadiongracht

Museum Tramlijn

Schinkel

△ Amsterdamse Bos

△ Amsterdamse Bos

△ Amsterdamse Bos

| 0 | Metres | 300 |

from the historicism that had dominated nineteenth-century Dutch architecture, opting instead for a chunky Expressionism, but after his death his two successors departed from Berlage's sobriety altogether, in preference for the playful touches – turrets and bulging windows, sloping roofs and frilly balustrades – that you see in the buildings of the New South today. Neither was this architectural virtuosity confined to the houses of the well-to-do. In 1901, a reforming Housing Act forced the city council into a concerted effort to clear Amsterdam's slums, a principal result being several quality public housing projects designed by De Klerk and Kramer. There's one extant example near the Western Islands (see p.99) and another here in the New South, **De Dageraad**, though neither is as fanciful as the duo's Scheepvaarthuis (see p.68). Cutbacks in the city's subsidy meant that the more imaginative aspects of Berlage's original scheme for the New South were toned down, but the area's wide boulevards and narrower side streets were completed as conceived. In this, Berlage wanted to reinterpret the most lauded feature of the city's seventeenth-century canals: their combination of monumental grandeur and picturesque scale.

Nowadays the New South is one of Amsterdam's most sought-after addresses. **Apollolaan**, **Stadionweg** and, a little way to the east, **Churchilllaan** are especially favoured and home to some of the city's most sumptuous properties – huge idiosyncratic mansions set back from the street behind trees and generous gardens. Locals pop to the shops on **Beethovenstraat**, the main drag running south right through the district from the Noorder Amstel canal. Nonetheless, posh residential areas are rarely much fun for the casual visitor and the New South is no exception. More enticing is the languid greenery of the **Beatrixpark**, and, slightly further out beyond the railway tracks, the sprawling parkland of the **Amsterdamse Bos** – both providing a pleasant interlude from the network of suburban streets.

Meidi-Ya, Beethoven-straat 18, is the premier Japanese supermarket in town, with every imaginable speciality on display; there's also a daytime snack bar for sushi and hot take-aways.

Apollolaan and around

Apollolaan, a wide residential boulevard just south of the Noorder Amstel canal, is representative of Berlage's intended grand design, but despite its obvious gracefulness, the New South was far from an instant success with the native Dutch bourgeoisie. Indeed, in the late 1930s the district became something of a Jewish enclave – the family of Anne Frank, for example, lived on Merwedeplein just off Churchilllaan. This embryonic community was swept away during the German occupation, their sufferings retold in Grete Weil's (Dutch-language) novel *Tramhalte Beethovenstraat*, and a memorial to those terrible times, when the New South witnessed some of the worst German excesses, may be found at the intersection of Apollolaan and Beethovenstraat; the **monument** commemorates the reprisal shooting of 29 people here in 1944. Another reminder is the school just off Apollolaan on Rubenstraat – itself named after an Amsterdam Resistance fighter who was shot for organizing false identity papers – which was once the headquarters of the Gestapo, and where the Frank family were brought after their capture.

On a different note, Apollolaan is also known for the **Amsterdam Hilton** at no. 138, where John Lennon and Yoko Ono staged their famous week-long "Bed-In" for peace in 1969. Part celebrity farce, part skilful publicity stunt, the couple's anti-war proclamations were certainly heard far and wide, though the episode also sparked as many revelations in the British press about the supposed "bad" influence of Yoko on the ex-Beatle.

Beatrixpark to De Dageraad

Trams #5 and #24 travel along Beethoven-straat, but only tram #5 crosses the Amstel canal to run past Cornelius Dopperkade, a handy entrance for the Beatrix-park.

From Apollolaan, head south down Beethovenstraat, and having passed the Amstel canal, take the first left, Cornelius Dopperkade, for the nearest of several entrances into the **Beatrixpark** (daily dawn to dusk; free). Recently renovated, this appealing park, with its footpaths and walled garden, is latticed by narrow waterways fed by the Amstel canal. It's a pleasant place for a stroll and in summer you may catch a free open-air concert. The park's eastern perimeter is marked by the Boeren Wetering canal, beyond which rises the clumpy **RAI exhibition centre**, a trade and conference complex that was built as part of the city's plan to attract more business trade. It's of little general interest, but if you're at a loose end, you might want to check out one of the centre's many exhibitions. To get there, leave the Beatrixpark at Boerenweteringpad and follow Wielingenstraat across the canal.

A rather more appealing option is to take a left down Haringvlietstraat, which leads – after about 350m – to the west end of **Churchilllaan**. This wide and well-heeled boulevard leads, in its turn, to Waalstraat, which, after crossing the Amstel canal, becomes Pieter Lodewijk Takstraat, a short narrow street home to **De Dageraad** ("The Dawn") housing project, completed in 1923 and one of the most successful examples of the Amsterdam School of architecture. Architects De Klerk and Kramer used a reinforced concrete frame as an underlay to the structure, thus permitting folds, tucks and curves in the brick exterior – a technique known as "apron architecture" (*Schortjesarchitectuur*). The facades are punctuated by strong, angular doors, sloping roofs and turrets, and you'll find a corner tower at the end of every block.

From De Dageraad, you can either walk up to the Albert Cuypstraat market (see p.131), or take a couple of tram rides (tram #12 northwest via Churchilllaan to the Concertgebouw, and then tram #16 heading west) to the Haarlemmermeer Station for the Amsterdamse Bos.

The Amsterdamse Bos

With 2000 acres of woodland park, the **Amsterdamse Bos**
(Amsterdam Forest) is the city's largest open space. Planted during
the 1930s, the park was a laudable, large-scale attempt to provide
gainful work for the city's unemployed, whose numbers had risen
alarmingly following the Wall Street Crash of 1929. Originally a
bleak area of flat, marshy fields, it combines a rural feel with that of
a well-tended city park: frankly, the "forest" part of its name is a little exaggerated. In the north of the park, the **Bosbaan**, a kilometre-
long dead-straight canal, is used for boating and swimming, and
there are children's playgrounds and spaces for various sports,
including ice skating. There's also a reserve in the south containing
bison, buffalo and deer, or you can simply walk or jog your way
around a choice of fourteen planned trails.

The main entrance to the Bos is at the junction of
Amstelveenseweg and Van Nijenrodeweg, beyond the railway lines
directly south of the Vondelpark. It can be reached by bus #170,
#171 or #172 from Raadhuisstraat, just west of the Dam, or from
Leidseplein. From the bus stop on Amstelveenseweg, it's a couple of
hundred metres to the east end of Bosbaan, where you can rent a
bike (March–Oct), much the best way of getting round the Bos.
Canoes, pedaloes and motorboats can also be rented here. It's a little more convoluted, but you can also get to this same entrance on
the antique trams of the **Museum Tramlijn** (April–Oct Sun
10.30am–5pm; May–Sept also Wed, same times; every 20min; ƒ5):
take any of the three buses mentioned or trams #6 and #16 to the
Haarlemmermeer Station tram terminus, at the north end of
Amstelveenseweg. From here, the old trams, imported from as far
away as Vienna and Prague, clank south to the Bos and beyond. The
Bosmuseum, also at the eastern end of the Bosbaan at Koenenkade
56 (daily 10am–5pm; free), provides maps and basic information on
the park's facilities, and has an exhibition on its history and function.

The East

Amsterdam East (Oost), a rough and ready working class quarter
stretching out beyond the Singelgracht, is not the city's most
enchanting area. Its boundary is marked by Amsterdam's eastern
gate, the **Muiderpoort** (pronounced "mao-der-port"), overlooking
the canal at the end of Plantage Middenlaan. In the 1770s, the gate
was revamped in pompous style, a neoclassical refit complete with a
flashy cupola and grandiosely carved pediment. Napoleon staged a
triumphal entry into the city through the Muiderpoort in 1811, but
his imperial pleasure was tempered by his half-starved troops, who
could barely be restrained from helping themselves in a city of (what
was to them) amazing luxury. Despite its general lack of appeal the

The East

Oost district does have one obvious attraction: the Museum of the Tropics, or **Tropenmuseum**, which sits on the corner of another of the city's municipal parks, the **Oosterpark**.

The Tropenmuseum

Across the Singelgracht canal on Mauritskade rises the gabled and turreted **Royal Tropen Instituut** – formerly the Royal Colonial Institute – a sprawling complex which contains the **Tropenmuseum** (Museum of the Tropics: Mon–Fri 10am–5pm, Sat & Sun noon–5pm; ƒ12,50), whose entrance is round the side at Linnaeusstraat 2. With its cavernous central hall and three floors of gallery space, the museum has room to focus on all the world's tropical and sub-tropical zones and impresses with its applied art. Amongst many artefacts, there are Javanese stone friezes, fancy carved wooden boats from the Pacific, a whole room of masks and, perhaps strangest of all, ritual totem poles cut from giant New Guinea mangroves. The collection is imaginatively presented through a variety of media – slides, videos and sound recordings – and there are creative and engaging displays devoted to such subjects as music-making and puppetry, as well as traditional storytelling. There are also reconstructions, down to sounds and smells, of typical streets in India, China or Africa, plus candid expositions on the problems besetting the developing world, both urban – the ever-expanding slum dwellings of cities like Bombay – and rural, examining such issues as the destruction of the world's tropical rainforests. The permanent collection is enhanced by an ambitious programme of temporary exhibitions.

To get to the Tropenmuseum take tram #9 or #14 and alight at Mauritskade, or hop on the Canal Bus (see p.530).

While you're here, be sure to look in on the **bookshop**, which has a good selection of titles on the developing world, and try the inex-

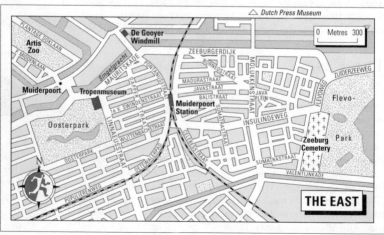

pensive **restaurant**, the *Ekeko*, which serves tropical snacks and lunches. Downstairs, the **Tropen Instituut Theater** specializes in Third World cinema, music and dance (see p.239). Part of the Tropenmuseum is also geared up for children under the age of twelve. This section, the **Kindermuseum** (Children's Museum), takes a hands-on approach to the same themes as the main museum but operates restricted opening hours (see p.282); call ☎568 8233 for details.

The Oosterpark and beyond

Behind the Royal Tropen Instituut, the manicured greenery of the **Oosterpark** is a gentle introduction to the area that extends south and east. A working-class district for the most part, particularly on the far side of Linnaeusstraat, the area also has a high immigrant presence, and the street names – Javastraat, Balistraat, Borneostraat – recall Holland's colonial past. This is one of the city's poorer neigh-bourhoods, with a sea of ageing terraced houses, though whole streets have been torn down to make way for new and better public housing. One of the few reasons to venture out this way is the **Dapperstraat market** (Mon–Sat 9am–5pm), one block east of Linnaeusstraat. This Eastern equivalent to the Albert Cuypstraat market (see p.131) is a diverse affair, with robed Arab men mingling with Dutch women in jeans, and where you can pick up a quarter-kilo of Edam at one stall and a fragrant Vietnamese *loempia* at the next.

A second specific attraction, slightly further east, is the **Nederlands Persmuseum** (Dutch Press Museum; Mon–Fri 9am–5pm; free), housed in the International Institute for Social History at Cruquiusweg 31. This tidy museum focuses on the history of the Dutch press since 1618, as revealed in newspapers, leaflets, posters and political cartoons. The collection of the Institute itself holds original letters and writings from many of the leading figures of the left including Marx, Lenin and Bakunin.

To reach the Dutch Press Museum, take tram #7 or #10 to Javaplein, follow Molukkenstraat north over the canal and along Veelaan to the east end of Cruquiusweg – a distance of about 1.5km.

The West

Of all Amsterdam's outer central districts, Amsterdam **West** is prob-ably the least interesting for the visitor, as it's primarily a residential area with only a couple of nondescript parks as possible attractions. The **Old West**, beyond the Singelgracht and above the Vondelpark, has a busy Turkish and North African immigrant-based street life that can be worth checking out if you find yourself in the vicinity: trams #7 and #17 run down **Kinkerstraat**, which is a good place to bar-gain-hunt if you're not after anything fancy, and there's also the vig-orous **Katestraat market**, about halfway down Kinkerstraat on the right. Outside of this zone, in the New West districts of Bos en Lommer, De Baarsjes and Overtoomse Veld, there's little other than the large but run-of-the-mill **Rembrandtpark** to draw you out this far.

The North

Solidly residential, Amsterdam **north**, on the far side of the River IJ, has flourished since the construction of the IJ tunnel in the 1960s linked it with the city centre. Unfortunately, the area is blighted by crass modern planning: you'll have to be pretty determined to weather the aesthetic storm that precedes the countryside. That said, if you've been in Amsterdam for a while, the prospect of wide open spaces can be a real fillip and the area to head for is the **Waterland**, an expanse of peat meadows, lakes, polders and marshland to the northeast of the built-up area. Until the turn of the twentieth century, this parcel of land was a marshy fen, whose scattered population made a healthy living raising and grazing cattle to be sold in Amsterdam. The Waterland was then made much more tractable by the digging of drainage canals, prompting wealthy Amsterdammers to build their summer residences here. These myriad waterways still pattern the district today and are home to a wide range of waterfowl, as are the many lakes, the largest of which – abutting the Markermeer – is the **Kinselmeer**.

Given the relative paucity of public transport this far out of the centre, easily the best way to explore the Waterland is by **bike**. Before you catch the ferry (see below), visit the VVV and pick up their Waterland leaflet (f3,50), which outlines a circular, 38km-long bike tour. The recommended route begins at the **Adelaarswegveer ferry dock** on the north side of the IJ, from where you follow Meeuwenlaan to the big roundabout at the start of Nieuwendammerdijk. This long thin lane leads east, running parallel to the river, before it meets Schellingwoudedijk and then Durger Dammerdijk at the southern tip of the long dike stretching up the coast, with the polders and a scattering of tiny villages just inland.

GVB operates two **ferries** across the IJ from Pier 8 behind Centraal Station. Neither ferry (*veer*) takes cars but both carry foot passengers, bicycles and motorbikes for free. Of the two, the Buiksloterwegveer – like a huge mobile air-traffic control tower – shuttles back and forth every ten minutes or so, 24 hours a day, running to the foot of Buiksloterweg. The smaller Adelaarswegveer (Mon–Sat 6.20am–8.50pm) connects with the southern end of Meeuwenlaan, the starting point of the Waterland bike tour.

Chapter 8

Day-trips from Amsterdam

lthough Amsterdammers may try to persuade you that there's nothing remotely worth seeing outside their own city, the truth is very much the opposite – indeed, you're spoilt for choice. Fast and efficient, the Dutch railway network puts a whole swathe of the Netherlands within easy reach, including all of the Randstad, a sprawling conurbation that stretches south and east of Amsterdam and encompasses the country's other big cities, The Hague, Utrecht and Rotterdam. Close to Amsterdam, amidst this urban pile-up, are two delightful medium-sized towns – Haarlem, whose attractive centre is home to the outstanding Frans Hals Museum, and Leiden, a proud university town with leafy canals and several first-rate museums. In between the two lie the best of the Dutch bulbfields, a blaze of colour from March to May, whilst Haarlem is the briefest of train rides from the wide sandy beaches of Zandvoort, one of Holland's most popular resorts.

A map of Amsterdam and the surrounding area appears in the colour insert at the back of this book.

To the north of Amsterdam, there's more countryside and less city. The most obvious targets are the old seaports bordering the fresh-water **Markermeer**, which forms part of the Ijsselmeer, created when the Afsluitdijk dam cut the former Zuider Zee off from the North Sea in 1932. No trains venture out along this coast, but it's an easy bus ride from Amsterdam to the nearest three: the former fish-ing village of **Marken**, the port of **Volendam** and – best of the lot – the beguiling, one-time shipbuilding centre of **Edam**. Edam is, of course, famous for its cheese, but its open-air **cheese market** is not a patch on that of **Alkmaar**, itself an amiable small town forty min-utes by train north from Amsterdam. On the way, most trains pause at Koog-Zaandijk, the nearest station to the windmills and canals of the recreated Dutch village of **Zaanse Schans**, which illustrates rural life as it was in the eighteenth century.

Public transport to all these destinations from Amsterdam is fast, frequent and inexpensive. In the case of Alkmaar, the longest train ride, it is, however, worth asking about discounted fares.

Haarlem and around

Though only fifteen minutes from Amsterdam by train, **Haarlem** has a quite different pace and feel from the capital. Founded on the banks of the River Spaarne in the tenth century, the town first prospered as a place where the counts of Holland levied tolls on local shipping, but later developed as a clothmaking centre. In 1572, the town sided with the Protestant rebels against the Habsburgs, a decision they came to regret when a large Spanish army led by Frederick of Toledo besieged them in December of the same year; it was a desperate affair that lasted for eight months, but finally the town surrendered after receiving various assurances of good treatment – assurances which Frederick promptly broke, massacring over 2000 of the Protestant garrison and all their Calvinist ministers. Recaptured in 1577 by the Protestants under William the Silent, Haarlem went on to enjoy its greatest prosperity in the seventeenth century, becoming a centre for the arts and home to a flourishing school of painters. Nowadays, Haarlem is an easily absorbed town of around 150,000 people, its good-looking centre studded with fine old buildings and containing the outstanding **Frans Hals Museum**, located in the almshouse where the artist spent his last, and for some his most brilliant, years. Well worth an afternoon in itself – maybe even an overnight stay if you're tired of the crowds and grime of Amsterdam – Haarlem is also a short train ride from two coastal resorts: the clumsy modern town of **Zandvoort-aan-Zee**, redeemed by its long sandy beach, and the **Bloemendaal-aan-Zee** beach resort, both of which allow easy access to the undeveloped dunes and seashore of the nearby **Nationaalpark de Kennemerduinen**.

Accommodation Prices

Throughout these listings we've used a code system to denote the price of the cheapest double room per night available in high season, including breakfast. For hostel accommodation we've used the code if they have doubles, otherwise we've specified the actual price per person for dorm beds.

① up to ƒ100/€45   ⑤ ƒ250–300/€112.50–135

② ƒ100–150/€45–67.50   ⑥ ƒ300–400/€135–180

③ ƒ150–200/€67.50–90   ⑦ ƒ400–500/€180–225

④ ƒ200–250/€90–112.50   ⑧ ƒ500+/€225+

Haarlem

At the heart of **HAARLEM** is the **Grote Markt**, a wide and attractive open space flanked by an appealing ensemble of Gothic and Renaissance architecture, including an intriguing if exceptionally garbled **Stadhuis**, whose turrets and towers, balconies and galleries were put together in piecemeal fashion between the fourteenth and the seventeenth centuries. At the other end of the Grote Markt stands a **statue** of a certain Laurens Coster (1370–1440), who, Haarlemmers insist, is the true inventor of printing. Legend tells of him cutting a letter "A" from the bark of a tree, dropping it into the sand by accident, and, hey presto, realising how to create the printed word. The statue shows him holding the wooden letter up triumphantly, but most historians agree that it was actually the German Johannes Gutenberg who invented printing, in the early 1440s.

The statue stands in the shadow of the **Grote Kerk** or **Sint Bavokerk** (Mon–Sat 10am–4pm; ƒ2,50), a mighty Gothic structure supported by heavy buttresses. The church is surmounted by a good-looking lantern tower directly above the transept crossing, which is actually made of wood, but clad in lead – the original stone version had to be dismantled when, in 1514, it proved too heavy for its supports and was about to crash down. Finally finished in 1538, after 150 years of work, the church dwarfs the surrounding clutter of streets and houses, and serves as a landmark from almost anywhere in the town. If you've been to the Rijksmuseum in Amsterdam (see p.115), the Grote Kerk may seem familiar, at least from the outside, since it was the principal focus of the seventeenth-century painter Gerrit Berckheyde's many views of Haarlem's Grote Markt – only the black-coated burghers are missing. The **interior** is breathtakingly cavernous, its beauty enhanced by the stark, white power of the vaulting. The present entrance (round the back on Oude Groenmarkt) leads to the east end of the church, where the southern ambulatory contains the tombstone of the painter Pieter Saenredam, and the choir that of Frans Hals. Nearby, next to the south transept, is the Brewers' Chapel, where the central pillar bears two black marks – one showing the height of a local giant, the 2.64m-tall Daniel Cajanus, who died in 1749, the other the 0.84m-high dwarf Simon Paap from Zandvoort. Further west still, on the north side of the nave, is the Dog Whippers' Chapel, built – curiously enough – for the men employed to keep dogs out of the church, and now separated from the nave by an iron grille. At the west end of the church, the mighty Christian Müller **organ** was four years in the making, completed in Amsterdam in 1738. It is said to have been played by Handel and Mozart (the latter on his tour of the country in 1766, at the age of ten) and is one of the biggest in the world, with over five thousand pipes and loads of snazzy Baroque embellishment; if you can make it to one of the organ recitals (mid-May to mid-September Tues 8.15pm, July & Aug also Thurs 3pm; free), it's well worth the

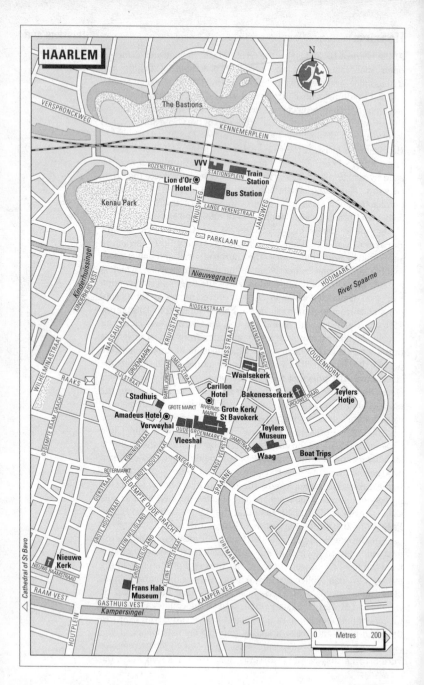

effort. Beneath the organ, Jan Baptist Xavery's lovely group of draped marble figures represent Poetry and Music offering thanks to the town, which is depicted as a patroness of the arts – in return for its generous support in the purchase of the organ.

Back outside, just beyond the western end of the church, the old meat market, the **Vleeshal** (Mon–Sat 11am–5pm, Sun noon–5pm; ƒ7,50, including Verweyhal) boasts a flashy Dutch Renaissance facade and serves as an annexe to the Frans Hals Museum (see below), holding temporary exhibitions of modern art. Just along the square, the **Verweyhal** (same details) serves much the same purpose, with special attention given to the local artist Kees Verwey (1900–1995).

The Frans Hals Museum

Haarlem's chief attraction, the **Frans Hals Museum** at Groot Heiligland 62 (Mon–Sat 11am–5pm, Sun noon–5pm; ƒ10), is a five-minute stroll south from the Grote Markt – just follow the signs. It's housed in an old almshouse complex, a much modified red-brick *hofje* with a central courtyard, where the aged Hals is supposed to have lived out his last destitute years on public funds. Little is known about **Frans Hals** (c1580–1666). Born in Antwerp, the son of Flemish refugees who settled in Haarlem in the late 1580s, his extant oeuvre is relatively small – some two hundred paintings and nothing like the number of sketches and studies left behind by Rembrandt. This is largely because Hals wasn't fashionable until the nineteenth century, and a lot of his work was lost before it became collectable. His outstanding gift was as a portraitist, showing a sympathy with his subjects and an ability to capture fleeting expression that some say even Rembrandt lacked. Seemingly quick and careless flashes of colour characterize his work, blended into a coherent whole to leave us a set of marvellously animated seventeenth-century figures.

The museum begins with the work of other artists: first a small group of sixteenth-century paintings, the most prominent a triptych by Gérard David and a polished *Adam and Eve* by Jan van Scorel. Afterwards, Room 10 features a good group of paintings by the **Haarlem mannerists**, including works by **Carel van Mander** (1548–1606), leading light of the Haarlem School and mentor of many of the other painters represented here. There's also a curious painting by Haarlem-born **Jan Mostaert** (1475–1555), his *West Indian Scene* depicting a band of naked, poorly armed natives trying to defend themselves against the cannon and sword of their Spanish invaders; the comparison with the Dutch Protestants is obvious. Moving on to Room 11, **Cornelis Cornelisz van Haarlem** (1562–1638) best followed van Mander's guidelines: his *Wedding of Peleus and Thetis* is an appealing rendition of what was then a popular subject, though Cornelisz gives as much attention to the arrangement of his elegant nudes as to the subject. This marriage

A combined ticket covering admission to the Frans Hals Museum, the Verweyhal and the Vleeshal costs ƒ12,50, and is sold at all three venues.

Haarlem and around

precipitated civil war amongst the gods and was used by the Dutch as a warning against discord, a call for unity during the long war with Spain. Similarly, the same artist's *Massacre of the Innocents* connects the biblical story with the Spanish siege of Haarlem in 1572.

Frans Hals was a pupil of van Mander too, though he seems to have learned little more than the barest rudiments from him. The Hals paintings begin in earnest in Room 21 with a set of "Civic Guard" portraits – group portraits of the militia companies initially formed to defend the country from the Spanish, but which later became social clubs for the gentry. Getting a commission to paint one of these portraits was a well-paid privilege – Hals got his first in 1616 – but their composition was a tricky affair and often the end result was dull and flat. With great flair and originality, Hals made the group portrait a unified whole instead of a static collection of individual portraits, his figures carefully arranged, but so cleverly as not to appear contrived. For a time, Hals himself was a member of the Company of St George, and in the *Officers of the Militia Company of St George* he appears in the top left-hand corner – one of his few self-portraits.

Further on in the museum, Hals' later paintings are darker, more contemplative works, closer to Rembrandt in their lighting. In Room 26, the *Governors* and *Governesses of St Elizabeth Gasthui*, painted in 1641, are good examples, as are the portraits of the *Regents* and *Regentesses of the Oudemannenhuis*, in Room 28. The latter were commissioned when Hals was in his eighties, a poor man despite a successful painting career, hounded for money by the town's tradesmen and by the mothers of his illegitimate children. As a result he was dependent on the charity of people like those depicted here: their cold, self-satisfied faces staring out of the gloom, the women reproachful, the men only slightly more affable. The character just right of centre in the *Regents* painting has been labelled (and indeed looks) drunk, although it is inconceivable that Hals would have depicted him in this condition; it's more likely that he was suffering from some kind of facial paralysis, and his jauntily cocked hat was simply a popular fashion of the time. There are those who claim Hals had lost his touch by the time he painted these pictures, yet their sinister, almost ghostly power as they face each other across the room, suggests quite the opposite. Van Gogh's remark that "Frans Hals had no fewer than 27 blacks" suddenly makes perfect sense.

The most famous portrait of a militia company is Rembrandt's The Night Watch, housed in the Rijksmuseum (see p.120).

Haarlem's other sights

Beyond the Frans Hals Museum, at the end of Groot Heiligland, turn left along the canal and it's a short walk east to the River Spaarne, whose gentle curves mark the eastern periphery of the town centre. Turn left again, along Turfmarkt and its continuation Spaarne, to reach the surly stonework of the **Waag** (Weigh House)

and then the country's oldest museum, the **Teylers Museum**, located in a grand old building at Spaarne 16 (Tues–Sat 10am–5pm, Sun
noon–5pm; ƒ10). Founded in 1774 by a wealthy local philan-
thropist, one Pieter Teyler van der Hulst, the museum should
appeal to scientific and artistic tastes alike. It contains everything
from fossils, bones and crystals, to weird, H.G. Wells-type technology (including an enormous eighteenth-century electrostatic gen-
erator) and sketches and line drawings by Michelangelo, Raphael,
Rembrandt and Claude, among others. The drawings are covered to
protect them from the light, but don't be afraid to pull back the curtains and peek. Look in, too, on the rooms beyond, filled with work
by eighteenth- and nineteenth-century Dutch painters, principally
Breitner, Israëls, Weissenbruch and, not least, Wijbrand Hendriks,
who was once the keeper of the art collection here. Teyler also
bestowed his charity on the riverside **Teylers Hofje**, a little way
east around the bend of the Spaarne at Koudenhorn 64. With none
of the cosy familiarity of the town's other *hofjes*, this is a grandiose
affair, a neoclassical edifice dating from 1787 and featuring solid
columns and cupolas. Nearby, the elegant fifteenth-century tower
of the **Bakenesserkerk**, on Vrouwestraat, is a flamboyant, vaguely
oriental protrusion on the Haarlem skyline.

*The
Bakenesserkerk
is not open to
the public.*

Two other sights that may help structure your wanderings are on
the opposite side of town. Van Campen's **Nieuwe Kerk**, just west of
Grote Houtstraat, was added – rather unsuccessfully – onto Lieven
de Key's bulbed, typically Dutch tower in 1649, though the interior
possesses a crisp soberness that acts as an antidote to the soaring
heights of the Grote Kerk. Just beyond, and much less self-effacing,
the Roman Catholic **Cathedral of St Bavo** (April–Oct Mon–Sat
10am–noon & 2–4.30pm; free) is one of the largest ecclesiastical
structures in Holland. Designed by Joseph Cuypers, son of P.J.
Cuypers (see p.58), and built on the west bank of the Leidsevaart
canal between 1895 and 1906, it is broad and spacious inside, with
cupolas and turrets crowding around an apse reminiscent of
Byzantine churches, the whole surmounted by a distinctive copper
dome.

Practicalities

Connected to Amsterdam by fast and frequent services, Haarlem's
splendid **train station** is located on the north side of the town centre, about ten minutes' walk from the Grote Markt. The **bus station**
is in front of the train station and the VVV (April–Sept Mon–Sat
9am–5.30pm; Oct–March Mon–Fri 9am–5.30pm, Sat 9am–4pm;
☎0900/616 1600) is next door. The latter issues free town maps and
brochures and has a small supply of **private rooms**, which cost
around ƒ35 per person per night pluš a ƒ10 room reservation fee,
but they are mostly on the outskirts of town. Haarlem has three central **hotels**, the pick of which is the homely *Amadeus*, a low-key spot

with plain but perfectly comfortable en-suite rooms at Grote Markt 10 (☎532 4530, fax 2328; ②); also on the Grote Markt, at no. 27, is the *Carillon* (☎531 0591, fax 4909; ②), another inexpensive place with frugal rooms, while the four-star *Golden Tulip Lion d'Or* is a smart chain hotel housed in a sturdy nineteenth-century building close to the train station at Kruisweg 34 (☎532 1750, fax 9543; ③). There's a **youth hostel**, near the sports stadium a couple of kilometres to the north of the town centre at Jan Gijzenpad 3 (April–Dec; ☎537 3793, fax 1176), where dorm beds cost around ƒ25 per night; bus #2 or #6 runs frequently from the station – a ten-minute journey. **Campsites** are dotted along the coast in and around Zandvoort – see below. Woltheus Cruises, by the river at Spaarne 11 (☎535 7723), operate several **boat trips** from Haarlem, the most interesting of which is a twice-weekly excursion to Zaanse Schans (July–Aug; 7hr; ƒ25).

The Haarlem's area telephone code is ☎023.

Haarlem's best **restaurants** are conveniently clustered around the Grote Markt and on Oude Groenmarkt. Excellent options include the *Applause*, a chic little place at Grote Markt 23a (☎531 1425), where main courses hover around the ƒ35 mark, and the slightly more expensive and equally smart *De Componist*, at Korte Veerstraat 1 (☎532 8853); both serve Dutch cuisine. The moderately priced *Quatre Mains*, Grote Markt 4 (☎542 4258) specializes in fondues and the eccentric *Haarlem aan Zee*, Oude Groenmarkt 10 (☎531 4884), whose interior is done out like a Dutch beach, serves a splendid range of seafood, with main dishes averaging between ƒ30 and ƒ40. The very popular and inexpensive *Restaurant La Plume*, Lange Veerstraat 1 (☎531 3202), offers a range of tasty dishes from pasta through to traditional Dutch. For a **drink**, *In Den Uiver*, just off the Grote Markt at Riviervismarkt 13, is a lively and extremely appealing bar offering occasional live music, while the *Grand Café Fortuyn*, Grote Markt 21, is a quieter, cosier spot, as is the laidback and typically Dutch *'t Ouwe Proef*, an intimate bar at Lange Veerstraat 7. Alternatively, there's the long-established and boisterous *Café Mephisto*, Grote Markt 29, and *Café 1900*, Barteljorisstraat 10, a fashionable locals' hangout serving drinks and light meals in a pleasant turn-of-the-century interior. Finally, *Ze Crack*, at the junction of Lange Veerstraat and Kleine Houtstraat, is a dim, smoky bar with good sounds.

Haarlem is also just a quick bus ride from the Keukenhof Gardens (see p.154), about 13km south of town.

Zandvoort and Bloemendaal-aan-Zee

Haarlem is just 7km from the coast at **ZANDVOORT**, a major seaside resort whose agglomeration of modern apartment blocks strings along the seashore behind a wide and sandy beach. As resorts go it's pretty standard – packed in summer, dead and gusty in winter – but the **beach** is excellent and the place also musters a casino and a car racing circuit. What's more, Zandvoort is one of the few places on the Dutch coast with its own train station (see opposite): the journey from Amsterdam to Zandvoort only takes twenty-five minutes, which makes it an easy day-trip – ideal for a spot of sunbathing.

Some 3km north along the coast from Zandvoort are the beachside shacks, dunes and ice cream stalls of **BLOEMENDAAL-AAN-ZEE**, a pocket-sized resort (not to be confused with Bloemendaal) which possesses several campsites (see below). It is also located on the southern edge of the **Nationaalpark de Kennemerduinen**, whose pine woods and dunes cover 1250 hectares of coastline. Maps of the park are widely available – petrol stations and local VVVs will, for example, oblige – and are useful if you intend to negotiate its network of footpaths and cycle trails – cycle hire is available in Zandvoort (see below). The park's **visitor centre** is in its southeast corner, just off the N200. To the north of the park is the gritty ferry port and eminently missable industrial town of Ijmuiden.

Practicalities

Zandvoort is well served by train: from June to August there are five trains hourly from Haarlem and three from Amsterdam Centraal, as well as one every half hour from Haarlem the rest of the year – the **train station** is only a five-minute walk (if that) from the beach. There are buses from Haarlem too – the **bus station** is in the centre of the resort on Louis Davidsstraat. There's no real reason to stay overnight in Zandvoort, but the VVV (April to mid-July & mid-Aug to Sept Mon–Sat 9am–5pm; mid-July to mid-Aug Mon–Sat 9am–7pm; Oct Mon–Sat 10am–12.30pm & 1.30–5pm; Nov–March Tues–Sat 10am–12.30pm & 1.30-4.30pm; ☎571 7947), a short, signposted walk west of the train station at Schoolplein 1, has a full list of local accommodation. This includes several four-star tower-block **hotels** dotted along the seashore, amongst which the slick 120-room *Gran Dorado Strandhotel*, Trompstraat 2 (☎572 0000, fax 573 0000; ④) is probably the most appealing. At the other end of the market, the VVV books **private rooms** for ƒ30 per person per night, but in summer these fill up fast – so ask early or telephone ahead. **Cycle hire** is available at the Rent-a-bike centre, Passage 20, in Zandvoort (May–Aug; ☎571 3343), and at several local campsites.

Bloemendaal-aan-Zee has two good **campsites**, both among the dunes within comfortable reach of the beach: the sprawling De Lakens, at Zeeweg 60 (☎573 2266, fax 2288; April–Oct), and Bloemendaal at Zeeweg 72 (☎573 2178, fax 2174; April to late Sept). Bus #81 runs from Haarlem train station to Bloemendaal-aan-Zee – and Zandvoort – along the N200; both campsites are just to the north of, and within easy walking distance of, this road.

Leiden

Some 30km southwest of Amsterdam, **LEIDEN** may well have been founded by the Romans as a forward base on an important trade

Leiden

route running behind the dunes; it was certainly fortified in the ninth century when the local lords added a castle, among the marshes on an artificial mound. After Flemish weavers migrated here in the fourteenth century the town prospered as a clothmaking centre, though it only became famous on the back of its **university**, a gift from William the Silent as a reward for enduring a year-long siege by the Spanish. The town emerged victorious on October 3, 1574, when William cut through the dykes around the town and sailed in with his fleet for a dramatic last-minute rescue. The event is still commemorated with an annual fair, fireworks, and the consumption of two traditional dishes: herring and white bread, which the fleet was supposed to have brought with them, and *hutspot*, a vegetable and potato stew, a cauldron of which was apparently found simmering in the abandoned Spanish camp outside the town walls.

Ideal for a day-trip from Amsterdam, from where there are fast and frequent trains, Leiden possesses a string of good museums – too many in fact to see in one day, so be selective – and has lots of good bars and restaurants. A lively and energetic place (largely due to its students), the town centre has real charm, its maze of narrow

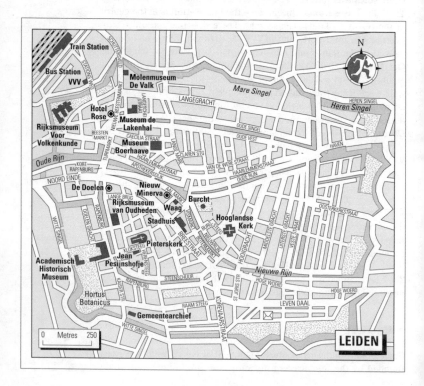

The Town

A good place to start an exploration of the town centre is the **Rapenburg**, a slender canal lined by some of Leiden's grandest mansions. In one of the largest, at no. 28, is the town's best-known attraction, the **Rijksmuseum Van Oudheden** (National Museum of Antiquities; Tues–Fri 10am–5pm, Sat & Sun noon–5pm; f7). This is also Holland's principal archeological museum, the speciality of which is its Egyptian and classical collections. You can see one of its major exhibits, the *Temple of Taffeh*, for free. Situated in a courtyard near the museum entrance, it was a gift from the Egyptian government in gratitude for the part the Dutch played in the 1960s UNESCO excavations, which succeeded in uncovering a number of Nubian monuments. Dating back to the first century AD, the temple was adapted in the fourth century to the worship of Isis, eventually being sanctified as a Christian church four hundred years later. The Egyptians placed very firm conditions on their legacy: no one should have to pay to see it, and the temperature and humidity must be carefully regulated, with the lights overhead simulating the passage of the sun.

Inside the museum proper, the first exhibit is the remains of a temple dedicated to Nehellania – a goddess of sailors – which was uncovered in Zeeland. Next comes classical Greek and Roman sculpture, leading chronologically through Hellenistic works to busts, statues and friezes from Imperial Rome. The most enjoyable collection, though, is the Egyptian one, beginning with wall reliefs, statues and sarcophagi from tombs and temples, and continuing in the rooms immediately above with a set of mummies and sarcophagi as complete as you're likely to see outside Egypt. The *Three Figures of Maya*, to name just one exhibit, are exceptionally well preserved. The third floor is devoted to the Netherlands: an archeological history of the country from prehistoric, Roman and medieval times, which is, perhaps inevitably, less interesting than the rest of the museum.

Further along Rapenburg, at no. 73, parts of the medieval monastery that became the university's first home still stand and hold the **Academisch Historisch Museum** (Sept–June Wed–Fri 1–5pm; free), detailing the university's history. Through the courtyard, the **Hortus Botanicus** (Botanical Gardens; Mon–Fri 9am–5pm, Sun 10am–5pm; April–Sept also Sat 9am–5pm; f5) is a lovely spot, lushly planted and subtly landscaped across to the Witte Singel canal. Planted in 1587, this is one of the oldest botanical gardens in Europe, a mixture of carefully tended beds of shrubs and hothouses full of tropical foliage.

Leiden

Pieterskerk

Cross Rapenburg from the Academisch Historisch Museum, and you're in the network of narrow streets that constitutes the medieval town, converging on a central square and the Gothic **Pieterskerk** (daily 1.30–4pm), Leiden's principal church. Deconsecrated now, it has an empty warehouse-like feel, but among the fixtures that remain are a simple and beautiful Renaissance rood screen and a host of memorials to the sundry notables buried here – including one to **John Robinson** (1575–1625), leader of the Pilgrim Fathers. Robinson lived in a house on the site of what is now the **Jean Pesijnshofje** at Kloksteeg 21, right beside the church. A curate in England at the turn of the seventeenth century, he was suspended from preaching in 1604, later fleeing with his congregation to pursue his Puritan form of worship in the more amenable atmosphere of Calvinist Holland. Settling in Leiden, Robinson acted as pastor to growing numbers, but still found himself at odds with the establishment. In 1620, a hundred of his followers – "The Pilgrim Fathers" – sailed via Plymouth for the untrammelled wilderness of America, though Robinson died before he could join them; he's buried in the church.

You'll also find the best of the Gemeente-archief's documents online at www.leiden.nl/gemeente-archief

If you want to find out more about the Pilgrim Fathers, stroll down to Leiden's municipal archives, the **Gemeentearchief** (Mon–Fri 9.30am–5pm, Sat 9am–12.15pm; free) at Boisotkade 2A, which have an outstanding collection of documents relating to the settlers. Alternatively, head east to Breestraat.

The Stadhuis and the Waag

Just east of Pieterskerk, pedestrianized **Breestraat** marks the edge of Leiden's commercial centre, but is undistinguished except for the **Stadhuis**, an imposing edifice whose Renaissance facade is a copy of the late sixteenth-century original destroyed by fire in 1929. Behind the Stadhuis, the canals that cut Leiden's centre into pocket-sized islands converge at the busiest point in town, the site of a vigorous general **market** on Wednesdays and Saturdays. Here, a tangle of narrow bridges is flanked by a number of buildings, from overblown Art Nouveau department stores to modest terrace houses. On the south side – on Aalmarkt – is the **Waag** (Weigh House), a replacement for a previous Gothic structure, built to a design by Pieter Post (1608–1669) and fronted with a naturalistic frieze showing a merchant watching straining labourers. Pieter Post was a successful architect, but his artist brother, Frans, was much better-known. Frans made a major contribution to the *Historia Naturalis Brasiliae*, a natural and ethnographic study of eastern Brazil (in Dutch hands from 1630 to 1654) that was to influence many such similar works.

The Hooglandsekerk and the Burcht

The general market sprawls right over the bridges and extends southeast along one of the town's prettiest canals, the **Nieuwe Rijn**.

Strolling along its north bank, take the first left, Burgsteeg, and turn

Strolling along its north bank, take the first left, Burgsteeg, and turn right at the end for the **Hooglandsekerk**, on Nieuwstraat (mid-May to mid-Sept Mon 1–5pm, Tues–Fri 11am–3.30pm & Sat 11am–4pm; free). A light and lofty Gothic structure built in stages over a couple of hundred years, the church holds a monument to Pieter van der Werff, the heroic burgomaster of Leiden at the time of the 1573–74 siege. When the situation became so desperate that most people were all for giving up, the burgomaster, no doubt remembering the massacre of Haarlem, offered his own body to them as food. His invitation was rejected, but – the story goes – it succeeded in instilling new determination in the flagging citizens.

Doubling back to the end of Burgsteeg, follow the alley and you'll soon reach the **Burcht** (daily 10am–10pm; free), the heavily restored stone shell of a medieval fortress that perches high above the town centre on an artificial mound. Dating back to the ninth century, the mound was where Leiden began, home to an isolated stronghold amongst the marshes that provided locals with some security; it's worth climbing up to the fort for a panoramic view of Leiden's roofs and towers. At the far end of the alley is the **Oude Rijn** canal, on the other side of which lies the blandly pedestrian **Haarlemmerstraat**, the town's main shopping street.

Museum Boerhaave and the Municipal Museum

A few metres to the north of Haarlemmerstraat, the **Museum Boerhaave** – the National Museum of the History of Science and Medicine – at Lange Agnietenstraat 10 (Tues–Sat 10am–5pm, Sun noon–5pm; ƒ5) is named after a seventeenth-century Leiden surgeon, Herman Boerhaave. It gives a brief but fairly absorbing overview of scientific and medical developments over the last five centuries, with particular reference to Dutch achievements, and including some gruesome surgical implements, pickled brains and suchlike.

Five minutes' walk north from here, Leiden's municipal museum, the **Stedelijk Museum de Lakenhal** (Tues–Sat 10am–5pm, Sun noon–5pm; ƒ8), housed in the old Cloth Hall at Oude Singel 32, has a similarly engaging exhibition. Downstairs, on the ground floor, amongst a healthy sample of local sixteenth- and seventeenth-century paintings, are examples of the work of Jacob van Swanenburgh (first teacher of the young Rembrandt), Jan Lievens (with whom Rembrandt shared a studio), and **Gerrit Dou** (1613–1675), whose exquisite *Astrologer* is in Room 8. Rembrandt's first pupil, Dou began by imitating his master, but soon developed his own style, pioneering the Leiden tradition of small, minutely detailed pictures of enamel-like smoothness. Prosperous and well regarded, Dou was, however, impossible to work with, forever trying to remove every speck of dust from his studio. There's also Lucas van Leyden's (1494–1533) alarming and spectacularly unsuccessful *Last*

Judgement triptych in Room 6, several paintings devoted to the siege of 1574 and the heroics of burgomaster Werff, plus mixed rooms of furniture, silver, tiles, glass and ceramics. **Rembrandt** himself, despite being born in Leiden, is poorly represented; he left his home town at the tender age of fourteen, and, although he returned in 1625, it was only for six years, after which he settled permanently in Amsterdam. Only a handful of his Leiden paintings survive, but there's one here, *Agamemnon before Palamedes*, a stilted and rather unsuccessful rendition of the classical tale, painted in 1626. The other floors of the museum are of cursory interest only: the first floor holds several old guild rooms moved here from other parts of Leiden, the second floor temporary exhibitions and the top floor a series of modest displays on the town's history.

The Windmill and Ethnology museums

At the west end of Oude Singel turn right and it's a couple of hundred metres to the **Molenmuseum De Valk** (The Valk Windmill Museum; Tues–Sat 10am–5pm, Sun 1–5pm; *f*5), a restored grain mill and the last survivor of the twenty-odd windmills built on the town's outer fortifications in the eighteenth century. Inside, there are seven floors. On the ground floor are the millers' living quarters, furnished in simple, period style, and upstairs are a variety of displays, the most interesting of which is a slide show and exhibition recounting the history and development of Dutch windmills.

From the windmill, it's a five-minute walk west along Binnenvestgracht to the **Rijksmuseum voor Volkenkunde** at Steenstraat 1 (National Museum of Ethnology; Tues–Fri & Sun 10am–5pm, Sat noon–5pm; *f*10). This museum has comprehensive sections on Indonesia and the Dutch colonies, along with reasonable ones on the South Pacific and Far East. However, it gives most other parts of the world a less than thorough showing and is far from being an essential stop.

Practicalities

Leiden's ultra-modern **train station** is next to the **bus station** on the northwest edge of town, a five- to ten-minute walk from the centre along Stationsweg. Halfway, at no. 210, is the **VVV** (Mon–Fri 11am–7pm & Sat 11am–3pm; ☎0900/222 2333), which has useful maps and brochures detailing walking tours of the town as well as a wide range of regional information. Of the town's **hotels** easily the most enjoyable is the excellent *Nieuw Minerva*, which occupies several old canalside houses in the centre at Boommarkt 23 (☎512 6358, fax 514 2674, *www.nieuwminerva.nl*; ②), and whose rooms range from the attractive and tastefully decorated to the top-range "honeymoon" room, complete with four-poster and fancy drapes (⑤). A good second choice is the three-star, fifteen-room *De Doelen*, by another of the town's canals at Rapenburg 2 (☎512 0527, fax

512 8453; ②). Finally, there's also the bargain-basement *Hotel Rose*, an inexpensive haunt at Beestenmarkt 14 (☎514 6630, fax 521 7096; ①). **Canal trips** around the town centre depart between three and five times daily from the Beestenmarkt, between April and September; tickets cost ƒ9 per person and the trip lasts forty minutes.

Many of Leiden's choicest **cafés** and **restaurants** are concentrated around Pieterskerk. It's here you'll find *M'n Broer*, Kloksteeg 7, an agreeable, low-key café-bar offering a tasty range of light meals, and the rather more polished *Bistro La Cloche*, a French restaurant just up the street at no. 3 (☎512 3053). Nearby, *La Bota*, at Herensteeg 9, has some of the best-value local food in town as well as an excellent array of beers, while *Koetshuis de Burcht*, at Burgsteeg 13 (☎512 1688), is a fashionable French/Dutch bistro working to an imaginative and well-wrought menu. Another excellent choice is the smart, bistro-style *Restaurant de Gouvernante*, Kort Rapenburg 17 (☎514 8818; closed Mon), which serves such delicacies as steak with truffles – for a reasonable ƒ40; it's a popular spot, so reservations are advised. There's no shortage of places to **drink**. *Hebes*, Oude Rijn 1, is a traditional neighbourhood bar with a low-key atmosphere, and quite the opposite of the lively *North End English Pub* at Noordeinde 55, on the corner with Rapenburg. Close by, opposite the old university building, *Barrera* is a fashionable café-bar, a student favourite offering light meals and a good range of beers. Otherwise, *Jazzcafé The Duke*, on the corner of Oude Singel and Nieuwe Beestenmarkt, has a friendly bar and live jazz several nights of the week, and *Café Jazzmatazz*, round the corner on Lange Scheistraat, also features live music and attracts an expat crowd.

Around Leiden: the bulbfields

The pancake-flat fields extending north from Leiden towards Haarlem are the heart of the Dutch **bulbfields**, whose bulbs and blooms support a billion-guilder industry and some ten thousand growers, as well as attracting tourists in their droves. Bulbs have flourished here since the late sixteenth century, when one Carolus Clusius, a Dutch botanist and one-time gardener to the Habsburg emperor, brought the first tulip bulb over from Vienna, where it had – in its turn – been brought from modern-day Turkey by an Austrian aristocrat. The tulip flourished in Holland's sandy soil and was so highly prized that it fuelled a massive speculative bubble. At the height of the boom – in the mid-1630s – bulbs were commanding extraordinary prices: the artist Jan van Goyen, for instance, paid ƒ1900 and two paintings for ten rare bulbs, while another set of one hundred bulbs were swapped for a coach and pair of horses. The bubble burst in 1636, thanks to the intervention of the government, and the bulb industry returned to normal, though it left hundreds of investors ruined, much to the satisfaction of the country's Calvinist ministers who had railed against the excesses.

Other types of bulbs were introduced after the tulip and today the **spring** flowering sequence begins in mid-March with crocuses, followed by daffodils and yellow narcissi in late March, and hyacinths and tulips in mid- and late April through to May. Gladioli flower in August. The view from any of the trains heading south to – or north from – Leiden can often be sufficient in itself, the fields divided into stark geometric blocks of pure colour. However, with your own transport you can take in the full beauty of the bulbfields by way of special routes marked by hexagonal signposts – local VVVs sell pamphlets listing the best vantage points – or you can reach the bulb growers' showcase, the **Keukenhof Gardens**, easily enough by bus from Leiden or Haarlem. Bear in mind also that there are any number of local **flower festivals** and **parades** in mid- to late April – every local VVV has the details.

The Keukenhof Gardens

The small town of **Lisse**, halfway between Leiden and Haarlem, is home to the **Keukenhof Gardens** (late March to late May daily 8am–7.30pm; ƒ18), the largest flower gardens in the world. The Keukenhof was set up in 1949, designed by a group of prominent bulb growers to convert people to the joys of growing flowers from bulbs in their own gardens. Literally the "kitchen garden", its site is the former estate of a fifteenth-century countess, who used to grow herbs and vegetables for her dining table here – hence the name. Some seven million flowers are on show for their full flowering period, complemented, in case of especially harsh winters, by 5000 square metres of glasshouses holding indoor displays. You could easily spend a whole day here, swooning among the sheer abundance of it all, but to get the best of it you need to come early, before the tour buses pack the place. There are several restaurants in the 28 hectares of grounds, and well-marked paths take you all the way through the gardens, which specialize in daffodils, narcissi, hyacinths and tulips. To get to the Keukenhof by public transport from Leiden, take **bus #54** from the bus station (every 30min; 30min). There are no direct bus services from Haarlem – you have to change in Lisse; details at the Haarlem VVV or bus station.

Aalsmeer

You can see the flower industry in action in **AALSMEER**, 23km northeast of Leiden, towards Amsterdam. The **flower auction** here, again the largest in the world, is held daily in a building approximately the size of 75 football fields (Mon–Fri 7.30–11am; ƒ5). The dealing is fast and furious, and the turnover staggering. In an average year around ƒ2.5 billion worth of plants and flowers are traded, many of them arriving in florists' shops throughout Europe on the same day. In case it all seems a mystery, there are headphones with recorded information in English placed strategically around. Be sure to arrive well before 10am or you won't see a single flower.

Marken, Volendam and Edam

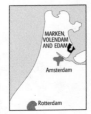

The turbulent waters of the **Zuider Zee** were once busy with Dutch trading ships plying to and from the Baltic. This Baltic trade was the lynchpin of Holland's prosperity in the Golden Age, revolving around the import of huge quantities of grain, the supply of which was municipally controlled to guarantee against famine. The trade was immensely profitable and its proceeds built a string of prosperous seaports – including Volendam, Enkhuizen and Hoorn – and nourished market towns like Edam, while the Zuider Zee itself supported numerous fishing villages such as Marken. In the eighteenth century the Baltic trade declined, leaving the ports economically stranded, and, with the rapid increase in the Dutch population during the nineteenth century, plans were made to reclaim the Zuider Zee and turn it into farmland. The first part of the scheme was the completion of a dam, the **Afsluitdijk**, across the mouth of the Zuider Zee in 1932, but by the time a second, complementary barrier linking Enkhuizen with Lelystad was finished in 1976, the steam had gone out of the project. The old Zuider Zee was never completely drained and most has remained water, with the two dams creating a pair of freshwater lakes – the **IJsselmeer** and **Markermeer**.

These placid, steel-grey lakes are popular with day-tripping Amsterdammers, who come here in their hundreds to sail their boats and visit a string of pretty little towns and villages. These begin on the west shore just a few kilometres north of Amsterdam with the picturesque old fishing village of **Marken** and the former seaport of **Volendam**. In the summer, it's possible to travel between these two by boat, but the trip can also be made – if a little less conveniently – by bus. Buses also link Volendam with **Edam**, a far prettier proposition and much less swamped by tourists. You don't necessarily need to make a choice though, since all three places can comfortably be visited in a day.

Marken

Once an island in the Zuider Zee, **Marken** was, until its road connection to the mainland in 1957, pretty much a closed community, supported by a small fishing industry. Despite its proximity to Amsterdam, its biggest problem was the genetic defects caused by close and constant intermarrying; now it's how to contain the tourists, whose numbers increase yearly. That said, there's no denying the picturesque

Marken, Volendam and Edam

charms of the island's one and only village – also called **MARKEN** – where the immaculately maintained houses, mostly painted in deep green with white trimmings, cluster on top of artificial mounds raised to protect them from the sea. There are two main parts to the village, **Havenbuurt**, behind the harbour, and **Kerkbuurt** around the church (mid-May to Oct Mon–Sat 10am–5pm; free), an ugly 1904 replacement for its longstanding predecessor. Of the two Kerkbuurt is the less touristy, its narrow lanes lined by ancient dwellings and a row of old eel-smoking houses, now the **Marken Museum**, Kerkbuurt 44 (April–Oct Mon–Sat 10am–4.30pm, Sun noon–4.30pm; free), devoted to the history of the former island and its fishing industry. Across in the Havenbuurt, one or two of the houses are open for tourists, proclaiming themselves to be "typical" of Marken, and the waterfront is lined by snack bars and souvenir shops, often staffed by locals in traditional costume. It's all a tad prosaic, but now and again you get a hint of how hard life used to be – most of the houses on the waterfront are raised on stilts, allowing the sea to roll under the floors in bad weather, enough to terrify most people half to death.

Practicalities

Marken is accessible direct from Amsterdam on **bus #111**. This departs from the bus stop across the street from St Nicolaaskerk, close to Centraal Station (every 15–30min; 30min) and drops you beside the car park on the edge of Marken village, from where it's a five-minute walk to the centre. Marken does not have a VVV and neither is there anywhere **to stay**. In season, a passenger **ferry** links Marken with Volendam (March–Oct daily every 30min 11am–6pm; 30min; ƒ10; information ☎0299/363 331), but at other times it's a fiddly **bus** trip: take bus #111 back towards Amsterdam, but get off at the Swaensborch stop on the edge of Monnickendam village. At Swaensborch, change to bus #110, which runs from Amsterdam to Volendam and Edam. If you're planning to use more than a bus or two, buy a timetable in Amsterdam, before you set out.

Volendam

Larger but not nearly as quaint as Marken, the old fishing village of **VOLENDAM** has had, by comparison with its neighbour, some riproaring cosmopolitan times. In the early years of the twentieth century it became something of an artists' retreat, with both Picasso and Renoir spending time here. The artists are, however, long gone and nowadays Volendam heaves with day-tripping tourists bobbing in and out of the souvenir stalls that run the length of the main street. Quiet places, never mind pretty ones, are hard to find, but narrow **Meerzijde**, one street back from the harbour, does have its moments in its mazy alleys and mini-canals. One curiosity to look out for is a plaque at the corner of Berend Demmerstraat and Josefstraat marking how high the floodwaters of 1916 rose here.

Practicalities

Bus #110 from Amsterdam and Monnickendam (for Marken – see above) drops passengers on Zeestraat, just along the street from the Volendam VVV, at no. 37 (April–Sept daily 10am–5pm; Oct–March Mon–Sat 10am–3pm; ☎0299/363 747). From the VVV, it's a couple of minutes' walk to the waterfront. With Amsterdam just a short bus ride away and Edam even nearer (see below), there's absolutely no reason to stay overnight here, but if you do, the long-established *Best Western Spaander* on the waterfront at Haven 15 (☎0299/363 595, fax 369 615; ③) is the most attractive option. In the summertime, there is a regular **passenger ferry** to Marken (March–Oct daily every 30min 10am–5pm; 30min; ƒ10; information ☎0299/363 331).

Edam

Further on down the #110 bus route from Amsterdam, just 3km from Volendam, you might expect **EDAM** to be jammed by tourists considering the international fame of the rubbery red balls of cheese that bear its name. In fact, Edam generally lacks the crowds and is a delightful, good-looking and prosperous little town of neat brick houses, swing bridges and slender canals. Founded by farmers in the twelfth century it boomed in the seventeenth as a shipbuilding centre with river access to the Zuider Zee. The excellent pasture land surrounding the town is still grazed by large herds of cows, but nowadays most Edam cheese is produced elsewhere, even in Germany – "Edam" is the name of a type of cheese and not its place of origin. This does, of course, rather undermine the authenticity of Edam's open-air **cheese market**, held every Wednesday in July and August on the Kaasmarkt (10.30am–12.30pm), but it's still a popular attraction and the only time the town heaves with tourists. Edam's cheese market is a good deal more humble than Alkmaar's (see p.161), but it follows the same format, with the cheeses laid out in rows before the buyers sample them. Once a cheese has been purchased, the cheese porters, dressed in the traditional white costumes and straw boaters, spring into action, carrying them off on their gondola-like trays.

At the heart of Edam is the **Damplein**, a pint-sized main square where an elongated humpbacked bridge has long vaulted in the Voorhaven canal, which once used to flood the town with depressing regularity. Also on the square is Edam's eighteenth-century **Stadhuis**, a severe Louis XIV-style structure whose plain symmetries culminate in a dinky little tower, and the **Edams Museum** (April–Oct Tues–Sat 10am–4.30pm, Sun 1.30–4.30pm; ƒ3,50), housed in a pretty building whose crow-stepped gables date from 1530. Inside, a modest assortment of local bygones is redeemed by the curious floating cellar, supposedly built by a retired sea captain who could not bear the thought of sleeping on dry land. From Damplein, it's a short walk along Grote Kerkstraat to the rambling **Grote Kerk** (April–Oct daily 2–4.30pm; free), on the edge of the fields to the north of the village. This is the largest three-ridged church in Europe, with a huge organ built in 1663 and a vaulted ceiling constructed in wood in an attempt to limit the subsidence caused by the building's massive weight. A handsome, largely Gothic structure, it contains several magnificent **stained-glass windows** dating from 1606 to 1620, mostly heraldic but including historical scenes too. Unfortunately, the church's strong lines are disturbed by the almost comically stubby spire, which was shortened to its present height after a lightning strike started a bad fire in 1602.

Strolling back from the church, take Matthijs Tinxgracht – one street west of Grote Kerkstraat – along the canal and you'll soon reach the Kaasmarkt, site of both the cheese market and the **Kaaswaag** (Cheese Weigh House), whose decorative panels celebrate – you guessed it – cheese-making and bear the town's coat-of-arms, a bull on a red field with three stars. From here, it's a couple of hundred metres to the sixteenth-century **Speeltoren**, the elegant tower visible from all over town, and roughly the same distance again – south along Lingerzijde – to the impossibly picturesque bridge of **Kwakelbrug**. This leads over to one of Edam's most charming streets, **Schepenmakersdijk**, a cobbled, canalside lane flanked by immaculate gardens and the quaintest of houses.

To explore Edam's every architectural nook and cranny, pop into the VVV, in the Stadhuis (see below), and buy their *A Stroll through Edam* (ƒ4,95).

Practicalities

Leaving Amsterdam every half hour from near St Nicolaaskerk, **bus #110** takes thirty-five minutes to reach Volendam and ten minutes more to get to Edam. Edam's **bus station** is on the southwest edge of town, on Singelweg, a five-minute walk from Damplein. There are no signs, but aim for the easily spotted Speeltoren tower: cross the distinctive swing-bridge, turn right and follow Lingerzijde as it jinks left and right. From the Speeltoren, it's a few metres east to the Damplein, where the VVV (April–Oct Mon–Sat 10am–5pm; Nov–March Mon–Sat 10am–2pm; ☎0299/315 125) issues town maps and has the details of **boat trips** both along the local canals and out into the Markermeer. **Bike hire** is available at Ronald Schot, in the town centre by the Speeltoren at Kleine Kerkstraat 9 (☎0299/372 155); a one-day rental costs ƒ10.

The VVV also has a number of **private rooms** (ƒ30–40 per person including breakfast), which they will book on your behalf for free. Otherwise, there are three **hotels**, the pick being the charming *De Fortuna*, just round the corner from the Damplein at Spuistraat 7 (☎0299/371 671, fax 469; ③). This three-star hotel, with its immaculate garden flowing down to a canal, has just thirty comfortable rooms distributed amongst six cosy little houses. An appealing second choice is the *Damhotel*, which occupies a modernized old inn opposite the VVV (☎0299/371 766, fax 374 031; ②). The third hotel is the rather more modest, one-star *Harmonie*, in a plain but pleasant canalside house a couple of hundred metres east of the VVV at Voorhaven 92 (☎0299/371 664; ②). The nearest **campsite** is east of town near the lakeshore at Zeevangszeedijk 7 (☎0299/371 994) – a twenty-minute walk east along the canal from Damplein.

For **eating**, *De Fortuna* has the best restaurant in town, but eating at the *Damhotel* is hardly a hardship – and it's a good deal cheaper; both serve Dutch cuisine.

Zaandam and Zaanse Schans

Every few minutes one of the many trains heading north out of Amsterdam passes through the build-up of settlements collectively known as **Zaanstad**, which trails northwest of the city on the far side of the River IJ. Amongst them, two in particular are worth visiting – **Zandaam**, the urban core of Zaanstad, and the museum-village of **Zaanse Schans**, complete with its old wooden cottages and windmills.

Zaandam

From the train it's not an especially enticing prospect, but unassuming **ZAANDAM** is an amiable, largely modern town that merits a brief stop. It was a popular tourist hangout in the nineteenth century, when it was known as "La Chine d'Hollande" for the faintly oriental appearance of its windmills, canals, masts, and row upon row of brightly painted houses. Claude Monet spent some time here in the 1870s, and, despite being suspected of spying and under constant police surveillance, immortalized the place in a series of paintings.

Follow the main street, Gedempte Gracht, from the train station for five minutes (the VVV is at no. 76; Mon–Fri 9am–5.30pm, Sat 9am–4pm; ☎075/616 2221), turn right down Damstraat, right again, and left down Krimp, and you can see something of Monet's Zaandam, the harbour spiked with masts beyond a little grouping of wooden houses. On Krimp itself, at no. 23, is the town's main modern claim to fame, the **Czaar Petershuisje** (Tues–Fri 10am–1pm & 2–5pm, Sat & Sun 1–5pm; ƒ3,50), a house in which the Russian Tsar Peter the Great stayed when he came to study shipbuilding here. In those days Zaandam was an important shipbuilding centre, and the tsar made four visits to the town, the first in 1697 when he arrived incognito and stayed in the simple home of one Gerrit Kist, who had formerly served with him. A tottering wooden structure enclosed within a brick shelter, the house is little more than two tiny rooms, decorated with a handful of portraits of a benign-looking emperor and the graffiti of tourists going back to the mid-nineteenth century. Among the few things to see is the cupboard bed in which Peter is supposed to have slept, together with the calling cards and pennants of various visiting Russian delegations; around the outside of the house is an exhibition on the shipbuilding industry in Zaandam. Napoleon is said to have remarked on visiting the house, "Nothing is too small for great men."

Zaanse Schans

Most visitors to Zaanstad are, however, here to visit the recreated Dutch village of **Zaanse Schans**. The village is made up of cottages, windmills and workshops assembled from all over the region, in an energetic and endearing attempt to reproduce a Dutch village as it would have looked in the eighteenth and early nineteenth century. Spread over a network of narrow canals beside the River Zaan, it's a pretty spot and deservedly popular, with the particular highlight being the working **windmills**, giant industrial affairs used – amongst other things – to cut wood, grind mustard and produce oil. This is the closest place to Amsterdam to see working windmills and there is a scattering of other attractions too, notably a **Kaasmakerij** (Cheese-making workshop) and a **Klompenmakerij** (Clog-making workshop), where you can watch the village's employees practising traditional skills. You can walk round the village at any time, but the windmills and workshops are only open during the day, mostly from 9am to 5pm in winter, 6pm in summer; admission is around ƒ2 per person per attraction. There are also enjoyable hour-long **boat trips** on the River Zaan from the jetty near De Huisman mustard windmill (April–Sept daily 10am–5pm, every hour; ƒ8).

It's about 1km to Zaanse Schans from the nearest train station, **Koog-Zaandijk**, two stops up the line from Zaandam. To get there from Zaandam, take bus #88 (every 30min; 10min).

Alkmaar

Forty minutes from Amsterdam by train and thirty from Koog-Zaandijk, the little town of **ALKMAAR** was founded in the tenth century in the middle of a marsh, and takes its name from the auk diving bird which lived here, as in *alkeen meer*, or auk lake. Just like Haarlem, the town was besieged by Frederick of Toledo, but heavy rain flooded its surroundings and forced the Spaniards to withdraw in 1573, an early Dutch success in the Eighty Years' War. Alkmaar's agreeable, partially canalized centre is still surrounded by its medieval moat, part of which has been incorporated into the Noordhollandskanaal, itself part of a longer network of waterways running north from Amsterdam to the Waddenzee, beyond the Afsluitdijk.

Alkmaar has a cluster of impressive medieval buildings, but is best known for its much-touted **cheese market** (mid-April to mid-Sept Fri 10am–noon), an ancient affair that these days ranks as one of the most extravagant tourist spectacles in Holland. Cheese has been sold on the main square here since the 1300s, and although it's no longer a serious commercial concern, the market remains popular and continues to draw the crowds. If you want to see it be sure to get there early, as by opening time the crowds are already thick on the ground. The ceremony starts with the buyers sniffing, crumbling, and finally tasting each cheese, followed by intensive bartering. Once a deal has been concluded, the cheeses – golden discs of Gouda mainly, laid out in rows and piles on the square – are borne away on ornamental carriers by four groups of porters (*kaasdragers*) for weighing. The porters wear white trousers and shirt plus a black hat whose coloured bands – green, blue, red or yellow – represent the four companies that comprise the cheese porters' guild. Payment for the cheeses, tradition has it, takes place in the cafés around the square.

The Town

Even if you've only come for the cheese market, it's worth seeing something of the rest of the town before you leave. On the main square, the **Waag** (Weigh House) was originally a chapel dedicated to the Holy Ghost, but was converted and given its delightful east gable – an ostentatious Dutch Renaissance affair bedecked with allegorical figures – shortly after the town's famous victory against the Spanish. Nowadays the Waag houses the VVV (see p.162) and the **Kaasmuseum** (Cheese Museum; April–Oct Mon–Thurs & Sat 10am–4pm, Fri 9am–4pm; *f*5), with displays on the history of cheese, cheese-making equipment and suchlike. Just off the north side of the square, the **Biermuseum de Boom**, housed in the old De Boom brewery at Houttil 1 (Tues–Sat 10am–4pm, Sun 1–4pm; *f*4), has displays tracing the brewing process from the malting to the bottling stage, aided by authentic props from this and other breweries the world over. There's lots of technical equipment, enlivened by mannequins and empty bottles from once innumerable Dutch brewers – though few, curiously, from De Boom itself. It's an engaging little museum, lovingly put together by enthusiasts, and there's a shop upstairs where you can buy a huge range of beers and associated merchandise, as well as a downstairs bar serving some eighty varieties of Dutch beer.

Heading south from the Waag along Mient, it's a few metres to the jetty from where boat trips (see p.163) leave for a quick zip round the town's central canals – an enjoyable way to spend forty-five minutes. At the south end of Mient, the open-air **Vismarkt** (Fish Market; Fri 9am–noon) marks the start of the **Verdronkenoord** canal, whose dignified facades lead down to the spindly **Accijnstoren** (Excise Tower), part harbour master's office, part fortification built during the long struggle with Spain in 1622. Turn left at the tower along Bierkade and you'll soon reach **Luttik Oudorp**, another attractive corner of the old centre, a slender canal leading back to the Waag.

One block south of the Waag, pedestrianized **Langestraat** is Alkmaar's main, mundane, shopping street, whose only notable building is the **Stadhuis**, a florid affair, half of which (the eastern side and tower) dates from the early sixteenth century. At the west end of Langestraat lurks **St Laurenskerk** (mid-April to mid-Sept Fri 9am–5pm; June–Aug also Tues–Thurs & Sat noon–5pm), a Gothic church of the late fifteenth century whose pride and joy is its huge organ, commissioned at the suggestion of the diplomat and political big-wheel Constantijn Huygens in 1645. The case was designed by Jacob van Campen, the architect who was later to design Amsterdam's town hall (see p.61), and decorated with paintings illustrating the triumph of David by Caesar van Everdingen (1617–1678). The artist's seamless brushstrokes and willingness to kow-tow to the tastes of the burgeoning middle class were soon to make him a wealthy man. In the apse is the tomb of Count Floris V, penultimate in the line of medieval counts of North Holland, who did much to establish the independence of the towns hereabouts and for his trouble was murdered by jealous nobles in 1296.

Across from the church, in the newly enlarged cultural centre, the **Stedelijk Museum** (Municipal Museum; Tues–Fri 10am–5pm, Sat & Sun 1–5pm; ƒ3), displays pictures and plans of the siege of 1573, along with an assortment of seventeenth-century paintings. Amongst the latter is a striking *Holy Family* by Gerard van Honthorst (1590–1656), a Mannerist who specialized in glossy portraits of high officials. There's also work by Pieter Saenredam and Maerten van Heemskerck (1498–1574), a transitional figure who was tutored in the Dutch Mannerist style before a visit to Italy in 1532 changed the direction of his work. Greatly impressed by the Italians, Heemskerck returned home to paint in the style of Michelangelo, populating his large canvases with muscular men-of-action and buxom women.

Practicalities

From Alkmaar's **train** and **bus station**, it's about ten minutes' walk to the centre of town: keep straight outside the station, turn right down Snaarmanslaan and then left at busy Geesterweg, which leads over the old city moat to St Laurenskerk. From the church, it's another five minutes' walk east along Langestraat to the **VVV**, housed in the Waag on Waagplein (Mon 10am–5.30pm, Tues & Wed 9am–5.30pm, Thurs 9am–9pm, Fri 9am–6pm & Sat 9.30am–5pm; ☎072/511 4284). Alkmaar only takes an hour or two to explore, but if you decide to stay the VVV have plenty of **private rooms** for about ƒ30 per person per night, including breakfast, though most places are on the outskirts of town and en-suite rooms are rare. Failing that, Alkmaar has one recommendable central **hotel**, the *Motel Stad en*

Land, a plain and simple two-star establishment near the train station at Stationsweg 92 (☎072/512 3911, fax 511 8440; ③).

Boat trips leave from the jetty on Mient (May–Aug daily on the hour 11am–5pm; April, Sept & Oct same times Mon–Sat only; during the cheese market on Fri 9.30am–noon, every 20min; ƒ6). There are also longer trips to Zaanse Schans (mid-May to late Oct 2–3 weekly; 6hr; ƒ17,50 single, ƒ27,50 return) and even to Amsterdam (mid-June to mid-Sept 1 weekly; 9hr; ƒ22,50 single, ƒ37,50 return); ask at the VVV for further details or contact the operators, Woltheus Cruises, at the Kanaalkade jetty, on the north side of the centre (☎072/511 4840).

For **food**, Alkmaar is well-served by *'t Waegh-Stuck*, just off the Waagplein at Fnidsen 101, a smart restaurant serving tasty and traditional Dutch cuisine at reasonable prices. Otherwise, *'t Gulden Vlies*, Koorstraat 30, is a recommended grand café with a good line in light meals, and *Porto Fino*, close to the Waag at Mient 5, is a traditional Italian place serving delicious pizzas from ƒ10. **Drinking**, too, is also well catered for. There are two groups of bars, one on Waagplein, the other around the Vismarkt, at the end of the Verdronkenoord canal. Among the former, the pick is *Proeflokaal 't Apothekertje*, an old-style bar, open until 2am, with an antique-cluttered interior and a laid-back atmosphere. Metres away, *Café Corridor* is younger and plays loud music late into the night. On Verdronkenoord, *De Pilaren* is another noisy place, though catering to a rather cooler crowd, some of whom take refuge in the *Café Stapper*, next door, if the music gets too much.

Part 3

Listings

Chapter 9

Accommodation

Accommodation in Amsterdam is extremely difficult to find, and can be a major expense: even hostels are pricey for what you get, and the hotels are among the most expensive in Europe. The city's compactness means that you'll inevitably end up somewhere central, but if you arrive without a reservation you'll still need to search hard to find a decent place to stay. At peak times of the year – July and August, Easter and Christmas – it's extremely advisable to book ahead; hotel rooms and even hostel beds can be swallowed up remarkably quickly, and if you leave finding a room to chance, you may well be disappointed (and/or out of pocket). Most of the places we've listed – even the larger hostels – will accept bookings from abroad by fax or email (in fact a lot of hostels will not accept phone bookings during peak season), although the cheaper ones may require some guarantee of payment (such as a credit card number). You can also reserve rooms in advance by contacting the **Netherlands Reservations Centre** (☎0031/704 195500), who coordinate three Web sites where you can view availability and prices and make hotel and apartment bookings online. The three sites are: *www.hotelres.nl*, *www.amsterdam.nl* and *www.visitholland.com*. Once you've arrived, VVs all over the country will make advance hotel reservations for a ƒ6 fee (see *Introducing the city*, p.49, for locations and opening times of the Amsterdam

VVs); they will also book accommodation on the spot for the same fee, or simply sell you a booklet on hotels in Amsterdam (ƒ5). Several shops on Damrak will also book accommodation for you, again usually for a ƒ5 fee; of these Sunro Change is open till late, but also charges ten percent of your hotel bill in advance, for which you are discounted when you hand in the booking form to the hotel.

To help you choose a place to stay, we've divided our listings by **area**, using the same headings as in the guide chapters – "The Old Centre", "Grachtengordel", etc. This gives a rough pointer as to what you can expect in terms of surroundings. However, bear in mind that while some of the hotels in the Old Centre are on quiet canals, many are on or close to busy traffic or pedestrian streets; you'll be right in the middle of things, but if you're looking for peace and quiet you're probably better off scanning the Grachtengordel West or South listings for a canalside location. Similarly, hotels ideally situated for the major museums (in the "Museum Quarter" section) might be a tram ride or a half-hour's walk from the city-centre restaurants and bars. All the hostels, hotels and B&Bs we describe are marked on a **map** of the relevant area. We've also pinpointed specifically **gay** or gay-friendly hotels in the listings, although it's illegal for a hotel or hostel to refuse entry to anyone on the grounds of sexual orientation.

Accommodation

If, like most visitors, you arrive in town via Centraal Station, you'll probably be approached by **touts** outside offering rooms or beds in hostels and cheap hotels. Usually they walk you to the place and claim a fee from the management. Despite the fact that most of them are genuine enough, our advice is to steer clear. If the place they're offering is in our listings you can phone it directly yourself, and if it isn't, it's probably been left out for a reason. Although the possibility of encountering unpleasantness is small, it does exist; there are plenty of good, cheap and reliable places listed here that are within five minutes' walk of Centraal Station. Check out our recommendations first.

Something to bear in mind when choosing a hotel is the fact that many of Amsterdam's buildings have narrow, very steep **staircases**, and not all hotels have installed lifts: in the older houses, construction of lifts is actually illegal. If this is a consideration for you, check before you book.

Note that all directions given are from Centraal Station (abbreviated as "CS"). For information on **camping**, see p.187.

HOSTELS

The bottom line for most travellers is taking a dormitory bed in a **hostel**, and there are plenty to choose from: official Hostelling International places, unofficial private hostels, even Christian hostels; in fact, you'll probably be accosted outside the train station with numerous offers of beds. Most hostels will either provide (relatively) clean bed linen or charge a few guilders for it; your own sleeping bag might be a better option. Many hostels also lock guests out for a short period each day, both for security reasons and to clean the place; some set a nightly curfew, though these are usually late enough not to cause too much of a problem. Many hostels don't accept reservations from June to August.

The cheapest deal you'll find is around ƒ25 per person per night; at better-furnished and/or more central hostels the average is closer to ƒ35. Much more and you might as well be in a hotel room. A few otherwise friendly, good-value places have a policy of charging more at the weekends than during the week: the price hike on Friday and Saturday nights can be as much as ƒ5. Despite their protestations, there seems little excuse for this, and if you're planning a weekend stay it might be worthwhile moving somewhere else on Friday morning, just to bring the point home. Note that you can pay the same for a bed in a sixteen-person dorm as you'd pay to be in a four-person dorm elsewhere: any place that won't allow you to see the dorm before you pay is worth avoiding. If you want a little extra privacy, many hostels also offer triples, doubles and singles for much less than you'd pay in a regular hotel, though the quality and size of rooms can leave a lot to be desired.

HOTELS AND B&BS

Apart from a couple of ultra-cheap places, most of Amsterdam's **hotels** start at around ƒ90 for a double, and although some form of breakfast – "Dutch" (bread and jam) or "English" (bacon and eggs) – is normally included in the price at all but the cheapest and the most expensive hotels, some places can give the barest value for money. Amsterdam has a huge number of what might be called comfortable family hotels, with basic double rooms with private bathroom hovering more or less around the ƒ150 (£45/$72) mark: the ones listed here have something particular to recommend them – location, value for money or ambience. Don't be afraid to ask to see the room first, and to refuse it if you don't like it.

There are very few **bed-and-breakfasts** in Amsterdam, although Holiday Link, PO Box 70160, 9704 AD Groningen (☎050/313 4545, fax 3177, *www.holidaylink.com*), can send you a book for ƒ14,75 that lists reputable B&Bs throughout the country.

APARTMENTS AND HOUSEBOATS

For groups or families especially, short-term **apartment** rentals can work out cheaper than staying in a hotel, with the further advantages of privacy and the convenience of self-catering. Apartments sleeping four or five can often be found for the same price as a double room in a hotel. Many places dotted all the way down the main tourist strip of Damrak advertise short- and long-term apartment rentals – although their prices can seem reasonable, check what's included (and what isn't), and insist on seeing the place yourself before you hand over any money. **Houseboat** rentals are often organized by the same people and

tend to be significantly more luxurious and expensive. Apartment and houseboat rental agencies recommended by the VVV include the following:

Amsterdam House, Amstel 176a, 1017 AE Amsterdam ☎626 2577, fax 626 2987, *amshouse@euronet.nl*

Gasthuismolen Apartments, Gasthuismolensteeg 10, 1016 AM Amsterdam ☎624 0736, fax 420 9991, *gasthuismolen@flash.A2000.nl*

Riverside Apartments, Weteringschans 187E, 1017 XE Amsterdam ☎627 9797, fax 9858, *geuje@worldonline.nl*

The Old Centre

If you choose to stay in the Old Centre, you'll never have to search for nightlife. Cheap hotels abound in the Red Light District, as you might expect – and this is the first place to start looking if money is tight – but there's also a good selection of quiet, reasonably priced places on and off the canals, close to restaurants and shopping areas.

Hostels

Bob's Youth Hostel, Nieuwezijds Voorburgwal 92 ☎623 0063, fax 675 6446; 10min from CS. An old favourite of backpackers and a grungy crowd, *Bob's* is lively and smoky. Small dorms at ƒ26 per person, including breakfast in the coffeeshop on the ground floor (which also does cheap dinners). They also let four apartments (ƒ150 for two people, ƒ175 for three).

Budget Youth Hostel, Warmoesstraat 87 ☎625 5974, fax 422 0885; 5min from CS. Unremarkable, scruffy hostel amidst the porn merchants, which nevertheless gets full very quickly. One-armed bandits and cheeseburgers downstairs; sheets cleaned weekly upstairs. Prices for dorms ƒ35, doubles (①).

Bulldog Low Budget Hotel, Oudezijds Voorburgwal 220 ☎620 3822, fax 627 1612, *www.bulldog.nl*; tram #4, #9, #16 or #24 to Dam, then a 3min walk. Part of the Bulldog coffeeshop chain, with

Accommodation

To call Amsterdam from abroad, dial your international access code, followed by ☎31 for Holland, then ☎20 (the area code for Amsterdam, minus its initial 0), followed by the number.

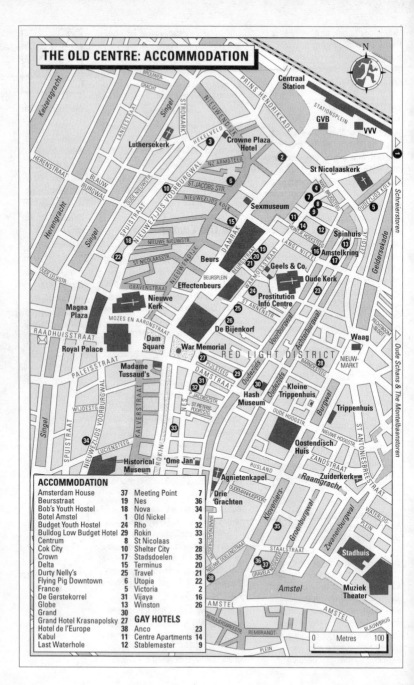

THE OLD CENTRE: ACCOMMODATION

Centraal Station
GVB
VVV
Lutersekerk
Crowne Plaza Hotel
St Nicolaaskerk
Sexmuseum
Spinhuis
Beurs
Amstelkring
Geels & Co.
Oude Kerk
Effectenbeurs
Prostitution Info Centre
Nieuwe Kerk
Magna Plaza
De Bijenkorf
Waag
Dam Square
War Memorial
Royal Palace
RED LIGHT DISTRICT
NIEUW-MARKT
Madame Tussaud's
Hash Museum
Kleine Trippenhuis
Trippenhuis
Historical Museum
'Ome Jan'
Oostendisch Huis
Agnietenkapel
Drie Grachten
Zuiderkerk
Stadhuis
Muziek Theater
Amstel

ACCOMMODATION

Amsterdam House	37	Meeting Point	7
Beursstraat	19	Nes	36
Bob's Youth Hostel	18	Nova	34
Botel Amstel	1	Old Nickel	4
Budget Youth Hostel	24	Rho	32
Bulldog Low Budget Hotel	29	Rokin	33
Centrum	8	St Nicolaas	3
Cok City	10	Shelter City	28
Crown	17	Stadsdoelen	35
Delta	15	Terminus	20
Durty Nelly's	25	Travel	21
Flying Pig Downtown	6	Utopia	22
France	5	Vijaya	16
De Gerstekorrel	31	Winston	26
Globe	13		
Grand	30	**GAY HOTELS**	
Grand Hotel Krasnapolsky	27	Anco	23
Hotel de l'Europe	38	Centre Apartments	14
Kabul	11	Stablemaster	9
Last Waterhole	12		

0 Metres 100

dorms sleeping up to sixteen people, at
ƒ35 per night. Double rooms (②) during
the summer. No breakfast.

The Crown, Oudezijds Voorburgwal 21
☎626 9664, no fax; 3min from CS.
Friendly hostel-cum-hotel overlooking a
canal. Recently revamped clean six-per-
son dorms for around ƒ40 per night, plus
double rooms (②), some with a view (for
which you pay an extra ƒ5). Be warned
though that their prices can go up considerably when it's busy. Very safe,
despite the location. Late bar until 5am;
breakfast extra.

Durty Nelly's, Warmoesstraat 115 ☎638
0125, no fax, nellys@xs4all.nl; 5min from
CS. Good quality partitioned dorms
above a packed Irish pub, with a cooked
breakfast, sheets and lockers included.
ƒ35 per person. Street-side dorms are
lighter and airier.

Flying Pig Downtown, Nieuwendijk 100
☎420 6822, fax 624 9516, www.flying-
pig.nl; 5min from CS. Clean, large and
well-run by ex-travellers familiar with the
needs of backpackers. Free use of
kitchen facilities, no curfew, and there's a
late-night coffeeshop, Twin Pigs, next
door. Hostel bar open all night. Justifiably
popular, and a very good deal, with a
dorm bed priced between ƒ26,50 and
ƒ38,50 depending on the size of the
dorm. During the peak season you'll
need to book well in advance. See also
the Flying Pig Palace, p.183.

Kabul, Warmoesstraat 38 ☎623 7158,
fax 620 0869; 3min from CS. Huge,
famous and bustling, with an international clientele and multilingual staff. Rooms
sleep between one and sixteen people.
Higher dorm rates than usual – ƒ40 in
peak season, including use of all facilities. Given the extra cost, it's not always
as clean as it should be, but it's safe,
there's no lockout or curfew, and there's
a late bar next door. Groups are no
problem, and you can book in advance.

Last Waterhole, Oudezijds Armsteeg 12
☎624 4814, fax 427 4985, www.last-
waterhole.nl; 3min from CS. Long-established friendly Amsterdam dosshouse.

Large dorms, with sheets and towels
included, for ƒ30 per person during the
week (watch out for the weekend price
hike). The dorm price includes storage
space, but no lock, so make sure you
bring your own. Live blues and rock
bands most nights.

Meeting Point, Warmoesstraat 14 ☎627
7499, fax 7499; 2min from CS. Warm
and cosy central hostel with space in
ten-bed dorms going for ƒ30 per person.
Check-out 10am.

The Shelter City, Barndesteeg 21 ☎625
3230, fax 623 2282, www.shelter.nl;
metro Nieuwmarkt. A non-evangelical
Christian youth hostel smack in the middle of the Red Light District. At ƒ28 these
are some of the best-value beds in
Amsterdam, with bed linen, shower and
sizeable breakfast included. Dorms are
single-sex, lockers require a ƒ10 deposit
and there's a midnight curfew (1am at
weekends). You might be handed a
booklet on Jesus when you check in, but
you'll get a quiet night's sleep and the
sheets are clean.

Stadsdoelen, Kloveniersburgwal 97
☎624 6832, fax 639 1035; metro
Nieuwmarkt, or tram #4, #9, #16, #24 or
#25 to Muntplein. The closest to the sta-
tion of the two official hostels, with
clean, semi-private dorms at ƒ30,50 for
members, who get priority in high season; non-members pay a ƒ5 supplement.
Sheets cost a steep ƒ6,50. Guests get a
range of discounts on activities in the
city; you can also book Eurolines bus
tickets here. The bar serves good-value if
basic food, and there's a 2am curfew
(though the door opens for three 15min
intervals between 2am and 7am). The
other HI hostel is the Vondelpark, which
is better equipped for large groups (see
p.183).

Hotels

Amsterdam House (Eureka), 's-
Gravelandseveer 3 ☎624 6607, fax
1346; tram #4, #9, #16, #24 or #25 to
Muntplein. Considering it's just across the
Amstel from Rembrandtplein, this is a
surprisingly quiet part of town. Rooms

Accommodation

Accommodation

are small but clean and pleasant, the staff are friendly, and you're perfectly positioned for the nightlife. ③–④

Beursstraat, Beursstraat 7 ☎626 3701, fax 690 9012; 5min from CS. Basic but very cheap hotel (no breakfast or bar) nestling behind Berlage's Stock Exchange. However, there have been some complaints about surly management, and the raising of room prices after bookings is confirmed. ①

Botel Amstel, moored at Oosterdokskade 2 ☎626 4247, fax 639 1952; 2min from CS. Despite the seeming romance of a floating hotel, the rooms are all identically poky, connected by claustrophobic corridors. Something a bit different certainly, but, in-house movies or not, staying here is like spending your holiday on the cross-Channel ferry. ③

Centrum, Warmoesstraat 15 ☎624 3535, fax 420 1666, centrum@xs4all.nl; 3min from CS. On a tatty street in the Red Light District, but, considering the location, some rooms (high up and at the back) are very quiet and light (in contrast to the bar). Choice of large and small rooms, with or without bath/shower. Friendly and accommodating. ②

Cok City, Nieuwezijds Voorburgwal 50 ☎422 0011, fax 420 0357; 10min from CS. A three-star hotel which is sparkling clean, but nevertheless a rather soulless place to stay. En-suite rooms with TV, plus a kitchenette on each floor. There are two more Cok hotels down near the Vondelpark. Has a no-smoking floor. ⑤

Delta, Damrak 42 ☎620 2626, fax 3513; 10min from CS. If you really want to stay on Damrak, try this place first – uninspired, plain and characterless, but comfortable enough, it's one of the better options on a bad street. ④

France, Oudezijds Kolk 11 ☎422 3311, fax 3925; 2min from CS. Basic hotel on a tiny, very beautiful and little-used canal in the heart of the medieval centre. Small, comfortable rooms, if a little characterless. ④

De Gerstekorrel, Damstraat 22 ☎624 1367, fax 623 2640, gersteko@euronet.nl; tram #4, #9, #16, #24 or #25 to Dam square. Small, simple hotel, steps away from the Dam, with large, brightly decorated and well-lit rooms. Pleasant staff and good breakfast. On a noisy, bustling street (ask for a back room). Recommended. ④

The Globe, Oudezijds Voorburgwal 3 ☎421 7424, fax 421 7423, manager@theglobe.demon.nl; 5min from CS. A well set-up hotel, specializing in one-off "theme" nights. The bar is also equipped with a multitude of screens showing all-day sports. In addition to rooms they have dorm beds at around ƒ45–50. Breakfast is an extra ƒ7. ③

Grand, Oudezijds Voorburgwal 197 ☎555 3111, fax 3222, hotel@degrandwestin.nl; tram #4, #9, #16, #24 or #25 to Dam square. Originally a Royal Inn dating from 1578, and after that the Amsterdam Town Hall, this extraordinary building is a centrepiece of the city's medieval district. It claims to offer "a sublime combination of luxury, warm hospitality and unrivalled grandeur". ƒ650 or so for a double. ⑧

Grand Hotel Krasnapolsky, Dam 9 ☎554 9111, fax 622 8607, www.krasnapolsky.nl; tram #4, #9, #16, #24 or #25 to Dam square. A huge midnineteenth-century building occupying an entire side of Dam square, this is a luxuriously grand place to stay. If you can't afford the ƒ500 or more a double room costs, scrape together enough to have a coffee in the fabulous Winter Garden, occupying a spectacular atrium space in the centre of the hotel. ⑧

Hotel de l'Europe, Nieuwe Doelenstraat 2 ☎531 1777, fax 1778, www.leurope.nl; tram #4, #9, #16, #24 or #25 to Muntplein. Very central hotel which retains a wonderful fin-de-siècle charm, with large, well-furnished rooms and a very attractive riverside terrace. A liveried flunkey and red carpet on the pavement outside complete the picture. ⑧

Nes, Kloveniersburgwal 137 ☎624 4773, fax 620 9842, hotel.nes@wxs.nl;

49/30

tram #4, #9, #16, #24 or #25 to Muntplein. Extremely pleasant and quiet, with a lift; well-positioned away from noise but close to shops and nightlife. Helpful staff. Prices vary, depending on the view. ⑥

Nova, Nieuwezijds Voorburgwal 276 ☎623 0066, fax 627 2026, *novahtl@pi.net*; tram #1, #2 or #5 to Spui. Spotless rooms, all en suite and with fridge and TV; friendly staff, a lift and secure access. Perfect, quiet location. Winter discounts. ④

Old Nickel, Nieuwe Brugsteeg 11 ☎624 1912, fax 620 7683; 2min from CS. Homely pub with simple rooms above, run by the same family for twenty years. ②

Rho, Nes 5 ☎620 7371, fax 7826; tram #4, #9, #16, #24 or #25 to Dam square. A very comfortable hotel in a quiet alley off Dam square, with an extraordinary high-ceilinged lounge, originally built as a theatre in 1908. The place looks a bit run-down from the outside, but it's still a fine city-centre option, with helpful and welcoming staff. ④

Rokin, Rokin 73 ☎626 7456, fax 625 6453; tram #4, #9, #16, #24 or #25 to Dam or Spui. Something of a bargain considering the location, with doubles from ƒ110, including breakfast. ②

St Nicolaas, Spuistraat 1a ☎626 1384, fax 623 0979, *www.hotelnicolaas.nl*; 3min from CS. Very pleasant, well-run little hotel housed in a former mattress factory (with a king-size lift to prove it). All-wood decor throughout, all rooms are en suite, comfortable and scrupulously clean; the only minus is the traffic noise. Recommended. ③

Terminus, Beursstraat 11 ☎622 0535, fax 627 2216, *ath@terminus.nl*; 10min from CS. Small rooms in a rather gloomy hotel on seedy Beursstraat. There's a lift, but you still need to climb the stairs to get to some rooms. ④

Travel, Beursstraat 23 ☎626 6532, no fax; 10min from CS. Small, simple hotel on a dingy street; very clean and comfortable inside, with a quiet 24-hr bar

and no curfew. Light years away from the backpacker style of nearby places. ②

Utopia, Nieuwezijds Voorburgwal 132 ☎626 1295, fax 622 7060; 10min from CS. Self-confessed "smokers' hotel" above a coffeeshop – tiny, musty rooms over the street, reached by a near-vertical staircase. Basic, and generally welcoming, though we've had complaints about unhelpful staff during peak season. ②

Victoria, Damrak 1 ☎623 4255, fax 625 2997, *victoria@euronet.nl*; opposite CS. The *Victoria* is one of the landmarks of the city – a tall, elegant building, wonderfully decorated throughout – and one of the classiest hotels, with every possible amenity. ⑧

Vijaya, Oudezijds Voorburgwal 44 ☎626 9406, fax 620 5277; 10min from CS. Stately old canal house in the heart of the Red Light District, with accommodating management and plain rooms. Clean, but no lift. Ten percent discount in winter. ②

Winston, Warmoesstraat 123 ☎623 1380, fax 639 2308, *www.winston.nl*; 10min from CS. Hotel designed for an arty crowd, which is safe and affordable, but popular (and noisy). Light and airy rooms (sleeping from one to six), some en suite, some with a communal balcony, twenty of which are specially commissioned "art" rooms, including the Durex Room, Heineken Room and Schiffmacher Room (the management plans to refurbish all the rooms in this way over the next few years). Lift and full disabled access. Recommended. ②

Gay hotels

Anco, Oudezijds Voorburgwal 55 ☎624 1126, fax 620 5275, *info@ancohotel.nl*; 10min from CS. Small and friendly hotel, catering exclusively to leather-wearing gay men, in the Red Light District. ③

Centre Apartments, Heintje Hoeksteeg 27 ☎627 2503, fax 625 1108; 5min from CS. Studios and apartments for rent in the middle of the Old Centre. The same people also run a small, less

Accommodation

Accommodation

expensive guesthouse out in the Jordaan, with singles and doubles. ③

Stablemaster, Warmoesstraat 23 ☎625 0148, fax 624 8747; 5min from CS. Small, exclusively male gay hotel above a popular leather bar in the heart of the Red Light action; English-speaking staff. ③

Grachtengordel West

The western section of the canal ring, while only a few minutes' walk from the bustle of Dam square, has a number of quiet canalside hotels; the Anne Frank House and some of the smaller museums are also close by. There are cheaper options to be found in the strip of hotels on Raadhuisstraat, one of the city's busiest traffic streets.

Hotels

Ambassade, Herengracht 341 ☎626 2333, fax 624 5321, *www.ambassade-hotel.nl*; tram #1, #2 or #5 to Spui. Elegant canalside hotel made up of ten seventeenth-century houses, with antique-furnished lounges and comfortable en-suite rooms. Breakfast is an extra ƒ22,50 but is well worth it. A good middle-of-the-range option. ⑥

Aspen, Raadhuisstraat 31 ☎626 6714, fax 620 0866; tram #13, #14 or #17 to Westermarkt. One of a number of inexpensive hotels situated in the Art Nouveau crescent of the Utrecht Building. Basic but tidy rooms, which are checked every day. ①

Blakes, Keizersgracht 384 ☎530 2010, fax 3020, *hotel@blakes.nl*; tram #1, #2 or #5 to Keizersgracht. The latest Anouchka Hempel hotel (there are already two in London), housed in a seventeenth-century building, centred on a beautiful courtyard and terrace. Both the décor and the restaurant menu combine Oriental and European styles. ⑦–⑧

Brian, Singel 69 ☎624 4661, no fax; 10min from CS. A tatty, cheap hotel in a good spot; ƒ90 for a very basic double, including breakfast, but you'll have to take a leap over the laundry to get to it

(equally inexpensive triple and quadruple rooms also available). Not the best place if you're looking for somewhere peaceful. ①

Canal House, Keizersgracht 148 ☎622 5182, fax 624 1317, *canalhousehotel@compuserve.com*; tram #13, #14 or #17 to Westermarkt. Magnificently restored seventeenth-century building, centrally located on one of the principal canals. American family-run hotel with a friendly bar and cosy rooms, towards the top of this price bracket. ⑤

Clemens, Raadhuisstraat 39 ☎626 9658, fax 624 6089; tram #13, #14 or #17 to Westermarkt. Just one of the options on this hotel strip. Clean, neat and good value for money. This is one of the city's busiest streets, so ask for a room at the back. ②

Estherea, Singel 303 ☎624 5146, fax 623 9001, *estherea@xs4all.nl*; tram #1, #2 or #5 to Spui. Chic, standard hotel converted from a row of canal houses; though they lack the personal touch, the rooms are all of a high quality. ⑥

Galerij, Raadhuisstraat 43 ☎624 8851, fax 622 6975; tram #13, #14 or #17 to Westermarkt. One of the Raadhuisstraat budget options. Basic rooms (ask for a quieter one at the back) with clean sheets but well-worn blankets supplied. ②

Hegra, Herengracht 269 ☎623 7877, fax 8159; tram #1, #2 or #5 to Spui. Welcoming atmosphere and relatively cheap for the location, on a beautiful stretch of the canal. Rooms are small but comfortable. ②

Hoksbergen, Singel 301, ☎626 6043, fax 638 3479, *hotelhoksbergen@wxs.nl*; tram #1, #2 or #5 to Spui. Friendly, standard hotel, with a light and open breakfast room overlooking the canal. Basic en-suite rooms, all with telephone and TV. ③

Keizersgracht, Keizersgracht 15 ☎625 1364, fax 620 7347; 5min from CS. Terrific location on a major canal close to the station, with a good mixture of singles and doubles, plus rooms sleeping

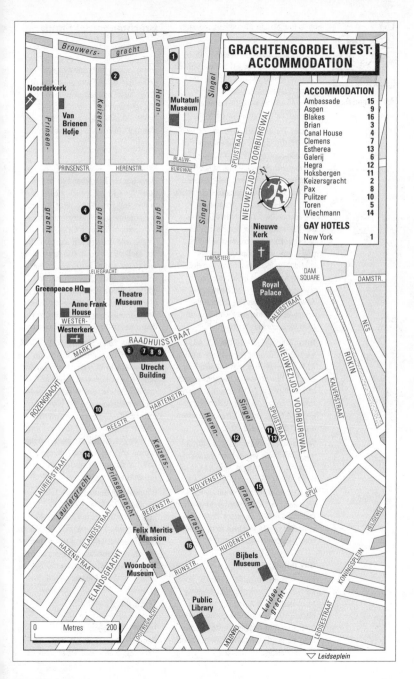

GRACHTENGORDEL WEST: ACCOMMODATION

Noorderkerk

Van Brienen Hofje

PRINSENSTR.   HERENSTR.

Multatuli Museum

BLAUW- BURGWAL

TORENSTEEG

Nieuwe Kerk

ACCOMMODATION

Ambassade	15
Aspen	9
Blakes	16
Brian	3
Canal House	4
Clemens	7
Estherea	13
Galerij	6
Hegra	12
Hoksbergen	11
Keizersgracht	2
Pax	8
Pulitzer	10
Toren	5
Wiechmann	14

GAY HOTELS

New York	1

LELIEGRACHT

DAM SQUARE   DAMSTR.

Greenpeace HQ

Theatre Museum

Anne Frank House

WESTER- MARKT

Westerkerk

Royal Palace

RAADHUISSTRAAT

MARKT

Utrecht Building

ROZENGRACHT

REESTR.   HARTENSTR.

HERENGRACHT

SINGEL

SPUISTRAAT

NIEUWEZIJDS VOORBURGWAL

PALEISSTRAAT

ROKIN

KALVERSTRAAT

NES

LAURIERSTRAAT

Lauriergracht

PRINSENGRACHT

KEIZERSGRACHT

WOLVENSTR.

BERENSTR.

SPUI

HEILIGEWEG

ELANDSSTRAAT

HAZENSTRAAT

ELANDSGRACHT

Felix Meritis Mansion

Woonboot Museum

RUNSTR.

HUIDENSTR.

Bijbels Museum

Public Library

Leidse- gracht

LEIDSESTRAAT

KONINGSPLEIN

0   Metres   200

▽ Leidseplein

Accommodation

up to four people, all spotless. Breakfast not included. ②

Pax, Raadhuisstraat 37 ☎624 9735, no fax; tram #13, #14 or #17 to Westermarkt. Basic city-centre cheapie with fair-sized rooms – breakfast is brought to your room. As with most of the hotels along here, ask for a room at the back. ①

Pulitzer, Prinsengracht 315 ☎523 5235, fax 627 6753, *sales_amsterdam@ sheraton.com*; tram #13, #14 or #17 to Westermarkt. An entire row of seventeenth-century canal houses converted into a determinedly luxurious hotel that's often rated the best in Amsterdam. Subsidence over the centuries means that the inside of the hotel is a warren of steep stairs and crooked corridors, which only adds to its character. Individually decorated rooms are delightful and some have lift access; you're also spoilt for choice between canal views and windows overlooking the sumptuous internal courtyard. Around ƒ500 for a double. ⑧

Toren, Keizersgracht 164 ☎622 6352, fax 626 9705, *hotel.toren@tip.nl*; tram #13, #14 or #17 to Westermarkt. Fine example of a seventeenth-century canal house, once the home of a Dutch prime minister. En-suite rooms are comfortable and well-furnished, and the hotel retains a good deal of grace. ④

Wiechmann, Prinsengracht 328 ☎626 3321, fax 8962, *www.channels.nl/amsterdam/wiechman.html*; tram #13, #14 or #17 to Westermarkt. Another canal-house restoration project, family-run for fifty years, with dark wooden beams and restrained style throughout. Rooms kept in perfect condition. Close to the Anne Frank House. ③–④

Gay hotels

New York, Herengracht 13 ☎624 3066, fax 620 3230; 5min from CS. Recently renovated, this is a popular, two-star, exclusively gay hotel, consisting of three modernized seventeenth-century houses. High standards throughout, with a good Dutch breakfast. No lift. ④

Grachtengordel South

The southern section of the canal circle is an appealing area to stay, whether you're looking for bustling nightlife or peace and quiet. There are plenty of hotels for all budgets close to the bars and restaurants of Leidseplein and Rembrandtplein, plus a number of very pleasant options along the surrounding canals.

Hostels

Hans Brinker, Kerkstraat 136 ☎622 0687, fax 638 2060; tram #1, #2 or #5 to Prinsengracht. Well-established and raucously popular Amsterdam cheapie, with dorm beds going for around ƒ40. Singles and doubles (②) also available. The facilities are good, dorms are basic and clean, and it's very close to the Leidseplein buzz. One to head for if you're out for a good time (and not too bothered about getting a good night's sleep), though be prepared to change dorms several times during your stay.

Euphemia, Fokke Simonszstraat 1 ☎ & fax 622 9045, *euphjm@pi.net*; tram #16, #24 or #25 to Weteringcircuit. Situated a shortish walk from Leidseplein and the major museums, with a likeable laid-back atmosphere and big, basic rooms with TVs. They're pricey though: doubles (②–③), plus three- and four-bed rooms for a very steep ƒ85 per person in high season and at weekends, dropping to half that during low season. Breakfast not included.

International Budget Hotel, Leidsegracht 76 ☎624 2784, fax 626 1839 *euphjm@pi.net*; tram #1, #2 or #5 to Prinsengracht. An excellent budget option on a peaceful little canal in the heart of the city, with the same owners as the *Euphemia*. Small, simple rooms sleeping up to four (from ƒ40 per person), with singles and doubles (③) available. Young, friendly staff.

Hotels and B&Bs

Agora, Singel 462 ☎627 2200, fax 627 2202, *agora@worldonline.nl*; tram #1, #2

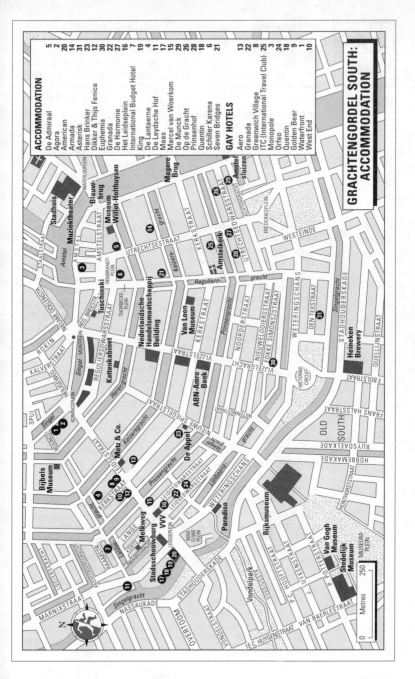

GRACHTENGORDEL SOUTH: ACCOMMODATION

ACCOMMODATION

De Admiraal	5
Agora	2
American	20
Armada	14
Asterisk	31
Hans Brinker	23
Dikker & Thijs Fenice	12
Euphemia	22
Granada	30
De Harmonie	27
Het Leidseplein	16
International Budget Hotel	7
King	19
De Lantaerne	4
De Leydsche Hof	11
Maas	17
Marcel van Woerkom	15
De Munck	29
Op de Gracht	28
Prinsenhof	18
Quentin	6
Schiller Karena	21
Seven Bridges	

GAY HOTELS

Aero	13
Granada	22
Greenwich Village	8
ITC (International Travel Club)	25
Monopole	3
Orfeo	24
Quentin	18
Golden Bear	9
Waterfront	1
West End	10

Accommodation

or #5 to Koningsplein. Nicely located, small and amiable hotel right near the flower market; doubles cost upwards of ƒ150, three- and four-bed rooms proportionately less. Many rooms have canal views, and the wood-beam decor is delightful. ③

De Admiraal, Herengracht 563 ☎626 2150, fax 623 4625; tram #4, #9 or #14 to Rembrandtplein. Friendly hotel close to the nightlife, with wonderful canal views. Breakfast an extra ƒ10. ②

American, Leidsekade 97 ☎556 3000, fax 3001; tram #1, #2 or #5 to Leidseplein. Landmark Art Deco hotel dating from 1902 (and in pristine, renovated condition), right on Leidseplein and the water. Large, double-glazed, modern doubles from around ƒ500. If you can't afford to stay, don't leave Amsterdam without soaking up some of the atmosphere at the popular and superbly decorated *Café Americain* overlooking the square. ⑧

Armada, Keizersgracht 713 ☎623 2980, fax 5829; tram #4 to Keizersgracht. Large if slightly tatty rooms close by the Amstel; at the low end of the price band. ③

Asterisk, Den Texstraat 16 ☎624 1768, fax 638 2790; tram #16, #24 or #25 to Weteringcircuit. Good-value budget hotel on the edge of the city centre, just across the canal from the Heineken Brewery. ②

Dikker & Thijs Fenice, Prinsengracht 444 ☎626 7721, fax 625 8986; tram #1, #2 or #5 to Prinsengracht. Small and stylish hotel on a beautiful canal close to all the shops. Rooms vary in decor but all include a minibar, telephone and TV – those on the top floor give a good view of the city (there's a lift, but it's small and old-fashioned). Breakfast not included. ⑥

Granada, Leidsekruisstraat 13 ☎623 6711, fax 622 8143, *granada@xs4all.nl*; tram #1, #2 or #5 to Leidseplein. Small, unremarkable rooms near Leidseplein in this gay- and lesbian-friendly hotel. ②

De Harmonie, Prinsengracht 816 ☎625

0174, fax 622 8021; tram #4 to Prinsengracht. A basic hotel not far from the Rembrandtplein. Some of the rooms are very plain, and rather small, plus the shared shower and toilet are on alternate floors, but it's friendly and central. Breakfast is brought to your room. ③

Het Leidseplein, Korte Leidsedwarsstraat 79 ☎627 2505, fax 623 0065; tram #1, #2 or #5 to Leidseplein. Scruffy, low-maintenance hotel handily placed for frenetic Leidseplein, but on a noisy and tacky street. Steep and narrow staircase. ④

King, Leidsekade 85 ☎624 9603, fax 620 7277; tram #1, #2 or #5 to Leidseplein. Nicely situated hotel on the water next to the *American Hotel*; unremarkable doubles from ƒ135. ②

De Lantaerne, Leidsegracht 111 ☎623 2221, fax 2683, *reservations@hotellantaerne.com*; tram #1, #2 or #5 to Leidseplein. Well located for the Melkweg and all the nightlife, but rather seedy, despite the elegant building. It can get noisy too, and the management aren't overly friendly. ②

De Leydsche Hof, Leidsegracht 14 ☎623 2148, no fax; tram #1, #2 or #5 to Keizersgracht. Stately privately-run canal house on one of the smaller and quieter waterways, which only operates during high season. It looks a bit run-down but the rooms are comfortably sized, each with en-suite shower. Closed October 1 to April 1. ②

Maas, Leidsekade 91 ☎623 3868, fax 622 2613, *www.hotelmaas.nl*; tram #1, #2 or #5 to Leidseplein. Modern hotel on a quiet stretch of water; clean, nicely decorated and well-equipped en-suite rooms – ask for one with a waterbed! ⑤

De Munck, Achtergracht 3 ☎623 6283, fax 620 6647; tram #4 to Frederiksplein. Fine hotel in a quiet spot steps from the Amstel, with clean, light and well maintained rooms. The Sixties-style breakfast room sports a Wurlitzer jukebox with a good collection of 1960s hits. Bear in mind, however, that the owner is quite strict about his house rules. ③

Op de Gracht, Prinsengracht 826 ☎626 1937, no fax; tram #4 from the RAI centre or CS to Prinsengracht. B&B in a stately canalhouse on one of the main canals, run by Jolanda Schipper. Two rooms tastefully decorated, both with en-suite bathroom. Minimum stay two nights. ③

Prinsenhof, Prinsengracht 810 ☎623 1772, fax 638 3368, *prinshof@xs4all.nl*; tram #4 to Prinsengracht. Tastefully decorated, this is one of the city's top budget options; the best rooms are at the back. ②

Quentin, Leidsekade 89 ☎626 2187, fax 622 0121; tram #1, #2 or #5 to Leidseplein. Very friendly small hotel, often a stopover for artists performing at the Melkweg. Welcoming to all, and especially well-regarded among gay and lesbian visitors, but families with children might feel out of place. ②

Schiller Karena, Rembrandtplein 26 ☎554 0700, fax 624 0098, *sales@gtschiller.goldentulip.nl*; tram #4, #9 or #14 to Rembrandtplein. Once something of a hangout for Amsterdam's intellectuals, this still has one of the city's best-known and most atmospheric bars on its ground floor. Named after the painter and architect Schiller, whose works are liberally sprinkled throughout the hotel. Wonderful Art Deco furnishings in all the public areas. The drawback is its location on tacky Rembrandtplein. ⑤

Seven Bridges, Reguliersgracht 31 ☎623 1329; tram #4 to Prinsengracht. Perhaps the city's most charming hotel – and certainly one of its better-value ones – so-called because its canalside location affords a view of seven bridges in a row. Beautifully decorated, spotless rooms, which are permanently upgraded. Small and popular, so often booked solid. Breakfast is served in your room. ④–⑤

Marcel van Woerkom, Leidsestraat 87 ☎ & fax 622 9834, *www. marcelamsterdam.nl*; tram #1, #2 or #5 to Prinsengracht. Well-known, popular B&B run by an English-speaking graph-ic designer and artist, in a stylish restored house, with four en-suite doubles available for two, three or four people sharing. A haven of peace surrounded by the buzz of the city, with regulars returning year after year, so you'll need to ring well in advance in high season. Breakfast not included, but there are tea- and coffee-making facilities. ④

Accommodation

Gay hotels

Aero, Kerkstraat 49 ☎622 7728, fax 638 8531; tram #1, #2 or #5 to Prinsengracht. Sixteen clean enough rooms, many with shower and/or toilet. Off-season discounts a possibility. No single rooms. ②

Golden Bear, Kerkstraat 37 ☎624 4785, fax 627 0164, *www.goldenbear.nl*; tram #1, #2 or #5 to Prinsengracht. Solid budget option, recently given a modern-style makeover, with a good range of clean, comfortable rooms, some en suite. ②

Granada, Leidsekruisstraat 13 ☎623 6711, fax 622 8143, *granada@xs4all.nl*; See main listings opposite. ②

Greenwich Village, Kerkstraat 25 ☎626 9746, fax 625 4081; tram #1, #2 or #5 to Prinsengracht. A well-kept, if slightly down-at-heel hotel surrounded by gay bars and clubs on Amsterdam's main gay street. Rooms sleeping from one to six people, all ƒ75 per person. Helpful and friendly staff. ②

ITC (International Travel Club), Prinsengracht 1051 ☎623 0230, fax 624 5846, *office@itc-hotel.com*; tram #4 to Prinsengracht. A little way away from the major gay areas, close to the Amstelveld on a tranquil section of canal, and perhaps the least expensive gay hotel of this quality. Off-season discounts. ③

Monopole, Amstel 60 ☎ & fax 624 6271, *arad@monopole.demon.nl*; tram #4, #9 or #14 to Rembrandtplein. Overlooking the Amstel, very close to the Muziektheater, and right next door to the *Monopole Taverne* and all the Rembrandtplein nightlife. Singles, doubles, triples and quadruples. ③

Accommodation

Orfeo, Leidsekruisstraat 14 ☎623 1347, no fax; tram #1, #2 or #5 to Prinsengracht. Very pleasant hotel round the back of Leidseplein, with a small Finnish sauna for guests and decent breakfasts served until midday. ②–③

Quentin, Leidsekade 89 ☎626 2187, fax 622 0121. See main listings, p.179. ③

Waterfront, Singel 458 ☎623 9775, fax 620 7491; tram #1, #2 or #5 to Koningsplein. Smart value-for-money hotel on a major canal, close to the shopping and nightlife, with decent rooms and service. ③

West End, Kerkstraat 42 ☎624 8074, fax 622 9997. Another conveniently located hotel for the Kerkstraat area, if a little musty, with the late-night *Cosmo* bar downstairs as its main attraction; breakfast not included, but rooms come with coffee- and tea-making facilities. ②

The Jordaan

Staying in the Jordaan puts you in among the locals and well away from the hustle and bustle of the tourist centres. There's no shortage of bars and restaurants in this up-and-coming area – and some of the most beautiful of the city's canals – but you'll be at least fifteen minutes' walk from the bright lights. Beware that Marnixstraat and Rozengracht are busy traffic streets.

Hostels

The Shelter Jordan, Bloemstraat 179 ☎624 4717, fax 627 6137, *www.shelter.nl*; tram #13, #14 or #17 to Marnixstraat. The second of Amsterdam's two Christian youth hostels (the other is the *Shelter City*), which is great value at ƒ28 per bed, with breakfast and bed linen included. Dorms are single-sex, lockers require a ƒ10 deposit and there's a 2am curfew. Friendly and helpful staff, plus a decent café. Sited in a particularly beautiful part of the Jordaan, close to the Lijnbaansgracht canal.

Hotels and B&Bs

Acacia, Lindengracht 251 ☎622 1460, fax 638 0748, *acacia@wxs.nl*; 15min from CS. Amicable hotel run by a young married couple, which was one of the filming locations for the *Heimat* TV series. Situated right on a corner, so some of the rooms have a great panoramic view. They also let self-catering apartments. ②

Arrivé, Haarlemmerstraat 65 ☎622 1439, fax 1983; 10min from CS. Hotel which is basically a spruced-up hostel with one four-bed dorm, plus singles and doubles. Friendly enough, but nothing to write home about. ②

De Bloeiende Ramenas, Haarlemmerdijk 61 ☎624 6030, fax 420 2261, *myhotel@ibn.net*; 15min from CS. Welcoming and friendly hotel with comfortable rooms at sensible prices. A peaceful location to the northwest of the centre, away from the nightlife, but with good access to the city's markets. ②

La Bohème, Marnixstraat 415 ☎624 2828, fax 627 2897, *boheme@dxs.nl*; tram #1, #2 or #5 to Leidseplein. One of the best of the many, many hotels spreading up the Marnixstraat from Leidseplein, this small hotel with super-friendly staff has en-suite doubles for ƒ180. ③

Calendula Goldbloom's, Goudsbloemstraat 132 ☎428 3055, fax 776 0075, *www.calendulas.com*; bus #18 to Willemstraat. Comfortable and well-furnished B&B close to the Noordermarkt, which has a couple of spacious double rooms, each with TV, and a shared bathroom. ③

Johanna's, Van Hogendorpplein 62 ☎684 8596, fax 682 3013, *j.sleeswijk@speed.a2000.nl*; tram #10 from Leidseplein to Van Limburg Stirumplein. A privately-run B&B, which is very friendly and helpful to newcomers. A little difficult to get to, situated out near the Westergasfabriek, but with excellent prices. Places for five people only, so call before you arrive. ②

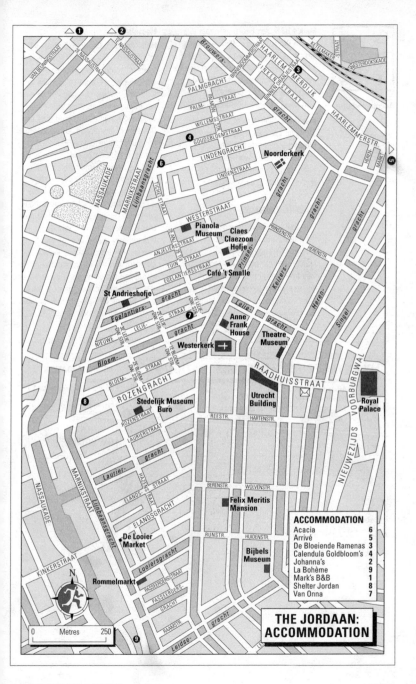

THE JORDAAN:
ACCOMMODATION

ACCOMMODATION

Acacia	6
Arrivé	5
De Bloeiende Ramenas	3
Calendula Goldbloom's	4
Johanna's	2
La Bohème	9
Mark's B&B	1
Shelter Jordan	8
Van Onna	7

Accommodation

Mark's B&B, Van Beuningenstraat 80a ☎776 0056, fax 681 5060, *www.geocities.com/CollegePark/Plaza/3686*; tram #10 to de Wittenkade, or a 5min taxi ride from CS. Comfortable and stylishly decorated B&B, with one double and one twin, plus a pleasant garden terrace. ③

Van Onna, Bloemgracht 102 ☎626 5801, no fax; tram #13, #14 or #17 to Westermarkt. A quiet, comfortable family-run place on a tranquil canal. Rooms sleeping up to four people for ƒ70 per person, including all services. ②

Plantagebuurt

Very few tourists venture out this way: the streets and canals off the main traffic arteries of Weesperstraat and Plantage Middenlaan are purely residential, with very few bars or restaurants. While you're pretty much guaranteed a quiet night's sleep here, you'll be a tram ride away from any of the main sights.

Hostels

Hotel Arena, 's-Gravesandestraat 51 ☎694 7444, fax 663 2649, *www.hotelarena.nl*; metro Weesperplein, then walk, or tram #6 from Leidseplein to Korte 's-Gravensandestraat. A little way out of the centre to the east, in a renovated old convent on the edge of the Oosterpark, this place is a major centre for youth culture. Simply furnished dorms in the attic provide some of the best hostel accommodation in the city, which, from ƒ37,50 per person, is relatively expensive but it's worth it: the lively and fun atmosphere more than compensates. It also has en-suite doubles (②). Breakfast isn't included. Women-only dorms at peak times. Lockers available. Facilities include an excellent and varied programme of live music and dance nights, a great bar and restaurant, the convent gardens, and even parking facilities. Open year-round; no curfew; wheelchair access.

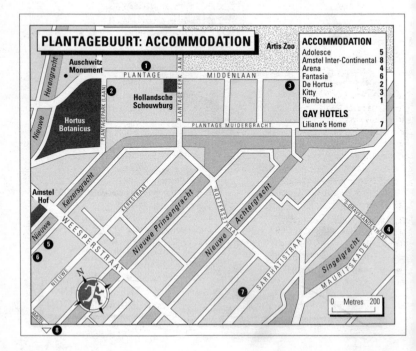

PLANTAGEBUURT: ACCOMMODATION

Artis Zoo

Herengracht
Nieuwe
Auschwitz Monument
PLANTAGE ❶ MIDDENLAAN
PLANTAGEPARK (LAAN)
PLANTAGE KERK LAAN
❷
Hollandsche Schouwburg
Hortus Botanicus
❸
PLANTAGE MUIDERGRACHT
Keizersgracht
KERKSTRAAT
Nieuwe Prinsengracht
ROETERSSTRAAT
Nieuwe Achtergracht
's-GRAVESANDESTRAAT
Amstel Hof
Nieuwe
WEESPERSTRAAT
❺
❻
NIEUWE
AMSTEL
SARPHATISTRAAT
Singelgracht
MAURITSKADE
❹
N
❼
0 Metres 200
❽

ACCOMMODATION
Adolesce 5
Amstel Inter-Continental 8
Arena 4
Fantasia 6
De Hortus 2
Kitty 3
Rembrandt 1

GAY HOTELS
Liliane's Home 7

Hotels

Adolesce, Nieuwe Keizersgracht 26 ☎626 3959, fax 627 4249; tram #9 or #14 to Waterlooplein. Large, popular and welcoming hotel, with neat if unspectacular rooms and a large dining room and bar. ②

Amstel Inter-Continental, Professor Tulpplein 1 ☎622 6060, fax 5808, *www.interconti.com*; metro Weesperplein. The absolute top-of-the-range; by far the best and most luxurious hotel in the country. Favoured by visiting celebrities and renovated a few years ago in sumptuous style to the tune of ƒ60 million. If you have the money, splash out on a night of ultimate style and class; cheapest doubles from ƒ850. If you're in a regal mood, check out the Royal Suite from ƒ4250 per night. ⑧

Fantasia, Nieuwe Keizersgracht 16 ☎623 8259, fax 622 3913, *reservation@fantasia_hotel.com*; tram #9 or #14 to Waterlooplein. Nicely situated hotel on a broad, quiet canal just off the Amstel; the rooms are well maintained, connected by quaint, narrow corridors, and there are also some very attractive attic rooms for ƒ135. ②–③

De Hortus, Plantage Parklaan 8 ☎625 9996, fax 416 4785, *d.colle@wxs.nl*; tram #9 to Artis Zoo. Smoker-friendly hotel close to the Hortus Botanicus. Rooms vary in size and maintenance is kept to a minimum but they're clean, and the common room, equipped with pool table and coffee machine, has a good atmosphere. We have recently, however, had complaints about the reliability of their booking service. All rooms ƒ45 per person. ①

Kitty, Plantage Middenlaan 40 ☎622 6819, no fax; tram #9 or #14 to Plantage Badlaan. Hotel run by an elderly lady, a little out from the centre, but in an interesting neighbourhood close to the Zoo. Decent-sized rooms for ƒ120 a double, including as much breakfast as you can eat from 8.30am to 10am. We've had some complaints about the service however. ②

Rembrandt, Plantage Middenlaan 17 ☎627 2714, fax 638 0293. Tram #9 to the Artis Zoo. Elegant hotel with a dining room dating from the sixteenth century, though the building itself is nowhere near as old. The plain rooms pale somewhat by comparison, but are clean enough. ②

Gay hotels

Liliane's Home, Sarphatistraat 119 ☎627 4006, no fax; metro Weesperplein. A privately run B&B for women only. Liliane runs the place herself, and doesn't have many rooms, so call first. Single ƒ75, double from ƒ130, with triples and quads available. She also rents out two nearby apartments. ②

Museum Quarter and the Vondelpark

The main reason for staying this far out of the centre is to be within spitting distance of the three main museums – although the nightlife around Leidseplein is also close by. There are no canals in the area, and Overtoom and 1e Constantijn Huygensstraat constantly rumble with traffic, but there are plenty of quiet and comfortable hotels in the smaller side streets, as well as two of the city's best hostels on the edges of the gorgeous Vondelpark.

Hostels

Flying Pig Palace, Vossiusstraat 46 ☎400 4187, fax 4105, *www.flyingpig.nl*; tram #1, #2 or #5 to Leidseplein, then walk. The better of the two *Flying Pig* hostels, facing the Vondelpark and close to the most important museums. Immaculately clean and well maintained by a staff of travellers, who well understand their backpacking guests. Free use of kitchen facilities, no curfew and good tourist information. Dorms start at ƒ26,50 per person, with double rooms (①–②) available too. Great value.

Vondelpark, Zandpad 5 ☎589 8996, fax 8955, *fit.vondelpark@njhc.org*; tram #1, #2 or #5 to Leidseplein, then walk. Well

Accommodation

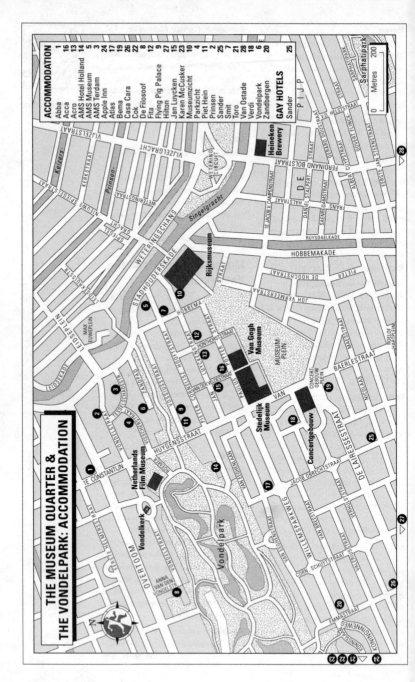

THE MUSEUM QUARTER & THE VONDELPARK: ACCOMMODATION

ACCOMMODATION

Abba	1
Acca	16
Acro	13
AMS Hotel Holland	14
AMS Museum	5
AMS Terdam	3
Apple Inn	24
Atlas	17
Bema	19
Casa Cara	26
Cok	22
De Filosoof	8
Fita	12
Flying Pig Palace	9
Hilton	27
Jan Luycken	15
Karen McCusker	23
Museumzicht	10
Parkzicht	4
Piet Hein	11
Prinsen	2
Sander	25
Smit	7
Toro	21
Van Ostade	28
Verdi	18
Vondelpark	6
Zandbergen	20

GAY HOTELS

Sander	25

located and, for facilities, the better of the two HI hostels, with a bar, restaurant, TV lounge, free Internet access and bicycle shed, plus various discount facilities for tours and museums. HI members have priority in high season; non-HI members pay an extra ƒ5. Rates are ƒ38 per person in the dorms, including use of all facilities, shower, sheets and breakfast. Singles, doubles (②) and rooms sleeping up to six are available. Secure lockers; lift; no curfew. To be sure of a place in high season you'll need to book at least two months ahead.

Hotels and B&Bs

Abba, Overtoom 122 ☎ 618 3058, fax 685 3477; tram #1 to 1e Constantijn Huygensstraat. Recently renovated rooms, each with TV and telephone. Friendly, helpful staff; winter discounts. Busy street location, though. ②

Acca, Van der Veldestraat 3a ☎ 662 5262, fax 679 9361; tram #2 or #5 to Van Baerlestraat. Intimate little hotel barely a minute from the Stedelijk and Van Gogh museums. The rooms are a little tatty given the price. ③

Acro, Jan Luyckenstraat 44 ☎ 662 0526, fax 675 0811; tram #2 or #5 to Van Baerlestraat. Excellent, modern hotel with stylish rooms, a plush bar and self-service restaurant (breakfast only). Well worth the money. ③

AMS Hotel Holland, P.C. Hooftstraat 162 ☎ 676 4253, fax 5956, *www.ams.nl*; tram #2 or #5 to Hobbemastraat. Comfortable, quiet and welcoming hotel at the end of the street near the Vondelpark. ③–④

AMS Museum, P.C. Hooftstraat 2 ☎ 662 1402, fax 673 3918, *www.ams.nl*; tram #2 or #5 to Hobbemastraat. Large, standard hotel which is very well maintained. Next door to the Rijksmuseum. ③–④

AMS Terdam, Tesselschadestraat 23 ☎ 612 6876, fax 683 8313, *www.ams.nl*; tram #1, #2, #5 or #11 to Leidseplein, then walk. Large, clean, comfortable hotel close to the museums,

with a relatively pleasant interior and helpful enough staff. ⑤

Apple Inn, Koninginneweg 93 ☎ 662 7894, fax 675 5235, *mail@hotel-apple-inn. A2000.nl*; tram #2 from CS to Emmastraat. Recently redecorated hotel with 35 basic and clean rooms, most of which are en suite and several also with an entrance to the garden. Breakfast buffet. Close to the Vondelpark. ③

Atlas, Van Eeghenstraat 64 ☎ 676 6336, fax 671 7633; tram #2 to Jacob Obrechtstraat. Situated just to one side of the Vondelpark, this Art Nouveau building houses a personable modern hotel with every convenience and comfort, plus an à la carte restaurant. Small, tranquil and very welcoming. ④

Bema, Concertgebouwplein 19b ☎ 679 1396, fax 662 3688, *postbus@hotel_bema.demon.nl*; tram #5 to Museumplein. Small but friendly place, kept very clean by the English-speaking manager. The rooms aren't modern (the beds can be a bit uncomfortable), but they're full of character. Handy for concerts and museums. ②

Casa Cara, Emmastraat 24 ☎ 662 3135, fax 676 8119; tram #2 or #16 to Emmastraat. Homely hotel a few minutes from the Concertgebouw and major museums. ②

Cok, Koninginneweg 34–36 ☎ 664 6111, fax 5304, *www.cokhotels.nl*; tram #2 to Valeriusplein. Actually two hotels on one site: Superior Tourist Class and Business Class, with doubles ranging from ƒ200 to ƒ450 depending on which you choose. Both are packed with facilities, but, like their more central counterpart Cok City, have little character. The majority of trade comes from package holidaymakers, which means it's crammed during summer months. ④–⑦

De Filosoof, Anna van den Vondelstraat 6 ☎ 683 3013, fax 685 3750, *filosoof@xs4all.nl*; tram #1 to Jan Pieter Heijestraat. Hospitable hotel on a charming little street off the Vondelpark, whose owner has a passion for philosophy: each room, small but comfortable, is

Accommodation

Accommodation

named after a different philosopher, and furnished with relevant period pieces, paintings and, of course, their books. There's also a small library. Unique and attractive. No lift. ③

Fita, Jan Luyckenstraat 37 ☎679 0976, fax 664 3969, *hotel@fita.demon.nl*; tram #2 or #5 to Van Baerlestraat. Mid-sized, friendly hotel in a quiet spot between the Vondelpark and the museums. Comfortable en-suite doubles (extra bed ƒ50). ④

Jan Luycken, Jan Luyckenstraat 58 ☎573 0730, fax 676 3841, *info@janluycken.nl*; tram #2 or #5 to Van Baerlestraat. Elegant, privately-run hotel in imposing nineteenth-century town-houses. Stylish and comfortable. ⑥–⑦

Karen McCusker, Zeilstraat ☎679 2753, fax 670 4578 (9am–noon only); tram #2 to Amstelveenseweg. Small B&B run by an Englishwoman who moved to Amsterdam in 1979; cosy and clean, Laura Ashley-style double rooms in her home, close to the Vondelpark, cost around ƒ110 (ƒ150 for the room with a roof-terrace). Ring first, because the owner isn't always there (you'll need to call well in advance). ②

Museumzicht, Jan Luyckenstraat 22 ☎671 5224, fax 3597; tram #2 or #5 to Hobbemastraat. Overlooking the Rijksmuseum, with fourteen plain-ish rooms on the upper floors of a Victorian house. ②

Parkzicht, Roemer Visscherstraat 33 ☎618 1954, fax 618 0897; tram #1 to 1e Constantijn Huygensstraat. Quiet unassuming little hotel on a pretty back-street near the Vondelpark and museums, with an appealingly lived-in look – clean and characterful. ②

Piet Hein, Vossiusstraat 53 ☎662 7205, fax 1526, *info@hotelpiethein.nl*; tram #2 or #5 to Hobbemastraat. Calm, low-key and clean, tucked away on a quiet street running past the Vondelpark, midway between Leidseplein and the Concertgebouw – ask for the double room with waterbed. At the lower end of this price bracket. ④

Prinsen, Vondelstraat 38 ☎616 2323, fax 6112, *manager@prinsenhotel.demon.nl*; tram #1 to 1e Constantijn Huygensstraat. Family-style hotel on the edge of the Vondelpark; quiet and with a large, secluded garden at the back. ④

Sander, Jacob Obrechtstraat 69 ☎662 7574, fax 679 6067, *htlsandr@xs4all.nl*; tram #16 to Jacob Obrechtstraat. Right behind the Concertgebouw, a spacious, pleasant hotel, welcoming to gay men and women, and everyone else too. ④

Smit, P.C. Hooftstraat 24 ☎671 4785, fax 662 9161, tram #2 or #5 to Hobbemastraat. Welcoming hotel with a lunch and breakfast bar on the corner of the street. En-suite twins and doubles for around ƒ200. ③

Toro, Koningslaan 64 ☎673 7223, fax 675 0031; tram #2 to Emmastraat. Lovely hotel in two very comfortably furnished turn-of-the-century townhouses on a peaceful residential street by the southern reaches of the Vondelpark. Has its own garden and terrace overlooking a lake in the park. The service isn't overly friendly though. ⑤

Verdi, Wanningstraat 9 ☎676 0073, fax 673 9070; tram #5 to Museumplein. Small and simple hotel with basic but comfortable rooms near the Concertgebouw. ③

Zandbergen, Willemsparkweg 205 ☎676 9321, fax 1860; tram #2 to Jacob Obrechtstraat. Light, airy, family-run hotel on a busy street near the Vondelpark; the rooms are clean and spacious. ③

Gay hotels

Sander, Jacob Obrechtstraat 69 ☎662 7574, fax 679 6067, *htlsandr@xs4all.nl*. See main listings above. ④

The South

The only reason you'll be staying so far away from the sights is the specific appeal of one of the following places, which are marked off the Museumplein and Vondelpark map on p.184.

Hilton, Apollolaan 138 ☎710 6000, fax 710 6080; tram #5 or #24 to Apollolaan. Way outside the centre in the distinctly upmarket New South, with everything you'd expect, including a Yacht Club, health club and a fine Italian restaurant. Doubles hover around the ƒ400 mark, but it's only really worth considering if you can afford to soak up a bit of 1960s nostalgia in its (admittedly stunning) Lennon and Ono suite, where the couple held their notorious 1969 "Bed-In" for peace; one night here will set you back ƒ1750. ⑦

Van Ostade, Van Ostadestraat 123 ☎679 3452, fax 671 5213, *bicyclehotel@capitol.online.nl*; tram #25 to Ceintuurbaan. Friendly, youthful place not far from the Albert Cuyp market in the Pijp; bills itself as a "bicycle hotel", renting bikes (ƒ10 per day) and giving advice on routes and such. Basic but clean rooms. Good breakfast. Garage parking for cars, though you'll need to book in advance. ②

Accommodation

CAMPSITES

There are several **campsites** in and around Amsterdam, most of them easily accessible by car or public transport. The four listed below are recommended by the VVV, which divides them into "youth campsites", which are self-explanatory, and "family campsites", which are more suitable for those seeking some quiet, or touring with a caravan or camper (for information on city campsites throughout the Netherlands take a look at *www.stadscampings.nl*).

YOUTH CAMPSITES

Vliegenbos, Meeuwenlaan 138 ☎636 8855, fax 632 2723; bus #32, #36 or nightbus #73 from CS. April–Sept. A relaxed and friendly site, just a 10-min bus ride into Amsterdam North from the station. Facilities include a general shop, bar and restaurant. Rates are ƒ14,75 per night per person, with tent-rental at ƒ5 per person; hot showers are included. There are also huts with bunk beds and basic cooking facilities, for ƒ85 per night for four people; phone ahead to check availability. Under-18s need to be accompanied by an adult; pets forbidden.

Zeeburg, Zuiderzeeweg 29 ☎694 4430, fax 694 6238, *camping@xs4all.nl*; train from CS (or tram #10 from Leidseplein) to Muiderpoort Station, then bus #37. Open all year. Slightly better equipped than the *Vliegenbos*, but more difficult to get to. Rates are ƒ7,50 per person, plus ƒ5 for a tent, ƒ5 for a motorbike and ƒ7,50 for a car. Hot showers are an extra ƒ1.50. Cabins sleeping two and four are ƒ25 per person per night, including bed-linen. A sleep-in tent, which includes several bunkbeds, costs ƒ17,50.

FAMILY CAMPSITES

Amsterdamse Bos, Kleine Noorddijk 1, Aalsmeer ☎641 6868, fax 640 2378; yellow NZH bus #171 from CS. April–Oct. Facilities include a bar, shop and restaurant, but this is a long way out, on the southern reaches of the lush and well-kept Amsterdam Forest. Rates are ƒ8,75 per night (ƒ4,50 for four- to twelve-year-olds, ƒ3 for dogs), hot showers included, plus ƒ4,75 for a car, ƒ11 for a camper and ƒ6,75 for a caravan. Huts sleeping up to four cost ƒ65 a night, which includes a gas stove.

Gaasper Camping, Loosdrechtdreef 7 ☎696 7326, fax 696 9369; metro Gaasperplas. March 15–Dec 31. Campsite just the other side of the Bijlmermeer housing complex in Amsterdam Zuidoost (Southeast), and easily reached from Centraal Station by metro. Very close to the wonderful open-air Gaasperplas park, which has facilities for all sorts of outdoor activities. Rates are ƒ6,50 (ƒ3,50 for under-12s, ƒ4 for dogs), plus ƒ7,25 per tent, ƒ6,25 for a car, ƒ9,25 for a caravan. Hot showers ƒ1,50.

Chapter 10

Eating and Drinking

Amsterdam is better-known for **drinking** than eating, and with good reason: its selection of bars is one of the real pleasures of the city. As for **eating**, this may not be Europe's culinary capital, but there's a good supply of ethnic restaurants, especially Indonesian and Chinese, and the prices (by big-city standards) are hard to beat. And there are any number of *eetcafés* and bars serving increasingly adventurous food, quite cheaply, in a relaxed and unpretentious setting. This said however, it's worth bearing in mind that Dutch service is not known for its speed, and isn't always the most friendly.

Dutch **mealtimes** are a little idiosyncratic. Breakfast tends to be later than you might expect, and other meals tend to be eaten earlier. If you choose to eat breakfast out of your hotel, you'll find few cafés open before 8 or 8.30am. The standard Dutch lunch hour is from noon to 1pm, and most restaurants are at their busiest between 7 and 8pm (and may stop serving altogether by 10pm).

For such a small city, Amsterdam is filled with places to eat and drink, and you should have no trouble finding somewhere convenient and enjoyable to suit your budget. While the Red Light District area has more than its fair share of tacky, low-quality establishments, there are plenty of good restaurants scattered all over the city, and in much of the centre you can find a bar on almost every corner. With Amsterdam's singular approach to the sale and con-

sumption of marijuana, you might choose to enjoy a joint after your meal rather than a beer: we've included in this chapter a selection of coffeeshops where you can buy and smoke grass.

In this chapter you will find full **listings** and reviews of Amsterdam's bars, cafés, coffeeshops, tearooms and restaurants, the last of these listed by type of cuisine rather than area. We've also given general information about what to expect from Amsterdam's eating, drinking and smoking establishments.

BREAKFAST, FAST FOOD AND SNACKS

In all but the very cheapest hostels and the most expensive hotels, **breakfast** (*ontbijt*) will be included in the price of the room. Though usually nothing fancy, it's always very filling: rolls, cheese,

Dutch cheese

Holland's **cheeses** have an unjustified reputation abroad for being bland and rubbery, possibly because they only export the nastier products and keep the best for themselves. In fact, Dutch cheese can be delicious, although there isn't the variety you get in, say, France or Britain. Most are based on the same soft, creamy *Goudas*, and differences in taste come with the varying stages of maturity – young, mature or old (*jong*, *belegen* or *oud*). *Jong* cheese has a mild flavour, *belegen* is much tastier, while *oud* can be pungent and strong, with a flaky texture not unlike Italian Parmesan. Generally, the older they get, the saltier they are. Among the other cheeses you'll find are the best-known round, red *Edam*, made principally for export and (quite sensibly) not eaten much by the Dutch; *Leidse*, which is simply *Gouda* with cumin seeds; *Maasdammer* and *Leerdammer*, strong, creamy and full of holes; and Dutch-made *Emmentals* and *Gruyères*. The best way to eat cheese here is the way the Dutch do it, in thin slices cut with a special cheese knife (*kaasschaaf*) rather than large hunks.

Eating and Drinking

ham, hard-boiled eggs, jam and honey or peanut butter are the principal ingredients. If you're not eating in your hotel, many bars and cafés serve breakfast, and those that don't invariably offer rolls and sandwiches.

For the rest of the day, eating cheaply and well, particularly on your feet, is no real problem, although those on the tightest of budgets may find themselves dependent on the dubious delights of **Dutch fast food**. This has its own peculiarities. Chips – *frites* – are the most common standby (*Vlaamse* or "Flemish" are the best), either sprinkled with salt or smothered with huge gobs of mayonnaise (sometimes known as *fritesaus*); some alternative toppings are curry, goulash, peanut or tomato sauce. Chips are often complemented with *kroketten* – spiced meat (usually either veal or beef) in hash covered with breadcrumbs and deep-fried – or *fricandel*, a frankfurter-like sausage. All these are available over the counter at evil-smelling fast-food places (FEBO is the most common chain), or, for one or two guilders, from heated glass compartments outside. As an alternative there are also a number of **Indonesian fast-food** places, serving *sateh* and noodle dishes in a McDonald's-type atmosphere.

Tastier, and good both as a snack and a full lunch, are the **fish specialities** sold from street kiosks: salted raw herrings, smoked eel, mackerel in a roll, mussels,

and various kinds of deep-fried fish; tip your head back and dangle the fish into your mouth, Dutch-style. Other, though far less common street foods are **pancakes** (*pannekoeken*), sweet or spicy (more widely available at sit-down restaurants, see p.219), **waffles** (*stroopwafels*) doused with maple syrup, and, in November and December, *oliebollen*, deep-fried dough balls with raisins and candied peel, traditionally eaten on New Year's Eve. Dutch **cakes and biscuits** are always good and filling, best eaten in a *banketbakkerij* with a small serving area; or buy a bag and eat them on the go. Apart from the ubiquitous *appelgebak* – a wedge of apple tart flavoured with cinnamon – and waffles, other things to try include *spekulaas*, a cinammon biscuit with a gingerbread texture, and *amandelkoek*, cakes with a biscuity outside and melt-in-the-mouth almond paste inside.

As for the kind of food you can expect to encounter in bars, there are **sandwiches and rolls** (*boterhammen* and *broodjes*) – often open, and varying from a slice of tired cheese on old bread to something so embellished it's a complete meal – as well as more substantial fare. In the winter, *erwtensoep* (aka *snert*) is available in most bars, and at about ƒ7,50 a shot it makes a great buy for lunch: thick pea soup with smoked sausage, served with a portion of smoked bacon on pumpernickel. Or there's *uitsmijter* (literally, "bouncer"):

GLOSSARY OF DUTCH FOOD AND DRINK TERMS

Although most menus in Amsterdam include full English translations, the list below will help you to make specific requests.

BASICS

Boter	Butter	*Pindakaas*	Peanut butter
Boterham/broodje	Sandwich/roll	*Sla/salade*	Salad
Brood	Bread	*Smeerkaas*	Cheese spread
Dranken	Drinks	*Stokbrood*	French bread
Eieren	Eggs	*Suiker*	Sugar
Gerst	Barley	*Vis*	Fish
Groenten	Vegetables	*Vlees*	Meat
Honing	Honey	*Voorgerechten*	Starters/
Hoofdgerechten	Main courses		hors d'oeuvres
Kaas	Cheese	*Vruchten*	Fruit
Koud	Cold	*Warm*	Hot
Nagerechten	Desserts	*Zout*	Salt
Peper	Pepper		

STARTERS AND SNACKS

Erwtensoep/ snert	Thick pea soup with bacon or sausage		cheese, bread, and perhaps soup
Huzarensalade	Potato salad with pickles	*Patates/frites*	Chips/French fries
		Soep	Soup
Koffietafel	A light midday meal of cold meats,	*Uitsmijter*	Ham or cheese with eggs on bread

MEAT AND POULTRY

Biefstuk (hollandse)	Steak	*Karbonade*	Chop
Biefstuk (duitse)	Hamburger	*Kip*	Chicken
Eend	Duck	*Kroket*	Spiced veal or beef
Fricandeau	Roast pork		in hash, coated
Fricandel	A frankfurter- like sausage		in breadcrumbs
		Lamsvlees	Lamb
Gehakt	Minced meat	*Lever*	Liver
Ham	Ham	*Rookvlees*	Smoked beef
Kalfsvlees	Veal	*Spek*	Bacon
Kalkoen	Turkey	*Worst*	Sausages

FISH

Forel	Trout	*Oesteren*	Oysters
Garnalen	Prawns	*Paling*	Eel
Haring	Herring	*Schelvis*	Haddock
Haringsalade	Herring salad	*Schol*	Plaice
Kabeljauw	Cod	*Tong*	Sole
Makreel	Mackerel	*Zalm*	Salmon
Mosselen	Mussels		

Eating and Drinking

TERMS

Belegd	Filled or topped, as in *belegde broodjes* – small rolls topped with cheese, etc	*Geraspt*	Grated
		Gerookt	Smoked
		Gestoofd	Stewed
		Half doorbakken	Medium-done
Doorbakken	Well-done	*Hollandse saus*	Hollandaise (a milk and egg sauce)
Gebakken	Fried/baked		
Gebraden	Roast		
Gegrild	Grilled	*Rood*	Rare
Gekookt	Boiled		

VEGETABLES

Aardappelen	Potatoes	*Rijst*	Rice
Bloemkool	Cauliflower	*Sla*	Salad, lettuce
Bonen	Beans	*Stampot Andijvie*	Mashed potato and endive
Champignons	Mushrooms		
Erwten	Peas	*Stampot Boerenkool*	Mashed potato and cabbage
Hutspot	Mashed potatoes and carrots		
		Uien	Onions
Knoflook	Garlic	*Wortelen*	Carrots
Komkommer	Cucumber	*Zuurkool*	Sauerkraut
Prei	Leek		

INDONESIAN DISHES AND TERMS

Ajam	Chicken	*Nasi Rames*	Rijsttafel on a single plate
Bami	Noodles with meat/chicken and vegetables		
		Pedis	Hot and spicy
		Pisang	Banana
Daging	Beef	*Rijsttafel*	Collection of different spicy dishes served with plain rice
Gado gado	Vegetables in peanut sauce		
Goreng	Fried	*Sambal*	Hot, chilli-based sauce
Ikan	Fish	*Satesaus*	Peanut sauce to accompany meat grilled on skewers
Katjang	Peanut		
Kroepoek	Prawn crackers		
Loempia	Spring rolls	*Seroendeng*	Spicy shredded and fried coconut
Nasi	Rice		
Nasi Goreng	Fried rice with meat/chicken and vegetables	*Tauge*	Bean sprouts

SWEETS AND DESSERTS

Appelgebak	Apple tart or cake	*Pannekoeken*	Pancakes
Drop	Dutch liquorice, available in *zoet* (sweet) or *zout* (salted) varieties – the latter an acquired taste	*Pepernoten*	Dutch ginger nuts
		Poffertjes	Small pancakes, fritters
		(Slag)room	(Whipped) cream
		Speculaas	Spice and honey-flavoured biscuit
Gebak	Pastry		
IJs	Ice cream	*Stroopwafels*	Waffles
Koekjes	Biscuits	*Taai-taai*	Dutch honey cake
Oliebollen	Doughnuts	*Vla*	Custard
			Continues over

Eating and Drinking

Eating and Drinking

one, two or three fried eggs on buttered bread, topped with a choice of ham, cheese or roast beef – at about ƒ12, another good budget lunch.

RESTAURANT FOOD

Dutch **restaurant food** tends to be higher in protein content than imagination: steak, chicken and fish, along with filling soups and stews, are staple fare. Where possible stick to *dagschotels* (dish of the day, generally available as long as the restaurant is open), a meat and two vegetable combination for which you pay around ƒ17,50 bottom-line, for what tend to be enormous portions. The fish is generally high-quality but not especially cheap (ƒ20 and up, on average). Many places advertise "tourist menus" costing an average of ƒ17,50 which are usually extremely dull.

A wide selection of **vegetarian** restaurants offer full-course set meals for around ƒ17, or hearty dishes for ƒ15 or less. Bear in mind that they often close early. Another cheap stand-by is **Italian** food: pizzas and pasta dishes start at a fairly uniform ƒ12–14 in all but the ritziest places. **Chinese** restaurants are also common, as are (increasingly) **Spanish** ones, and there are a handful of **Tex-Mex** eateries, all of which serve well-priced, filling food. But Amsterdam's real speciality is its **Indonesian** restaurants, a consequence of the country's imperial adventures and well worth checking out. You can eat à la carte – *Nasi Goreng* and *Bami Goreng* (rice or noodles with meat) are ubiquitous dishes, and chicken or beef in peanut sauce (*sateh*) is available everywhere too. Alternatively, order a *rijsttafel*: boiled rice and/or noodles served with a number of spicy side dishes and hot *sambal* sauce on the side. Eaten with the spoon in the right hand, fork in the left, and with dry white or rosé wine or beer, this doesn't come cheap, but it's delicious and is normally more than enough for two.

DRINKS

Dutch **coffee** is black and strong, and comes in disappointingly small cups. It is often served with *koffiemelk* (evaporated milk); ordinary milk is offered only occasionally. If you want white coffee (*café au lait*), ask for a *koffie verkeerd*. Most bars also serve cappuccino, although bear in mind that many stop serving coffee altogether around 11pm. **Tea** generally comes with lemon, if anything; if you want milk you have to ask for it. **Hot chocolate** is also popular, served hot or cold: for a real treat drink it hot with a layer of fresh whipped cream on top.

The beverage drunk most often in Amsterdam's bars is **beer**. This is usually served in small measures, around half a pint (ask for *een pils*), much of which will be a frothing head – requests to have it poured English-style meet with various responses, but it's always worth trying. **Jenever**, Dutch gin, is not unlike English gin but a bit weaker and a little oilier; it's made from molasses and flavoured with juniper berries. It's served in small glasses and is traditionally drunk straight, often knocked back in one gulp with much hearty back-slapping. There are a number of varieties: *oud* (old) is smooth and mellow, *jong* (young) packs more of a punch – though neither is terribly alcoholic. Ask for a *borreltje* (straight *jenever*), a *bitterje* (with angostura bitters), or, if you've a sweeter tooth, try a *bessenjenever* – blackcurrant-flavoured gin; for a glass of beer with a jenever chaser, ask for a *kopstoot*. Other drinks you'll see include numerous Dutch **liqueurs**, notably *advocaat* (eggnog), and the sweet blue *curaçao*; and an assortment of lurid-coloured **fruit brandies**, which are best left for experimentation at the end of an evening. There's also the Dutch-produced brandy, *Vieux*, which tastes as if it's made from prunes but is in fact grape-based.

Beer and *jenever* are both dirt-cheap if bought by the bottle from a shop or supermarket: the commonest beers, all local brews – Amstel, Grolsch and Heineken – cost around ƒ1,50 for a half-litre (about a pint), although a small deposit on the bottle will be added (and given back when it's returned). A bottle of *jenever* sells for around ƒ20. Imported spirits are considerably more expensive. **Wine**, too, is very reasonable – expect to pay around ƒ4–5 for plonk, and ƒ7–8 or so for a fairly decent bottle.

BARS AND CAFÉS

Amsterdam is well known for its drinking, and with good reason: the selection of **bars** is one of the real pleasures of the city, fuelled by Holland's proximity to two of the premier beer-drinking nations in Europe – Belgium, where monks more or less invented modern beer, and Germany, famous for its beer consumption. The three leading brands of Dutch beer – Amstel, Grolsch and Heineken – are worldwide best-sellers, but are available here in considerably more potent formats than the insipid varieties shunted out for export. Dutch gin, or *jenever*, has a kick all its own, and, in addition, the selection of imported beers and spirits on offer in Amsterdam's bars is exceptionally good, with almost limitless possibilities for experimentation.

There are, in essence, two kinds of Amsterdam bar. The traditional, old-style bar is the **brown café** – a *bruin café* or *bruine kroeg*; these are cosy places so called because of the dingy colour of their walls, stained by years of tobacco smoke. As a backlash, slick, self-consciously modern **designer bars** have sprung up, many of them known as "grand cafés", which tend to be as un-brown as possible and geared towards a largely young crowd. We've included details of the more established ones, although these places come and go – something like seventy percent are said to close down within a year of opening. Bars, of either kind, open at around 10am or 5pm; those that open in the

Eating and Drinking

For the story of the weed, check out the Hash Marihuana Hemp Museum – see p.69. For more dope on dope, see pp.70–71.

morning do not close at lunchtime, and both stay open until around 1am during the week, 2am at weekends (sometimes until 3am). Another type of drinking spot – though there are very few of them left – are the **tasting houses** (*proeflokalen*), originally the sampling rooms of small private distillers, now tiny, stand-up places that sell only spirits and close around 8pm.

One growing trend in Amsterdam drinking is **Irish pubs**: at the last count there were ten in and around the city centre, all featuring Guinness and other stouts on tap, Gaelic music of varying quality, and English football live via satellite most weekends. The clue to their success seems to lie much more in the football than the fiddlers – all have rapidly become "locals" for the relatively large numbers of British and Irish living and working in Amsterdam, and although at quiet times the clientele might include a smattering of Amsterdammers, most of the (generally male) drinkers in these places are expats rather than locals.

Prices are fairly standard everywhere, and the only time you'll pay through the nose is when there's music, or if you're foolish (or desperate) enough to step into the obvious tourist traps around Leidseplein and along Damrak. Reckon on paying roughly ƒ2,75 for a standard-measure small beer, called a *pils* (or, if you get it in a straight glass, a *fluitje*). A tiny beer chaser, called a *kleintje pils*, costs the same. Apart from these, different beers come in different glasses – *Oranjeboom*, for instance, is served in a *vasje*; white beer (*witbier*), which is light, cloudy and served with lemon, has its own tumbler, and most of the speciality Belgian beers have special stemmed glasses. Most places should be able to come up with a pint if you really want one (at roughly ƒ7), but bear in mind that a quarter of the glass, whether large or small, always comes as foam.

You can also use cafés as a place for **budget eating**. Many – often designated *eetcafés* – offer a complete menu, and most will make you a sandwich or a

bowl of soup; at the very least you can snack on hard-boiled eggs from the counter for a guilder or so each. Some bars that specialize in food are listed in the "Restaurants" section.

There are around 1400 bars and cafés in Amsterdam – which works out at roughly one every 50m (or so it seems) – and what follows is inevitably very selective. It does, however, cover a very broad cross-section of places across the city, so wherever you are, and, whatever your tastes, you should be able to find something nearby to suit you.

COFFEESHOPS

Art, architecture and canals aside, a large proportion of visitors to Amsterdam have come for one thing: the **drugs**. Amsterdam remains just about the only city in the world where you can stand in a public place and announce in a loud, clear voice that you intend to buy and smoke a large, well-packed joint, and then do just that in front of the watching police. In theory, purchases of up to 5g of cannabis, and possession of up to 30g (the legal limit), are tolerated; in practice, most coffeeshops around the city offer discounted bulk purchases of 50g with impunity (though bear in mind that if the police do search you they're entitled to confiscate any amount they find). No one will ever call the police on you in Amsterdam for discreet, personal dope-smoking, but if in doubt about whether smoking is OK in a given situation, ask somebody – the worst you'll get will be a "no".

The first thing you should know about Amsterdam's **coffeeshops** is that locals use them too. The second thing you should know is that the only ones locals use are outside the Red Light District. Practically all the coffeeshops you'll run into in the centre are worth avoiding, either for their decor, their deals or their clientele. Plasticky, neon-lit dives abound, pumping out mainstream varieties of house, rock or reggae at ear-splitting level; the dope on offer is usually limited and of poor quality – and, since they're

Eating and Drinking

Bar, café, coffeeshop or tearoom?

You might expect a place describing itself as a "café" to be open only during the day, selling simple food, cups of tea and no alcohol. In Amsterdam, though, a "café" – **brown** or **grand** – is just a type of bar. One way to distinguish between brown cafés and grand cafés – apart from the ambience – is in the main activity going on. In a grand café, people might be eating full meals, or drinking coffee, wine or beer; in a brown café, like an English pub, the single main activity is alcohol consumption. Don't worry, though: they both serve more or less the same kind of fare, and if one place doesn't have what you want, somewhere just down the road will.

There is, however, a more fundamental difference between coffeeshops and tearooms. To foreigners, a **coffeeshop** brings to mind a quiet daytime place serving coffee and cakes. Far from it. In Amsterdam, somewhere calling itself a "coffeeshop" is advertising just one thing: cannabis. You might sometimes be able to get coffee and cake, but the main activity in a coffeeshop is smoking. If you want to avoid dope-smoke, there are plenty of places throughout the city where you can sit in the afternoon with a cup of coffee and a sandwich; they tend to shy away from the connotations of "coffeeshop", and have taken to calling themselves **tearooms** instead. Non-smokers should beware that wherever you go it's almost impossible to avoid cigarette smoke.

mostly serving tourists, they can rig the deals without fear of comeback. A short time exploring the city will turn up plenty of more congenial, high-quality outlets for buying and enjoying cannabis, light years away from the tack of the city centre.

When you first walk into a coffeeshop, how you buy the stuff isn't immediately apparent – it's illegal to advertise cannabis in any way, which includes calling attention to the fact that it's available at all. What you have to do is ask to see the **menu**, which is normally kept behind the counter. This will list all the different hashes and grasses on offer, along with (if it's a reputable place) exactly how many grammes you get for your money. Most of the stuff is sold either per gramme, or in bags worth ƒ10 or ƒ25 (the more powerful it is, the less you get). The in-house dealer will be able to help you out with queries.

Hash you may come across originates in various countries and is pretty self-explanatory, apart from *Pollem*, which is compressed resin and stronger than normal. **Marijuana** is a different story, and the old days of imported Colombian, Thai and sensimelia are fading away; taking their place are limitless varieties of Nederwiet, Dutch-grown

under UV lights and more potent than anything you're likely to have come across. Skunk, Haze and Northern Lights are all popular types of Dutch weed, and should be treated with caution – a smoker of low-grade British draw will be laid low (or high) for hours by a single spliff of Skunk. You would be equally well advised to take care with **space-cakes**, which are widely available: you can never be sure exactly what's in them; they tend to have a delayed reaction (up to two hours before you notice anything strange – don't get impatient and gobble down another one!); and once they kick in, they can bring on an extremely intense, bewildering high – 10–12 hours is common. Some large coffeeshops, such as the *Bulldog*, refuse to sell them, and advise you against buying elsewhere. You may also come across cannabis seeds for growing your own. While Amsterdammers are permitted to grow five small marijuana plants for "domestic consumption", the import of cannabis seeds is illegal in any country – don't even think about trying to take some home.

However, for dabblers and committed stone-heads alike, Amsterdam is full of possibilities. The coffeeshops we list are better than average; most of them open

Eating and Drinking

around 10am or 11am and close around midnight.

TEAROOMS

Amsterdam's **tearooms** roughly correspond to the usual concept of a café – places that are generally open all day, might serve alcohol but definitely aren't bars, don't allow dope-smoking, but serve good coffee, sandwiches, light snacks and cakes. Along with *eetcafés* – which are listed in amongst the bars – tearooms make good places to stop off for lunch, or to spend a quiet time reading or writing without distractions.

The Old Centre

All the following places are marked on the map on pp.198–199.

Bars and cafés

Belgique, Gravenstraat 2. Tiny bar behind the Nieuwe Kerk that specializes in brews from Belgium.

Bern, Nieuwmarkt 9. Casual and inexpensive brown café patronized by a predominantly arty clientele. Run by a native of Switzerland, its speciality is, not surprisingly, cheese fondue.

Blarney Stone, Nieuwendijk 29. Packed and central Irish pub.

Blincker, St Barberenstraat 7. Squeezed between the top end of Nes and Oudezijds Voorburgwal, this hi-tech theatre bar, all exposed steel and hanging plants, is more comfortable than it looks.

De Brakke Grond, Nes 43. Modern, high-ceilinged bar full of people discussing the performances they've just seen at the adjacent theatre.

De Buurvrouw, St Pieterspoortsteeg 29. Dark, noisy bar with a wildly eclectic crowd; a great alternative place to head for in the centre.

Carel's Café, Voetboogstraat 6. Large, youth-oriented bar serving slightly overpriced food – though the *dagschotels* are a good buy. Also at Frans Halsstraat 76. The dimly-lit late-night version, *Carel's nacht café* at Saenredamstraat 32

is open until 6am at the weekend and 4am during the week.

Cul de Sac, Oudezijds Achterburgwal 99. Down a long alley in what used to be a seventeenth-century spice warehouse, this is a handy retreat from the Red Light District. Small, quiet and friendly.

Café Dante, Spuistraat 320. Is it a bar? Is it an art gallery? It's both and there are just as many people sitting drinking as there are perusing the walls.

Dantzig, Zwanenburgwal 15. Easy-going grand café, right on the water behind Waterlooplein, with comfortable chairs, friendly service and a low-key, chic atmosphere. Food served at lunchtime and in the evenings.

De Drie Fleschjes, Gravenstraat 16. Tasting house for spirits and liqueurs, which once would have been made on the premises. No beer, and no seats either; its clients tend to be well heeled or well soused (often both). Closes 8pm.

Droesem, Nes 41. On a thin, theatre-packed alley behind the Dam, this is a highly recommended wine bar. Wine comes in carafes filled from the barrel, along with a high-quality choice of cheeses and other titbits to help it on its way.

Durty Nelly's, Warmoesstraat 115. Irish pub in the heart of the Red Light action. With a clean and well-run hostel above, this is one of the better expat Brit/Irish meeting places, packed for the weekend football shown live by satellite.

De Engelbewaarder, Kloveniersburgwal 59. Once the meeting place of Amsterdam's bookish types, this is still known as a literary café. It's relaxed and informal, with live jazz on Sunday afternoons.

De Engelse Reet, Begijnensteeg 4. More like someone's front room than a bar – indeed, all drinks mysteriously appear from a back room. Photographs on the wall record generations of sociable drinking.

Fiddlers, Warmoesstraat 55. Good enough Irish pub, but you'd do better to walk down the road to *Durty Nelly's*.

Frascati, Nes 59. Theatre bar, elegantly brown with mirrors and a pink marble bar, popular with a young, media-type crowd. Good, too, for both lunchtime and informal evening eating, with full meals for around *f*20, snacks and soups for less. Recommended.

Gaeper, Staalstraat 4. Convivial brown café packed during the school year with students from the university across the canal. Good food and seating outside watching the locals pass by.

't Gasthuis, Grimburgwal 7. Another brown café popular with students. Both this place and *Gaeper* are run by brothers, so it's in more or less the same style.

Gollem, Raamsteeg 4. Small, noisy bar with a huge array of different beers. A genial barman dispenses lists to help you choose.

Hard Rock Café, Oudezijds Voorburgwal 246. Not the overblown burger joint found in London, but a small, crowded (smoking) bar showing 1970s-style videos to similarly styled customers. Patronized mainly by those in Amsterdam for the weed. The real thing can be found at Max Euweplein.

Harry's American Bar, Spuistraat 285. One of a number of would-be sophisticated hangouts at the Spui end of Spuistraat, *Harry's* is primarily a haunt for Amsterdam's more elderly *bons vivants*, with easy-listening jazz and an unhealthily wide selection of cocktails.

Het Kantoor, Waterlooplein. The best place to run to if the market gets too much – situated on the first floor, overlooking the mayhem below. Popular with the traders.

Het Paleis, Paleisstraat 16. Bar that's a favourite with students from the adjoining university buildings. Laid-back and likeable.

De Hoogte, Nieuwe Hoogstraat 2a. Small alternative bar on the edge of the Red Light District. Good music, engaging atmosphere, and beers a little cheaper than usual.

Hoppe, Spui 18. One of Amsterdam's longest-established and best-known bars, and one of its most likeable, frequented by the city's dark-suited office crowd on their wayward way home. Summer is especially good, when the throngs spill out onto the street.

De Jaren, Nieuwe Doelenstraat 20. One of the grandest of the grand cafés, but without a trace of pretentiousness. Overlooking the Amstel next to the university, with three floors, two terraces and as much elegance as you could wish for. There's all kinds of English reading material, too – this is one of the best places to nurse the Sunday paper. Serves reasonably priced food and has a great salad bar. From 10am.

Kabul, Warmoesstraat 38. Bar of the adjacent budget hotel, open late.

Karpershoek, Martelaarsgracht 2. Old-fashioned bar which is a relic among Amsterdam pubs because of its corner-side location facing Centraal Station. A loyal and varied (often hard-drinking) clientele, no music, and it also serves coffee.

De Koningshut, Spuistraat 269. In the early evening, at least, it's standing room only in this small, spit-and-sawdust bar, popular with office people on their way home or to dinner. For middle-aged swingers only.

Lokaal 't Loosje, Nieuwmarkt 32. Quiet old-style local brown café that's been here for two hundred years and looks it. Wonderful for late breakfasts and pensive afternoons.

Luxembourg, Spui 22. The prime watering-hole of Amsterdam's advertising and media brigade. If you can get past the crowds, it's actually an elegant bar with a good (though pricey) selection of snacks. Overlooks the Singel at the back.

Café Mono, Oudezijds Voorburgwal 2. Lively brown café where musicians drop in to have a chat or do some DJ-ing. Open all day during the summer, with a terrace at the front, and from 5pm in the winter. Weekends feature blues, jungle and hip-hop DJs.

Eating and Drinking

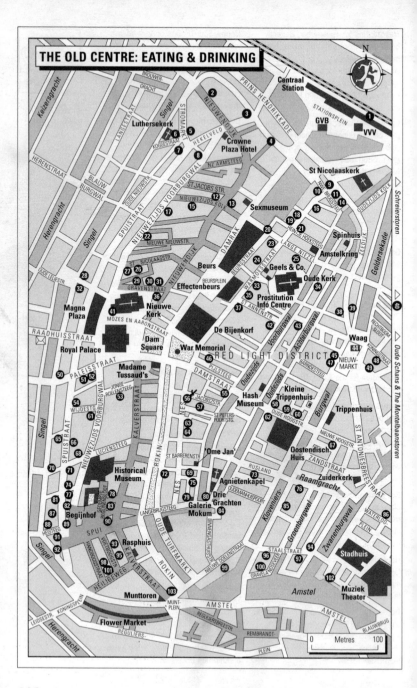

THE OLD CENTRE: EATING & DRINKING

N

Centraal Station

GVB
VVV

Lecturserk
Crowne Plaza Hotel

St Nicolaaskerk

Sexmuseum

Spinhuis

Amstelkring

Beurs

Geels & Co.

Effectenbeurs

Oude Kerk

Magna Plaza

Nieuwe Kerk

Prostitution Info Centre

De Bijenkorf

Waag

Royal Palace

Dam Square

War Memorial

RED LIGHT DISTRICT

Madame Tussaud's

Hash Museum

Kleine Trippenhuis

Trippenhuis

Historical Museum

'Ome Jan'

Oostendisch Huis

Zuiderkerk

Agnietenkapel

Drie Grachten

Raamgracht

Begijnhof

Galerie Mokum

Rasphuis

Stadhuis

Munttoren

Muziek Theater

Amstel

Flower Market

Amstel

0   Metres   100

BARS AND CAFÉS

Anco	34	Het Paleis	50
Argos	35	De Hoogte	67
Belgique	31	Hoppe	91
Bern	49	De Jaren	99
Blarney Stone	2	Kabul	19
Blincker	69	Karpershoek	3
De Brakke Grond	63	De Koningshut	71
De Buurvrouw	57	Lokaal 't Loosje	47
Carel's Café	93	Luxembourg	92
Casa Maria	23	Café Mono	14
Club Jaecques	33	't Nieuwe Kafé	41
Cuckoo's Nest	15	O'Reilly's	51
Cul de Sac	43	Oininio	4
Café Dante	87	't Pakhuys	95
Dantzig	102	De Pilserij	36
De Drie Fleschjes	30	De Pool	62
Droesem	56	Scheltema	61
Durty Nelly's	37	Schuim	54
The Eagle	24	De Schutter	98
De Engelbewaarder	85	Shako's	100
De Engelse Reet	78	Stablemaster	16
Fiddlers	21	Tapvreugd	59
Frascati	64	Tara	72
Gaeper	96	Ter Kuile	28
't Gasthuis	79	Van Daele	52
Gollem	70	Vrankrijk	65
Hard Rock Café	55	The Web	12
Harry's American Bar	77	Why Not	8
Het Kantoor	86	Wynand Fockink	46
		De Zwart	89

RESTAURANTS

1e Klas	1	Luden	81
Bredero	75	Mensa Atrium	84
Centra	25	New King	39
Haesje Claes	74	Oud Holland	27
Hemelse Modder	40	Café Pacifico	18
Het Beeren	48	Palmers	11
Hoi Tin	38	Pannekoekhuis Upstairs	80
In de Waag	44	Poco Loco	45
Kam Yin	9	Sie Joe	29
Kantjil en de Tijger	82	De Silveren Spiegel	5
Keuken van 1870	7	Stereo Sushi	53
De Klaes Compaen	76	Tom Yam	97
Kopke Adega	6	Vasso	83
La Place	103	De Vergulde Lantaarn	13
Lana Thai	10	Werkendam	26
Lucius	66		

COFFEESHOPS

The Bulldog	42
Dampkring	101
Extase	58
Grasshopper (NZ Voorburgwal)	17
Grasshopper (Oudebrugsteeg)	20
Homegrown Fantasy	22
Josephine Baker	60
Kadinsky	68
Rusland	73
De Tweede Kamer	88

TEAROOMS

Café Esprit	90
Puccini	94
Villa Zeezicht	32

Eating and Drinking

't Nieuwe Kafé, adjoining the Nieuwe Kerk, facing Gravenstraat. Smart bistro-style café popular with shoppers, serving good, reasonably priced lunches.

O'Reilly's, Paleisstraat 103. Cavernously vast Irish pub right by Dam square; light on atmosphere.

Oininio, Prins Hendrikkade 20. Airy, relaxed bar attached to a thriving new-age centre (which also has a restaurant, see p.227) – remarkably peaceful for being seconds from Centraal Station.

't Pakhuys, Voetboogstraat 10. An inviting place serving cheapish food; one of a clutch of bars that line this tiny street.

De Pilserij, Gravenstraat 10. Roomy bar behind the Nieuwe Kerk that has a comfortable back room and plays good jazz. Above all, though, it's the authentic nineteenth-century surroundings that appeal – little has changed, even down to the cash register.

De Pool, Oude Hoogstraat 8. Pleasant bar, somewhat quieter than most of the others along this stretch.

Scheltema, Nieuwezijds Voorburgwal 242. Journalists' bar, now only frequented by more senior newshounds and their occasionally famous interviewees, since all the newspaper headquarters along here have now moved to the suburbs. Faded turn-of-the-century feel, with a reading table and meals.

Schuim, Spuistraat 189. Popular and spacious alternative grand café, which, though not chic (it's full of secondhand furniture) nevertheless has a trendy enough clientele who rate it one of the best places in town.

De Schutter, Voetboogstraat 13. Former folk music hangout, now simply a spacious upstairs bar, full of people munching on the cheap and basic food.

Tapvreugd, Oude Hoogstraat 11. Far and away the most amicable of the loud, crowded music bars on this and surrounding streets.

Tara, Rokin 89. Excellent Irish bar with regular live music. The location does it down, but it's worth taking the time to find.

Ter Kuile, Torensteeg 8. A brown café with a new polished look, and a pleasant place from which to view this stretch of the Singel. Serves food at the usual *eetcafé* prices.

Van Daele, Paleisstraat 101. Worth mentioning more for what it was than what it is, this used to be the city's most infamous punk bar, called *No Name*; it later became a squatters' bar, then a women's restaurant. Today it's a fairly ordinary bar.

Vrankrijk, Spuistraat 216. The best and most central of Amsterdam's few remaining squat bars. Cheap drinks, hardcore noise, and almost as many dogs-on-strings as people. Buzz to enter. From 10pm.

Wynand Fockink, Pijlsteeg 31. Hidden just behind Dam square. One of the older *proeflokalen*. Frequented by local street musicians.

De Zwart, Spuistraat 334. Less businesslike neighbour of the more famous *Hoppe* across the alley, but similarly crowded.

Gay bars

Anco, Oudezijds Voorburgwal 55. Late-night hotel leather bar with a large darkroom.

Argos, Warmoesstraat 95. Europe's oldest leather bar, with two bars and a raunchy cellar. Not for the faint-hearted. From 10pm.

Casa Maria, Warmoesstraat 60. Mixed gay bar in the heart of the Warmoesstraat scene. Over-25s only.

Club Jaecques, Warmoesstraat 93. A meeting place for locals, but appropriate (leather- and denim-clad) visitors are made welcome.

Cuckoo's Nest, Nieuwezijds Kolk 6. A cruisey leather bar with a long reputation, this is described as "the best place in town for chance encounters". Vast and infamous darkroom. From 1pm.

The Eagle, Warmoesstraat 90. Long-established leather bar popular with men of all ages. Gets very busy after 1am.

Shako's, 's Gravelandseveer 2. Friendly, studentish bar in a quiet street on the Amstel.

Stablemaster, Warmoesstraat 23. A leather bar with hotel attached; English-speaking staff and a British following.

The Web, St Jacobsstraat 6. Strict rubber, leather and denim bar with a dance floor, darkrooms and a pool table. From 2pm.

Why Not, Nieuwezijds Voorburgwal 28. Long-standing, intimate bar with a porno cinema above.

Coffeeshops

The Bulldog, Oudezijds Voorburgwal 90 and 132 and 218; Singel 12. The biggest and most famous of the coffeeshop chains; see p.208 for details.

Dampkring, Handboogstraat 29. Colourful coffeeshop with loud music and laid-back atmosphere, known for its good-quality hash.

Extase, Oude Hoogstraat 2. Part of a chain run by the initiator of the Hash Museum. Considerably less chichi than the better-known coffeeshops.

Grasshopper, Oudebrugsteeg 16; Nieuwezijds Voorburgwal 57. One of the city's more welcoming coffeeshops, though at times overwhelmed by tourists.

Homegrown Fantasy, Nieuwezijds Voorburgwal 87a. Attached to the Dutch Passion seed company, this sells the widest selection of marijuana in Amsterdam, most of it local.

Josephine Baker, Oude Hoogstraat 27. Once known as the *Café de Dood* – "Café of the Dead", after the studiously wasted youth who patronize it – this is the loudest and most squalid hangout in the area.

Kadinsky, Rosmarijnsteeg 9. Strictly accurate deals weighed out to a background of jazz dance. Chocolate chip cookies to die for.

Rusland, Rusland 16. One of the first Amsterdam coffeeshops, a cramped but vibrant place that's a favourite with both dope fans and tea addicts (it has 43 different kinds). A cut above the rest.

De Tweede Kamer, Heisteeg 6. A busy coffeeshop that's more "brown" than most of its rivals. In a tiny alley off Spui.

Tearooms

Café Esprit, Spui 10a. Swish modern café, with wonderful sandwiches, rolls and superb salads.

Puccini, Staalstraat 21. Lovely cake and chocolate shop-cum-café, with wonderful handmade pastries and good coffee. Close to Waterlooplein.

Villa Zeezicht, Torensteeg 3. Small and central, this all-wood café serves excellent rolls and sandwiches, plus some of the best apple cake in the city, fresh-baked every 10min or so.

Grachtengordel West

All the following places are marked on the map on p.202.

Bars and cafés

Aas van Bokalen, Keizersgracht 335. Unpretentious local bar with good food. Great collection of Motown tapes. Very small, so go either early or late.

De Admiraal, Herengracht 319. Large and uniquely comfortable *proeflokaal*, with a vast range of liqueurs and spirits to explore.

De Beiaard, Herengracht 90. Light and airy 1950s-style bar for genuine beer aficionados. There's a wide selection of bottled and draught beers, selected with true dedication by the owner, who delights in filling you in on the relative properties of each.

Belhamel, Brouwersgracht 60. Kitschy bar/restaurant with an Art Nouveau-style interior and excellent, though costly, French food. The main attraction in summer is one of the most picturesque views in Amsterdam.

De Doffer, Runstraat 12. Small, affable bar with food and a billiards table.

Eating and Drinking

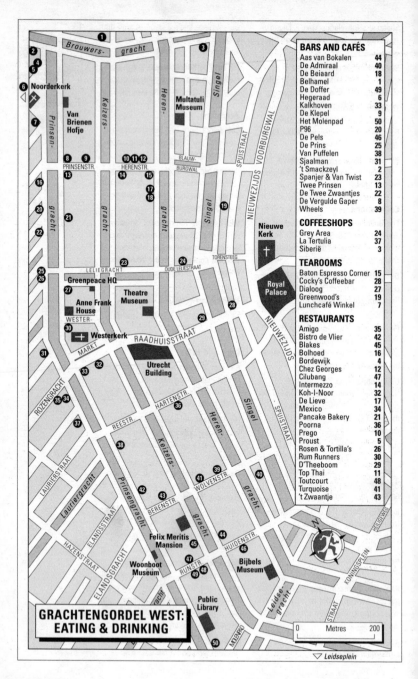

BARS AND CAFÉS

Aas van Bokalen	44
De Admiraal	40
De Beiaard	18
Belhamel	1
De Doffer	49
Hegeraad	6
Kalkhoven	33
De Klepel	9
Het Molenpad	50
P96	20
De Pels	46
De Prins	25
Van Puffelen	38
Sjaalman	31
't Smackzeyl	2
Spanjer & Van Twist	23
Twee Prinsen	13
De Twee Zwaantjes	22
De Vergulde Gaper	8
Wheels	39

COFFEESHOPS

Grey Area	24
La Tertulia	37
Siberië	3

TEAROOMS

Baton Espresso Corner	15
Cocky's Coffeebar	28
Dialoog	27
Greenwood's	19
Lunchcafé Winkel	7

RESTAURANTS

Amigo	35
Bistro de Vlier	42
Blakes	45
Bolhoed	16
Bordewijk	4
Chez Georges	12
Cilubang	47
Intermezzo	14
Koh-I-Noor	32
De Lieve	17
Mexico	34
Pancake Bakery	21
Poorna	36
Prego	10
Proust	5
Rosen & Tortilla's	26
Rum Runners	30
D'Theeboom	29
Top Thai	11
Toutcourt	48
Turquoise	41
't Zwaantje	43

GRACHTENGORDEL WEST: EATING & DRINKING

0 Metres 200

▽ Leidseplein

Hegeraad, Noordermarkt 34. Lovingly maintained old-fashioned brown café with a fiercely loyal clientele. The back room, furnished with red plush and paintings, is the perfect place to relax with a hot chocolate.

Kalkhoven, Prinsengracht 283. One of the city's most characteristic brown cafés. Nothing out of the ordinary, but warm and welcoming.

De Klepel, Prinsenstraat 22. Quiet bar where people come to play chess. English newspapers.

Het Molenpad, Prinsengracht 653. This is one of the most appealing brown cafés in the city: long, dark and dusty. Also serves remarkably good food. Fills up with a young, professional crowd after 6pm. Recommended.

P96, Prinsengracht 96. A late-opening bar a little way down the canal from *De Prins*; there's a dartboard, should you feel like a game.

De Pels, Huidenstraat 25. Few surprises here – one of Amsterdam's quieter but more pleasant bars.

De Prins, Prinsengracht 124. Boisterous student bar, with a wide range of drinks and a well-priced menu. A great place to drink in a nice part of town. Food served from 10am to 10pm.

Van Puffelen, Prinsengracht 377. A café and restaurant adjacent to each other. The café is an appealing place to drink, with a huge choice of international beers and a reading room; the restaurant (daily 6–11pm) serves French food, which, though not cheap, is usually well worth it.

Sjaalman, Prinsengracht 178. Small bar with a pool table and Thai food. Good in the summer when the church tower is lit up.

't Smackzeyl, Brouwersgracht 101. Uninhibited drinking hole on the fringes of the Jordaan (corner of Prinsengracht). One of the few brown cafés to have Guinness on tap; also an inexpensive menu of light dishes.

Spanjer & van Twist, Leliegracht 60. A gentle place, which comes into its own

on summer afternoons, with chairs lining the most peaceful stretch of water in the city centre.

Twee Prinsen, Prinsenstraat 27. Cornerside people-watching bar that's a useful starting place for touring the area. Its heated terrace makes it possible to sit outside, even in winter.

De Twee Zwaantjes, Prinsengracht 114. Tiny Jordaan bar whose live accordion music and raucous singing you'll either love or hate. Fun, in an oompah-pah sort of way.

De Vergulde Gaper, Prinsenstraat 30. Opposite the *Twee Prinsen*, this offers much the same kind of low-key attraction – though it's somewhat larger and there's a wider choice of food. Has a heated terrace should you fancy sitting outside.

Wheels, Wolvenstraat 4. Deceptively like any other brown café to look at, but actually the confirmed haunt of a number of British expats. Expect to be served by a friendly north London soul boy.

Coffeeshops

Grey Area, Oude Leliestraat 2. High-class coffeeshop with menu (and prices) to match.

La Tertulia, Prinsengracht 312. Tiny corner coffeeshop, complete with indoor rockery and tinkling fountain. Much better outside, though, as it's on a particularly beautiful stretch of the canal.

Siberië, Brouwersgracht 11. Set up by the former staff of *Rusland* and notable for the way it's avoided the over-commercialization of the larger chains. Very relaxed, very friendly, and worth a visit whether you want to smoke or not.

Tearooms

Baton Espresso Corner, Herengracht 82. Convivial tearoom with a huge array of sandwiches. In a central location, handy for cheap lunches.

Cocky's Coffeebar, Raadhuisstraat 8. Good no-nonsense place with a wide variety of sandwiches.

Eating and Drinking

Eating and Drinking

Dialoog, Prinsengracht 261a. A few doors down from the Anne Frank House, one long room filled with paintings, restrained classical music, and downstairs, a gallery of Latin American art. Good choice of sandwiches and salads, too.

Greenwood's, Singel 103. Small, English-style teashop in the basement of a canal house. Pies and sandwiches, pots of tea – and a decent breakfast.

Lunchcafé Winkel, Noordermarkt 43. A popular café on the corner with Westerstraat; something of a rendezvous on Saturday mornings, with the Boerenmarkt in full flow, and some of the most delicious apple cake in the city going like, well, hot apple cake.

Grachtengordel South

All the following places are marked on the map on pp.206–207.

Bars and cafés

Café Americain, *American Hotel*, Leidseplein 28. The terrace bar here was the gathering place for Amsterdam media people for years, and it's worth coming at least once, if only for the decor: Art Nouveau frills coordinated down to the doorknobs. A place to be seen, with prices not surprisingly above average. Good fast lunches, though.

De Balie, Kleine Gartmanplantsoen 10. Big high-ceilinged haunt of the city's trendy left, part of the Balie cultural centre. Not especially inspiring, but if you're stuck on Leidseplein on a Saturday night, it provides a welcome change of atmosphere.

't Balkje, Kerkstraat 46. Snacky meeting place: eggs, eggs and bacon, and eggs, bacon and ham. Beer too.

Black & White, Leidseplein 18. No-nonsense bar, whose "rolling stone" emblem at the front is a good indicator of the loud rock music within. A large good-time crowd on Saturday night.

De Duivel, Reguliersdwarsstraat 87. Tucked away on a street of bars and coffeeshops, this is the only hip-hop café in Amsterdam, with continuous beats and a clientele to match. Opposite the hip-hop coffeeshop *Free I*.

Eetcafé 't Lieverdje, Singel 415. Quiet, rather ordinary café that's a good bet for a simple meal. Open from 4pm. Closed Mon & Tues.

De Geus, Korte Leidsedwarsstraat 71. Cheerful place with a limited but tasty menu of Dutch food.

Het Hok, Lange Leidsedwarsstraat 134. Games bar, where you can play backgammon, chess or draughts, or just drink against a backdrop of clicking counters. Pleasingly unpretentious after the plastic restaurants of the rest of the street, though women may find the overwhelmingly male atmosphere off-putting.

Het Land van Walem, Keizersgracht 449. One of Amsterdam's nouveau-chic cafés: cool, light, and vehemently un-brown. The clientele is stylish, and the food is a kind of hybrid French-Dutch; there's also a wide selection of newspapers and magazines, including some in English. Breakfast in the garden during the summer is a highlight. Usually packed.

Huyschkaemer, Utrechtsestraat 137. Attractive small local bar-restaurant on a street renowned for its eateries, which is a favourite watering-hole of arty students. At weekends the restaurant space is turned into a dance floor.

Café Klein Wiener Wad, Utrechtsestraat 135. Small, self-consciously modern café; trendy and unavoidably intimate.

De Koe, Marnixstraat 381. A fine, popular café amidst the many in this area, and, being slightly further out from the Leidseplein, one of the less busy options, too.

L & B, Korte Leidsedwarsstraat 82. A cosy bar, rather misplaced among the touristy restaurants and clubs of this part of town. Has a selection of two hundred different whiskies and bourbons from around the world. Open until 3am.

Lux, Marnixstraat 403. The most trendy option among this stretch of cafés, draw-

ing a young alternative crowd. Loud
music. Open late.

Morlang, Keizersgracht 451. Bar/restaurant of the new wave, yuppie variety
(much like the *Walem* next door), serving
good food for around ƒ20. Occasional
live music.

Mulligan's, Amstel 100. By far the best
Irish pub in the city, with an authentic
atmosphere, superb Gaelic music and
good service.

Mulliners Wijnlokaal, Lijnsbaansgracht
267. Upmarket wine bar (around ƒ6 a
glass, ƒ25 a bottle), serving food as well.
Good atmosphere.

Oosterling, Utrechtsestraat 140. Stone-
floored local bar-cum-off-licence that's
been in the same family since the middle of the last century. Very quiet –
home to some serious drinkers.

Reynders, Leidseplein 6. The last real
option if you want to sit out on the
Leidseplein. A remnant of days long
gone, with aproned waiters and an elegant interior.

Café Schiller, Rembrandtplein 26. Art
Deco bar of the upstairs hotel, authentic
in both feel and decor, and offering a
genteel escape from the tackiness of
much of Rembrandtplein.

De Tap, Prinsengracht 478. Roomy bar
with a balcony and more individuality than
you'd expect this close to Leidseplein.

Terzijde, Kerkstraat 59. Within a stone's
throw of Leidsestraat, this is a peaceful
little bar used by the locals and students.

Vive la Vie, Amstelstraat 7. Small, campy
bar, patronized mostly, but not exclusively, by women and transvestites.

Café de Wetering, Weteringstraat 37.
Tucked away out of sight off the
Spiegelgracht, this is a wonderfully
atmospheric local brown café, complete
with wood beams, sleeping cat and, during the winter, an open fire.

De Zotte Proeflokaal, Raamstraat 29.
Belgian hangout on the edge of the
Jordaan. Food, liqueurs and hundreds of
different types of beer.

Gay bars

Amstel Taveerne, Amstel 54. Well-
established, traditional gay bar with regular singalongs. Always packed, and at
its most vivacious in summer when the
crowds spill out onto the street.

April, Reguliersdwarsstraat 37. On the itin-
erary of almost every gay visitor to
Amsterdam. Lively and cosmopolitan,
with a good selection of foreign newspapers, cakes and coffee, as well as booze.

Camp Café, Kerkstraat 45. Pleasant mix
of friendly regulars and foreign visitors.
Worth a visit for the ceiling alone, which
is covered with a collection of beer
mugs from around the world.

Company, Amstel 106. Western-style
leather bar. Fills up later in the evening.

Cosmo Bar, Kerkstraat 42. Comfortable,
quiet bar, part of the *West End Hotel*
(see p.180). Daily midnight to 3am.

Downtown, Reguliersdwarsstraat 31. A
favourite with visitors. Relaxed and
friendly, with inexpensive meals.

Entre Nous, Halvemaansteeg 14. Just
down the road from *De Steeg*, and with
much the same campy ambience.

Fellows, Amstel 50. Civilized and immaculately clean bar on the river. An ideal
location in summer.

Gaiety, Amstel 14. Small gay bar with a
warm welcome. One of the most popular young gay haunts in Amsterdam.

Havana, Reguliersdwarsstraat 17. Stylish
and would-be sophisticated hangout
patronized by those who like to be seen
out on the town.

Krokodil, Amstelstraat 34. Amiable, noisy
bar in between the discos and clubs.

Lellebel, Utrechtsestraat 4. A gay-friendly
café featuring drag acts, with a lively and
cheerful atmosphere.

Mankind, Weteringstraat 60. Quiet, non-
scene bar with its own terrace and landing stage. Lovely in summer.

Meia Meia "66", Kerkstraat 63. Good if
you like Guinness; popular with the
clone regulars.

Eating and
Drinking

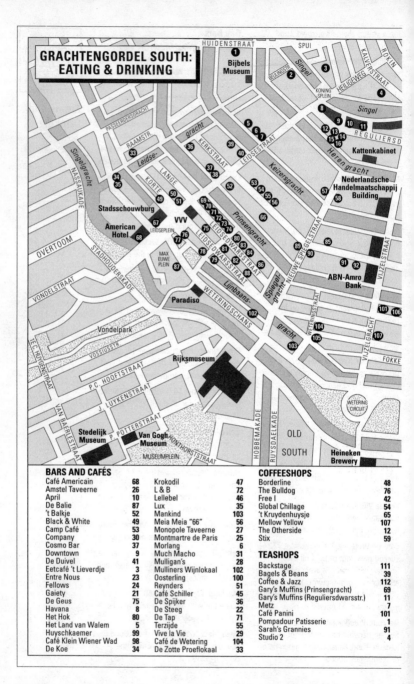

GRACHTENGORDEL SOUTH: EATING & DRINKING

BARS AND CAFÉS

Café Americain	**68**	Krokodil	**47**
Amstel Taveerne	**26**	L & B	**72**
April	**10**	Lellebel	**46**
De Balie	**87**	Lux	**35**
't Balkje	**52**	Mankind	**103**
Black & White	**49**	Meia Meia "66"	**56**
Camp Café	**53**	Monopole Taveerne	**27**
Company	**30**	Montmartre de Paris	**25**
Cosmo Bar	**37**	Morlang	**6**
Downtown	**9**	Much Macho	**31**
De Duivel	**41**	Mulligan's	**28**
Eetcafé 't Lieverdje	**3**	Mulliners Wijnlokaal	**102**
Entre Nous	**23**	Oosterling	**100**
Fellows	**24**	Reynders	**51**
Gaiety	**21**	Café Schiller	**45**
De Geus	**75**	De Spijker	**36**
Havana	**8**	De Steeg	**22**
Het Hok	**80**	De Tap	**71**
Het Land van Walem	**5**	Terzijde	**55**
Huyschkaemer	**99**	Vive la Vie	**29**
Café Klein Wiener Wad	**98**	Café de Wetering	**104**
De Koe	**34**	De Zotte Proeflokaal	**33**

COFFEESHOPS

Borderline	**48**
The Bulldog	**76**
Free I	**42**
Global Chillage	**54**
't Kruydenhuysje	**65**
Mellow Yellow	**107**
The Otherside	**12**
Stix	**59**

TEASHOPS

Backstage	**111**
Bagels & Beans	**39**
Coffee & Jazz	**112**
Gary's Muffins (Prinsengracht)	**69**
Gary's Muffins (Reguliersdwarsstr.)	**11**
Metz	**7**
Café Panini	**101**
Pompadour Patisserie	**1**
Sarah's Grannies	**91**
Studio 2	**4**

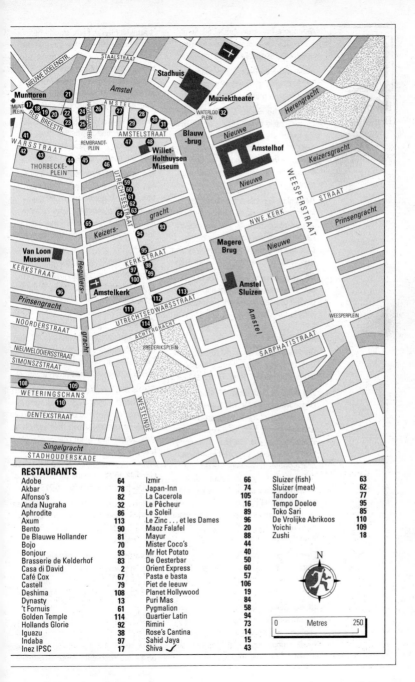

RESTAURANTS

Adobe	64	Izmir	66	Sluizer (fish)	63
Akbar	78	Japan-Inn	74	Sluizer (meat)	62
Alfonso's	82	La Cacerola	105	Tandoor	77
Anda Nugraha	32	Le Pêcheur	16	Tempo Doeloe	95
Aphrodite	86	Le Soleil	89	Toko Sari	85
Axum	113	Le Zinc . . . et les Dames	96	De Vrolijke Abrikoos	110
Bento	90	Maoz Falafel	20	Yoichi	109
De Blauwe Hollander	81	Mayur	88	Zushi	18
Bojo	70	Mister Coco's	44		
Bonjour	93	Mr Hot Potato	40		
Brasserie de Kelderhof	83	De Oesterbar	50		
Casa di David	2	Orient Express	60		
Café Cox	67	Pasta e basta	57		
Castell	79	Piet de leeuw	106		
Deshima	108	Planet Hollywood	19		
Dynasty	13	Puri Mas	84		
't Fornuis	61	Pygmalion	58		
Golden Temple	114	Quartier Latin	94		
Hollands Glorie	92	Rimini	73		
Iguazu	38	Rose's Cantina	14		
Indaba	97	Sahid Jaya	15		
Inez IPSC	17	Shiva	43		

Eating and Drinking

Monopole Taveerne, Amstel 60. Semi-leather bar, popular with both tourists and locals, especially on hot afternoons.

Montmartre de Paris, Halvemaansteeg 17. A convivial brown café, with the emphasis on music and entertainment.

Much Macho, Amstel 102. Bar with an older clientele in the early evening, shifting towards a younger public later at night. Music varies from Dutch and German *schlagers* to house music. Occasional live performances and strippers.

De Spijker, Kerkstraat 4. Leather and jeans bar which made a name for itself with its twice-monthly, safe sex jack-off parties. These are now a thing of the past, but they do show porn movies and there's still a darkroom. Open from 1pm.

De Steeg, Halvemaansteeg 10. Camp and often outrageous small bar. Can be packed at peak times, when everyone joins in the singalongs.

Coffeeshops

Borderline, Amstelstraat 37. Opposite the *iT* disco, with gently bouncing house beats. Open until 2.30am Fri & Sat.

The Bulldog, Leidseplein 15; Korte Leidsedwarsstraat 49. The biggest and most famous of the coffeeshop chains, and a long way from its pokey Red Light District dive origins. The main Leidseplein branch (the Palace), housed in a former police station, has a large cocktail bar, coffeeshop, juice bar and souvenir shop, all with separate entrances. It's big and brash, not at all the place for a quiet smoke, though the dope they sell (packaged up in neat little brand-labelled bags) is reliably good.

Free I, Reguliersdwarsstraat 70. Tiny place that looks and feels like an African mud hut, except for the hip-hop beats. Grass specialists.

Global Chillage, Kerkstraat 51. Celebrated slice of Amsterdam dope culture, always comfortably filled with tie-dyed stoneheads propped up against the walls, so chilled they're horizontal.

't Kruydenhuysje, Keizersgracht 665. One of the best general coffeeshops in the city – in an old canal house on a quiet stretch of the Keizersgracht near Rembrandtplein, with a welcoming atmosphere, good dope and a wonderful little terrace. Highly recommended.

Mellow Yellow, Vijzelgracht 33. Sparse but bright coffeeshop with a small but good-quality dope list. A little out of the way, but makes up for it in friendliness.

The Otherside, Reguliersdwarsstraat 6. Gay coffeeshop (in Dutch, "from the other side" is a euphemism for gay). Despite stiff competition from its more established neighbours, it's managed to find a niche. Mostly men, but women welcome.

Stix, Utrechtsestraat 21. The quietest branch of an Amsterdam institution in dope-smoking; other locations in the Red Light District.

Tearooms

Backstage, Utrechtsedwarsstraat 67. Run by former cabaret stars the Christmas Twins (Greg and Gary), this offbeat place also sells knitwear and African jewellery.

Bagels & Beans, Keizersgracht 504. The latest bagel eatery, *B&B* makes some of the most creative and delicious snacks, attracting a young public: their version of strawberries and cream cheese is a big favourite in the summer. The "Beans" part of the name refers to the coffee you can have to accompany your bagel. Also a branch in the South (see p.213).

Coffee & Jazz, Utrechtsestraat 113. Small, soulless café serving small rolls and coffee, with a selection of jazz playing in the background.

Gary's Muffins, Prinsengracht 454; Reguliersdwarsstraat 53. The first New York bagels in town, with big, American-style cups of coffee (and half-price refills) and wonderful fresh-baked muffins. Reguliersdwarsstraat branch open until 3am.

Metz, Keizersgracht 455. Wonderful café on the top floor of the Metz department store, giving panoramic views over the canals of Amsterdam. Pricey, but then in Metz you're not supposed to care.

Café Panini, Vijzelgracht 3. Tearoom-cum-restaurant with good sandwiches, plus pasta dishes in the evening.

Pompadour Patisserie, Huidenstraat 12. A great patisserie specializing in hand-made chocolates.

Sarah's Grannies, Kerkstraat 176. Quiet and elegant place with a small gallery, serving good breakfasts and lunches. Caters mostly, but not exclusively, for women. Sunday mornings are a delight.

Studio 2, Singel 504. Pleasantly situated, airy tearoom with a delicious selection of rolls and sandwiches. Recommended.

The Jordaan

All the following places are marked on the map on p.210.

Bars and cafés

Chris, Bloemstraat 42. Very proud of itself for being the Jordaan's (and Amsterdam's) oldest bar, dating from 1624. Comfortable, homely atmosphere.

Daalder, Lindengracht 90. A drinking place, normally filled with locals, which makes a good alternative to *De Tuin*.

Doll's Place, Vinkenstraat 57. A mixed bar popular with anyone who wants a late-night drink.

Duende, Lindengracht 62. Wonderful little tapas bar, with regular flamenco perfor-mances.

Du Lac, Haarlemmerstraat 118. Very appealing Art Deco grand café, with plenty of foliage.

Gambit, Bloemgracht 20. Chess bar, with boards laid out all day until midnight.

De Kat in de Wijngaert, Lindengracht 160. Hefty *bessenjenevers* and an entic-ing name, "Cat in the Vineyard".

Koophandel, Bloemgracht 49. Empty before midnight, this is the early-hours bar you've dreamed of, in an old ware-house on one of Amsterdam's most pic-turesque canals. Open until at least 3am, often later.

't Monumentje, Westerstraat 120. Unspectacular Jordaan local haunt that plays good music. Likeable and inexpen-sive.

Nol, Westerstraat 109. Probably the epit-ome of the jolly Jordaan singing bar, a luridly lit dive, popular with Jordaan gangsters and ordinary Amsterdammers alike. Opens and closes late, especially at weekends, when the back-slapping joviality and drunken singalongs keep you here until closing time.

De Reiger, Nieuwe Leliestraat 34. The Jordaan's main meeting place, an old-style café filled with modish Amsterdammers. Affordable food.

Saarein, Elandsstraat 119. Notorious for years for its stringent women-only policy, *Saarein* has recently opened its doors to men. Though some of the former glory of this café is gone, it's still a warm, relaxing place to take it easy, with a cheerful atmosphere. Also a useful starting point for contacts and information. Closed Mon.

Café SAS, Marnixstraat 79. An artists' bar and café backing onto a canal, open all day, with couches, armchairs and all kinds of cosiness, enhanced after dark by candlelight.

't Smalle, Egelantiersgracht 12. Candle-lit and comfortable, with a barge out front for relaxed summer afternoons. One of the highlights of the city.

Soundgarden, Marnixstraat 164. Alternative grunge bar, packed with peo-ple and noise, with a canalside terrace as a retreat.

De Tuin, 2e Tuindwarsstraat 13. The Jordaan has some marvellously unpre-tentious bars, and this is one of the best: agreeably unkempt and always filled with locals.

Café West Pacific, Westergasfabriek, Haarlemmerweg 8; tram #10 to Van Limburg. Large bar-restaurant with an open fireplace, attracting a hip young crowd of Amsterdammers. Mutates into a disco after 11pm.

Eating and Drinking

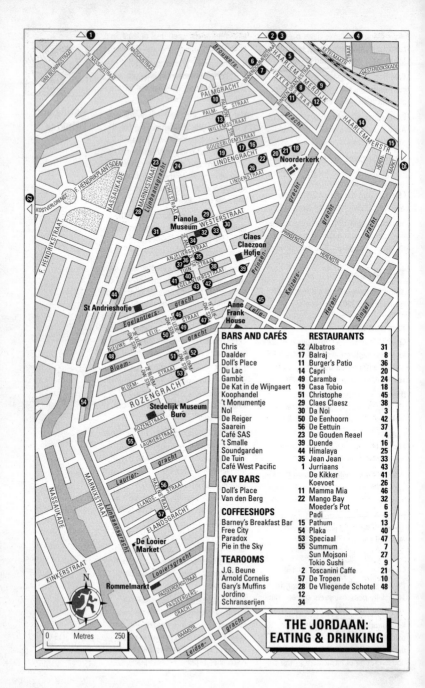

BARS AND CAFÉS

Chris	52
Daalder	17
Doll's Place	11
Du Lac	14
Gambit	49
De Kat in de Wijngaert	19
Koophandel	51
't Monumentje	29
Nol	30
De Reiger	50
Saarein	56
Café SAS	23
't Smalle	39
Soundgarden	44
De Tuin	35
Café West Pacific	1

GAY BARS

Doll's Place	11
Van den Berg	22

COFFEESHOPS

Barney's Breakfast Bar	15
Free City	54
Paradox	53
Pie in the Sky	55

TEAROOMS

J.G. Beune	2
Arnold Cornelis	57
Gary's Muffins	28
Jordino	12
Schranserijen	34

RESTAURANTS

Albatros	31
Balraj	8
Burger's Patio	36
Capri	20
Caramba	24
Casa Tobio	18
Christophe	45
Claes Claesz	38
Da Noi	3
De Eenhoorn	42
De Eettuin	37
De Gouden Reael	4
Duende	16
Himalaya	25
Jean Jean	33
Jurriaans	43
De Kikker	41
Koevoet	26
Mamma Mia	46
Mango Bay	32
Moeder's Pot	6
Padi	5
Pathum	13
Plaka	40
Speciaal	47
Summum	7
Sun Mojsoni	27
Tokio Sushi	9
Toscanini Caffe	21
De Tropen	10
De Vliegende Schotel	48

THE JORDAAN: EATING & DRINKING

Gay bars

Doll's Place, Vinkenstraat 57. See main listings, p.209. A little off the beaten "gay" track.

Van den Berg, Lindengracht 95. Likeable local café with good food and a billiard table. Frequented mainly by gays and lesbians.

Coffeeshops

Barney's Breakfast Bar, Haarlemmerstraat 102. Not exactly a coffeeshop, but not exactly a café either, *Barney's* is simply the most civilized place in town to enjoy a big joint with a fine breakfast.

Free City, Marnixstraat 233. Crowded coffeeshop done up in *Mad Max* style and favoured by local "professional" smokers.

Paradox, 1e Bloemdwarsstraat 2. If you're fed up with the usual coffeeshop food offerings of burgers, cheeseburgers or double cheeseburgers, *Paradox* satisfies the munchies with outstanding natural food, including spectacular fresh fruit concoctions. Closes 8pm.

Pie in the Sky, 2e Laurierdwarsstraat 64. Beautiful canal-corner setting, great for outside summer lounging.

Tearooms

J.G. Beune, Haarlemmerdijk 156. Age-old chocolatier with a tearoom attached.

Arnold Cornelis Elandsgracht 78. Confectioner with a snug tearoom.

Gary's Muffins, Marnixstraat 121. Branch of the New York bagel-and-muffin teashop, with the biggest cups of coffee around. Sunday newspaper heaven.

Jordino, Haarlemmerdijk 25. Small tearoom with an enormous variety of chocolates, pastries and ice cream – heaven for anyone with a sweet tooth.

Schranserijen, 2e Anjeliersdwarsstraat 6. Small place with very tasty hot chocolate.

The Old Jewish Quarter and Plantagebuurt

All the following places are marked on the map on p.212.

Bars and cafés

De Druif, Rapenburgerplein 83. Possibly the city's first bar, and one of its most beguiling, yet hardly anyone knows about it. Its popularity with the locals lends it a village pub feel.

East of Eden, Linnaeusstraat 11. A wonderfully relaxed little place right near the Tropenmuseum. Appealing combination of high-ceilinged splendour and gently waving palm trees, with James Dean thrown in on top. Well worth a sunny afternoon.

Entredok, Entrepotdok 64. Perhaps the best of a growing number of bars in this up-and-coming area. The clientele hails from the surrounding hi-tech offices, though increasingly from the residential blocks in between, too.

De Groene Olifant, Sarphatistraat 126. Metres from the Muiderpoort, this is a characterful old wood-panelled brown café, with floor-to-ceiling windows and an excellent, varied menu.

't IJ, in the De Gooyer windmill, Funenkade 7. The beers (*Natte*, *Zatte* and *Struis*), brewed on the premises, are extremely strong. A fun place to drink yourself silly. Wed–Sun 3–8pm.

Café 't Sluyswacht, Jodenbreestraat 1. A tiny, leaning hut with water on three sides, which has somehow survived the upheavals to hit the Jodenbreestraat. Opposite the Rembrandt House.

Tisfris, St Antoniesbreestraat 142. Colourful, split-level café and bar near the Rembrandt House, and minutes from Waterlooplein. Youthful and popular.

The Museum Quarter and the Vondelpark

All the following places are marked on the map on p.214.

Bars and cafés

't Blauwe Theehuis, Vondelpark 5. Beautiful tearoom/café housed in a circular building from the De Stijl period. Serves a decent range of rolls, pies etc to accompany your tea, as well as beer

Eating and Drinking

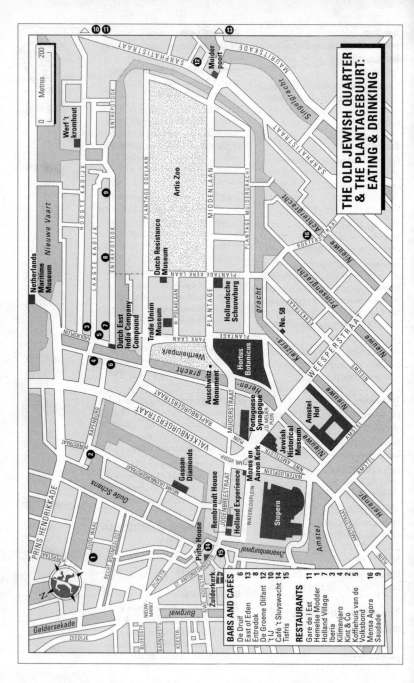

THE OLD JEWISH QUARTER & THE PLANTAGEBUURT: EATING & DRINKING

BARS AND CAFÉS

De Druif	6
East of Eden	13
Entredok	8
De Groene Olifant	12
't IJ	10
Café 't Sluyswacht	14
Tisfris	15

RESTAURANTS

Gare de l'Est	11
Hemelse Modder	7
Holland Village	3
Iberia	4
Kilimanjaro	2
Kint & Co	5
Koffiehuis van de Volksbond	16
Mensa Agora	9
Saudade	9

and nachos. The most relaxing of the terraces in the Vondelpark, open from 9am till late.

Café Ebeling, Overtoom 52. Alternative, but not overly raucous, bar within a few minutes of Leidseplein, housed in an old bank – with the toilets in the vaults.

Helfensteyn, Overtoom 28. Popular and agreeable *eetcafé* about a 5min walk from Leidseplein. Food is a little pricey though.

Kasbah, Amstelveenseweg 134. Squat bar, part of the OCCII venue (see p.232), with candles, atmosphere and cheap drinks.

Keyser, Van Baerlestraat 96 ☎671 1441. In operation since 1905, and right next door to the Concertgebouw, this café/restaurant exudes *fin-de-siècle* charm, with ferns, gliding bow-tied waiters, and a dark, carved-wood interior. Prices are slightly above average, especially for the food, but a wonderful place nonetheless. You'll need to make bookings for the restaurant, and dress accordingly. Closed Sun.

Café Vertigo, Vondelpark 3. Attached to the Film Museum, this is a wonderful place to while away a sunny afternoon (or take refuge from the rain), with a spacious interior and a large terrace overlooking the park.

Welling, J.W. Brouwersstraat 32. Supposedly the traditional haunt of the gloomy Amsterdam intellectual, *Welling* is usually packed solid with performers and visitors from the Concertgebouw next door.

Wildschut, Roelof Hartplein 1. Large and congenial bar famous for its Art Deco trimmings. Not far from the Concertgebouw, with the Amsterdam School architecture all around.

The South

All the following places are marked on the map on p.214.

Bars and cafés

Duvel, 1e van der Helststraat 59. An *eetcafé* on a pedestrianized street adjacent to Albert Cuypstraat. Handy if you've come to shop in the market.

Hesp, Weesperzijde 130. Quite a way out, but with a real old-fashioned atmosphere and rarely any tourists. Frequented by hacks from the nearby *Volkskrant, Trouw* and *Parool* newspapers.

Café Krull, Sarphatipark 2. On the corner of 1e van der Helststraat, a few metres from the Albert Cuyp, this is an atmospheric place on a lively corner, serving drinks, snacks and jazz all day long from 11am.

O'Donnells, Ferdinand Bolstraat 5. The best Guinness in town, in an established Irish pub just behind the Heineken brewery. A seemingly limitless interior worms its way back into the building.

Coffeeshops

Greenhouse, Tolstraat 4; Waterlooplein 345. Consistently sweeps the boards at the annual Cannabis Cup, with medals for its dope as well as "Best Coffeeshop". Tolstraat is a way down to the south (tram #4), but worth the trek: if you're only buying once, buy here.

Katsu, 1e van der Helststraat 70. Tatty, neighbourhood coffeeshop just off the Albert Cuyp market, with excellent weed and a 1970s music collection.

Yo-Yo, 2e Jan van der Heijdenstraat 79. About as local as it's possible to get. Down in the Pijp, to the east of the Sarphatipark, a small, airy little place to seek out smoking solitude.

Tearooms

Granny, 1e van der Helststraat 45. Just off the Albert Cuyp market, with terrific *appelgebak* and *koffie verkeerd*.

Bagels & Beans, Ferdinand Bolstraat 70. The southern branch of this popular bagel joint, just opposite the Albert Cuyp – see p.208 for more details.

Restaurants

Amsterdam may not be Europe's culinary capital – Dutch cuisine is firmly rooted in the meat, potato and cabbage school of

Eating and Drinking

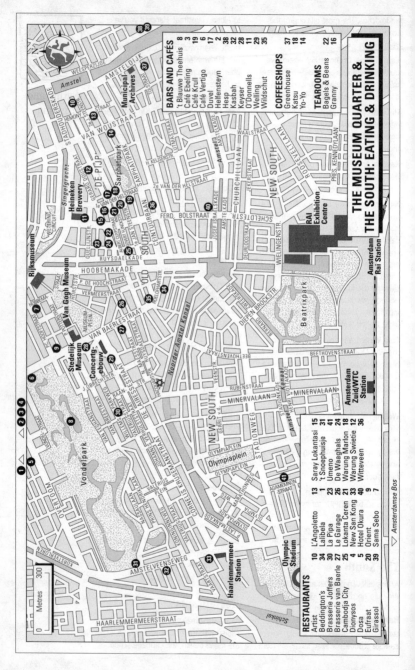

THE MUSEUM QUARTER & THE SOUTH: EATING & DRINKING

BARS AND CAFES

't Blauwe Theehuis	8
Café Ebeling	3
Café Krull	19
Café Vertigo	6
Duvel	17
Helfensteyn	2
Hesp	38
Kasbah	32
Keyser	28
O'Donnells	11
Welling	29
Wildschut	35

COFFEESHOPS

Greenhouse	37
Katsu	18
Yo-Yo	14

TEAROOMS

Bagels & Beans	22
Granny	16

RESTAURANTS

Artist	10	Saray Lokantasi	15
Beddington's	34	't Snoephuisje	1
Brasserie Joffers	23	Umeno	41
Brasserie van Baerle	27	De Waaghals	24
Cambodja City	25	Warung Marlon	18
Dionysos	4	Warung Swietie	12
Dosa	20	Witteveen	36
Eufraat	9		
Girassol	39		

L'Angoletto	10	
Lalibela	34	
La Pipa	23	
Le Garage	26	
Lokanta Ceren	21	
New San Kong	33	
Hotel Okura	5	
Orient	20	
Sama Sebo	39	

Budget eating

Listed here are a few places where it's possible to fill up for under ƒ13 per person, which is the least you can expect to pay for a meal in Amsterdam. Check out, too, the pancake places on p.219 and the food delivery box on p.227.

Eating and Drinking

Amigo, p.226. Surinamese.

Bojo, reviewed on p.224. Indonesian.

Het Beeren, p.218. Dutch.

Keuken van 1870, p.218. Dutch.

Mensa Agora, Roeterstraat 11 ☎525 2699 (map p.212). Self-service student cafeteria, with all that that entails. Mon–Fri noon–2pm & 5–7pm.

Mensa Atrium, Oudezijds Achterburgwal 237 ☎525 3999 (map pp.198–199). Central self-service cafeteria attached to the University of Amsterdam (but open to all) – full meals for under ƒ10, though the quality leaves a little to be desired. Mon–Fri noon–2pm & 5–7pm.

Maoz Falafel, Reguliersbreestraat 45 ☎624 9290 (map pp.206–207). The best street-food in the city – mashed chickpea balls deep-fried and served in Middle Eastern bread, with as much salad as you can eat, for the grand sum of ƒ6. Other branches at Leidsestraat and Ferdinand Bolstraat. Mon–Thurs & Sun 11am–2am, Fri & Sat 11am–3am.

Mr Hot Potato, Leidsestraat 44 ☎623 2301 (map pp.206–207). The only place in town for baked potatoes – nothing fancy, but cheap at around ƒ5. Daily 10am–8pm.

New King, p.218. Chinese.

La Place, part of Vroom & Dreesman department store, Kalverstraat 201 ☎622 0171 (map pp.198–199). Self-service buffet-style restaurant, where it's easily possible to fill up for under ƒ12. Daily 10am–9pm.

Rimini, p.225. Italian.

Suzy Creamcheese, p.228. Vegetarian.

Toko Sari, p.224. Indonesian takeaway.

---

cooking – but as a recompense, the country's colonial adventures have ensured there's a wide range of non-Dutch **restaurants**: Amsterdam is acclaimed for the best Indonesian food outside Indonesia, at prices which – by big-city standards – are hard to beat. Other cuisines from around the world are also well represented: aside from close-at-hand French, Spanish and Italian influences, there are some fine Chinese and Thai restaurants, and a growing number of Moroccan and Middle Eastern places, as well as many covering the range of Indian cuisine. Amsterdam also excels in the quantity and variety of its *eetcafés* and bars, which serve increasingly adventurous food, quite cheaply, in a relaxed and unpretentious setting.

The reviews of restaurants and *eet-cafés* that follow are grouped alphabetically by cuisine. We've indicated the average cost for a main course without drinks within each listing, but as a broad guide, very few places charge more than ƒ35 for a main dish; in fact you can often get a sizeable, quality meal at many *eetcafés* and smaller restaurants for ƒ20 or less. Bars and cafés are also worth checking out: many serve food, and at lunchtime it's possible to fill up cheaply with a bowl of soup or a French bread sandwich.

The majority of *eetcafés* are **open** all day; most restaurants open at 5 or 6pm. The Dutch eat out early – very rarely later than 9pm – and restaurants normally close their doors at 10 or 11pm, though you'll still be served if you're already installed. Times can vary a little according to season or how busy things are that night. Vegetarian restaurants tend to close even earlier than this. Unless indicated otherwise, all the places we've listed are open seven days a week, from 5 or 6pm until 10 or 11pm.

Eating and Drinking

At anywhere we've described as Moderate or Expensive, it's sensible to call ahead and reserve a table. Larger restaurants will probably take major credit cards, but eetcafés and smaller restaurants almost certainly won't. All restaurant and café bills include 17.5 percent sales tax as well as a fifteen percent service charge. **Tipping** on top of this is completely optional, though usually expected – if service merits it, the custom is generally to hand some change directly to your server rather than adding it to the bill.

One thing all visitors to the city should be aware of is the practice of several restaurants in and around the tourist centre of Leidseplein of refusing to serve a glass of ordinary water with a meal, insisting that you pay for mineral water instead. This is a policy of, among others, the famous, and otherwise worthwhile, Indonesian restaurant *Bojo*. If this is important to you, check with the staff before you sit down: there is absolutely no reason why any restaurant shouldn't give you a glass of water, and ones that refuse to do so don't deserve your money or goodwill.

Budget: Under ƒ20/€9
Inexpensive: ƒ20–30/€9–13.50
Moderate: ƒ30–40/€13.50–18
Expensive: Over ƒ40/€18

Prices are the average cost per person for a main course without drinks.

African and Middle Eastern

Artist, 2e Jan Steenstraat 1 ☎671 4264 (map p.214). A small Lebanese restaurant just off Albert Cuypstraat. Inexpensive.

Axum, Utrechtsedwarsstraat 85 ☎622 8389 (map pp.206–207). Small Ethiopian eetcafé, open from 2pm, with a choice of fifteen authentic dishes. Budget.

Beyrouth, Kinkerstraat 18 ☎616 0635. Small Lebanese place out in the Old

West and well off any beaten tracks; lacking in atmosphere, but the food is highly regarded. Tram #3 or #12 to Kinkerstraat, or #7 or #17 to Bilderdijkstraat. Closed Tues. Inexpensive.

Eufraat, 1e van der Helststraat 72 ☎672 0579 (map p.214). Basic eetcafé in the midst of the cosmopolitan Pijp district, serving Syrian food which just about translates to the very un-Syrian setting. Daily 11am–midnight. Inexpensive.

Indaba, Utrechtsestraat 96 ☎421 3852 (map pp.206–207). Authentic South African interior, and, with the likes of zebra, ostrich and kudu on the menu, authentic flavours too; the cook brings the food to your table. Popular so make a reservation. Moderate.

Kilimanjaro, Rapenburgerplein 6 ☎622 3485 (map p.212). Bright African restaurant in a bedraggled part of town, serving such delicacies as Tanzanian antelope, Moroccan *tajine* and Ethiopian pancakes. Small, simple and super-friendly. Closed Mon. Moderate.

Lalibela, 1e Helmersstraat 249 ☎683 8332 (map p.214). Another excellent Ethiopian restaurant, with a well-balanced menu and attentive service. Tram #1 or #6 to Jan Pieter Heyenstraat. Inexpensive.

Pygmalion, Nieuwe Spiegelstraat 5a ☎420 7022 (map pp.206–207) Good spot for both lunch and dinner, popular among locals. South African dishes include crocodile steaks, and there's a good selection of sandwiches. Moderate.

The Americas

Alfonso's, Korte Leidsedwarsstraat 69 ☎627 0580 (map pp.206–207). Substantial helpings of relatively bland Mexican food; vegetarian dishes. Good value for Leidseplein, and not too touristy, but avoid the margaritas as they're watery and overpriced. Mon–Fri 5–10.30pm, Sat & Sun noon–10.30pm. Inexpensive.

Caramba, Lindengracht 342 ☎627 1188 (map p.210). Steamy, busy Mexican restaurant in the heart of the Jordaan.

The margaritas are almost on a par with *Rose's* (see below). Inexpensive.

Castell, Lijnbaansgracht 252 ☎622 8606 (map pp.206–207). Cosy restaurant with an old brown hearth and homely atmosphere, serving barbecued food. The cocktails certainly hit their mark. Fri & Sat until 1.30am. Moderate.

Iguazu, Prinsengracht 703 ☎420 3910 (map pp.206–207). For carnivores only: a superb Argentinian–Brazilian restaurant, with perhaps the best fillet steak in town. Daily noon–midnight. Moderate.

Mexico, Prinsengracht 188 ☎624 6538 (map p.202). A cheaper and more amiable alternative to the glossier central eateries. Jolly owners, excellent food. Inexpensive.

Mister Coco's, Thorbeckeplein 8 ☎627 2423 (map pp.206–207). Bustling, determinedly youthful American restaurant that lives up to its own slogan of "lousy food and warm beer". Cheap, though (try the all-you-can-eat spare ribs), and very lively. Inexpensive.

Café Pacifico, Warmoesstraat 31 ☎624 2911 (map pp.198–199). Quality array of Mexican (and Mexican–Californian) food, in a cramped and crowded little joint only minutes from Centraal Station. Moderate.

Planet Hollywood, Reguliersbreestraat 35 ☎427 4277 (map p.000). Amsterdam outlet of the jazzed up burger joint, though not one of the city's better deals at around ƒ25 for a burger. A last resort option. Inexpensive.

Poco Loco, Nieuwmarkt 24 ☎624 2937 (map pp.198–199). Cajun split-level restaurant with a friendly, cheerful atmosphere, and a menu including burritos, steaks and jambalaya. Inexpensive.

Rose's Cantina, Reguliersdwarsstraat 38 ☎625 9797 (map pp.206–207). In the heart of trendy Amsterdam, this Mexican restaurant qualifies as possibly the city's most crowded, which includes the garden terrace at the back. No bookings, and you'll almost certainly have to wait; but it's no hardship to sit at the bar nursing a cocktail and watching the would-be cool bunch. The margaritas

should carry a public health warning. Moderate.

Rosen & Tortilla's, Prinsengracht 126 ☎620 6525 (map p.202). Atmospheric Mexican restaurant serving the usual main courses, as well as a good range of tapas. Its location right by the water makes it a good place to eat in the summer. Open 10am–1am. Inexpensive.

Chinese, Thai, Filipino and Korean

Adobe, Utrechtsestraat 42 ☎625 9251 (map pp.206–207). A good introduction to Korean cooking. Closed Mon. Moderate.

Cambodja City, Albert Cuypstraat 58–60 ☎671 4930 (map p.214). Thai and Vietnamese restaurant serving delicious meat fondues, soups and prawn dishes, run by a friendly, but no-nonsense, lady who provides good service. Inexpensive–Moderate.

Dynasty, Reguliersdwarsstraat 30 ☎626 8400 (map pp.206–207). Festive choice of Indo-Chinese food, with Vietnamese and Thai options; not for the shoestring traveller. Subdued atmosphere suits the prices (average ƒ75). Closed Tues. Expensive.

Hoi Tin, Zeedijk 122 ☎625 6451 (map pp.198–199). One of the best places to choose in Amsterdam's rather dodgy Chinatown, this is a constantly busy place with an enormous menu (in English too) including some vegetarian dishes. Worth a try. Daily noon–midnight. Moderate.

De Klaes Compaen, Raamgracht 9 ☎623 8708 (map pp.198–199). Good Thai food at affordable prices. Daily 5–9.45pm. Moderate.

Lana Thai, Warmoesstraat 10 ☎624 2179 (map pp.198–199). Among the best Thai restaurants in town, with seating overlooking the water of Damrak. Quality food, chic surroundings but high prices (ƒ40–50). Closed Tues. Expensive.

Mango Bay, Westerstraat 91 ☎638 1039 (map p.210). Small, intimate Filipino restaurant with laid-back service and fairly reasonable prices (there's a set three-course menu for just over ƒ40). Moderate.

Eating and Drinking

Eating and Drinking

New King, Zeedijk 115 ☎ 625 2180 (map pp.198–199). Extraordinary range of cheap Chinese dishes – don't count on quality, but your wallet will approve. Free limitless jasmine tea. Daily noon–midnight. Budget.

New San Kong, Amstelveenseweg 338 ☎ 662 9370 (map p.214). Don't be put off by the ranch-style decor; the Cantonese food is excellent and not too pricey (try the dim sum). Take tram #24 to the end of the line. Daily noon–10pm. Moderate.

Pathum, Willemsstraat 16 ☎ 624 4936 (map p.210). Cheap and cheerful Thai place, out in the Jordaan. Closed Tues. Inexpensive.

Tom Yam, Staalstraat 22 ☎ 622 9533 (map pp.198–199). High-quality Thai restaurant in the middle of town. Branches at Prinsengracht 42 and Utrechtsestraat 55 do takeaways. Moderate–Expensive.

Top Thai, Herenstraat 22 ☎ 623 4463 (map p.202) and 2e Const. Huygenstraat 64 ☎ 683 1297. A popular pair of restaurants that boast some of the best Thai food in Amsterdam, with spicy, authentic dishes at a good price, and a friendly atmosphere. For complete burn-out try one of their chilli salads. Inexpensive.

Dutch

De Blauwe Hollander, Leidsekruisstraat 28 ☎ 623 3014 (map pp.206–207). Dutch food in generous quantities – something of a boon in an otherwise touristy, unappealing part of town. Expect to share a table. Inexpensive.

Claes Claesz, Egelantiersstraat 24 ☎ 625 5306 (map p.210). Exceptionally friendly Jordaan restaurant that attracts a good mixed crowd and serves excellent Dutch food. Live music from Thursday to Saturday, and Sunday's "theatre-dinner" sees various Dutch theatrical/musical acts between the courses. Often has (pricey) special menus to celebrate occasions like Easter or the Queen's Birthday. Closed Mon. Moderate.

De Eenhoorn, 2e Egelantiersdwarsstraat 6 ☎ 623 8352 (map p.210). A less

attractive alternative to *De Eettuin* (see below) but just down the road, so handy if it's full. Inexpensive.

> **Budget**: Under ƒ20/€9
> **Inexpensive**: ƒ20–30/€9–13.50
> **Moderate**: ƒ30–40/€13.50–18
> **Expensive**: Over ƒ40/€18
>
> *Prices are the average cost per person for a main course without drinks.*

De Eettuin, 2e Tuindwarsstraat 10 ☎ 623 7706 (map p.210). Hefty portions of Dutch food, with salad from a serve-yourself bar. Non-meat eaters can content themselves with the large, if dull, vegetarian plate, or the delicious fish casserole. Inexpensive.

Haesje Claes, Spuistraat 275 ☎ 624 9998 (map pp.198–199). Dutch cuisine at its best. Extremely popular – go early to get a table. Daily noon–10pm. Moderate.

Het Beeren, Koningsstraat 15 ☎ 622 2329 (map pp.198–199). Daily 5.30–9.30pm. Huge portions of the simplest Dutch fare – cabbage, mashed potato and steaming stew. Budget.

Hollands Glorie, Kerkstraat 220 ☎ 624 4764 (map pp.206–207). Welcoming place with a good selection of Dutch dishes and attentive service. Inexpensive.

Keuken van 1870, Spuistraat 4 ☎ 624 8965 (map pp.198–199). Former soup kitchen in the heart of the city, still serving Dutch meat-and-potato staples. Frill-free. Mon–Fri 12.30–8pm, Sat & Sun 4–9pm. Budget.

Koevoet, Lindenstraat 17 ☎ 624 0846 (map p.210). The "Cow's-Foot" – or, alternatively, the "Crowbar" – is a traditional Jordaan *eetcafé* serving unpretentious food at good prices. Closed Mon. Budget.

Moeder's Pot, Vinkenstraat 119 ☎ 623 7643 (map p.210). Ultra-cheap, basic Dutch food, the quality of which is a rather hit-and-miss affair. Vegetarians should steer clear of the touted vegetarian dish. A good place if you're looking

Pancakes

In the tradition of simple cooking, **pancakes** are a Dutch speciality – for fillers and light meals, you'd be hard pushed to find better. Although there are plenty of places dotted around town, those listed below are recommended.

Bredero, Oudezijds Voorburgwal 244 ☎622 9461 (map pp.198–199). On the edge of the Red Light District, one of the city's best-value pancake places. June–Sept daily noon–10pm, Oct–May times vary according to the number of customers, often only open at weekends. Budget.

Le Soleil, Nieuwe Spiegelstraat 56 ☎622 7147 (map pp.206–207). Pretty little restaurant (once visited by the Queen) which makes some great pancakes – try one with ginger and raisins. Open until 6pm. Budget.

The Pancake Bakery, Prinsengracht 191 ☎625 1333 (map p.202). Open all day, in a beautiful old house on the canal. A large selection of (filled) pancakes from ƒ10, many big enough to count as a meal. Daily noon–9.30pm. Budget.

Pannekoekhuis Upstairs, Grimburgwal 2 ☎626 5603 (map pp.198–199). Minuscule place in a tumbledown house opposite the university buildings, with sweet and savoury pancakes at low prices. Student discount. Wed–Fri noon–7pm, Sat & Sun noon–6pm. Budget.

't Snoephuisje, Vondelpark 7 ☎664 5091 (map p.214). Peaceful pancake eatery on the Amstelveen side of the Vondelpark, which has a lovely terrace in the summer where you can eat pancakes and watch the kids in the nearby playground. April–Oct daily 11am–8pm; Nov–March Sat & Sun noon–5pm. Budget.

De Vergulde Lantaarn, Niewendijk 145 ☎624 5413 (map pp.198–199). Old-fashioned pancake house, which isn't perhaps the best, but handy if you're shopping at the Nieuwendijk. Also serves steaks, omelettes and rolls. Daily 9am–7pm. Inexpensive.

for authentic atmosphere though. Mon–Sat 5–9.30pm. Budget.

Oud Holland, Nieuwezijds Voorburgwal 105 ☎624 6848 (map pp.198–199). Basic, down-the-line Dutch staples (cabbage-and-potato stew, pea soup, etc) in a seventeenth-century building. Mon–Sat noon–9.30pm. Inexpensive.

Piet de Leeuw, Noorderstraat 11 ☎623 7181 (map pp.206–207). Amsterdam's best steakhouse, dating from the Forties. Excellent steaks, and a mouthwatering Dame Blanche dessert. Mon–Fri noon–11pm, Sat & Sun 5–11pm. Inexpensive.

De Silveren Spiegel, Kattengat 4 ☎624 6589 (map pp.198–199). There's been a restaurant in this location since 1614, and 'The Silver Mirror" is one of the best in the city, with a delicately balanced menu of Dutch cuisine. The proprietor lives on the coast and brings in the fish himself. Spectacular food, with a cellar of 350 wines to complement it. Four-course dinner for two at a table set with silver is a cool ƒ200, though you can get away with around ƒ77,50 each. Closed Sun. Expensive.

Witteveen, Ceintuurbaan 256 ☎662 4368 (map p.214). Held in high regard by locals, this is a thoroughly Dutch, highly atmospheric place for Amsterdam cooking, though not cheap at upwards of ƒ35. Also has a bar if you just want to go for a drink. Moderate–Expensive.

't Zwaantje, Berenstraat 12 ☎623 2373 (map p.202). Old-fashioned Dutch restaurant with a nice atmosphere and well-cooked, reasonably priced food. Moderate.

Fish

Albatros, Westerstraat 264 ☎627 9932 (map p.210). Family-run restaurant serving

Eating and Drinking

some mouth-wateringly imaginative fish dishes. A place to splash out and linger over a meal. Closed Wed. Expensive.

Brasserie de Kelderhof, Lange Leidsedwarsstraat 53 ☎622 0682 (map pp.206–207). Extension of the well-known Prinsengracht restaurant, serving delicious fish dishes in a modern and light Mediterranean setting. Daily noon–10.30pm. Moderate.

Kopke Adega, Koggestraat 1 ☎622 4587 (map pp.198–199). Another Mediterranean-style fish restaurant, which also has a bar serving tapas from 4pm. Moderate.

Le Pêcheur, Reguliersdwarsstraat 32 ☎624 3121 (map pp.206–207). Beautiful restaurant with a well-balanced menu (the four-course set menu is good value at around ƒ70). Lovely garden terrace in the summer. Open for lunch. Closed Sun. Moderate.

Lucius, Spuistraat 247 ☎624 1831 (map pp.198–199). Pricey at around ƒ60 for two courses, but one of the best fish restaurants in town. Their speciality is seafood, but the diverse menu includes wonderful smoked salmon and a vast array of all kinds of fish, delicately prepared. Very popular. Closed Sun. Expensive.

De Oesterbar, Leidseplein 10 ☎626 3463 (map pp.206–207). Veteran restaurant overlooking the Leidseplein action, popular with a largely older clientele. Worth it if everywhere else is full, particularly, of course, if you're an oyster fan. Daily noon–midnight. Moderate.

Sluizer, Utrechtsestraat 45 ☎626 3557 (map pp.206–207). Next door to its trendy meat-based partner (see p.222), serving simply prepared fish (though not always of the highest quality). Moderate.

Werkendam, St Nicolaasstraat 43 ☎428 7744 (map pp.198–199). Stylish, affordable restaurant in one of the alleys running from Nieuwzijds Voorburgwal to Nieuwendijk, largely frequented by local professionals. Efficient and friendly staff. Inexpensive.

French and Belgian

1e Klas Grand Café Restaurant, Platform 2b, Centraal Station ☎625 0131 (map pp.198–199). An unlikely setting, but offering good-value (ƒ40 and up) gourmet French cuisine from a well-balanced menu in this deeply atmospheric, restored late nineteenth-century restaurant. Expensive.

Beddington's, Roelof Hartstraat 6 ☎676 5201 (map p.214). Refined French cuisine blended with Japanese delicacy – always original, never disappointing. The subtlety of flavours is matched by Japanese-inspired presentation (especially for the fish dishes), and a meal here can be memorable, though not cheap at ƒ90 or so for a couple of courses. Closed Sun. Expensive.

Bistro de Vlier, Prinsengracht 422 ☎623 2281 (map p.202). Fairly basic cooking in an affable atmosphere. Inexpensive.

Bonjour, Keizersgracht 770 ☎626 6040 (map pp.206–207). Classy French cuisine in a romantic setting; particularly good charcoal-grilled dishes. Set menus from ƒ45. Closed Mon & Tues. Moderate.

Bordewijk, Noordermarkt 7 ☎624 3899 (map p.202). A chic restaurant serving stylish French cuisine – a favourite of Johannes van Dam, Amsterdam's most famous food critic. Moderate–Expensive.

Brasserie Joffers, Willemsparkweg 163 ☎673 0360 (map p.214). Small café-like brasserie with a terrace at the front, serving delicious soups and poultry dishes. Mon–Fri 8am–10pm, Sat 8am–6pm, Sun 9am–6pm. Moderate.

Brasserie van Baerle, Van Baerlestraat 158 ☎679 1532 (map p.214). Light and airy restaurant serving good food; set up by a couple of ex-KLM flight attendants. Very popular, especially on Sun. Closed Sat. Moderate–Expensive.

Café Cox, Marnixstraat 427 ☎620 7222 (map pp.206–207). Stylish but amicable bar and restaurant underneath the Stadsschouwburg, serving a wide range of dishes. Inexpensive.

Chez Georges, Herenstraat 3 ☎626 3332 (map p.202). A highly-rated upmarket Belgian eatery, with all the meat that entails; dishes ƒ45 and up. Closed Wed & Sun. Expensive.

Budget: Under ƒ20/€9
Inexpensive: ƒ20–30/€9–13.50
Moderate: ƒ30–40/€13.50–18
Expensive: Over ƒ40/€18

Prices are the average cost per person for a main course without drinks.

Christophe, Leliegracht 46 ☎625 0807 (map p.210). Classic Michelin-starred restaurant on a quiet and beautiful canal, drawing inspiration from the olive-oil-and-basil flavours of southern France and the chef's early years in North Africa. His aubergine terrine with cumin has been dubbed the best vegetarian dish in the world. Reservations far outstrip capacity. Expect to pay ƒ50–60 for two courses. Closed Sun. Expensive.

't Fornuis, Utrechtsestraat 33 ☎626 9139 (map pp.206–207). A slightly cheaper alternative to *Orient Express* (see p.222), though it's usually very busy. Moderate.

Gare de l'Est, Cruciusweg 9 ☎463 0620 (map p.212). Restaurant with one set menu only (with a vegetarian option) which is proving a popular new idea in Amsterdam. Enchanting candle-lit interior, with solid dark wooden tables. Way out in the eastern district: tram #10 to Zeeburgerdijk, then a 5min walk over the bridge to Panamaweg. Expensive.

De Gouden Reael, Zandhoek 14 ☎623 3883 (map p.210). Fine French food (ƒ40 and up) in a unique setting up in the western harbour. The bar, as described in the novel of the same name by Jan Mens, has a long history of association with the dockworkers. Mon–Fri noon–10pm, Sat 5–10pm. Expensive.

Hemelse Modder, Oude Waal 9 ☎624 3203 (map pp.198–199). Tasty meat, fish and vegetarian food in French–Italian style at reasonable prices in an informal

atmosphere. Highly popular (especially among the gay community). Closed Mon. Moderate.

Holland Village, Entrepotdok 7 ☎421 5393 (map p.212). A huge, friendly restaurant which caters for large groups (though smaller groups and couples are also welcome) and so tends to be very lively, with plenty of folk singing and dancing. The three-course set menu consists of high-quality French cuisine, and, though it's not cheap at ƒ135 per person, this includes as many drinks as you can handle. Fri & Sat (booking only).

Intermezzo, Herenstraat 28 ☎626 0167 (map p.202). Good French–Dutch cooking at above-average prices, but worth every penny. Closed Sun. Moderate.

In de Waag, Nieuwmarkt ☎422 7772 (map pp.198–199). Comfortable and stylish Belgian café-restaurant with uniformed staff. Daily 10am–12am. Moderate.

Jean Jean, 1e Anjeliersdwarsstraat 12 ☎627 7153 (map p.210). Simple, local Jordaan restaurant, with sizeable portions and friendly service. Inexpensive.

Jurriaans, Egelantiersgracht 72 ☎622 7887 (map p.210). Friendly French-Belgian restaurant serving steaks and grilled fare to a mixed clientele. Also has a bar with seven draught beers on tap. Inexpensive.

De Kikker, Egelantiersstraat 128 ☎627 9198 (map p.210). Two-tier, top quality restaurant that has a downstairs *eetcafé*. Upstairs is only really accessible to the well-dressed, wealthy and committed gourmet. Well equipped for dining in groups. Moderate.

Kint & Co, Peperstraat 10 ☎627 0280 (map p.212). Very attractive restaurant slightly out of the way in a relatively unexplored corner of Amsterdam. Well presented Mediterranean food. Closed Wed. Inexpensive–Moderate.

Koffiehuis van de Volksbond, Kadijksplein 4 ☎622 1209 (map p.212). Formerly a Communist Party café and apparently the place where the local

Eating and Drinking

Eating and Drinking

dockworkers used to receive their wages, this is now an Eastern Islands neighbourhood restaurant, with variable food. Budget–Inexpensive.

Le Garage, Ruysdaelstraat 54 ☎679 7176 (map p.214). This elegant restaurant is popular with a media crowd and their hangers-on, since it's run by a well-known Dutch TV cook. An eclectic French and Italian menu; call to reserve a week ahead, dress to impress and bring at least ƒ60 or so per person. Daily 6–11pm, Mon–Fri also noon–2pm. Expensive.

Le Zinc . . . et les Dames, Prinsengracht 999 ☎622 9044 (map pp.206–207). Wonderfully atmospheric little place serving good quality, simple fare for an average of ƒ45; there's a particularly good wine list. Closed Mon & Sun. Expensive.

De Lieve, Herengracht 88 ☎624 9635 (map p.202). Belgian restaurant with a pleasant atmosphere, although reports of the food (from ƒ40 upwards) are mixed. Expensive.

Luden, Spuistraat 304 ☎622 8979 (map pp.198–199). Excellent French restaurant that does fine value *prix fixe* menus, for which you can expect to pay ƒ40–55, as well as a more moderately priced à la carte menu and brasserie. Moderate.

Orient Express, Utrechtsestraat 29 ☎620 5129 (map pp.206–207). Not cheap, but very good French food; you can choose from the monthly menu of French-flavoured dishes from each of the countries the Orient Express train passes through. Closed Mon. Moderate.

Proust, Noordermarkt 4 ☎623 9145 (map p.202). Another *eetcafé* in the Jordaan. The food is average, but they do cater for vegetarians and the location is wonderful. Daily 11am–1pm & 6–11pm. Inexpensive.

Quartier Latin, Utrechtsestraat 49 ☎622 7419 (map pp.206–207). Small, cosy place, good for a quiet, romantic dinner. Undemanding food and service. Closed Mon. Moderate.

Sluizer, Utrechtsestraat 43 ☎622 6376 (map pp.206–207). French-oriented food,

in one of Amsterdam's most atmospheric restaurants. There's a fish restaurant of the same name next door – see p.220. Daily noon–3pm & 5pm–midnight. Moderate.

D'Theeboom, Singel 210 ☎623 8420 (map p.202). Classic, ungimmicky French cuisine – around ƒ50 for two courses. Moderate–Expensive.

Toutcourt, Runstraat 13 ☎625 8637 (map p.202). Restaurant run by one of the Fagel brothers, whose refined French cuisine is renowned in Holland. Try the calf's sweetbread and tongue in carrot-ginger mousse. Expensive.

Fusion cuisine

Blakes, Keizersgracht 384 ☎530 2010 (map p.202). Overpriced restaurant in the newly-opened *Blakes* hotel, which is open to the public. Japanese-style decorated interior, with some Dutch extras, while the food is a fusion of Japanese, Thai and European styles. Expensive.

Inez IPSC, Amstel 2 ☎639 2899 (map pp.206–207). Glitzy first-floor restaurant overlooking the flower market, Munt and Amstel and frequented by arty professionals. Deliciously sweet fusion menu. Daily noon–3pm & 7–11.30pm. Expensive.

Palmers, Zeedijk 4 ☎427 0551 (map pp.198–199). French fusion restaurant (set up, according to the menu, by an ex-aviator who crashed over Greenland and married an Eskimo) with such dishes as grilled salmon in coriander and soy sauce. Inexpensive.

Summum, Binnendommersstraat 13 ☎770 0407 (map p.210). Another fusion menu, this time mixing North African and Asiatic spices with French/Italian flavours – try the ricotta limecake with sugared tomatoes dessert. Closed Mon. Moderate.

De Tropen, Palmgracht 39 ☎421 5528 (map p.210). A small French fusion restaurant, with a menu to match, but the food is perfectly flavoured, using ingredients from all over the world. An open kitchen, so you can view the action. Closed Mon & Tues. Budget–Inexpensive.

Greek, Balkan and Turkish

Aphrodite, Lange Leidsedwarsstraat 91 ☎ 622 7382 (map pp.206–207). Refined Greek cooking in a street where you certainly wouldn't expect it. Fair prices too. Daily 5pm–midnight. Inexpensive.

Dionysos, Overtoom 176 ☎ 689 4441 (map p.214). Good Greek restaurant a little to the south of Leidseplein, with the distinct added advantage of serving until 1am. Phone ahead if you're going to turn up after midnight. Daily 5pm–1am. Inexpensive.

Izmir, Kerkstraat 66 ☎ 627 8239 (map pp.206–207). Cosy, family-run little Turkish place; welcoming atmosphere and fine kebabs. Daily 5pm–midnight. Inexpensive.

Lokanta Ceren, Albert Cuypstraat 40 ☎ 673 3524 (map p.214). Authentic and well-populated local Turkish place, with a welter of *meze* to suit all tastes and fine kebab dishes. Let the *raki* flow. Daily 2pm–1am. Inexpensive.

Ouzeri, De Clercqstraat 106 ☎ 618 1412. Greek *eetcafé* in the Old West where you can compose your own meal and make it as cheap – or as expensive – as you like. Tram #12, #13 or #14 to E. Wolffstraat. Daily 5pm–12.30am.

Plaka, Egelantiersstraat 124 ☎ 627 9338 (map p.210). Enormous plates of greasy Greek grub; vegetarian dishes too. Popular (either book ahead or turn up early) and friendly. Daily 5pm–midnight. Inexpensive.

Saray Lokantasi, Gerard Doustraat 33 ☎ 671 9216 (map p.214). Excellent Turkish eatery down in the Pijp neighbourhood. Popular with students. Moderate.

Budget: Under ƒ20/€9
Inexpensive: ƒ20–30/€9–13.50
Moderate: ƒ30–40/€13.50–18
Expensive: Over ƒ40/€18

Prices are the average cost per person for a main course without drinks.

Turquoise, Wolvenstraat 22 ☎ 624 2026 (map p.202). Good Turkish restaurant with a beautiful long bar, giving it a café-like atmosphere. Inexpensive.

Indian

Akbar, Korte Leidsedwarsstraat 33 ☎ 624 2211 (map pp.206–207). Fabulous South Indian food, especially strong on tandoori, with a fine choice across the board. Plenty for veggies. Friendly service. Daily 5–11.30pm. Moderate.

Balraj, Binnen Oranjestraat 1 ☎ 625 1428 (map p.210). Small, old musty place serving reasonable food for a good price. Budget.

Dosa, Overtoom 146 ☎ 616 4838 (map p.214). Halfway along the Vondelpark, a cheap restaurant on the corner serving Southern- as well as the more usual Northern-style cuisine. Budget.

Himalaya, Haarlemmerstraat 11 ☎ 622 3776 (map p.210). Cosy and welcoming atmosphere, with a good selection to choose from. Inexpensive.

Koh-I-Noor, Westermarkt 29 ☎ 623 3133 (map p.202). One of the city's better Indian restaurants, deservedly popular, though recently they've suffered a bit of a decline. Take-away too. Inexpensive.

Mayur, Korte Leidsedwarsstraat 203 ☎ 623 2142 (map pp.206–207). Decent traditional restaurant in a tacky part of town. The chefs, hailing from New Delhi, have set up a well-balanced menu, which thankfully compensates for the slightly inattentive service. Moderate.

Poorna, Hartenstraat 29 ☎ 623 6772 (map p.202). The speciality here is spicy tandoori; they also sell Indian silk paintings. Inexpensive.

Shiva, Reguliersdwarsstraat 72 ☎ 624 8713 (map pp.206–207). The city's most outstanding Indian restaurant in terms of quality and price, with a wide selection of dishes, all expertly prepared. Vegetarians well catered for. Highly recommended. Inexpensive.

Tandoor, Leidseplein 19 ☎ 623 4415 (map pp.206–207). Doesn't live up to its

Eating and Drinking

Eating and Drinking

reputation, but pretty good nonetheless. The tandoori dishes are very tasty, and won't break the bank. Inexpensive.

Indonesian

Anda Nugraha, Waterlooplein 339 ☎626 6064 (map pp.206–207). Lively restaurant serving moderately spicy Indonesian food. Well prepared dishes using fresh ingredients, but the selection is small. There's a very pleasant terrace in the summer. Inexpensive.

Bojo, Lange Leidsedwarsstraat 51 ☎622 7434 (map pp.206–207). Also round the corner at Leidsekruisstraat 12. Possibly the best-value – though certainly not the best – Indonesian place in town. Recommended for the young, lively atmosphere, but the food is very much a hit-and-miss affair, and you'll have to wait a long time both for a table and service. Mon–Wed 4pm–2am, Thurs & Sun noon–2am, Fri & Sat noon–4am. Budget.

Cilubang, Runstraat 10 ☎626 9755 (map p.202). Small restaurant, with a friendly atmosphere, serving well-presented spicy dishes. Moderate.

Kantjil en de Tijger, Spuistraat 291 ☎620 0994 (map pp.198–199). High-quality food averaging around ƒ55 per person, served in a stylish wood-panelled grand café. Moderate–Expensive.

Orient, Van Baerlestraat 21 ☎673 4958 (map p.214). Excellently prepared dishes, with a wide range to choose from; vegetarians are very well taken care of, and the service is generally good. Expect to pay around ƒ45 for a *rijsttafel*. Moderate–Expensive.

Padi, Haarlemmerdijk 50 ☎625 1280 (map p.210). Small Indonesian *eetcafé* with a small selection and rather tacky ambience, but very reasonable prices. Inexpensive.

Puri Mas, Lange Leidsedwarsstraat 37 ☎627 7627 (map pp.206–207). Exceptionally good value for money, on a street better known for rip-offs. Friendly and informed service preludes spectacular *rijsttafels*, both meat and vegetarian. Recommended. Moderate.

Sahid Jaya, Reguliersdwarsstraat 26 ☎626 3727 (map pp.206–207). Excellent restaurant where you can eat outside surrounded by a beautiful flower garden. Helpful and friendly staff. Moderate.

Sama Sebo, P.C. Hooftstraat 27 ☎662 8146 (map p.214). Amsterdam's best-known Indonesian restaurant, especially for its *rijsttafel* – although the prices may initially put you off, it's easy to eat quite reasonably by choosing à la carte dishes, and the food is usually great. Closed Sun. Inexpensive–Moderate.

Sie Joe, Gravenstraat 24 ☎624 1830 (map pp.198–199). Small café-restaurant which is great value for money. The menu is far from extensive, but made of well-prepared, simple dishes such as *gado gado, sateh, rendang* and soups. Mon–Sat 11am–7pm, Thurs till 8pm. Budget.

Speciaal, Nieuwe Leliestraat 142 ☎624 9706 (map p.210). Generally agreed to be one of the better Indonesian places in this price range. Inexpensive.

Tempo Doeloe, Utrechtsestraat 75 ☎625 6718 (map pp.206–207). Reliable, quality place close to Rembrandtplein. As with all Indonesian restaurants, be guided by the waiter when choosing – some of the dishes are very hot indeed. Moderate.

Toko Sari, Kerkstraat 161 ☎623 2364 (map pp.206–207). Fabulous Indonesian takeaway. Tues–Sat 11am–6pm. Budget.

Italian

Burger's Patio, 2e Tuindwarsstraat 12 ☎623 6854 (map p.210). Despite the name (the site used to be occupied by a butcher's), there isn't a burger in sight in this young and convivial vegetarian Italian restaurant where you compose your own main course from several given options. Inexpensive.

Capri, Lindengracht 61 ☎624 4940 (map p.210). Good café-restaurant with much of the joyful atmosphere of the neighbouring market. Inexpensive.

Casa di David, Singel 426 ☎624 5093 (map pp.206–207). Solid-value dark wood Italian restaurant with a long-standing reputation, although we have had some complaints about the service. Pizzas from wood-fired ovens, fresh hand-made pasta, and more substantial fare. Best seats are by the window. Moderate.

Da Noi, Haarlemmerdijk 128 ☎620 1409 (map p.210). A friendly open-kitchen restaurant where two chefs prepare three- or five-course dinners, from an à la carte menu. A place to settle down for the evening and enjoy Italian food beyond pasta and pizza. Expensive.

L'Angoletto, Hemonystraat 2 (map p.214). Everyone's favourite Italian, always packed out – as you'll see from the condensation on the two big windows; the long wooden tables and benches create a very sociable atmosphere. Not everything they make is on the card so keep an eye on the glass showcase in front of the kitchen for any specials. No bookings, so just turn up and hope for the best. Closed Sat. Inexpensive.

Mamma Mia, 2e Leliedwarsstraat 13 ☎638 7286 (map p.210). Good selection of pizzas, in a pleasant, family atmosphere. Budget–Inexpensive.

Pasta e basta, Nieuwe Spiegelstraat 8 ☎422 2229 (map pp.206–207). Fresh pasta dishes only; the staff, all singers and musicians, belt out various arias as they go about their business. Expensive.

Prego, Herenstraat 25 ☎638 0148 (map p.202). Small restaurant serving exceptionally high-quality Mediterranean cuisine for ƒ65 or so for two courses. Polite and friendly staff. Daily 6–10pm. Expensive.

Budget: Under ƒ20/€9
Inexpensive: ƒ20–30/€9–13.50
Moderate: ƒ30–40/€13.50–18
Expensive: Over ƒ40/€18

Prices are the average cost per person for a main course without drinks.

Rimini, Lange Leidsedwarsstraat 75 ☎622 7014 (map pp.206–207). Surprisingly cheap pizza and pasta, most of it well prepared. Daily 3–11.30pm. Budget.

Toscanini Caffe, Lindengracht 75 ☎623 2813 (map p.210). Authentic food prepared in front of your eyes; very popular, so book ahead. At least ƒ55 per person for two courses. Expensive.

Vasso, Roozenboomsteeg 12 ☎626 0158 (map pp.198–199). Authentic, creative restaurant on the corner of het Spui, housed in three curvy sixteenth-century buildings. Polite and attentive service. Moderate.

Japanese

Bento, Kerkstraat 148 ☎422 4248 (map pp.206–207). Superbly prepared vegetarian and vegan macrobiotic dishes, with fish options. Choice of authentic *tatami* seating (cross-legged at a low table) or a boring table-and-chair. Closed Mon. Moderate–Expensive.

Hotel Okura, Ferdinand Bolstraat 333 ☎678 7111 (map p.214). The two restaurants in this five-star hotel – the sushi restaurant *Yamazato*, and the grill-plate restaurant *Teppan-Yaki Sazanka* – serve the finest Japanese cuisine in the city. Reckon on at least ƒ95 per person. Both are also open for lunch noon–2.30pm. Expensive.

Japan-Inn, Leidsekruisstraat 4 ☎675 9892 (map pp.206–207). Warm and welcoming restaurant in the middle of the Leidseplein buzz. Inexpensive.

Stereo Sushi, Jonge Roelensteeg 4 ☎777 3010 (map pp.198–199). Funky sushi restaurant whose accessories include tip-up chairs to make space for a dance-floor and small TV screens in the toilets showing cult movies and Manga films. DJ until 3am on Fridays and Saturdays, otherwise till 1am. Open from 7pm. Inexpensive.

Tokio Sushi, Haarlemmerdijk 28 ☎638 5677 (map p.210). Good-quality fresh-sushi restaurant, with very competitive prices (starting from ƒ2,75). Also does takeaway. Mon–Sat noon–9pm. Inexpensive.

Eating and Drinking

Eating and Drinking

Umeno, Agamemnonstraat 27 ☎676
6089 (map p.214). Down in the residential New South, but with cooking and
prices that are well worth the journey.
Closed Mon. Tram #24. Moderate.

Yoichi, Weteringschans 128 ☎622 6829
(map pp.206–207). High-class (at least
ƒ45 per person) Japanese cuisine in an
improbable dark-brown, old Dutch
atmosphere. Closed Wed. Expensive.

Zushi, Amstel 20 ☎330 6882 (map
pp.206–207). High-tech sushi bar, serving
colour-coded dishes on a conveyor belt
running along the bar. Daily noon–midnight. Inexpensive.

Spanish and Portuguese

Casa Tobio, Lindengracht 31 ☎624
8987 (map p.210). Small Jordaan restaurant that doles out vast servings of
Spanish food; cut costs and risk annoy-
ing the management by sharing a paella
for two among three – a good general
rule for all Spanish places. There have
been reports of surliness, though. Closed
Wed. Inexpensive.

Centra, Lange Niezel 29 ☎622 3050
(map pp.198–199). Cantina with a wonderful selection of Spanish food, master-
fully cooked, genially served and in the
running for Amsterdam's best. Daily
1–11pm. Inexpensive.

Duende, Lindengracht 62 ☎420 6692
(map p.210). Wonderful little tapas bar
up in the Jordaan, with good, cheap
tapas (ƒ3–8 each) to help your drink go
down. Also includes a small venue in
the back for live dance and music performances. Mon–Thurs 4pm–1am, Fri
4pm–2am, Sat 2pm–2am, Sun
2pm–1am. Budget.

Girassol, Weesperzijde 135 ☎692 3471
(map p.214). Close to Amstel Station, this
place is a fair hike out from the centre,
but easily merits the journey. A friendly,
family-run Portuguese restaurant that
Amsterdam foodies have cottoned on to.
Inexpensive.

Iberia, Kadijksplein 16 ☎623 6313 (map
p.212). A little more expensive than
some of the others listed here, but good

service and great food. Moderate.

La Cacerola, Weteringstraat 41 ☎626
5397 (map pp.206–207). Small and
secluded, with likeable if eccentric service – and erratic opening hours.
Wed–Fri 6.30–10pm. Moderate.

La Pipa, Gerard Doustraat 50 ☎679
2318 (map p.214). A great favourite with
the Spanish community in Amsterdam
with good food, sometimes accompanied by spontaneous flamenco performances.

Saudade, Entrepotdok 36 ☎625 4845
(map p.212). Portuguese restaurant out
to the east of the centre, with authentic
cooking in an appealing canalside setting. Mon & Wed–Sun noon–10pm.
Moderate.

Budget: Under ƒ20/€9
Inexpensive: ƒ20–30/€9–13.50
Moderate: ƒ30–40/€13.50–18
Expensive: Over ƒ40/€18

*Prices are the average cost per
person for a main course without
drinks.*

Surinamese and Caribbean

Amigo, Rozengracht 5 ☎623 1140 (map
p.202). Basic, but good value-for-money
Surinamese restaurant close to the
Westerkerk. Tues–Sun 2–10pm. Budget.

Kam Yin, Warmoesstraat 6 ☎625 3115
(map pp.198–199). Cheap, if not terribly
cheerful, Surinamese–Chinese diner close
to Centraal Station. Daily noon–midnight.
Budget.

Riaz, Bilderdijkstraat 193 ☎683 6453.
Out in the Old West, an excellent
Surinamese restaurant. Tram #3 or #12
to Kinkerstraat or #7 or #17 to
Bilderdijkstraat. Mon–Fri 1–9pm, Sun
2–9pm. Inexpensive.

Rum Runners, Prinsengracht 277 ☎627
4079 (map p.202). Caribbean-style
bar/restaurant situated in the old
Westerkerk hall. Expensive cocktails but
well-priced if not always devastatingly
tasty food. Moderate.

Warung Marlon, 1e van der Helststraat 55 ☎671 1526 (map p.214). Surinamese takeaway and popular hangout for lunch, rapidly gaining a loyal clientele. Lively atmosphere. Mon & Wed–Sun 11am–8pm. Budget.

Warung Swietie, 1e Sweelinckstraat 1 ☎671 5833 (map p.214). Cheap and cheerful Surinamese–Javanese *eetcafé*. Closed Wed. Daily 11am–9pm. Budget.

Vegetarian and natural

Bento, Kerkstraat 148 ☎622 4248 (map pp.206–207). See "Japanese" listings, p.225. Book ahead. Closed Mon. Moderate–Expensive.

Bolhoed, Prinsengracht 60 ☎626 1803 (map p.202). Something of an Amsterdam institution. Familiar vegan and vegetarian options from the daily

changing menu, with organic beer to wash it down. More expensive than you might imagine. Daily noon–10pm. Moderate.

Burger's Patio, 2e Tuindwarsstraat 12 ☎623 6854 (map p.210). See "Italian" listings, p.224. Inexpensive.

Deshima, Weteringschans 65 ☎625 7513 (map pp.206–207). A little difficult to spot (it's in the basement), this is actually a macrobiotic food store, with a small restaurant attached. Mon–Fri noon–2pm. Inexpensive.

Golden Temple, Utrechtsestraat 126 ☎626 8560 (map pp.206–207). Laid-back place with a little more soul than the average Amsterdam veggie joint. Well-prepared, lacto-vegetarian food (without sugar and milk) and pleasant, attentive service. Walk out satisfied. No

Eating and Drinking

Food Delivery

Having food **delivered** to your door is still far from the norm in Amsterdam, and so something of a rarity. As well as the places listed below, there are many **pizza lines**, which deliver pizza for free in response to a telephone call. However, the quality of these varies dramatically, and you shouldn't expect anything better than basic. Pizzas usually start at around ƒ14; phone numbers include ☎623 5539 and ☎675 0736. All food delivery lines open in the late afternoon, and most close down by 10pm.

Belgenlijn (☎468 8805, fax 8806) are a Belgian food delivery service, including various starters, main courses and desserts, plus a wine list. The telephone number is frequently engaged, so try faxing – once you get through it is well worth it.

Koh-I-Noor (☎623 3133) deliver good-quality, reasonably priced Indian food (see p.223).

Mousaka Express (☎675 7000) are just what you'd expect, with a long delivery menu of Greek speciality dishes; mousaka starts at ƒ15 (vegetarian from ƒ13.50), but they've got everything from ƒ6 taramasalata to a ƒ55 mixed grill for two.

Ontbijt Service (☎616 1613; orders taken 24hr; daily delivery 6am–1pm) have a range of breakfasts for home or

hotel delivery, ranging from ƒ49 for two people for standard fare (bread, cheese, egg, orange juice, tea/coffee, fruit etc), up to ƒ99 for lots of everything for two, with meat, fish and a bottle of champagne on top.

Porto Ercole (☎624 7654) have a wide range of all kinds of Italian food for delivery, from cold and hot *antipasti* through twenty styles of pizza, fresh home-made pasta and lasagne, to fillet steak and a fine tiramisu. Drop by Vijzelstraat 97 to pick up a menu.

Terang Boelan (☎620 9974) will deliver a *rijsttafel* and other Indonesian specialities to your door for around ƒ25.

Two in One (☎612 8488) have excellent, reasonably priced Indian and Surinamese food for delivery, at a rough average of ƒ15 per person.

Eating and Drinking

alcohol and non-smoking throughout. Inexpensive.

Oininio, Prins Hendrikkade 20 ☎553 9328 (map pp.198–199). Vegetarian restaurant in a new-age centre, serving dishes made of fresh ingredients brought in daily. The menu changes according to season. Inexpensive–Moderate.

Sun Mojsoni, van Hallstraat 8 ☎682 8496 (map p.210). Family restaurant set up by a group of health-conscious friends, serving wholesome and affordable vegetarian food. Includes a gallery and play area for children. Daily 10am–10pm. Budget.

Suzy Creamcheese, Cliffordstraat 36 ☎682 0411. You can get a full, three-course meal here for ƒ14. The menu changes weekly. Part of a less-than-mainstream community centre up near the Westergasfabriek. Tram #10 to Van Hallstraat. Friday only 6–9pm. Budget.

De Vliegende Schotel, Nieuwe Leliestraat 162 ☎625 2041 (map p.210). Perhaps the best of the city's cheap and whole-some vegetarian restaurants, the "Flying Saucer" serves delicious food in large portions. Lots of space, a peaceful ambience and a good noticeboard. Budget.

Budget: Under ƒ20/€9
Inexpensive: ƒ20–30/€9–13.50
Moderate: ƒ30–40/€13.50–18
Expensive: Over ƒ40/€18

Prices are the average cost per person for a main course without drinks.

De Vrolijke Abrikoos, Weteringschans 76 ☎624 4672 (map pp.206–207). All ingredients, produce and processes are organic or environmentally friendly in this restaurant that serves fish and meat as well as vegetarian dishes. Closed Tues. Inexpensive–Moderate.

De Waaghals, Frans Halsstraat 29 ☎679 9609 (map p.214). Well-prepared organic dishes in this co-operative-run restaurant near the Albert Cuyp. Tues–Sun 5–9.30pm. Inexpensive.

Chapter 11

Entertainment and Nightlife

Although Amsterdam is not generally considered one of the world's major cultural centres, the quality and quantity of music, dance and film on offer here are high – largely thanks to the government's long-term subsidy to the arts. With its uniquely youthful population, the city is at the cutting edge in many ways, though its strengths lie in the graphic arts and new media rather than the performing arts. In fact, there can be a marked lack of daring in Dutch performance, which may have something to do with the stable and homogeneous nature of Dutch society, and its high standard of living. If you spend any time in Amsterdam you're bound to come across plenty of fringe and mainstream events, many of them spontaneous and entertaining, though lacking perhaps the inventiveness or perspective of New York and London. That said, though, Amsterdam buzzes with places offering a wide range of affordable entertainment and you'll never find yourself at a loss for something to do.

INFORMATION AND TICKETS

For information about **what's on**, a good place to start is the **Amsterdam Uitburo**, or **AUB**, the cultural office of the city council, which is housed in a corner of the Stadsschouwburg theatre on Leidseplein (daily 10am–6pm, Thurs until 9pm; ☎ 0900/0191). You can get advice here on anything remotely cultur-

al, as well as tickets and copies of what **listings magazines** there are. Non-Dutch readers have to grapple with the hole left by *Time Out Amsterdam*'s 1996 decision to switch to Internet publication – which has left the city without a single English-language magazine in print. *Time Out*'s weekly updated entertainment pages can now be found at *www.timeout.nl*. Critical paper-printed listings of clubs, live music gigs and film screenings are hard to find, and your best bet, until some enterprising publisher fills the obvious gap, is to keep an eye out for posters, billboards, notices, slips of paper stuck on windows, *anything* advertising upcoming events in the city. One possibility is to try and decipher the bare listings in the AUB's own monthly *Uitkrant*, which is comprehensive and free, but in Dutch; or you could settle for the VVV's bland and uncontroversial English-language *What's On In Amsterdam* (ƒ4). The newspaper *Het Parool*'s Wednesday entertainment supplement, *Uit en Thuis*, is one of the most up-to-date reference sources. Take a look, too, at the AUB's *Uitlijst* noticeboards, which include a weekly update on pop music events, or grab a copy of the *Camel uitlijst* from any café for the latest live music gigs. Any cinema can provide the long, thin, fold-out "Week Agenda", which gives details of all films showing in the city that week (Thursday to Wednesday). Bars and restaurants

Entertainment and Nightlife

often stock similar fortnightly or monthly listings leaflets, most of them sponsored by cigarette companies. *SHARK*, a photocopied pamphlet listing Amsterdam's clubs, bars and cafés, each with a personal review, and including a gay supplement, is available at the Atheneum News Centre at Spui and a few other cafés and bookshops around town.

Tickets for most performances can be bought at the Uitburo (for a ƒ3 fee) and VVV offices, or reserved by phone through the AUB Uitlijn (☎0900/0191) for a one-percent booking fee. You can also buy tickets for any live music event in the country at the GWK bureau de change offices at the Leidseplein and larger train stations, and the post office at Singel 250, again for around a one-percent fee. Obviously the cheapest way to obtain tickets is turn up at the venue itself. Some major performance venues – the Carré, Muziektheater, Stadsschouwburg and others – sell tickets for each other's productions at no extra cost through the Kassadienst plan. If you're under 26, the AUB is the place to go for a **Cultureel Jongeren Passport (CJP)**, which costs ƒ22,50 and gets you reductions on entry to theatres, concerts and *filmhuizen*. Generally the only people eligible for **discounts** at cultural events are students, over-65s (though most places will only take Dutch ID) and CJP cardholders.

Rock, Folk and World Music

As far as **live music** goes, Amsterdam is a regular tour stop for many major artists, and something of a testing ground for current rock bands. Until recently, **Dutch rock** was almost uniformly dire, divided fairly evenly between the traditional songs being belted out in cafés in the Jordaan – a brash and sentimental adaptation of French *chansons* – and anaemic Dutch imitations of English and American groups, singing (unconvincingly) in English. The best place to hear the former – if you must – is still the Jordaan, at cafés such as *Nol* and

the *Twee Zwaantjes*, detailed in the *Eating and Drinking* chapter. As for modern pop and rock, times have mercifully changed, and Dutch groups nowadays can lay claim to both quality and originality. Look out for the celebrated Urban Dance Squad, the Osdorp Posse and other members of the dance/hip-hop scene, or try to catch rock bands like Bettie Serveert. Mathilde Santing is a popular draw whenever she plays. Bear in mind, too, that Amsterdam is often on the tour circuit of up-and-coming British bands – keep a sharp eye on the listings.

With the construction of the brand-new 50,000-seat ArenA out in the southeastern suburbs of the city, Amsterdam has finally gained the stadium **rock venue** it has craved for years. However, the ArenA is taking some time to catch on, and, aside from the Tina Turner/Michael Jackson brand of superstar, most major touring acts still choose to play at Rotterdam's Ahoy sports hall. The three dedicated music venues in Amsterdam city centre – the Paradiso, the Melkweg and the Arena (not to be confused with the ArenA) – are all much smaller, and supply a constantly changing seven-days-a-week programme of music to suit all tastes (and budgets). Alongside the main venues, the city's clubs, bars and multimedia centres sporadically host performances by live bands. As far as **prices** go, for big names you'll pay anything between ƒ40 and ƒ60 a ticket; ordinary gigs cost ƒ10–25, although some places charge a membership (*lidmaatschap*) fee on top. If no price is listed, entrance is usually free.

The Dutch **folk music** tradition in Amsterdam is virtually extinct, although interest has been revived of late by the new duo, Acda and de Munnik, and there are still one or two touring folk singers who perform traditional Jordaan *smartlappen* ("torchsongs") at the Carré theatre. Outside of this however, your best bet is to try and catch the small but thriving scene continuing in a few sympathetic cafés. More accessible is **world music**, for which there are a couple of good venues: the Utrecht-based Network for Non-Western Music (☎030/231 9676) is an organization that regularly brings world music performers to Amsterdam, to play at the Tropenmuseum theatre; and music from around the world is also a regular feature of the Melkweg's programme.

Aside from summer Sundays in the Vondelpark, Amsterdam doesn't have many **outdoor music festivals**; the biggest events are the Drum Rhythm and Racism Beat it Festivals, held in May and August respectively (see p.292), which are multi-venue extravaganzas attracting world-class acts, and of course, for classical music, the Grachtenfestival in the last week of August (see p.292). Of the festivals outside the city, the most famous is the Pink Pop Festival in June, down in the south at the Draf en Renbaan in Landgraaf, near Maastricht. Others include the spring Halfweg Festival in Spaarnwoude, halfway between Amsterdam and Haarlem; the May Goffert Pop in Nijmegen; and the June Park Pop, in The Hague. Dates are variable, so check with the VVV before making plans.

Major venues

Melkweg ("Milky Way"), Lijnbaansgracht 234a ☎624 1777, www.melkweg.nl. Probably Amsterdam's most famous entertainment venue, and these days one of the city's prime arts centres, with a young, hip clientele. A former dairy (hence the name) just round the corner from Leidseplein, it underwent a four-year renovation programme between 1995 and 1999, and now has two separate halls for live music, putting on a broad range of bands covering everything from reggae to rock, all of which lean towards the "alternative". Late on Friday and Saturday nights, excellent off-beat disco sessions go on well into the small hours, sometimes featuring the best DJs in town. As well as the gigs, there's also a fine monthly film programme, a theatre, gallery, and bar and restaurant (Marnixstraat entrance) open Wed–Sun 2–9pm (dinner from 5.30pm).

Concerts start between 9pm and 11pm. **Paradiso**, Weteringschans 6–8 ☎626 4521, www.paradiso.nl. A converted church near the Leidseplein, with bags of atmosphere, featuring bands ranging from the up-and-coming to the Rolling Stones. It has been known to host classical concerts, as well as debates and multimedia events (often in conjunction with the nearby Balie centre). Bands usually get started around 9pm.

Arena, 's-Gravensandestraat 51 ☎694 7444, www.hotelarena.nl. Part of the major reorganization of what used to be the *Sleep-In* hostel, the Arena is a multi-media centre featuring live music and cultural events, and has a bar, coffeeshop and restaurant, while remaining one of the better hostels in the city. Awkwardly located out to the east of the centre (trams #6 and #10), the Arena's intimate hall tends to feature underground bands from around the world. Start time around 9.30pm.

Smaller venues

Akhnaton, Nieuwezijds Kolk 25 ☎624 3396. A "Centre for World Culture", specializing in African and Latin American music and dance parties. On a good night, the place heaves with people.

AMP, KNSM-laan 13 ☎418 1111. Way out in the eastern harbour district, this rehearsal space and recording studio now features live bands at the weekends.

De Buurvrouw, Pieterspoortsteeg 29 ☎625 9654. Eclectic alternative bar featuring loud local bands.

Cruise Inn, Zeeburgerdijk 271 ☎692 7188. Off the beaten track, but with great music from the 1950s and 1960s. Saturday is R&B night.

De Kikker, Egelantiersstraat 130 ☎627 9198. A chic Art Deco place in the middle of the Jordaan, where easy-listening music accompanies the pricey French cuisine. Smooth trios playing bossa nova and French *chansons*; weekends only.

Korsakoff, Lijnbaansgracht 161 ☎625 7854. Late-night performances by some

Entertainment
and Nightlife

Entertainment and Nightlife

All the Irish bars in the city feature live Gaelic music; see Eating and Drinking for details.

of the better-known local grunge bands, in a lively setting with cheap drinks and a post-punk clientele. Free admission.

Last Waterhole, Oudezijds Armsteeg 12 ☎624 4814. In the depths of the Red Light District, this is the favoured spot for Amsterdam's biker set; however, the Dutch variety lacks bark as well as bite, and travellers from the hostel upstairs are welcome at the pool tables or to join the jam sessions onstage.

Maloe Melo, Lijnbaansgracht 163 ☎420 4592. Next door to the *Korsakoff*, a dark, low-ceilinged bar, with a small back room featuring local bluesy acts.

Meander Café, Voetboogstraat 5 ☎625 8430. Daily live music of the soul, funk and blues variety.

Mulligans, Amstel 100 ☎622 1330. Irish bar head and shoulders above the rest for atmosphere and authenticity, with Gaelic musicians and storytellers most nights for free.

OCCII, Amstelveenseweg 134 ☎671 7778. Cosy former squat bar at the far end of the Vondelpark, with occasional live alternative music.

Tropen Instituut Theater, Linnaeusstraat 2 ☎568 8500, *www.kit.nl.theater*. Part of the Tropical Institute, this formal theatre specializes in the drama, dance, film and music of the developing world. A great place for ethnic music and to pick up on acts that you wouldn't normally get to see.

Winston Kingdom, Warmoesstraat 123 ☎623 1380. Adventurous small venue, next to the hotel, featuring everything from live Ghanean percussion and symphonic rock to R&B, punk/noise and club nights. Poetry night once a month on Monday.

Jazz and Latin

For **jazz** fans, Amsterdam can be a treat. Since the 1940s and 1950s, when American jazz musicians began moving to Europe to escape discrimination back home, the city has had a soft spot for jazz (although Paris stole much of the

limelight). Chet Baker lived and died in Amsterdam; he and any number of legendary jazzbos could once be found jamming into the small hours at the *Casablanca* on Zeedijk. Although Zeedijk has been dragged into the 1990s, there's still an excellent range of jazz venues for such a small city, varying from tiny bars staging everything from Dixieland to avant-garde, to the *Bimhuis* – the city's major jazz venue – which plays host to both international names and homegrown talent. Saxophonists Hans Dulfer, Willem Breuker and Theo Loevendie, and percussionist Martin van Duynhoven, are among the **Dutch musicians** you might come across – and they're well worth catching if you get the chance.

It's worth remembering, too, that the Netherlands has one of the best jazz **festivals** in the world, the North Sea Jazz Festival, held in the Congresgebouw in The Hague during July – information from PO Box 87840, 2508 DE The Hague (☎015/215 7756, fax 8393, *www.northseajazz.nl*). Comprising three days and nights of continuous jazz on twelve stages, the festival regularly involves over 700 musicians, among them world-class performers from Oscar Peterson to James Brown, Chuck Berry to Guru's Jazzmatazz. Tickets cost from about ƒ100 a day, with supplements for the big names – although, considering the music on offer, this is still a bargain. Special late-night trains are laid on to bring revellers back to Amsterdam after the gigs – hotel rooms in The Hague are booked up months in advance. October is also a good time to catch jazz, with extra concerts and small festivals held all over the country. If your Dutch is up to it, you can get **information** on jazz events all over Holland by phoning Jazzline on ☎626 7764.

The Dutch connection with Surinam – a former colony tucked in between Venezuela and Brazil – means that there is a sizeable **Latin American** community in the city, and, while some of the Andean buskers on the Leidseplein may verge on the yawn-worthy, there is plenty of authentic salsa and other Latin sounds to be discovered.

Venues

Akhnaton, Nieuwezijds Kolk 25 ☎624 3396. A crowded, lively venue that often puts on Latin music.

Café Alto, Korte Leidsedwarsstraat 115 ☎626 3249. It's worth hunting out this legendary little jazz bar just off Leidseplein for the quality modern jazz every night from 10pm until 3am (and often much later). It's big on atmosphere, though slightly cramped, but entry is free, and you don't have to buy a (pricey) beer to hang out and watch the band.

Bamboo Bar, Lange Leidsedwarsstraat 66 ☎624 3993. Legend has it Chet Baker used to live upstairs and jam onstage to pay his rent. These days the *Bamboo* is an unpretentious, friendly bar with blues and jazz, plus occasional salsa nights. Free entry, but you need to buy a drink. Open from 9pm.

Bimhuis, Oude Schans 73–77 ☎623 1361. The city's premier jazz venue for almost 28 years, with an excellent auditorium and ultra-modern bar. Concerts Thurs–Sat, free sessions Mon–Wed. There's also free live music in the bar on Sun at 4pm. Concert tickets are for sale on the day only.

Bourbon Street, Leidsekruisstraat 6 ☎623 3440. Friendly bar with a relaxed atmosphere and quality blues and jazz nightly until 3am.

Canecao, Lange Leidsedwarsstraat 68 ☎638 0611. A wonderful little place filled with the sounds of samba and salsa – not entirely for the tourists.

Casablanca, Zeedijk 26 ☎625 5685. A shadow of its former self, though still hosting live jazz every night.

De Engelbewaarder, Kloveniersburgwal 59 ☎625 3772. Excellent live jazz sessions on Sunday afternoon and evening.

IJsbreker, Weesperzijde 23 ☎693 9093. Principally a venue for contemporary music (see p.234), but with occasional avant-garde and free-jazz evenings.

Le Maxim, Leidsekruisstraat 35 ☎624 1920. Intimate piano bar that's been going since the Sixties, with live music nightly.

Winston Kingdom, Warmoesstraat 123 ☎625 3912. Theatre-café attached to the *Winston Hotel*, with spoken word and jazz-poetry evenings attracting occasional semi-big-name acts from the US.

Entertainment and Nightlife

Classical Music, Opera and Contemporary Music

There's no shortage of **classical music** concerts in Amsterdam, with two major orchestras based in the city, plus regular visits by other Dutch orchestras. The **Royal Concertgebouw Orchestra** remains one of the most dynamic in the world, and occupies one of the finest concert halls to boot. The other resident orchestra is the **Netherlands Philharmonic**, based at the Beurs van Berlage concert hall, which has a wide symphonic repertoire and also performs with the Netherlands Opera at the Muziektheater. Among visiting orchestras, the Rotterdam Philharmonic and the Utrecht Symphony have world-class reputations, as does the Radio Philharmonic Orchestra, based in Hilversum outside Amsterdam.

As far as **smaller classical ensembles** go, Dutch musicians pioneered the use of period instruments in the 1970s, and Ton Koopman's Amsterdam Baroque Orchestra and Frans Brüggen's Orchestra of the 18th Century are two internationally renowned exponents. Koopman's Amsterdam Baroque Choir and the Amsterdam Bach Soloists are also preeminent. As well as the main concert halls, a number of Amsterdam's churches (and former churches) host regular performances of classical and chamber music – both types of venue are listed below.

The most prestigious venue for **opera** is the Muziektheater (otherwise known as the Stopera) on Waterlooplein, which is home to the Netherlands Opera company – going from strength to strength under the guidance of Pierre Audi – as

Entertainment and Nightlife

well as the National Ballet. Visiting companies sometimes perform here, but more often at the Stadsschouwburg and the Carré theatre.

As far as **contemporary music** goes, the IJsbreker centre on the Amstel is a leading showcase for musicians from all over the world. Local talent is headed by the Asko and Schoenberg Ensembles, as well as the Nieuw Ensemble and the Volharding Orchestra. Look out also for Willem Breuker and Maarten Altena, two popular musicians who successfully combine improvised jazz with composed new music.

The most prestigious multi-venue Dutch festival by far is the annual **Holland Festival** every June (info ☎530 7111), which attracts the best domestic mainstream and fringe performers in all areas of the arts, as well as an exciting international line-up. Otherwise, one of the more interesting music-oriented events is the **piano recital** held towards the end of August on a floating stage outside the *Pulitzer Hotel* on the Prinsengracht – with the whole area floodlit and filled with small boats, and every available spot on the banks and bridges taken up, this can be a wonderfully atmospheric evening. Also around this time – and from two ends of the musical spectrum – Utrecht plays host to the internationally renowned **Early Music Festival**, and Amsterdam holds the **International Gaudeamus Music Week**, a forum for debate and premier performance of cutting-edge contemporary music.

All the major venues listed below, as well as some of the churches, have wheelchair access, though you should call ahead if you need assistance.

Venues

Beurs van Berlage, Damrak 213 ☎627 0466. The splendid interior of the former stock exchange (see p.59 has been put to use as a venue for theatre and music. The resident Netherlands Philharmonic and Netherlands Chamber Orchestra perform in the huge but comfortable Yakult Zaal and the AGA Zaal, the latter a very strange, glassed-in room-within-a-room.

Carré Theatre, Amstel 115–125 ☎622 5225. A splendid hundred-year-old structure (originally built for a circus) which represents the ultimate venue for Dutch folk artists, and hosts all kinds of top international acts: anything from Russian folk dance to *La Cage aux Folles*, with reputable touring orchestras and opera companies squeezed in between.

Concertgebouw, Concertgebouwplein 2–6 ☎671 8345. After a facelift and the replacement of its crumbling foundations in the early 1990s, the Concertgebouw is now looking – and sounding – better than ever. The acoustics of the Grote Zaal (Large Hall) are unparalleled, and a concert here is a wonderful experience. The smaller Kleine Zaal regularly hosts chamber concerts, often by the resident Borodin Quartet. Though both halls boast a star-studded international programme, prices are on the whole very reasonable, rarely over ƒ35, and ƒ20 for Sunday morning events. Free Wednesday lunchtime concerts are held from Sept to May (doors open 12.15pm, arrive early), and in July and August there's a heavily subsidized series of summer concerts. Look out also for occasional swing/jazz nights.

IJsbreker, Weesperzijde 23 ☎668 1805. Out of the town centre by the Amstel, with a delightful terrace on the water. Has a large, varied programme of international modern, chamber and experimental music, as well as featuring obscure, avant-garde local performers. Concerts are occasionally held in the Planetarium of the Artis Zoo.

Marionette Theatre, Nieuwe Jonkerstraat 8 ☎620 8027. A repertoire of Mozart and Offenbach operas performed by marionettes.

Muziektheater, Waterlooplein ☎625 5455. Part of the ƒ306 million complex that includes the city hall. The theatre's resident company, Netherlands Opera, offers the fullest, and most reasonably priced, programme of opera in Amsterdam. Tickets go very quickly. Look out for free lunchtime concerts Sept–May.

Stadsschouwburg, Leidseplein 26 ☎624 2311. These days somewhat overshadowed by the Muziektheater, but still staging significant opera and dance (it's the home theatre of the Netherlands Dance Theatre – see p.237), as well as visiting English-language theatre companies.

The **churches** (and former churches) listed below have regular programmes of chamber and baroque music; others, including the huge **Nieuwe Kerk** on Dam Square, the **Westerkerk**, the **Noorderkerk**, the **Mozes en Aaronkerk** on Waterlooplein, and the tiny **Amstelkerk** on Kerkstraat, as well as numerous small churches out in the residential south and west, occasionally put on one-off concerts, often with very reasonable prices.

Engelse Kerk, Begijnhof 48 ☎624 9665. The church with the biggest programme – three to four performances a week, lunchtime, afternoon and evening, with an emphasis on period instruments.

Oude Kerk, Oudekerksplein 23 ☎625 8284. Hosts organ and carillon recitals, as well as occasional choral events. In summer, in conjunction with the Amstelkring Museum, the church organizes a series of "walking" concert evenings, consisting of three separate concerts at different venues, with time for coffee and a stroll between each.

Waalse Kerk, Oudezijds Achterburgwal 157; information from the Old Music Society on ☎030/236 2236. Weekend afternoon and evening concerts of early music and chamber music.

Theatre and Cabaret

Surprisingly for a city that functions so much in English, there is next to no **English-language drama** to be seen in Amsterdam. The *Stalhouderij* is the only company working in English, performing in a broom-cupboard of a theatre in the Jordaan, although the Theater de Bochel, converted from a bath house, often

hosts visiting productions. Apart from these, a tiny handful of part-time companies put on two or three English productions during the summer; there are also performances by touring groups at the theatres listed below and at other venues dotted around town.

English-language **comedy** and **cabaret**, on the other hand, has become a big thing in Amsterdam, spearheaded by the resident and extremely successful Boom Chicago comedy company. During the summer in particular, a number of small venues host mini-seasons of English-language stand-up comedy and cabaret, with touring British performers (Eddie Izzard played the Nieuwe de la Mar in 1996), and material that's generally targeted at visitors to the city.

Most of Amsterdam's larger theatre companies concentrate either on foreign works in translation or Dutch-language theatre, neither of which is likely to be terribly interesting for the non-Dutch speaker. However, there are plenty of **avant-garde** theatre groups in the city, much of whose work relies on visual rather than verbal impact, as well as one or two companies devoted to **mime** (including the famous Griftheater). We've listed the most likely venues below. Look out also for performances at the Amsterdam Marionette Theatre.

The main **event** to watch out for, apart from the mainstream Holland Festival (see opposite), is the summer-long **Over Het IJ Festival** (info ☎636 1083), a showcase for all kinds of theatre and performance arts at big, often outdoor locations in Amsterdam North (thus "over the IJ"). With a great many interesting fringe companies taking part, including the celebrated Dogtroep, productions are often surprising and exciting. In June, there is also the **International Theatre School Festival** (info ☎626 1241), when the four theatres on Nes, a tiny alley running from Dam Square parallel to Rokin, host productions by local and international theatre schools.

Entertainment and Nightlife

Entertainment and Nightlife

Following is a list of the more important venues that put on **avant-garde and mime** productions. Check the usual listings and information sources for details.

Bellevue, Leidsekade 90 ☎ 624 7248.

De Brakke Grond, Nes 45 ☎ 626 6866. Many Flemish productions.

Cosmic Theater, Nes 75 ☎ 622 8858.

De Engelenbak, Nes 71 ☎ 624 0394.

Felix Meritis, Keizersgracht 324 ☎ 623 1311.

Frascati, Nes 63 ☎ 626 6866.

De Nieuw Amsterdam, Spuistraat 2 ☎ 627 8672. Multicultural focus on non-western productions.

Nieuwe de la Mar, Marnixstraat 404 ☎ 623 3462.

Storkfabriek, Csaar Peterstraat 213 ☎ 419 3088.

Westergasfabriek, Haarlemmerweg 8–10 ☎ 627 9070. Hosts eclectic productions of all kinds.

Venues

Badhuis-Theater de Bochel, Andreas Bonnstraat 28 ☎ 668 5102. A former bath house out near the Oosterpark, this is now a low-profile forum for all kinds of visiting productions and guest directors.

De Balie, Kleine Gartmanplantsoen 10 ☎ 623 2904. A multimedia centre for culture and the arts, located off the Leidseplein, which often plays host to drama, debates, international symposia and the like, sometimes in conjunction with the Paradiso next door.

Boom Chicago, Korte Leidsedwarsstraat 12 ☎ 423 0101. Something of a phenomenon in Amsterdam in recent years, this rapid-fire improv comedy troupe performs nightly to crowds of both tourists and locals, and has received rave reviews from *Rough Guide* readers, the Dutch press and *Time* magazine alike. With inexpensive food, the cheapest beer in town (in pitchers, no less!), and a Smoke Boat Cruise following the show at 10.30pm, the comedy need not be funny – but it is.

Carré Theatre, Amstel 115–125 ☎ 622 5225. A chunky old building on the eastern bank of the Amstel that, aside from its folk associations, hosts all kinds of top international acts, with the emphasis on hit musicals.

Comedy Café, Max Euweplein 29 ☎ 638 3971. Small cabaret theatre with a bar that sometimes hosts English-language acts.

Kleine Komedie, Amstel 56 ☎ 624 0534. One of Amsterdam's oldest theatres, established in 1786, with occasional English-language shows, and performances by the odd pop megastar.

Marionette Theatre, Nieuwe Jonkerstraat 8 ☎ 620 8027. Continues an old European tradition with its performances of operas by Mozart and Offenbach. Although they're touring Holland and the rest of Europe for most of the year, the wooden marionettes return to Amsterdam around May, October and Christmas. Call for details of performances, and to find out about their opera dinners.

Melkweg, Lijnbaansgracht 234a ☎ 624 1777 after 1pm. At the centre of the city's cultural scene, this is often the first-choice venue for foreign touring companies.

Stadsschouwburg, Leidseplein 26 ☎ 624 2311. Often hosts productions on tour from London or New York.

Stalhouderij, Bloemgracht 57/1 ☎ 626 4088. Amsterdam's only non-subsidized English-language theatre company, mounting new productions every six weeks or so in one of the city's smallest, most intimate theatre spaces. Contemporary and modern works, Shakespeare, readings, classes and workshops.

Storkfabriek, Csaar Peterstraat 213
☎ 419 3088. Old factory featuring dance, mime and various theatre groups.

Dance

Of the major **dance companies** based in Amsterdam, the largest and most prestigious is the Muziektheater's National Ballet, under Wayne Eagling – though their critics say they lack verve and imagination. Also working regularly in Amsterdam are the noted Dutch choreographers Toer van Schayk and Rudi van Dantzig, while for **folk dance** fans the excellent Folkloristisch Danstheater is based in the city. However, a constant feature of dance in Holland is the prevalence of non-Dutch choreographers and dancers, and the work of William Forsyth, Lloyd Newson, Saburo Teshigawara and others is regularly on show.

Of the other major Dutch dance companies, which can be seen on tour in Amsterdam – or in nearby Rotterdam and The Hague – the most innovative is The Hague's Netherlands Dance Theatre, with a repertoire of ballet and modern dance featuring inspired choreography by Jiri Kylian and Hans van Manen. The oldest company in the country, the Scapino Ballet (based in Rotterdam), has spruced up its image and is gathering a new generation of admirers.

On a smaller scale, Amsterdam is particularly receptive to the latest trends in **modern dance**, and has many experimental dance groups, often incorporating other media into their productions; small productions staged by dance students also abound. Look out for performances by the Dans Werkplaats Amsterdam and the extraordinary Cloud Chamber company, as well as the mime specialists Griftheater, and Shusaku Takeuchi's vast, open-air water-based extravaganzas. Modern dance and movement theatre companies from outside Amsterdam that often perform in the city include the Rotterdamse Dansgroep, who mainly focus on New

York modern dance; Introdans, similar in style to the Netherlands Dance Theatre; and Djazzex, fine exponents of jazz dance.

Dance festivals are a little thin on the ground: **Julidans**, which is held in the Stadsschouwburg every July, is the leading event in the city. Two festivals in The Hague to watch for are the **Holland Dance Festival** (info ☎ 070/361 6142), which takes place every two years (October 2001 and 2003) and attracts many leading international companies; and **CaDance** (info ☎ 070/363 7540), which premiers contemporary dance works. The Hague is just 45 minutes away from Amsterdam by regular trains from Centraal Station.

Listed below are the theatres that solely host dance productions; dance is sometimes also on the bill at a number of general venues and theatres around the city – check the usual listings sources.

Venues

Cosmic Theater, Nes 75 ☎ 622 8858. A modern dance and theatre company featuring young professionals with a multicultural background.

Dans Werkplaats Amsterdam, Arie Biemondstraat 107 ☎ 689 1789. A dance studio staging occasional productions at the Westergasfabriek and other locations in the city.

Folkloristisch Danstheater, Kloveniersburgwal 87 ☎ 623 9112. Original folk dance from around the world, with international choreographers brought in to work with the dancers.

Former Storkfabriek, Csaar Peterstraat 213 ☎ 419 3088. Old factory featuring dance, mime and various theatre groups.

Het Veem, Van Diemenstraat 410 ☎ 626 0112. Old warehouse converted into dance studios and a small theatre. Good for mime.

Muziektheater, Waterlooplein ☎ 625 5455. Home of the National Ballet, but with a third of its dance schedule given over to international companies.

Entertainment and Nightlife

Entertainment
and Nightlife

*Two
Amsterdam
cinemas are
worth a visit
no matter
what's show-
ing: the
extravagantly
Art Deco
Tuschinski
(see p.86) and
the atmospher-
ic The Movies
(see p.97).*

*For details of
gay and les-
bian film
programmes,
see p.274.*

Film

Most of Amsterdam's commercial **cine-mas** are huge, multiplex picture palaces showing a selection of general releases – and are interesting for just that. There's also a scattering of film houses (*filmhuizen*) showing **revival and art films** and occasional retrospectives; and Amsterdam's multimedia centres often organize film and video programmes, too. Pick up a copy of the **"Week Agenda"** from any cinema for details of all films showing in the city. Weekly pro-grammes change on Thursdays.

All foreign movies playing in Amsterdam (almost no Dutch movies turn up anyway) are shown in their **orig-inal language** and subtitled in Dutch – which is fine for British or American fare, but a little frustrating if you fancy Tarkovsky or Pasolini. If you're interested in seeing a non-English-language movie, check with the venue whether it's been **subtitled** in English (*Engels Ondertiteld*) before you go. Films are almost never dubbed into Dutch: if they are, *Nederlands Gesproken* will be printed in the listings. Most major cinemas have four showings a day: two in the after-noon, two in the evening; some also have midnight shows on Fridays and Saturdays. In all the mainstream cine-mas, an ancient and deeply irritating pol-icy of sticking a fifteen-minute **interval** (*pauze*) in the middle of the movie per-sists, although you could use this time to buy yourself a beer – as John Travolta pointed out in *Pulp Fiction*, you can drink while watching the movie without a problem.

As a guide, **tickets** can cost more than ƒ15 for an evening show Friday to Sunday, though it's not hard to find a ticket for ƒ11 during the week. Prices at the *filmhuizen* are slightly lower, and can drop to as little as ƒ6 for a 10am Sunday showing. Aside from occasional film fes-tivals held by the likes of Amnesty International, Amsterdam's only regular event is the fascinating **International Documentary Film Festival** in December (info ☎627 3329). Whereas the Dutch

Film Festival, held each September in Utrecht, features only homegrown pro-ductions, January's **Rotterdam Film Festival** (info ☎010/411 8080) is truly international, with screenings of well over 100 art movies from all parts of the world, as well as the usual accompany-ing lectures and seminars.

Filmhuizen and Revival Cinemas

De Balie, off Leidseplein ☎553 5100. Cultural centre for theatre, politics, film and new media, showing movies on Friday and Saturday nights, often with English subtitles.

Cavia, Van Hallstraat 52 ☎681 1419. Incongruously sited above a martial arts centre, this is one of the best of the small *filmhuizen*, with an eclectic and non-commercial programme of interna-tional movies. Tram #10.

Cinecenter, Lijnbaansgracht 236 ☎623 6615. Opposite the Melkweg, this shows independent and quality commercial films, the majority originating from non-English-speaking countries.

Desmet, Plantage Middenlaan 4a ☎627 3434. *Filmhuis* on the border between mainstream and arthouse cinema, and still showing a lot of European films, which tend to have a long run in Amsterdam. ƒ5 entry Monday nights. Tram #7, #9 or #14.

Filmmuseum, Vondelpark 3 ☎589 1400. Subsidized by the government since the 1940s, the Filmmuseum holds literally tens of thousands of prints. Dutch films show regularly, along with all kinds of movies from all corners of the world. Silent movies often have live piano accompaniment, and on summer weekend evenings there are free open-air screenings on the terrace. Also many cheap matinees. Most movies have English subtitles. There is talk of plans to move to Rotterdam, but not before Spring 2001.

Het Ketelhuis, Westergasfabriek, Haarlemmerweg 8–10 ☎684 0090. Stylish cinema hall in an old nineteenth-century industrial building, which shows

Dutch productions and co-productions only (though not necessarily Dutch-spoken, since a number of films are made by ethnic groups in their own language). Tram #10 to Van Limburg Stirumplein or bus #18 to Vredenhof.

Kriterion, Roeterstraat 170 ☎623 1708. Stylish duplex cinema close to Weesperplein metro. Shows arthouse and quality commercial films, with late-night cult favourites. Friendly bar attached. Tram #6, #7, #10.

Melkweg, Lijnbaansgracht 234a ☎624 1777 after 1pm. As well as music, art and dance, the Melkweg manages to maintain a consistently good monthly film and video programme, ranging from mainstream fodder through to obscure imports. Tram #1, #2 or #5 to Leidseplein.

The Movies, Haarlemmerdijk 161 ☎624 5790. A beautiful Art Deco cinema, and a charming setting for independent films. Worth visiting for the bar and restaurant alone, fully restored to their original sumptuousness. Late shows at the weekend. Tram #3.

Rialto, Ceintuurbaan 338 ☎675 3994. The only fully authentic arthouse cinema in Amsterdam, showing an enormously varied programme of European and World movies, supplemented by themed series and classics. Refurbished in 1999 the cinema now boasts a large café open to the public, and, thanks to the set-up of volunteer staff, the place has a friendly and welcoming atmosphere. On Saturday afternoons there's a talk entitled "Documentaire Salon", in which documentary film-makers discuss their work (tickets ƒ12,50). Tram #3, #24 or #25 from the centre.

Tropen Instituut Theater, Linnaeusstraat 2 ☎568 8500. Attached to the Tropenmuseum, this theatre concentrates mostly on music and dance, but puts on ad hoc film shows and themed film festivals from around the world. Tram #6, #9 and #10.

De Uitkijk, Prinsengracht 452 ☎623 7460. The oldest cinema in the city (pro-nounced "out-kike"), in a converted canal house with no bar, no ice cream and no popcorn – but low prices. Shows popular movies for months on end.

Clubs and Discos

Clubbing in Amsterdam is not the exclusive, style-conscious business it is in many other capitals. There is no one really extravagant night spot, especially since the closure of the *Roxy* in 1999, which was a big loss to the city's nightlife, and most Amsterdam clubs – even the hip ones – aren't very expensive or difficult to get into; with the exception of *iT*, you go more to dance than to people-watch. As for the music itself, as in so many other things, Amsterdam is not at the cutting edge of experimentation: **house** is definitely the thing. Hip-hop has its devotees, as do modern and retro funk, jazz and underground trance and trip-hop, but unless you go looking for something special, a random dip into a club will probably turn up mellow, undemanding house beats.

That said, though, there's a recent craze for pumped-up, 200bpm+ **"gabber"** (pronounced the Dutch way, with a throaty "kh" at the beginning), laid on at vast arenas for thousands of shaven-headed speed-freaks. If you can find a gabber event (check for flyers at Midtown Records, Nieuwendijk 104 ☎638 4252), expect to pay a hefty ƒ60 or more for entry, although it'll go on until dawn and flyers for after-hours parties will circulate during the rave. Unlike many other places around Europe, there are now practically no **illegal raves** or parties in and around Amsterdam, and the last squat venues in the harbour areas have finally made way for apartment buildings; the old days of acid warehouse parties are well and truly over.

Most clubs have very reasonable **entry prices**, hovering between ƒ15 and ƒ20 at weekends and then dropping to between ƒ7,50 and ƒ10 during the week, sometimes going as low as ƒ5, especially in the gay scene. A singular feature of

Entertainment
and Nightlife

Entertainment and Nightlife

Amsterdam clubbing however is that you tip the bouncer: if you want to get back into the same place next week, ƒ2 or ƒ5 in the palm of his hand will do very nicely thank you. Drinks prices are just slightly more expensive than in cafés at around ƒ4–5 but not excessively hiked up, and, as in the rest of the city, toilets cost money (25c or 50c). **Dress codes** are minimal or nonexistent, except where we've noted in the listings below. As far as **drugs** go, smoking joints is generally fine – though if you can't see or smell the stuff, ask the barman if it's OK. Should you need reminding, Ecstasy, acid and speed are all completely illegal, and you can expect less than favourable treatment from the bouncers (and the law) if you're spotted with anything.

Although all the places listed below **open** at either 10pm or 11pm, there's not much point turning up anywhere before midnight; unless stated otherwise, everywhere stays open until 5am on Friday and Saturday nights, 4am on other nights.

For **news** and flyers about clubs, upcoming parties and raves, drop in to places like Clubwear House, at Herengracht 265 (☎622 8766), and the Hair Police and Conscious Dreams, next door to each other at Kerkstraat 115 and 117. Alternatively, pick up the *Camel uitlijst* in any café, which gives just about the definitive listing of live music venues and clubs.

Finally, there are a couple of clubs **outside Amsterdam** that you might see advertised around town. *Stalker*, in Haarlem (☎023/531 4652), is a small place with a dedicated following and a consistently adventurous music policy, while the equally popular *De Waakzaamheid*, in Koog aan de Zaan (☎075/628 5829), attracts British and European DJs to its weekend parties.

Mainstream Clubs

Arena, 's-Gravensandestraat 51 ☎694 7444. Part of a large hostel-cum-multimedia centre, with popular dance parties on Fri and Sat.

Club 114, Herengracht 114 ☎622 7685. One of the longest-established club locations in Amsterdam, recently reborn and playing all kinds of non-housey music, from hip-hop to R&B, with heavy trance nights. Nightly; prices vary.

Club de Ville, Westergasfabriekterrijn. An old, vast industrial hall with a few wooden tables, a bar and plenty of people out for a good time. Large house, gabber, jungle and clubhouse beats mean the noise level is often high.

Dansen bij Jansen, Handboogstraat 11 ☎620 1779. Founded by – and for – students, and very popular. Open nightly; ƒ4, but officially you need student ID to get in.

Du Lac, Haarlemmerstraat 118 ☎624 4265. Rather trendy bar with R&B and soul DJs from Thurs till Sun.

Escape, Rembrandtplein 11 ☎622 3542. What once used to be a tacky disco is now home to Amsterdam's hottest Saturday night, "Chemistry", every so often featuring Holland's top DJ, Dimitri. A vast hangar, with room for 2000 people (although you may still have to queue). Closed Sun.

iT, Amstelstraat 24 ☎625 0111. Large disco with a superb sound system, often featuring well-known live acts. Has popular and glamorous gay nights (see opposite), but Thursday, Friday and Sunday are mixed gay/straight and attract a dressed up, uninhibited crowd.

Korsakoff, Lijnbaansgracht 161 ☎625 7854. Small, dark grunge club, featuring live bands as well as alternative rock and noise nights. Free.

Mazzo, Rozengracht 114 ☎626 7500. One of the city's hippest and most laid-back discos, with a choice of music to appeal to all tastes. Perhaps the easiest-going bouncers in town. Open nightly.

Melkweg, Lijnbaansgracht 234a ☎624 1777 after 1pm. After the bands have finished, this multimedia centre plays host to some of the most enjoyable theme nights around, everything from

African dance parties to experimental jazz-trance.

The Ministry, Reguliersdwarsstraat 12 ☎623 3981. A new club trying to catch a wide brand of party people and featuring quality DJs. Speed garage, house and R&B. Monday night jam session with the local jazz talent. Open late.

Odeon, Singel 460 ☎624 9711. This converted seventeenth-century building is one of the oldest venues in the city – during the 1940s, 50s and 60s it was Amsterdam's premier gay nightspot. Its heady days have passed, though, and now its stylishly elegant interior plays host to an invariably studentish gang, although on Wednesday nights the basement reverts to being the *DOK* gay night club (see below). Open nightly.

Paradiso, Weteringschans 6–8 ☎623 7348. One of the principal venues in the city, which on Fridays turns into the unmissable VIP (Vrijdag In Paradiso) Club, from midnight onwards. Also hosts one-off events – check listings.

Sinners in Heaven, Wagenstraat 3 ☎620 1375. Rembrandtplein club churning out lots of R&B and house, with a dressed-up clientele consuming long drinks.

Soul Kitchen, Amstelstraat 32a ☎620 2333. Relaxed club that's refreshingly oriented towards 1960s and 70s soul and funk rather than the usual housey stuff.

Time, Nieuwezijds Voorburgwal 163 ☎423 3792. Friendly, no-nonsense club playing reggae, fusion, drum-and-bass and house. Weekdays open until 4am (free before 11pm).

West Pacific, Westergasfabriek, Haarlemmerweg 8–10 ☎597 4458. After playing host to many an acid rave in the late 1980s, this converted gas factory is now *the* up-and-coming location in the city. An on-site café with an open fireplace attracts a trendy crowd of young Amsterdammers, who stay late to party.

Winston Kingdom, Warmoesstraat 129 ☎6231380. Small venue with a club night on Sundays. See p.233.

Lesbian and Gay Clubs

The places listed below cater either predominantly or exclusively to a **gay** clientele. Some venues have both gay only and mixed gay/straight nights, as noted. Lesbian-only nights are on the increase and many venues run gay nights for both men and women. Gay men should also check out posters and flyers for the monthly Club Trash and Wasteland events.

COC, Rozenstraat 14 ☎626 3087. Very popular women-only disco and café every Sat from 8pm called "Just Girlsz", popular with younger lesbians. Pumping on Friday nights too (mixed men/women).

Cockring, Warmoesstraat 96 ☎623 9604. Currently Amsterdam's most popular – and very cruisey – gay men's disco. Light show and bars on two levels. Get there early at the weekend to avoid queuing. Nightly; free.

DOK, Singel 460 ☎624 9711. Housed in the *Odeon*, this was once Amsterdam's premier gay nightspot, which is now enjoying something of a revival; gay parties being held in the basement on Wednesday evenings have started the rumours around in town – *DOK* is back.

Exit, Reguliersdwarsstraat 42 ☎625 8788. Along with *iT* (see p.242), the city's most popular gay club. Current sounds play nightly to an upbeat, cruisey crowd. Predominantly male, though women are admitted. Free.

Getto Girls, Warmoesstraat 51 ☎421 5151. Women-only night on Tuesdays at the *Getto* with plenty of music, plus a bar serving vegetarian food and cocktails. Transforms into a dance club later on in the evening.

Havana, Reguliersdwarsstraat 17 ☎620 6788. Small dance floor above a bar slap in the middle of a buzzing gay area. Very popular with a mixed clientele (gay, yuppie, art crowd); mostly men, but women admitted. Also perhaps the only place in town to cater for people who want to dance but still get up for work

Entertainment
and Nightlife

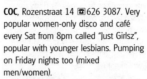

Entertainment
and Nightlife

the next day. Mon–Thurs & Sun
11pm–1am, Fri & Sat 11pm–2am; free.

De Huyschkaemer, Utrechtsestraat 137
☎ 627 0575. More like a local café shifting its dinner tables at night to make
space for a dance floor, but a fun night
all the same, run by a gay man and
attracting a somewhat serious, but nevertheless cheerful clientele. Not exclusively gay.

iT, Amstelstraat 24 ☎ 625 0111.
Saturday night here really is IT, as the
city's most glamorous transvestites come
out to play and the place gets packed
out (men only). Thursday night is free if
you're gay, and Sunday is a popular
gay/straight night.

Lellebel, Utrechtsestraat 4 ☎ 427 5139.
A gay-friendly café featuring drag shows
and live acts, with a colourful, cheerful
atmosphere.

Liplickers Club, at *Sinners in Heaven*,
Wagenstraat 3 ☎ 620 1375. Female-only
dance night every first Sunday of the
month, with changing themes and
music.

De Trut, Bilderdijkstraat 165 (no phone).
Housed in a former factory building, this
squat venue holds a Sunday night, gay-
only dance party: there's a large dance
floor, cheap drinks, and non-commercial
music. Very popular with both men and
women – the doors are closed at midnight and if you arrive after 11pm you
may not get in. Gets very hot as it's in a
basement.

Vive la Vie, Amstelstraat 7 ☎ 624 0114.
Café mainly for women, which shifts its
tables at the weekend to make room for
a dance space.

The Web, St Jacobsstraat 6 ☎ 623 6758.
Somewhat underground leather and
denim club, held every last Friday of the
month; for both men and women
(though the amount of women can vary
considerably).

You II, Amstel 178 ☎ 421 0900.
Amsterdam's first and long-awaited lesbian dance club, which opened its doors
in the summer of 1999. Men are in fact
welcome, as long as they're under
female supervision.

Chapter 12

Museums and Galleries

The Netherlands has had a strong and active tradition of government support for the arts since World War II, and the effect on Amsterdam in particular has been dramatic: the city is absolutely full of art. In addition to three world-class **museums**, there are well over 200 private **commercial art galleries**, showcasing art of all kinds. In addition, most bars and cafés have changing exhibitions of photographs or small artworks, many public spaces are decorated with sculptures of one kind or another (some official, but just as many unofficial), and there are schemes to help members of the public hang original works in their own home – through purchase or long-term rental. For active support and mainstream interest in art of all kinds, Amsterdam is unparalleled in Europe.

Galleries

The **contemporary art** scene in Amsterdam is enormous and incredibly

diverse. Partly due to a long-standing (but now terminated) system of direct government subsidies to individual artists, and partly due to the Dutch tradition of encouraging individual expression, Amsterdam has long attracted artists from all parts of the world. This active international community has had a marked influence on Amsterdam's galleries, which are eclectic, all-encompassing, and about as unstuffy as it's possible to be.

Galleries are scattered all over the city centre rather than confined to any specific area, though because of the space the older houses offer, you'll often find galleries along the major canals. In general opening times are Tuesday to Saturday noon to 6pm, plus noon to 5pm on the first Sunday of the month, with the smaller and less commercial galleries open from Thursday to Saturday. Your best bet for **information** to supplement our brief listings (which cover both galleries and art dealers) is the gallery guide *Alert*,

The Dutch tend to use the words "museum" and "gallery" slightly differently from how you might expect. For the Dutch, an art **museum** displays works of art (most often fine art) that are not for sale – they are either national treasures, or they have been purchased directly by the museum for its own collection. Thus the Rijksmuseum, which in Britain or America would be called the National Gallery, here translates as the National Museum. A **galerie** is a much smaller operation, which neither buys nor sells art for itself. Most often rooted in the contemporary art scene, a *galerie* acts as a showcase for changing exhibits by different artists, and also as an agent, selling works on to third parties for a commission. A further complication is that many art dealers (*kunsthandel*), who buy and sell works of art – generally from better-known artists, while often keeping a stock of prints – have taken to calling themselves galleries, in an attempt to elevate themselves from the purely commercial.

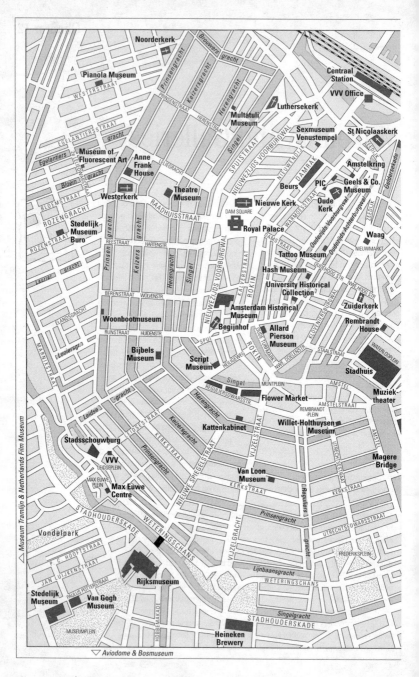

Noorderkerk
Pianola Museum
WESTERSTRAAT
EGELANTIERSTRAAT
gracht
Egelantiers
Museum of
Fluorescent Art
Bloem gracht
BLOEMSTRAAT
Westerkerk
ROZENGRACHT
ROZENSTRAAT
Stedelijk
Museum
Buro
Laurier gracht
ELANDSGRACHT
Looiersgr.
MARNIXSTRAAT

Brouwers gracht
Prinsengracht
Keizersgracht
Herengracht
PRINSENSTRAAT
HERENSTRAAT
Multatuli
Museum
LELIEGRACHT
Anne
Frank
House
Theatre
Museum
RAADHUISSTRAAT
BEESTRAAT
HARTENSTR.
Prinsen gracht
Keizers gracht
Herengracht
Singel
BERENSTRAAT
WOLVENSTR.
Woonbootmuseum
RUNSTRAAT
HUIDENSTR.
SPUI
Bijbels
Museum
Script
Museum

Singel
SPUISTRAAT
NIEUWEZIJDS VOORBURGWAL
NIEUWENDIJK
Luthersekerk
Sexmuseum
Venustempel
Beurs
Nieuwe Kerk
DAM SQUARE
Royal Palace
DAMSTRAAT
Tattoo Museum
Hash Museum
University Historical
Collection
KALVERSTRAAT
ROKIN
NIEUWEZIJDS VOORBURGWAL
Amsterdam Historical
Museum
Begijnhof
Allard
Pierson
Museum
ROKIN
NWE. DOELENSTR.
OUDE TURFMARKT
HEILIGEWEG
Singel
MUNTPLEIN
Flower Market
REGULIERSDWARSSTR.

Centraal
Station
VVV Office
St Nicolaaskerk
Amstelkring
DAMRAK
Geels & Co.
Museum
PIC
Oude
Kerk
WARMOESSTRAAT
Oudezijds Voorburgwal
Oudezijds Achterburgwal
OUDEHOOG STR.
ZEEDIJK
NWE.HOOG STR.
Waag
NIEUWMARKT
Zuiderkerk
KLOVENIERSBURGWAL
Rembrandt
House
STAALSTRAAT
WATERLOOPLEIN
Stadhuis
Muziek-
theater
AMSTEL
AMSTELSTRAAT
REMBRANDT-
PLEIN

Stadsschouwburg
Leidse gracht
Leidse
EIDSESTRAAT
VVV
LEIDSEPLEIN
MAX EUWE
PLEIN
Max Euwe
Centre
STADHOUDERSKADE
Vondelpark
P. C. HOOFTSTRAAT
JAN LUIJKENSTRAAT
Stedelijk
Museum
PAULUS POTTERSTRAAT
Van Gogh
Museum
MUSEUMPLEIN
HOBBEMAKADE
Rijksmuseum

Herengracht
Keizersgracht
Prinsengracht
NIEUWE SPIEGELSTRAAT
KERKSTRAAT
Kattenkabinet
VIJZELSTRAAT
Van Loon
Museum
KERKSTRAAT
VIJZELGRACHT
Prinsengracht
WETERINGSCHANS
Lijnbaansgracht
WETERINGSCHANS
Heineken
Brewery

Willet-Holthuysen
Museum
AMSTEL
Magere
Bridge
UTRECHTSESTRAAT
Reguliers gracht
UTRECHTSEDWARSSTRAAT
FREDERIKSPLEIN
KERKSTRAAT
Singelgracht
STADHOUDERSKADE

◁ Museum Tramlijn & Netherlands Film Museum

▽ Aviodome & Bosmuseum

244   LISTINGS: CHAPTER 12

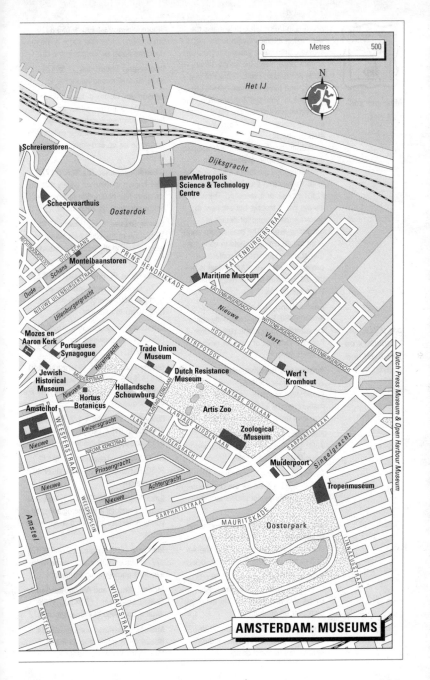

AMSTERDAM: MUSEUMS

Het IJ

Schreierstoren

Dijksgracht

newMetropolis Science & Technology Centre

Scheepvaarthuis

Oosterdok

PRINS HENDRIKKADE

OUDE SCHANS

Montelbaanstoren

Oude Schans

NIEUWE UILENBURGERGRACHT

Uilenburgergracht

KATTENBURGERSTRAAT

Maritime Museum

KATTENBURGERGRACHT

Nieuwe

HOOGTE KADIJK

Vaart

WITTENBURGERGRACHT

OOSTENBURGERGRACHT

Mozes en Aaron Kerk

Portuguese Synagogue

Herengracht

ENTREPOTDOK

Trade Union Museum

Dutch Resistance Museum

Werf 't Kromhout

Jewish Historical Museum

MUIDERSTRAAT

Nieuwe

Hortus Botanicus

Hollandsche Schouwburg

PLANTAGE KERKLAAN

PLANTAGE DOKLAAN

Amstelhof

Nieuwe

WEESPERSTRAAT

Keizersgracht

PLANTAGE MIDDENLAAN

PLANTAGE MUIDERGRACHT

Artis Zoo

Zoological Museum

SARPHATISTRAAT

NIEUWE KERKSTRAAT

Nieuwe

Prinsengracht

Muiderpoort

Singelgracht

Nieuwe

WEESPERPLEIN

Achtergracht

Tropenmuseum

Amstel

Nieuwe

SARPHATISTRAAT

MAURITSKADE

Oosterpark

LINNAEUSSTRAAT

WIBAUTSTRAAT

AMSTELDIJK

0   Metres   500

N

△ Dutch Press Museum & Open Harbour Museum

Museums and Galleries

See p.311, for a rundown on Dutch art and artists.

which is in Dutch but clearly marks the locations of all the galleries in the city; it's available from some galleries themselves or from larger magazine shops. *What's On In Amsterdam* carries listings of major shows, and more informed entries can be found in *Time Out Amsterdam*, on the Internet at *www.timeout.nl*. For dedicated art bookshops, see the *Shops and Markets* chapter.

A distinctive feature of the Amsterdam art scene are **open ateliers**, where neighbourhood groups of artists and galleries throw open their doors to the public for a week or a weekend. These are always worth visiting, but are hard to predict – ask around for details of upcoming events. The mainstream annual art fair, **KunstRai**, is held in early summer at the enormous RAI conference centre. The alternative **Kunstvlaai** is held the week before or after this in the Westergasfabriek.

Galerie Akinci, Lijnbaansgracht 317 ☎638 0480. Eclectic, constantly changing exhibits, often at the cutting edge. Part of a complex of galleries next door to each other.

Amsterdams Beeldhouwers Kollektief, Zeilmakerstraat 15 ☎625 6332. Amsterdam Sculptors' Collective: a permanent exhibit of contemporary Dutch sculptors up in the Western Islands.

Animation Art, Berenstraat 39 ☎627 7600. Comic art specialist, with hand-inked Disney cels for sale.

De Appel, Nieuwe Spiegelstraat 10 ☎625 5651. Centre for the contemporary arts, with regular shows by newcomers.

Arti, Rokin 112 ☎623 3508. Impressive nineteenth-century exhibition space showing art by the members of the *Arti et Amicitae* (Arts and Friendship) society.

AYAC'S 22, Keizersgracht 166 ☎638 5240. The Amsterdam Young Artists Circuit, showing paintings and drawings by recent art graduates.

Galerie Binnen, Keizersgracht 82 ☎625 9603. The premier gallery for industrial and interior (*binnen*) design.

Bloom, Bloemstraat 150 ☎638 8810. Small gallery presenting some of the most unconventional exhibitions in the city.

Boomerang, Boomstraat 12 ☎420 3516. Australian and Aboriginal art.

Consortium, Oostelijke Handelskade 29a ☎421 2408. Contemporary art shows held in a former warehouse called Kunstpakhuis Wilhelmina, a collective of ateliers in an up-and-coming neighbourhood.

D'Eendt, Spuistraat 272 ☎626 5777. Well-known modern art gallery that critics claim has declined in recent years. Still, it shouldn't be overlooked.

Galerie Delaive, Spiegelgracht 23 ☎622 1295. One of the city's best-known galleries, showing the work of established Dutch artists.

Donkersloot, PC Hooftstraat 127 ☎572 2722. Gallery showing work by predominantly famous young Dutch painters. Daily 10am to midnight.

Espace, Keizersgracht 548 ☎624 0802. Paintings and drawings from the 1960s and 1970s.

Galerie Fons Welters, Bloemstraat 140 ☎423 3046. One of the city's best, tending towards sculpture, always of the highest quality.

Fotogalerie 2 1/2 bij 4 1/2, Prinsengracht 356 ☎626 0757. Exceptionally high-quality photographic exhibitions.

Go Galerie, Prinsengracht 64 ☎422 9580. Paintings reflecting the diversity of different cultures.

Jurka, Singel 28 ☎626 6733. Up-to-the-minute paintings and photographs, by young American and Dutch avant-garde artists.

Melkweg, Lijnbaansgracht 234a ☎624 1777. Premier multimedia centre, with excellent photographic exhibitions.

Modern African and African-Related Art Gallery, Kerkstraat 123 ☎620 1958. What it says. Also at Prinsengracht 472.

Mokum, Oudezijds Voorburgwal 334 ☎624 3958. Interesting art from the New Dutch Realism School.

Montevideo/Time Based Arts, Keizersgracht 264 ☎623 7101. The best-known centre for video and media arts in the contemporary scene.

Nanky de Vreeze & Living Stone, Lange Leidsedwarsstraat 200 ☎627 3808. Large, mainstream gallery with very accessible shows.

Parade, Prinsengracht 799 ☎427 6446. Commercial gallery specializing in pop- and minimalist art, plus contemporary photography.

Galerie Paul Andriesse, Prinsengracht 116 ☎623 6237. Major showcase for the Amsterdam avant-garde.

Psychedelic Gallery, Marnixstraat 255 ☎638 4334, *www.xs4all.nl/~seeds*. Psychedelic photography, and various other "far out" artefacts.

Reflex, Weteringschans 79a ☎627 2832. Excellent exhibitions of modern art, changing monthly. Also at Weteringschans 83 and Spiegelgracht 8.

Scheltema Holkema Vermeulen, Koningsplein 20 ☎523 1411. The stair-case of this large bookshop features changing exhibits of often excellent photography.

Stedelijk Museum Buro Amsterdam, Rozenstraat 59 ☎422 0471. Gallery connected to the museum and devoted to showing the work of young Amsterdam artists.

Taller, Keizersgracht 607 ☎624 6734. Group of Latin American artists who have been working and exhibiting in this converted coach house for thirty years or more.

Torch, Lauriergracht 94 ☎626 0284. Reliable exhibitions of modern art in this sought-after gallery space.

W139, Warmoesstraat 139 ☎622 9434. Enormous space right in the heart of the Red Light District, showing work by students and new graduates.

Galerie XY, 2e Laurierdwarsstraat 42 ☎625 0282. Forward-thinking Jordaan gallery, with shows from unknowns cheek-by-jowl with international grandees.

Museums

Museums and Galleries

For a relatively small city, Amsterdam has a vast array of **museums** catering to all tastes. Although it may be that you find more than enough visual stimulation in the mansions and canals, even the most reluctant museum-goer will be intrigued by the sights and sounds of the world offered by the **Tropenmuseum**, or by the brand-new interactive **newMetropolis Science and Technology Centre**. Failing those, the rather less dynamic **Hash Marihuana Hemp Museum** or the newly opened **Tattoo Museum** might appeal. Amsterdam has a superb concentration of art museums, of which three – the **Rijksmuseum**, the **Van Gogh** and the **Stedelijk** – rank among the finest in the world. Add to these over thirty small historical museums – including the **Anne Frank House**, an excellent **Jewish Historical Museum**, and the beautiful hidden church of the **Amstelkring** – and you get some idea of just how impressive the range is. The listings below, combined with the map on pp.244–245 and the accounts in the guide chapters, should help you choose.

If you intend to visit more than three or four museums (or the same museum three or four times), you'd be well advised to buy a **museumjaarkaart** (museum year-card), either from the VVV or direct from a museum – take a passport photo and they can issue it on the spot. It costs ƒ55, or ƒ25 for under-24s and ƒ45 for senior citizens, and gives free (or occasionally reduced) entry to around 400 museums throughout the country for a full year – although it doesn't relieve you of the burden of queuing up to get in every time. Considering it would normally cost you a hefty ƒ27,50 to visit the essential Rijksmuseum and Van Gogh Museum alone, the *museumjaarkaart* is a real bargain: if you have one, practically all the places listed below let you in for free. Bear in mind, though, that some museums (most notably the Anne Frank House) *don't* give reductions for museumcard-holders;

Museums and Galleries

Page references relate to the relevant guide chapter where the museum is usually described in more detail.

we've indicated this in the listings. An alternative for those under 26 is the **Cultureel Jongeren Passport** or **CJP**, which for ƒ20 gets you reductions on entry to museums, as well as to theatres, concerts and *filmhuizen* (art-house cinemas) – though these reductions can vary, and are sometimes not that substantial. Valid throughout the Netherlands and in Belgium too, the CJP can be bought from the AUB Uitburo in the Stadsschouwburg theatre on Leidseplein. Entry charges for **children** are usually about half the price of adult admission, although the larger museums may offer even better-value **family tickets**, usually covering two adults and two children, where one person gets in free. Many museums also offer **group-rate discounts**, although the number of people required for a group varies from eight in some places to twenty or more in others; call ahead for details, and also call the museums direct for information about in-house **guided tours** – although these can be expensive, they're not a bad option if you have limited time, or would like expert information on what you're looking at.

Opening times, particularly for state-run museums, tend to follow a pattern: closed on Monday, open from 10am to 5pm Tuesday to Saturday and from 1 to 5pm on Sunday and public holidays. However, this pattern has begun to change in recent years, and many larger museums are now open on Monday as well. Bear in mind that Dutch primary schools tend to take Wednesday afternoons off, so this might be a bad time to try and find some peace and quiet in the Zoo (see p.281) or the Tropenmuseum.

Almost all Amsterdam museums offer at least basic **information** in English or a written English guide. Most have temporary special exhibitions or *tentoonstellingen*, and the best way to find out what's on is to pick up a free copy of the English *Museum Magazine* from any museum. "Museum Agenda" in the *Uitkrant* and *What's On In Amsterdam* are also useful for up-to-

date listings, as is *Time Out Amsterdam* on the World Wide Web at *www.time-out.nl*. However, perhaps your best bet would be to drop into the AUB Uitburo on the Leidseplein and scan the leaflets.

Finally, if you like to take your museums the easy way, the **Museumboot** (museum-boat) runs a regular daily service once every half-hour (45min in winter) from 10am to 5.30pm, calling at six jetties located at or near eighteen of the city's major museums; from the jetties it's a short walk to the Anne Frank House, the Amsterdam Historical Museum, Rijksmuseum, Van Gogh and Stedelijk museums, Rembrandt House, Jewish Historical Museum and the Maritime Museum, among others. However, since the larger museums can take some hours to explore (using up valuable time on your day ticket), the Museumboot is perhaps best used for spending a day cruising between the smaller museums. A hop-on, hop-off day ticket will cost you ƒ25. The office and main boarding point is in front of Centraal Station, although you can also buy tickets from the jetty opposite the Rijksmuseum; for more details call ☎530 1090. For gentle canal hops between museums, there's also the **Canal Bus** service, which takes in just the central museums (see *Introducing the City*, p.53).

Allard Pierson Museum

Oude Turfmarkt 127 ☎ *525 2556. Tram #4, #9, #14, #16, #20, #24, #25 (stop Spui); Tues–Fri 10am–5pm, Sat, Sun & holidays 1–5pm. ƒ9,50; over-65s, CJP, students ƒ7; under-15s ƒ3; under-12s ƒ1. Wheelchair access.*
The city's premier archeological museum. See p.71.

Amstelkring Museum

Oudezijds Voorburgwal 40 ☎ *624 6604. Mon–Sat 10am–5pm, Sun & holidays 1–5pm. ƒ7,50; under-19s, over-65s, CJP ƒ6, under-5s free. No wheelchair access.*
A beautiful and well-preserved seventeenth-century clandestine Catholic

church and house in the heart of the Red Light District. See p.65.

Amsterdam Historical Museum
Entrances at Kalverstraat 92 and Nieuwezijds Voorburgwal 357 ☎ *523 1822. Tram #1, #2, #4, #5, #9, #14, #16, #24, #25 (stop Spui). Mon–Fri 10am–5pm, Sat & Sun 11am–5pm. f11; under-17s f5,50. Guided tours by appointment only. Limited wheelchair access.*

Modern and engaging collection of arte-facts relating to the history of the city, with a library, lectures and concerts. Beautiful surroundings in the heart of Amsterdam. See p.72.

Anne Frank House
Prinsengracht 263 ☎ *556 7100, www.annefrank.nl. Tram #13, #14, #17, #20 (stop Westermarkt). Daily: April–Aug 9am–9pm; Sept–March 9am–7pm. Closed Yom Kippur. f10; under-17s, over-65s, CJP f5; under-10s free; no museumcards. No wheelchair access.*

The secret annexe where Anne Frank and her family hid during the occupation, now a museum. See p.79.

Aviodome
Schiphol Centre ☎ *406 8000, www.aviodome.com. Train to Schiphol Airport, then walk or bus from stop B12. April–Sept daily 10am–5pm; Oct–March Tues–Fri 10am–5pm, Sat & Sun noon–5pm. f12,50; over-65s f11.50; 4- to 12-year-olds f10; no museumcards. Wheelchair access.*

Huge, hands-on exhibition for buffs and kids alike, with over thirty historic aircraft to examine and clamber onto, including the first motorized plane from 1903 and the latest flight-simulators. Ask for an all-in ticket from Centraal Station, which includes the train fare, entry to the museum, and a coffee and apple cake at Schiphol train station.

Bijbels Museum
Herengracht 366 ☎ *624 2436. Tram #1, #2, #5 (stop Spui). Mon–Sat 10am–5pm, Sun 1–5pm. f5; over-65s, CJP f3,50; under-16s f2,50. Limited wheelchair access.*

Ecumenical museum of life in biblical times, housed in two wonderful canal houses. See p.82.

Bosmuseum
Koenenkade 56, in the Amsterdamse Bos ☎ *643 1414. At the end of the Museum Tramline from Haarlemmermeer Station, or bus #170, #171 or #172. Daily 10am–5pm. Free. Wheelchair access.*

Information centre for the Amsterdam Forest, in the south of the city. See p.135.

CoBrA Museum of Modern Art
Sandbergplein 1, Amstelveen ☎ *547 5050. Tram #5, #51 (stop Binnenhof or Oranjebaan), or bus #170, #171, #172 (stop Plein 1960). Tues–Sun 11am–5pm. f7,50; over-65s, CJP, 5- to 16-year-olds f3,50. Wheelchair access.*

Museum way out in the southern sub-urbs dedicated to the CoBrA movement of the 1950s and 60s; well worth the journey. For more on the CoBrA movement, see p.318.

Dutch Press Museum
International Institute for Social History, Cruquiusweg 31 ☎ *668 5866. Tram #7, #10 (stop Javaplein), or bus #22. Mon–Fri 9am–5pm. Free.*

The history of the Dutch press since 1903, as revealed in newspapers, leaflets, posters and political cartoons. See p.137.

Electric Ladyland – Museum of Fluorescent Art
2e Leliedwarstraat 5 ☎ *420 3776, www.electric-lady-land.com. Tram #13, #14, #17 or #20 (stop Westermarkt). Tues–Sat 1–6pm (by appointment). f5, children free.*

A small fluorescent "cave" built by the proprietor in his basement, comprising mirrors and kaleidoscopes to give you a varied perspective on the fluorescent minerals and crystals he has collected through the years. Short- and longwave UV lamps further your insight into the structure of the rocks.

Geels & Co. Museum
Warmoesstraat 67 ☎ *624 0683. Tues & Fri 2–4pm, Sat 2–4.30pm. Free. No wheelchair access.*

Museums and Galleries

Museums and Galleries

Museum of coffee- and tea-related displays above a shop selling the same. Call in advance to be sure it's open (Saturday is the best day). See p.64.

Hash Marihuana Hemp Museum

Oudezijds Achterburgwal 148 ☎ 623 5961. Tram #4, #9, #16, #24, #25 (stop Dam), or metro Nieuwmarkt. Daily 11am–10pm. f8; no discount for museumcards. Limited wheelchair access.

The story of the weed, with a growing garden and even a Bible made of hemp. There's a handy head shop next door for hands-on experience. See p.69.

Hollandsche Schouwburg

Plantage Middenlaan 24 ☎ 626 9945. Tram #7, #9, #14 (stop Plantage Kerklaan). Daily 11am–4pm. Free. Limited wheelchair access.

Sober exhibition on the role of this theatre building during World War II as a holding point for Jews about to be transported to concentration camps. See p.109.

Hortus Botanicus

Plantage Middenlaan 2a ☎ 625 9021. Tram #7, #9, #14, or #20 (stop Plantage Kerklaan). April–Sept Mon–Fri 9am–5pm, Sat & Sun 11am–5pm; Oct–March Mon–Fri 9am–4pm, Sat & Sun 11am–4pm. f7,50; 5- to 14-year-olds f4,50. Guided tours on Sunday at 2pm.

A Botanical Garden since 1682 with 6000 plant species. The nineteenth-century palm-filled greenhouses make the perfect place to take a break from the city buzz. See p.109.

Jewish Historical Museum

J.D. Meijerplein ☎ 626 9945. Tram #9 or #14 (stop Waterlooplein), or metro Waterlooplein. Daily 11am–5pm; closed Yom Kippur. f8; over-65s, students f4; 10- to 16-year-olds f2; under-10s free. Wheelchair access.

Innovative and award-winning museum on the history of the Jews in the Netherlands, with many fascinating side exhibits. A cassette tour of the museum is available (f2,50). Also operates walking tours of the district (f55) and visits to the nearby Portuguese Synagogue. See p.108.

Kattenkabinet

Herengracht 497 ☎ 626 5378, www.kattenkabinet.nl. Tram #16, #24, #25 (stop Muntplein), or tram #1, #2, #5 (stop Koningsplein). Mon–Fri 10am–2pm, Sat & Sun 1–5pm. f10; no museumcards. No wheelchair access.

Hundreds of paintings and art objects related to cats, on display in an old canal house. See p.85.

Kromhout Shipyard

Hoogte Kadijk 147 ☎ 627 6777. Bus #22 or #32.

Though it has in fact given up its official museum function, visitors are still welcome to this old shipyard, which is an historic place to go and see. They still restore vessels, and the authenticity of the place makes a refreshing change from some of the more tacky museums in the city. See p.114.

Maritime Museum (Scheepvaartsmuseum)

Kattenburgerplein 1 ☎ 523 2222. Bus #22, #32. Tues–Sun 10am–5pm, mid-July to mid-Sept also Mon 10am–5pm. f14,50; 6- to 17-year-olds f8; under-6s free. Wheelchair access.

Impressive collection of maritime objects, large and small, including a replica of a VOC ship, one of a fleet used by the largest European trade company in the seventeenth century. See p.112.

Max Euwe Centre

Max Euweplein 30, www.maxeuwe.nl. Tram #1, #2, #5, #6, #7, #10 (stop Leidseplein). Tues–Fri, plus the first Sat of the month 10.30am–4pm. Free. Limited wheelchair access.

Eponymous museum of the only Dutch chess champion, full of chess-related bits and pieces.

Multatuli Museum

Korsjespoortsteeg 20 ☎ 638 1938. Tram #1, #2, #5, #13, #17 (stop Nieuwezijds Kolk). Tues 10am–5pm, Sat & Sun noon–5pm; free. No wheelchair access.

Museum in the former home of the eighteenth-century Dutch writer. See p.78.

Museum Tramlijn

Amstelveenseweg 264 ☎ 673 7538.
Tram #6, #16 (stop Haarlemmermeer
station). April–Oct Sun 10.30am–5pm;
May–Sept also Wed (same times); rides
every 20min. f5; 4- to 11-year-olds
f2,50; under-4s free; no museumcard.
No wheelchair access.

Not so much a museum as a set of
working antique trams, maintained by
volunteers, that run along old railway
tracks down to the other side of the
Amsterdamse Bos. Your ticket allows you
to get off anywhere and spend some
time in the Bos before catching a later
tram back into town.

Netherlands Film Museum

Vondelpark 3, next to Roemer
Visscherstraat ☎ 589 1400. Tram #1, #6
(stop 1e Constantijn Huygensstraat), or
tram #3, #12 (stop Overtoom). Box office
open Mon–Fri 9am–10pm, Sat & Sun
1–10pm; films screened nightly, plus
Wed matinees; tickets f10. Library and
documentation centre at Vondelstraat 69
☎ 589 1435; Tues–Fri 10am–5pm, Sat
11am–5pm. Free. Wheelchair access.

Less a museum than a restored showcase for obscure films on a variety of
subjects – not always Dutch and usually
organized by theme. See p.127.

newMetropolis, Science and Technology Centre

Oosterdok, near entrance to IJ tunnel
☎ 531 3233, www.newmet.nl. 5min
walk from CS, or bus #22 or #32.
Tues–Sun 10am–6pm. f24; under-16s
f16; after 4pm f14.

Interactive "centre for human creativity",
with the latest cutting-edge hi-tech displays, perfect for hands-on exploration.
The building, shaped like a ship's bow,
sits on top of the IJ tunnel, affording a
mesmerizing view to the city: bring a picnic and sit out on the terrace. See p.113.

Open Harbour Museum

KNSM-laan 311 ☎ 418 5522. Bus #32 or
#59. Wed–Sun 1–5pm. Free if no special
exhibition, otherwise f5; over-65s, CJP,
museumcard holders f3,50. Wheelchair
access.

History of the harbour of Amsterdam,
from a social viewpoint, with interesting
and broadly alternative historical analysis. For about six months of the year
they arrange special exhibitions on specific topics relating to the harbour or its
new architectural surroundings.

Pianola Museum

Westerstraat 106 ☎ 627 9624. Tram #3,
#10 (stop Marnixplein). Sun 1–5pm;
other times by appointment. f7,50; no
museumcards. Limited wheelchair
access.

Tiny and fascinating private collection of
working pianolas, with occasional weekend concerts. See p.95.

Prostitution Information Centre (PIC)

Enge Kerksteeg 3 (next to the Oude Kerk)
☎ 420 7328, www.pic_amsterdam.com.
Tues, Wed, Fri & Sat 11.30am–7.30pm,
guided tour Sun 10am. Free.

For a slightly more enlightening visit to
the Red Light District, find out how the
women in the windows are improving
their working conditions and campaign-
ing for greater legal and social provi-
sions. Includes a small exhibition, plus
book and souvenir shop. See p.64.

Rembrandt House

Jodenbreestraat 4–6 ☎ 520 0400,
www.rembrandthuis.nl. Tram #9, #14,
#20 (stop Mr Visserplein), or metro
Waterlooplein. Mon–Sat 10am–5pm, Sun
1–5pm. f7,50; 10- to 15-year-olds f5;
over-65s f6; museumcard holders free.
Limited wheelchair access.

The home of Rembrandt at the height of
his fame and popularity, with a wonderful display of his engravings. See p.104.

Resistance Museum (*Verzetsmuseum*)

Plantage Kerklaan 61a ☎ 620 2535,
www.verzetsmuseum.nl. Tram #7, #9, #14,
#20 (stop Plantage Kerklaan). Tues–Fri
10am–5pm, Sat & Sun noon–5pm. f8;
under-15s, over-65s, CJP f4; under-5s free.
Limited wheelchair access.

Excellent display on the rise of the
Resistance from the invasion in May
1940 to the liberation in 1945, with
additional displays on contemporary
neo-Nazism. See p.110.

Museums and
Galleries

Museums and Galleries

For details of museums that specifically appeal to children, see the Kids' Amsterdam chapter.

Rijksmuseum

Stadhouderskade 42 (South Wing entrance at Hobbemastraat 19) ☎ *674 7000, www.rijksmuseum.nl. Tram #2, #5, #20 (stop Hobbemastraat), or tram #6, #7, #10 (stop Spiegelgracht). Daily 10am–5pm. f15; under-18s, over-65s f7,50; CJP f5. Wheelchair access.*

The country's national museum, with a marvellous collection of Dutch painting up to 1850, as well as decorative arts, furniture, oriental ceramics and more, spread over 200 rooms. To supplement the brief descriptions, you can take a CD audio tour, which gives instant information on over 550 works in the museum – pick one up at the Front Hall desk or the South Wing entrance for f7,50. See pp.115–123.

Script Museum

University Library, Singel 425. Tram #1, #2, #5 (stop Koningsplein). Mon–Fri 9.30am–5pm, Tues & Thurs till 8pm, Sat 9.30am–1pm. Free. Limited wheelchair access.

Offbeat collection of different writing materials and alphabets from around the world.

Sexmuseum Venustempel

Damrak 18 ☎ *622 8376. Daily 10am–11.30pm. f4,50, no museumcards. Wheelchair access.*

Sober but varied exhibition of sex-related art and artefacts. See p.59.

Stedelijk Museum of Modern Art

Paulus Potterstraat 13 ☎ *573 2737, www.stedelijk.nl. Tram #2, #3, #5, #12, #20 (stop Van Baerlestraat), or tram #16 (stop Museumplein). Daily: April–Sept 10am–6pm; Oct–March 11am–5pm. f9; 7- to 16-year-olds, CJP f4,50; under-7s free. Wheelchair access.*

The city's prime venue for modern art. Clear displays from its excellent permanent collection, as well as regular temporary exhibitions. Also has a library and programme of lectures and events. See p.125.

Stedelijk Museum Buro

Rozenstraat 59 ☎ *422 0471. Tram #13, #14, #17, #20 (stop Marnixstraat).* *Tues–Sun 11am–5pm. Free. Wheelchair access.*

Annexe of the main museum devoted to cutting-edge exhibitions and multimedia installations by Amsterdam artists. See p.94.

Tattoo Museum

Oudezijds Achterburgwal 130 ☎ *625 1565, www.tattoomuseum.com. Tram #4, #9, #16, #24, #25 (stop Dam), or metro Nieuwmarkt. Tues–Sun noon–5pm, f7,50; no museumcards. Limited wheelchair access.*

The history of the art form, with hundreds of drawings, photos and tools, and even some preserved tattooed skin.

Theatre Museum

Herengracht 168 ☎ *551 3300. Tram #13, #14, #17, #20 (stop Westermarkt). Tues–Fri 11am–5pm, Sat & Sun 1–5pm. f7,50; under-16s, over-65s, students, CJP free. Resource centre open Tues–Fri 11am–5pm; free.*

Recreations of contemporary stage sets alongside models that trace the earlier days of the theatre in the Netherlands, fabulously located in a canal house dating from 1638. See p.81.

Trade Union Museum

Henri Polaklaan 9 ☎ *624 1166. Tram #7, #9, #14 (stop Plantage Kerklaan). Tues–Fri 11am–5pm, Sun 1–5pm. f5. Limited wheelchair access.*

A small collection of documents, cuttings and photos relating to the Dutch labour movement. See p.110.

Tropenmuseum

Linnaeusstraat 2 ☎ *568 8200, www.kit.nl/tropenmuseum. Tram #3, #7, #9, #10, #14 (stop Mauritskade). Mon–Fri 10am–5pm, Sat & Sun noon–5pm. f12,50; 6- to 17-year-olds, over-65s, students, CJP f7,50; museumcard holders f5; under-5s free. Wheelchair access. Adjacent "Kindermuseum" open at different times; see Kids' Amsterdam, p.282.*

Entertaining exhibits on the realities of life in the developing world, imaginatively displayed through a variety of media. See p.136.

University Historical Collection

Oudezijds Voorburgwal 231 ☎ 525 3339. Tram #4, #9, #14, #16, #24, #25 (stop Spui). Mon–Fri 9am–5pm. Free. No wheelchair access.

Collections of books, prints, letters and suchlike, related to the history of the University of Amsterdam – the buildings beat the exhibits hands-down. See p.69.

Van Gogh Museum

Paulus Potterstraat 7 ☎ 570 5200. Tram #2, #3, #5, #12, #20 (stop Van Baerlestraat), or tram #16 (stop Museumplein). Daily 10am–6pm. f12,50; over-65s f7,50; 13- to 17-year-olds f5; under-12s free. Wheelchair access.

An extensive and well-presented collection covering all periods and styles of Van Gogh, with a good representative sample of works of contemporaries such as Toulouse-Lautrec and Gauguin. For f7 you can take an audio tour (the machine is shaped like a portable phone – you dial in the number of the painting). Regular lunchtime lectures in English, open symposia and films on relevant art and art-history topics. See p.124.

Van Loon Museum

Keizersgracht 672 ☎ 624 5255. Tram #16, #20, #24, #25 (stop Keizersgracht). Fri–Mon 11am–5pm; f7.50; over-65s f5; no museumcards. No wheelchair access.

Golden Age canal house with a classically furnished interior; there's also a garden in the eighteenth-century French style. See p.87.

Museum Willet-Holthuysen

Herengracht 605 ☎ 523 1822. Tram #4, #9, #14, #20 (stop Rembrandtplein). Mon–Fri 10am–5pm, Sat & Sun 11am–5pm. f7,50; over-65s, CJP f5,50; under-16s f3,50. No wheelchair access.

Rococo-style, period canal house, somewhat more pristinely restored than the Van Loon. See p.85.

Woonbootmuseum

Elandsgracht/Prinsengracht ☎ 427 0750, home.wxs.nl/~houseboatmuseum. Tues–Sun 10am–5pm. f4, children f2,50.

As a step into the past this houseboat could have been better chosen: compared to others in Amsterdam it's quite small and the interior, consisting more or less of an armchair, table and some bookshelves, is not very well preserved. Nonetheless you do get some idea of the cramped living conditions.

Museums and Galleries

Chapter 13

Shops and Markets

Variety is the essence of **shopping** in Amsterdam. Whereas in other capitals you can spend days trudging around in search of something interesting, here you'll find every kind of store packed into a relatively small area that's nearly always pleasant to wander around. Throw in a handful of great **street markets**, and Amsterdam's shopping possibilities look even better. There are, of course, the obligatory generic malls and pedestrianized shopping streets, where you can find exactly the same stuff you'd see at home (only more expensive), but where Amsterdam scores is in some excellent, unusual **speciality shops** – designer clocks, rubber stamps, Indonesian arts, and condoms, to name just a few.

Shopping in Amsterdam can be divided roughly by **area**, with similar shops often huddled together in neighbouring streets. While exploring, bear in mind that the major canals are mostly given over to homes and offices, and it's along the small radial streets that connect them that many of the most interesting and individual shops are scattered. Broadly, the **Nieuwendijk/Kalverstraat** strip running through Dam square is where you'll find mostly dull, high-street fashion and mainstream department stores – Saturday afternoon here can be a hellish experience. **Magna Plaza**, just behind the Royal Palace, is a marvellous, striped castle of a building that

used to be the main post office, but has now been transformed into a covered mall on five floors, complete with Virgin Megastore, pricey espressos, and teenagers on the escalators. The southern edge of the Red Light District, along **Damstraat** and **Oude Doelenstraat**, although popular, has little to recommend it, and you'd do well to keep one hand on your wallet while window-shopping here. **Koningsplein** and **Leidsestraat** used to be home to the most exclusive of shops; these days many of them have fled south, though there's still a surprisingly good selection of affordable designer shoe and clothes stores. The **Jordaan**, to the west, is where many local artists ply their wares: you can find individual items of genuine interest here, as well as more specialized and adventurous clothes shops and some affordable antiques. Less affordable antiques – the cream of Amsterdam's renowned trade – can be found in the Spiegelkwartier, centred on **Nieuwe Spiegelstraat**, while to the south, **P.C. Hooftstraat, Van Baerlestraat** and, further south still, **Beethovenstraat** play host to designer clothiers, upmarket ceramics stores, confectioners and delicatessens.

The consumer revolution is noticeably absent from Amsterdam's cobbled alleys, and the majority of shops you'll come across are individual small businesses rather than chains: in Amsterdam, it's the shopworker, not the consumer, who reigns supreme, as borne out by both the limited **opening hours** of most shops and the relatively high prices. The majority of shops take Monday morning off, not opening up until noon or 1pm and closing again at 6pm. On Tuesday, Wednesday and Friday, hours are the standard 9am to 6pm, while Thursday is late-opening night (*koopavond*), with most places staying open from 9am until 9pm. Saturday hours are normally 8.30 or 9am to 5 or 5.30pm, and all except the larger shops on the main streets are closed on Sunday. A few "night shops" are open between roughly 4pm and 1am; see the box on p.264.

Most small and medium-sized shops – and even some of the larger ones – won't accept **payment** by credit card: don't take it for granted in anywhere but the biggest or most expensive places. Shops that do will accept the range of major cards (American Express, Visa, Access/Mastercard, etc), but never travellers' cheques. Practically everywhere, however, takes Eurocheques, with the appropriate card as guarantee.

Antiques

By necessity, this is only a sample of what's on offer – you'll find many more **antiques** shops in every corner of Amsterdam.

Affaire D'Eau, Haarlemmerdijk 150 ☎422 0411. Antique bathtubs, taps, sinks and toilets.

Blitz, Nieuwe Spiegelstraat 37a ☎623 2663. Chinese ceramics.

Couzijn Simon, Prinsengracht 578 ☎624 7691. Antique toys and dolls.

Dick Meijer, Keizersgracht 539 ☎624 9288. Egyptian, Roman and pre-Columbian antiquities.

Eduard Kramer, Nieuwe Spiegelstraat 64 ☎638 8740. Specialists in fifteenth- to twentieth-century Dutch tiles, with a marvellous selection.

Elisabeth Hendriks, Nieuwe Spiegelstraat 61 ☎623 0085. Snuffbottles.

Gallery de Munt, in the Munttoren,

Muntplein 12 ☎623 2271. The best outlet for gifts of antique delftware, pottery, hand-painted tiles and the like.

Jan Beekhuizen, Nieuwe Spiegelstraat 49 ☎626 3912. European pewter from the fifteenth century onwards.

De Looier, Elandsgracht 109 ☎624 9038. A rambling indoor market selling moderately priced antiques.

Thom & Lenny Nelis, Keizersgracht 541 ☎623 1546. Medical antiques and spectacles.

Tóth Ikonen, Nieuwe Spiegelstraat 68 ☎420 7359. Antique Russian icons.

Van Dreven & Toebosch, Nieuwe Spiegelstraat 33 ☎625 2732. Antique clocks, barometers and music boxes.

Van Hier tot Tokio, Prinsengracht 262 ☎428 2682. Japanese furniture, crafts, kimonos etc. A split-level store with a good variety of quality items.

De Vredespijp, 1e Van der Helststraat 5–11 ☎676 4855. Art Deco furniture and decorative pieces.

Art Supplies, Postcards and Posters

The card and gift shops in the main tourist areas mostly sell items of highly questionable taste, ranging from the tacky to the openly pornographic. In the shops listed below you can get cards that are a cut above the usual dross.

Art Unlimited, Keizersgracht 510 ☎624 8419. Enormous card and poster shop, with excellent stock. All kinds of images: good for communiqués home that don't involve windmills.

De Lach, 1e Bloemdwarsstraat 14 ☎626 6625. Fairy-tale movie poster shop, "from *Casablanca* to *Pulp Fiction*".

Paper Moon, Singel 419 ☎626 1669. Well-stocked card shop.

Quadra, Herengracht 383 ☎626 9472. Original advertising posters from 1900 onwards.

Van Beek, Stadhouderskade 63 ☎662 1670. Long-established outlet for art

Shops and Markets

Shops and Markets

For more on cycling in the city, see Introducing the City, pp.51–52.

materials. Graphic arts supplies are sold at the Weteringschans 201 branch.

Van Ginkel, Bilderdijkstraat 99 ☎618 9827. Supplier of art materials, with an emphasis on print-making.

Vlieger, Amstel 52 ☎623 5834. Every kind of paper downstairs, every kind of paint upstairs.

Bikes

Bikes can be **rented** from Centraal Station (and other train stations), or from a number of private outlets all over town – see *Directory*, p.294. When **buying** a bike, don't be tempted by anything you're offered on the street or in a bar – more often than not you'll end up with a stolen bike. Try instead the shops listed below, which rent, sell and repair bikes of all qualities. If you find that no one in the shop speaks English, check out the glossary of basic bike terms on p.335.

Bike City, Bloemgracht 70 ☎626 3721. The best of the sale-and-rental crowd for service and quality – try here first.

Fietsenmakerij Damstraat, Damstraat 20 ☎625 5092. Bike repair and rental.

Freewheel, Akoleienstraat 7 ☎627 7252. Bike repairs and sales in a shop run by women.

Lohman, De Clercqstraat 70 ☎618 3906. New and used racing bikes.

MacBike, Mr Visserplein 2 ☎620 0985. Also MacBike Too at Marnixstraat 220 ☎626 6964. Well-respected rental-and-sales firm a little out of the centre.

P. Jonkerk, Lange Leidsedwarsstraat 145 ☎623 2542. Good selection of used bikes.

Ton Kroonenberg, Van Woustraat 59 ☎671 6466. Repairs and sales; service is helpful and courteous.

Zijwind, Ferdinand Bolstraat 168 ☎673 7026. Wide stock of bikes to buy or rent in a shop run by women.

Books and Magazines

Virtually all Amsterdam bookshops stock at least a small selection of English-language books, though prices are always inflated (sometimes dramatically). In the city centre it's possible to pick up most English **newspapers** the day they come out, and English-language **magazines** are available, too, from newsstands and bookshops. The **secondhand** and **antiquarian** booksellers listed below are only the most accessible; for a comprehensive list, pick up from any of them the leaflet *Antiquarian & Secondhand Bookshops of Amsterdam*.

General bookstores

American Book Center, Kalverstraat 185 ☎625 5537. Vast stock, all in English, with lots of imported US magazines and books. Especially good gay section. Students get ten percent discount.

Athenaeum, Spui 14 ☎623 3933. Excellent all-round bookshop with an adventurous stock. Also the best source of international newspapers and magazines.

The English Bookshop, Lauriergracht 71 ☎626 4230. A small but quirky collection of titles, many of which you won't find elsewhere.

Martyrium, Van Baerlestraat 170 ☎673 2092. Mostly remaindered stock, but none the worse for that – English-language paperbacks and hardbacks galore.

Scheltema Holkema Vermeulen, Koningsplein 20 ☎523 1411. Amsterdam's biggest and best bookshop. Six floors of absolutely everything. Open late and on Sundays.

De Slegte, Kalverstraat 48 ☎622 5933. The Amsterdam branch of a nationwide chain specializing in new and used books at a discount.

Waterstone's, Kalverstraat 152 ☎638 3821. Dutch branch of the UK high-street chain, with four floors of books and magazines. A predictable selection, but prices are sometimes cheaper here than elsewhere.

Zwart op Wit, Utrechtsestraat 149 ☎622 8174. Small but well-stocked store. Open on Sunday afternoons and until 7pm during the week.

Secondhand and antiquarian

A. Kok, Oude Hoogstraat 14 ☎623 1191. Antiquarian stock, especially strong on prints and maps.

Boekenmarkt, Spui. Open-air book market every Friday – see p.268.

The Book Exchange, Kloveniersburgwal 58 ☎626 6266. Rambling old shop with a crusty proprietor. Huge, dark and dusty.

Book Traffic, Leliegracht 50 ☎620 4690. An excellent and well-organized selection, run by an American.

Brinkman, Singel 319 ☎623 8353. Stalwart of the Amsterdam book trade, Brinkman has occupied the same premises for forty years. Worldwide mail order service.

Egidius, Haarlemmerstraat 87 ☎624 3255. A good selection of literature, art, poetry, plus a gallery selling lithographs.

Esoro, Oudemanhuispoort kast 1 ☎626 5783. Fictional titles, as well as books on philosophy and modern art. Friendly, chatty owner. Fri & Sat only.

Fenix, Frans Halsstraat 88 ☎673 9459. Irish literature, and a good range of books on Celtic history and culture, as well as general prehistory.

De Kloof, Kloveniersburgwal 44 ☎622 3828. Enormous higgledy-piggledy used bookshop on four floors. Great for a rummage.

Magic Galaxies, Oude Schans 140 ☎627 6261. Run by a couple whose spare time is spent collecting Science Fiction, fantasy and other esoteric books, many of which are in English. Run from home, so call first.

Oudemanhuispoort Book Market. See p.269.

Timboektoe & Wonderbook, Verversstraat 4 ☎ 6200 568. English paperbacks, travel literature and books on technical innovation.

Vrouwen In Druk, Westermarkt 5 ☎624 5003. Secondhand books, all by women authors.

Art and architecture

Architectura & Natura, Leliegracht 44 ☎623 6186. Books on architecture and interior design.

Art Book, Van Baerlestraat 126 ☎644 0925. The city's best source of high-gloss art books. Check out also the shops of the main museums, particularly the Stedelijk.

Boekie Woekie, Berenstraat 16 ☎639 0507. Books by and on Dutch artists and graphic designers.

Lankamp & Brinkman, Spiegelgracht 19 ☎623 4656. Art and applied arts, antiques and collectables, plus a good general stock.

Nijhoff en Lee, Staalstraat 13a ☎620 3980. Art and design titles, specializing in books on the art of printing, typography and lithography.

Comics and graphic novels

CIA (Comic Import Amsterdam), Zeedijk 31a ☎620 5078. What it says.

Lambiek, Kerkstraat 78 ☎626 7543. The city's largest and oldest comic bookshop and gallery, with an international stock.

Stripwinkel Kapitein Rob, 2e Egelantiersdwarsstraat 7 ☎622 3869. Cartoon books old and new.

Vandal Com-x, Rozengracht 31 ☎420 2144. US comic imports, as well as related toys, games and masks.

Computer

Boek N Serve, Ferdinand Bolstraat 151 ☎664 3446. Good range of computer literature and travel guides. You can get coffee and surf the Internet too.

Computer Collectief, Amstel 312 ☎638 9003. Vast collection of books, software and magazines, and an eminently knowledgeable staff.

Cookery

Kookboekhandel, Runstraat 26 ☎622 4768. Cookery books in a variety of languages, mostly English; also some out-of-print treasures. The owner is a well-known Dutch cookery journalist,

Shops and Markets

Shops and Markets

and can be grumpy if you don't display enough knowledge.

Gay, lesbian and women's issues

Intermale, Spuistraat 251 ☎625 0009. Gay men's bookshop.

Vrolijk, Paleisstraat 135 ☎623 5142. Self-billed as "the largest gay and lesbian bookstore on the continent".

Xantippe, Prinsengracht 290 ☎623 5854. General bookstore with a decent selection of books on women studies.

Language

Intertaal, Van Baerlestraat 76 ☎671 5353. Teach-yourself books and dictionaries in every language you can think of.

Politics and society

El Hizjra, Singel 300a ☎420 1517. Books on the Middle East and the Arab world.

Fort van Sjakoo, Jodenbreestraat 24 ☎625 8979. Anarchist bookshop stocking a wide selection of radical political publications.

Milieuboek, Plantage Middenlaan 2H ☎624 4989. Right next to the Hortus Botanicus, and specializing in books on green and environmental issues.

Pantheon, St Antoniesbreestraat 132 ☎622 9488. General bookshop with a strong politics and Middle East section.

Pegasus, Singel 367 ☎623 1138. The best politics collection in the city.

Tropenmuseum Bookstore, Linnaeusstraat 2 ☎568 8295. Books on Third World politics and culture, many in English.

Religion, occult and New Age

Au Bout du Monde, Singel 313 ☎625 1397. Astrology, philosophy, psychology and mysticism, with classical music playing while you browse.

Himalaya, Warmoesstraat 56 ☎626 0899. Cosy New Age bookshop with a marvellous café out the back.

International Evangelist Bookshop, Raadhuisstraat 14 ☎620 1859. Bibles and Christian books.

Oininio, Prins Hendrikkade 20 ☎553 9344. Bookshop attached to a large New Age centre.

De Roos, Vondelstraat 35 ☎689 0436. Delightful New Age centre with a wide selection of esoteric books and the most peaceful café in Amsterdam.

Theatre and film

Cine-Qua-Non, Staalstraat 14 ☎625 5588. Mostly English titles on film and cinema history.

International Theatre and Film Books, Leidseplein 26a ☎622 6489. Books and magazines on all aspects of the stage and screen.

Travel

A la Carte, Utrechtsestraat 110 ☎625 0679. Large and friendly travel bookshop.

Evenaar, Singel 348 ☎624 6289. Concentrates more on travel literature than guidebooks.

Jacob van Wijngaarden, Overtoom 97 ☎612 1901. The city's best travel bookshop, with knowledgeable staff and a huge selection of books and maps.

Pied-à-Terre, Singel 393 ☎627 4455. Hiking maps for Holland and beyond, most in English.

Scheltema Holkema Vermeulen, Koningsplein 20 ☎523 1411. A multistorey general bookshop with a comprehensive travel section.

Stadsboekwinkel, Waterlooplein 18 ☎622 4537. The shop for all books on Amsterdam: architecture, transport, history, urban planning, geography, etc.

Clothes and Accessories

When it comes to **clothes**, Amsterdam is in many ways an ideal place to shop: prices aren't through the roof and the city is small enough that a shopping trip doesn't have to destroy your feet. However, don't expect the huge choice of, say, London or New York. The city's department stores (see p.261) tend to be conservative, and the Dutch disapproval of ostentation means that the big international designers stay out of the limelight. What you will find are good-value, if dull, mainstream styles along Kalverstraat and Nieuwendijk, with better stuff along Rokin and Leidsestraat, and the really fancy goods down in the south of the city on P.C. Hooftstraat, Van Baerlestraat and Beethovenstraat. More interestingly, there's a fair array of one-off youth-oriented and secondhand clothing shops dotted around in the Jordaan, on Oude and Nieuwe Hoogstraat, and along the narrow streets that connect the major canals west of the city centre. For **secondhand clothes** the Waterlooplein flea market (see p.269) is a marvellous hunting ground. What follows is a brief rundown of some of the more exciting outlets.

New and designer clothes

Agnès B, Rokin 126 ☎ 627 1465. Shop of the French designer.

America Today, in Magna Plaza mall ☎ 638 8447; also at Sarphatistraat 48. Hugely popular outlet for classic US brands, imported direct and sold cheap.

Antonia, Gasthuismolensteeg 12 ☎ 627 2433. A gathering of adventurous Dutch designers under one roof. Good on shoes and bags too.

Confetti, Prinsenstraat 11 ☎ 622 3178. Bright, fun, easy to wear and affordable women's clothes.

Cora Kemperman, Leidsestraat 72 ☎ 625 1284. Well-made designer clothes that won't break the bank.

Diversi, 1e Leliedwarsstraat 6 ☎ 625 0773. Small but inspired collection of reasonably priced, mainly French clothes for women.

Edgar Vos, P.C. Hooftstraat 134 ☎ 662 6336. Amsterdam shop of the Dutch *haute couture* designer; power styles for women.

Exota, Nieuwe Leliestraat 32 ☎ 420 6884; also at Hartenstraat 10. Good,

fairly priced selection of simple, new and used clothing.

Fever, Prinsengracht 192 ☎ 623 4500. Elegant, exclusive designs for women. Phone ahead.

G & G, Prinsengracht 514 ☎ 622 6339. Men's clothing in larger sizes.

Hemp Works, Nieuwendijk 13 ☎ 421 1762. Not all hemp is like sackcloth – check out these silky hemp shirts and jeans.

Hobbits, Van Baerlestraat 34 and 42 ☎ 664 0779. High prices but a good and varied selection of women's and men's clothes. Keep an eye out for sales.

Kamikaze, Kalverstraat 158 ☎ 626 1194. Pretty standard Kalverstraat clothing outlet.

Local Service, Keizersgracht 400 ☎ 626 6840. Men's and women's fashions. Ultra-trendy and expensive.

Look Out, Utrechtsestraat 91 ☎ 625 5032. Colourful coats and knits – not cheap.

Mateloos, Bilderdijkstraat 62 ☎ 683 2384. Clothes for women in larger sizes.

De Mof, Haarlemmerdijk 109 ☎ 623 1798. Basically an industrial clothier, selling heavy-duty shirts, baggy overalls and the like for rock-bottom prices.

Pauw, Leidsestraat 16 ☎ 626 5698; also at Heiligeweg 10, and branches all over town. Mainstream and often unexceptional separates for women.

Raymond Linhard, Van Baerlestraat 50 ☎ 679 0755. Cheerful, well-priced separates.

Reflections, P.C. Hooftstraat 66 ☎ 664 0040. The absolute *crème de la crème*, with price tags to match.

Robin & Rik, Runstraat 30 ☎ 627 8924. Handmade leather clothes and accessories for men and women.

Robin's Bodywear, Nieuwe Hoogstraat 20 ☎ 620 1552. Affordable lingerie store with a wide stock.

Sissy Boy, Leidsestraat 15 ☎ 623 8949; also at Van Baerlestraat 12 and

Shops and Markets

For where to buy children's clothes, see Kids' Amsterdam.

Shops and Markets

Kalverstraat 210. Simply-designed but pricey clothes.

Street and clubwear

Clubwear House, Herengracht 265 ☎622 8766. The place for everything to do with clubbing in Amsterdam, from flyers to fabulous clothes. DJs play in-store on Saturdays.

Hair Police, Kerkstraat 113 ☎620 8567. Well-known for its colourful, dreadlocked hairdresser at the back (and now also its all-female team of tattooists), this shop has a selection of eclectic, interesting styles from both sides of the Atlantic.

Punch, St Antoniesbreestraat 73 ☎626 6673. Doc Martens and Lonsdale.

Rodolfo's, in Magna Plaza mall ☎623 1214; also at Sarphatistraat 59. Huge collection of in-line skates and skateboards and the latest styles to go with them.

Spunge, Leidsestraat 50 ☎423 6008. Futuristic designer gear.

Stilett, Damstraat 14 ☎625 2854. A cut above the regular T-shirt shop, with a jealously protective owner – no pictures!

Secondhand clothes

Daffodil, Jacob Obrechtstraat 41 ☎679 5634. Designer labels only in this posh secondhand shop down by the Vondelpark.

The End, Nieuwe Hoogstraat 26 ☎625 3162. Unspectacular but inexpensive.

Jojo, Huidenstraat 23 ☎623 3476; also at Runstraat 9. Decent secondhand clothes from all eras. Particularly good for trench coats and 1950s jackets.

Kelere Kelder, Prinsengracht 285 (no phone). Goldmine for used alternative clothing. Fri–Sun 1–6pm.

Lady Day, Hartenstraat 9 ☎623 5820. Good-quality secondhand fashion at reasonable prices.

Laura Dols, Wolvenstraat 7 ☎624 9066. Vintage clothing and lots of hats.

Rose Rood, Kinkerstraat 159 ☎618 2334. Period women's clothing – Victorian undergarments and the like.

Second Best, Wolvenstraat 18 ☎422 0274. Classy cast-offs.

Waterlooplein market – see p.269.

Zipper, Huidenstraat 7 ☎623 7302; also at Nieuwe Hoogstraat 10. Used clothes selected for style and quality – strong on jeans and flares. Prices are high, but it's very popular, and everything is in good condition.

Shoes and accessories

Abracadabra, Sarphatipark 24 ☎676 6683. Beautiful little shop selling jewellery and bric-a-brac from India.

Big Shoe, Leliegracht 12 ☎622 6645. All designs and styles for larger-sized feet of either sex.

Body Sox, Leidsestraat 35 ☎627 6553. Socks, tights and stockings in every conceivable colour and design.

Bonnier, Haarlemmerstraat 58 ☎622 1641. Very reasonably priced bag and umbrella shop.

Dr Adam's, Oude Doelenstraat 5 ☎622 3734; also at Leidsestraat 25 and P.C. Hooftstraat 90. One of the city's broadest selections of shoes.

The English Hatter, Heiligeweg 40 ☎623 4781. Ties, hats and various other accessories, alongside classic menswear from shirts to cricket sweaters.

Fleco, Haarlemmerstraat 8 ☎624 6447. Hats, ties and socks for men.

Fred de la Bretonière, St Luciesteeg 9 ☎623 4152; also at Utrechtsetstraat 77. Designer famous for his high-quality handbags and shoes, sold at reasonable prices.

Freelance Shoes, Rokin 86 ☎420 3205. Attractive designer shoes in all styles.

De Grote Tas D'Zaal, Oude Hoogstraat 6 ☎623 0110. Family-run store now in the third generation, selling a wide selection of serious bags, briefcases and suitcases.

Hoeden M/V, Herengracht 422 ☎626 3038. Designer hats galore, from felt Borsalinos to straw Panamas. Gloves and umbrellas too; intimidating prices, though.

Jan Jansen, Rokin 42 ☎625 1350. Famous Dutch designer selling hand-made shoes with frivolous designs.

Kenneth Cole, Leidsestraat 20 ☎627 6012. One of the better options on Shoe Street: affordable funky styles and solid, hardwearing boots.

Shoebaloo, Koningsplein 7 ☎626 7993; also at P.C. Hooftstraat 80. Unisex shoes in trendy styles. Check out also Bagbaloo around the corner.

Tie Rack, Heiligeweg 7 ☎627 2978; also at Kalverstraat 138 and Centraal Station. Amsterdam branches of the ubiquitous UK chain.

Tulips, Nieuwe Leliestraat 25 ☎627 5595. Tights and socks – a vast array.

Department Stores

Amsterdam's **department stores**, like many of the city's shops, err on the side of safety. Venture inside only if you have an unfulfilled urge to shop; otherwise save them for specifics. More exciting is **Magna Plaza**, in the old post office building at Nieuwezijds Voorburgwal 182, behind Dam square, which is not a department store but a covered mall sheltering all kinds of out-lets, from stationery to underwear. Alternatively, try the **Kalvertoren**, anoth-er covered mall on Kalverstraat, close to the Munt, with a range of general high-street outlets. The glass lift in the centre takes you up to the HEMA restaurant, a wonderful belvedere and a good place for coffee and simple lunches.

De Bijenkorf, Dam 1 ☎621 8080. Dominating the northern corner of Dam square, this is the city's top shop, a huge bustling place (the name means bee-hive) that has an indisputably wide range and little snobbishness. Departments to head for include house-hold goods, cosmetics and kidswear; there's also a good range of newspapers and magazines.

HEMA, Nieuwendijk 174 ☎623 4176; also in the Kalvertoren and branches out of the centre. A kind of Dutch Woolworth's, but of a better quality: good for stocking up on toiletries and other essentials, and occasional designer delights – it's owned by De Bijenkorf, and you can sometimes find the same items at knockdown prices. Surprises include wine and salami in the back of the shop.

Maison de Bonneterie, Rokin 140 ☎626 2162. Apart from the building, which rises through balustraded bal-conies to a high central dome, nothing special: very conservative and, on the whole, extremely expensive. By appoint-ment to Her Majesty.

Marks & Spencer, Kalverstraat 66 ☎620 0006. The place to head for if you're feeling homesick; it's got exactly the same stock, only priced with a ƒ not a £.

Metz & Co., Keizersgracht 455 ☎624 8810. By far the city's swishest shop, with the accent on Liberty prints (it used to be owned by Liberty's of London), stylish ceramics and designer furniture of the kind that's exhibited in modern art museums: just the place to pick up a Rietveld chair. If your funds won't stretch quite that far, settle for a cup of coffee in the top-floor Rietveld restaurant, which gives great views over the city.

Peek & Cloppenberg, Dam 20 ☎623 2837. Less a department store than a multistorey clothes shop with some painfully middle-of-the-road styles. Nonetheless, an Amsterdam institution.

Vroom & Dreesmann, Kalverstraat 203 (entrance also from Rokin) ☎622 0171. The main Amsterdam branch of a mid-dle-ground nationwide chain, just near Muntplein. It's pretty unadventurous, but take comfort from the fact that the restaurant is quite outstanding (for a department store), and they bake fresh bread on the premises as well. Check out also the listening stands in the CD section on the top floor – the best place for a free Mozart recital with a canal view.

Shops and Markets

Shops and Markets

Food and Drink

Amsterdam's talent for small specialist outlets extends to food as much as anything else. While the city's supermarkets may not impress, there's a whole host of **speciality food** stores where you can buy anything from local fish to imported Heinz beans. We've also listed a selection of **wine and spirits shops**, chosen for their location, specialities or simply because they're good value.

Supermarkets

For home cooking and economical eating and drinking, **supermarkets** are the place to go. Unfortunately, they're rather thin on the ground in the city centre, and most are throwbacks to the 1970s; going supermarket shopping in Amsterdam will probably be the only occasion when you'll long for the impersonal efficiency of back home. Aisles are narrow, trolleys are battered (you need a guilder coin to de-chain them), there are too many people and not enough choice. If you're buying fruit or vegetables, you'll need to weigh and price them yourself (unless a price is given per item, *per stuk*) – put them on the scale, press the little picture, then press *BON* to get a sticky barcode. If you're buying beer, juice or water in **bottles** (glass or plastic), a deposit of 15c–ƒ1 will be added on at the checkout; you get it back when you return the empties – to a different store, if you like. Unless you have a bag for all your stuff, you'll have to pay about 35c for an own-brand one. Most supermarkets conform to regular shop hours (see p.255).

Albert Heijn, Koningsplein 4 ☎624 5721. Variable opening hours, currently Mon–Sat 10am–10pm, Sun noon–6pm. Amsterdam's main branch of a nationwide chain but still small, crowded and expensive. There are other central branches at Nieuwmarkt 18 and Waterlooplein 131, but prices are lower in those further out of the centre: Haarlemmerdijk 1, Overtoom 454, Vijzelstraat 117 and Westerstraat 79.

Dirk van den Broek, Heinekenplein 25 ☎611 0812. Beats *Albert Heijn* hands down in everything except image. Cheaper across the board; bigger too. Trams #16, #24 or #25. Mon–Sat roughly 9am–9pm. More branches dotted around the suburbs.

Marks & Spencer, Kalverstraat 66 ☎620 0006. Delectable food section, full of choice goodies, ready to cook or ready to munch.

De Natuurwinkel, Weteringschans 133 ☎638 4083. Main branch of a chain selling only organic food (thus a little more expensive). Much better tasting fruit and vegetables than anywhere else, also grains, pulses and Bon Bon Jeanette chocolates. Superb bread. Smaller branches around town. Mon–Sat 7am–8pm, Thurs till 9pm, Sun 11am–6pm.

Beer, wine and spirits

The **legal age** at which you can be sold beer is sixteen; for wines and spirits you need to be eighteen. The Dutch word for an off-licence (liquor store) is *slijterij*.

De Bierkoning, Paleisstraat 125 ☎625 2336. The "Beer King" is aptly named: 850 different beers, with matching glasses to drink them from.

Chabrol, Haarlemmerstraat 7 ☎622 2781. All kinds of alcohol from all parts of the world. A fine selection of wines, and the staff are extremely knowledgeable.

Chateau P.C. Hooft, Honthorststraat 1 ☎664 9371. Extensive but expensive: fifty malt whiskies, forty champagnes, and Armagnac from 1886.

Cheers, O.Z. Achterburgwal 142 ☎624 2969. Red Light District booze.

Drinkland, Spuistraat 116 ☎638 6573. Largest off-licence in the centre of the city.

Elzinga Wijnen, Frederiksplein 1, corner of Utrechtsestraat ☎623 7270. High-quality wines from around the world.

Gall & Gall, Nieuw Zijds Voorburgwal 226 ☎421 8370. Most central branch of the largest off-licence chain in Amsterdam. Other outlets at Van Baerlestraat 85, 1e van der Helststraat 82, Rozengracht 72 and Utrechtsestraat 67.

D'Oude Gekroonde, Rosmarijnsteeg 10 ☎623 7711. International beer shop.

Vintner Otterman, Keizersgracht 300 ☎625 5088. Small, exclusive selection of French wines to weep for.

Breads, pastries and sweets

Along with the outlets selling cholesterol- and sugar-packed goodies, we've listed some places where you can buy healthier baked goods. Note that a *warme bakkerij* sells bread and rolls; a *banketbakkerij* sells pastries and cream cakes.

Bonbon Atelier Lawenda, 1e Anjeliersdwarsstraat 17 ☎420 5262. Dreamily wonderful chocolates.

Bon Bon Jeanette, Centraal Station ☎421 5194. Organic, handmade, additive-free, preservative-free, low-sugar chocolates – surprisingly delicious.

Gary's Muffins, Prinsengracht 454 ☎420 1452. The best, most authentic New York bagels (and muffins) in town. Branches at Marnixstraat 121 and at Reguliersdwarsstraat 53, the latter open until 3am.

Hartog's, Ruysschstraat 56 ☎665 1295. Fat-free, 100-percent-wholegrain breads, rolls and croissants. From 7am. Metro Wibautstraat.

J.G. Beune, Haarlemmerdijk 156 ☎624 8356. Handmade cakes and chocolates in an old-style interior.

Kwekkeboom, Reguliersbreestraat 36 ☎623 1205. One of the city's most famous pastry shops, showered with awards. Not cheap, but you're paying for the chocolatier's equivalent of Gucci. Also at Ferdinand Bolstraat 119 and Linnaeusstraat 80.

Lanskroon, Singel 385 ☎623 7743. Another famously good pastry shop, with a small area for on-the-spot consumption.

Mediterrané, Haarlemmerdijk 184 ☎620 3550. Famous for their croissants; also North African pastries, French bread, etc.

Paul Année, Runstraat 25 ☎623 5322. The best wholegrain and sourdough breads in town, bar none – all made from organic grains.

Pompadour Chocolaterie, Huidenstraat 12 ☎623 9554. Chocolates and lots of home-made pastries (usually smothered in or filled with chocolate).

Runneboom, 1e van der Helststraat ☎673 5941. Wonderful selection of breads from around the world – fitting, given its location in the multicultural Pijp district. Open from 7am.

Cheese

Arxhoek, Damstraat 19 ☎622 9118. Centrally situated general cheese shop.

Comestibles Kinders, Westerstraat 189 ☎622 7983. Excellent selection of cheeses and other goodies.

Robert & Abraham Kef, Marnixstraat 192 ☎626 2210. A wide range of French cheeses – and facilities for tasting. Closed Mon & Tues.

Wegewijs, Rozengracht 32 ☎624 4093. Majestic selection and expert advice, with sampling possibilities.

Coffee and tea

The Coffee Company, Leidsestraat 60 ☎622 1519. More of an espresso bar, but with some whole and ground beans for sale as well.

Geels & Co., Warmoesstraat 67 ☎624 0683. Oddly situated among Warmoesstraat's porn shops, this is one of the city's oldest and best-equipped specialists, with low prices on beans and utensils.

Levelt, Prinsengracht 180 ☎624 0823. A specialist tea and coffee company has occupied this shop for over 150 years, and much of the original decor remains. Sound advice and friendly service.

Delis and imported foods

Eichholtz, Leidsestraat 48 ☎622 0305. Specialists in imported foods from Britain

Shops and Markets

Shops and Markets

Night shops (*avondwinkels*)

Most of these places open when everyone else is starting to think about closing up, and they stay open until well into the night – which sounds great, but you have to pay for the privilege: essentials can cost a barefaced three times the regular price – and at 1am there's nowhere else to go. Most of them, too, are not immediately accessible from the centre of town, and may take a little looking for. Once you're there, though, and if you can suspend your money worries, night shops are like heaven. There are more in the outskirts, too – look in the *Gouden Gids* (Yellow Pages) under "*avondverkoop*". Before you embark upon the search though, bear in mind that Albert Heijn Supermarkets are open until 10pm.

Avondmarkt, De Wittenkade 94 ☎ 686 4919. The biggest, best and cheapest of the night shops, just west of the city centre. Tram #10. Daily 4pm–midnight.

Big Bananas, Leidsestraat 73 ☎ 627 7040. Well stocked and convenient, but absurdly expensive and not known for the kindly treatment of their customers. Mon–Fri & Sun 11am–1am, Sat 11am–2am.

Dolf's, Willemsstraat 79 ☎ 625 9503. One of the better night shops: expensive, but reasonably central, tucked in a corner of the Jordaan. Mon–Sat 3pm–1am, Sun 10am–1am.

Heuft's, Rijnstraat 62 ☎ 642 4048. Way down in the south, and too expensive to bother about – unless, that is, you fancy a late-night champagne blow-out at home: this is the only night shop to deliver. Accepts major credit cards (they need to). Mon–Sat 5pm–1am, Sun 3pm–1am.

Sterk, Vijzelstraat 127 ☎ 420 2687. Unremarkable, expensive, and unrelated to the institution below, but nonetheless of fair quality. Daily 5pm–1am.

Sterk, Waterlooplein 241 ☎ 626 5097. Less a night shop than a city centre institution, with all kinds of fresh breads and pastries baked on the premises, a large fresh produce section, friendly staff – this place pulls something over on regular supermarkets; daily 9–1am. Smaller, lower-key branch out west at De Clercqstraat 3 ☎ 618 1727; daily 8am–1am.

and the US. The only place to find Oreo cookies, Pop Tarts, Velveeta and Heinz beans.

Ithaka, 1e Bloemdwarsstraat 18 ☎ 638 4665. Greek deli with snacks and take-away meals, in the heart of the Jordaan. Open daily.

La Tienda, 1e Sweelinckstraat 21 ☎ 671 2519. Musty old Spanish deli, with chorizos, hams and cheeses galore. Also all kinds of Latin American spices.

Meidi-Ya, Beethovenstraat 20 ☎ 673 7410. Comprehensively stocked Japanese supermarket, with a takeaway section and sushi bar.

Olivaria, Hazenstraat 2a ☎ 638 3552. Olive oil, and nothing but. Incredible range of oils, all self-imported from small- and medium-sized concerns around the world. Expert advice and a well-stocked tasting table.

Oriental Commodities, Nieuwmarkt 27 ☎ 626 2797. Warren-like Chinese supermarket. All sorts of stuff squirrelled away in corners – seaweed, water-chestnuts, spicy prawn crackers. Get there early for the handmade tofu.

Renzo, Van Baerlestraat 67 ☎ 673 1673. Everything freshly made on the premises – from pastas to sandwiches and some exquisite desserts.

Taste of Ireland, Herengracht 228 ☎ 625 6704. Irish sausages, draught Guinness and freshly baked soda bread, to name just the most obvious items.

Tjin's Toko, 1e van der Helststraat 64 ☎ 671 7708. Small Asian–American supermarket and deli counter.

Fish and seafood

Although there are lots of fresh herring and seafood stalls dotted around the city at strategic locations, including one or two excellent ones in the Albert Cuyp market, perhaps the best is the award-winning **Bloemberg**, on Van Baerlestraat, on the corner of the Stedelijk Museum. To eat your herring the Dutch way, tilt back your head and dangle the fish head-first into your mouth whole. The following are a couple of good fish shops.

Viscenter Volendam, Kinkerstraat 181 ☎618 7062. Out of the centre, but with consistently high-quality fresh and cured fish. Owned and run by a family from Volendam, a fishing village north of Amsterdam.

Volendammer Vishandel, Nieuwe Spiegelstraat 54, on the corner with Kerkstraat ☎623 2962. Volendam is obviously a name that sells. A good, central fish shop with friendly service.

Organic and natural food

De Aanzet, Frans Halsstraat 27 ☎673 3415. Organic supermarket co-operative, next to *De Waaghals* restaurant (see p.228) in the Pijp.

De Belly, Nieuwe Leliestraat 174 ☎624 5281. Small and very friendly shop stocking all things organic.

Boerenmarkt. Weekly organic farmers' market – see p.268.

Deshima, Weteringschans 65 ☎625 7513. A little difficult to spot (it's in the basement), this is a macrobiotic food store with a small restaurant attached – see p.227.

Gimsel, Huidenstraat 19 ☎624 8087. Very central, with a good selection of fruit and vegetables and excellent bread.

De Groene Weg, Huidenstraat 11 ☎627 9132. Organic butcher.

De Natuurwinkel. See "Supermarkets", p.262. By far the best selection.

De Weegschaal, Jodenbreestraat 20 ☎624 1765. Small, friendly shop near the Waterlooplein flea market.

Music

The price of CDs in Amsterdam is higher than in Britain – and outrageous compared to the US. Where the city scores is in the selection available: there are lots of small, low-key shops specializing in one type of music, where you can turn up classic items unavailable elsewhere. If it's vinyl you're after, you've come to the wrong country. Some places still sell records, but it's very much taken for granted that music comes on CDs. However, the **Waterlooplein flea market** (see p.269) has stacks of old records (and CDs) on offer, and some shops – particularly jazz and reggae outlets – do maintain sections devoted to used vinyl.

Backbeat Records, Egelantiersstraat 19 ☎627 1657. Small specialist in soul, blues, jazz, funk, etc, with a helpful and enthusiastic owner.

Blues Record Centre, Hendrik Jacobszstraat 12 ☎679 4503. What it says. Tram #2. Opens at 1pm.

Boudisque, Haringpakkersteeg 10, in an alley off the top end of Damrak ☎623 2603. Well known for its wide selection of rock, house and world music.

Charles, Weteringschans 193 ☎626 5538. Concentrates on classical and folk.

Concerto, Utrechtsestraat 54 ☎623 5228. New and used records and CDs in all categories; equally good on baroque as on grunge. The best all-round selection in the city, with the option to listen before you buy.

Dance Tracks, Nieuwe Nieuwestraat 69 ☎639 0853. Imported dance music, hip-hop, jazz, dance, soul and house.

Distortion Records, Westerstraat 72 ☎627 0004. Secondhand independent vinyl.

Fame, Kalverstraat 2 ☎638 2525. Large and predictable selection of CDs and tapes.

Fat Note, Nieuwezijds Voorburgwal 332 ☎626 5142. Amercian garage, jazzy house, breakbeats and experimental dance.

Shops and Markets

Shops and Markets

Forever Changes, Bilderdijkstraat 148 ☎612 6378. New wave and collectors' items, secondhand and new.

Free Record Shop, Kalverstraat 32 & 230 ☎626 5808. One of the better pop/rock chains. Also at Centraal Station, Leidsestraat 24 and Nieuwendijk 229. No records.

Get Records, Utrechtsestraat 105 ☎622 3441. Sizeable selection of independent and alternative CDs, plus some vinyl. Check out also the deceptively small R&B section in the back of the shop.

Midtown, Nieuwendijk 104 ☎638 4252. House of all kinds from ambient to 200bpm. Also tickets and flyers.

Musiques du Monde, Singel 281 ☎624 1354. As the name suggests, world music, both new and used. Listen before you buy.

Outland, Zeedijk 22 ☎638 7576. Another good house selection, in a bright and breezily decorated environment.

Record Palace, Weteringschans 33 ☎622 3904. Opposite the *Paradiso* (see p.231), a small shop specializing in records from the 1950s and 1960s.

The Sound of the Fifties, Prinsengracht 669 ☎623 9745. Small place near the Leidsegracht with stacks of 1950s and 1960s pop and jazz.

Staalplaat, Jodenbreestraat 24 ☎625 4176. Noise, avant-garde and obscure music. Good range of cassettes.

Virgin Megastore, in the Magna Plaza mall ☎622 8929. The widest range of everything in the worst buying environment.

New Age and Natural Remedies

The Body Shop, Kalverstraat 157 ☎623 9789. The same the world over.

Dela Rosa, Staalstraat 10 ☎421 1201. One of the better shops for vitamins and dietary supplements, with friendly, expert advice.

Ego-Soft, Nieuwe Kerkstraat 67 ☎626 8069. Approaches New Age from a hi-tech standpoint, with brain machines (including free demonstration), self-awareness programmes on cassette and video, and a selection of natural stimulants.

Erica, Centraal Station ☎626 1842. Located in the unlikeliest of surroundings, this little shop is part of a chain selling a sizeable array of herbal remedies, teas, cosmetics and vitamins.

Himalaya, Warmoesstraat 56 ☎626 0899. Something of an oasis of calm in the midst of Warmoesstraat's porn shops, this cosy shop has a wide selection of books and magazines from around the world, with New Age music, tarot cards and bric-a-brac, as well as readings, a changing photo/art exhibit, and a marvellous café with a terrace and canal view out the back.

Jacob Hooij, Kloveniersburgwal 10 ☎624 3041. In business at this address since 1778, and the shop and its stock are the same now as then. Homeopathic chemist with any amount of herbs and natural cosmetics, as well as a huge stock of *drop* (Dutch liquorice).

Kruiderij De Munt, Vijzelstraat 1 ☎624 4533. A very wide range of herbal remedies, essential oils, teas and dietary supplements.

Oininio, Prins Hendrikkade 20 ☎553 9355. A remarkably peaceful place, given the scale of the building. This multi-floored centre has a huge modern bar with a vegetarian restaurant attached, a large shop selling all kinds of ecological clothes, vitamins and cosmetics, a bookshop, and a sauna on the roof.

De Roos, Vondelstraat 35 ☎689 0081. Delightful New Age centre, with a warm, intimate atmosphere. The bookshop has a wide selection of esoteric books, and the ground-floor café, with its own rambling garden, is the most peaceful in Amsterdam. A wide range of courses and workshops are available, including daily open sessions in yoga, meditation and so on.

Smart Shops

Riding on the coat-tails of Amsterdam's liberal policy towards cannabis are a number of what have become known as **"smart shops"**, ostensibly established as outlets for "smart" drugs (memory enhancers, concentration aids, and so on), while doing most of their business selling natural alternatives to hard drugs such as LSD, speed or Ecstasy. These substitutes often have many or all of the effects of the real thing, but with greatly reduced health risks – and the added bonus of legality. A consistently popular alternative to LSD are psychotropic or "magic" mushrooms, which grow wild all over northern Europe, but when processed or dried are classified as hard drugs and thus illegal. Conscious Dreams was recently forced to fight a court case over its sale of magic mushrooms; by reclassifying its business as a greengrocery, it was permitted to continue its sale of fresh magic mushrooms (dried ones remain illegal), and retains its role at the centre of a knowledgeable Amsterdam underground devoted to exploring the ramifications of altered states of consciousness.

Conscious Dreams, Kerkstraat 117 ☎ 626 6907. The oldest and best smart shop in Amsterdam.

The Magic Mushroom Gallery, Spuistraat 249 ☎ 427 5765; also on Singel 524. Most central of the three,

with an art exhibit as an added draw.

When Nature Calls, Leidsestraat corner Keizersgracht 508 ☎ 330 0700. Another shop selling cannabis products like Hemp chocolate and beer, plus seeds, and, of course, mushrooms.

Shops and Markets

Miscellaneous Shops

Perhaps more than any other place in Europe, Amsterdam is a great source of odd little shops devoted to one particular product or interest. What follows is a selection of favourites.

Abracadabra, Sarphatipark 24 ☎ 676 6683. Plastic chandeliers, silver jewellery, and colourful Indian cloths. Just off Albert Cuyp market.

Absolute Danny, Stromarkt 13 ☎ 421 0915. Bills itself as an "erotic lifestyle store", with everything that implies.

Akkerman, Kalverstraat 149 ☎ 623 1649. Vast array of pens, inks and writing implements.

Art d'Eco, Haarlemmerdijk 130 ☎ 622 1210. Accessories, clothing and stationery made of remaindered materials.

Baobab, Elandsgracht 128 ☎ 626 8398. Textiles, jewellery and ceramics from Indonesia and the Far East.

Body Soap, Haarlemmerdijk 178. Soaps made of natural oils and plants – cinnamon, ginger & mandarin, tea tree etc. – sold in cake slices.

Gamekeeper, Hartenstraat 14 ☎ 638 1579. The place to go if you're into games. All kinds of "fantasy" games from Games Workshop to role-play games, collectible cards, backgammon, magic accessories, etc, mainly for adults.

Condomerie Het Gulden Vlies, Warmoesstraat 141 ☎ 627 4174. Condoms of every shape, size and flavour imaginable. All in the best possible taste.

D. Eberhardt, Damstraat 16 ☎ 624 0724. Chinese and southeast Asian crafts, ceramics, clothes and jewellery.

Demmenie Sports, Marnixstraat 2 ☎ 624 3652. Sports shop selling everything you might need for hiking, camping and survival.

Donald E. Jongejans, Noorderkerkstraat 18 ☎ 624 6888. Hundreds of old spectacle frames, all of them without a previous owner. Supplied the specs for Bertolucci's *The Last Emperor*.

Fair Trade, Heiligeweg 45 ☎ 625 2245. Crafts from – and books about – the developing world.

Gerda's, Runstraat 16 ☎ 624 2912. Amsterdam is full of flower shops, but

For general toy shops, see Kids' Amsterdam, p.283.

Shops and Markets

this one is the most imaginative and sensual. An aesthetic experience.

Harrie van Gennip, Govert Flinckstraat 402 ☎ 679 3025. A huge collection of old and antique stoves from all parts of Europe, lovingly restored and all in working order.

The Head Shop, Kloveniersburgwal 39 ☎ 624 9061. Every dope-smoking accessory you could possibly need, along with assorted marijuana memorabilia.

Heimwee & Nu, Haarlemmerstraat 85 ☎ 622 5295. Antiques, but painted in colourful "punkish" style. Inexpensive.

Hera Candles, Overtoom 402 ☎ 616 2886. A wonderful little all-wood shop

selling nothing but handmade candles of all shapes, sizes and scents.

Jan Best, Keizersgracht 357 ☎ 623 2736. Famed antique lamp shop, with some wonderfully kitsch examples.

't Japanse Winkeltje, Nieuwezijds Voorburgwal 177 ☎ 627 9523. Japanese arts and crafts.

Joe's Vliegerwinkel, Nieuwe Hoogstraat 19 ☎ 625 0139. Kites, frisbees, boomerangs, diabolos, yo-yos, juggling balls and clubs.

Kitsch Kitchen, 1e Bloemdwarsstraat 21 ☎ 622 8261. Crammed full of bowls, spoons and other kitchen stuff in Day-Glo colours.

Markets

Albert Cuypmarkt Albert Cuypstraat, between F. Bolstraat and Van Woustraat Mon–Sat 9am–5pm. *The city's principal general goods and food market, with some great bargains to be had – check out Hilten's stall partway down on the right for the best deals on vegetables. Amsterdammers in their natural habitat.*

Amstelveld Prinsengracht, near Utrechtsestraat Mon 10am–3pm. *Flowers and plants, but much less of a scrum than the Bloemenmarkt. Friendly advice on what to buy, and the location is a perfect spot to enjoy the canal.*

Antiekmarkt Nieuwmarkt Sun 9am–5pm. *A low-key antiques market, with some good-quality books, furniture and* objets d'art *dotted in amongst the tat. May–Sept only.*

Bloemenmarkt Singel, between Koningsplein and Muntplein Mon–Sat 9am–5pm. *Flowers and plants, ostensibly for tourists, but regularly frequented by locals. Bulbs for export (with health certificate). Some stalls open on Sunday as well.*

Boekenmarkt Spui Fri 10am–3pm. *Wonderful rambling collection of sec-* *ondhand books, with many a priceless gem lurking in the unsorted boxes.*

Boerenmarkt Noordermarkt, next to the Noorderkerk Sat 9am–5pm. *Organic farmers' market selling all kinds of organically grown produce, plus amazing fresh breads, exotic fungi, fresh herbs and home-made mustards.*

Dapperstraat Dapperstraat, south of Mauritskade Mon–Sat 9am–5pm. *Covers about the same ground as the Albert Cuyp, but with not a tourist in sight. Bags of atmosphere, exotic snacks on offer, and generally better prices.*

Kunstmarkt Spui Sun 10am–3pm Thorbeckeplein, south of Rembrandtplein Sun 10am–3pm. *Low-key but high-quality art market in two locations, with much lower prices than you'll find in the galleries; prints and occasional books as well. Neither operates during the winter.*

Lindengracht Lindengracht, south of Brouwersgracht Sat 8am–4pm. *Rowdy, raucous general household supplies market, a complete switch from the jollity of the neighbouring Boerenmarkt.*

't **Klompenhuisje**, Nieuwe Hoogstraat 9a ☎ 622 8100. Amsterdam's best and brightest array of clogs.

Knopenwinkel, Wolvenstraat 14 ☎ 624 0479. Buttons in every conceivable shape and size.

Kramer and **Pontifex**, Reestraat 20 ☎ 626 5274. On one side of the shop, Mr Kramer repairs old broken dolls and teddies; on the other, Pontifex sell all kinds of candles, oils and incense.

Nieuws Innoventions, Prinsengracht 297 ☎ 627 9540. Specialists in modern designer items for the home – projector clocks, remote control lamps, Philippe Starck vases, etc. Also round dice, chocolate body-paint and shark laundry pegs.

1001 Kralen, Rozengracht 54 ☎ 624 3681. "Kralen" means beads, and 1001 would seem a conservative estimate in this place, which sells nothing but.

P.G.C. Hajenius, Rokin 92 ☎ 623 7494. Old, established tobacconist selling its own and other brands of cigars, tobacco, smoking accessories, and every make of cigarette you can think of.

Pakhuis Amerika, Prinsengracht 541 ☎ 639 2583. Secondhand Americana – take home a US mailbox on a pole, crates for Coke bottles, or a real American trashcan.

Partyhouse, Rozengracht 93b ☎ 624 7851. Every conceivable funny item – masks, rentable costumes and wigs,

Shops and Markets

De Looier Elandsgracht 109 daily except Fri 11am–5pm, Thurs till 9pm. *Indoor antiques market, with a whole variety of dealers selling everything from 1950s radios to sixteenth-century Delftware. Generally good quality.*

Nieuwmarkt Nieuwmarkt Sat 9am–5pm. *One of the last remnants of the Nieuwmarkt's ancient market history, and a rival to the more popular and better-stocked Boerenmarkt, with organic produce, breads, cheeses, and arts and crafts.*

Noordermarkt Noordermarkt, next to the Noorderkerk Mon 9am–1pm, Sat 8am–3pm. *Junk-lover's goldmine, with a general market on Mondays full of all kinds of bargains, tucked away beneath piles of useless rubbish. Get there early. There's also a farmers' produce market (Sat 9am–3pm) and a bird market (Sat 8am–1pm), though the latter is best avoided.*

Oudemanhuispoort
Oudemanhuispoort, off O.Z. Achterburgwal Mon–Sat 10am–4pm. *Charming little book market held in a university corridor since 1876, with new and used books of all kinds, many in Dutch but some in English. You can*

sit and read your purchases in the university hall, with a coffee and sandwich.

Rommelmarkt Looiersgracht 38 Mon–Thurs, Sat & Sun 11am–5pm. *A vast, permanent indoor flea market and jumble sale, with things turning up here that were left unsold at the city's other street markets.*

Stamp and Coin Market N.Z. Voorburgwal, south of Dam square Wed & Sat 11am–4pm. *For collectors of stamps, coins and related memorabilia, organized by the specialist shops crowded in the nearby alleys.*

Waterlooplein Waterlooplein, behind the Stadhuis Mon–Sat 9am–5pm. *A real Amsterdam institution, and the city's best flea market by far. Sprawling and chaotic, it's the final resting place for many a pair of yellow corduroy flares; but there are more wearable clothes to be found, and some wonderful antique/junk stalls to root through. Secondhand vinyl too.*

Westermarkt Westerstraat, from the Noorderkerk onwards Mon–Sat 9am–5pm. *Another general goods market, very popular with the Jordaan locals.*

Shops and Markets

talking clocks, crazy feet, streamers and hats. You name it.

Peter Doeswijk, Vijzelgracht 11 ☎420 3133. Phones – hundreds of identical, old rotary-dial phones, each painted with a different design (and they all work). It's chutzpah, if nothing else.

Posthumus, Sint Luciensteeg 23 ☎625 5812. Posh stationery, cards and, best of all, a choice of hundreds of rubber stamps. By appointment to Her Majesty.

Santa Jet, Prinsenstraat 7 ☎427 2070. Hand-made Latin American items, from collectibles to humorous knick-knacks, and plenty of religious icons. You can visit a palm-reader by appointment after the shop has closed.

Schaak en Go Het Paard, Haarlemmerdijk 147 ☎624 1171. Many different – and very beautiful – types of chessboards and figures; also the Japanese game "Go". Books too.

Shalimar, Utrechtsestraat 25 ☎639 2037. Tiny shop with a wonderful array of antique and modern Indian jewellery.

Taste of Ireland, Herengracht 228 ☎625 6704. Imported food and drink for the homesick.

3-D Holograms, Grimburgwal 2 ☎624 7225. All kinds of holographic art, big and small.

Tibet Shop, Spuistraat 185a ☎420 5438. Books, music, jewellery and more, all made by Tibetan refugees in Nepal and India. The Tibet Support Group (☎623 7699) can give travel advice, information on Tibetan restaurants in Holland, and on anything else concerned with Tibet.

Tikal, Hartenstraat 2a ☎623 2147. Colourful textiles and jewellery from Mexico and Guatemala.

Waterwinkel, Roelof Hartstraat 10 ☎675 5932. The only thing on offer here is water – over 100 different bottled mineral waters from all over the world. Try the wonderful German *Statl Fasching*.

't Winkeltje, Prinsengracht 228 ☎625 1352. Jumble of cheap glassware and crockery, candlesticks, antique tin toys, kitsch souvenirs, old apothecaries' jars and flasks. Perfect for browsing.

Witte Tandenwinkel, Runstraat 5 ☎623 3443. The White Teeth Shop sells wacky toothbrushes and just about every dental hygiene accoutrement you could ever need.

Chapter 14

Gay and Lesbian Amsterdam

In keeping with the Dutch reputation for tolerance, no other city in Europe accepts **gay people** as readily as Amsterdam. Here, more than anywhere, it's possible to be openly gay and accepted by the straight community. Gays are prominent in business and the arts, the age of consent is sixteen, and, with the Dutch willingness to speak English, French and just about any other language, Amsterdam has become a magnet for the international gay scene – a city with a dense sprinkling of advice centres, bars, clubs and cinemas. The COC (pronounced "say-oh-say"), the national gay and lesbian pressure group, celebrated its fiftieth birthday in 1996 – one of the longest-lived, and largest, groups of its kind in the world.

The practice of homosexuality was decriminalized in the Netherlands as long ago as 1811; a century later – still sixty years ahead of the UK – the gay **age of consent** was reduced to 21, and in 1971 it was brought into line with that of heterosexuals at 16. The most recent legal development was in 1998, with the the legislation of **same-sex marriages**.

Gay couples have full legal rights these days, and it is maybe a mark of the level of acceptance of gay lifestyles in mainstream Dutch society that every year there is a party in Amsterdam for Holland's gay and lesbian civil servants. It also says much for the strength of the gay community that the arrival of **AIDS** was not accompanied by the homophobia seen in many other places. Rather than close down clubs and saunas, the city council funded education programmes, encouraged the use of condoms, and has generally conducted an open policy on the issue; today there are a number of well-established organizations and foundations devoted to HIV prevention and support for HIV/AIDS sufferers.

However, gay men in Amsterdam are much better catered for than **lesbians**. Although there is a sizeable lesbian community in Amsterdam, there are no strictly women-only establishments – even the *Saarein*, previously the city's single women-only café, has finally opened its doors to men. A new club for women, *You II*, did open in 1999, but it too does in fact welcome men, as long as they are accompanied by a female. In many ways, London, New York or San Francisco have more nightlife options for gay women than Amsterdam, whose lesbian scene is really limited to a few women-only nights held in otherwise

---

Condoms specifically designed for gay sex are available in a large number of bars and sex shops, specifically those geared towards gay men. Brand names include: Duo, Gay Safe, Hot Rubber and Mondos Yantra.

Gay and Lesbian Amsterdam

male or mixed clubs. With the strength and achievements of the mainstream Dutch feminist movement, many of the battles currently being fought by women around the world have already been won in the Netherlands: women are fully integrated into policy-making at national and local levels, the degree of sexism in society is low, gay and lesbian lifestyles are openly presented and discussed in schools, and so on. In the last ten or fifteen years, there seems to have been less and less general need for exclusively women-only activities in Amsterdam, and exclusively lesbian entertainment has also largely been subsumed into the mainstream. Although there are a number of lesbian-owned businesses in the city, many lesbian support organizations have been forced to close for economic reasons. Amsterdam's politically active lesbians tend to move within tight circles, and it can take time to find out what's happening.

The city has four recognized **gay areas**: the most famous and most lively centres, populated as much by locals as visitors, are **Kerkstraat** and **Reguliersdwarsstraat**, the latter with a more outgoing, international scene. The streets just north of **Rembrandtplein** are a camp focus, as well as being home to a number of rent-boy bars, while **Warmoesstraat**, in the heart of the Red Light District, is cruisy and mainly leather- and denim-oriented.

As far as the attitude of the general public goes, the bottom line is that, if you're **discreet** about it, you can do what you like. Same-sex couples holding hands and kissing in the streets are no more worthy of comment than straight couples. **Cruising** is generally tolerated in places where it's not likely to cause offence; if you're new to the city, take some time to get acquainted with what's what. Many bars and clubs have **darkrooms**, which are legally obliged to provide safe sex information and condoms.

You'll find descriptions of gay **bars and nightclubs** scattered throughout Chapters 10 and 11, while recommended **gay hotels** are reviewed in Chapter 9.

If you want more information, get hold of a copy of the widely available **Columbia Fun Map** of Amsterdam produced by the *SAD-Schorerstichting* (see opposite). You could also invest in a copy of the *Best Guide to Amsterdam*, a comprehensive gay **guidebook** (in English) available from any of the shops listed below and most gay bookshops around the world. Britain's *Gay Times* carries **listings** for Amsterdam; among the many local gay newspapers and magazines, the fortnightly *Gay Krant* has all the details you could conceivably need, including up-to-the-minute listings, though it is in Dutch only (alternatively you could look up their Web site, *www.gaykrant.nl*). *De Regenbooggids* is a gay/gay-friendly version of the Yellow Pages.

Resources and contacts

In addition to the organizations and centres listed below, two important sources of information on the gay and lesbian scenes are the **Gay and Lesbian Switchboard** (☎623 6565; daily 10am–10pm; *www.dds.nl/~glswitch*), an English-speaking service which also provides help and advice, and **MVS Radio**, Amsterdam's gay and lesbian radio station (office ☎620 0247) which broadcasts daily from 6pm to 9pm on 106.8FM (or 103.8 via cable) – try and catch the English-language talk show *Aliens*, on Sunday. National Radio 5 (1008kHz MW) also broadcasts *Het Roze Rijk* ("The Pink Empire") on Saturday 6–7pm.

COC, Rozenstraat 14; office ☎626 3087 (Mon–Fri 9am–5pm), information ☎623 4079 (till 10pm). Amsterdam branch of the national gay and lesbian organization, offering advice, contacts and social activities (including an English-speaking group; info ☎420 3068), plus a coffeeshop (Mon–Sat 1–5pm) and a large noticeboard. The general COC café (Wed 8pm–midnight, Fri 10pm–3am) is also the venue for more specific "themed" nights: an HIV café (Thurs 8pm–midnight), a youth café (Wed 8pm–midnight) and multicultural night (Sun 8pm–midnight). One of the most popular women-only nights in Amsterdam is held regularly on Saturday in both the café (10pm–3am) and the nightclub (10pm–3am).

Gala, P.O. Box 15815, 1001 NH Amsterdam ☎616 1979, *www. gayamsterdam.net/gala*. Organization responsible for various Homomonument-Festivals, including those on Queensday and World Aids Day, which also has an information point at the Homo-monument itself called the Pink Point of Presence, where you can get general info and flyers etc.

Homodok (The Documentation Centre for Lesbian and Gay Studies), Nieuwpoortkade 2a, 1055 RX Amsterdam ☎606 0712, fax 0713, *www.homodok.nl*. Mon–Fri 10am–4pm. A major archive of all forms of literature, as well as videos and photographs, relating to lesbian and gay studies, contemporary and historical. It's recommended that prospective visitors write several weeks ahead detailing areas of interest: they'll write back to tell you what they can offer. See also the IIAV archive in the *Women's Amsterdam* chapter.

The Long Yang Club, Postbus 1172, 1000 BD Amsterdam ☎673 3551. International organization for Asian gays, which holds regular parties in Amsterdam, as well as publishing a monthly magazine called *Oriental Express*.

SAD Schorerstichting, P.C. Hooftstraat 5 ☎662 4206, *info@sadschorer.nl*; Mon–Fri 9am–5.30pm. Gay and lesbian counselling centre offering professional and politically conscious advice on identity, sexuality and lifestyle.

Sjalhomo ("Shalom-o"), Postbus 2536, 1000CM, Amsterdam ☎679 3898. National organization for Jewish gays and lesbians.

Stichting Tijgertje, Tigertje 10521, 1001 EM Amsterdam ☎673 2458, *tijgertj@xs4all.nl*. Gay and lesbian sports club.

Wildside, COC, Rozenstraat 14 ☎071/512 8632, *wildside@dds.nl*. A les-bian SM group which has regular open meetings at the COC (see opposite).

Bookstores

American Book Centre, Kalverstraat 185 ☎625 5537. Large general bookstore, with a fine gay and lesbian section.

Intermale, Spuistraat 251 ☎625 0009. Well-stocked gay bookshop, with a wide selection of English, French, German and Dutch literature, as well as cards, newspapers and magazines. They have a worldwide mail order service.

Vrolijk, Paleisstraat 135 ☎623 5142, *www.xs4all.nl/~vrolijk*. "The largest gay and lesbian bookstore on the continent", with a vast stock of new and second-hand books and magazines, as well as music and videos.

Xantippe, Prinsengracht 290 ☎623 5854. An impressively wide range of books and resources by, for and about women, with a large lesbian section.

Health

The two main telephone numbers for anyone needing confidential advice or information on AIDS are the **AIDS Helpline** (freephone ☎0800/022 2220; Mon–Fri 2–10pm) and the **HIV Plus Line** (☎685 0055; Mon, Wed & Fri 1–4pm, Tues & Thurs 8–10.30pm), which counsels people who are HIV-positive. See also the "Health and Insurance" section of Basics, p.25.

HIV Vereniging, 1e Helmersstraat 17 ☎616 0160, *www.hivnet.org/hvn*; clinic Mon–Fri 9am–5pm. The Netherlands HIV Association, which provides the main point of contact for anyone HIV-positive, supplying up-to-date information, as well as running a clinic, the above HIV Plus Line and an HIV Café. Call first to make an appointment.

NVSH, Blauwburgwal 7–9 ☎623 9359; Mon–Sat 11am–6pm. The Amsterdam branch of the Netherlands Society for Sexual Reform, with booklets on safe sex and general health information, as well as leather accessories and sex toys. The adjacent bar often has nights exclusively

Gay and Lesbian Amsterdam

Gay and Lesbian Accommodation

Listed below are the city's gay-friendly hotels, cross-referenced to the reviews in the *Accommodation* chapter. There are no women-only hotels, although two unofficial, privately run bed-and-breakfasts – *Johanna's* (p.180) and *Liliane's Home* (p.183) – cater for gay women, the latter exclusively so. Hotels *Quentin* and *Granada* are particularly popular with lesbians, though all the hotels listed below are lesbian-friendly. Note that it's illegal for a hotel to refuse entry to anyone on the grounds of sexual orientation.

Aero (p.179)

Anco (p.173)

Centre Apartments (p.173)

Golden Bear (p.179)

Granada (p.179)

Greenwich Village (p.179)

ITC (p.179)

Monopole (p.179)

New York (p.176)

Orfeo (p.186)

Quentin (p.179)

Sander (p.186)

Stablemaster (p.174)

Waterfront (p.180)

West End (p.1180)

for transsexuals or bisexual men; call or visit for details.

SAD Schorerstichting, GG&GD (Municipal Health Department), Groenburgwal 44 ☎662 4206; Fri 7–9pm. Weekly clinic for gay men run by the counselling centre (see p.273), offering STD (including HIV) tests and treatment. Call SAD Schorerstichting to make an appointment.

Women's Healthcentre, Obiplein 4 ☎693 4358; Mon–Fri 10am–1pm (closed for three weeks between July and August). Information and advice for women – given by women – on all health matters. Can recommend non-sexist, non-homophobic doctors, dentists and therapists.

Nightlife and entertainment

The main gay areas in the Old Centre and Grachtengordel South are dotted with numerous **gay bars**, reviewed in detail in *Eating and Drinking* – see pp.200–211. Of the late-night bars in and around Kerkstraat and Warmoesstraat, *Cockring* (p.241), *Spijker* (p.208) and many others are exclusively **male**; watch also for posters for Wasteland and Club Trash once a month. *Havana* (p.241), *You II* (p.242)

and *De Trut* (p.242) have mixed gay nights. There are currently no clubs exclusively for **lesbians** in Amsterdam. The most popular women-only night at present is "Just Girlsz" on Saturday at the COC (see p.272) although *De Trut*'s mixed gay and lesbian parties on Sunday nights (p.242) also have people queuing round the block. At a pinch, check out *Havana* or *Vive la Vie*. The Vrouwenhuis (see "Women's Amsterdam") also organizes occasional women-only nights at different venues: "Liplickers" at *Sinners in Heaven* (see p.242) and "Pussy Night", adopted by *De Melkweg* from the once famous *Roxy*, are two of the best, but currently the hottest place for women to go is *You II* (see p.242) which, though it has both a lesbian and heterosexual clientele, is strongly oriented towards the former, and only allows men in if they're with a female friend.

The only cinema left that shows **gay films** on a regular basis is The Filmhuis Cavia (☎681 1419; Tues–Fri) which also hosts an annual event in December called De Roze Filmdagen ("The Pink Film Days"), a mini-season of gay and lesbian movies. Het Ketelhuis (☎684 0090) also shows gay and lesbian movies every last Sunday afternoon of the month, and the Desmet (☎627 3434) occasionally features mainstream gay films. Call these, or the Gay and Lesbian Switchboard (see p.272), for details of gay movies showing around town, or take a look at the AUB's *Uitlijst*.

Events

The three long-standing major events in Amsterdam's gay calendar are **Coming Out Day** (Sept 5), **World AIDS Day** (Dec 1) and **Remembrance Day** (May 4), all of which occasion ceremonies and happenings around the Homo-monument, the symbolic focus of the city's gay community (see p.81). Other events occur on a less regular basis.

The first **Amsterdam Pride** took place in 1996, organized by the Gay Business Association (☎620 8807), with street parties and performances, as well as a "Canal Pride" flotilla of boats parading along the Prinsengracht. If you're in the city in August, keep an eye out for parties around this annual event.

Finally, the old Amsterdam tradition of **Hartjesdag** ("Day of the Hearts"), which ceased to be observed just before World War II, was uncovered during research a few years ago by a lecturer in Gay and Lesbian Studies at the University of Amsterdam. Apparently, at some time in August, people who so desired would spend the day in the clothes of the opposite sex. Unfortunately, the tradition seems to have vanished as far as the general public goes, but Amsterdam's nightclubs often have themed drag weekends in August to keep the old values alive.

Shops and services

Beach Boy Holidays (Ticketlijn), Amstel 24 ☎428 2428, *ticketlijn@euronet.nl*. Gay travel agent.
Black Body, Lijnbaansgracht 292 ☎626 2553, *www.blackbody.nl*. Huge selection of rubber and leather, new and second-hand, plus toys and much more.
Bronx, Kerkstraat 55 ☎623 1548. Strictly porno books, magazines and videos for men.

Demask, Zeedijk 64 ☎492 1323. Expensive rubber and leather fetish store for men and women.
Drake's, Damrak 61 ☎627 9544. Gay porn cinema.
Expectations, Warmoesstraat 32 ☎624 5573. Rubber, leather and latex wear – made on the premises.
Female and Partners, Spuistraat 100 ☎620 9152, *www.femaleandpartners.nl*. Shop selling plain and kinky sex toys for women, with probably the widest variety of vibrators in the city.
Fenomeen, 1e Schinkelstraat 14 ☎671 6780. Laid-back, inexpensive sauna in an open-plan setting, with café and chill-out room, attracting a faithful lesbian clientele on Monday 1–11pm. ƒ11 if you leave before 6pm, ƒ13,50 after. Closed for six weeks during July and August.
De Gay Krant Travel Service, Kloveniersburgwal 40 ☎421 0000, *travel@gaykrant.nl*. All kinds of information for travel in Amsterdam and worldwide.
De Leertent, Sarphatistraat 61 ☎627 8090. Huge collection of leather wear.
Mail and Female, Prinsengracht 489 ☎623 3916, *coolboys@euronet.nl*. A wide range of erotica for women in a classy scarlet environment, with helpful (female) staff.
Mandate, Prinsengracht 715 ☎625 4100. Exclusively gay male gym, which also has a sauna and café. Mon–Fri 11am–10pm, Sat noon–6pm, Sun 2–6pm.
Manstore, Max Euweplein 52 ☎626 9802. Designer underwear, swimwear and nightclothes.
Mister B, Warmoesstraat 89 ☎422 0003, *www.mrb.nl*. Rubber and leather clothing and sex toys, spread over three floors. Piercing by appointment.
RoB gallery, Weteringschans 253 ☎625 4686, *www.rob.nl*. Top-quality made-to-measure leather wear, with a worldwide mail order service. Also in London and San Francisco.
Robin and Rik, Runstraat 30 ☎627 8924. Handmade leather clothes and accessories.
Sauna Damrak, Damrak 54 ☎622 6012. Centrally located gay sauna.

Gay and Lesbian Amsterdam

f23,50, including towels. You can also get a private sauna for two for f60. Mon–Fri 10am–11pm, Sat & Sun noon–8pm. Women are also welcome on Saturday and Sunday.

Splash, Looiersgracht 26 ☎ 624 8404. Gay-friendly gym. Daily 7am–midnight.

Thermos Day Sauna, Raamstraat 33 ☎ 623 9158. Modern gay men's sauna, with steam room, whirlpool, cinema and coffee bar spread out over five floors. (Mon–Fri noon–11pm, Sat & Sun noon–10pm; f30).

Thermos Night Sauna, Kerkstraat 58–60 ☎ 623 4936. Much the same facilities as the day sauna, with the addition of a jacuzzi and dark steamroom. Cruisy atmosphere. Daily 11pm–8am; f30.

Chapter 15

Women's Amsterdam

Just over a century ago, the only women out at night in Amsterdam were prostitutes, and a respectable woman's place was firmly in the home; after voting rights were extended to women in 1919, Dutch feminism largely faded out of sight until the radical upheavals of the late 1960s. During the 1970s, though, while in many other countries feminist movements were struggling for recognition, in the Netherlands assimilation of feminist values into the mainstream came by leaps and bounds. A law was passed on abortion in 1981, and four years later abortions became available through the national health service. The controversial morning-after pill is now also available, and every town in the country has a Commissioner for Women's Affairs taking part in policy decisions. Today, Amsterdam has an impressive **feminist infrastructure**: support groups, health centres and businesses run by and for women, and there's a good range of bars and discos too. Unless you're here for an extended stay, however, or are positively seeking out information, much of this can remain invisible: feminist circles are generally indifferent to travellers, and most of the contacts you'll make will be with other visitors to the city.

As far as **safety** on the streets is concerned, Amsterdam is relatively problem-free for women travellers. As always, when exploring by yourself, it helps to project a confident attitude. The brashness of the main **Red Light District** around Oudezijds Achterburgwal can be very intimidating, and walking with a friend is a good idea here, if only to ward off unwelcome leers. However, the smaller backstreet red-light areas, such as those around the northern end of Spuistraat, are best avoided altogether, as is the southern district of "De Pijp" after dark. As for **nightclubs and bars**, the men who hang around them pose no greater or lesser threat than similar operators at home.

Resources and contacts

Het Vrouwenhuis, Nieuwe Herengracht 95 ☎625 2066. Information by phone (Mon–Fri 11am–4pm); call for other services. The "Women's House" is an organizing centre for women's activities and cultural events. There's a well-stocked library of books by and about women, a bar open weekday evenings, and a whole range of classes.

IIAV, Obiplein 4 ☎665 0820; Mon noon–5pm, Tues–Fri 10am–5pm, Tues till 7pm. The International Archives of the Women's and Lesbian Movement has a wealth of literature of all kinds detailing the history of the feminist movement in the Netherlands, and information regarding the current status of women in Dutch society. There is also an elaborate historical collection from international sources, and a referral service for Women's Studies.

Vrouwenstudies UVA, University of Amsterdam, O.Z. Achterburgwal 237 ☎525 2148. Monthly meeting of the

For specifically lesbian information, see Gay and Lesbian Amsterdam.

Women's Amsterdam

women studies group at the university, who get together for a drink somewhere in a university bar. Open to all visitors – look for notes in the hallway.

Vrouwen in Druk, Westermarkt 5 ☎ 624 5003; Mon–Fri 11am–6pm, Sat 11am–5pm. "Women in Print" stocks second-hand books by female authors, with a large English selection.

Xantippe, Prinsengracht 290 ☎ 623 5854; Mon 1–7pm, Tues–Fri 10am–7pm, Sat 10am–6pm, Sun 10am–5pm. Amsterdam's foremost women's bookshop, with a wide selection of new feminist titles in English.

Health

Aletta Jacobshuis, Overtoom 323, office ☎ 616 6222 (Mon–Fri 9am–4.30pm, Tues & Thurs also 7.30–9pm, Sat emergencies only); helplines ☎ 0900/9398 (Mon–Fri 9am–5pm; ƒ1 per min). Named after the country's first female doctor, the Jacobshuis offers sympathetic information and help on sexual problems and birth control. It's possible to get cheap but reliable condoms here, as well as prescriptions for contraceptive pills and the morning-after pill, IUD fitting and cervical smear tests.

GG&GD clinic, Groenburgwal 44 ☎ 555 5822; Mon–Fri 8–10.30am & 1.30–3.30pm, Thurs also 7–8.30pm. Municipal Health Department STD clinic; they have women-only days – phone for

details and an appointment.

MR '70, Sarphatistraat 620–626 ☎ 624 5426; Mon–Thurs 9am–4pm, Fri 9am–1pm. Centre for consultation on birth control and abortion, offering help and advice. Call first for an appointment.

Polikliniek Oosterpark, Oosterpark 59 ☎ 693 2151 (24hr). Sympathetic information and advice on contraception and abortion.

Women's Healthcentre, Obiplein 4 ☎ 693 4358; Mon–Fri 10am–1pm. Information and advice for women – given by women – on all health matters. Can recommend non-sexist, non-homophobic doctors, dentists and therapists.

Women's centres and groups

Clara Wichmann Institute, Ambonplein 73 ☎ 668 4069, www. clara-wigman.nl; office Mon–Fri 9am–5pm. Foundation providing advice and guidance for lawyers and journalists on points of law involving women. They have a nationwide list of legal practices specializing in womens' rights, and a library that's open to the public by appointment only.

Eastern Bathhouse Hammam, Zaanstraat 88 ☎ 681 4818. Tues–Sat noon–10pm (women), Sat & Sun noon–10pm (men); closed Aug. Admission ƒ15. A unique and wonderful institution, formerly for women only but, since 1999, now open to men at the weekends. Comprises hot and cold rooms and top-to-toe washing; full body scrub and massage costs a little more. Emerge feeling cleaner and more alive than you ever thought possible.

De Hippe Heks, Confuciusplein 10 ☎ 611 2268. Mon–Fri 9.30am–4.30pm. Women's meeting place, running, amongst others, Dutch-language courses.

Proscecutors Bonnema & De Boer, Willemstraat 24 ☎ 624 0323; Mon–Fri 9am–5pm. Legal help for women (but not over the phone), especially in cases involving women's rights; ring for an appointment. Walk-in session on Thurs 10am–noon.

Prostitution Information Centre, Enge Kerksteeg 3 ☎420 7328, *www.pic_amsterdam.com*; Tues & Wed, Fri & Sat 11.30am–7.30pm. See box on p.64; the centre welcomes all visitors and questions, and includes a small exhibition and shop.

De Rode Draad, Kloveniersburgwal 47 ☎624 3366. Prostitutes' trade union.

Xenia Intercultural Women's Centre, Pieter Callandlaan 230 ☎619 8765. Mon–Fri 9am–10pm. Classes and courses of all kinds for women from all backgrounds.

Feminist businesses

Freewheel, Akoleienstraat 7 ☎627 7252; Tues–Fri 9am–6pm, Sat 9am–5pm. Bike repairs and sales.

Kast 5, Oudemanhuispoort. One of the very few purely feminist businesses left –

a bookstore run by two women, with a seriously female-oriented collection.

Het Lokaal, behind Gelderlandplein/De Kamp ☎642 0361. Tues–Fri 9.30am–noon, Tues, Thurs & Fri also 1.30–5pm. ƒ12,50 per session (2hr 30min); call first to make a reservation. Fully equipped workshop for women, with tools and materials for working in wood, glass, clay, plaster, paint or linoleum. No previous experience necessary.

Vrouwen In Druk, Westermarkt 5 ☎624 5003; Mon–Fri 11am–6pm, Sat 11am–5pm. Bookstore run by women, selling secondhand books by women authors.

Zijwind, Ferdinand Bolstraat 168 ☎673 7026; Tues–Fri 9am–6pm, Sat 9am–5pm. Another bicycle repair shop run by women; they also rent bikes.

Women's Amsterdam

Chapter 16

Kids' Amsterdam

With its unique canals, tiny cobbled alleys and – above all – trams, Amsterdam in itself can be entertaining enough for some **kids**. Still, the Dutch take their children seriously and provide plenty of opportunities for them to satisfy their curiosities through play – practically all the city's parks and most patches of green have some form of playground, and the play area in the Vondelpark is heaven for kids and parents alike. There's also a multitude of attractions specifically aimed at children, ranging from circuses, puppet theatres, urban farms and rides on old trams to one of the best zoos in Europe, with a planetarium attached.

The Dutch attitude towards children is as understanding as you'd expect. If museums don't allow prams then they provide snugglies to carry small children in; most restaurants provide high chairs and special children's menus (though they're not always that great); and bars don't seem to mind accompanied kids, as long as they're reasonably under control. In short, it's very rare that having a small child in your care will close doors to you. Teenagers, while less welcome in bars, should have enough to gawk at in the city streets to keep them amused.

Babyminding

It's worth noting that not all hotels welcome young children (they'll make this clear when you book), but many of those that do also provide a **babyminding** service. If yours doesn't, try contacting **Babysit Agency Kriterion**, Roeterstraat 170 (☎624 5848 5–7pm), a long-established agency with a high reputation, which uses students at least eighteen years old, all of whom are vetted. Between 8pm and midnight rates run at ƒ10 per hour, at any other time it's ƒ12,50 per hour. Add to this a ƒ6 administration charge, plus a supplement of ƒ5 on Friday and Saturday evenings and ƒ5 for any hotel residences. The minimum charge is ƒ20. For babyminding at the weekend it's best to book in advance.

Parks, playgrounds and farms

The city's most central green spot, the **Vondelpark** (info ☎570 5411), has an

One area where Amsterdammers fall flat on their face is in keeping **dog-shit** off the streets. They just don't seem able to do it, and the stuff is a major hazard, especially for kids. Although there are teams of street-cleaners armed with high-power hoses to regularly blast the stuff off the pavement, wait another hour or two and there's fresh to replace it. Any patch of green space is obviously susceptible to contamination, too, despite poop-scoop technology, and unless an area is marked as being dog-free, you'd do well to keep one eye on your offspring and the other on your next step.

excellent playground with all sorts of stuff to do, as well as sandpits, paddling pools, ducks to feed, and even a couple of cafés where you can take a break (*'t Snoephuisje*, a pancake eatery on the Amstelveen side of the park, is perfectly situated opposite the playground – see p.219). During the summer there's always some free entertainment put on for kids – mime, puppets, acrobats and the like.

Most other city parks offer something to keep children entertained, and the best is the **Gaasperpark**, outside the centre (metro stop Gaasperplas; buses #60, #61, #157, #158, #174), which has terrific play facilities and paddling pools. In the **Amsterdamse Bos** (see p.135) you'll find playgrounds, lakes, and herds of wild deer; you can also rent canoes to explore the waterways, or visit the worthwhile Bosmuseum (see p.135) and the **Geitenhouderij Ridammerhoeve** (☎645 5034; March–Oct daily except Tues 10am–5pm; Nov–Feb also closed Mon), a very entertaining little farm with hundreds of goats and kids kept for their milk.

There are also plenty of **urban farms** dotted around the city itself – look in the phone book under *Kinderboerderij* for a full list, but worthwhile ones include the **Artis Zoo Children's Farm** (which could easily be visited as part of an Artis day out; see below for details of the zoo itself) and **De Dierenpijp** (Lizzy Ansinghstraat 82 ☎664 8303; afternoons only, closed Tues), in the south of the Pijp district.

City trips and activities

For older children, a good introduction to Amsterdam might be one of the **canal trips** that start from Centraal Station or Damrak. Much more fun, though, is a ride on a **canal bike**. This can get tiring, but jetties where boats can be picked up and dropped off are numerous, and it's quite safe; see p.53 for details. If your kids enjoy being on the water, you could also take them on a **free ferry ride** to Amsterdam North

(only 5–10min away). The best ferry to take is the *Adelaarswegveer*, a small tug-like craft with a partly exposed deck, which leaves every 10min or so from Pier 8 behind Centraal Station (Mon–Sat 6.20am–8.50pm); once there, you could either come straight back, or walk a few hundred metres west along the riverfront and take the larger, closed-in *Buiksloterwegveer* back to Centraal Station. For details of inexpensive **canal and bus tours** of Amsterdam, see p.54.

For a great view of the city, try a trek up the **towers** of the Oude Kerk or the Westerkerk (open summer only; see p.65 and p.80).

It's possible to take the kids along when you're **cycling** around the city, by renting either a bike with a child-seat attached, or a tandem, depending on the size of the child. Bike City at Bloemgracht 70 (☎626 3721) rents both kinds and gives friendly advice. In the winter, there's **ice-skating** at the Sporthal Jaap Eden (see p.288), which has indoor and outdoor rinks, open at different times. If the canals are frozen and you don't have any skates, just skeeter along on the ice with everybody else.

The best **swimming pool** for kids is the indoor, tropical-style Mirandabad (De Mirandalaan 9 ☎642 8080), which has all sorts of gimmicks like wave machines, slides and whirlpools; there's also a separate toddlers' pool. In summer, the most popular outdoor pool is in the Flevopark; for details of this and other outdoor pools, see p.289.

Museums and the Zoo

Artis Zoo, Plantage Kerklaan 40 ☎523 3400. Tram #7, #9 or #14. April–Sept daily 9am–6pm; Oct–March daily 9am–5pm; adults ƒ23,50, 4- to 11-year-olds ƒ15,50; during September admission is reduced by fifty percent. No other discounts and no dogs. The ticket includes entry to the zoo and its gardens, the Zoological Museum, the Geological Museum and the Planetarium.

Kids' Amsterdam

For a full list of Amsterdam's parks, see the Directory, p.296.

Kids'
Amsterdam

Pushchairs can be rented for ƒ2,50, and an English guidebook to the whole complex costs ƒ7,50. The café and restaurant are handily situated between the flamingo pool and the kids' playground.

Opened in 1838, this is the oldest **zoo** in the country, and it's now one of the city's top tourist attractions, though thankfully its layout and refreshing lack of bars and cages mean that it never feels overcrowded. The huge aquariums are one of the main features of the zoo. On top of the usual creatures and creepy-crawlies, there is also a Children's Farm where kids can come nose-to-nose with sheep, calves, goats, etc. Feeding times – always popular – are as follows: 11am birds of prey; 11.30am and 3.45pm seals and sea-lions; 2pm pelicans; 2.30pm crocodiles (Sun only); 3pm lions and tigers (not Fri); 3.30pm penguins. The on-site **Planetarium** (same hours, except Mon when it opens at 1pm) has five or six shows daily, all in Dutch – you can pick up a leaflet with an English translation from the desk. All in all, this is one of the best days out in the city. You can also combine an Artis day out with a canal cruise: the Artis Express runs daily 10am–5pm every 30min between Centraal Station and the zoo, including a little detour through the city (return ƒ15, 4- to 11-year-olds ƒ10; information on ☎622 2181).

Aviodome, Schiphol Centre ☎406 8000, *www.aviodome.com*. Train to Schiphol Airport, then walk or take a bus from stop B12. April–Sept daily 10am–5pm; Oct–March Tues–Fri 10am–5pm, Sat & Sun noon–5pm; ƒ12,50, over-65s ƒ11,50, 4- to 10-year-olds ƒ10; no museumcards. A huge, hands-on exhibition for buffs and kids alike – see p.249.

Kindermuseum, in the Tropenmuseum, Linnaeusstraat 2 ☎568 8233, *www.kit.nl/kindermuseum*. Tram #9, #10 or #14. Daily during school holidays, otherwise Wed afternoon, Sat & Sun (3–4 shows, 1hr 30min; call to reserve). Adults ƒ12 (though you are only allowed in for a post-"show" party), children ƒ10. Designed especially for children between the ages of six and twelve, the Kindermuseum's aim is to promote international understanding through exhibitions on other cultures. It's nowhere near as dry as it sounds, and although the show is in Dutch only, this is more than compensated for by the lively exhibits, which are expertly presented, incorporating art and music and dance performances, all designed to fascinate children (which it does). There are lots of things for kids to get their hands on, but it's best to go on Sunday, when school groups aren't visiting. Exhibits tend to have a two-year run.

Madame Tussaud's, Dam 20 ☎622 9239. Daily 10am–5.30pm. Adults ƒ19.50; 5- to 14-year-olds, over-65s ƒ16; family ticket 1 (2 adults, 2 children and a guidebook) ƒ63,75; family ticket 2 (2 adults, 3 children and a guidebook) ƒ71,75. Very large waxwork collection that's similar to the one in London, with the usual smattering of famous people and rock stars, plus some Amsterdam peasants and merchants thrown in for local colour. Hardly the high point of anyone's trip to the city, but there are parts that might excite the kids.

Museum Tramlijn, Amstelveenseweg 264 ☎673 7538. Tram #6 or #16 (stop Haarlemmermeer Station). April–Oct Sun 10.30am–5pm; May–Sept also Wed; rides every 20min. ƒ5, 4- to 11-year-olds ƒ2,50, under-4s free. No museumcards. A set of working antique trams, which run down to the Amsterdamse Bos – see p.251.

newMetropolis Science and Technology Centre, Oosterdok, near entrance to IJ tunnel ☎531 3233, *www.newmet.nl*. 5min walk from CS, or bus #22 or #32. Tues–Sun 10am–6pm. ƒ24, under-16s ƒ16; after 4pm ƒ14. Interactive "centre for human creativity" – see p.251.

Theatres, circuses and funfairs

A number of **theatres** put on inexpensive (around ƒ5) entertainment for children in the afternoon, a fair proportion of which gets around the language problem by being **mime**- or **puppet**-based: check the children's section ("Jeugdagenda") of the monthly *Uitkrant* (see p.229), and look for the words *mimegroep* and *poppentheater*. For general information on children's theatre in Amsterdam, call ☎622 2999. Public holidays and the summer season bring touring **circuses** and the occasional mobile **funfair** (*kermis*) to the city, the latter usually setting up on Dam square and thus hard to miss. Lastly, check out the **festivals** listings on p.291: many of them, such as the Queen's Birthday celebrations, can be enjoyable for kids.

Carré Theatre, Amstel 115–125 ☎622 5225. Occasionally books internationally famous circuses.

Circustheater Elleboog, Passeerdersgracht 32 ☎626 9370. For around ƒ15 or so, kids from ten to seventeen can spend the day learning how to juggle and unicycle, do conjuring tricks, be a clown, and practise face-painting. At the end of the day they put on a little show for the parents. Phone for full details of times and prices – some days are members-only sessions.

Deridas, Hobbemakade 68 ☎662 1588. Excellent weekly puppet theatre, wonderful for the under-6s. The shows are every Sunday at 11am, but the doors open at 10.15am so that the tots can play first. Booking essential.

Kids go Paradiso, Weteringschans 6–8 ☎626 4521. About three times a year the famous music venue Paradiso (see p.231) gives concerts for kids, with anything from bands playing high-tempo versions of nursery rhymes to chart music discos complete with make-up artists. Tickets around ƒ15.

De Krakeling, Nieuwe Passeerdersstraat 1 ☎624 5123. Permanent children's theatre, with shows for over- and under-12s. The emphasis is often on full-scale audience participation. Phone for a schedule.

Restaurants

Enfant Terrible, De Genestetstraat 1 ☎612 2032. Near *De Geboortewinkel* (see "Shops", below), this is the only Amsterdam café intended for families. Its wooden interior is surprisingly calm;

there is a supervised play area (ƒ2.50 per hour), so you can relax for a few minutes yourself if you need to. They will also mind your child for you for up to three hours (ƒ25), while you take off. Aside from anything else, the food is remarkably good. Open from morning until after dinner, this is a wonderful idea, and it works very well.

KinderKookKafé, Oudezijds Achterburgwal 193 ☎625 3257. Adults ƒ15, 5- to 12-year-olds ƒ10, under-5s ƒ5. Another fabulous idea – a whole restaurant entirely run by children, from cooking to waitering to dishwashing (though there are adult staff on hand). The food is simple but well done, and the whole experience is worth it just for the novelty. Booking is essential, as the café is only open to the public for weekend dinners, while on weekdays the kids can attend cookery courses and hold birthday parties.

Sun Mojsoni, van Hallstraat 8 ☎682 8496. A family restaurant run by a group of friends, with a gallery and a play area for children – see p.227.

Shops

Azzurro Kids, P.C. Hooftstraat 122 ☎673 0457. Perhaps the city's chicest kids' clothes store.

De Beestenwinkel, Staalstraat 11 ☎623 1805. Stuffed toy animals, priced from 50c to ƒ100.

Bell Tree, Spiegelgracht 10 ☎625 8830. A beautiful shop full of old-fashioned toys, mobiles, models and kids' books.

Berend Botje, Zocherstraat 87 ☎618 3349. Secondhand clothes for children, near the Vondelpark.

De Bijenkorf, Dam 1 ☎621 8080. This department store has one of the best (and most reasonable) toy sections in town.

Boon, Gravenstraat 11 ☎620 8438. One of the flashiest clothes stores for kids you'll ever see, with their own designer label, Boontje.

De Geboortewinkel, Bosboom Toussaint-straat 22 ☎683 1806. Specialists in all kinds of stuff for new or expectant parents.

Kids'
Amsterdam

**Kids'
Amsterdam**

Intertoys, Heiligeweg 26 ☎ 622 1122. Amsterdam's largest toy shop, with branches throughout the city.
De Kinderboekwinkel, Nieuwezijds Voorburgwal 344 ☎ 622 7741. Also at Rozengracht 34. Children's books, arranged by age, some of them in English.
De Kinderbrillenwinkel, Nieuwezijds Voorburgwal 129 ☎ 626 4091. Shop specializing in spectacles for children.
Kleine Nicolaas, Cornelis Schuytstraat 19 ☎ 676 9661. Handmade toys.

Chapter 17

Sports and Activities

Most visitors to laid-back Amsterdam tend to confine their exercise to walking around the major sights. But if you get the urge to stretch your muscles, there's a range of **participatory sports** to get into. In winter, skating on the frozen waterways is the most popular and enjoyable activity; other sports are generally based in private, health or sports clubs, to which you can usually get a day pass, though many are outside the centre of town. There are also a number of less energetic activities you can get involved in, whether your tastes run to chess, blackjack, or relaxing in a flotation tank.

As a **spectator**, you're limited mainly to cheering on the talented and successful local football (soccer) team Ajax (pronounced "eye-axe") in their spanking new ArenA stadium out in the suburbs – though their Rotterdam rivals Feyenoord, and the equally talented PSV team from Eindhoven, are just a train ride away. Less mainstream offerings include Holland's own *korfbal* and the weird spectacle of pole sitting. For up-to-the-minute details on all the sports listed here, or to find out where you can partake in your own favourite sporting activity, call the City Hall sports information service on ☎ 552 2490.

Baseball (Honkbal)

The local team is the **Amsterdam Pirates**, based at Sportpark Jan van Galenstraat (tram #13) ☎ 616 2151.

Matches take place on Saturday afternoons in the summer, and are free while the Pirates languish in a lower division. To **play**, you need only wander into the Vondelpark on any summer afternoon – impromptu baseball games spring up all over.

Beaches

The Netherlands has some great **beaches**, although the weather is unreliable and the infamous North Sea water is often murky and full of jellyfish. For swimming or sunbathing, the nearest resort is **Zandvoort** (see *Day-trips*, p.146), a short train-ride from Amsterdam – though be warned that it attracts large crowds in season. Otherwise, there are low-key resorts and long sandy beaches all the way up the dune-filled western coastline: Katwijk and Noordwijk can be reached by bus from Leiden, Castricum-aan-Zee, Bergen-aan-Zee and Egmond-aan-Zee by bus from Alkmaar. With your own vehicle, or a willingness to hike, it's possible to find any number of deserted spots in between.

Bowling

Knijn Bowling Centre, Scheldeplein 3, opposite the RAI complex ☎ 664 2211. The closest bowling alley to the city centre, with eighteen lanes, a bar and a pool. Lanes cost between ƒ30 and ƒ45 per hour, with a maximum of six people per lane. Reservations recommended. Fridays and Saturdays have "night bowling",

Sports and Activities

accompanied by a DJ playing club music. Mon–Sat 10am–1am, Sun noon–midnight.

Bungee Jumping

For one of the most unlikely bungee jumps imaginable, a new permanent **jump site** opened four years ago behind Centraal Station. Here you can throw yourself from a height of 75m into the Amsterdam skies, and even request a masochistic dip in the River IJ. The site is thoroughly legal and operated by Bungee Jump Holland (☎070/310 6242), part of the Dutch Federation of Bungee Jumping. The first jump costs ƒ100, the second ƒ75; you can also buy a ten-jump season ticket for a mere ƒ400. April–Oct daily noon–9pm; Oct–March Sat & Sun only noon–6pm.

Chess and Draughts

There are three **cafés** in Amsterdam where chess and draughts are played to the exclusion of (almost) everything else: *Gambit* at Bloemgracht 20, *Het Hok* at Lange Leidsedwarsstraat 134, and *Domino*, Leidsekruisstraat 19. There's a small charge for a board. See *Eating and Drinking* for more details.

Climbing

Despite the flat landscapes of the Netherlands, the Dutch love mountain walking and climbing. In Amsterdam the only substitute for the real thing is a climbing wall (*klimhal*) at Klimmuur Centraal, De Ruyterkade160 ☎427 5777, squeezed in between a rail track, a main road and a canal, so that the only way, literally, is up. A couple of hours' climbing costs ƒ22,50 per person.

Floating

Koan Float, at Herengracht 321 (☎625 4970), is the only place in Amsterdam currently offering floating as a relaxation technique. The idea is to float in a large bath of warm water, to which magnesium and sodium salt have been added to aid muscular relaxation and provide buoyancy. Because the water is the same temperature as your body, the sensation is of floating freely, and you don't have to move to stay afloat, allowing your mind and body to release pent-up stress. There are two lockable individual floating cabins, each with its own shower, so you don't even need to bring a swimming costume; once you're inside, lights, music and clothing are optional. Advance reservations are essential. Current charges are ƒ55 per 45min though you can float as long as you like, and there are discounts for return visits. Towels and bathrobes are provided. Daily 9.30am–10pm, Fri–Sun till 11pm.

Football

It's a mark of the local dominance of **Ajax**, **Feyenoord** and **PSV** that most foreigners would be hard pushed to name any other Dutch teams – indeed, in recent years Ajax have been Dutch champions three years running. After their 1995 European Cup and World Club Championship victories, Ajax also remain at or near the top of the European game, and the Dutch style of play – based on secure passing with sudden, decisive breaks – has made Dutch players highly sought-after all over Europe. Despite all this, with the building of the extraordinary new all-seater ArenA stadium in the suburbs, it's become more than a little difficult to get to see Ajax play. You can't buy a ticket without a "clipcard", and although these only cost ƒ10 for two years, you must apply in advance (fax 311 1480) and wait six weeks for your application to be processed. Having done all that, ticket prices are around ƒ35 (and more or less the same for Feyenoord and PSV). The season runs from September to May, and matches are generally on Sunday at 2.30pm, with occasional games at 8pm on Wednesday. For a full list of all league matches, consult the VVV.

Ajax Amsterdam, ArenA stadium, Bijlmer; metro Bijlmer ☎311 1450, *www.ajax.nl.*

A talented and entertaining team currently at the peak of its power, although as
far as crowd trouble goes Ajax's "F-side"
mob are every bit as bad as anything
British fans can come up with.
Feyenoord Rotterdam, Olympiaweg 50,
Rotterdam ☎010/492 9499. One of the
country's major teams. Trains stop near
the ground.
PSV Eindhoven, Frederiklaan 10a,
Eindhoven ☎040/250 5505. Talented
and friendly club, always in the running
for major honours.

Gambling

If you're itching to strike it rich with your
last few guilders, Amsterdam will prove a
disappointment. There's no horse racing
to speak of and there's just one legal
casino in the city. You can, however,
place bets on British horse races at
Hippo Toto, at Leidsestraat 101 (☎623
8583) and 1e Constantijn Huygensstraat
43 (☎683 6758). The only legal place to
play the tables in Amsterdam is the
Holland Casino, Max Euweplein 62
(daily 1.30pm–2am; over-18s only; cover
charge ƒ6; ☎521 1111). Men need to
wear a jacket, and you should be prepared to show some sort of ID. For the
really desperate, there's another Holland
Casino inside Schiphol Airport
(☎023/574 0574), but since it's beyond
passport control you've got to show a
boarding card to get in.

Gyms and Saunas

Deco, Herengracht 115 ☎623 8215. In
the running for Amsterdam's most stylish
sauna and steam bath, with a magnificent Art Deco interior and a nice café. A
great place to hang out for the day without a stitch on. Highly recommended.
Entry costs ƒ17,50. Mon–Fri before 2pm,
at other times it's ƒ27,50 for 5hr.
Mon–Sat 11am–11pm, Sun 1–6pm.
Garden Gym, Jodenbreestraat 158
☎626 8772. Weight-training and dance-
workout studio, with saunas, solarium,
massage and self-defence classes.
Mainly, but not exclusively, for women. A

sauna costs ƒ18,50; a day pass for all
activities ƒ23,50 (including a sauna).
Mon, Wed & Fri 9am–11pm, Tues &
Thurs noon–11pm, Sat 11am–6.30pm,
Sun 10am–7pm.
Oininio, Prins Hendrikkade 20 ☎553
9311. Sauna attached to a large New
Age centre – one of the best places to
sink into a bath of hot mud. ƒ23 before
5pm, ƒ27,50 thereafter. Daily 10am–midnight.
Sauna Damrak, Damrak 54 ☎622 6012.
Centrally located gay sauna, though
women are also welcome at weekends
– see p.275.
Splash, Looiersgracht 26 ☎624 8404.
Very popular hi-tech fitness centre with
sauna, tanning salon and Turkish bath.
Daily aerobic classes and single-sex
training rooms. Day pass ƒ35, week pass
ƒ87,50. Daily 7am–midnight.
De Stokerij, 1e Rozendwarsstraat 8
☎625 9417. Council fitness centre with
facilities for football, tennis, volleyball,
etc, plus a gym. ƒ3,50 for a lesson, otherwise you must buy a month's pass for
ƒ60. Daily 8am–11pm.

Hockey

Amsterdam, Wagener Stadium, Nieuwe
Kalfjeslaan, Amstelveen ☎640 1141;
bus #170, #171 or #172. The major
club in the area; its stadium, set in the
Amsterdamse Bos, also plays host to
international matches. The season runs
from September to May, with matches
on Sunday afternoon; tickets to domestic
games are free.

Horse Riding

Amsterdamse Manege, Nieuwe
Kalfjeslaan, Amstelveen ☎643 1342.
The place for a ride in the Amsterdamse
Bos – but only with supervision. You
need your own boots and riding hat,
and you must reserve ahead. ƒ28,50
per hour.
Hollandsche Manege, Vondelstraat 140,
☎618 0942. A manege built in 1882 in
neo-Renaissance style on the rim of the
Vondelpark. Again, your own boots and

Sports and
Activities

Sports and Activities

hat are required, and a lesson costs ƒ32,50.

Ice-skating

When it's really cold, skaters can get spoiled in Amsterdam: almost every drop of available water is utilized, and the **canals** provide an exhilarating way to whizz round the city – much more fun than going round a rink. Surprisingly, the canal cruises continue even when the ice is solid, with the boats crunching their way up and down the Prinsengracht; happily, though, they leave the Keizersgracht alone, and the full sweep of it becomes a fairy-tale scene, with whole families of bundled-up Amsterdammers taking to the ice. Before you venture out, however, take note of a few **safety points**:

• If no one's on the ice, don't try skating – locals have a better idea of its thickness.

• To gain confidence, start off on the smaller ponds in the Vondelpark.

• Be careful under bridges, where the ice takes longest to freeze.

• If the ice gives way and you find yourself in the water, head for the darkest spot you can see in the ice above – that's the hole.

It's also possible to skate out of Amsterdam and into surrounding towns – through the Waterland or to Muiderslot and Naarden, for example. One of the great events in Holland's sporting calendar is the annual **Elfstedentocht**, a race across eleven towns and 200km of frozen waterways in Friesland. Though the race had to be suspended for twenty years, a recent spate of cold winters has meant a number of competitions and an increasing number of participants –16,000 is now the maximum number. For more details, call the organizers, De Friese Elfsteden, in the town of Leeuwarden (☎058/215 5020; 11am–2pm). If you're around in January and the ice is good, you'll hear talk of little else.

Rinks and skate rental

Most Amsterdammers have their own skates, and there are surprisingly few places where you can **rent** a pair. If Dutch friends can't help, you can rent some at a rink or sports hall, but they won't allow you to take them away. De Meesterslijpers at Kinkerstraat 271 (☎612 2824) is one of the few shops that does rent skates for use outside, at a cost of ƒ25 per day plus a ƒ75 deposit. **Buying** a pair from a department store or sports shop will cost close to ƒ125; the best way is to find a second-hand pair by keeping an eye on noticeboards in bars and suchlike.

Sporthal Jaap Eden, Radioweg 64 ☎694 9894. Tram #9. Large complex with an indoor and outdoor rink. ƒ7, ƒ4,50 for under-15s. You can rent skates for ƒ9 from Waterman Sport next door (☎694 9884), but you can only use them at Jaap Eden, and you must leave your passport or driving licence as a deposit. Oct–March only: outdoor rink Mon–Wed & Fri 8.30am–4.30pm & 8–10pm, Thurs 8.30am–4.30pm, Sat 2–4pm, Sun 11am–4pm; indoor rink Mon–Wed & Fri 2–4pm & 8–10pm, Thurs 2–4pm.

In-line skating

If you're equipped with skates, or a skateboard, there is a free public ramp at the northeastern edge of Museumplein. Check out also the car park of the huge RAI conference centre. A few places to **rent** skates, gear and boards are: 't Snoephuisje at the Amstelveen entrance in the Vondelpark (☎664 5091); The Old Man, Damstraat 16 ☎627 0043; Rodolfo's, in the Magna Plaza mall on Nieuwezijds Voorburgwal ☎623 1214, and also at Sarphatistraat 59 ☎622 5488; and Vibes, Singel 10 ☎622 3962. If you're renting to skate around town – and many do – take care not to get stuck in the tram-tracks.

Korfbal

This is a home-grown sport, cobbled together from netball, basketball and volleyball, and played with mixed teams and a high basket. **Blauw Wit** play at the Sportpark Joos Banckersweg, off Jan van Galenstraat (☎616 0894), on Sunday at 2pm from September to June (free).

Pole Sitting

Every year in July or early August, there's the chance to witness the offbeat spectator sport of pole sitting. In Noorderwijkerhout, just north of Scheveningen on the coast near The Hague, there's a **pole sitting marathon** that lasts about five days. Although not exactly a dynamic sport, it generates a fair amount of excitement as some fifteen braves sit it out on poles perched in the North Sea. The last one left is the winner.

Running and Jogging

The main circuits are in the **Vondelpark** and **Amsterdamse Bos**, the latter with routes of varying distances signposted throughout. The **Amsterdam Marathon**, should you be up for it (a little over 42km – info on ☎663 0781), takes place in late September – 2000 will see the 25th running of the event; the start and finish lines are in front of the RAI building. A week beforehand, there is the easier-going **Dam to Dam Race**, covering the 16km between Amsterdam and Zaandam.

Snooker and Carambole

There are plenty of bars and cafés across the city where you can find a game of **pool**, although you may have to go to a hall to play **snooker**. A popular local variation on billiards (*biljart*) is **carambole**, played on a table without pockets. You score by making cannons, and the skill of some of the locals, often spinning the ball through impossible angles, is unbelievable. You'll find tables in many cafés, and get plenty of advice on how to play if you so much as look at a ball.

Snooker and pool halls

Snooker and Pool Centre Bavaria, Van Ostadestraat 97. The first, third and fourth floors comprise the **pool centre** (Mon–Thurs & Sun 2pm–1am, Fri & Sat 2pm–2am; ☎676 7903), with 26 tables costing a flat rate of ƒ13,75 per hour plus drinks. The second floor is the **snooker centre** (Mon–Thurs & Sun 11am–1am, Fri & Sat 11am–2am; ☎676 4059), which has seven tables at ƒ10 per hour before 2pm, ƒ15 after 2pm. There's also one carambole table, charged at ƒ10 per hour.

Snooker Centre, Rokin 28 ☎620 4974. Twelve tables at ƒ16 per hour. Mon–Thurs & Sun 11am–2am, Fri & Sat 11am–3am.

Snooker Centre de Keizer, Keizersgracht 256 ☎623 1586. Eight high-quality tables in a seventeenth-century canal house. Charges are ƒ10 per hour before 7pm, ƒ16 after 7pm; members pay a little less. Mon–Thurs noon–1am, Fri & Sat noon–2am, Sun 1pm–1am.

Swimming pools (Zwembaden)

Flevoparkbad, Zeeburgerdijk 630 ☎692 5030. Tram #3 or #10. The best outdoor pool in the city; gets very busy on sunny days. Mid-May to mid-Sept daily 10am–5pm, until 7pm on warm days.

Jan van Galenbad, Jan van Galenstraat 315 ☎612 8001. Outdoor pool in the west of the city. May–Sept.

Marnixbad, Marnixplein 9 ☎625 4843. Central 25m indoor pool complete with slides and whirlpools. ƒ5, with discounts for repeat visits.

De Mirandabad, De Mirandalaan 9 ☎644 6637. Superbly equipped swimming centre (outdoor and indoor pools), with wave machine, whirlpools and slides. Adults ƒ5,75, kids ƒ4,50. As with all the pools, you should call before you set out, since certain times are set aside for small children, family groups etc.

Zuiderbad, Hobbemastraat 26 ☎679 2217. Lovely old pool that's been around for close on a hundred years and is thus refreshingly free of the gimmicks that clutter up the others. That said, they have a naturist hour on Sunday from 2.30 to 3.30pm. ƒ5.

Sports and Activities

Sports and Activities

Table Tennis (Tafeltennis)

Tafeltennis Centrum Amsterdam, Keizersgracht 209 ☎624 5780. Very central table tennis hall, with a bar. ƒ14 per table per hour. Reservations essential after 6pm. Mon 3–6pm, Tue–Sat 4pm–1am, Sun 1–7pm.

Tennis and Squash

Most outdoor **tennis** courts are for members only, and those that aren't need to be reserved well in advance. Your best bets for getting a game at short notice are either at the open-air tennis courts in the Vondelpark, or at one of the following.
Frans Otten Stadion, Stadionstraat 10 ☎662 8767. Five indoor tennis courts and twenty squash courts. Tennis courts are charged at ƒ25 per hour before 5pm,

ƒ30 after 5pm; squash courts are ƒ30 then ƒ37,50 per hour. Racket rental ƒ5. Call ahead to reserve a court in the evenings. Mon–Fri 9am–midnight, Sat & Sun 9am–8pm.
Gold Star Tennis, K. Lotsylaan 20, near Vrije Universiteit (next to Station Zuid) ☎644 5483. Tram #5. Twelve indoor and 24 outdoor tennis courts, for ƒ35–45 per hour. Racket rental ƒ5. Daily 9am–10pm, with longer hours in summer.
Squash City, Ketelmakerstraat 6 ☎626 7883. Fifteen squash courts at ƒ14 per person for 45min, rising to ƒ18,50 after 5.15pm (a third person costs ƒ12,50); all prices include use of the sauna and fitness area. Racket rental ƒ5. Call ahead to reserve courts. Mon–Fri 8.45am–midnight, Sat & Sun 8.45am–10pm.

Chapter 18

Festivals and Events

Most of Amsterdam's **festivals** aren't so much street happenings as music and arts events, in addition to which there are a sprinkling of religious celebrations. Most, as you'd expect, take place in the summer; the Queen's Birthday celebration at the end of April is the city's most touted and exciting annual event, with a large portion of the city given over to an impromptu flea market. On a more cultural level, the Holland Festival, held throughout June, attracts a handful of big names. Check with the VVV for further details, and remember that many other interesting events, such as the Easter performance of Bach's *St Matthew Passion* in Naarden and the North Sea Jazz Festival in The Hague, are only a short train ride away.

The following is a diary of events held throughout the year.

February

Carnaval. Six weeks before Easter. Though the three-day Catholic celebrations are more or less confined to the south of the Netherlands, centring on Breda, 's-Hertogenbosch and Maastricht, there is a parade through Amsterdam itself (information ☎ 623 2568).

Chinese New Year. First or second week. Dragondance and fireworks, held at Nieuw Markt.

Commemoration of the February Strike. Feb 25. Speeches held around the Docker Statue on J.D. Meijerplein (see p.108).

March

Stille Omgang. Sunday closest to March 15. "Silent procession" by local Catholics through the Red Light District to the Oude Kerk (info on ☎ 023/524 5415; and see p.165).

Blues Festival. Third week. Held at the Meervaart Theatre.

"Head of the River" rowing competition. Last week. On the River Amstel.

April

Vondelpark Open Air Theatre. April–Aug. Free theatre, dance and music performances throughout the summer.

Nationaal Museumweekend. Second week. Free entrance to all the museums in the Netherlands.

Paasopenstelling. Second or third week. The Royal Palace open day.

Koninginnedag (the Queen's Birthday). April 30. Celebrated by a fair on the Dam, street markets throughout the city, and fireworks in the evening. A street event par excellence, which seems to grow annually and is almost worth planning a visit around, though some people claim it has become too commercialized over recent years. There are also special club nights and parties the night before and/or after which are well worth it if you can get into them – you'll need to book in advance, either from the club itself or from selected record stores.

Festivals and Events

May

World Press Photo Exhibition. Throughout May. A collection of some of the best photographs from newspapers around the world, held in the Nieuwe Kerk.

Herdenkingsdag (Remembrance Day). May 4. There's a wreath-laying ceremony and two-minute silence at the National Monument in Dam square, commemorating the Dutch dead of World War II, as well as a smaller event at the Homomonument in Westermarkt.

Bevrijdingsdag (Liberation Day). May 5. The country celebrates the 1945 liberation from Nazi occupation with bands, speeches and impromptu markets around the city.

Oosterparkfestival. First week. Held in the large park near the Tropenmuseum, this free festival celebrates the mix of cultures living in the area, with live music and numerous food stands.

Drum Rythm Festival. Second week. Amsterdam's first real summer event held over a weekend at the Westergasfabriek and very popular with a lot of locals. Famous musicians from all over the world take part, from Salif Keita to Lauryn Hill.

KunstRAI. Third week. The annual mainstream contemporary arts fair, held in the RAI conference centre. A less commercially-oriented alternative is the Kunstvlaai at the Westergasfabriek, always held the week before or after KunstRAI.

June

Holland Festival. Throughout June. The largest music, dance and drama event in the Low Countries; see the *Entertainment and Nightlife* chapter (p.229) for details.

Over het IJ Festival. Last week. Modern theatre and dance festival in various locations at the docklands in Amsterdam-Noord. Bus #35, or you can take a festival boat from behind Centraal Station. There's a restaurant and bar on the premises. See p.235.

July

Woodstock. Throughout July and August. Live percussion, dance acts and plenty of beach parties at the Bloemendaal beach (close to Zandvoort), with a friendly atmosphere. Weekends only.

Kwakoe festival. Second week of July to second week of August; weekends only; *www.dds.nl/~kwakoe*. A Surinam and Antillian festival held at a playground close to the Amsterdam ArenA in the southeastern suburbs, showing lots of music, dance acts and stand-up comedy. There are also workshops, and even prayer services on Sunday morning. In the middle of the festival there's a football competition between several "tropical" teams. Roti and bakabana is widely available from stalls around the festival.

August

Amsterdam Pride. First or second weekend. The city's gay community celebrates, with street parties and performances, as well as a "Canal Pride" flotilla of boats parading along the Prinsengracht.

Dance Valley. First week; *www.dancevalley.nl*. Held over a weekend at the natural amphitheatre in the hills of Spaarnwoude, just north of Haarlem, with all the techno, drum-and-bass, house and ambient DJs you could possibly wish for.

The Parade. First two weeks. An excellent travelling theatrical fair with various short theatre performances given in or in front of the artists' tents (they all work independently). Held in the Martin Luther-King park.

Racism Beat it Festival. Second Week. Bands from all over the world perform at Spaarnwoude, highlighting the racism issue. Special buses leave from Sloterdijk station.

Uitmarkt. Last week. A weekend where every cultural organization in the city advertises itself with performances either on Museumplein or by the Amstel.

Grachtenfestival. Last week. International musicians perform classical music at twenty historical locations around the three main canals. Includes the Prinsengrachtconcert, one of the world's most prestigious free open-air concerts, held opposite the *Pulitzer Hotel*.

YCity. Last week. Floating square on Oosterdok, next to the New Metropolis museum. Architectural experiment in combination with contemporary art, theatre and dance performances.

September

Open Monumentendag. Throughout September most of the state-owned monuments have an open day.

Bloemencorso. First week. The Aalsmeer–Amsterdam flower pageant in the city centre, celebrating every kind of flower except tulips, which are out of season. Vijzelstraat is the best place to see things, since the events in Dam square are normally packed solid.

Chinatown festival. Second weekend. Tong and Soeng musicians, acrobatics, Kung-Fu and Tai-Chi demonstrations at the Nieuwmarkt.

Hiswa te Water. Second week. State-of-the-art boat show at the Oosterdok. Illuminated canoe-row at night.

World Wide Video Festival. Mid-Sept to mid-Oct. Celebrating small-screen culture, starting with seminars on media art in September and then showing exhibitions in October. Held in five major places: the Stedelijk Museum, Melkweg, Het Veem, Montevideo and W139.

The Jordaan Festival. Second or third week. A street festival in a friendly neighbourhood. There's a commercial fair on Palmgracht, talent contests on Elandsgracht, a few street parties and a culinary fair on the Sunday afternoon at the Noordermarkt.

Amsterdam City Marathon. Last week.

November

Triple X. Usually first week; *www.triplex.nl*. Festival in the Westergasfabriek exploring and crossing artistic boundaries, with performances and installations by multidisciplinary international artists.

Parade of Sint Nicolaas. Second or third week. The traditional parade of *Sinterklaas* (Santa Claus) through the city on his white horse, with his helpers (called *Zwarte Pieten*, "Black Peters" – so called because of their blackened-out faces) handing out sweets and little presents.

December

Pakjesavond. Dec 5. Though it tends to be a private affair, Pakjesavond, rather than Christmas Day, is when Dutch kids receive their Christmas presents. If you're here on that day and have Dutch friends, it's worth knowing that it's traditional to give a present together with an amusing poem you have written caricaturing the recipient.

The Winter Parade. Last two weeks. Winter version of the Parade in August (see opposite), except this one is held at the Westergasfabriek.

New Year's Eve. Dec 31. New Year's Eve is big in Amsterdam, with fireworks and crazy celebration everywhere. Most bars and discos stay open until morning – make sure you get tickets in advance. A word of warning, though: Amsterdammers seem to love the idea of throwing lit fireworks around and won't hesitate to chuck one at you: in 1995 two people died and over 800 were injured because of it, half of them bystanders. To preserve your sanity (and looks), stay away, but this might qualify as the wildest and most reckless street partying in Europe.

Festivals
and Events

Chapter 19

Directory

AIRLINES at Schiphol airport: Aer Lingus
☎601 0265; Alitalia ☎577 7444;
British Airways ☎601 0245; British
Midland ☎604 1075; Delta Airlines
☎316 1676; Easyjet ☎653 2598; KLM
☎649 9123; KLM uk ☎474 7747;
Martinair ☎601 1222; Northwest
Airlines ☎649 2229; Singapore Airlines
☎316 3266; United Airlines ☎653
4620.

BABIES Some hotels don't accommodate babies, or will do so only during
the low season, so you'll need to check
when booking rooms. For details of
babysitting services, see *Kids'
Amsterdam* (p.280).

BBC WORLD SERVICE On 648kHz medium wave 24 hours a day.

BIKE RENTAL You can rent bikes at the
following outlets: Bike City, Bloemgracht
70 ☎626 3721; Holland Rent-a-Bike,
Damrak 247 ☎622 3207; Koenders
Take-a-Bike, Stationsplein 12 ☎624
8391; MacBike, Mr Visserplein 2 ☎620
0985; Macbike Too, Marnixstraat 220
☎626 6964; Take-a-bike rentservice
Zijwind, Van Ostadestraat 108 ☎673
7026.

BRING . . . Toiletries, film and English-
language books, all of which are expensive in Amsterdam.

CAR PARKS The following are all 24hr
city-centre car parks: De Bijenkorf,
Beursplein, off Damrak; Byzantium,
Tesselschadestraat 1, near Leidseplein;
De Kolk, Nieuwezijds Kolk 20;
Muziektheater, Waterlooplein (under City
Hall); Parking Plus Amsterdam Centraal,

Prins Hendrikkade 20, east of Centraal
Station.

CAR RENTAL Selected car rental agencies (*auto-verhuur*): Adams, Nassaukade
346 ☎685 0111; Avis, Nassaukade 380
☎683 6061; Budget, Overtoom 121
☎612 6066; Diks, Van Ostadestraat
278 ☎662 3366; Europcar, Overtoom
51 ☎683 2123; Hertz, Overtoom 333
☎612 2441; Ouke Baas, van
Ostadestraat 366 ☎679 4842.

CONTRACEPTIVES Condoms are widely
available from *drogists* or the
Condomerie (see p.267) – generally
they're on view but behind the counter,
so you have to point to what you want.
To get the pill you need a prescription –
see *Women's Amsterdam*, p.277.

DIAMONDS The industry was founded
here in the late sixteenth century by
refugee diamond workers from Antwerp,
but since World War II it has depended
on tourists for a livelihood. Currently
around twenty diamond firms operate in
Amsterdam. All are working factories,
but many open their doors to the public
for viewing the cutting, polishing and
sorting practices, and (most importantly)
for buying. City tours often include diamond factories (see p.105), but a few
can be visited individually. Among them
are Coster, Paulus Potterstraat 2–4
☎676 2222, Van Moppes, Albert
Cuypstraat 2–6 ☎676 1242, the
Amsterdam Diamond Centre, Rokin 1
☎624 5787, Stoeltie, Wagenstraat
13–17 ☎623 7601, and the famous
Gassan, Nieuwe Uilenburgerstraat

173–175 ☎ 622 5333. Admission is free.

DOG SHIT With so little green space in the centre of Amsterdam, this is a major problem. Unfortunately, dog-owners seem unwilling or unable either to train their animals to use the gutter or to clear up after them. Every time some form of legislation is proposed, the dog lobby shouts it down. Until something gets done, keep one eye on where you're walking.

ELECTRIC CURRENT 220v AC – effectively the same as British, although with round two- (or occasionally three-) pin plugs. British equipment will need either an adaptor or a new plug; American requires both a transformer and a new plug.

FREE AMSTERDAM Larger branches of Albert Heijn supermarkets often have free **coffee** for shoppers (and occasionally nibbles of this and that too), and many bakeries around town offer bite-sized bits of fresh gourmet **bread** or pastries (although generally as an incentive to buy at least something). The **markets** on Albert Cuypstraat and Dapperstraat close at 5pm, when over-juicy tomatoes and bruised apples go begging. Fine wines and cheeses can be found on offer at the opening of a new exhibition at one of Amsterdam's many **galleries**; just try and look interested in the art as well. There are no restrictions on listening to your favourite **CDs** all day long on the top floor of Vroom and Dreesman (Kalverstraat) or in the Virgin Megastore, where you can also play the latest **video games** to your heart's content. Many larger cafés trust you with today's English **newspapers**, so long as you leave them behind for the next free-loader. The café in De Bijenkorf is next to their magazine department; they allow you to pick any magazine off the shelf, peruse it at your leisure over a (paid-for) cup of coffee, then put it back. There is also free **art** (the Schuttersgallerij outside the Amsterdam Historical Museum on Kalverstraat), a free **boat-ride** across the IJ to Amsterdam North and back (the "IJveer" boats leave Pier 8 behind Centraal Station roughly every 10min), free lunchtime **concerts** at the Concertgebouw (October to June only), free **jazz** nightly at Bourbon Street, Café Alto and the Bamboo Bar (all near Leidseplein), even free **postcards** in café racks that are sometimes worth sending.

ISIC CARDS Student ID won't help gain reduced admission to anything in the city – for this you need a museumcard, a "culture and leisure pass" or a CJP (see p.247).

LAUNDRY (wassalons) The Clean Brothers, Kerkstraat 56 (daily 7am–9pm) is the best self-service launderette, with a sizeable load currently ƒ8 to wash, 25c per five minutes in the drier; they also do service-washes, dry-cleaning, ironing, etc; branches at Jacob van Lennepkade 179 and Westerstraat 26. Other launderettes are to be found at: Oudebrugsteeg 22 (off Damrak), Elandsgracht 59 (Jordaan), Warmoesstraat 30, Monnikenstraat 8 and Oude Doelenstraat 12 (Red Light District) and Herenstraat 24.

LIBRARIES No one will stop you from using any of the public libraries, or Openbare Bibliotheken, for reference purposes, but to borrow books you'll need to show proof of residence and pay around ƒ38 for a year's membership (less for under-18s). The main branch at Prinsengracht 587 (Mon 1–9pm, Tues–Thurs 10am–9pm, Fri & Sat 10am–5pm; Oct–March also Sun 1–5pm; ☎ 523 0900) has English newspapers and magazines and a cheap snack bar; there's also a CD library and a piano for rent (ƒ3 per hour, no library card needed). The American Institute Library is at Plantage Muiderstraat 12 (Mon, Wed & Fri 10am–4pm; ☎ 525 4380).

LOST PROPERTY For items lost on the trams, buses or metro, contact GVB Head Office, Prins Hendrikkade 108–114 (Mon–Fri 9am–4pm; ☎ 460 5858). For property lost on a train, go to the Gevonden Voorwerpen office at the nearest station; Amsterdam's is at Centraal Station, near the left luggage lockers (☎ 557 8544; 24hr). If you collect your property within two days there is no charge, but after two days each item

Directory

Directory

costs ƒ5, and after three days all unclaimed property goes to the Central Lost Property Office at 2e Daalsedijk 4, Utrecht ☎030/235 3923, and costs ƒ7,50 per item to pick up; the leaflet *Verloren Voorwerpen* has a map showing the location of the office. If you lose something in the street or a park, try the police lost property at Stephensonstraat 18 (Mon–Fri noon–3.30pm; ☎559 3005). Schiphol Airport's lost and found number is ☎601 2325. The Hook of Holland ferry terminal has no central lost property office: if you lose something here, try contacting the ferry company.

MOPED RENTAL Moped Rental Service, Marnixstraat 208 ☎422 0266.

MOSQUITOES These thrive in Holland's watery environment, and bite their worst in the canal-filled city centre and at the campsites. Muggenmelk, with DEET, is very powerful: a little smear will keep the critters well away for a good night's sleep. Other popular brands include the Autan range. For more sensitive skins, Prrrikweg (honestly) contains pungent citronella oil. After the event, an antihistamine cream such as Phenergan helps. All these and more are available all over Amsterdam.

NOTICEBOARDS Most "brown cafés" have noticeboards with details of concerts, events and the like, occasionally displaying personal notices too. The main library (see p.295) and all Albert Heijn supermarkets have noticeboards useful for apartment- and job-hunting, sharing lifts, and the like. Small neighbourhood cafés or restaurants often have thriving boards; try *Gary's Muffins* or the *Vliegende Schotel*; also the American Book Center. There's a travellers' noticeboard in the Tropenmuseum if you're looking for companions or rides to other parts of the world.

NUCLEAR ALERT On the first Monday of every month, at exactly noon, wailing klaxons start up all over the city as Amsterdam's nuclear early-warning system is tested. Amsterdammers make a show of ignoring the noise, but it is deeply sinister and unsettling. If klaxons start up at any other time, you'd be well

advised to run with everybody else.

PARKING CONTROL OFFICES The main parking control offices (Dienst Stadstoezicht) are at: Bakkerstraat 13, near Rembrandtplein (Mon–Sat 8am–11pm, Sun noon–11pm; ☎639 2469); Kinkerstraat 17 in the Jordaan (Mon–Sat 8am–11pm); and Cruquiuskade 25, Eastern Islands (24hr; ☎553 0165).

PARKS Amstelpark, beyond ring road to the south (bus #69 or #169 from Amstel station); Amsterdamse Bos (bus #170, #171 or #172 from Raadhuisstraat); Beatrixpark, next to RAI exhibition centre (tram #5); Oosterpark (tram #3, #6, #9, #10 or #14); Sarphatipark, De Pijp (tram #3); and Westerpark (tram #3 or #10).

PHOTO BOOTHS Scattered around town, but most reliably on the stairway at Vroom & Dreesmann on Kalverstraat, or at Centraal Station. You'll pay around ƒ5 for four black-and-white pictures.

PHOTOCOPYING Places like the central library and main post office have clunky old machines that cost 25c per page to use – Albert Heijn rates are cheaper at 10c per page. Specialist copy shops, whose prices mostly start at around 6c, are cheaper and better, and have all kinds of fancy paper and colour copying as well. The most people-friendly place is Copy-Copy, at Keizersgracht 306; also try Printerette (Spuistraat 128, Vijzelstraat 76). Kinko's (Overtoom 62) is open 24 hours daily, but has higher prices and a corporate attitude to match. All these places also let you use computers running everything from simple wordprocessors to desktop publishing packages; all do laser-printing too.

PROSTITUTES The women in the windows set their own prices; some pay income tax and so charge more to their customers. Expect to pay a minimum of ƒ50 for either oral sex or intercourse, always with a condom. It won't take more than fifteen minutes.

RELIGIOUS SERVICES Christian in English: Sun 12.15pm, at St John and St Ursula (Catholic), Begijnhof 30 ☎622 1918; Sun 10.30am, at the Anglican Church, Groenburgwal 42 ☎624 8877; Sun 10.30am, at the English Reformed

Church, Begijnhof 48 ☎ 624 9665. **High Mass** in Latin: Sun 9.30am and 11am, at De Krijtberg, Singel 448 ☎ 623 1923. **Jewish** Liberal, Jacob Soetendorpstraat 8 ☎ 642 3562; Orthodox, Van der Boechorststraat 26 ☎ 646 0046. **Muslim** THAIBA Islamic Cultural Centre, Kraaiennest 125 ☎ 698 2526.

TELEPHONE HELPLINES AND SERVICES
Samaritans/Lifeline/Crisis Helpline ☎ 675 7575; Legal Advice Centre ☎ 626 4477, also free legal advice from student lawyers ☎ 444 6333; ACCESS (Administrative Committee to Co-ordinate English Speaking Services) ☎ 070/346 2525; public transport information ☎ 0900/9292; wake-up service ☎ 0900/8000 (choose option 4, then enter your telephone number).

TIME One hour ahead of Britain, six hours ahead of New York, nine hours ahead of Los Angeles. Daylight-saving operates from the end of March to the end of October. Dutch speaking clock ☎ 0900/8002.

TIPPING Restaurants, hotels, taxis, etc, must include a fifteen percent service charge by law, so anything over and above this is at your discretion. Generally a tip is expected in restaurants, particularly the more expensive ones, where it's considered proper to round up the bill to the nearest five guilders.

TOILETS are invariably spotlessly clean and well maintained, and equally invariably cost 25c or 50c. For men, there are evil-smelling pissoirs located all over the city.

WEATHER Changeable, with a good chance of rain later in the day. Recorded information in Dutch on ☎ 0900/8003.

WINDMILLS The most central windmill in Amsterdam is De Gooyer in the Eastern Islands district (see p.114), and the best-preserved one is in the south of Amstelpark (see opposite). But the best place to see windmills is Kinderdijk near Rotterdam; they're also very much part of the landscape in the polderlands north of Amsterdam. Some have been moved and reassembled in the open-air museums at Zaanse Schans, near Zaandam (see p.160), and just outside Arnhem.

Directory

Part 4

The Contexts

A History of Amsterdam

To a considerable extent, a history of Amsterdam is a history of the whole of the Netherlands. The city has been at the centre of national events since its sixteenth-century ascendancy: it was the most glorious cultural and trading centre throughout the Golden Age, and, after a brief downturn in the eighteenth century, picked itself up to emerge as a major metropolis in the nineteenth. In the 1960s, Amsterdam was galvanized by its youth, who took to hippy culture with gusto; their legacy is a social progressiveness – most conspicuously in drugs and prostitution – that still underpins the city's international reputation, or notoriety, today.

The Earliest Years

Amsterdam's earliest history is as murky as the marshes from which it arose. Legend asserts that two Frisian fishermen were the first inhabitants and, true or not, it is indeed likely that the city began as a fishing village at the mouth of the River **Amstel**. Previously, this area had been a stretch of peat bogs and marshes, but, with a fall in sea-level, settlement on the higher ground of river banks was finally possible. The village was first given some significance when the local lord built a castle here around 1204, and then, some sixty years later the Amstel was dammed (leading to the name Amstelredam) and it received its

municipal **charter** from a new feudal overlord, Count Floris V, in 1275. Designating the village a toll port for beer imported from Hamburg, the charter led to Amsterdam's flourishing as a trading centre from around 1300, when it also became an important transit port for Baltic grain, destined for the burgeoning cities of the Low Countries (modern-day Belgium and Netherlands).

As Amsterdam grew, its **trade** diversified. In particular, it made a handsome profit from the English wool trade: the wool was imported, transported onto Leiden and Haarlem – where it was turned into cloth – and then much of it came back to Amsterdam to be exported. The cloth trade drew workers into the town to work along Warmoesstraat and the Amstel, and ships were able to sail right up to Dam square to pick up the finished work and drop off imported wood, fish, salt and spices.

Though the city's **population** rose steadily throughout the sixteenth century to around 12,000, Amsterdam was relatively small compared to Antwerp or London: building on the waterlogged soil was difficult and slow, requiring timber piles to be driven into the firmer sand below. And with the extensive use of timber and thatch, fires were a frequent occurrence. A particularly disastrous blaze in 1452 resulted in such destruction that the city council made building with slate and stone obligatory – one of the few wooden houses that survived the fire still stands today at the entrance to the Begijnhof. In the mid-sixteenth century the city underwent its first major **expansion**, as burgeoning trade with the Hanseatic towns of the Baltic made the city second only to Antwerp as a marketplace and warehouse for northern and western Europe. The trade in cloth, grain and wine brought craftspeople to the city, and its merchant fleet grew: by the 1550s three-quarters of all grain cargo out of the Baltic was carried in Amsterdam vessels. The foundations were being laid for the wealth of the Golden Age.

The Rise of Protestantism

At the beginning of the sixteenth century the superstition, corruption and elaborate ritual of the established **Church** found itself under attack throughout northern Europe. First, Erasmus of Rotterdam promoted ideas of reformation and then, in 1517, **Martin Luther** went one step – or rather, leap – further, producing his 95 theses against the Church practice of indulgences, a prelude to his more comprehensive assault on the entire institution. His writings and Bible translations were printed in the Netherlands, but it was Calvin (who differed from Luther in his views on the roles of Church and State) who gained the most popularity in Amsterdam. The city's doughty Calvinists had little time for other, more egalitarian Protestant sects and matters came to a head when, in 1535, one of the radical split-off groups, the **Anabaptists**, rioted, occupying Amsterdam's town hall and calling on passers-by to repent. Previously the town council had tolerated the Anabaptists, but it acted swiftly when civic rule was challenged: the town hall was besieged and the surviving Anabaptists executed on the Dam.

In 1555, the fanatically Catholic **Philip II** succeeded to the Spanish throne. Through a series of marriages the Spanish monarchy – and Habsburg family – had come to rule over the Low Countries, and Philip was determined to rid his empire of its heretics – regardless of whether they were pure Calvinists or Anabaptists. However, in the Low Countries he came face to face with a rapidly spreading Calvinist movement, whose supporters could be found in every strata of society, even the aristocracy. In 1565 a winter crop failure caused a famine, prompting Calvinist workers to riot, their anger further fuelled by Philip's anti-Protestant edicts. Later that year, a wave of **iconoclasm** swept the country: in Amsterdam, Calvinist mobs ran riot in the churches, stripping them of their treasures and their rich decoration; only when promised the Franciscan church for their worship were they mollified. Many churches, particularly in North Holland, were never restored, leaving them with the plain whitewashed interiors still seen today. The ferocity of the outbreak shocked the nobility into renewed support for Spain; most of the radical Protestant leaders saw the strong possibility of repression and quietly slipped away, the majority abroad.

War with Spain

Philip's answer to the iconoclasm was to send in an army of 10,000 men, led by the **Duke of Alva**, to suppress the heresy absolutely; the duke's first act was to condemn to death 12,000 of those who had taken part in the rebellion the previous year. The Protestant revolt took time, but was eventually led by **William the Silent**, a prince of the House of Orange-Nassau and the country's largest landowner, who took Delft, Haarlem and Leiden from Alva's troops. Amsterdam, however, prudently remained on the side of the Habsburgs until it became clear that William was winning and his forces had surrounded the town, when it then plumped for the Protestants. On William's entry into the city, the Catholic clergy was expelled and Catholic churches and monasteries were handed over for Protestant use.

In 1579 the seven Dutch provinces signed the Union of Utrecht, bringing about the formation of the **United Provinces**, an alliance against Spain that was the first consolidation of the northern Low Countries into an identifiable country. The Utrecht agreement stipulated **freedom of religious belief**, ensuring that anti-Spanish sentiment wasn't translated into divisive anti-Catholicism. Though this tolerant measure didn't extend to freedom of worship, a blind eye was turned to the celebration of Mass if it was done privately and inconspicuously – a move that gave rise to "clandestine" Catholic churches (*schuilkerken*) like that of the **Amstelkring** on Oudezijds Voorburgwal (see p.65).

With the revolt against Spain concluded, Amsterdam was free to carry on with what it did best – trading and making money.

The Golden Age

The brilliance of Amsterdam's explosion onto the European scene is as difficult to underestimate as it is to detail. The size of its **merchant fleet** carrying Baltic grain into Europe had long been considerable. Even the determined Spaniards had been unable to undermine Dutch **maritime superiority**, and, following the effective removal of Antwerp as a competitor, Amsterdam became the emporium for the products of northern and southern Europe and the new colonies in the West Indies. The city didn't prosper from its market alone, though; Amsterdam ships also carried produce, a cargo trade that greatly increased the city's wealth.

Dutch **banking and investment** brought further prosperity, and by the mid-seventeenth century Amsterdam's wealth was spectacular. The

Calvinist bourgeoisie indulged themselves in fine and whimsically decorated canal houses, and commissioned images of themselves in group portraits. Civic pride knew no bounds as great monuments to self-aggrandizement, such as the new **town hall** (now the Royal Palace), were hastily erected, and, if some went hungry, few starved, as the poor were cared for in municipal almshouses.

The arts flourished and **religious tolerance** extended even to the traditional scapegoats, the Jews, and in particular the Sephardic Jews, who had been hounded from Spain by the Inquisition but were guaranteed freedom from religious persecution under the terms of the Union of Utrecht. By the end of the eighteenth century, Jews accounted for ten percent of the city's population. Guilds and craft associations thrived, and in the first half of the seventeenth century Amsterdam's population quadrupled. Agricultural workers were drawn to the city by the better wages offered in Dutch industry, along with Protestant refugees from across Europe.

To accommodate its growing populace, Amsterdam **expanded** several times during the seventeenth century. The grandest and most elaborate plan to enlarge the city was begun in 1613, with the building of the western stretches of the **Herengracht**, **Keizersgracht** and **Prinsengracht**, the three great canals of the *grachtengordel* that epitomize the wealth and self-confidence of the Golden Age. In 1663 the sweeping crescent was extended east and north beyond the River Amstel, but by this time the population had begun to stabilize, and the stretch that would have completed the ring of canals around the city was left only partially developed – an area that would in time become the Jodenbuurt or Jewish Quarter.

One organization that kept the city's coffers brimming throughout the Golden Age was the **East India Company**. Formed by the newly powerful Dutch Republic in 1602, this Amsterdam-controlled enterprise sent ships to Asia, Indonesia and as far away as China to bring back spices, wood and other assorted plunder. Given a trading monopoly in all lands east of the Cape of Good Hope, it also had unlimited military powers over the lands it controlled, and was effectively the occupying government in Malaya, Ceylon and Malacca. Twenty years later the **West Indies Company** was inaugurated to protect new Dutch interests in the Americas and Africa. Expending

most of its energies in waging war on Spanish and Portuguese colonies from a base in Surinam, it never achieved the success of the East India Company and was dismantled in 1674, ten years after its small colony of New Amsterdam had been ceded to the British – and renamed New York. Elsewhere, the Dutch held on to their colonies for as long as possible – Indonesia, its principal possession, only secured its independence in 1945.

Gentle Decline – 1650 to 1815

Amsterdam's rise to economic pre-eminence in the early seventeenth century was greatly assisted by the problems of its **rivals**: England was riven by Civil War, the French economy was in chaos and Germany was ravaged by the Thirty Years' War. By the second half of the century however, all three countries were recovering and the Dutch position was less secure; on different occasions, Louis XIV of France attempted an invasion of the Low Countries that all but reached Amsterdam, the troops of the Bishop of Münster occupied the east of the country, and on the high seas the English and Dutch navies fought two wars (1652–54 and 1665–67). The United Provinces survived – indeed **Admiral Michel Ruyter** inflicted an embarrassing defeat on the English fleet when he sailed up the Thames and caught his enemies napping in 1667 – but the need for carefully constructed alliances (paid for by the wealth of the country if necessary) was all too obvious.

Though the Dutch had seen off the French, Louis retained designs on the United Provinces. When his grandson succeeded to the Spanish throne, which brought with it control of the Spanish Netherlands (present-day Belgium), Louis forced him to hand the area over to French control. In response, England, Austria and the United Provinces formed an alliance against the French, and so began the **War of the Spanish Succession**, a haphazard conflict that dragged on until 1713. French ambitions were thwarted by the war, but the United Provinces gained little; the nation's wealth was drained and a slow decline in the city's fortunes began, the mood altered to one of conservatism. With the English ruling the commercial roost over the ensuing years, it was clear that the Golden Age was over.

Towards the end of the eighteenth century, Amsterdam and the United Provinces witnessed a rising tension between the pro-French ruling families (who styled themselves "Patriots") and Dutch loyalists. By the 1780s there was near-civil war, and in 1795, aided by the Patriots, the French invaded, setting up the **Batavian Republic** and administering it from Amsterdam. Under French control, the United Provinces were dragged into **war with England** and in 1806 Napoleon removed the last vestiges of Dutch independence by installing his brother **Louis** as King of The Netherlands in Amsterdam's town hall (giving it, incidentally, its title of **Royal Palace**), in an attempt to create a commercial gulf between the country and England. Once settled, however, Louis was not willing to allow the country to become a simple satellite of France and surprised his brother by showing a degree of independence, ignoring the more imperious of Napoleon's directives, until, after just four years, he was forced to abdicate. Following Napoleon's disastrous retreat from Moscow, French rule weakened and the country was returned to **Dutch control** under William I, who was installed as ruler of the ill-starred united **Kingdom of the Netherlands**, incorporating both present-day Belgium and Holland.

The Nineteenth Century

Amsterdam's status was dramatically eroded during the short-lived Kingdom of the Netherlands (1815–1830). Previously, the self-governing city, made bold by its wealth, could (and frequently did) act in its own self-interest, at the expense of the nation. From 1815, however, it was integrated within the country, with no more rights than any other city. The seat of government (and the centre for all decision-making) was The Hague, and it remained so after the southern provinces broke away and the present two countries of Belgium and The Netherlands were formed in 1830.

In the first years of the nineteenth century Amsterdam's economical decline was partly camouflaged by profitable colonial trade with the East Indies (Indonesia). This trade was hampered however by the **Zuider Zee**, whose shallows and sandbanks presented real problems given the increase in the size of merchant ships. The North Holland Canal, completed in 1824 to bypass the Zuider Zee, made little difference, and it was Rotterdam, strategically placed on the Rhine inlets between the industries of the Ruhr and

Britain, that prospered at Amsterdam's expense. Even the opening of the **North Sea Canal** in 1876 failed to push Amsterdam's trade ahead of Rotterdam's, though the capital did house the country's **shipbuilding industry**, remnants of which can still be seen at the 't Kromhout shipyard (see p.114).

Between 1850 and the turn of the century, the population of Amsterdam, which had remained static since the 1650s, doubled. Most of the newcomers to the city were poor, drawn here by the city's emergent industries, and the **housing** built for them reflected their lack of wealth: the humble homes around De Pijp in the Old South date from this period. However, the Jordaan, one of the city's most impoverished quarters, was cleared: its polluted canals were filled in and small, inexpensive homes were built, the most conspicuous of several large-scale schemes put together by philanthropic social organizations, and the council, to improve the city. The political climate was outstandingly liberal, influenced by cabinet leader **Jan Rudolf Thorbecke** and an increasingly socialist contingent on the Amsterdam city council.

Until the hard years of the depression, the city continued to grow. The rise in the standard of living among working people meant that they could afford better homes, usually under the auspices of housing associations or the city's own building programmes. The most interesting of these were the estates built in what came to be called the **New South**: designed by a group known as the **Amsterdam School** of architects, they combined Modernism and Expressionism with elements of home-grown styles – and were extremely successful.

The War Years

The Netherlands remained neutral during **World War I** and although it suffered indirectly as a result of the Allied blockade of German ports, this was offset by the high profits many of its merchants made by trading with both sides. Similar attempts to remain neutral in **World War II** soon failed: German troops invaded on May 10, 1940, and the Dutch were quickly overwhelmed. Queen Wilhelmina fled to London, and Arthur Seyss-Inquart was installed as the Nazis' puppet leader. Members of the **NSB**, the Dutch fascist party, which had welcomed the invaders, found themselves rapidly promoted to positions of authority, but, in the early years of the occupation at least, life for ordinary Amsterdammers went on much as usual. Even when the first roundups of the Jews began in 1941, most people pretended they weren't happening, the single large-scale demonstration against the Nazi actions being the quickly suppressed **February strike** of the same year.

The **Dutch Resistance** was instrumental in destroying German supplies and munitions and carrying out harassing attacks in the city, and as the Resistance grew, underground newspapers flourished – today's newspaper *Het Parool* (The Password) began life as an illegal newsletter. Around 13,000 Resistance fighters and sympathizers lost their lives during the war, and the city's old **Jewish quarter**, swollen by those who had fled Germany during the persecutions of the 1930s, was obliterated, leaving only the deserted Jodenhoek and the diary of a young girl – Anne Frank – as testaments to the horrors.

After the War

The years immediately after the war were spent patching up the damage of occupation and liberation. It was a period of intense **poverty** in the capital, as food, fuel and building materials were practically non-existent; a common sight on the streets was handcart burials of those who had died of hunger or hypothermia, black cardboard coffins being trundled to mass graves. As the Canadian army had moved nearer to Amsterdam, the Germans had blown up all the dikes and the sluices on the North Sea coast at IJmuiden, and repairing these further slowed the process of rebuilding. The sea itself claimed victims in 1953, when an unusually high tide swept over Zeeland's coastal defences, flooding 40,000 acres of land and drowning more than 1800 people. The subsequent **Delta Project** ensured the safety of cities to the south of Amsterdam, though Amsterdam itself had already been secured by the completion of the **Afsluitdijk** in 1932, a dike which separated the Zuider Zee from the North Sea and turned it into the freshwater IJsselmeer. The post-war opening of the **Amsterdam-Rhine canal** did much to boost the city's fortunes too, with massive cargo-handling facilities built to accommodate the import of grain and the supply of ore to the Ruhr furnaces. Steadily the rebuilding continued and giant suburbs such as **Bijlmermeer** to the southeast were

the last word in 1960s large-scale residential planning, with low-cost modern housing, play areas and traffic-free foot and cycle paths.

The 1960s and 1970s: Radical Movements

The radical and youthful mass movements that swept through the West in the 1960s transformed Amsterdam from a middling, rather conservative city into a turbo-charged hotbed of **hippy action**. In 1963, for example, one-time window cleaner and magician extraordinaire Jasper Grootveld won celebrity status by painting "K" – for *kanker* ("cancer") – on cigarette billboards throughout the city. Two years later, he proclaimed the statue of the *Lieverdje* ("Loveable Rascal") on the Spui (see p.73) the symbol of "tomorrow's addicted consumer" – since it had been donated to the city by a cigarette manufacturer – and organized large-scale gatherings there once a week.

The Provos and Kabouters

Grootveld wasn't the only interesting character around town: **Roel van Duyn**, a philosophy student at Amsterdam University and the initiator of a New Left movement known as the **Provos** (short for *provocatie* – "provocation"), participated in Grootveld's meetings, sparking a chain of rebellion that would influence events in the Netherlands for the next twenty years. The number of real Provos never exceeded about 25, but their actions and street "happenings" appealed to a large number of young people. The group had no coherent structure: they emerged into public consciousness through one common aim – to bring points of political or social conflict to public attention by spectacular means. More than anything they were masters of publicity, and pursued their "games" with a spirit of fun rather than grim political fanaticism. The reaction of the police, however, was aggressive: the first two issues of the Provos' magazine were confiscated and, in July 1965, they intervened at a Saturday night "Happening", setting a pattern for future confrontations. The magazine itself contained the Provos' manifesto, a set of policies which later appeared under the title "**The White Plans**". These included the famously popular **white bicycle plan**, which proposed that the council ban all cars in the city centre and supply 20,000 bicycles (painted white) for general public use – the idea being that you picked up a bike, rode it to your destination, and then left it for someone else to use.

There were regular police-Provo confrontations throughout 1965 and early 1966, but it was the action taken on March 10, 1966, the wedding day of Princess Beatrix and Claus von Amsberg, that provoked the most **serious unrest**. Amsberg had served in the German army during World War II and many Dutch were deeply offended by the marriage, not least because of its excessive cost to the public purse. Smoke bombs were thrown at the wedding procession and fights with the police broke out across the city. The following month Provo Hans Tuynman was arrested for handing a policeman a leaflet protesting against police actions. **Street demonstrations** followed, along with further arrests, and when Tuynman was sentenced to three months' imprisonment on May 11, anger spread. Throughout all this conflict, however, the Provos were winning increased public support: in the municipal elections of 1966 they received over 13,000 votes – two and a half percent of the total, and enough for a seat on the council. But this achievement didn't mean the end of the Provos' street actions. Indeed, the next event in which they were involved was one of the most violent of the 1960s. It started with a demonstration by city construction workers on June 13, during which one worker suddenly died. Such was the anti-police feeling that it was assumed he had been killed by police patrolling the protest, and the following day the workers staged a **strike** and marched through the city with thousands of supporters, including the Provos, who by now were regarded as the champions of the public versus the police. The worker actually died of a heart attack, but the mood had been set and there were clashes between police and rioters for four days. A month later the Hague government ordered the dismissal of Amsterdam's police chief and, a year later, that of the mayor. But by May 1967 the Provos' inspiration was waning, and at a final gathering in the Vondelpark they announced that they would disband, even though they still had a member on the city council.

The next phase in the Provo phenomenon was the creation of the "Oranje Free State", a so-called alternative society set up by Van Duyn in 1970 in the form of a mock government, with its own "ministers" and "policies". The new movement, whose members were named **Kabouters** after a helpful gnome in Dutch folklore, was successful if short-lived. It adopted some of the more reasonable "white policies" of the Provos and went so far as to win seats in six municipalities, including five in Amsterdam, on a vaguely socialist ticket. "No longer the socialism of the clenched fist, but of the intertwined fingers, the erect penis, the escaping butterfly . . . ", their manifesto proclaimed. But before long the Kabouter movement, too, faded, amid disputes over methodology.

Opposition to the metro

As the Provo and Kabouter movements disappeared, many of their members joined **neighbourhood committees**, set up to oppose certain plans of the city council. By far the most violently attacked scheme was the plan to build a **metro line** through the Nieuwmarkt to the new suburb of Bijlmermeer. The initial idea was conceived in 1968 and consisted of a plan to build a four-line network for an estimated ƒ250 million. By 1973, the cost had risen to ƒ1500 million – for just one line. It was the council's policy of compulsory re-housing and its enthusiasm for moving city dwellers into the Bijlmermeer that infuriated Amsterdammers. Many felt that their town was being sold off to big business, their homes flattened to make way for banks and offices. Consequently, when the opponents of the metro plan objected to the number of houses that would have to be demolished, they hit a raw and very popular nerve.

Official **clearance of the Nieuwmarkt** area was scheduled for February 1975, but by December 1974 confrontation between police and protesters had already begun. Many residents of the condemned houses refused to move, and further violent clashes were inevitable. The worst came on March 24, 1975, a day that became known as **Blue Monday**: the police began a clearing action early in the morning and their tactics were heavy-handed. Tear-gas grenades were fired through windows smashed by water cannons, armoured cars ripped through front doors, and the police charged in to arrest occupants (residents and supporters), who threw paint cans and powder bombs in retaliation. The fighting went on late into the night with thousands of demonstrators joining in. At the end of the day, 30 people – including 19 policemen – had been wounded, and 47 arrested; 450 complaints were filed against the police. A couple of weeks later came another big clash, but this time the demonstrators used different tactics, forming human barricades in front of the houses to be cleared. The police charged, armed with truncheons; it was an easy eviction. But the protesters had made their point, and afterwards showed their spirit by holding parties on the rubble-strewn sites. Despite continuing opposition, the metro eventually opened in 1980.

The 1980s: squatters and protesters

The radicalism of the 1960s had reached Amsterdam early, and word of the psychedelic revolution had been quick to catch on. Dam square and the Vondelpark became open-air urban campsites, and the pilgrims of alternative culture descended on the easy-going, dope-happy capital in their droves. The city's **housing problems**, however, became the focus of the counterculture and in the early 1980s the US deployment of **Cruise missiles** in the Netherlands added another popular target. In spite of large-scale protest (over four million people signed an anti-Cruise petition, the *volkspetitonnment*, and there were many demonstrations in the city), the missiles were scheduled to be deployed in 1985; the nearest missile base to Amsterdam, **Woensdrecht**, though seventy miles away, was frequently surrounded by protesters. However, arms negotiations between the US and USSR meant that the missiles never arrived – and that the buildings created to house them were all a waste of time and money. Meanwhile, the housing problem had brought about the emergence of a new movement – the **squatters**. At first the squatters' movement was peripheral, consisting mainly of independently operating neighbourhood committees. There was little sense of unity until joint actions to defend a handful of symbolic Amsterdam squats took place. These shaped the development of the squatters' movement, which became a political force, with clearly defined rights and the ear of the city council. Four events help explain how this transformation of the squatters' movement occurred: the actions at the key squats of Vondelstraat, Lucky Luyk and Wyers – and the national day of squatting on April 30, 1980.

Vondelstraat and the Coronation Day protests

The end of the **Vondelstraat** squat in Amsterdam's most prestigious neighbourhood was perhaps the most famous squatting event in the Netherlands. Three days after the empty office premises were occupied in March 1980, police armoured cars were deployed to remove the squatters. About 500 police took part and the resulting riots spread through the streets and reached the Leidseplein. Battles raged the whole day and fifty people were wounded. The squatters were evicted, but it wasn't long before they reoccupied the building. The significance of the Vondelstraat squat was that the attempted eviction and ensuing riots cost the council a considerable amount of money – thus making the authorities much more reluctant to undertake future evictions.

The next major event involved not a specific squat but protest actions on April 30, 1980 – the coronation day of Queen Beatrix. Squatters in Amsterdam and throughout the Netherlands staged protests against the huge amounts of money being spent on the festivities, in addition to the reputed *f*84 million spent on the rebuilding of her residence in The Hague. Two hundred buildings in 27 cities were squatted; half of these squats were cleared the same day, and it was at one of these clearances that the first of the day's battles began. Then, in the afternoon, a protest **demonstration** set off to march through the city to Dam square, where the crowning ceremony was taking place. Confrontation with the police began almost immediately on Waterlooplein, and from then on the city centre was turned into chaos. The squatters' ranks were swelled by other protesters angered by the coronation expenditure at a time when the city council claimed it could not afford to build homes. Public festivities came to an abrupt halt as fighting broke out in the streets and continued until the early hours. Tear gas enveloped the city, while Special Squad Police made repeated charges, and many revellers were caught up with the rebels as the police cordoned off the most militant groups.

Lucky Luyk and Wyers

The squatting movement was reaching its peak. After the success of the Vondelstraat squat in 1980, an estimated 10,000 squatters took over buildings across Amsterdam. The eviction of those who had occupied **Lucky Luyk**, a villa on Jan Luykenstraat, was the most violent and the most expensive the city had known to date, with damage running into millions of guilders. Lucky Luyk was originally squatted in July 1980 after standing empty for several years. In October squatters were forcibly evicted by the *knokploegen* – groups of heavies rented by property owners to protect their investments – but soon reoccupied the building. Two months later the owners of the villa won a court order for the eviction of the squatters, but the city council stepped in to pre-empt the inevitable violence: they bought the villa for ƒ350,000 – giving the owners an easy ƒ73,000 profit. The squatters weren't happy, but agreed to leave the building if it were used for young people's housing. On October 11, 1982, two days before a meeting between the council and the squatters, twelve policemen from the Special Squad broke into Lucky Luyk through the roof and arrested the occupants – a surprise attack that enraged squatters across the country and resulted in sympathy protests in many other cities.

In Amsterdam, rioting lasted for three days. Supporters of the Lucky Luyk, who included many non-squatters, built barricades, wrecked cars, destroyed property and set fire to a tram, while police retaliated with tear gas and water cannons. The mayor declared unprecedented emergency measures, permitting the police to arrest anyone suspected of disrupting public order.

In retreat, the squatters needed to develop a new defence tactic. They hit on politics, and found a new case to fight – **Wyers**. This building, a former distribution centre for a textile firm, had been occupied in October 1981 by about a hundred squatters from all over the city. They were soon informed that Hollandse Beton Maatschappij, one of the country's largest building companies, had just obtained permission to build luxury apartments and shops on the site. Trouble was postponed temporarily when HBM decided the time was not right for their financial investment and scrapped their plans. But in the spring of 1982 they reapplied for building rights, this time to put up a hotel on behalf of Holiday Inn. The initial application was turned down, but an amended plan was approved by the council in June 1983. An eviction order was presented to the Wyers inhabitants, but the squatters found legal loopholes in it and the clearance was delayed.

The squatters were meanwhile busy preparing an alternative plan to present to the council, in which the building would be used as a combined cultural-residential complex with space for small businesses and studios. This constructive alternative won the support of many people, and even the council considered it a viable idea. Dialogue between the council and the squatters continued, but in another act of bad faith, the council forcibly cleared the Wyers in February 1984, with the usual pictures of water cannons and tear gas spread across the front pages of Europe's newspapers. The eviction itself was relatively peaceful: the squatters had decided not to resist and instead linked arms around the site and waited for the police onslaught. Today the *Crowne Plaza* stands on Nieuwezijds Voorburgwal as a testament to the fact that the squatters failed here: but as banners proclaimed after the eviction, "You can demolish Wyers but you will never destroy the ideas behind Wyers".

Stopera

Nevertheless, in the late 1980s, under the socialist mayor, Ed van Thijn, new construction in the city firmly targeted Amsterdam's luxury hotel market rather than addressing its residential needs, and the city's squatting movement seemed defeated – its demise confirmed with the construction of the **Muziektheater/Stadhuis** complex on Waterlooplein. Historically the site chosen for the new opera building was sensitive, as it was part of the old Jodenhoek (Jewish Quarter) and had been a public space for centuries; politically, the building of a highbrow cultural centre was attacked as elitist; and architecturally the plans were a clumsy hybrid, with different designers responsible for each section.

The Muziektheater was bound to come in for flak, and got it from the **Stopera** campaign, whose name was a convenient contraction of "Stop the Opera". No doubt the fact that Amsterdam was angling for the 1992 Olympics was the reason the council railroaded the plans through, yet, compared to episodes from the past, protest was surprisingly slight – and the monstrosity went up as planned. Similarly, there was little fuss made over the casino that opened just off the Leidseplein in 1994, along with a neighbouring private residential and shopping development, all of massive and unappealing proportions. The developers were – and are – in command, though they do seem to have at least learnt a few lessons and now regularly consult with the public.

The 1990s

The decline of the squatting movement did not, however, signal a complete victory for the Right. Indeed, for a while at the end of the 1980s, some of the ideas (and idealism) of decades past seemed to be reappearing on a national level, although they were often thwarted by entrenched interests. In the elections of 1989 **Groen Links**, the Green-Left coalition of mainly small left and ecology parties, had a strong showing, and the previous year the Netherlands had become the first European country to officially adopt a **National Environment Plan**, a radical agenda of Green policies: as yet, however, the Plan has still to be implemented. In Amsterdam, the city council adopted a plan for a **traffic-free centre** after a narrow majority voted for the policy in an admittedly low turnout referendum, though again implementation of the plan has been stalled for years. Meanwhile, the far-right **Centrum Democratische** party had also won enough votes in 1989, and again in 1994, to gain unheard-of representation in the Lower House of the Dutch parliament, events which occasioned multiple demonstrations. As the most powerful group in the Social Democratic Party put it, the Nieuw Links (New Left) has largely given way to the era of the Nieuw Flinks (New Firm).

However, at the heart of the Dutch body politic lies **consensus**: in the **1994 elections**, although the Labour Party won the largest share of the vote, it took three months of high-level politicking to thrash out a deal forming an unprecedented "left-right" **coalition government** under Prime Minister Wim Kok, with the Labour Party sharing power with both the left-of-centre "66 Democrats" and the right-wing Liberal Party. This coalition excluded the previously influential Christian Democrats — but then it proceeded to embark on a largely Christian Democrat programme, keeping everybody happy. Another force in Dutch politics also emerged from the 1994 elections: **pensioners' parties** won eight seats in the Lower House, highlighting public dismay over government plans to freeze state old-age pensions, and raising the possibility that pensioners could be included in the government formation process.

For all parties, **Schiphol Airport** remains a problem. Essential to the national economy (it's Europe's most important airport, after Heathrow), it will need to grow still more in the next few years, which means the area around it will suffer further. Some doubts still exist about the airport's safety after the incident in October 1992, when an El Al Boeing 747 cargo plane crashed into the Bijlmermeer housing estate. Around fifty people were killed, though the exact total will never be known: the estate was crowded with people from Surinam and the Dutch Antilles, some of whom may well have been in the country illegally. The plane's cargo of kerosene and secret unspecified "military chemicals" destroyed a vast swathe of the estate, and it's fortunate that casualties were relatively low.

One consequence of the disaster was that the government ordered an amnesty on Surinamese and Antillian **immigrants** in order to allow a full death toll to be calculated; the tradition — and reality — of Dutch liberalism means that up to 50,000 or more people each year seek **asylum** in The Netherlands, where they generally get a much more positive reception than in most other countries.

Amsterdam in the year 2000

At the start of the new millennium, Amsterdam is increasingly **thinking big**; the days of "happenings" and helpful gnomes seem long gone. Tourism throughout the country generates a turnover of ƒ36 billion annually — in 1995, over two million people took canal trips in Amsterdam alone — and massive public and private works projects are an ongoing response to both the burgeoning tourism industry and a shift in locals' self-perception. The brand-new multimedia "Holland Experience" complex opened in Amsterdam four years ago, its aim to present to the world "a literally sensational view" of the country and its capital, in a vast, multimillion-guilder attempt to replace the parochial image of tulips and windmills with that of a modern, technology-driven society. The hard-headedly pragmatic city council under Mayor Schelto Patijn has embarked on a series of measures intended to bury Amsterdam's laid-back image and replace it with one more suited to a dynamic European capital: the notoriously liberal **drug laws** have been tightened up, crackdowns have begun on the more extreme forms of **pornography**, **squats** are pretty much a thing of the past, and **redevelopment** of empty areas of land in and around the city centre is proceeding apace, most notably with the high-income housing complexes shooting up on the long-derelict KNSM island. Throughout the mid-1990s, in Duivendrecht, an otherwise unremarkable southeastern commuter suburb, one of the most modern **stadiums** in Europe was quietly under construction, and in 1996 the 51,000-capacity Amsterdam ArenA finally opened. The new home of Ajax Amsterdam, one of Europe's most successful football teams, the ArenA is well on the way to becoming the large-scale venue for rock concerts and mass entertainments that the city has so sorely lacked.

And yet, throughout the turmoil, Amsterdam in the year 2000 still retains that idiosyncratic mix of single-minded commercialism and cosy domesticity that has characterized it for centuries. On the one hand, there are bodies such as the **Netherlands Foreign Investment Agency**, which has managed the remarkable feat of attracting over twenty percent of US and Japanese investment in Europe to this one tiny country. And on the other, sitting easily alongside the practical business of making money, the ghosts of Amsterdam's hippy past still survive in the tumble-down houseboats that throng its canals.

Dutch Art

This is the very briefest of introductions to the subject, designed to serve only as a quick reference on your way round the major galleries. For more in-depth and academic studies, see the recommendations in "Books" on p.332. For a list of where to find some of the paintings mentioned here, turn to the box at the end of this section.

Beginnings

Until the sixteenth century the area now known as the "Low Countries" was in effect one country, the most artistically productive part of which was Flanders in modern Belgium, and it was there that the solid realist base of later Dutch painting developed. Today the works of these **early Flemish painters** are pretty sparse in Holland, and even in Belgium few collections are as complete as you might expect; indeed, many ended up as the property of the ruling Habsburgs and were removed to Spain. Most Dutch galleries do, however, have a few examples.

Jan van Eyck (1385–1441) is generally regarded as the originator of Low Countries painting, and has even been credited with the invention of oil painting itself – though it seems more likely that he simply perfected a new technique by thinning his paint with the recently discovered turpentine, thus making it more flexible. His most famous work still in the Low Countries is the altarpiece in Ghent cathedral (debatably painted with the help of his lesser-known brother, Hubert), which was revolutionary in its realism, for the first time using elements of native landscape in depicting biblical themes.

Firmly in the Van Eyck tradition were the **Master of Flemalle** (1387–1444) and **Rogier van der Weyden** (1400–64). The Flemalle master is a shadowy figure: some believe he was the teacher of Van der Weyden, others that the two artists were in fact the same person. There are differences between the two, however: the Flemalle master's paintings are close to Van Eyck's, whereas Van der Weyden shows a more emotional and religious intensity. Van der Weyden influenced such painters as **Dieric Bouts** (1415–75), who was born in Haarlem but worked in Leuven, and is recognizable by his stiff, rather elongated figures. **Hugo van der Goes** (d. 1482) was the next Ghent master after Van Eyck, most famous for the Portinari altarpiece in Florence's Uffizi gallery; after a short painting career, he died insane. Few doubt that **Hans Memling** (1440–94) was a pupil of Van der Weyden: active in Bruges throughout his life, he is best remembered for the pastoral charm of his landscapes and the quality of his portraiture, much of which survives on the rescued side panels of triptychs. More renowned are **Hieronymus Bosch** (1450–1516), whose frequently reprinted and discussed religious allegories are filled with macabre visions of tortured people and grotesque beasts, and **Pieter Bruegel the Elder** (1525–69), whose gruesome allegories and innovative interpretations of religious subjects are firmly placed in Low Countries settings.

Meanwhile, there were movements based to the north of Flanders. **Geertgen tot Sint Jans** ("Little Gerard of the Brotherhood of St John"; d. 1490), a student of Albert van Ouwater, had been working in **Haarlem**, initiating – in a strangely naive style – an artistic tradition in the city that would prevail throughout the seventeenth century. **Jan Mostaert** (1475–1555) took over after Geertgen's death, and continued to develop a style that diverged more and more from that of the southern provinces. **Lucas van Leyden** (1489–1533) was the first painter to effect real changes in northern painting. Born in Leiden, his bright colours and narrative technique were refreshingly new at the time, and he introduced a novel dynamism into what had become a rigidly formal treatment of devotional subjects. There was rivalry, of course. Eager to publicize Haarlem as the artistic capital of the northern Netherlands, Carel van Mander (see below) claimed Haarlem native Jan van Scorel (1495–1562) as the better painter, complaining, too, of Van Leyden's dandyish ways.

Certainly Van Scorel's influence should not be underestimated. At this time every painter was expected to travel to Italy to view the works of Renaissance artists. When the Bishop of Utrecht became Pope Hadrian VI, he took Van Scorel with him as court painter, giving him the opportunity to introduce Italian styles into what had been a completely independent tradition. Hadrian died soon after, and Van Scorel returned north, combining the ideas he had picked up in Italy with Haarlem realism and passing them on to **Maerten van Heemskerck** (1498–1574), who went off to Italy himself in 1532, staying there five years before returning to Haarlem.

The Golden Age

The seventeenth century begins with **Carel van Mander**, Haarlem painter, art impresario and one of the few chroniclers of the art of the Low Countries. His *Schilderboek* of 1604 put Flemish and Dutch traditions into context for the first time, and in addition specified the rules of fine painting. Examples of his own work are rare – though Haarlem's Frans Hals Museum weighs in with several – but his followers were many. Among them was **Cornelius Cornelisz van Haarlem** (1562–1638), who produced elegant renditions of biblical and mythical themes; and **Hendrik Goltzius** (1558–1616), who was a skilled engraver and an integral member of Van Mander's Haarlem academy. These painters' enthusiasm for Italian art, combined with the influence of a late revival of Gothicism, resulted in works that combined Mannerist and Classical elements. An interest in realism was also felt, and, for them, the subject became less important than the way in which it was depicted: biblical stories became merely a vehicle whereby artists could apply their skills in painting the human body, landscapes, or copious displays of food. All of this served to break religion's stranglehold on

art, and make legitimate a whole range of everyday subjects for the painter.

In Holland (and this was where the north and the south finally diverged) this break with tradition was compounded by the **Reformation**: the austere Calvinism that had replaced the Catholic faith in the United (ie northern) Provinces had no use for images or symbols of devotion in its churches. Instead, painters catered to the burgeoning middle class, and no longer visited Italy to learn their craft; the real giants of the seventeenth century – Hals, Rembrandt, Vermeer – stayed in the Netherlands all their lives. Another innovation was that painting split into more distinct categories – genre, portrait, landscape – and artists tended (with notable exceptions) to confine themselves to one field throughout their careers. So began the greatest age of Dutch art.

Historical and Religious Painting

Italy continued to hold some sway in the Netherlands not through the Renaissance painters but rather via the fashionable new realism of Caravaggio. Many artists – Rembrandt for one – continued to portray classical subjects, but in a way that was totally at odds with the Mannerists' stylish flights of imagination. The Utrecht artist **Abraham Bloemaert** (1564–1651), though a solid Mannerist throughout his career, encouraged these new ideas, and his students – **Gerard van Honthorst** (1590–1656), **Hendrik Terbrugghen** (1588–1629) and **Dirck van Baburen** (1590–1624) – formed the nucleus of the influential **Utrecht School**, which followed Caravaggio almost to the point of slavishness. Honthorst was perhaps the leading figure, learning his craft from Bloemaert and travelling to Rome, where he was nicknamed "Gerardo delle Notti" for his ingenious handling of light and shade. In his later paintings, however, this was to become more routine technique than inspired invention, and though a supremely competent artist, Honthorst remains somewhat discredited among critics today. Terbrugghen's reputation seems to have aged rather better: he soon forgot Caravaggio and developed a more individual style, his later, lighter work having a great influence on the young Vermeer. After the obligatory jaunt to Rome, Baburen shared a studio with Terbrugghen and produced some fairly original work – work which also had some influence on Vermeer – but today he is the least studied member of the group and few of his paintings survive.

But it's **Rembrandt** who was considered the most original historical artist of the seventeenth century, painting religious scenes throughout his life. In the 1630s, the poet and statesman Constantijn Huygens procured for him his greatest commission – a series of five paintings of the Passion, beautifully composed and uncompromisingly realistic. Later, however, Rembrandt received fewer and fewer commissions, since his treatment of biblical and historical subjects was far less dramatic than that of his contemporaries and he ignored their smooth brushwork, preferring a rougher, darker and more disjointed style. It's significant that while the more conventional Jordaens, Honthorst and Van Everdingen were busy decorating the Huis ten Bosch near The Hague for patron Stadholder Frederick Henry, Rembrandt was having his monumental *Conspiracy of Claudius Civilis* (painted for the new Amsterdam Town Hall) rejected – probably because it was thought too pagan an interpretation of what was an important symbolic event in Dutch history. **Aert van Gelder** (1645–1727), Rembrandt's last pupil and probably the only one to concentrate on historical painting, followed the style of his master closely, producing shimmering biblical scenes well into the eighteenth century.

Genre Painting

Genre refers to scenes from everyday life, a subject that, with the decline of the church as patron, had become popular in Holland by the mid-seventeenth century. Many painters devoted themselves solely to such work. Some genre paintings were simply non-idealized portrayals of common scenes, while others, by means of symbols or carefully disguised details, made moral entreaties to the viewer.

Among early seventeenth-century painters, **Hendrik Terbrugghen** and **Gerard Honthorst** spent much of their time on religious subjects, but also adapted the realism and strong chiaroscuro learned from Caravaggio to a number of tableaux of everyday life. **Frans Hals**, too, is better known as a portraitist, but his early genre paintings no doubt influenced his pupil, **Adriaen Brouwer** (1605–38), whose riotous tavern scenes were well received in their day and collected by, among others, Rubens and Rembrandt. Brouwer spent only a couple of

years in Haarlem under Hals before returning to his native Flanders, where he influenced the younger **David Teniers**. **Adriaen van Ostade** (1610–85), on the other hand, stayed in Haarlem most of his life, skilfully painting groups of peasants and tavern brawls – though his later acceptance by the establishment led him to water down the realism he had learnt from Brouwer. He was teacher to his brother **Isaak** (1621–49), who produced a large number of open-air peasant scenes, subtle combinations of genre and landscape work.

The English critic E.V. Lucas dubbed Teniers, Brouwer and Ostade "coarse and boorish" compared with **Jan Steen** (1625–79), who, along with Vermeer, is probably the most admired Dutch genre painter. You can see what he had in mind: Steen's paintings offer the same Rabelaisian peasantry in full fling, but they go their debauched ways in broad daylight, and nowhere do you see the filthy rogues in shadowy hovels favoured by Brouwer and Ostade. Steen offers more humour, too, as well as more moralizing, identifying with the hedonistic mob and reproaching them at the same time. Indeed, many of his pictures are illustrations of well-known proverbs of the time – popular epithets on the evils of drink or the transience of human existence that were supposed to teach as well as entertain.

Gerrit Dou (1613–75) was Rembrandt's Leiden contemporary and one of his first pupils. It's difficult to detect any trace of the master's influence in his work, however, as Dou initiated a style of his own: tiny, minutely realized and beautifully finished views of a kind of ordinary life that was decidedly more genteel than Brouwer's – or even Steen's for that matter. He was admired, above all, for his painstaking attention to detail: and he would, it's said, sit in his studio for hours waiting for the dust to settle before starting work. Among his students, **Frans van Mieris** (1635–81) continued the highly finished portrayals of the Dutch bourgeoisie, as did **Gabriel Metsu** (1629–67) – perhaps Dou's greatest pupil – whose pictures often convey an overtly moral message. Another pupil of Rembrandt's, though a much later one, was **Nicholaes Maes** (1629–93), whose early works were almost entirely genre paintings, sensitively executed and again with an obvious didacticism. His later paintings show the influence of a more refined style of portrait, which he had picked up in France.

As a native of Zwolle, **Gerard ter Borch** (1619–81) found himself far from all these Leiden/Rembrandt connections; despite trips abroad to most of the artistic capitals of Europe, he remained very much a provincial painter all his life. He depicted Holland's merchant class at play and became renowned for his curious doll-like figures and his enormous ability to capture the textures of different cloths. His domestic scenes were not unlike those of **Pieter de Hooch** (1629–after 1684), whose simple depictions of everyday life are deliberately unsentimental, and, for the first time, have little or no moral commentary. De Hooch's favourite trick was to paint darkened rooms with an open door leading through to a sunlit courtyard, a practice that, along with his trademark rusty red colour, makes his work easy to identify and, at its best, exquisite. That said, his later pictures reflect the encroaching decadence of the Dutch Republic: the rooms are more richly decorated, the arrangements more contrived and the subjects far less homely.

It was, however, **Jan Vermeer** (1632–75) who brought the most sophisticated methods to painting interiors, depicting the play of natural light on indoor surfaces with superlative skill – and the tranquil intimacy for which he is now famous the world over. Another recorder of the better-heeled Dutch households and, like De Hooch, without a moral tone, he is regarded (with Hals and Rembrandt) as one of the big three Dutch painters – though he was, it seems, a slow worker. As a result, only about forty paintings can be attributed to him with any certainty. Living all his life in Delft, Vermeer is perhaps the epitome of the seventeenth-century Dutch painter – rejecting the pomp and ostentation of the High Renaissance to record quietly his contemporaries at home, painting for a public that demanded no more than that.

Portraits

Naturally, the ruling bourgeoisie of Holland's flourishing mercantile society wanted to record and celebrate their success, and it's little wonder that portraiture was the best way for a young painter to make a living. **Michiel Jansz Miereveld** (1567–1641), court painter to Frederick Henry in The Hague, was the first real portraitist of the Dutch Republic, but it wasn't long before his stiff and rather conservative figures were superseded by the more spontaneous renderings of **Frans Hals** (1585–1666). Hals is perhaps best-known for his "corporation pictures" – portraits of the members of the Dutch civil guard regiments that had been formed in most of the larger towns while the threat of invasion by the Spanish was still imminent. These large group pieces demanded superlative technique, since the painter had to create a collection of individual portraits while retaining a sense of the group, and accord prominence based on the importance of the sitter and the size of the payment each had made. Hals was particularly good at this, using innovative lighting effects, arranging his sitters subtly, and putting all the elements together in a fluid and dynamic composition. He also painted many individual portraits, making the ability to capture fleeting and telling expressions his trademark; his pictures of children are particularly sensitive. Later in life, his work became darker and more akin to Rembrandt's.

Jan Cornelisz Verspronck (1597–1662) and **Bartholomeus van der Helst** (1613–70) were the other great Haarlem portraitists after Frans Hals – Verspronck recognizable by the smooth, shiny glow he always gave to his sitters' faces, Van der Helst by a competent but unadventurous style. Of the two, Van der Helst was the more popular, influencing a number of later painters and leaving Haarlem while still young to begin a solidly successful career as portrait painter to Amsterdam's burghers.

The reputation of **Rembrandt van Rijn** (1606–69) is still relatively recent – nineteenth-century connoisseurs preferred Gerard Dou – but he is now justly regarded as one of the greatest and most versatile painters of all time. Born in Leiden, the son of a miller, he was apprenticed at an early age to Jacob van Swanenburgh, a then quite important, though uninventive, local artist. He shared a studio with Jan Lievens, a promising painter and something of a rival for a while (now all but forgotten), before going up to Amsterdam to study under the fashionable Pieter Lastman. Soon he was painting commissions for the city elite and became an accepted member of their circle. The poet and statesman Constantijn Huygens acted as his agent, pulling strings to obtain all of Rembrandt's more lucrative jobs, and in 1634 Rembrandt married Saskia van Ulenborch, daughter of the burgomaster of Leeuwarden and quite a catch for the still relatively humble artist. His self-portraits at the time show the confident face of security – on top of things and quite sure of where he's going.

Rembrandt would not always be the darling of the Amsterdam smart set, but his fall from grace was still some way off when he painted *The Night Watch*, a group portrait often – but inaccurately – associated with the artist's decline in popularity. Indeed, although Rembrandt's fluent arrangement of his subjects was totally original, there's no evidence that the military company who commissioned the painting was anything but pleased with the result. More likely culprits are the artist's later pieces, whose obscure lighting and psychological insight took the conservative Amsterdam burghers by surprise. His patrons were certainly not sufficiently enthusiastic about his work to support his taste for art collecting and his expensive house on Jodenbreestraat, and in 1656 possibly the most brilliant artist the city would ever know was declared bankrupt. He died thirteen years later a broken and embittered old man – as his last self-portraits show. Throughout his career Rembrandt maintained a large studio, and his influence pervaded the next generation of Dutch painters. Some – Dou and Maes – more famous for their genre work, have already been mentioned. Others turned to portraiture.

Govert Flinck (1615–60) was perhaps Rembrandt's most faithful follower, and he was, ironically, given the job of decorating Amsterdam's new town hall after his teacher had been passed over. However, he died before he could execute his designs, and Rembrandt was one of several artists commissioned to paint them – though his contribution was removed shortly afterwards. The work of **Ferdinand Bol** (1616–80) was so heavily influenced by Rembrandt that for a long time art historians couldn't tell the two apart. Most of the pitifully slim extant work of **Carel Fabritius** (1622–54) was portraiture, but he too died young, before he could properly realize his promise as perhaps the most gifted of all Rembrandt's students. Generally regarded as the teacher of Vermeer, he forms a link between the two masters, combining Rembrandt's technique with his own practice of painting figures against a dark background, prefiguring the lighting and colouring of the Delft painter.

Landscapes

Aside from Bruegel, whose depictions of his native surroundings make him the first true Low

Countries landscape painter, **Gillis van Coninxloo** (1544–1607) stands out as the earliest Dutch landscapist. He imbued the native scenery with elements of fantasy, painting the richly wooded views he had seen on his travels around Europe as backdrops to biblical scenes. In the early seventeenth century, **Hercules Seghers** (1590–1638), apprenticed to Coninxloo, carried on his mentor's style of depicting forested and mountainous landscapes, some real, others not: his work is scarce but is believed to have had considerable influence on the landscape work of Rembrandt. **Esaias van der Velde**'s (1591–1632) quaint and unpretentious scenes show the first real affinity with the Dutch countryside, but while his influence was likewise great, he was soon overtaken in stature by his pupil **Jan van Goyen** (1596–1656), a remarkable painter who belongs to the so-called "tonal phase" of Dutch landscape painting. Van Goyen's early pictures were highly coloured and close to those of his teacher, but it didn't take him long to develop a marked touch of his own, using tones of green, brown and grey to lend everything a characteristic translucent haze. His paintings are, above all, of nature, and if he included figures it was just for the sake of scale. A long neglected artist, Van Goyen only received recognition with the arrival of the Impressionists, when his fluid and rapid brushwork was finally appreciated.

Another "tonal" painter and a native of Haarlem, **Salomon van Ruisdael** (1600–70) was also directly affected by Van der Velde, and his simple and atmospheric, though not terribly adventurous, landscapes were for a long time consistently confused with those of Van Goyen. More esteemed is his nephew, **Jacob van Ruysdael** (1628–82), generally considered the greatest of all Dutch landscapists, whose fastidiously observed views of quiet flatlands dominated by stormy skies were to influence European painters' impressions of nature right up to the nineteenth century. Constable, certainly, acknowledged a debt to him. Ruysdael's foremost pupil was **Meindert Hobbema** (1638–1709), who followed the master faithfully, sometimes even painting the same views (his *Avenue at Middelharnis* may be familiar).

Nicholas Berchem (1620–83) and **Jan Both** (1618–52) were the "Italianizers" of Dutch landscapes. They studied in Rome and were influenced by the Frenchman Claude Lorraine, taking back to Holland rich, golden views of the world, full of steep gorges and hills, picturesque ruins and wandering shepherds. **Allart van Everdingen** (1621–75) had a similar approach, but his subject matter stemmed from travels in Norway, which, after his return to Holland, he reproduced in all its mountainous glory. **Aelbert Cuyp** (1620–91), on the other hand, stayed in Dordrecht all his life, painting what was probably the favourite city skyline of Dutch landscapists. He inherited the warm tones of the Italianizers, and his pictures are always suffused with a deep, golden glow.

Of a number of specialist seventeenth-century painters who can be included here, **Paulus Potter** (1625–54) is rated as the best painter of **domestic animals**. He produced a fair amount of work in a short life, the most reputed being his lovingly executed pictures of cows and horses. The accurate rendering of **architectural** features also became a specialized field, in which **Pieter Saenredam** (1597–1665), with his finely realized paintings of Dutch church interiors, is the most widely known exponent. **Emanuel de Witte** (1616–92) continued in the same vein, though his churches lack the spartan crispness of Saenredam's. **Gerrit Berckheyde** (1638–98) worked in Haarlem soon after, but he limited his views to the outside of buildings, producing variations on the same scenes around town.

In the seventeenth century another thriving category of painting was the **still life**, in which objects were gathered together to remind the viewer of the transience of human life and the meaninglessness of worldly pursuits. Thus, a skull would often be joined by a book, a pipe or a goblet, and some half-eaten food. Again, two Haarlem painters dominated this field: **Pieter Claesz** (1598–1660) and **Willem Heda** (1594–1680), who confined themselves almost entirely to painting these carefully arranged groups of objects.

The Eighteenth and Nineteenth Centuries

Accompanying Holland's economic decline was a gradual deterioration in the quality and originality of Dutch painting. The delicacy of some of the classical seventeenth-century painters was replaced by finicky still lifes and minute studies of flowers, or finely finished portraiture and religious scenes, as in the work of **Adrian van der Werff** (1659–1722). Of the era's big names, **Gerard de Lairesse** (1640–1711) spent most of his time

decorating a rash of brand new civic halls and mansions, but, like the buildings he worked on, his style and influences were French. **Jacob de Wit** (1695–1754) continued where Lairesse left off, and he also benefited from a relaxation in the laws against Catholics, decorating several of their (newly-legal) churches. The period's only painter of any true renown was **Cornelis Troost** (1697–1750) who, although he didn't produce anything really original, painted competent portraits and some neat, faintly satirical pieces that have since earned him the title of "The Dutch Hogarth". Cosy interiors also continued to prove popular and the Haarlem painter **Wybrand Hendriks** (1744–1831) satisfied demand with numerous proficient examples.

Johann Barthold Jongkind (1819–91) was the first important artist to emerge in the nineteenth century, painting landscapes and seascapes that were to influence Monet and the early Impressionists. He spent most of his life in France and his work was exhibited in Paris with the Barbizon painters, though he owed less to them than to the landscapes of Van Goyen and the seventeenth-century "tonal" artists. Jongkind's work was a logical precursor to the art of the **Hague School**, a group of painters based in and around that city between 1870 and 1900 who tried to re-establish a characteristically Dutch national school of painting. They produced atmospheric studies of the dunes and polders around The Hague, nature pictures that are characterized by grey, rain-filled skies, windswept seas, and silvery, flat beaches – pictures that, for some, verge on the sentimental. **J.H. Weissenbruch** (1824–1903) was a founding member, a specialist in low, flat beach scenes dotted with stranded boats. The banker-turned-artist **H.W. Mesdag** (1831–1915) did the same but with more skill than imagination, while **Jacob Maris** (1837–99), one of three artist brothers, was perhaps the most typical of the Hague School, with his rural and sea scenes heavily covered by grey, chasing skies. His brother **Matthijs** (1839–1917) was less predictable, ultimately tiring of his colleagues' interest in straight observation and going to London to design windows, while the youngest brother **Willem** (1844–1910), is best-known for his small, unpretentious studies of nature.

Anton Mauve (1838–88) is better-known, an exponent of soft, pastel landscapes and an early teacher of Van Gogh. Profoundly influenced by the French Barbizon painters – Corot, Millet et al – he went to Hilversum in 1885 to set up his own group, which became known as the "Dutch Barbizon". **Jozef Israëls** (1826–1911) has often been likened to Millet, though it's generally agreed that he had more in common with the Impressionists, and his best pictures are his melancholy portraits and interiors. Lastly, **Johan Bosboom**'s (1817–91) church interiors may be said to sum up the nostalgia of the "Hague School: shadowy and populated by figures in seventeenth-century dress, they seem to yearn for Holland's Golden Age.

Vincent van Gogh (1853–90), on the other hand, was one of the least "Dutch" of Dutch artists, and he lived out most of his relatively short painting career in France. After countless studies of peasant life in his native North Brabant – studies which culminated in the sombre *Potato Eaters* – he went to live in Paris with his art-dealer brother Theo. There, under the influence of the Impressionists, he lightened his palette, following the pointillist work of Seurat and "trying to render intense colour and not a grey harmony". Two years later he went south to Arles, the "land of blue tones and gay colours", and, struck by the harsh Mediterranean light, his characteristic style began to develop. A disastrous attempt to live with Gauguin, and the much-publicized episode when he cut off part of his ear and presented it to a local prostitute, led eventually to his committal in an asylum at St-Rémy, where he produced some of his most famous, and most expressionistic, canvases – strongly coloured and with the paint thickly, almost frantically, applied.

Like Van Gogh, **Jan Toorop** (1858–1928) went through multiple artistic changes, though he did not need to travel the world to do so; he radically adapted his technique from a fairly conventional pointillism through a tired Expressionism to Symbolism with an Art-Nouveau feel. Roughly contemporary, **G.H. Breitner** (1857–1923) was a better painter, and one who refined his style rather than changed it. His snapshot-like impressions of his beloved Amsterdam figure among his best work and offered a promising start to the new century.

The Twentieth Century

Most of the trends in the visual arts of the early twentieth century have, at one time or another, found their way to the Netherlands: of many minor names, **Jan Sluyters** (1881–1957) was the Dutch pioneer of Cubism. But only one movement was specifically Dutch – **De Stijl** – literally, "the Style".

Piet Mondriaan (1872–1944) was De Stijl's leading figure, developing the realism he had learned from the Hague School painters – via Cubism, which he criticized for being too cowardly to depart totally from representation – into a complete abstraction of form which he called **Neo-Plasticism**. He was something of a mystic, and this was to some extent responsible for the direction that De Stijl – and his paintings – took: canvases painted with grids of lines and blocks made up of the three primary colours and white, black and grey. Mondriaan believed this freed the work of art from the vagaries of personal perception, making it possible to obtain what he called "a true vision of reality".

De Stijl took other forms too: there was a magazine of the same name, and the movement introduced new concepts into every aspect of design, from painting to interior design and architecture. But in all these media, lines were kept simple, colours bold and clear. **Theo van Doesburg** (1883–1931) was a De Stijl co-founder and major theorist: his work is similar to Mondriaan's except for the noticeable absence of thick, black borders and the diagonals that he introduced into his work, calling his paintings "contra-compositions" – which, he said, were both more dynamic and more in touch with twentieth-century life. **Bart van der Leck** (1876–1958) was the third member of the circle, identifiable by white canvases covered by seemingly randomly placed interlocking coloured triangles. Mondriaan split with De Stijl in 1925, going on to attain new artistic extremes of clarity and soberness before moving to New York in the 1940s and producing atypically exuberant works such as *Victory Boogie Woogie* – named for the artist's love of jazz.

During and after De Stijl, a number of other movements flourished, though their impact was not so great and their influence largely confined to the Netherlands. The Expressionist **Bergen School** was probably the most localized, its best-known exponent **Charley Toorop** (1891–1955), daughter of Jan, who developed a distinctively glaring but strangely sensitive realism. **De Ploeg** (The Plough), centred in Groningen, was headed by **Jan Wiegers** (1893–1959) and influenced by

Kirchner and the German Expressionists; the group's artists set out to capture the uninviting landscapes around their native town, and produced violently coloured canvases that hark back to Van Gogh. Another group, known as the **Magic Realists**, surfaced in the 1930s, painting quasi-surrealistic scenes that, according to their leading light, **Carel Willink** (1900–83), revealed "a world stranger and more dreadful in its haughty impenetrability than the most terrifying nightmare".

Postwar Dutch art began with **CoBrA**: a loose grouping of like-minded painters from Denmark, Belgium and Holland, whose name derives from the initial letters of their respective capital cities. Their first exhibition at Amsterdam's Stedelijk Museum in 1949 provoked a huge uproar, at the centre of which was **Karel Appel** (b. 1921), whose brutal Abstract Expressionist pieces, plastered with paint inches thick, were, he maintained, necessary for the era – indeed, inevitable reflections of it. "I paint like a barbarian in a barbarous age", he claimed. In the graphic arts the most famous twentieth-century figure is **M.C. Escher** (1898–1970).

As for today, there's as vibrant an art scene as there ever was, best exemplified in Amsterdam by the rotating exhibitions of the Stedelijk and by the dozens of galleries and exhibition spaces throughout the city. Among contemporary Dutch artists, look out for the abstract work of **Edgar Fernhout** and **Ad Dekkers**, the reliefs of **Jan Schoonhoven**, the multimedia productions of **Jan Dibbets**, the glowering realism of **Marlene Dumas**, the imprecisely coloured geometric designs of **Rob van Koningsbruggen**, the smeary expressionism of **Toon Verhoef**, and the exuberant figures of **Rene Daniels** – to name only the most important figures.

Amsterdam Galleries: a hit list

Of the galleries in **Amsterdam**, the **Rijksmuseum** (see pp.115–123) gives the most complete overview of Dutch art up to the end of the nineteenth century, in particular the work of Rembrandt, Hals and the major artists of the Golden Age. The **Van Gogh Museum** (see p.124) is best for the Impressionists and, of course, Van Gogh; and for twentieth-century and contemporary Dutch art, there's the **Stedelijk** (see p.125). The **CoBrA Museum of Modern Art** (see p.249) is in **Amstelveen** on the southern outskirts of the city.

Within easy reach of Amsterdam, **Haarlem** possesses the **Frans Hals Museum** (see p.143), which holds some of the best work of Hals, Mander and the Haarlem School, whilst Leiden has the **Stedelijk Museum de Lakenhal** (see p.151) with a healthy sample of the work of lesser-known sixteenth- and seventeenth-century Dutch painters.

The City in Fiction

Amsterdam lives more frantically in fiction than in reality. It's the capital of Dutch literature not only in the sense that most Dutch writers have lived here or are living here now, but it also forms the backdrop to most contemporary Dutch novels. A fair amount of Dutch literature has been translated into English in recent years, notably the work of Cees Nooteboom, Marga Minco, Harry Mulisch and Simon Carmiggelt. There's also, of course, English-language fiction set in Amsterdam or the Netherlands, of which the detective writer Nicolas Freeling is perhaps the best-known exponent.

Simon Carmiggelt

Humour is a frequent theme of Dutch literature, and Simon Carmiggelt was one of the country's best-loved humorous writers. He moved to the capital during the war, working as a production manager and journalist on the then illegal newspaper, *Het Parool*. In 1946, he started writing a daily column in the paper entitled "Kronkel", meaning "twist" or "kink". It was an almost immediate success, and he continued to write his *Kronkels* for several decades, in the end turning out almost 10,000. They're a unique genre – short, usually humorous anecdotes of everyday life, with a strong undercurrent of melancholy and a seriousness at their heart. They concern ordinary people, poignantly observed with razor-sharp – but never cruel – wit and intelligence. Some of the strongest have been bundled together in anthologies, two of which – *A Dutchman's Slight Adventures* (1966) and *I'm Just Kidding* (1972) – were translated into English. Simon Carmiggelt died in 1989.

Corner

In a café in the Albert Cuypstraat, where the open-air market pulses with sounds and colour, I ran into my friend Ben.

"Did you know Joop Groenteman?" he asked.

"You mean the one who sold fruit?" I replied.

"Yes. You heard about his death?"

I nodded. A fishmonger had told me. "It's a shame," said Ben. "A real loss for the market. He had a nice stall – always polished his fruit. And he had that typical Amsterdam sense of humour that seems to be disappearing. He'd say "Hi" to big people and "Lo" to little ones. If somebody wanted to buy two apples, he'd ask where the party was. No one was allowed to pick and choose his fruit. Joop handed it out from behind the plank. Somebody asked him once if he had a plastic bag, and he said, 'I got false teeth. Ain't that bad enough?' He never lost his touch, not even in the hospital."

"Did you go see him there?" I enquired.

"Yes, several times," Ben said. "Once his bed was empty. On the pillow lay a note: 'Back in two hours. Put whatever you brought on the bed.' He had to go on a diet because he was too fat. They weighed him every day. One morning he tied a portable radio around his waist with a rope, put his bathrobe over it, and got on the scale. To the nurse's alarm he'd suddenly gained eight pounds. That was his idea of fun in the hospital. During one visit I asked him when he'd get out. He said, 'Oh, someday soon, either through the front door or the back.'"

Ben smiled sadly.

"He died rather unexpectedly," he resumed. "There was an enormous crowd at his funeral. I was touched by the sight of all his friends from the market standing round the grave with their hats on and each one of them shovelling three spadesful of earth on to his coffin. Oh well, he at least attained the goal of his life."

"What goal?" I asked.

"The same one every open-air merchant has," Ben answered, "a place on a corner. If you're on a corner, you sell more. But it's awfully hard to get a corner place."

"Joop managed it, though?"

"Yes – but not in the Albert Cuyp," said Ben. "That corner place was a sort of obsession to him. He knew his chance was practically nil. So then he decided that if he couldn't get one while he was alive, he'd make sure of it when he died. Every time the collector for the burial insurance came along, he'd say 'Remember, I want a corner grave.' But when he did die, there wasn't a single corner to be had. Well, that's not quite right. It just happened that there was one corner with a stone to the memory of someone who had died in the furnaces of a concentration camp. Nobody was really buried there. And the cemetery people gave permission to have the stone placed somewhere else and to let Joop have that plot. So he finally got what he wanted. A place on the corner."

Herring-man

It was morning, and I paused to buy a herring at one of those curious legged vending carts that stand along Amsterdam's canals.

"Onions?" asked the white-jacketed herring-man. He was big and broad-shouldered, and his hair was turning grey – a football believer, by the looks of him, who never misses Sunday in the stadium.

"No onions," I answered.

Two other men were standing there eating. They wore overalls and were obviously fellow-workers.

"There's them that take onions, and them that don't," one of the men said tolerantly. The herring-man nodded.

"Take me, now, I never eat pickles with 'em," said the other in the coquettish tone of a girl revealing some little charm that she just happens to possess.

"Give me another, please," I said.

The herring-man cut the fish in three pieces and reached with his glistening hand into the dish of onions.

"No, no onions," I said.

He smiled his apology. "Excuse me. My mind was wandering," he said.

The men in overalls also ordered another round and then began to wrangle about some futility or other on which they disagreed. They were still at it after I had paid and proceeded to a café just across from the herring-cart, where I sat down at a table by the window. For Dutchmen they talked rather strenuously with their hands. A farmer once told me that when the first cock begins to crow early in the morning, all the other roosters in the neighbourhood immediately raise their voices, hoping to drown him out. Most males are cut from the same cloth.

"What'll it be?" asked the elderly waitress in the café.

"Coffee." As she was getting it a fat, slovenly creature came in. Months ago she had had her hair dyed straw yellow, but later had become so nostalgic for her own natural brown that her skull was now dappled with two colours.

"Have you heard?" she asked.

"What?"

"The herring-man's son ran into a streetcar on his motorbike yesterday," she said, "and now he's good and dead. The docs at the hospital couldn't save him. They came to tell his pa about a half an hour ago."

The elderly waitress served my coffee.

"How awful," she said.

I looked across the street. The overalled quarrellers were gone, and the broad, strong herring-man stood cleaning his fish with automatic expertness.

"The kid was just seventeen," said the fat woman. "He was learning to be a pastry cook. Won third prize at the food show with his chocolate castle."

"Those *motorbikes* are rotten things," the waitress said.

"People are mysterious," a friend of mine once wrote, and as I thought of those words I suddenly remembered the onions the herring-man nearly gave me with my second fish, his smiling apology: "My mind was wandering."

Genius

The little café lay on a broad, busy thoroughfare in one of the new sections of Amsterdam. The barkeeper-host had only one guest: an ancient man who sat amiably behind his empty genever glass. I placed my order and added, "Give grandfather something, too."

"You've got one coming," called the barkeeper. The old man smiled and tipped me a left-handed military salute, his fingers at his fragile temple. Then he got up, walked over to me, and asked, "Would you be interested in a chance on a first-class smoked sausage, guaranteed weight two pounds?"

"I certainly would be," I replied.

"It just costs a quarter, and the drawing will take place next Saturday," he said.

I fished out twenty-five cents and put it on the bar, and in return he gave me a piece of cardboard on which the number 79 was written in ink.

"A number with a tail," he said. "Lucky for you."

He picked up the quarter, put on his homburg

hat, and left the café with a friendly "Good after-noon, gentlemen." Through the window I saw him unlocking an old bicycle. Then, wheeling his means of transport, he disappeared from view.

"How old is he?" I asked.

"Eighty-six."

"And he still rides a bicycle?"

The barkeeper shook his head.

"No," he replied, "but he has to cross over, and it's a busy street. He's got a theory that traffic can see someone with a bicycle in his hand better than someone without a bicycle. So that's the why and the wherefore. When he gets across, he parks the bike and locks it up, and then the next day he's got it all ready to walk across again."

I thought it over.

"Not a bad idea," I said.

"Oh, he's all there, that one," said the barkeep-er. "Take that lottery, now. He made it up himself. I guess he sells about a hundred chances here every week. That's twenty-five guilders. And he only has to fork over one sausage on Saturday evening. Figure it out for yourself."

I did so, cursorily. He really got his money's worth out of that sausage, no doubt of it.

"And he runs the drawing all by himself," the barkeeper went on. "Clever as all get out. Because if a customer says, 'I've bought a lot of chances from you, but I never win,' you can bet your boots he *will* win the very next Saturday. The old man takes care that he does. Gets the customer off his neck for a good long time. Pretty smart, huh?"

I nodded and said, "He must have been a busi-nessman?"

"Well no. He was in the navy. They've paid him a pension for ages and ages. He's costing them a pretty penny."

All of a sudden I saw the old man on the other side of the street. He locked his bicycle against a wall and wandered away.

"He can get home from there without crossing any more streets," said the barkeeper.

I let him fill my glass again.

"I gave him a drink, but I didn't see him take it," I remarked.

The barkeeper nodded.

"He's sharp as tacks about that, too," he said. "Here's what he does. He's old and spry, and nearly everybody buys him something. But he never drinks more than two a day. So I write all the free ones down for him." He glanced at a notepad that lay beside the cash register. "Let's

see. Counting the one from you, he's a hundred and sixty-seven to the good."

Cees Nooteboom

Cees Nooteboom is one of Holland's best-known writers. He published his first novel in 1955, but only really came to public attention after the publication of his third novel, *Rituals*, in 1980. The central theme of all his work is the phenomenon of time: *Rituals* in particular is about the passing of time and the different ways of controlling the process. Inni Wintrop, the main character, is an outsider, a "dilet-tante" as he describes himself. The book is almost entirely set in Amsterdam, and although it describes the inner life of Inni himself, it also paints a vivid picture of the decaying city. Each section details a decade of Inni's life; the one reprinted below describes an encounter from his forties.

Rituals

There were days, thought Inni Wintrop, when it seemed as if a recurrent, fairly absurd phenome-non were trying to prove that the world is an absurdity that can best be approached with non-chalance, because life would otherwise become unbearable.

There were days, for instance, when you kept meeting cripples, days with too many blind peo-ple, days when you saw three times in succes-sion a left shoe lying by the roadside. It seemed as if all these things were trying to mean some-thing but could not. They left only a vague sense of unease, as if somewhere there existed a dark plan for the world that allowed itself to be hint-ed at only in this clumsy way.

The day on which he was destined to meet Philip Taads, of whose existence he had hitherto been unaware, was the day of the three doves. The dead one, the live one, and the dazed one, which could not possibly have been one and the same, because he had seen the dead one first. These three, he thought later, had made an attempt at annunciation that had succeeded insofar as it had made the encounter with Taads the Younger more mysterious.

It was now 1973, and Inni had turned forty in a decade he did not approve of. One ought not, he felt, to live in the second half of any century, and this particular century was altogether bad. There was something sad and at the same time ridiculous about all these fading years piling on top of one another until at last the millennium arrived. And they contained a contradiction, too: in order to reach the hundred, and in this case the thousand, that had to be completed, one had to add them up; but the feeling that went with the process seemed to have more to do with subtraction. It was as if no one, especially not Time, could wait for those ever dustier, ever higher figures finally to be declared void by a revolution of a row of glittering, perfectly shaped noughts, whereupon they would be relegated to the scrap heap of history. The only people apparently still sure of anything in these days of superstitious expectation were the Pope, the sixth of his name already, a white-robed Italian with an unusually tormented face that faintly resembled Eichmann's, and a number of terrorists of different persuasions, who tried in vain to anticipate the great witches' cauldron. The fact that he was now forty no longer in itself bothered Inni very much.

"Forty," he said, "is the age at which you have to do everything for the third time, or else you'll have to start training to be a cross-tempered old man," and he had decided to do the latter.

After Zita, he had had a long-lasting affair with an actress who had finally, in self-preservation, turned him out of the house like an old chair.

"What I miss most about her," he said to his friend the writer, "is her absence. These people are never at home. You get addicted to that."

He now lived alone and intended to keep it that way. The years passed, but even this was noticeable only in photographs. He bought and sold things, was not addicted to drugs, smoked less than one packet of Egyptian cigarettes a day, and drank neither more nor less than most of his friends.

This was the situation on the radiant June morning when, on the bridge between the Herenstraat and the Prinsenstraat, a dove flew straight at him as if to bore itself into his heart. Instead, it smashed against a car approaching from the Prinsengracht. The car drove on and the dove was left lying in the street, a gray and dusty, suddenly silly-looking little thing. A blonde-haired girl got off her bicycle and went up to the dove at the same time as Inni.

"Is it dead, do you think?" she asked.

He crouched down and turned the bird onto its back. The head did not turn with the rest of the body and continued to stare at the road surface.

"Finito," said Inni.

The girl put her bike away.

"I daren't pick it up," she said, "Will you?"

She used the familiar form of you. As long as they still do that, I am not yet old, thought Inni, picking up the dove. He did not like doves. They were not a bit like the image he used to have of the Holy Ghost, and the fact that all those promises of peace had never come to anything was probably their fault as well. Two white, softly cooing doves in the garden of a Tuscan villa, that was all right, but the gray hordes marching across the Dam Square with spurs on their boots (their heads making those idiotic mechanical pecking movements) could surely have nothing to do with a Spirit which had allegedly chosen that particular shape in which to descend upon Mary.

"What are you going to do with it?" asked the girl.

Inni looked around and saw on the bridge a wooden skip belonging to the Council. He went up to it. It was full of sand. Gently he laid the dove in it. The girl had followed him. An erotic moment. Man with dead dove, girl with bike and blue eyes. She was beautiful.

"Don't put it in there," she said. "The workmen will chuck it straight into the canal."

What does it matter whether it rots away in sand or in water, thought Inni, who often claimed he would prefer to be blown up after his death. But this was not the moment to hold a discourse on transience.

"Are you in a hurry?" he asked.

"No."

"Give me that bag then." From her handlebar hung a plastic bag, one from the Athenaeum Book Store.

"What's in there?"

"A book by Jan Wolkers."

"It can go in there then," said Inni. "There's no blood."

He put the dove in the bag.

"Jump on the back."

He took her bike without looking at her and rode off.

"Hey," she said. He heard her rapid footsteps and felt her jumping on the back of the bike. In the shop windows he caught brief glimpses of something that looked like happiness. Middle-aged gentleman on girl's bicycle, girl in jeans and white sneakers on the back.

He rode down the Prinsengracht to the

Haarlemmerdijk and from a distance saw the barriers of the bridge going down. They got off, and as the bridge slowly rose, they saw the second dove. It was sitting inside one of the open metal supports under the bridge, totally unconcerned as it allowed itself to be lifted up like a child on the Ferris wheel.

For a moment Inni felt an impulse to take the dead dove out of the plastic bag and lift it up like a peace offering to its slowly ascending living colleague, but he did not think the girl would like it. And besides, what would be the meaning of such a gesture? He shuddered, as usual not knowing why. The dove came down again and vanished invulnerably under the asphalt. They cycled on, to the Westerpark. With her small, brown hands, the girl dug a grave in the damp, black earth, somewhere in a corner.

"Deep enough?"

"For a dove, yes."

He laid the bird, which was now wearing its head like a hood on its back, into the hole. Together they smoothed the loose earth on top of it.

"Shall we go and have a drink?" he asked.

"All right."

Something in this minimal death, either the death itself or the summary ritual surrounding it, had made them allies. Something now had to happen, and if this something had anything to do with death, it would not be obvious. He cycled along the Nassaukade. She was not heavy. This was what pleased him most about his strange life – that when he had gotten up that morning, he had not known that he would now be cycling here with a girl at his back, but that such a possibility was always there. It gave him, he thought, something invincible. He looked at the faces of the men in the oncoming cars, and he knew that his life, in its absurdity, was right. Emptiness, loneliness, anxiety – these were the drawbacks – but there were also compensations, and this was one of them. She was humming softly and then fell silent. She said suddenly, as if she had taken a decision, "This is where I live."

Translated by Adrienne Dixon;
© Louisiana State University Press, 1983.

Rudi van Dantzig

Rudi van Dantzig is one of Holland's most famous choreographers, and was, until 1991, artistic director of the Dutch National Ballet. For
a Lost Soldier, **published in 1986, is his debut novel, an almost entirely autobiographical account of his experiences as a child during the war years. It's an extremely well-written novel, convincingly portraying the confusion and loneliness of the approximately 50,000 Dutch children evacuated to foster families during the winter. The novel's leading character is Jeroen, an eleven-year-old boy from Amsterdam who is sent away to live with a family in Friesland. During the Liberation celebrations, he meets an American soldier, Walt, with whom he has a brief sexual encounter; Walt disappears a few days later. The extract below details Jeroen's desperate search for Walt shortly after his return to Amsterdam.**

For a Lost Soldier

I set out on a series of reconnoitring expeditions through Amsterdam, tours of exploration that will take me to every corner. On a small map I look up the most important streets to see how I can best fan out to criss-cross the town, then make plans on pieces of paper showing exactly how the streets on each of my expeditions join up and what they are called. To make doubly sure I also use abbreviations: H.W. for Hoofdweg, H.S. for Haarlemmerstraat. The pieces of paper are carefully stored away inside the dust-jacket of a book, but I am satisfied that even if somebody found the notes, they wouldn't be able to make head or tail of them. It is a well-hidden secret.

For my first expedition I get up in good time. I yawn a great deal and act as cheerfully as I can to disguise the paralysing uncertainty that is governing my every move.

"We're going straight to the field, Mum, we're going to build a hut," but she is very busy and scarcely listens.

"Take care and don't be back too late."

The street smells fresh as if the air has been scrubbed with soap. I feel dizzy with excitement and as soon as I have rounded the corner I start to run towards the bridge. Now it's beginning, and everything is sure to be all right, all my waiting and searching is about to come to an end; the solution lies hidden over there, somewhere in the clear light filling the streets.

The bright air I inhale makes me feel that I am about to burst. I want to sing, shout, cheer myself hoarse.

I have marked my piece of paper, among a tangle of crossing and twisting lines, with H.W, O.T, W.S, Hoofdweg, Overtoom, Weteringschans.

The Hoofdweg is close by, just over the bridge. It is the broad street we have to cross when we go to the swimming baths. I know the gloomy houses and the narrow, flowerless gardens from the many times I've walked by in other summers, towel and swimming trunks rolled under my arm. But beyond that, and past Mercatorplein, Amsterdam is unknown territory to me, ominous virgin land.

The unfamiliar streets make me hesitate, my excitement seeps away and suddenly I feel unsure and tired. The town bewilders me: shops with queues outside, people on bicycles carrying bags, beflagged streets in the early morning sun, squares where wooden platforms have been put up for neighbourhood celebrations, whole districts with music pouring out of loudspeakers all day. An unsolvable jigsaw puzzle. Now and then I stop in sheer desperation, study my hopelessly inadequate piece of paper, and wonder if it would not be much better to give up the attempt altogether.

But whenever I see an army vehicle, or catch a glimpse of a uniform, I revive and walk a little faster, sometimes trotting after a moving car in the hope that it will come to a stop and he will jump out.

Time after time I lose my way and have to walk back quite far, and sometimes, if I can summon up enough courage, I ask for directions.

"Please, Mevrouw, could you tell me how to get to the Overtoom?"

"Dear me, child, you're going the wrong way. Over there, right at the end, turn left, that'll take you straight there."

The Overtoom, when I finally reach it, seems to be a street without beginning or end. I walk, stop, cross the road, search: not a trace of W.S. Does my plan bear any resemblance to the real thing?

I take off my shoes and look at the dark impression of my sweaty foot on the pavement. Do I have to go on, search any more? What time is it, how long have I been walking the streets?

Off we sail to Overtoom,
We drink milk and cream at home,
Milk and cream with apple pie,
Little children must not lie.

Over and over again, automatically, the jingle runs through my mind, driving me mad.

As I walk back home, slowly, keeping to the shady side of the street as much as I can, I think of the other expeditions hidden away in the dust-jacket of my book. The routes I picked out and wrote down with so much eagerness and trust seem pointless and unworkable now. I scold myself: I must not give up, only a coward would do that. Walt is waiting for me, he has no one, and he'll be so happy to see me again.

At home I sit down in a chair by the window, too tired to talk, and when I do give an answer to my mother my voice sounds thin and weak, as if it were finding it difficult to escape from my chest. She sits down next to me on the arm of the chair, lifts my chin up and asks where we have been playing such tiring games, she hasn't seen me down in the street all morning, though the other boys were there.

"Were you really out in the field?"

"Ask them if you don't believe me!" I run onto the balcony, tear my first route map up into pieces and watch the shreds fluttering down into the garden like snowflakes.

When my father gets back home he says, "So, my boy, you and I had best go into town straightway, you still haven't seen the illuminations."

With me on the back, he cycles as far as the Concertgebouw, where he leans the bike against a wall and walks with me past a large green space with badly worn grass. Here, too, there are soldiers, tents, trucks. Why don't I look this time, why do I go and walk on the other side of my father and cling – "Don't hang on so tight!" – to his arm?

"Now you'll see something," he says, "something you've never even dreamed of, just you wait and see."

Walt moving his quivering leg to and fro, his warm, yielding skin, the smell of the thick hair in his armpits . . .

I trudge along beside my father, my soles burning, too tired to look at anything.

We walk through the gateway of a large building, a sluice that echoes to the sound of voices, and through which the people have to squeeze before fanning out again on the other side. There are hundreds of them now, all moving in the same direction towards a buzzing hive of activity, a surging mass of bodies.

There is a sweet smell of food coming from a small tent in the middle of the street in front of which people are crowding so thickly that I can't see what is being sold.

I stop in my tracks, suddenly dying for food,

dying just to stay where I am and to yield myself up to that wonderful sweet smell. But my father has already walked on and I have to wriggle through the crowds to catch up with him.

Beside a bridge he pushes me forward between the packed bodies so that I can see the canal, a long stretch of softly shimmering water bordered by overhanging trees. At one end brilliantly twinkling arches of light have been suspended that blaze in the darkness and are reflected in the still water. Speechless and enchanted I stare at the crystal-clear world full of dotted lines, a vision of luminous radiation that traces a winking and sparkling route leading from bridge to bridge, from arch to arch, from me to my lost soldier.

I grip my father's hand. "Come on," I say, "let's have a look. Come on!"

Festoons of light bulbs are hanging wherever we go, like stars stretched across the water, and the people walk past them in silent, admiring rows. The banks of the canal feel as cosy as candle-lit sitting-rooms.

"Well?" my father breaks the spell. "It's quite something, isn't it? In Friesland, you'd never have dreamed that anything like that existed, would you now?"

We take a short cut through dark narrow streets. I can hear dull cracks, sounds that come as a surprise in the dark, as if a sniper were firing at us.

My father starts to run.

"Hurry, or we'll be too late."

An explosion of light spurts up against the black horizon and whirls apart, pink and pale green fountains of confetti that shower down over a brilliant sign standing etched in the sky.

And another shower of stars rains down to the sound of muffled explosions and cheers from the crowd, the sky trembling with the shattering of triumphal arches.

I look at the luminous sign in the sky as if it is a mirage.

"Daddy, that letter, what's it for? Why is it there?" Why did I have to ask, why didn't I just add my own letters, fulfil my own wishful thinking?

"That W? You know what that's for. The W, the W's for Queen Wilhelmina . . ." I can hear a scornful note in his voice as if he is mocking me.

"Willy here, Willy there," he says, "but the whole crew took off to England and left us properly in the lurch."

I'm not listening, I don't want to hear what he has to say.

W isn't Wilhelmina: it stands for Walt! It's a sign specially for me . . .

Reprinted by permission of The Bodley Head.

Marga Minco

Marga Minco's *Empty House*, first published in 1966, is another wartime novel. During the occupation, the Germans deported her entire family, who were Jewish, to the concentration camps and none of them survived. Minco herself managed to escape this fate and spent much of the war in hiding in Amsterdam. In 1944 she moved to Kloveniersburgwal 49, which served as a safe house for various Dutch artists during the ensuing winter famine; it's this house – or, rather, the house next door – that is the model for the various empty houses in the novel. In the following extract, the main character, Sepha, meets Yona, another Jewish survivor and later to become a great friend, when travelling back from Friesland to the safe house.

An Empty House

As soon as we were in the centre Yona put on her rucksack and tapped on the window of the cab. We'd been delayed a lot because the lorry which had picked us up at our spot beyond Zwolle had to go to all kinds of small villages and made one detour after another. We sat in the back on crates. Yona had grazed her knee heaving herself up over the tail-gate. I'd not seen it because I'd been making a place for us to sit.

"What have you done?" I asked.

"Damn it," she cried, "I'm not as agile as you. I told you. I spent all my time holed up in a kind of loft." She tied a hanky round her knee. "One step from the door to the bed. Do you think I did keep-fit exercises or something?"

I thought of the fire-escape which I'd gone up and down practically every day. In the end I could do it one-handed.

"Have you somewhere to go to in Amsterdam?"

I expected her to say it was none of my business, but she seemed not to hear me. The lorry thundered along a road where they'd just cleared away barricades.

"Do you know," she said, "at first I didn't know where I was?" Suddenly her voice was much less sharp. "All I knew was that it was a low house with an attic window above the back door. "You don't live here," said the woman of the house. She always wore a blue striped apron. "But I am here though," I said. "No," she said, "you must remember that you're not here, you're nowhere." She didn't say it unpleasantly, she wished me no harm. But I couldn't get it out of my mind – you're nowhere. It's as if, by degrees, you start believing it yourself, as if you begin to doubt yourself. I sometimes sat staring at my hands for ages. There was no mirror and they'd white-washed the attic window. It was only by looking at my hand that I recognized myself, proved to myself that I was there."

"Didn't anybody ever come to see you?"

"Yes. In the beginning. But I didn't feel like talking. They soon got the message. They let me come downstairs in the evenings occasionally, the windows were blacked out and the front and back doors bolted. It didn't impress me as being anything special. Later on, I even began to dislike it. I saw that they were scared stiff when I was sitting in the room. They listened to every noise from outside. I told them that I'd rather stay upstairs, that I didn't want to run any risks. You can even get used to a loft. At least it was mine, my loft."

While talking, she had turned round; she sat with her back half turned towards me. I had to bend forward to catch her last words. Her scarf had slipped off. Her hair kept brushing my face. Once we were near Amsterdam, she started talking about her father who went with her to the Concertgebouw every week, accompanied her on long walks and ate cakes with her in small tea-rooms. She talked about him as if he were a friend. And again I had to hear details of the house. She walked me through rooms and corridors, showed me the courtyard, the cellar with wine-racks, the attic with the old-fashioned pulley. I knew it as if I had lived there myself. Where would she sleep tonight?

"If you want to, you can come home with me," I said. "I shan't have any time. I've so much to do. There's a case of mine somewhere as well. I can't remember what I put in it."

We drove across Berlage Bridge. It was still light. She'd fallen silent during the last few kilometres and sat with her chin in her hands. "The south district," I heard her say. "Nothing has changed here, of course."

I wrote my address on a little piece of paper

and gave it to her. She put it in the pocket of her khaki shirt without looking at it.

"You must come," I shouted after her when she had got out at Ceintuurbaan. She walked away without a backward glance, hands on the straps of her rucksack, hunched forward as if there were stones in it. I lost sight of her because I was looking at a tram coming from Ferdinand Bolstraat. The trams were running again. There were tiny flags on the front. Flags were hanging everywhere. And portraits of the Queen. And orange hangings. Everyone seemed to be in the streets. It was the last evening of the Liberation celebrations. The driver dropped me off at Rokin. I'd not far to go. If I walked quickly, I could be there in five minutes. The door was usually open, the lock was broken – less than half a minute for the three flights of stairs. I could leave my case downstairs.

People were walking in rows right across the full width of the street. The majority had orange buttonholes or red, white and blue ribbons. There were a lot of children with paper hats, flags and tooters. Two mouth-organ players and a saxophonist in a traditional Volendammer costume drifted with the mass, though far apart. I tried to get through as quickly as possible. I bumped into a child who dropped his flag, which was about to be trodden underfoot. I made room with my case, grabbed the flag from the ground and thrust it into his hand. Jazz music resounded from a bar in Damstraat. The door was open. Men and women were sitting at the bar with their arms around each other. Their bodies shook. All that was left in the baker's window were bread-crumbs. Here it was even busier. Groups of Canadians stood at the corners, besieged by whores, black-market traders and dog-end collectors.

I'd not seen much of the Liberation in the Frisian village. The woman I'd stayed with baked her own bread; she had done so throughout the war and she just went on doing it. When I was alone in the kitchen with her she asked with avid interest about my experiences in the hunger winter. She wanted to know everything about the church with corpses, the men with rattles, the people suffering from beriberi on the steps of the Palace, the emaciated children who went to the soup-kitchen with their pans. I spared her no details. About the recycled fat which gave us diarrhoea, the rotten fen potatoes, the wet, clay-like bread, about the ulcers and legs full of sores.

I saw it as a way of giving something back.

At last I was at the bridge. I looked at the house with the large expanses of window and the grimy door. At the house next door, the raised pavement and the neck gable. The windows were bricked up. The debris was piled high behind. All that was left were bare walls. I put down my case to change hands. It was as if, only then, that I felt how hungry I was, how stiff my knees were from sitting for hours on the crate. There was something strange about the houses, as if I'd been away for years. But it could have been that I'd never stopped on the bridge before, never looked at them from that angle. The barge was still there. An oil-lamp was burning behind the portholes.

Our front door was closed. The lock had been mended in the meantime. I ought to have had a key somewhere. I didn't want to ring. I'd never realized that the staircase was so dark when the front door was shut. Without thinking, I groped for the banister and banged my hand against the rough wall. "It's nice, soft wood," Mark had said as he sawed the banister into logs. "You can cut it nicely into pieces with a sharp knife." The steps on the upper flight grated as if there were sand on them. I pushed the door open with my case.

There was a black lady's handbag on the bed. A leather bag with a brass clasp. Who had a bag like that? The leather was supple and smooth, except for some creases on the underside. I walked to the table which was full of bottles and glasses. I saw a long dog-end lying in one of the ashtrays. The cigarette must have been carefully put out. Afterwards the burnt tobacco had been nipped off. I found the empty packet on the floor, Sweet Caporal. The divan was strewn with newspapers. Eisenhower standing in a car. Montgomery standing in a car. A new Bailey bridge built in record time.

I had to look among the piled-up crockery in the kitchen for a cup. I rinsed it a long time before I drank from it. I felt the water sink into my stomach; it gurgled as if it was falling into a smooth, cold hollow. The tower clock sounded the half-hour. The house became even quieter. There appeared to be nobody home on the other floors either. Half nine? It got dark quickly now. It was already dark under the few trees left along the canal. I opened one of the windows and leant outside. A man and a woman tottered along the pavement on the other side. They held each other firmly under the arm. They would suddenly lurch forward a few metres, slowly right themselves and start up again. The nine o'clock man always walked there too. I'd not heard him since the Liberation.

Reprinted by permission of Peter Owen Publishers, London.

Nicolas Freeling

Creator of the Dutch detective Van der Valk, Nicolas Freeling was born in England but has lived all his life in Europe, where most of his novels are set. He actually left Amsterdam over twenty years ago and nowadays rarely returns to the city. But in the Van der Valk novels he evokes Amsterdam (and Amsterdammers) as well as any writer ever has, subtly and unsentimentally using the city and its people as a vivid backdrop to his fast-moving action. The following extract is from A Long Silence, first published in 1972.

A Long Silence

Arlette came out into the open air and saw that spring had come to Amsterdam. The pale, acid sun of late afternoon lay on the inner harbour beyond the Prins Hendrik Kade: the wind off the water was sharp. It gave her a shock. A succession of quick rhythmic taps, as at the start of a violin concerto of Beethoven. That she noticed this means, I think, that from that moment she was sane again. But it is possible that I am mistaken. Even if insane one can have, surely, the same perceptions as other people, and this "click" is a familiar thing. Exactly the same happens when one takes a night train down from Paris to the Coast, and one wakes somewhere between Saint Raphael and Cannes and looks out, and there is the Mediterranean. Or was.

The pungent salt smell, the northern, maritime keynotes of seagull and herring, the pointed brick buildings, tall and narrow like herons, with their mosaic of parti-coloured shutters, eaves, sills, that gives the landscapes their stiff, heraldic look (one is back beyond Brueghel, beyond Van Eyck, to the primitives whose artists we do not know, so that they have names like the Master of the Saint Ursula Legend). The lavish use of paint in flat bright primary colours which typifies these Baltic, Hanseatic quay-sides is startling to the visitor from central Europe. Even the Dutch flags waving everywhere (there are no more determined flag-wavers) upset and worried Arlette: she had not realised how in a short time her eye had accustomed itself to the subtle and faded colourings of France, so that it was as though she had never left home. The sharp flat brightness of Holland! The painters' light which hurts the unaccustomed eye . . . Arlette never wore sunglasses in France, except on the sea, or on the snow, yet here, she remembered suddenly, she had practically gone to bed in them. It was all so familiar. She had lived here, she had to keep reminding herself, for twenty years.

She had no notion of where she wanted to go, but she knew that now she was here, a small pause would bring the spinning, whirling patterns of the kaleidoscope to rest. She crossed the road and down the steps to the little wooden terrace – a drink, and get her breath back! Everything was new – the pale heavy squatness of the Dutch café's cup-and-saucer, left on her table by the last occupant; the delightful rhythmic skyline across the harbour of the Saint Nicolaas church and the corner of the Zeedijk! Tourists were flocking into waterbuses, and now she was a tourist too. An old waiter was wiping the table while holding a tray full of empty bottles, which wavered in front of her eye.

"Mevrouw?"

"Give me a chocomilk, if at least you've got one that's good and cold."

Another click! She was talking Dutch, and as fluently as ever she had! He was back before she had got over it.

"Nou, mevrouwtje – cold as Finnegan's feet." His voice had the real Amsterdam caw to it. "You aren't Dutch though, are you now?"

"Only a tourist," smiling.

"Well now, by-your-leave: proper-sounding Dutch you talk there," chattily, bumping the glass down and pouring in the clawky chocomilk.

"Thank you very much."

"Tot Uw dienst. Ja ja ja, kom er aan" to a fussy man, waving and banging his saucer with a coin. Neem mij niet kwa-a-lijk; een be-hoor-lijk Nederlands spreekt U daar. Like a flock of rooks. Yah, yah ya-ah, kom er a-an. And she was blinded by tears again, hearing her husband's exact intonation – when with her he spoke a Dutch whose accent sometimes unconsciously – ludicrously – copied hers, but when with the real thing, the rasecht like himself his accent would begin to caw too as though in self-parody.

Next door to her were sitting two American girls, earnest, quiet, dusty-haired, looking quite clean though their jeans were as darkly greasy as the mud the dredger over there was turning up off the harbour bottom. Scraps of conversation floated across.

"She's a lovely person, ever so quiet but really mature, you know what I mean, yes, from Toledo." Arlette knew that Van der Valk would have guffawed and her eyes cleared.

I see her there, at the start of her absurd and terrifying mission. She has the characteristic feminine memory for detail, the naively earnest certainty that she has to get everything right. Had I asked what those two girls were drinking she would have known for sure, and been delighted at my asking.

I have not seen Amsterdam for four or five years, and it might be as long again before I shall. This is just as well. I do not want my imagination to get in the way of Arlette's senses. Piet, whose imagination worked like mine, saw things in an entirely different way to her. We were sitting once together on that same terrace.

"Look at that dam building," pointing at the Central Station, a construction I am fond of, built with loving attention to every useless detail by an architect of the last century whose name I have forgotten (a Dutch equivalent of Sir Giles Gilbert Scott). "Isn't it lovely?" Lovely is not the word I would have chosen but it is oddly right.

"The Railway Age," he went on. "Make a wonderful museum – old wooden carriages, tuff-tuff locos with long funnels, Madame Tussaud figures of station-masters with beards, policemen wearing helmets, huge great soup-strainer moustaches, women with bustle and reticules . . ." Yes, indeed, and children in sailor suits. Arlette's mind does not behave like this.

I am changed, thought Arlette, and unchanged. I am the same housewife, familiar with these streets, these people. I am not pricked or tickled by anything here, like a tourist. I see all this with the coolness and objectivity of experience. I am not going to rush into anything stupid or imprudent. This is a town I know, and I am going to find myself perfectly able to cope with the problem. I am not alone or helpless; I have here many friends, and there are many more who were Piet's friends and who will help me for his sake. But I am no longer the thoughtless and innocent little wife of a little man in a little job, standing on the corner with shopping bag wondering whether to have a cabbage or a cauli. I am a liberated woman, and that is going to make a difference.

A tout was circling around the cluster of tables, sizing up likely suckers. A year or so ago he would have been handing out cards for a restaurant or hotel, looking for a quickie trip around the sights, with waterbus, Anne Frank and the Rembrandthuis all thrown in for only ten guilders. Now – he had closed in on the two American girls and she could hear his pidgin-German patois that is the international language of the European tout – selling live sex-shows. The two girls glanced up for a second with polite indifference, and went back to their earnest, careful, intense conversation, paying no further attention to him at all. He broke off the patter, circled backwards like a boxer and gave Arlette a careful glance: Frenchwomen, generally fascinated by the immoralities and debaucheries of these English and these Scandinavians – a likely buyer, as long as they have first done their duty with a really good orgy at Marks and Spencer's. Arlette met his eye with such a chill and knowing look that he shuffled back into the ropes and made off sideways: cow has been to the sex-show and has no money left. Amsterdam too has changed and not changed, she thought.

"Raffishness" was always the first cliché tourists used, the Amsterdammers were always intensely, idiotically proud of their red-light district and since time immemorial a stroll to look at "the ladies behind the windows" was proposed to every eager tourist the very first night.

They have taken now with such relish to the new role of exhibitionist shop-window that it is hard not to laugh – the visitor's first reaction generally is roars of laughter. The Dutch have a belief that sex has made them less provincial somehow – for few attitudes are more provincial than the anxious striving to be modern-and-progressive. Paris doesn't exist any more, and London is slipping, they will tell one with a boastful pathos, and Holland-is-where-it's-at. A bit immature, really, as the two nineteen-year-olds from Dubuque were probably at that moment saying. Arlette was a humble woman. She saw herself as snobbish, narrow, rigid, French provincial bourgeois. Piet, born and bred in Amsterdam, used to describe himself as a peasant. This humility gave them both an unusual breadth, stability, balance. I remember his telling me once how to his mind his career if not his life had been an abject failure.

"But there," drinking brandy reflectively, being indeed a real soak and loving it, "what else could I have done?"

Arlette, walking through the lazy, dirty sunshine of late afternoon in Amsterdam, was thinking too, "What else could I have done?" She had come to lay a ghost. Not that she – hardheaded woman – believed in ghosts, but she had lived long enough to know they were there. Piet was a believer in ghosts. "I have known malign influences outside the bathroom door," he used to say. He was delighted when I gave him to read the finely-made old thriller of Mr A.E.W. Mason which is called *The Prisoner in the Opal*: he saw the point at once, and when he brought it back he said that he too, with the most sordid, materialistic, bourgeois of enquiries, always made the effort "to pierce the opal crust". Poor old Piet.

Once we were having dinner together in a Japanese restaurant. We had had three pernods, big ones, the ones Piet with his horrible Dutch ideas of wit which he took for *esprit* described as "*Des Grand Pers*". We were watching the cook slicing raw fish into fine transparent slices.

"There is poetry," said Piet suddenly, "in those fingers." I turned around suspiciously, because this is a paraphrase from a good writer, whom Piet had certainly not read. I used the phrase as an epigraph to a book I once wrote about cooks – which Piet had not read either. "Poetry in the fat fingers of cooks" – I looked at Piet suspiciously.

"So," with tactful calm, "is that a quotation?"

"No," innocent, "Just a phrase. Thought it would please you, haw." That crude guffaw; completely Piet. The stinker; to this day I don't know whether he was kidding me. A skilful user of flattery, but damn it, a friend.

The Damrak, the Dam, the Rokin. Squalid remnants of food, flung upon the pavements. The young were unable or unwilling to spend much on food, she thought, and what they got for their money probably deserved to be flung: one could not blame them too much, just because one felt revolted. But one did blame them: beastly children.

The Utrechtsestraat. The Frederickplein. And once out of the tourist stamping-ground, Arlette knew suddenly where she was going. She was heading unerringly and as though she had never been away straight towards the flat where she had lived for twenty years. It was a longish way to walk, all the way from the Central Station and carrying a suitcase too. Why had she done it? She would have said, "What else could I have done?" crossly, for when she got there she was very tired and slightly footsore, dishevelled, her hair full of dust, smelling of sweat and ready to cry.

"Arlette! My dear girl! What are you doing? – but come in! I'm so happy to see you – and at the same time, my poor child, I'm so sad! Not that we know anything – what one reads in the paper nowadays – Pah! And again Pah! come in, my dear girl, come in – you don't mean to say you walked . . . from the station? You didn't! You couldn't! Sit down child, do. The lavy? But of course you know where it is, that's not something you'll have forgotten. I'll make some coffee. My dear girl, marvellous to see you, and the dear boys? – no no, I must be patient, go and have a pee child, and a wash, do you good." The old biddy who had always had a ground floor flat, and still did . . . She taught the piano. It had been the most familiar background noise to Arlette's life throughout the boys' childhood; her voice carried tremendously.

"One, Two, not so hasty. Pedal there, you're not giving those notes their value, that's a sharp, can't you hear it?" And coming back from shopping an hour later another one was being put through its hoops. "Watch your tempo, not so much espressivo, you're sentimentalising, this is the Ruysdaelskade, not the Wiener Wald or something."

"Lumpenpack," she would mutter, coming out on the landing for a breather and finding Arlette emptying the dustbin.

Old Mother Counterpoint, Piet always called her, and sometimes in deference to Jane Austen "Bates" ("Mother hears perfectly well; you only have to shout a little and say it two or at the most three times"). A wonderful person really. A mine of information on the quarter, possessor of efficient intelligence networks in every shop, an endless gabble on the telephone, forever fixing things for someone else. She could find anything for you; a furnished room, a second-hand pram scarcely used, a boy's bike, a shop where they were having a sale of materials ever so cheap – even if she didn't have her finger on it she knew a man who would let you have it wholesale. Warm-hearted old girl. Gushing, but wonderfully kind, and gentle, and sometimes even tactful.

"You take yours black, dear, oh yes, I hadn't forgotten – you think I'd forget a thing like that? Not gaga yet, thank God. Good heavens, it must be seven years. But you haven't aged dear, a few lines yes – badges of honour my pet, that's what I call them. Tell me – can you bear to talk about it? Where are you staying? By the look of you you could do with a square meal."

"I don't know, I was wondering . . ."

"But my poor pet of course, how can you ask, you know I'd be more than pleased and I've plenty of room, it's just can you bear all the little fussinesses of a frightened old maid – oh nonsense child, now don't be tiresome. Now I'll tell you what, no don't interrupt, I'm going to the butcher, yes still the same awful fellow, all those terrible people, how they'll be thrilled, just wait till he hears, I'll frighten him, he gave me an escalope last week and tough . . . my poor girl, since you left he thinks everything is permitted him. I'll get a couple of nice veal cutlets and we'll have dinner, just you wait and I'll get something to drink too, I love the excuse and what's more I'll make pancakes. I never bother by myself, you take your shoes off and put your feet up and read the paper, nonsense you'll do no such thing, I want to and anyway I'll enjoy it: would you perhaps love a bath, my pet?" The voice floated off into the hallway.

"Where's my goloshes, oh dear, oh here they are now how did they get that way, oh wait till I tell the wretch the cutlets are for you, he'll jump out of his skin . . ." The front door slammed. Arlette was home.

It was a nice evening. Bates brought Beaujolais – Beaujolais! "I remember you used to buy it, child, I hope you still like it. Cutlets."

"He practically went on his knees when he heard, with the tears in his eyes he swore on his mother's grave you'd be able to cut them with a fork and I just looked and said 'She'd better', that's all."

"Bananas – I've got some rum somewhere, hasn't been touched in five years I'd say, pah, all dusty, do you think it'll still be all right dear, not gone poisonous or anything, one never knows now, they put chemicals in to make things smell better, awful man in the supermarket and I swear he squirts the oranges with an aerosol to make them smell like oranges, forlorn hope is all I can say."

The rum was tasted, and pronounced fit for pancakes.

"And how's Amsterdam?" asked Arlette, laughing.

It wasn't what it was; it wasn't what it had been. Arlette had been prepared to be bored with old-maidish gush about how we don't sleep safe in our beds of nights, not like when we had a policeman in the house, which did give someone a sense of security somehow. She ought to have known better really, because old mother Counterpoint had the tough dryness, the voluble energy, the inconsequent loquacity she expected – and indeed remembered, but the warm-hearted kindness was illuminated by a shrewd observation she had never given the old biddy credit for.

"Well, my dear, it would ill become me to complain. I'll have this flat for as long as I live and they can't put my rent up, I have to spread my butter thinner but I'm getting old and I need less of it. I have the sunshine still and the plants and my birds and they'll all last my time. I think it comes much harder on a girl your age, who can remember what things used to be, and who still has to move with the changes and accept them, whereas people expect me to be eccentric and silly. And I'm sorrier still for the young ones. They don't have any patterns to move by: it must give a terrible sense of insecurity and I think that's what makes them so unhappy. Everyone kowtows to them and it must be horrid really. Look at the word young, I mean it used to mean what it said and no more, young cheese or a young woman and that was that – and now they talk about a young chair or a young frock and it's supposed to mean good, and when you keep ascribing virtue to people, and implying all the time that they should be admired and imitated, well dear, it makes their life very difficult and wearisome; I used to know a holy nun and she said sometimes that everybody being convinced one was good made a heavy cross to carry. When the young do wicked things I can't help feeling that it's because they're dreadfully unhappy. Of course there's progress, lots and lots of progress, and it makes me very happy. I don't have many pupils now, but I'm always struck when they come, so tall and healthy and active, so unlike the pale little tots when I was a young woman, and I remember very hard times, my dear, all the men drunk always because their lives were so hard, but they don't seem to me any happier or more contented and they complain more because they expect much more. I can't really see what they mean talking about progress because that seems to me that people are good and get better and the fact is, my pet, as you and I know, people are born bad and tend to get worse and putting good before evil is always a dreadful struggle dear, whatever they say. One is so vain and so selfish."

And Arlette, who had had a good rest, a delicious bath, and a good supper, found herself pouring out her whole tale and most of her heart.

"Well," said Bates at the end with great commonsense, "that has done you a great deal of good my dear, and that's a fact, just like taking off one's stays, girls don't wear stays any more and they don't know what they miss."

Arlette felt inclined to argue that it was a good thing to be no longer obliged to wear stays.

"Of course dear, don't think I don't agree with you, healthy girls with good stomach muscles playing tennis, and no more of that fainting and vapouring. But I maintain that it was a good thing for a girl to know constraint. Sex education and women's lib, all dreadful cant. Girls who married without knowing the meaning of the word sex were sometimes very happy and sometimes very unhappy, and I don't believe they are any happier now. I married a sailor, dear, and learned how to go without."

"It doesn't make me any happier now," said Arlette dryly.

"No dear, and that's just what I felt in 1940 when my ship got torpedoed. So now let's be very sensible. You've come here very confused and embittered, and you don't want anything to do with the police, and you're probably quite right because really poor dears they've simply no notion, but at the present you've no notion either. You'd never of thought about asking my advice because I'm a silly old bag but I'll give it you, and it is that you probably can find out who killed your husband, because it's surprising what you can do when you try, but it's as well to have friends you can count on, and you can count on me for a start, and with that my dear we'll go to bed, your eyes are dropping out."

"Did you join the resistance, in 1940 I mean?" asked Arlette.

"Yes I did, and what's more once I threw a bomb at a bad man in the Euterpestraat, and that was a dreadful place, the Gestapo headquarters here in Amsterdam and it was very hard because I was horribly frightened of the bomb, and even more frightened of the bad man who had soldiers with him and most of all because I knew they would take hostages and execute them, but it had to be done, you see."

"I do see," said Arlette seriously, "it wasn't the moment to take off one's stays and feel comfortable."

"Right, my pet, right," said old mother Counterpoint.

Books

Most of the books listed below are in print and in paperback – those that are out of print (o/p) should be easy to track down in secondhand bookshops. Publishers are detailed with the British publisher first, followed by the US publisher, where both exist. Where books are published in only one of these countries, UK or US follows the publisher's name; where the book is published by the same company in both countries, the name of the company appears just once.

History and Society

Geoffrey Cotterell, *Amsterdam* (o/p). Popularized, offbeat history giving a highly readable account of the city up to the late 1960s.

Mike Dash, *Tulipomania* (Gollancz/Crown). An examination of the introduction of the tulip into the Low Countries at the height of the Golden Age, and the extraordinarily inflated and speculative market in the many varieties of bulbs and flowers that resulted from this. There's a lot of padding and scene-setting, but it's an engaging enough read, and has nice detail on seventeenth-century Amsterdam, Leiden and Haarlem.

Pieter Geyl, *The Revolt of The Netherlands 1555–1609; The Netherlands in the Seventeenth Century 1609–1648.* (Cassell; US, o/p). Geyl's history of the Dutch-speaking peoples is the definitive account of Holland's history during its formative years, chronicling the uprising against the Spanish and the formation of the United Provinces. Quite the best thing you can read on the period.

Mark Girouard, *Cities and People: A Social and Architectural History* (Yale). Has an informed and well-illustrated chapter on the city's social history.

Christopher Hibbert, *Cities and Civilisation* (Stewart, Tabori & Chang, US). Includes a chapter on Amsterdam in the age of Rembrandt. Some interesting facts about seventeenth-century daily life.

J.H. Huizinga, *Dutch Civilisation in the 17th Century* (o/p). Analysis of life and culture in the Dutch Republic by one of the country's most widely respected historians.

Geert Mak, *Amsterdam: A Brief Life of the City* (Harvill, UK). Recently published, this is a readable and evocative social history of Amsterdam written by a leading Dutch journalist. It's light and accessible enough to read from cover to cover, but its index of places makes it useful to dip into as a supplement to this guide, too.

J.L. Price, *Culture and Society in the Dutch Republic in the 17th Century* (Yale). An accurate, intelligent account of the Golden Age.

Simon Schama, *The Embarrassment of Riches: An Interpretation of Dutch Culture in the Golden Age* (Fontana; Vintage). Enthralling and highly readable account of the Golden Age, drawing on a vast range of archive sources.

Jan Stoutenbeek et al, *A Guide to Jewish Amsterdam* (o/p). Fascinating, if perhaps overdetailed, guide to just about every Jewish monument in the city. You can purchase a copy in better Amsterdam bookshops.

Sir William Temple, *Observations upon the United Provinces of The Netherlands* (o/p). Written by a seventeenth-century English diplomat, and a good, evocative account of the country at the time.

Art and Architecture

Pierre Cabanne, *Van Gogh* (o/p). Standard mix of art criticism and biography, drawing heavily on the artist's own letters.

Kenneth Clark, *Civilisation* (Penguin, UK). Includes a warm and scholarly rundown on the Golden Age, with illuminating insights on the way in which the art reflected the period.

Eugene Fromentin, *The Masters of Past Time: Dutch and Flemish Painting from Van Eyck to*

Rembrandt (Phaidon, UK). Entertaining essays on the major Dutch and Flemish painters.

R.H. Fuchs, *Dutch Painting* (Thames & Hudson). As complete an introduction to the subject – from Flemish origins to the present day – as you could wish for in just a couple of hundred pages.

Guus Kemme (ed.), *Amsterdam Architecture: A Guide* (o/p). Illustrated guide to the architecture of Amsterdam, with potted accounts of the major buildings.

Paul Overy, *De Stijl* (Thames & Hudson). Inventive reassessment of all aspects of the De Stijl movement. Clearly written and comprehensive.

Jacob Rosenberg et al, *Dutch Art and Architecture 1600–1800* (o/p). Full and erudite anthology of essays on the art and buildings of the Golden Age and after. For dedicated Dutch-art fans only.

Simon Schama, *Rembrandt's Eyes* (Penguin; Knopf). Published in 1999, this erudite work is an enchanting read, full of original insights into the life and times of one of the world's greatest artists.

Irving Stone, *Lust for Life* (Mandarin; New American Library). Everything you ever wanted to know about Van Gogh in a pop genius-is-pain biography.

Christopher White, *Rembrandt* (Thames & Hudson). The most widely available – and wide-ranging – study of the painter and his work, with wonderfully incisive commentary from the author.

Literature

Simon Carmiggelt, *Kronkels* (o/p). Second collection of Carmiggelt's "slight adventures", three of which are reprinted on pp.319–321.

Rudi van Dantzig, *For a Lost Soldier* (Gay Mens Press). Honest and convincing tale, largely autobiographical, that tells of a young boy's sexual awakening against a background of war and liberation. See the extract on pp.323–325.

Anne Frank, *The Diary of a Young Girl* (Penguin; Bantam). Lucid and moving, the most revealing thing you can read on the plight of Amsterdam's Jews during the war years.

Nicolas Freeling, *Love in Amsterdam* (Carroll & Graf, US); *Dwarf Kingdom* (Chivers; G.K. Hall). *A City Solitary*; *Strike Out Where Not Applicable*; *A Long Silence* (all o/p). Freeling writes detective novels, and his most famous creation is the rebel cop, Van der Valk, around whom a successful British TV series was made. Light, carefully crafted tales, with just the right amount of twists to make them classic cops 'n' robbers reading –

and with good Amsterdam (and Dutch) locations. There's an extract from *A Long Silence* on pp.327–331.

Etty Hillesum, *Etty: An Interrupted Life* (Persephone; Henry Holt). Diary of an Amsterdam Jewish young woman uprooted from her life in the city and taken to Auschwitz, where she died. As with Anne Frank's more famous journal, penetratingly written – though on the whole much less readable.

Margo Minco, *The Fall*; *An Empty House*; *The Glass Bridge* (all o/p). Prolific author and wartime survivor, Minco is one of Holland's leading contemporary authors. Her work (especially *The Fall*) focuses on the city's Jewish community, particularly in the war years. See the extract from *An Empty House* on pp.325–327.

Harry Mulisch, *The Assault* (Penguin; Random House). Set part in Haarlem, part in Amsterdam, this traces the story of a young boy who loses his family in a reprisal-raid by the Nazis. A powerful tale, made into an excellent and effective film.

Multatuli, *Max Havelaar: or the Coffee Auctions of the Dutch Trading Company* (Penguin, UK). Classic nineteenth-century Dutch satire of colonial life in the East Indies. Eloquent and, at times, amusing.

Cees Nooteboom, *Rituals* (Harvil; Harvest). An existentialist novel of the 1980s, mapping the empty existence of a rich Amsterdammer who dabbles in antiques. Bleak but absorbing. See the extract on pp.321–323.

Jona Oberski, *Childhood* (o/p). First published in 1978, this is a Jewish child's eye-witness account of the war years, the camps and executions. Written with feeling and precision.

Janwillem van de Wetering, *Hard Rain* (St Martins; Soho). An offbeat detective tale set in Amsterdam and provincial Holland. Like Van de Wetering's other stories, it's a humane, quirky and humorous story, worth reading for the characters and locations as much as for the inventive narrative.

David Veronese, *Jana* (Serpent's Tail, US). A hip thriller set in the underworld of Amsterdam and London.

Jan Wolkers, *Turkish Delight* (M Boyars, UK). Wolkers is one of The Netherlands' best-known artists and writers, and this is one of his early novels, a close examination of the relationship between a bitter, working-class sculptor and his young, middle-class wife. A compelling work, at times misogynistic and even offensive, by a writer who seeks reaction above all.

Language

It's unlikely that you'll need to speak anything other than English while you're in Amsterdam: the Dutch have a seemingly natural talent for languages, and your attempts at speaking theirs may be met with some amusement. Outside Amsterdam people aren't quite as cosmopolitan, but even so the following words and phrases of Dutch should be the most you'll need to get by; see also the detailed Food and Drink Glossary in *Eating and Drinking*.

Pronunciation

Dutch is pronounced much the same as English, but with a few differences:

v is like the English f in **f**ar
w like the v in **v**at
j like the initial sound of **y**ellow
ch and **g** are like the Scottish lo**ch**
(the word for canal – *gracht* – has two of these sounds)
ng is as in bri**ng**

nj as in o**nion**
y is not a consonant, but another way of writing **ij**

Otherwise, double consonants keep their separate sounds – **half**, for example, is pronounced "hul-uf", and **sch** is never like "shoe".

Doubling the letter lengthens the vowel sound:
a is like the English cat
aa like Ma or Pa
e like let
ee like late
ie as in see
o as in pop
oo in pope
oe as in soon
u is like wood
uu the French tu
ui, **au** and **ou** as in out
ei, **ij** and **y** as in fine
eu as in the French l**eu**r

Dutch numbers

When saying a number, the Dutch generally transpose the last two digits: for example, *drie guilden vijf en twintig* is ƒ3,25.

0	*nul*	18	*achttien*
1	*een*	19	*negentien*
2	*twee*	20	*twintig*
3	*drie*	21	*een en twintig*
4	*vier*	22	*twee en twintig*
5	*vijf*	30	*dertig*
6	*zes*	40	*veertig*
7	*zeven*	50	*vijftig*
8	*acht*	60	*zestig*
9	*negen*	70	*zeventig*
10	*tien*	80	*tachtig*
11	*elf*	90	*negentig*
12	*twaalf*	100	*honderd*
13	*dertien*	101	*honderd een*
14	*veertien*	200	*twee honderd*
15	*vijftien*	201	*twee honderd een*
16	*zestien*	500	*vijf honderd*
17	*zeventien*	1000	*duizend*

Dutch words and phrases

Basics and Greetings

Yes	*ja*
No	*nee*
Please	*alstublieft*
(No) Thank you	*(nee) dank u* or *bedankt*
Hello	*hallo* or *dag*
Good morning	*goedemorgen*
Good afternoon	*goedemiddag*
Good evening	*goedenavond*
Goodbye	*tot ziens*
See you later	*tot straks*
Do you speak English?	*spreekt u Engels?*
I don't understand	*Ik begrijp het niet*
Women/men	*vrouwen/mannen*
Children	*kinderen*
Men's/women's toilets	*heren/dames*

Other essentials

I want ...	*Ik wil ...*
I don't want ...	*Ik wil niet ...* (+verb) *Ik wil geen ...* (+noun)
How much is ...?	*Wat kost ...?*
Post office	*postkantoor*
Stamp(s)	*postzegel(s)*
Money exchange	*wisselkantoor*
Cash desk	*kassa*
How do I get to ...?	*Hoe kom ik in ...?*
Where is ...?	*Waar is ...?*
How far is it to ...?	*Hoe ver is het naar ...?*
When?	*Wanneer?*
Far/near	*ver/dichtbij*
Left/right	*links/rechts*
Straight ahead	*rechtuit gaan*
Platform	*spoor* or *perron*
Ticket office	*loket*
Here/there	*hier/daar*
Good/bad	*goed/slecht*
Big/small	*groot/klein*
Open/closed	*open/gesloten*
Push/pull	*duwen/trekken*
New/old	*nieuw/oud*
Cheap/expensive	*goedkoop/duur*
Hot/cold	*heet* or *warm/koud*
With/without	*met/zonder*

Useful cycling terms

Tyre	*band*
Puncture	*lek*
Brake	*rem*
Chain	*keting*
Wheel	*wiel*
Pedal	*trapper*
Pump	*pomp*
Handlebars	*stuur*
Broken	*kapot*

Days and Times

Sunday	*Zondag*
Monday	*Maandag*
Tuesday	*Dinsdag*
Wednesday	*Woensdag*
Thursday	*Donderdag*
Friday	*Vrijdag*
Saturday	*Zaterdag*
Yesterday	*gisteren*
Today	*vandaag*
Tomorrow	*morgen*
Tomorrow morning	*morgenochtend*
Year	*jaar*
Month	*maand*
Week	*week*
Day	*dag*
Hour	*uur*
Minute	*minuut*
What time is it?	*Hoe laat is het?*
It's ...	*Het is ...*
3.00	*drie uur*
3.05	*vijf over drie*
3.10	*tien over drie*
3.15	*kwart over drie*
3.20	*tien voor half vier*
3.25	*vijf voor half vier*
3.30	*half vier*
3.35	*vijf over half vier*
3.40	*tien over half vier*
3.45	*kwart voor vier*
3.50	*tien voor vier*
3.55	*vijf voor vier*
8am	*acht uur 's-ochtends*
1pm	*ein uur 's-middags*
8pm	*acht uur 's-avonds*
1am	*ein uur 's-nachts*

Glossary

Dutch terms

AMSTERDAMMERTJE Phallic-shaped objects placed alongside Amsterdam streets to keep drivers off pavements and out of the canals.

A.U.B. *Alstublieft* – "please" (also shown as **S.V.P.** from French).

BG *Begane grond* – "ground floor" ("basement" is **K** for *kelder*).

BEGIJNHOF Similar to a hofje but occupied by Catholic women (*begijns*) who led semi-religious lives without taking full vows.

BRUG Bridge.

BTW *Belasting Toegevoegde Waarde* – VAT.

FIETSPAD Bicycle path.

GASTHUIS Hospice for the sick or infirm.

GEEN TOEGANG No entry.

GEMEENTE Municipal, as in *Gemeentehuis* (town hall).

GEVEL Gable. Decoration on narrow-fronted canal houses – see opposite.

GEZELLIG A hard term to translate – something like "cosy", "comfortable" and "inviting" in one – which is often said to lie at the heart of the Dutch psyche. A long, relaxed meal in a favourite restaurant with friends is *gezellig*; grabbing a quick snack is not. The best brown cafés ooze *gezelligheid*; Kalverstraat on a Saturday afternoon definitely doesn't.

GILD Guild.

GRACHT Canal.

GROTE KERK Literally "big church" – the main church of a town or village.

HALLE Hall.

HIJSBALK Pulley beam, often decorated, fixed to the top of a gable to lift goods, furniture etc. Essential in canal houses whose staircases were narrow and steep, *hijsbalken* are still very much in use today.

HOF Courtyard.

HOFJE Almshouse, usually for elderly women who could look after themselves but needed small charities such as food and fuel; usually a number of buildings centred around a small, enclosed courtyard.

HUIS House.

JEUGDHERBERG Youth hostel.

KERK Church

KONINKLIJK Royal.

LAKENHAL Cloth hall. The building in medieval weaving towns where cloth would be weighed, graded and sold.

LET OP! Attention!

LUCHTHAVEN Airport.

MARKT Central town square and the heart of most Dutch communities, normally still the site of weekly markets.

MOKUM A Yiddish word meaning "city", originally used by the Jewish community to indicate Amsterdam; now in general usage as a nickname for the city.

NEDERLAND The Netherlands.

NEDERLANDS Dutch.

NOORD North.

OMMEGANG Procession.

OOST East.

PLEIN A square or open space.

POLDER An area of land reclaimed from the sea.

POSTBUS Post office box.

RAADHUIS Town hall.

RANDSTAD Literally "rim-town", this refers to the urban conurbation that makes up much of North and South Holland, stretching from Amsterdam in the north down to Rotterdam and Dordrecht in the south.

RIJK State.

SCHONE KUNSTEN Fine arts.

SCHOUWBURG Theatre.

SPIONNETJE Small mirror on a canal house enabling the occupant to see who is at the door without descending the stairs.

SPOOR Train station platform.

STADHUIS The most common word for a town hall.

STEDELIJK Civic, municipal.

STEEG Alley.

STEEN Fortress.

STICHTING Institute or foundation.

STRAAT Street.

T/M *Tot en met* – "up to and including".

TOEGANG Entrance.

UITGANG Exit.

V.A. *Vanaf* – "from".

V.S. *Verenigde Staten* – "United States".

VOLKSKUNDE Folklore.

WAAG Old public weighing-house, a common feature of most towns.

WEG Way.

WEST West.

WIJK District (of a city).

Z.O.Z. Please turn over (page, leaflet etc).

ZUID South.

Architectural Terms

APSE Semicircular protrusion at (usually) the east end of a church.

ART DECO Geometrical style of art and architecture popular in the 1930s.

ART NOUVEAU Style of art, architecture and design based on highly stylized vegetal forms. Popular in the early part of the twentieth century.

BAROQUE High Renaissance period of art and architecture, distinguished by extreme ornateness and exuberance.

CLASSICAL The term used to describe an architectural style incorporating Greek and Roman elements – pillars, domes, colonnades etc – at its height in the seventeenth century.

EXPRESSIONISTIC Artistic style developed at the beginning of the twentieth century, characterized by the use of symbolism and exaggeration.

GABLE The triangular upper portion of a wall – decorative or supporting a roof – which is a practical feature of many Amsterdam canal houses. Initially fairly simple, they became more ostentatious in the late seventeenth century, before turning to a more restrained classicism in the eighteenth and nineteenth centuries.

GOTHIC Architectural style of the thirteenth to sixteenth centuries, characterized by pointed arches, rib vaulting, flying buttresses and a general emphasis on verticality.

MISERICORD Ledge on choir stall on which occupant can be supported while standing; often carved with secular subjects.

NAVE Main body of a church.

NEOCLASSICAL A style of classical architecture (see above) revived in the nineteenth century, popular in the Low Countries during French rule.

NEOGOTHIC Revived Gothic style of architecture popular between the late eighteenth and nineteenth centuries.

RENAISSANCE Movement in art and architecture developed in fifteenth-century Italy.

RETABLE Altarpiece.

ROCOCO Highly florid, light and graceful eighteenth-century style of architecture, painting and interior design, forming the last phase of Baroque.

ROMANESQUE Early medieval architecture distinguished by squat forms, rounded arches and naive sculpture.

STUCCO Marble-based plaster used to embellish ceilings, etc.

TRANSEPT Arms of a cross-shaped church, placed at ninety degrees to nave and chancel.

TRIPTYCH Carved or painted work on three panels. Often used as an altarpiece.

VAULT An arched ceiling or roof.

Index

Stay in touch with us!

ROUGH*NEWS* is Rough Guides' free newsletter.
In four issues a year we give you news, travel
issues, music reviews, readers' letters and the
latest dispatches from authors on the road.

I would like to receive ROUGH*NEWS*: please put me on your free mailing list.

NAME . . . .

ADDRESS . . . .

Please clip or photocopy and send to: Rough Guides, 62–70 Shorts Gardens, London WC2H 9AB,
England or Rough Guides, 375 Hudson Street, New York, NY 10014, USA.

ROUGH GUIDES: Travel

Amsterdam
Andalucia
Australia

Austria
Bali & Lombok
Barcelona
Belgium &
  Luxembourg
Belize
Berlin
Brazil
Britain
Brittany &
  Normandy
Bulgaria
California
Canada
Central America
Chile
China
Corfu & the
  Ionian Islands
Corsica
Costa Rica
Crete
Croatia
Cyprus
Czech & Slovak
  Republics
Dodecanese &
  the East Aegean

Dominican
  Republic
Ecuador
Egypt
England
Europe
Florida
France
French Hotels &
  Restaurants
  1999
Germany
Goa
Greece
Greek Islands
Guatemala
Hawaii
Holland
Hong Kong &
  Macau
Hungary
India
Indonesia
Ireland
Israel & the
  Palestinian
  Territories
Italy
Jamaica
Japan
Jordan

Kenya
Lake District
Laos
London
Los Angeles
Malaysia,
  Singapore &
  Brunei
Mallorca &
  Menorca
Maya World
Mexico
Morocco
Moscow
Nepal
New England
New York
New Zealand
Norway
Pacific
  Northwest
Paris
Peru
Poland
Portugal
Prague
Provence & the
  Côte d'Azur
The Pyrenees
Rhodes & the
  Dodecanese

Romania
St Petersburg
San Francisco
Sardinia
Scandinavia
Scotland
Scottish
  highlands and
  Islands
Sicily
Singapore
South Africa
South India
Southwest USA
Spain
Sweden
Syria

Thailand
Trinidad &
  Tobago
Tunisia
Turkey
Tuscany &
  Umbria
USA
Venice
Vienna
Vietnam
Wales
Washington DC
West Africa
Zimbabwe &
  Botswana

AVAILABLE AT ALL GOOD BOOKSHOPS

ROUGH GUIDES: Mini Guides, Travel Specials and Phrasebooks

MINI GUIDES

Antigua
Bangkok
Barbados
Big Island of
  Hawaii
Boston
Brussels
Budapest

Dublin
Edinburgh
Florence
Honolulu
Jerusalem
Lisbon
London
  Restaurants
Madrid
Maui
Melbourne
New Orleans
Rome
Seattle
St Lucia

Sydney
Tokyo
Toronto

TRAVEL SPECIALS

First-Time Asia
First-Time
  Europe
Women Travel

PHRASEBOOKS

Czech
Dutch

Egyptian Arabic
European
French
German
Greek
Hindi & Urdu
Hungarian
Indonesian
Italian
Japanese

Mandarin
  Chinese
Mexican
  Spanish
Polish
Portuguese
Russian
Spanish
Swahili
Thai
Turkish
Vietnamese

ROUGH GUIDES:
Reference and Music CDs

REFERENCE
Classical Music
Classical:
  100 Essential CDs
Drum'n'bass
House Music
Jazz
Music USA

Internet
Millennium

ROUGH GUIDE MUSIC CDs
Music of the
  Andes
Australian
  Aboriginal
Brazilian Music
Cajun & Zydeco

Opera
Opera:
  100 Essential CDs
Reggae
Reggae:
  100 Essential CDs
Rock
Rock:
  100 Essential CDs
Techno
World Music
World Music:
  100 Essential CDs
English Football
European Football

Classic Jazz
Music of
  Colombia
Cuban Music
Eastern Europe

Music of Egypt
English Roots
  Music
Flamenco
India & Pakistan
Irish Music
Music of Japan
Kenya & Tanzania
Native American
North African
Music of Portugal

Reggae
Salsa
Scottish Music
South African
  Music
Music of Spain
Tango
Tex-Mex
West African
  Music
World Music
World Music Vol 2
Music of
  Zimbabwe

AVAILABLE AT ALL GOOD BOOKSHOPS

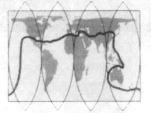
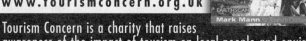

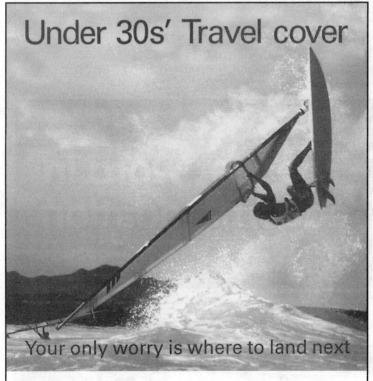 

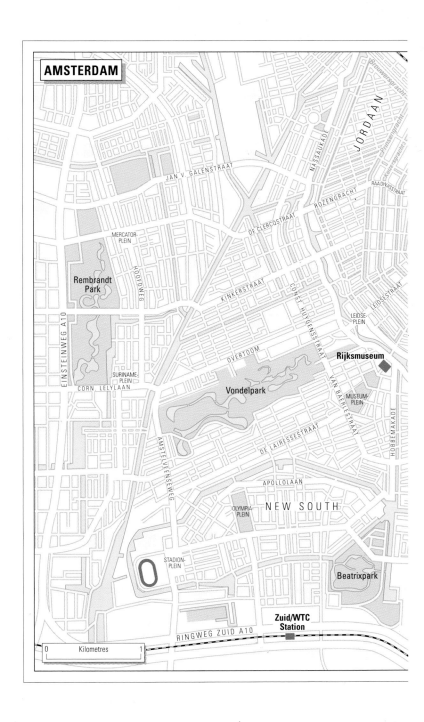

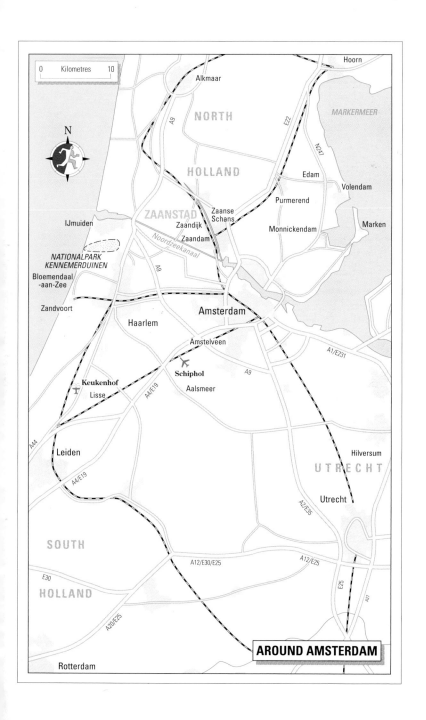

AROUND AMSTERDAM

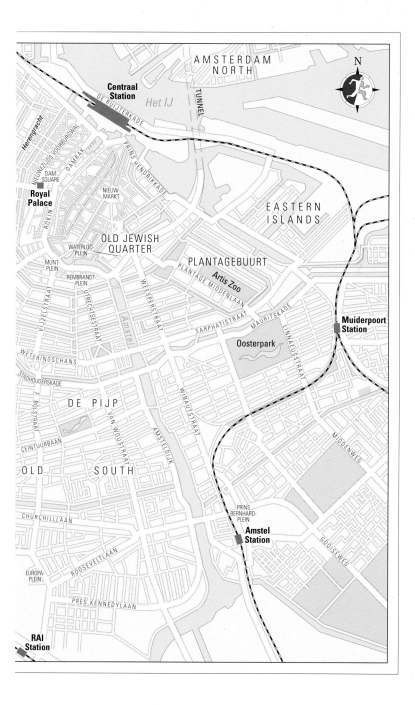

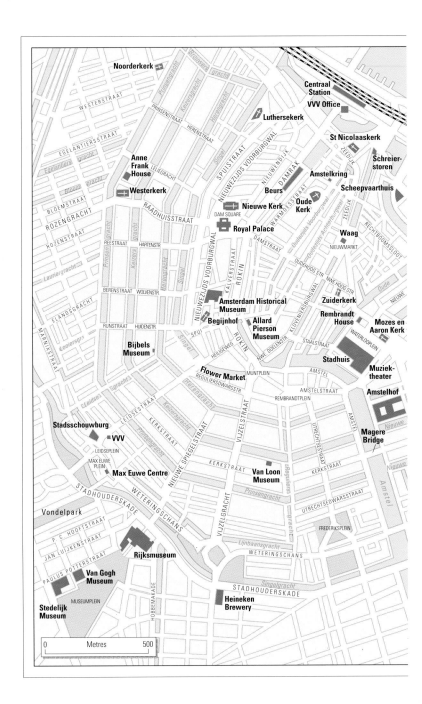

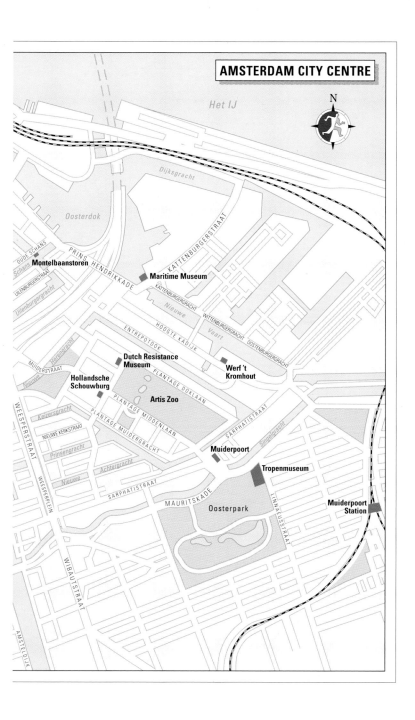

AMSTERDAM CITY CENTRE

N

Het IJ

Dijksgracht

Oosterdok

OUDE SCHANS

PRINS HENDRIKKADE

KATTENBURGERSTRAAT

Montelbaanstoren

ULENBURGERSTRAAT

Ulenburgergracht

Maritime Museum

KATTENBURGERGRACHT

Nieuwe

ENTREPOTDOK

HOOGTE KADIJK

WITTENBURGERGRACHT

OOSTENBURGERGRACHT

Vaart

MUIDERSTRAAT

Nieuwe

Herengracht

Dutch Resistance Museum

PLANTAGE DOKLAAN

Werf 't Kromhout

Hollandsche Schouwburg

PLANTAGE MIDDENLAAN

Artis Zoo

SARPHATISTRAAT

Singelgracht

WEESPERSTRAAT

Keizersgracht

PLANTAGE MUIDERGRACHT

NIEUWE KERKSTRAAT

Prinsengracht

Achtergracht

Muiderpoort

Nieuwe

Tropenmuseum

WEESPERPLEIN

SARPHATISTRAAT

MAURITSKADE

LINNAEUSSTRAAT

Muiderpoort Station

Oosterpark

WIBAUTSTRAAT

AMSTELDIJK

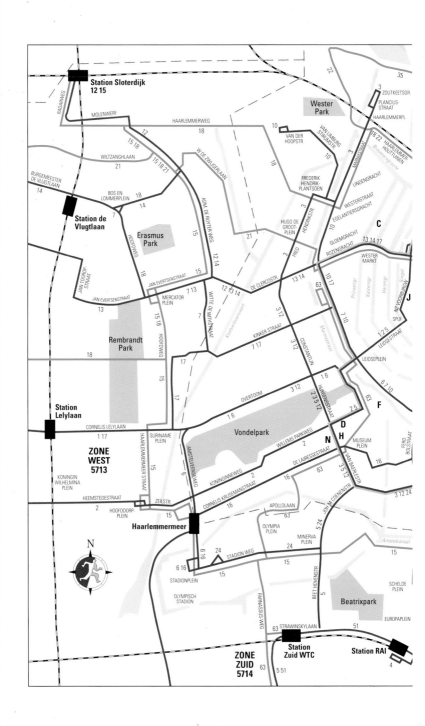

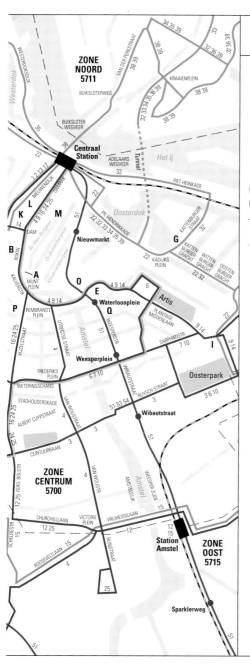

AMSTERDAM: TRAMS, BUSES & THE METRO

——————— Bus route
——————— Tram route
——————— Circle Tram 20
——————— Metro route
– – – – – Zone boundary
▭▭▭▭▭▭ Railway line
(reference only)

GVB Office
Opposite Centraal Station
April – Sept : Mon–Fri 7am – 9pm,
Sat & Sun 8am – 9pm
Oct – March : Mon–Fri 7am – 7pm,
Sat & Sun 8am – 7pm

A Allard Pierson Museum
B Amsterdam Historical Museum
C Anne Frank House
D Vincent van Gogh Museum
E Jewish Historical Museum
F Rijksmuseum
G Maritime Museum
H Stedelijk Museum
I Tropenmuseum
J Begijnhof
K Royal Palace
L Nieuwe Kerk
M Oude Kerke
N Concertgebouw
O Musiektheater
P Flower Market
Q Hortus Botanicus

THE OLD CENTRE

N

BROUWER.
GRACHT

Keizersgracht

Singel

LANGESTRAAT

STROMARKT

NIEUWEZIJDS VOORBURGWAL

NIEUWENDIJK

PRINS HENDRIKKADE

**Centraal
Station**

STATIONSPLEIN

GVB

VVV

HERENSTRAAT

BLAUW
BURGWAL

Herengracht

HEKELVELD

Luthersekerk

OUDE NIEUWSTR

SPUISTRAAT

**Crowne Plaza
Hotel**

NZ ARMSTEEG

ST.JACOBS STR.

NIEUWEZIJDS KOLK

NIEUWE NIEUWSTR.

Singel

ST NICOLAASSTR.

NIEUWENDIJK

Sexmuseum

DAMRAK

St Nicolaaskerk

OUDEZIJDS KOLK

ZEEDIJK

Schreierstoren

Oude Schans & The Montelbaanstoren

Geldersekade

LANGE NIEZEL

Amstelkring **Spinhuis**

BEURSSTRAAT

WARMOESSTRAAT

OUDE LEIESTR.

GRAVENSTRAAT

Beurs

BEURSPLEIN

Effectenbeurs

Geels & Co.

**Prostitution
Info Centre**

ST ANNENSTR.

Oude Kerk

OUDEZIJDS VOORBURGWAL

OUDEZIJDS ACHTERBURGWAL

ZEEDIJK

**Magna
Plaza**

**Nieuwe
Kerk**

MOZES EN AARONSTRAAT

De Bijenkorf

RAADHUISSTRAAT

Royal Palace

**Dam
Square**

War Memorial

R E D   L I G H T   D I S T R I C T

Waag

NIEUW-
MARKT

REGULIERSSLOOT

PALEISSTRAAT

**Madame
Tussaud's**

PIJLSTEEG

DAMSTRAAT

Oudezijds Voorburgwal

Oudezijds Achterburgwal

NIEUWEZIJDS VOORBURGWAL

WIJDSTEEG

SPUISTRAAT

Singel

NES

KALVERSTRAAT

P. JACOBSZSTR.

ST PIETERS-
POORTSTG.

**Hash
Museum**

**Kleine
Trippenhuis**

Trippenhuis

OUDE HOOGSTR.

NIEUWE HOOGSTR.

ST ANTONIESBREESTRAAT

LUCIENSTEEG

ROKIN

'Ome Jan'

**Oostendisch
Huis**

ZANDSTRAAT

Zuiderkerk

ZWANENBURGWAL

HEISTEEG

BEGIJNENSTEEG

**Historical
Museum**

Galerie Mokum

Agnietenkapel

**Drie
Grachten**

RUSLAND

OUDEMANHUISPOORT

Kloveniersburgwal

Raamgracht

Groenburgwal

WATERLOO-
PLEIN

Begijnhof

LANGEBRUGSTEEG

GRIMBURGWAL

**Allard
Pierson
Museum**

BINNENGASTHUISSTR.

SPUI

VOETBOOGSTR.

OUDE TURFMARKT

NIEUWE DOELENSTRAAT

STAALSTRAAT

Rasphuis

HANDBOOGSTRAAT

HEILIGEWEG

KALVERSTRAAT

ROKIN

Stadhuis

**Muziek
Theater**

LEIDSESTR.

KONINGSPLEIN

Munttoren

MUNT-
PLEIN

AMSTEL

Amstel

AMSTEL

BLAUWBRUG

Herengracht

Singel

Flower Market

REGULIERS-

REGULIERSBREESTRAAT

REMBRANDT
PLEIN

DWARSSTRAAT

0   Metres   100